T·H·E N·I·V

BIBLE

COMPANION

A BASIC COMMENTARY ON THE OLD AND NEW TESTAMENTS

ALISTER E. McGRATH

ZondervanPublishingHouse

Grand Rapids, Michigan

A Division of HarperCollinsPublishers

The NIV Bible Companion
Copyright © 1997 by Alister E. McGrath
First published as *NIV Bible Commentary* in the United Kingdom by Hodder and Stoughton
Limited.

Requests for information should be addressed to:

 ZondervanPublishingHouse
Grand Rapids, Michigan 49530

Library of Congress Cataloging-in-Publication Data

McGrath, Alister E., 1953–
    The NIV Bible companion : a basic commentary on the Old and New Testaments / Alister
E. McGrath.
       p.   cm.
    Includes bibliographical references.
    ISBN: 0-310-20547-6 (hardcover)
    1. Bible—Commentaries.   I. Title.
    BS491.2.M38   1997
    220.7—dc21   96-51874
                                                        CIP

This edition printed on acid-free paper and meets the American National Standards Institute
Z39.48 standard.

Interior design by Sherri Hoffman

Printed in the United States of America

98 99 00 01 02 03 04 /❖ DH/ 10 9 8 7 6 5 4 3 2

CONTENTS

THE NEW TESTAMENT

INTRODUCTION

Christianity is the best news the world has ever had. It focuses on the hope of eternal life and resurrection made possible through the life, death, and resurrection of Jesus Christ. Those who have discovered the joy of the gospel will know the sense of peace and delight which comes from knowing Christ.

The Bible—which Christians often refer to as "Scripture"—sets out the great historical events on which the Christian gospel is founded. It reassures us that the gospel is founded on the bedrock of historical truth. It gives substance to the hope and joy of the Christian life. It allows us to picture the figure of Jesus Christ and realize the enormous attraction he had for ordinary people. Reading the four Gospels fills out our understanding and appreciation of Jesus Christ. There is no better place to start reading Scripture than with one of the Gospels. The Acts of the Apostles also indicates the great joy and delight which the good news brought to men and women as it began its explosive expansion in the civilized world.

However, Scripture does more than allow us to appreciate the attraction of the gospel and its central figure, Jesus Christ. It goes behind the coming of Jesus Christ, and helps us understand the great sense of expectation which had built up within Judaism. By reading the Old Testament, we can understand the way in which God was preparing the way for Jesus Christ. We can go back in history and appreciate the hopes and expectations of the Old Testament community of faith as they looked to the future they knew would hold the coming of God's long-awaited Messiah. And as we read the gospel accounts of Jesus Christ, we can see how Christ fulfilled those great hopes.

Scripture also helps us to understand the difference which knowing Jesus Christ makes to the way Christians think and behave. The New Testament letters help us understand the basic ideas of the Christian gospel—the central doctrines which sum up the Christian understanding of the way things are, and the hope which the gospel brings to the world. They also help us learn the way in which knowing Christ should affect the way in which we behave. Paul's letters, for example, are full of wise advice on how Christians ought to live in a pagan world—advice which continues to be relevant and helpful today.

WHY A COMMENTARY? ————————————————

So why a commentary? Why not just read the Bible and soak in its wisdom? The simplest answer is that the Bible is best read in company. One of the reasons why Bible study groups are so popular is that they allow you to listen to other people talking about their insights into the meaning and relevance of the Bible. Commentaries are like that. They give you access to the wisdom of others.

Commentaries come in different forms. Some are very technical, dealing with the detailed historical backgrounds to the books and exploring the precise grammatical and theological meaning of the text in depth. Others are devotional, aiming to help their readers turn to prayer and adoration as a result of reading Scripture. Some devote entire volumes to a single book of the Bible. Others try to survey the Bible in a shorter space; this work is one of them.

This one-volume commentary is designed to introduce the reader to the main features of the Bible. It is written by a single author, which ensures that the same level and style of writing will be found throughout the book. Although there is not space in a single volume to deal with all the possible questions, such a book can whet its readers' appetites for more, and give them increasing confidence in their own ability to read and benefit from the Bible.

If you have been a Christian for some time, you will probably feel ready to begin reading the Bible immediately. If you're new to being a Christian, or feel that you could do with a little more information—read on!

WHAT'S IN THE BIBLE? ————————————————

The Bible is divided into two major sections, referred to as the Old Testament and the New Testament. The Old Testament consists of thirty-nine books, beginning with Genesis and ending with Malachi. This first section of the Bible deals with the history of the people of God before the coming of Jesus Christ. It helps us understand God's plans for his people, and the way in which he chose to redeem them. It introduces us to the great hopes of divine intervention in history, which will eventually be fulfilled through Jesus Christ. It is impossible to appreciate the full importance and wonder of the gospel without being aware of the preparation for the coming of Christ in the history of the people of God.

The Old Testament itself includes a number of different kinds of writings. Appreciating their different natures will help you get more out of reading them. The main sections of the Old Testament are the following:

The Five Books of the Law

The five books of the Law are sometimes also referred to as the Five Books of Moses, or the Pentateuch. They are: Genesis, Exodus, Leviticus, Numbers, and Deuteronomy. These deal with the creation of the world, the calling of Israel as a people and its early history, including the exodus from Egypt. The story they tell ends with the people of Israel about to cross over the Jordan and enter the promised land. One of the most important themes of these books is the giving of the Law to Moses, and its implications for the life of Israel.

The Historical Books

The historical books of Joshua, Judges, Ruth, 1 and 2 Samuel, 1 and 2 Kings, 1 and 2 Chronicles, Ezra, Nehemiah, and Esther deal with various aspects of the history of the people of God, from their entry into the promised land of Canaan to the return of the people of Jerusalem from exile in the city of Babylon. It includes detailed accounts of the conquest of Canaan, the establishment of a monarchy in Israel, the great reigns of kings David and Solomon, the breakup of the single nation of Israel into two parts (the northern kingdom of Israel and the southern kingdom of Judah), the destruction of Israel by the Assyrians, the defeat of Judah and exile of her people by the Babylonians, and the final return from exile and the rebuilding of the temple. The books are arranged in historical order.

The Prophets

This major section of the Old Testament contains the writings of a group of individuals, inspired by the Holy Spirit, who sought to make the will of God known to their people over a period of time. There are sixteen prophetic writings in the Old Testament, which are usually divided into two categories. First, there are the four Major Prophets: Isaiah, Jeremiah, Ezekiel, and Daniel. These are followed by the twelve Minor Prophets: Hosea, Joel, Amos, Obadiah, Jonah, Micah, Nahum, Habakkuk, Zephaniah, Haggai, Zechariah, and Malachi. The use of the words *major* and *minor* does not imply any judgment about the relative importance of the prophets. It refers simply to the length of the books in question. The prophetic writings are arranged roughly in historical order.

Other Books of the Old Testament

Other types of books can be noted, including the Wisdom Writings: Job, Proverbs, Ecclesiastes. These works deal with the question of how true wisdom may be found, and often provide some practical examples of wisdom. Another category of writings that lies outside the Old Testament should also be noted—the Apocrypha. This is also sometimes referred to as the "deuterocanonical writings." It includes a number of later writings from Old Testament times which, although informative, have not been regarded as of binding importance by Christians. Some Bibles include this section of writings; others, like the NIV, do not.

The Gospels

The New Testament is of vital importance to Christians, as it sets out the basic events and beliefs of the Christian gospel. The New Testament, which consists of twenty-seven books, is considerably shorter than the Old Testament. It is strongly recommended that new readers of the Bible begin by reading one of the four Gospels: Matthew, Mark, Luke, and John. The word *gospel* basically means "good news." Each of the four gospel writers—or "evangelists," as they are sometimes known—sets out the basic events lying behind the good news. These four books describe, from different viewpoints, the life of Jesus Christ, which reaches its glorious climax in his resurrection, as well as presenting his teachings.

The four Gospels have distinctive characteristics—for example, Matthew is concerned to present Jesus' teaching, whereas Mark is more interested in focusing on the last week of his earthly life. Taken together, all four build up to give a comprehensive account of the life, death and resurrection of Jesus Christ. They provide the main building blocks of the Christian faith, allowing readers to understand why Christians believe that Jesus Christ is indeed the Lord and Savior of the world. You will sometimes find the term synoptic Gospels used to refer to the first three Gospels (Matthew, Mark, and Luke); this term refers to their similar literary structure. The Gospels are usually referred to simply by the name of their author—such as "Mark"—rather than the more lengthy phrase "the Gospel according to Mark."

The Acts of the Apostles

The Gospels are followed by an account of the expansion of Christianity. How were events described in the Gospels received at the time? How did the gospel spread from Palestine to Europe? These questions are addressed in the Acts of the Apostles, which is almost always referred to simply as Acts. The Gospel of Luke and Acts were written by the same person—Luke.

The Letters

The next major section of material in the New Testament is the Letters, sometimes still referred to by the older English word *Epistles*. These letters provide teaching concerning both Christian beliefs and behavior, as important today as they were when they were first written. Some of the false teachings that arose in the early period of the church's history continue to arise in present times, and these letters provide important resources for defending the integrity of the Christian faith today.

Most of the letters were written by Paul, whose conversion to the Christian faith led him to undertake a major program of evangelism and church planting. Many of his letters were written to churches he had planted, giving them advice. All of Paul's letters are written to individuals (such as Timothy or Titus) or churches (such as the churches at Rome, Corinth, and Philippi).

Although the letters are sometimes referred to using the form "Paul's first letter to Timothy" or "Paul's second letter to the church at Corinth," they are much more usually referred to simply as 1 Timothy or 2 Corinthians.

Other letter writers include the apostles Peter and John, as well as the unknown author of the letter to the Hebrews (possibly Barnabas or Apollos). Often, the letters describe the hardship being faced for the gospel, or the joy which it brings to the writer and to those he is writing. This reminds us that Christianity is not just about ideas. It is about changed lives! The letters are not dull doctrinal textbooks, but living testimonies to faith, which include doctrinal teaching. Note that all these letters are identified by the person who wrote them, rather than the people to whom they are written. Although the full titles are sometimes used—such as "the first letter of Peter"—it is more common to refer to them by shorter forms, such as 1 Peter.

Two terms should be noted here. The letters of James, John, Jude, and Peter are sometimes referred to as the "general letters" or "the catholic epistles," to indicate that they have a general readership. Unlike Paul, they do not seem to be written to a specific audience, but were meant for wide reading. The term *Pastoral Letters* is sometimes used to refer to Paul's two letters to Timothy and his letter to Titus, which deal particularly with issues of pastoral importance (that is, care of people in the church).

The Revelation

The New Testament ends with "the Revelation of John"—almost always referred simply as Revelation, which stands in a class of its own. It represents a vision of the end of history in which the writer is allowed to see into heaven and gain a glimpse of the new Jerusalem that is prepared for believers.

WHERE DO I START?

One possibility might be to start with Genesis—the first book in the Old Testament—and work your way right through to the last book in the New Testament. This is not such a good idea, however. The most appropriate way of reading Scripture is to begin by reading a Gospel. By doing this, you will focus on Jesus Christ and become familiar with the historical bedrock of the Christian faith. It is often said that "Christianity is Jesus Christ." Reading one of the four Gospels will bring you face to face with the central figure of the Christian faith.

So which of the four Gospels should you begin with? Each has a distinctive character. Matthew is especially concerned to bring out how the life, death, and resurrection of Jesus Christ fulfill the great Old Testament prophecies of the coming Savior and Messiah. Mark is brief and fast-moving, bringing out clearly the remarkable impact Jesus had upon those around him. Luke is especially interested in bringing out the importance of Jesus for those who are not Jews. John is the most reflective of all the

Gospels and will give you substantial food for thought. The choice is yours. However, whichever of the Gospels you begin by reading, make sure that you read the other three, in whole or part, at some point.

Where do you go next? You might like to read of the rapid expansion of the gospel by looking at the Acts of the Apostles. This is an especially appropriate thing to do if you have just read Luke's gospel, as the two works dovetail together. You might also like to try reading one of the letters, to see how the gospel can change people's lives and hopes. Paul's letter to the Philippians is an especially appropriate choice for the next step. It is brief and very easy to read. For those wanting more doctrinal input, the letters to the Romans and Galatians are particularly important.

Having gained an understanding of the gospel, you might then like to go back to the Old Testament and explore the background to the coming of Jesus Christ. Many translations and editions of the Bible make this easier by providing footnotes or center-column references (see next section) to relevant passages in other parts of the Bible.

The best advice, however, is to study the Bible with other people, especially in groups that include older and more experienced Christians. They will be able to explore both the meaning and the implications of biblical passages for Christian life today. Your local church, college, or even place of work, will probably have a Christian Bible study group attached to it. Find it, and join up! If you haven't started going to a church—do so. Try to find one which takes the Bible seriously. This kind of church will have sermons that examine important Biblical passages, and will also have Bible study groups as an integral part of its teaching and support program.

REFERRING TO BIBLICAL BOOKS

One final point needs to be looked at. How do you identify the biblical passage about which you want to study or talk? To make this as easy as possible, a kind of shorthand way of referring to biblical passages has evolved over the years. Once you understand it, you are set for the rest of your Christian life. In what follows, we will explore this very briefly.

To locate a verse in the Bible, you need to identify three things: the book of the Bible, the chapter of that book, and the verse of that chapter. To make sure you understand this, turn to the Acts of the Apostles, chapter 27, verse 1. What is the name of the centurion mentioned in this verse? If your answer is not Julius, check your reference again. Now try turning to Paul's letter to the Romans, chapter 16, verse 5. Who was the first convert to Christ in Asia? If you answer is not Epenetus, check it again.

The above system is cumbersome. Writing out everything—"Paul's letter to the Romans, chapter 16, verse 5"—takes up too much space. So it is abbreviated as follows: Ro 16:5. This is the standard form of reference, with the following features:

1. An abbreviation of the book of the Bible being referred to, usually two or three letters in length (such as 1Ki for 1 Kings, Mt for Matthew, Ro for Romans, and 1Co for 1 Corinthians);
2. The number of the chapter of that book, followed by a colon (:);
3. The number of the verse in that chapter. A full list of the books of the Bible and their standard abbreviations may be found in a table following this introduction.

To check that you have learned how to use this system, try the following test. Match the following Biblical verses with the towns or cities they refer to. You will find the answers at the end of this section.

2Ti 4:12	Ephesus
Lk 24:50	Bethsaida
Jn 1:44	Bethany
2Ki 24:16	Jerusalem
Isa 51:17	Babylon

Now match the following Biblical verses with the individuals they refer to:

1Co 16:19	Paul
Ac 18:1	Aquila and Priscilla
Ro 4:1	Abraham
Eph 6:21	Silas
1Pe 5:12	Melchizedek
Heb 7:15	Tychicus

Now that you are familiar with this system, there are some minor points that need mentioning.

First, some biblical books are so brief that they consist only of one chapter (Obadiah; Philemon; 2 John; 3 John; Jude). In this case, only the verse number is cited. Thus Phm 2 is a reference to the second verse of Philemon.

Second, a commentary dealing with a passage in a specific biblical book (such as Genesis) may need to refer to another passage in the same book. In this case, the book name will be omitted. Thus, in a commentary on Genesis, a reference to Ge 12:1 would appear simply as 12:1.

Third, individual Psalms are treated as chapters of the Psalter. Thus a reference to Ps 23:1 is a reference to the first verse of the twenty-third Psalm.

You will also need to know how to refer to a passage of more than one verse. This is very simple. Look at the following reference:

Mt 3:13–17

This reference is to the passage which begins with Mt 3:13, and ends at Mt 13:17. To indicate a passage within a single chapter of a biblical book, you need only identify the opening and closing verse in this way. Sometimes the passage will include material from two or more chapters. The following reference is of this kind:

> 1Th 4:13—5:11

This refers to a passage which begins at 1Th 4:13 and ends at 1Th 5:11.

ANSWERS TO THE REFERENCE SELF-CHECKS——

(a)   Towns and Cities

2Ti 4:12	Ephesus
Lk 24:50	Bethany
Jn 1:44	Bethsaida
2Ki 24:16	Babylon
Isa 51:17	Jerusalem

(b) Individuals

1Co 16:19	Aquila and Priscilla
Ac 18:1	Paul
Ro 4:1	Abraham
Eph 6:21	Tychicus
1Pe 5:12	Silas
Heb 7:15	Melchizedek

ABBREVIATIONS FOR BOOKS OF THE BIBLE

THE OLD TESTAMENT

Genesis	Ge	2 Chronicles	2Ch	Daniel	Da
Exodus	Ex	Ezra	Ezr	Hosea	Hos
Leviticus	Lev	Nehemiah	Ne	Joel	Joel
Numbers	Nu	Esther	Est	Amos	Am
Deuteronomy	Dt	Job	Job	Obadiah	Ob
Joshua	Jos	Psalms	Ps	Jonah	Jnh
Judges	Jdg	Proverbs	Pr	Micah	Mic
Ruth	Ru	Ecclesiastes	Ecc	Nahum	Na
1 Samuel	1Sa	Song of Songs	SS	Habakkuk	Hab
2 Samuel	2Sa	Isaiah	Isa	Zephaniah	Zep
1 Kings	1Ki	Jeremiah	Jer	Haggai	Hag
2 Kings	2Ki	Lamentations	La	Zechariah	Zec
1 Chronicles	1Ch	Ezekiel	Eze	Malachi	Mal

THE NEW TESTAMENT

Matthew	Mt	Ephesians	Eph	Hebrews	Heb
Mark	Mk	Philippians	Php	James	Jas
Luke	Lk	Colossians	Col	1 Peter	1Pe
John	Jn	1 Thessalonians	1Th	2 Peter	2Pe
Acts	Ac	2 Thessalonians	2Th	1 John	1Jn
Romans	Ro	1 Timothy	1Ti	2 John	2Jn
1 Corinthians	1Co	2 Timothy	2Ti	3 John	3Jn
2 Corinthians	2Co	Titus	Tit	Jude	Jude
Galatians	Gal	Philemon	Phm	Revelation	Rev

THE OLD TESTAMENT

GENESIS

With the book of Genesis, the curtain lifts over the stage of world history. As the book unfolds, its readers will begin to learn about the great story of God's redemption of his people. Just as an operatic overture will introduce the themes of the opera to its waiting audience, so Genesis introduces its readers to the great themes that will dominate Scripture. We learn of God's creation of the world and of its rebellion against him. We learn of God's decision to restore his creation to fellowship with him and of his calling of a people to serve him and bring this good news to the ends of the earth. In short, Genesis sets the scene for the great drama of redemption that forms the subject of Scripture.

GENESIS 1:1 – 2:3

The First Creation Account

1:1–25 The Beginning. The title of this book means "origins," and it is hence no surprise that Genesis deals with the origins of humanity, especially its relationship to the God who created it. There are two accounts of the creation of the world, each told from different perspectives and with different points of focus. The first creation account in Genesis 1:1–2:3 opens with its famous declaration that God created the heavens and the earth (1:1). Everything has its origins from God. During the six days of creation, everything that is now a familiar part of the world is surveyed and declared to owe its existence to a sovereign act of creation on the part of God.

The account of the creation of the sun, moon, and stars is of special interest. For many ancient peoples, these heavenly bodies represented divine or supernatural powers and were the object of worship and superstition. Genesis puts them firmly in their place: they are parts of God's creation and thus subject to his power. They should not be worshiped and need not be feared. God has authority and dominion over them. No part of God's creation is to be worshiped, for the entire creation is the work of the creator God himself, and he only is to be worshiped.

In a powerful series of affirmations, Genesis declares the goodness of God's creation (1:4, 10, 18, 21). The work of creation is brought to a close with the affirmation that it is "very good" (1:31), perhaps referring to humanity as the climax of the work of creation or to the completion of this work as a whole. The theme of the goodness of creation is of central importance. The origin of sin is not due to God, but to the rebellion of his creation against him. The only thing that Genesis explicitly declares *not* to be good is Adam's loneliness (2:18). Yet even this is remedied immediately, through the creation of woman.

1:26–31 Humanity Created in the Image of God. The creation of humanity is of special importance. The first creation account places the creation of humanity at the end of God's work of creation (1:26–27). This is the high point of creation in which the only creature to bear the image of the creator God is introduced. The passage just cited is unusual in that it opens with something like a fanfare, a declaration that something major is about to take place. It is clear that humanity is meant to be seen as the summit of God's creative action and power. The Hebrew word often translated "man" is here to be understood as humanity in general, rather than as a male human being in particular.

Humanity, male and female, is created in the image or likeness of God (1:26–27). What does this mean? Two ideas may be noted as being of particular importance. First, being created in the image of God implies a likeness between God and humanity. There is the basis of a relationship here at the origins of the human race. To be made in God's image is to be created with the potential to relate to God personally. Humanity alone, out of all of

God started with nothing. Then he created everything, starting with the heavens and the earth. When he was finished, he declared that all was "very good."

God's good creation, has the distinctive possibility of being able to enter into a mutual relationship with its creator.

Second, the image of God suggests his ownership and authority over his creation. In the ancient world, kings often set up images of themselves throughout their lands in order to assert their authority over them. (There is an important reference to this practice in the book of Daniel, which relates how King Nebuchadnezzar set up a golden image of himself at Babylon that he commanded to be worshiped, Da 3:1–6.) Being made in the image of God is an assertion of God's ultimate authority over his creation and a reminder that all human beings are ultimately responsible to God.

2:1–3 God Rests. The first creation account concludes by declaring that God rested on the seventh day (2:2). This does not mean that God was physically tired; it is simply an affirmation that his work of creation was completed. Nothing remained to be done. This theme of rest will recur throughout Scripture. Just as God rested from his work of creation, so his people should rest from their labors on the seventh day (2:3). The Sabbath rest is thus an important reminder of God's work and affords an opportunity to reflect on his work of creation and redemption. The image of rest also becomes an image of the salvation God offers his people after they have served him in this life (Rev 14:13).

GENESIS 2:4 – 25

The Second Creation Account

2:47 The Breath of Life Breathed Into Humanity. The second creation account (2:4–25) takes a different form from the first account, yet makes many of the same points. The second account opens with the creation of humanity (2:7), affirming that humanity is the most important aspect of the creation. It is made absolutely clear that human life is totally dependent upon God. The reference to God breathing the "breath of life" into humanity (2:7) is of particular importance in that it both emphasizes the God-given origins of life and also anticipates the important life-giving role of the Holy Spirit. (The Hebrew term *ruach* can mean "spirit," "wind," or "breath," pointing to the close connections between these ideas.) It is only when God breathes upon humanity that it comes to life.

2:8–17 The Garden of Eden. We are now introduced to the celebrated Garden of Eden (2:8) into which the man is placed. This garden is described in glowing terms (2:9–14). It is not something that humanity has created. Rather, it is something that God has created and entrusted to humanity. Man is placed in this wonderful garden "to work it and take care of it" (2:15). The man's responsibility is that of being a steward of God's good creation. This delegated authority extends to the animals and birds. Genesis notes that the man was allowed to give names to "all the livestock, the birds of the air and all the beasts of the field" (2:20). (In the ancient world, naming someone or something was an assertion of authority over that person or thing. Parents named their children as an expression of authority over them.) Humanity does not own the garden and all that is in it, but is simply placed in it and asked to care for it. Yet, as will become clear only too soon, the man fails totally in this responsibility.

2:18–25 Woman Is Created. The first Genesis creation account could give rise to the impression that male and female are simply alternative versions of humanity without necessarily possessing any distinctive characteristics. The second Genesis creation account adds another important insight: male and female are created to complement one another:

> The LORD God said, "It is not good for the man to be alone. I will make a helper suitable for him" (2:18).

For some people, speaking of the female as a "helper" may seem to imply that the female is subordinate to the male. Yet according to Genesis 1 and 2, the female was created, not to serve the male, but to serve *with* the male. Male and female are entrusted with the task of being stewards of God's good creation. It must be remembered that God himself is referred to as a helper at several points in the Old Testament!

This is an extremely important passage. Up to now, God had pronounced his creation to be good. Notice how the refrain "and God saw that it was good" recurs in Genesis 1. But now God declares that an aspect of his creation is *not* good. A humanity without distinction between the sexes is seen as inadequate. The creation of male and female thus produces a complementarity within creation. The Hebrew word translated "suitable" implies a correspondence between male and female. Their complementarity is an inbuilt aspect of creation. Male and female are distinct and are meant to be distinct. Yet both bear the image of God, and both are charged with being stewards of God's creation.

This point is brought out clearly later in this chapter, when Genesis speaks of the male being "united" to the female:

> For this reason a man will leave his father and mother and be united to his wife, and they will become one flesh (2:24).

God created Adam and Eve last and gave them a perfect home— the Garden of Eden. But Satan convinced them to disobey God. And the world changed forever.

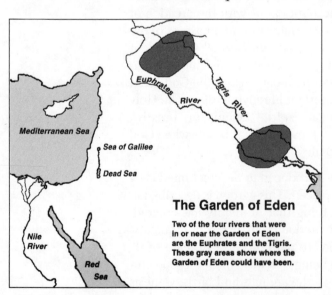

The Garden of Eden

Two of the four rivers that were in or near the Garden of Eden are the Euphrates and the Tigris. These gray areas show where the Garden of Eden could have been.

This passage clearly refers to a committed personal relationship between the male and the female and their union together in emotional and physical love. The passage explicitly uses the Hebrew words for male and female, making it unambiguously clear that sexual differences within humanity are to be seen as a good and God-given thing.

It is often pointed out that there are similarities between the Genesis accounts of creation and some of the other creation stories of the ancient Near East. Yet an important point should be noted here. Genesis 2 presents us with an account of the creation of woman that has no real parallel in any such story.

GENESIS 3:1–24

The Fall

3:1–5 The Serpent Deceives. Having given two complementary accounts of how the world came into being, Genesis now moves on to deal with the origins of sin. How could God's good creation turn into something fallen and sinful, requiring redemption? The answer is provided by Genesis 3, which gives a vivid and powerful account of the rebellion of humanity against its creator. Adam and Eve are treated as representatives of the human race as a whole as they seek to break free from the authority of their creator.

The story of the Fall opens with the man and the woman enjoying close fellowship with God and with one another in the Garden of Eden. It will not last. The figure of the serpent is introduced (3:1), possibly as a symbol either of Satan or of the lure of worldly wisdom and power. Part of the serpent's strategy is to misrepresent God (3:1). Did God *really* say that Adam and Eve were not to eat of the fruit of that special tree? The woman's reply is also interesting. While the serpent calls God's word into question, the woman adds to it (3:3): the command not to touch the tree in the middle of the garden was not part of God's original command.

But the real power of the serpent's approach lies in offering them the tantalizing possibility of being "like God" (3:4). The thought of being immortal and divine has been a constant temptation to humanity throughout its long history. The man and the woman do not want to be told by God what is right and what is wrong. They want to make their own rules. They come to believe that God is trying to keep them in their place by withholding vital information from them. And so they disobey their creator.

3:6–15 Man and Woman Disobey God. Once their disobedience has been discovered, both the man and the woman try to place the blame on someone else. The man blames the woman; the woman blames the serpent (3:12–13). The woman is deceived first, and she subsequently deceives the man. The passage indicates that God places the primary responsibility for the disobedience on the man, rather than the woman. It is not clear how important the order of this deception is. However, the passage is quite clear on one point: both were deceived, and both consented to the deception. It is quite proper to argue that they were deceived in different ways and at different times. Nevertheless, the passage makes it clear that both were deceived.

3:16–20 Relationships With God and Between Man and Woman Are Disrupted. The result of man and woman's disobedience is clear. The relationship between God and humanity is disrupted. The original intimate relationship of trust is destroyed and is replaced by one of hostility and suspicion. Notice also how the original intimate and cooperative relationship between the man and woman is shattered. Mutual recrimination makes its appearance. The command to reproduce remains, yet now childbearing will be a painful matter (3:16). The command to tend God's creation remains, yet this will now be a painful and tedious matter. In both cases, an existing task that is good and part of God's intention for his creation—that is, manual labor (3:19) and the bearing of children—become difficult. Work was originally intended to be something pleasurable and enjoyable. It now becomes a burden.

A new theme, which appears to be a direct result of the Fall, now makes its appearance: the domination of the female by the male. There is no explicit statement anywhere in Genesis 1 or 2 to the effect that woman was intended or created to be subordinate to man. The theme of complementarity dominates the first two chapters of Genesis. But as a result of the Fall, this situation changes drastically:

> To the woman he said,
> "I will greatly increase your pains in childbearing;
>   with pain you will give birth to children.
> Your desire will be for your husband,
>   and he will rule over you" (3:16).

As a result of the Fall, man will "rule over" woman. There are two main ways of understanding this development.

1. *Subordination (that is to say, males "lording it over" or ruling females) is a direct result of the Fall.* As such, it is one aspect of the influence of sin in the world and is to be regarded as something that is not itself God's will for his creation and is thus to be opposed by Christians. The female has become subservient and the male dominant as a consequence of the entry of sin into the world. Thus it is significant that Adam does not name Eve (3:20) until after the Fall, suggesting that the authority over her that this implies did not exist before the Fall.

2. *A particular form of subordination is a direct result of the Fall—namely, subordination based on force or oppression.* According to this view, woman is naturally subordinate to man in some sense of the word; the new

element introduced by the Fall is that this subordination was enforced or imposed by unacceptable means.

The second position has some points in its favor. For example, the Hebrew verb here translated as "rule" has overtones of domination. There are Hebrew words for the right kind of subordination and the wrong kind of subordination. The word used here points to the new element being not the idea of domination itself, but the kind of domination that results. An additional consideration is the context in which this verse is located. We noted above that the Fall made existing obligations (such as work and childbearing) a pain rather than a pleasure. By extension of this analogy, it would seem that the new element introduced by the Fall is that an existing obligation (the subordination of female to male) is made unpleasant through the introduction of the element of force. The kind of domination envisaged would seem to be that between a master and a slave or between a conquering power and a conquered people, where the latter is forcibly obliged to do things they would otherwise not choose to do.

3:21–24 Adam and Eve Banished From the Garden of Eden. Genesis 3 depicts other new things as happening as a direct result of the Fall. For example, as a result of their disobedience, the man and the woman experience shame at their nakedness for the first time (3:7, 10–11). Their naked state was already in existence; the new element is their shame at this state. There is an easy and natural parallel between shame and subordination by which another new element is introduced to an existing situation. Complementarity between male and female becomes polarized into domination by the male and submissiveness by the female. Thus the idea of inferiority of women within the created order cannot be traced back to the Genesis creation accounts, but is explained by the story of the Fall.

It is interesting to notice the strong parallels within Scripture concerning sin and redemption. Through the disobedience of Adam, humanity lost its fellowship with God; through the obedience of Jesus Christ, the possibility of that fellowship was restored. Eve was a disobedient woman; Mary, the mother of Jesus Christ, was obedient to God. Adam's disobedience took place in a garden (Eden); Christ's obedience to God was made evident in another garden (Gethsemane). Adam's tree of life ended up becoming a tree of death; Christ's tree of death (the cross) ended up becoming a tree of life. In all these respects, Christ's work of salvation can be seen as undoing the damage caused by the disobedience in Eden.

The overall emphasis of the passage under discussion is clear. God did not intend his creation to be spoiled by sin. Nor is God in any way the author of sin. Sin arises directly from the abuse of the freedom and responsibility God entrusted to humanity as the height of his creation. The creation rebels against its loving and caring Creator and decides to go its own way—with tragic results. The essence of this original sin is wanting to be like God. It is not long before the consequences of that sin become clear. The first disobedience is soon followed by the first murder.

GENESIS 4:1 – 26

Cain and Abel

4:1–7 The Children of Adam and Eve. The effect of sin is to disrupt the ordering of God's good creation and cause it to begin to fall apart. Genesis 3 documented the introduction of sin, distrust, and domination. Genesis 4 follows on from this by introducing further symptoms of this breakdown within creation. By the end of this chapter, we shall have encountered the introduction of jealousy, the deliberate killing of human beings, and the denial of responsibility for others.

Cain and Abel are the children of Adam and Eve. Cain's sin demonstrates the manner in which the disobedience of Adam and Eve has now become deeply rooted in human nature. It is not clear why God looks with favor on Abel but not on Cain (4:4–5). Both bring offerings to God as an acknowledgment that everything they possess owes its origins to God. Yet for some reason, Cain's offering does not find favor. The real significance of the story lies in Cain's reaction to this development. He was angry (4:5). God affirms his own integrity and justice. If Cain does what is right, he will be accepted; if he refuses to do what is right, he will end up being overcome by sin (4:7). What follows confirms the wisdom of these words.

4:8–16 Cain Murders Abel. Cain begins his deliberate rebellion against God by deceiving Abel (4:8) and then by attempting to deceive God (4:9). The deliberate murder of an innocent man illustrates the devastating effect of sin on humanity. Cain tries to deny any responsibility for the deed: why should he be responsible for his brother? Yet the deed and its motives are known to God, who condemns them in no uncertain terms (4:11–12). Cain recognizes that the penalty due for this sin is death (4:14). However, by intervening to prevent its full and just penalty being carried out, God moves to limit the effects of this sin. Cain loses any right to stand in the presence of God, but he is spared from death (4:15–16).

4:16–24 Cain's Descendants. The catalogue of sin continues in Cain's descendants. Lamech adds polygamy to the list of sins (4:19) and boasts about killing someone who had injured him (4:23–24). He calls this taking of human life vengeance for Cain's disgrace, which can be seen as an act of further defiance against God. Lamech wants to be his own master. By doing so, he furthers the spiral of sin into which humanity has descended.

4:25–26 People Begin to Call on the Lord. A note of hope is injected into this account of sin and violence. "At that time," we are told, people "began to call on the name of the LORD" (4:26). The writer uses here the special personal name for God, "the LORD," which was revealed much later on to Moses (Ex 3:14). Some seem to have realized that there was no hope of salvation in human violence, power, or strength. Salvation means turning to the Lord, and trusting in him.

GENESIS 5:1 – 32

From Adam to Noah

The following section opens with a reaffirmation that men and women are created in the likeness of God and were blessed by him (5:1–2). In many ways, the material in this section can be seen as bridging the period between Adam's disobedience and God's decision to eradicate sin and start all over again. The passage includes a number of points of interest. Some of the persons mentioned (such as Kenan and Jared, 5:12–14, 18–20) are described simply as having lived. Others, such as Enoch, are described as having "walked with God" (5:24). There is a clear distinction being made between simply living at the biological level and living for God. The fact that so few are singled out in this way is an important indicator of the continuing rebellion of humanity against God during this period.

The aspect of this section that attracts most comment, however, is the ages recorded for the individuals. For example, Methuselah is recorded as having lived for 969 years (5:27), which means that he would have died in the year of the Flood, which is described in the following chapter. Scholars are divided as to whether these figures are to be taken literally or whether they are symbolic. There are certainly indications that the figures may have a deeper meaning. For example, Enoch's age of 365 years (5:23) could well be a symbol of fullness or completion, based on the 365 days in a year. However, the figures are of relatively little importance in understanding the significance of this passage, which is concerned to bring out the direct line of continuity between Adam and Noah. The latter is introduced at the end of this section (5:29) and will be the subject of considerable attention for the next few chapters.

GENESIS 6:1 – 8

Human Wickedness

6:1–7 God Is Grieved by Humanity. The account of the Flood opens with a powerful description of human wickedness and sin. Evil has triumphed, corrupting the goodness of God's creation to its very foundations. The meaning of the opening verses (6:1–4) is unclear. One possibility is that the passage refers to the corruption of angelic beings (a possible interpretation of the "sons of God"); another is that it refers to the spread of intermarriage and the breakdown of traditional family structures. But whatever the explanation of these verses, its spiritual meaning is unambiguous: God's creation is in ruins.

The paradox of all this is that human beings were created in the image of God and thus with the freedom and ability to love and respect God. Yet this God-given freedom is abused, as human beings turn against their creator. Both in their acts and in the underlying motivation (6:5), humanity has fallen a willing victim to evil. With remarkable candor, the writer of this section describes God's reaction to this situation: God regrets having created humanity. Painful and distressing though this clearly is to him, God feels that he has to bring his creation to an end (6:7).

6:8 Noah. At the end of this account of human wickedness, a small word intervenes: *but* (6:8). The use of *but* in Scripture can often be dramatic, signaling a new development that opens the way to something that would otherwise be but a dream. And here we find exactly this kind of thing. "But Noah found favor in the sight of God." God's forlorn search for a righteous human being, which will find its climax when he himself provides that righteous person in Jesus Christ, focuses on Noah, who now becomes a sign of hope and redemption.

GENESIS 6:9 – 8:22

The Flood

Many ancient Near Eastern civilizations knew of a flood at the dawn of civilization. What is distinctive about the Genesis account of the Flood is its interpretation. The Flood is God's means of purging sinful humanity from the face of his earth. It is to cleanse his creation from the stain of human evil and sin (6:11–12). Many early Christian writers saw a powerful parallel between the Flood and baptism: just as the Flood cleansed the world of its sin, so baptism symbolizes the cleansing of human sin through the blood of Christ.

6:9–17 Noah Instructed to Build an Ark. Noah is identified as a "righteous man, blameless among the people of his time, and he walked with God" (6:9). It is clear that he is not contaminated by the wickedness and sin of the world. There is an important biblical principle here: the obedience of one righteous person can be the means of the salvation of others. The issue at stake is finding that righteous person—or, if none can be found, providing one. Noah is the means of salvation of the human race. Noah is directed to construct an ark, which is to bear him and his family, along with the male and female of every living creature, to safety. As the account of the Flood progresses, additional points emerge. For example, Noah is ordered to take on board seven of various kinds of creatures (7:2–3), such as those which will be offered as sacrifices in the future. Noah obeys (6:22; 7:5).

6:18–7:10 God's Covenant With Noah. A major theme of importance should not be overlooked here. God promises to establish a covenant with Noah (6:18). Here we encounter a biblical theme that will resonate throughout Scripture and reach its climax in Jesus Christ. A *covenant* is basically a set of promises made by God that require an appropriate response of trust and obedience on the part of those with whom the covenant is established.

7:11–24 The Flood Waters Rise. The Flood comes, as it rains for forty days, (7:17). The phrase "forty days and forty nights" is often found linked in Scripture with events of major importance in relation to God's redemption of humanity—such as the period of Moses' encounter with God (Dt 9:11) and Christ's temptation in the wilderness (Mt 4:1–11). The Flood continues for a further 150 days after the rains end (7:24). Everything and everyone, except the ark and its occupants, is wiped out. (Interestingly, no mention is made of any form of aquatic life; it is clearly assumed that these can and should survive, without the need for special assistance.)

8:1–22 The End of the Flood. As the Flood ends, God "remembers" Noah (8:1). The Hebrew original of this expression conveys far more than just mentally recalling someone or something. It means acting in such a way as to express care and concern. This beautiful phrase sums up God's attitude towards his people. They may forget about God, but he remembers them. Their faithlessness does not cancel his faithfulness. In his wrath, God remembers his covenant with those who remain faithful to him. And so the floods begin to abate, and hope dawns once more. God's judgment has been executed; now the process of reconstruction may begin.

When it is clear that the floods have receded, God commands Noah and the entire company of occupants of the ark to come out. They are told to go and multiply on the earth—a renewal of the creation commandment (1:22). The theme of the renewal of creation emerges as important at this point. There are to be no more floods (8:21–22). If sin emerges once more as a threat to his creation, God will deal with it in another manner.

GENESIS 9:1 – 29 ─────────────────────

God's Covenant With Noah

9:1–17 The Covenant and Its Sign. The covenant that God had promised to establish with Noah is now formally pledged. (As becomes clear later, the covenant is actually made with all life on the earth [9:17], and not just with Noah and his family.) God commands Noah and his sons to increase and fill the earth (9:1, 7). Everything is to be entrusted to the faithful remnant of humanity (9:3). The sacredness of human life is affirmed (9:5–6). Then the covenant is proclaimed: never again will there be a flood that will destroy the earth. As a sign of this covenant, God set his rainbow in the clouds

(9:13). The idea of a covenant sign is of major importance; it brings to mind God's compassion for his people, his promises towards them, and the obligations the covenant places on them.

9:18–29 Noah's Sin. It might be thought that the account of Noah could end happily at this point. Noah has been established as a righteous and obedient human being through whose righteousness a faithful remnant was preserved. Yet human weakness begins to become apparent almost immediately. Noah plants a vineyard and becomes drunk on the wine it produces (9:20–21). In this story, the potential weakness of human nature to sin is powerfully exposed. What will happen when other forms of temptation come the way of Noah and his descendants? Even as the account of Noah's triumph reaches its conclusion, we are being forewarned that sin continues to crouch at the door (Ge 4:7), awaiting opportunities to master those who foolishly believe that they can master sin.

GENESIS 10:1 – 32

From Noah to Babel

The command to Noah and his descendants was simple: "Go forth and multiply." The following section of Genesis provides details of how that command was fulfilled. The precise details of the descendants of Noah are not of vital importance to an understanding of the central themes of Genesis. A detailed examination of the information provided indicates that the descendants of Noah spread out over a wide geographical area, probably embracing the eastern Mediterranean region and extending as far east as the Persian Gulf and the Caspian Sea.

GENESIS 11:1 – 32

The Tower of Babel

11:1–5 A City and Tower Are Built. The repopulation of the world leads to a renewed confidence on the part of humanity. They all speak the same language and are able to collaborate on various ventures. Sin begins to express itself in their actions. Once more, the same basic human instincts emerge. There is a desire to become famous, to achieve immortality, and to gain total security (11:4). And these aspirations lead to the building of a city on the plain of Shinar (a term used to refer to what was later known as Babylonia). There is a pun here between the Hebrew word for Babylon (*Babel*) and the Hebrew word for "to confuse," which sound like each other. The tower in question would probably have taken the form of a ziggurat, typical of the region, consisting of a square base with a series of stepped layers built on top. It was a symbol of defiance. Here was what humanity could do without God! We can even reach heaven by ourselves!

11:6–9 God Confuses Their Language and Scatters the People. Once more, sin threatens to frustrate God's purposes for his creation. The tower is a potent symbol of human pride and rebellion against God. Yet God has promised never to destroy the world again. To check the power of sin, God scatters the people, and confuses their languages. The collective power of sin is reduced by the simple expedient of limiting the sinful human ability to collude together:

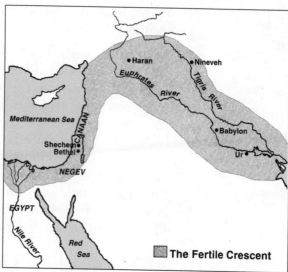

> Let us go down and confuse their language (11:7).

The "royal we" of this phrase is an expression of authority and dominion in the face of this human attempt at rebellion against God and of a refusal to accept the limitations placed on humanity in the created order.

11:10–32 From Shem to Abram. After the Babel episode, we are taken back to consider the further descendants of Noah through his son Shem. The importance of this account lies primarily in the fact that it introduces us to a man named Abram, who had settled in the town of Haran about 400 kilometers west of Nineveh. Abram was married to Sarai (later to be renamed Sarah, Ge 17:15), who was barren (11:27–30). With these spare details, we are introduced to the first patriarch, later to be renamed Abraham (Ge 17:5), who is a central figure in the history of Israel. (The term *patriarch* is used to refer to Abram, Isaac, and Jacob, who are seen as being the great forefathers of the people of Israel.)

Abraham was called by God to take his family from Ur, near the Persian Gulf, to Canaan to establish "a great nation." They traveled more than a thousand miles, first to Haran and finally to Shechem. Abraham built an altar to the Lord in the area of Bethel.

GENESIS 12:1–20

The Call of Abram

12:1–9 Abram Called to Go to Canaan. Without any reason being given, Abram is called to leave Haran and go to Canaan. The call of Abram is linked to a promise: that God will make him into a great nation through whom all the nations on earth will be blessed (12:2–3). Although no explanation of this call was given, Abram clearly feels that he can and should trust and obey this call. So he and his extended household set out for the land of Canaan (12:4–5).

They eventually arrive at Shechem, an important site in the central region of Canaan. At this time, Canaan was the center of various pagan religious cults. Yet Abram does not worship any of the local gods. Instead, in response to the LORD's promise that the region will belong to his descendants, he builds an altar to the Lord in the region of Bethel and calls on his name (12:8).

12:10–20 Abram in Egypt. Abram does not settle in the region of Canaan. He continues his wanderings, moving further south and west as he passes through the Negev into Egypt. (Although a famine had settled over Canaan, Egypt continued to enjoy fertility on account of the annual flooding of the River Nile, which ensured fertile and moist land in the neighborhood of its banks.) On account of local customs which are not entirely clear, Abram asks his wife to pose as his sister. The Egyptian monarch, invariably referred to by the royal title of Pharaoh (literally meaning "a great house"), is attracted to Sarai and treats Abram kindly as a result (12:14–16). On discovering that Sarai is actually Abram's wife, Pharaoh expels the entire household from Egypt (12:20) on their way back to Canaan.

GENESIS 13:1 – 14:24

The Further History of Abram

13:1–18 Abram and Lot Separate. By the time Abram leaves Egypt, he has become quite wealthy. This is especially evident from the references to his large holdings of livestock (13:2). The large number of animals involved leads to friction with his colleague Lot over grazing rights. Lot was introduced earlier in the narrative and identified as the son of Haran, one of Abram's brothers (Ge 11:27). Lot and Abram were thus relatives ("brothers" in the biblical sense of the term, 13:8). Perhaps it was inevitable that they should go their separate ways. In any case, Lot chooses to settle near the cities of the plain, already noted for their sinful behavior (13:10–13).

Bedouin tents in the Judean desert today are similar to those used by Abraham on his trip from Ur to Canaan.

However, Abram, receiving a fresh assurance from the Lord that the land about him will be his inheritance, pitches his tents in the area. Once more, Abram responds by building an altar to the Lord, this time at Hebron (13:18).

14:1–24 Abram Rescues Lot. Whereas God reassures Abram, Lot finds himself in difficulty. A series of shifting alliances among local kings leads to a major confrontation in the region in which he has settled (14:1–11). In the course of their abortive military action against neighboring kings, Sodom and Gomorrah and their allies are defeated and their goods seized and carried off. Lot, living in Sodom at this time (14:12), is also taken captive. Learning of the capture of his kinsman, Abram sets off in pursuit with 318 men and manages to defeat Lot's captors and release him (14:13–16).

Abraham built an altar to the Lord at Hebron. He went with his armed servants to rescue Lot, his nephew, who lived in Sodom and had been captured by neighboring kings.

Abram's victory attracts considerable attention, most notably from Melchizedek, probably a Canaanite king-priest (14:18–20). Melchizedek probably intended his "God most high" to refer to a local Canaanite deity. Abram, however, takes it as a reference to the Lord (14:22) and refuses to do anything that might have placed him under an obligation to anyone else.

GENESIS 15:1 – 17:27

God's Covenant With Abram

15:1–21 The Covenant. Abram's act of obedience is immediately followed by God's establishing a covenant with him and his descendants that goes beyond that established earlier with Noah. Abram is still childless and has designated his servant Eliezer (15:2) as his legal heir. God, however, promises that Abram will have a son and that this son will be his heir (15:4). In one of the most poignant moments in this book, God leads Abram outside his tent and asks him to contemplate the starry heavens. Abram's descendants, he promises, will be as numerous as those stars (15:5). Abram trusts God and puts his faith in this astonishing promise (15:6). Faith is thus seen as the natural and proper response to God's promises and counts as righteousness in the sight of God.

The promise of a son is followed by the reassurance that Abram will possess the land about him (15:7). Abram asks for reassurance on this point (15:8) and is granted a vision of the future of his people, including the coming exile in Egypt (15:9–16). God then marks the covenant in a variety of ways which, though perhaps strange to modern readers, would have been recognized at the time as involving the most solemn and binding oaths. God's covenant with Abram is for real (15:18) and may be totally relied upon. The covenant will be confirmed and amplified presently. The narrative now switches to the women in Abram's life.

16:1–16 Hagar and Ishmael. Sarai continues to be childless (16:1). Following an ancient Near Eastern custom, she suggests to Abram that he ought to sleep with Hagar, a maidservant whom they may have acquired during their period in Egypt. Abram concurs, and Hagar becomes pregnant (16:2–4). A certain degree of personal hostility now develops between Hagar and Sarai, with the result that Hagar leaves home. However, God speaks to her in a vision, reassuring her of her future. Her son is to be called Ishmael (16:11) and will be the fulfillment of God's promise to Abram. Yet, as becomes clear in the following chapter, God has intentions for Sarai as well.

17:1–27 The Covenant of Circumcision. The next major section introduces the next stage of the covenant between God and Abram. The first stage of this covenant involved the promise of land. Now, God affirms that he will be the God of both Abram and his descendants (17:7). As a token of this new relationship, Abram's name is formally changed to Abraham (17:5), just as Sarai is now to be known as Sarah (17:15). Both Abraham and Sarah will be blessed by God; and despite their advanced years, they will have a son, who is to be called Isaac (17:15–20). God's covenant with Abraham's successors will be through Isaac, not Ishmael (17:19–21). This clear statement that Ishmael is not the child of the promise is, however, tempered by God's evident kindness and mercy towards both Hagar and Ishmael.

The covenant that God now makes with Abraham and Sarah is conditional. Its privileges and benefits are linked with certain obligations that must be observed if the covenant is to remain in force. Its central feature is circumcision, which is the external sign of this covenant (17:9–14). Circumcision (which is basically the removal of the foreskin of the penis) is to be restricted to male children and is regarded as an essential sign of being a member of the covenant people of God. Abraham is obedient to this demand and arranges for himself, his son Ishmael, and all the males within his household to be circumcised as a sign of their new relationship with God (17:23–27).

GENESIS 18:1 – 19:38

Sodom and Gomorrah

18:1–15 The Three Visitors. The next section opens with an account of a visit to Abraham by the Lord, in the form of three visitors who turn out to be the Lord and two angels. (The visit is seen by many commentators as an early hint at the Christian doctrine of the Trinity.) Although he has no idea who they are, Abraham looks after his visitors with traditional Near Eastern courtesy, ensuring that their feet are washed and that they are provided with food and drink. The purpose of the visit is to reassure Abraham that his wife Sarah will indeed have a son. Sarah, who knows that both she and her husband are getting old, finds this amusing. But the Lord is adamant: "Is anything too hard for the LORD?" (18:14).

18:16–33 Abraham Pleads for Sodom. As the visitors prepare to leave, they look down on the city of Sodom, notorious for its sinfulness (18:16–22). It is clear that the city is marked for destruction. However, as a matter of justice, two of the three visitors will go on to the city to find out for themselves whether things really are that bad. In the dialogue between Abraham and the Lord which follows (18:23–33), the theme of the preservation of the righteous emerges as being of major importance. The Lord will spare a people for the sake of the righteous remnant within it. Abraham is convinced that God, the judge of all the earth, is righteous (18:25) and finds this confirmed in God's repeated affirmation that the presence of a small number of righteous people, even in a city as notoriously sinful as Sodom, will ensure its preservation.

19:1–29 Sodom and Gomorrah Destroyed. The narrative then moves to Sodom itself. Abraham's kinsman Lot is sitting in the gate of the city when the angels arrive. This suggests that he was a figure of some importance within the city, because the city gate was the traditional location for the dispensing of justice and handling of local issues. Lot takes them to his house and offers them the same traditional hospitality as had earlier been shown by Abraham (19:2–3). The visitors then find that their fears about Sodom are confirmed, for they nearly become the victims of homosexual rape (19:4–11). What follows brings out clearly the LORD's concern for the safety of the righteous. Lot and his family are bundled out of Sodom to escape its destruction and find safety in the nearby town of Zoar (19:20–22), which is spared on account of their presence. The story of Lot's wife looking back seems to have become proverbial and is even referred to by Jesus (Lk 17:32).

19:30–38 Lot's Daughters. It soon becomes clear that Lot and his relatives are as weak and fallible as anyone else. The story of how Lot's daughters seduced their father on two successive nights (19:30–38) in order to ensure the continuation of the family line is a forceful reminder of the continuing presence of sin in the world and the temptations to which God's people are prone.

GENESIS 20:1 – 25:11

The Later Life and Death of Abraham

20:1–34 Isaac Is Born. The following section of Genesis focuses on the later period of Abraham's life. The account of Abraham's meeting with Abimelech (20:1–17, and further developed at 21:22–32) is followed by a brief account of the fulfillment of God's promise to Abraham and Sarah: Isaac is born (21:1–7). In response to God's faithfulness, Abraham circumcises his son. Just as God has been faithful to his covenant, so Abraham honors his side of that same covenant. The birth of Isaac leads to growing alienation between Sarah and Hagar, with the result that Hagar and her son Ishmael leave Abraham's home (21:8–21). Yet despite Sarah's hostility towards them, they continue to be watched over and cared for by God.

22:1–24 Abraham Tested. After the birth of Isaac, Abraham's commitment to God is put to the test in one of the most famous incidents in the Old Testament. God requires Abraham to take his son Isaac and sacrifice him as an act of obedience. Earlier, Abraham had declared his faith that the judge of all the earth would do right; this faith is now put to the test. The story is powerful, moving, and disturbing, with strong parallels to the final days of Christ's life. For example, Isaac carries the wood for his own burnt offering (22:6), just as Christ carried his own cross to the place of crucifixion. Abraham is about to sacrifice his son, when he is prevented from doing so. His trust in and obedience to God are now beyond doubt. As Abraham looks around, he notices a ram caught in some thorns (22:13). This ram is then offered as a sacrifice to God in place of Isaac. Christians can hardly read this passage without being reminded of the way in which Jesus Christ as the Lamb of God was crowned with thorns and offered himself as a sacrifice to God in the place of sinful humanity (Mk 15:17; Jn 1:29). As a result of Abraham's obedience, God confirms his promises to him. Abraham's descendants will be as numerous as the stars of the sky and the grains of sand on the seashore (22:17). The news of the birth of sons to Abraham's brother Nahor (22:20–23) can be seen as the beginning of the fulfillment of this promise.

23:1–20 The Death of Sarah. Sarah and Abraham are now both very old. Sarah dies in the region of Canaan occupied by Hittites at the time. Abraham, who as a "stranger and alien" has no land rights, buys some land from the Hittites as a burial site for his wife. Sarah is finally laid to rest in a cave in a field in Canaan.

24:1–25:11 Isaac and Rebekah; Abraham's Death. Aware that his own death cannot be far away, Abraham begins to make arrangements for his son Isaac to take a wife. He dispatches the chief servant in his household (possibly Eliezer of Damascus, who had been considered as his heir prior to the birth of Isaac) to find a suitable woman. Although they currently live in Canaan, Abraham does not want Isaac to marry a Canaanite woman with all the dangers of syncretism that would imply. He wishes him to marry someone from his own home region, so he sends his servant to this region (24:1–11).

While preparing to water his camels outside the town of Nahor, the servant meets Rebekah (24:15), who has come to draw water for her family. Convinced that this is the right person, the servant arranges for himself to be introduced to her family (which includes her brother Laban), identifies himself as Abraham's servant, and explains why he believes God has guided him in this matter (24:12–49). Both Rebekah and her family are persuaded. Rebekah and her maids prepare for the long journey to Canaan with Abraham's servant. Finally, Isaac and Rebekah are married (24:50–66). Shortly afterwards, Abraham himself dies and is buried with Sarah at the cave near Hebron (25:1–11). The era of the first patriarch has ended.

GENESIS 25:12 – 28:9 ────────────────

Isaac and His Sons

25:12–34 Ishmael's Sons and Isaac's Sons, Jacob and Esau. After listing the sons of Ishmael (25:12–18), the following section focuses on the history of Isaac. Initially, Rebekah is barren; but after Isaac prays for her, she conceives and gives birth to twin boys. The first to be born is Esau, so called on account of his hairy appearance; the second is called Jacob, because he emerges from the womb clinging to his brother's heel. As the first to be born, Esau gains the privilege of the birthright—the right to inherit Isaac's property on his death. However, he evidently regards this as of little importance, for, in a moment of hunger, he gives it to Jacob in exchange for a bowl of red lentil stew (25:31–34).

26:1–33 God Renews His Covenant With Isaac. During a famine in the following years, the Lord renews his covenant with Isaac (26:1–6), confirming that the same promises made to Abraham were now extended to Isaac. The promise is confirmed once more soon afterwards (26:24), when Isaac settles in the Valley of Gerar.

26:34–27:40 Jacob Gets Isaac's Blessing. Relations between Esau and his parents deteriorate. At the age of 40, he marries two Hittite women (26:34); a third wife is mentioned later (28:9). This action is the source of much concern to Isaac and Rebekah; later, they would try to prevent Jacob from marrying a Hittite or Canaanite woman, insisting that he marry someone from their own home region (27:46–28:2). Nevertheless, Esau is the firstborn and thus has certain rights, including the right to receive his father's blessing. As Isaac's sight begins to fail him, he feels the need to bless Esau. Rebekah, however, is disgusted with Esau and decides that Jacob will seize this privilege. By disguising Jacob in such a way as to be taken for Esau, Isaac is deceived and blesses Jacob (27:5–29). On Esau's return from hunting, the deception is uncovered. Relations between the two brothers become severely strained (27:30–46).

27:41–28:9 Jacob Flees to Laban. Relations between Isaac and Jacob also deteriorate. Perhaps partly with a view to getting him away from home for a while, Isaac sends Jacob off to Rebekah's home region of Paddan Aram with instructions to find a wife from among the daughters of Rebekah's brother Laban (28:1–5). Rebekah has already advised him to go and stay with her brother to avoid Esau until his anger towards his younger brother has subsided (27:42–45). Her advice is to stay for a while until things calm down. In fact, Jacob stays there for twenty years (seven years for Leah, seven for Rachel, and six for livestock). The narrative now focuses on Jacob, who emerges as a major figure in his own right.

GENESIS 28:10 – 36:40

Jacob

Jacob's son Isaac tricked his father into giving him the blessing that rightfully belonged to the firstborn son, Esau. When Esau found out, he said he would kill Isaac. Jacob sent Isaac to relatives in Paddan Aram, telling him to find a wife there. Isaac did, but was himself tricked and returned with two wives.

28:10–22 Jacob's Dream at Bethel. So Jacob sets out for Haran, Abraham's hometown. During the course of this journey, he pauses at a place hitherto known as Luz, but which would from then on be known as Bethel. While sleeping, Jacob dreams of a stairway (not a runged wooden ladder as is sometimes suggested, but probably a brick staircase) on which angels are ascending and descending. In the course of this dream, the Lord extends the covenant he made with Abraham and Isaac to Jacob, promising him land and descendants (28:10–22). Despite all his deceptions, God is prepared to bless Jacob. Thus assured of the LORD's blessing, Jacob continues on his journey to Haran.

29:1–25 Jacob in Paddan Aram. On arriving in the region, Jacob asks if anyone knows Laban. Laban is clearly well known in the region. However, the first member of Laban's family that Jacob meets is the younger and more beautiful of Laban's two daughters, Rachel (29:1–12). After being welcomed into Laban's household, Jacob begins to work to earn his keep. When Laban asks him how much wages he would like, Jacob replies that he would like Rachel's hand in marriage in return for seven years work (29:18). Laban consents, but clearly has other plans. On the night of Jacob's wedding feast, Laban gives him his older daughter Leah in place of Rachel. Perhaps it was very dark, and perhaps large quantities of wine flowed at the wedding feast. At any rate, Jacob does not notice the substitution. He sleeps with Leah and only discovers the deception in the morning (29:25). There is a subtle irony here: having left a trail of deception behind him in Canaan, Jacob himself is now well and truly deceived. As later events concerning the possession of flocks (30:25–43) make clear, both Laban and Jacob will continue to try to deceive each other.

29:26–30:24 Jacob Marries Rachel and Has Children. Laban informs Jacob that he can have Rachel in return for a further seven years of work. The text makes it clear (29:28–30) that Jacob is not required to wait a further seven years before being given Rachel; he is allowed to sleep with her immediately in return for a promise of seven years of further work. The fact that Jacob has two wives simultaneously is not regarded as unusual or unacceptable. It is only when God establishes his covenant with Moses at Sinai that monogamy becomes the norm for his people. Through Leah, Jacob has a series of sons; Rachel, however, is barren. By sleeping with Rachel's maidservant (and later with Leah's, when Leah becomes too old to bear children), Jacob fathers several more sons (30:1–21). Then finally, Rachel conceives and bears a son. His name is Joseph (30:24).

30:25–31:21 Jacob Flees From Laban. After an incident involving mutual deception over flocks (30:25–43), tensions develop between Jacob and Laban and his family. Jacob is obliged to flee from Laban, taking his wives, children and livestock with him (31:1–55). They will return to Isaac. By failing to tell him of his intentions (31:20), Jacob continues to deceive Laban. Interestingly, without Jacob's knowledge, Rachel takes Laban's household gods with her (31:19), possibly reflecting her continuing pagan beliefs or a belief that the possession of these items would deter Laban from taking lethal action against them.

31:22–55 Laban Pursues Jacob. Laban, angry that his daughters and grandchildren have been taken away from him without his knowledge or permission, pursues Jacob and his party and eventually catches up with them. Yet Laban, despite being a pagan, has a dream in which God tells him not to harm Jacob (31:24). However, he is angry over the theft of his household gods and demands to have them returned. Jacob, ignorant of Rachel's theft, suggests that they search for them. Rachel, who has concealed the gods in her camel's saddle, tells Laban that she cannot move on account of her period. As a result, the gods remain undetected. After some explanation on the part of Jacob, he and Laban agree to patch up their differences. Jacob swears that he will take care of Rachel, Leah, and their children, and that he will have no more wives. They part reconciled, Laban to return home and Jacob to visit his brother Esau, who had settled in the region of Edom.

32:1–33:20 Jacob Prepares to Meet Esau. Jacob sends messengers to Esau to let him know of their arrival; the messengers duly report back that Esau is on his way to meet them with 400 men. Fearing the worst, Jacob divides his party into two groups, hoping that one might survive any ensuing attack (32:1–21). As he waits to meet Esau, Jacob has a night meeting with an angel at Peniel (32:22–32). For the first time, the name *Israel* is used to refer to Jacob and ultimately to his descendants. The angel refuses to disclose his own name. (Only at Sinai will God allow his name to be known to Moses; at this stage, Israel is not ready to learn more of the Lord who has called her into being.) Finally, Jacob and Esau meet (33:1–20). They have not seen each other for twenty years and had parted on very hostile terms. Esau, however, is overjoyed to see his brother (33:4). When they part once more, it is as friends.

34:1–35:15 Jacob Returns to Bethel. Trouble now arises on a different front. Dinah, Jacob's daughter by Leah, is raped by Shechem, a local ruler. Jacob and his family are outraged. Two of Jacob's sons suggest that if Shechem and his people agree to be circumcised (a very painful process), they will allow Dinah to marry him, and they will settle in the region. However, while the men are recovering from the pain of their circumcision and incapable of resistance, Simeon and Levi put them to the sword and plunder their possessions (34:1–29). Jacob is appalled, both at the deception and its possible implications. It will no longer be safe for them to live in the region. So they begin the move to Bethel, scene of Jacob's earlier dream, at which the Lord once more reaffirms his commitment to Jacob and his descendants (34:30–35:15).

35:16–36:43 The Deaths of Rachel and Isaac. At this stage, Jacob has eleven sons: six by Leah, two by Rachel's maidservant Bilhah, two by Leah's maidservant Zilpah, and one—Joseph—by Rachel (for the details, see 35:23–26). In the final stages of their journey to the city of Ephrath (also known as Bethlehem), Rachel dies while giving birth to another son, whom Jacob names Benjamin (35:16–18). Rachel is buried near Bethlehem. Jacob returns to the home of his father Isaac near Hebron (35:27–29). Finally, Isaac himself dies and is buried in the family tomb in the field near Machpelah (see 49:29–32). After listing the various descendants of Esau and the rulers of the land of Edom in which Esau resided (36:1–43), the narrative now shifts decisively to focus on one of Jacob's twelve sons: Joseph.

GENESIS 37:1 – 50:26

Joseph

37:1–38:30 Joseph Sold by His Brothers. Joseph was Jacob's son by Rachel, whom Jacob had loved. As a result, Jacob seems to have been especially fond of this son, to the intense irritation of his other sons (37:1–4). Joseph himself does little to help his brothers to like him. His dreams, which suggest that they are inferior to him, merely anger them further (37:5–11). Eventually, when they can bear him no longer, they sell him to a group of passing Midianite traders. Having dipped Joseph's richly ornamented coat in goat's blood, they bring it to Jacob, who concludes that his son has been killed by a wild animal (37:12–35). In fact, Joseph has been sold into slavery in Egypt (37:36). (At this point, the narrative about Joseph is interrupted to give an account of the marriage of Jacob's son Judah to a Canaanite woman and his subsequent involvement with his daughter-in-law Tamar: 38:1–30.)

39:1–23 Joseph and Potiphar's Wife. When the story of Joseph resumes, Joseph is a slave in the household of Potiphar, one of Pharaoh's senior officials. God grants Joseph success in his responsibilities with the result that he gains advancement within the house (39:1–6). However, his attractive features soon get him into trouble with Potiphar's wife, who, failing to seduce him, accuses him of attempted rape (39:7–18). As a result, Joseph is thrown into prison. Yet God remains with him, even in this seemingly hopeless situation (39:20–23).

This pyramid at Giza in Egypt was built as a tomb for a pharaoh, as the early rulers of Egypt were called. The Sphinx, a lion with a human head, represented the pharaoh. These huge monuments were built long before Joseph arrived in Egypt.

40:1–23 The Cupbearer and the Baker. Joseph is soon joined in prison by two men from Pharaoh's household, a cupbearer and a baker. Each has dreams, which they are unable to interpret. Joseph interprets the former's dream as a prophecy of restoration and the latter's as a prophecy of condemnation. He asks the cupbearer to remember him when he is restored to his post. In due course, the cupbearer is restored to Pharaoh's favor, and the baker is executed. Yet the cupbearer fails to remember Joseph, who continues to languish in prison, forgotten by all except God.

41:1–57 Pharaoh's Dreams; Joseph in Charge of Egypt. Now Pharaoh himself begins to dream and finds that there is no one who can give a satisfactory interpretation of his dreams. Finally, the cupbearer remembers Joseph, who is summoned from prison and proves able to interpret the dreams. There will be seven years of rich harvest, followed by seven years of famine. All this has been foretold by God, who has decided that this will take place. Convinced that God has singled out Joseph for this task, Pharaoh places him in charge of Egypt's preparations for the forthcoming famine. As a result, while other nations around languish under a severe famine, Egypt suffers no shortage of food.

42:1–38 Joseph's Brothers Go to Egypt. The famine seems to have been especially severe in Canaan, and Jacob and his household are affected. Eventually, hearing that there is grain in Egypt, Jacob sends all his sons except Benjamin, Rachel's second son, to buy grain there. On their arrival in Egypt, Joseph recognizes them, accuses them of spying, and throws them in prison (42:1–17). After three days, he sets them free on condition that they return with their youngest brother, Benjamin. However, Jacob refuses to allow Benjamin to travel to Egypt. It is too dangerous. He has already lost one of Rachel's two sons, and he has no desire to lose the other as well (42:18–38).

43:1–44:34 The Second Journey to Egypt; the Silver Cup. The famine persists, and Jacob and his household become dangerously short of food. Finally, the decision is taken; they will have to return to Egypt for more food. This time, Benjamin will have to travel with them (43:1–25). On their arrival, Joseph sees his brother Benjamin for the first time in many years and is deeply moved (43:29–31). However, as they prepare to return to Canaan, Joseph plants his own special cup in Benjamin's sack of food. As they are leaving, Joseph accuses one of them of stealing his cup. He demands that their sacks be searched. When it is found in Benjamin's sack, the brothers return to Joseph and offer themselves to him as his slaves. They implore him not to take Benjamin away from them. Their father had two sons by his wife; he has lost one of them and could not bear to lose the second (44:1–34).

45:1–47:27 Jacob Goes to Egypt. Joseph then reveals his identity to the astonished brothers and embraces them (45:1–15). He tells them of how God has blessed him. Pharaoh, fascinated by these developments, orders transport to be made available so that Jacob and his household can be moved to Egypt and allowed to settle in the land

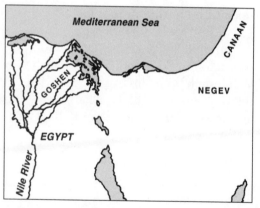

A famine in Canaan forced Jacob and his family to go to Egypt, where Joseph, the son Jacob thought was dead, was in charge of the food supplies.

as welcome and honored guests (45:16–24). The brothers return to Canaan and tell their overjoyed father that Joseph is not merely alive, but he is now ruler of all Egypt (45:25–28). So Jacob and his entire family move down to Egypt and are settled, with Pharaoh's blessing, in one of the richest parts of Goshen (46:1–47:12). Even though the famine continues in Egypt, Joseph ensures that seed grain is available to all, including the Israelites (47:13–27).

47:28–48:22 Manasseh and Ephraim. Jacob is by now very old. Knowing he must die soon, he asks to be buried in the family tomb in Canaan (47:28–31). He tells Joseph and his two sons of how God had established a covenant with him. After blessing Joseph's two sons, Manasseh and Ephraim, Jacob tells Joseph that God will one day take him back to the land of his fathers (48:1–22). God has given Canaan to his descendants. Yet Joseph will die in Egypt. The story of how the people of Israel returned to Canaan has only begun.

49:1–50:21 Jacob Blesses His Sons and Dies. Finally, Jacob blesses each of his twelve sons individually and the tribes which will bear their names (49:1–28). He repeats his request to be buried in the family grave in the field of Machpelah in Canaan beside Abraham, Sarah, Isaac, Rebekah, and Leah. (Rachel, it will be remembered, was buried near Bethlehem.) After these words, Jacob dies (49:33). Joseph ensures that his father's dying wishes are honored and accompanies the entire family as they return to Canaan to bury him. Afterwards, they go back to Egypt to remain there permanently (50:1–21).

50:22–26 The Death of Joseph. Jacob's dying words had included reference to Canaan as the Promised Land, which one day his offspring would inherit. In the same way, as Joseph himself is dying, he speaks of a day when God will take his people out of Egypt into the land that he had promised to Abraham, Isaac, and Jacob. Joseph asks that, when this great day comes, his remains be buried in that land. Genesis ends by recording the death of Joseph and his burial in Egypt.

And so the reader is left wondering: Will the people of Israel ever return to the Promised Land? Or will they remain permanently in Egypt? Will Joseph's remains ever be reburied in Canaan? Will God remain faithful to his promises to Abraham, Isaac, and Jacob? Exactly these questions are answered in the next book of the Old Testament, to which we now turn.

EXODUS

The word *exodus* literally means "departure" or "leaving," and focuses on the way the people of Israel were delivered by God from captivity in Egypt. Genesis closed with an account of the burial of Joseph and his hope that he would one day be buried in the land God had promised to Abraham, Isaac, and Jacob. Exodus takes up the story and sets the scene for Israel's return to Canaan to enter into this Promised Land.

EXODUS 1:1 – 22

Introduction

Exodus opens by describing how the Israelites (as the descendants of Jacob are now known) have flourished in the period after Joseph's death. God's promise to the patriarchs of many descendants is more than abundantly fulfilled, to the alarm of the native Egyptians. Increasingly, the Israelites come to be seen as a threat. The memory of Joseph and his work in Egypt seems to have been forgotten during the period of roughly two hundred years which separates the death of Joseph and the events which will be described in this book.

Finally, a "new king who did not know about Joseph" (1:8) comes to power. The pharaoh in question is often thought to be Ahmose, who is known to have been hostile to Semites. (The term *Semites*, which derives from Shem, is often used to refer to peoples of the region of Palestine, and especially to the Israelites.) Alarmed at the growing power of the Israelites, Pharaoh sets about limiting their numbers and influence. In the first place, the Israelites are forced into slavery (1:11–14); in the second, he attempts to have every male Israelite child killed at birth (1:15–22). Yet the strategy fails; the midwives, fearing God, will not carry out his wishes.

EXODUS 2:1 – 2

The Birth of Moses

In the midst of this attempt to eliminate all Israelite male children, a boy is born to a Levite family. Under Pharaoh's edict, he must be drowned in the

Moses, after killing an Egyptian, fled from Egypt to Midian, north of the Red Sea. There he married and settled down for years, until God called him.

river Nile. Unable to bear this thought, his mother places him in a basket among the reeds by the bank of the river. (The word used for *basket* is the same as that used at Genesis 6:14 to refer to Noah's ark, which was also a means of deliverance from death by drowning.) By the grace of God, the future deliverer of Israel is saved from death by a member of Pharaoh's own household—Pharaoh's daughter.

The princess recognizes that the child is Israelite. She uses the distinctive term *Hebrew* (2:6) to refer to the Israelites. The child's sister, who we later learn is called Miriam, offers to find someone from among the "Hebrew women" to nurse the child for the princess. Astutely, she finds her mother and thus achieves reunion of mother and son. When the child is older, he is adopted into Pharaoh's household, and given the name Moses.

As the story moves on (2:11–24), Moses is now grown, probably having reached the age of forty. Although raised in Pharaoh's household, he has not forgotten his own people. After accidentally killing an Egyptian who was abusing an Israelite, Moses is forced to flee from Egypt (2:15). He settles in the region of Midian, a desolate area to the east of the Gulf of Aqabah, several hundred kilometers from Egypt. There he marries a local woman, the daughter of Jethro, a Midianite priest, and settles down in that region with his family for many years.

Back in Egypt, the oppression of Israel continues (2:23–25). Yet God has not forgotten his people. The great theme of the covenant between God and Abraham, Isaac, and Jacob begins to make its appearance. God's promise to his people remains open. But how can it be realized? What can be done? The following chapter begins to set the scene for the great act of deliverance that will soon take place.

EXODUS 3:1 – 6:30

The Calling of Moses

3:1–22 Moses and the Burning Bush. Moses is tending the flocks of Jethro in the land of Midian when God calls him by name. In what follows (3:5–10), God reaffirms his commitment to the covenant he made with Abraham, Isaac, and Jacob, and his determination to deliver them from slavery in Egypt. He will lead them into "a land flowing with milk and honey" (3:8). And he has chosen Moses to go to Pharaoh and to bring Israel out of Egypt.

Moses is hesitant about this commission. Why him? And what will the Israelites say when he tries to enlist their support? God reassures him. Moses is to call God by name: "I AM WHO I AM" (3:14). This is not a name that Moses has chosen for God. It is the name by which God wishes to be known by his people. In the Old Testament, to name someone is to have or to claim authority over them. Just as nobody has authority over God, so nobody has the right to name God. God chooses to reveal his name. He is "the LORD" (3:15). The Hebrew word *Yahweh*, sometimes referred to as the *tetragrammaton* (the four letters YHWH, sometimes written Yahweh, and often written incorrectly as *Jehovah* in older English translations), is also a personal name for God. The name must not be confused with the general title *Lord*, which merely refers to the authority of God. "The LORD" is a special personal name for God by which he is to be known and addressed in worship and prayer. To avoid confusion, the NIV prints this name in capital letters, like this: LORD. God also affirms that he is the same God who was worshiped and obeyed by Abraham, Isaac, and Jacob. His promises to these great patriarchs still stand. He is thus the "God of Abraham, Isaac and Jacob" (3:16).

Moses is then commanded to return to Egypt, summon the elders (literally, the "old men"—in the Old Testament, wisdom and age are often regarded as closely linked) of Israel, and tell them of what has happened. Their moment of deliverance is not far away. Israel will be liberated from her bondage (3:18–22).

4:1–17 Signs for Moses. Moses, however, still hesitates. He can foresee his authority being challenged (4:1–9). He lacks confidence in his ability to speak well (4:10–12). He doesn't want to do it anyway (4:13–17). But God is adamant. Moses is the man of his choice. If he is worried about his ability to speak, he will use Aaron, Moses' brother, as a mouthpiece (see Ex 4:27–31). But Moses is to be the deliverer of his people Israel. He must get on with the task at hand.

4:18–5:23 Moses Returns to Egypt. So Moses obtains Jethro's permission to take his family back to Egypt (4:18–23). Yet, although Moses now clearly stands within the covenant between God and Abraham, he has not yet fulfilled one of its central demands: circumcision of his son (Ge 17:9–14). His wife, more alert to this than her husband, performs the operation on their son (4:24–26). After Moses' arrival in Egypt, he and Aaron call together the elders of Israel and assure them that the Lord has not forgotten them.

The scene now moves to the confrontation with Pharaoh. Moses and Aaron make their famous demand on behalf of God: "Let my people go!" Pharaoh is not interested. Who is this Lord that demands that he should act in this way? Irritated at their demands, Pharaoh decides to make life more difficult for the Israelites. No longer will they be given straw to help them make bricks. They will have to find their own (5:1–21). The Israelites are furious with Moses and Aaron for provoking Pharaoh like this. Moses is disconsolate. Why has God treated him in this way? (5:22–23).

These mud bricks are being made in Thebes, Egypt, in much the same way as the ancient Israelites made them when they were slaves of the pharaohs.

6:1–30 God Promises Deliverance. God reveals himself to Moses once more and reassures him of his presence and power (6:1–27). The same God who appeared to Abraham, Isaac, and Jacob makes himself known again to Moses. He has heard the groaning of his people, and he will remain faithful to his covenant. The theme of the covenant faithfulness of God, which is of such importance throughout the Old Testament, makes its presence felt strongly in chapters 19 to 24 of Exodus. Yet other themes also figure—such as the refusal of God's people to listen to his chosen servants and the lack of confidence of those servants both in themselves and in the God who has chosen them. For example, when Moses is told to speak to Pharaoh, he quibbles: he won't listen to me (6:28–30). Yet in the end, God is able to use even those with "faltering lips."

EXODUS 7:1 – 11:10

The Judgment Against Pharaoh

If Pharaoh will not listen to Moses' words, then he will have to deal with God's actions instead. The major section that now opens deals with Pharaoh's persistent rejection of God and his obstinate refusal to allow the Israelites to leave their captivity in Egypt. A theme that becomes important in this section is the hardening of Pharaoh's heart. This should not be understood to mean that God deliberately makes Pharaoh reject Moses' words or the will of God. Rather, it should be taken to mean that God confirms what is already present within Pharaoh's own heart. For every text that speaks of God hardening Pharaoh's heart (e.g., Ex 7:3; 9:12; 10:20) there is another that speaks of Pharaoh's heart being hardened (e.g., Ex 7:13, 22; 8:15, 32; 9:7). God brings out into the open the secret inner motives and desires of Pharaoh.

7:14–11:10 A Series of Plagues. It is clear that Pharaoh has not the slightest intention of allowing the Israelites to leave, despite the obvious signs of the Lord's presence and power (7:1–13). A series of plagues follows, each of which severely disrupts life in Egypt. Each of these plagues can be seen in terms of natural events. For example, the plague of blood (7:14–24) may have been a severe volcanic eruption discharging volcanic ash into the Nile and thus polluting the drinking water of both animals and human beings, as well as darkening the sky. The Israelites, who were localized in the region of Goshen, far away from the Nile, would have been unaffected. Behind these natural phenomena lay the hand of God in judgment. In the order in which they occurred, the plagues are blood (7:14–24), frogs (8:1–15), gnats (8:16–19), flies (8:20–32), a plague on livestock (9:1–7), boils (9:8–12), hail (9:13–35), locusts (10:1–20), and darkness (10:21–29). In each case, the same refrain occurs: Pharaoh hardened his heart, and would not let God's people go.

The scene is thus set for the final assault on Pharaoh's total obstinacy, as the events which would henceforth be celebrated in the Passover festival take place.

EXODUS 11:1 – 12:30

The Passover

11:1–10 The Plague on the Firstborn. The final judgment on Egypt parallels one of the most repressive measures adopted by Pharaoh against the Israelites. Pharaoh had ordered that all newborn male Israelite children be killed. Now that same judgment is executed against Egypt, from the royal household downwards. Yet even here, God's judgment is tempered by mercy. Whereas Pharaoh took the life of every male Israelite child, only the firstborn of each Egyptian family is to suffer the same fate. Israel, however, will not suffer from this judgment. She will be marked out as God's own people and spared from this act.

12:1–13 The Passover Meal. As a sign of the fact that something new is about to happen, Moses is commanded to begin a new religious calendar, based on what now takes place. (The time of year that is identified here corresponds to the period of March or April in modern calendars.) Each household or group of households is to sacrifice a perfect lamb or goat and to daub its blood across the sides and tops of their doorframes. This will mark them as God's own people. They are to eat a meal to remind them of their time in Egypt, which is now coming to an end. Both the type of food eaten and the way in which it is to be eaten will remind the people of their bitter years in Egypt as they waited for their redemption. The eating of "bitter herbs" (12:8)—herbs native to Egypt—symbolizes the bitterness of their bondage, just as the "bread made without yeast" points to the haste with which the people are being asked to prepare to leave Egypt. The festival is named "the LORD's Passover," which refers to the fact that God will "pass over" the houses of his own people as he brings vengeance against the Egyptians.

12:14–28 Commemoration of the Passover. In commemoration of this act of deliverance, the Passover is to be celebrated every year as a lasting ordinance. Further regulations concerning its celebration are mentioned later (12:43–49). It is no accident that in the New Testament the Last Supper of Jesus Christ is a Passover meal (Mt 26:17–29; Mk 14:12–25; Lk 22:7–20). In celebrating God's great act of deliverance in the past, Jesus Christ prepares for the great act of deliverance that will take place through his death upon the cross. God's judgment against sin, initially made against the firstborn of the Egyptians (12:29–30), eventually leads to the atoning death of his one and only firstborn son.

EXODUS 12:31 – 18:27

The Exodus

This final act of judgment breaks Pharaoh's resolve. Israel may leave Egypt. Fearful of further calamities, the Egyptians wish the Israelites to get away from their land as quickly as possible (12:31–39). Later (14:5–6) they will change their minds and decide to force them back into slavery.

13:1–16 Consecration of the Firstborn. As the Israelites prepare to leave, the custom is established of offering every firstborn male (whether animal or human) to the Lord. Once Israel has settled in the Promised Land, she will continue this custom as a means of recalling her imprisonment in Egypt and the LORD's great power and love in bringing Israel out of that captivity into a "land flowing with milk and honey." The custom is there as a reminder, in case Israel should ever forget that the Lord brought her out of Egypt with his mighty hand. The theme of remembering all that God has done for his people occurs frequently throughout Scripture.

13:17–15:21 Crossing the Sea. A further theme that will occur frequently in the account of Israel's journey to and entry into the Promised Land is that of the faithfulness of God to his promises. God promised to give the descendants of Abraham the land of Canaan. He will remain faithful to that promise despite his people's frequent disobedience and rebellion against him. As a token of this faithfulness of God to his promises, Moses has the bones of Joseph exhumed and brought with them as they travel (13:19) so that Joseph may share in the promise of resting in Canaan.

But how are they to reach Canaan? The most direct route would involve heading from Goshen to the coast and following the coastline through Philistia into Canaan. This, however, was a possible invasion route for Egypt's enemies. As a result, it was defended by a series of fortresses. Guided by a "pillar of cloud" by day and a "pillar of fire" by night, the Israelites journeyed southeast, rather than northeast, avoiding the much-used trade routes of the Sinai peninsula. The road they take leads them to what is traditionally known as the Red Sea, although the Hebrew words *yam suth* really mean "sea of reeds." It is not known for certain where this sea was located. The reference need not be to a *sea* in the strict sense of the term; it is possible that an inland lake may be intended.

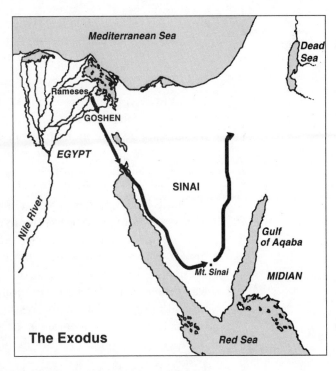

The Exodus

By now, the Egyptians are regretting their decision to allow the Israelites to leave unhindered (14:1–9). The realization dawns that they have lost a substantial pool of cheap slave labor. The decision is made: the Israelites will be pursued and recaptured. The search parties set out, tracking the fleeing Israelites down to Pi Hahiroth (14:9). Panic breaks out inside the Israelite camp, and recriminations flow fast and thick against Moses (14:10–12). However, Moses urges the people to trust God. In one of the most dramatic and best-known incidents in Scripture, a strong east wind divides the waters of this sea, allowing the people of Israel to pass through to the other side. The Egyptians, however, are swallowed up in the sea. Again, there is a strong element of irony here. The Egyptians wanted to drown every firstborn male child of Israel. They ended up by being drowned themselves. This great act of divine deliverance brings the Israelites to their senses. They now fear and trust God and are prepared to listen to his servant Moses (14:13–31). In a great song of triumph, Israel exults in the glorious triumph of a God who is faithful to his promises and who will guide them safely into the Promised Land of Canaan (15:1–21). For a while, Israel trusts her God and his servant.

Although Moses, at God's command, demanded that the Pharaoh allow the Israelites to leave Egypt, the Pharoah refused. He changed his mind only after God sent ten plagues that did not affect the Israelites. The map shows the first part of the Israelites' trip to the Promised Land.

15:22–27 The Waters of Marah and Elim. But it does not last. Sinful human nature soon tires of trusting and adoring God and turns back to concentrating on its purely physical needs. Shortly afterwards, the people are grumbling about the quality of their water supply. The problem is soon remedied. However, the reader of Exodus has been introduced to a theme which will recur throughout the story of the wanderings of Israel on her way to the Promised Land: the grumbling of an impatient people who demand instant gratification and are tempted to abandon God when the going gets tough. As will become clear, Israel is a people who need to be refined and tested before they are ready to enter that Promised Land.

16:1–36 Manna and Quail. The grumbling soon starts again (16:1–3). This time, the problem is the food. Israel misses her pots of meat. "We were better off in Egypt!" becomes something of a recurring theme in the people's long list of complaints against God. God's providential care for his people has already been demonstrated in the way in which they were saved from slavery in Egypt. Yet that care is far from exhausted, as what follows makes clear. For example, God provides quail (16:11–13) for meat. He also ordains that Israel will have "bread from heaven" (16:4), an aspect of God's goodness that finds its ultimate expression in the coming of Jesus Christ (Jn 6:32–33). The word *manna* is used to refer to this bread (16:31). It is not entirely clear what manna was. Some have suggested that it may have been a form of honeydew. However, the elaborate provisions concerning the gathering and keeping of the manna suggests that it was not something natural, but rather was ordained by God for the nourishment of his people at this crucial moment in their history. Interestingly, the idea of rest on the seventh day begins to make its appearance (16:23), even though it will not be formally imposed as a covenant requirement until Sinai itself.

17:1–7 Water From the Rock. Having had its food sorted out, Israel now begins to complain about the water again (17:1–2). In a marvelous passage,

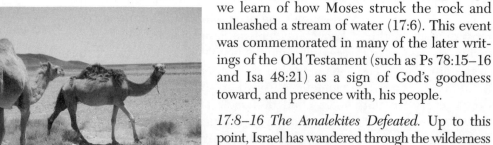

we learn of how Moses struck the rock and unleashed a stream of water (17:6). This event was commemorated in many of the later writings of the Old Testament (such as Ps 78:15–16 and Isa 48:21) as a sign of God's goodness toward, and presence with, his people.

17:8–16 The Amalekites Defeated. Up to this point, Israel has wandered through the wilderness without facing much in the way of opposition. There have been complaints from within the people about the food and water, but no external threats. Now this situation alters as Israel finds herself attacked by the Amalekites. The account of how the marauding Amalekites were defeated is of particular importance in

Moses and the Israelites may have used camels as they crossed the desert, like these in the Negev. Today's traveler can load everything into trucks and jeeps.

that it introduces us to Joshua, who will eventually lead Israel into the Promised Land after the death of Moses. Yet even at this early stage, he is singled out as an obedient and competent person. Later, he will be identified as Moses' assistant (24:13), who ascends Mount Sinai with Moses.

18:1–27 Jethro Visits Moses. The account of this early period of the wilderness wanderings comes to a close with the meeting between Moses and his father-in-law Jethro. Midian was not far from the region in which Moses had chosen to camp, and it seems that he sent his wife and children on to Midian to greet Jethro and arrange a meeting. Jethro, being a priest of Midian, was not a worshipper of the Lord. However, the news of the great deeds that the Lord has done for his people makes a deep impression on him. He acknowledges that the Lord is God and offers a sacrifice to him (18:9–12). Jethro, who is now to be regarded as a follower of the Lord, then teaches Moses the essence of the skill of delegation, something which Moses had, by all accounts, yet to master (18:13–27). Moses could not do everything for Israel, and the administration of justice was becoming burdensome and impractical. The beginnings of an organized system of government and law can be seen to be taking shape. It will be consolidated in the future as Israel presses on towards Sinai. It has been three months since she left Egypt.

EXODUS 19:1 – 24:18 ───────────────────────

The Covenant at Sinai

Israel encamps at the foot of Mount Sinai in the southeastern region of the Sinai peninsula. God summons Moses to the mountain and declares his intention to make Israel into a "kingdom of priests and a holy nation" (19:6). She will be set apart from other peoples and nations and will be dedicated to the service of the Lord. The New Testament picks up on both these ideas, affirming that Christian believers are now God's royal priesthood and people (1Pe 2:5, 9). The distinctiveness of Israel will be safeguarded by the covenant between God and his people, which will establish her distinctive identity as a people.

Moses and Israel prepare to hear God's covenant. In a series of ritual acts, they purify themselves (19:10–25). There is an important insight in this passage: sinners cannot stand before a holy God. Something has to be done if they are to come into God's presence. This idea is developed in the sacrificial system, which stresses the need for purification and holiness on the part of those who wish to draw near to God; however, it reaches its climax in the New Testament. Through faith in the atoning blood of Christ, sinners are finally enabled to come with confidence and joy into the presence of a holy God.

20:1–17 The Ten Commandments. God now delivers the covenant between himself and his people Israel. The basic structure is usually referred to as the *Decalogue* or Ten Commandments. There are important similarities between the covenant between God and Israel, and ancient Near Eastern covenants between monarchs and their peoples, which often opened with a declaration of the identity and achievements of the king in question. The Decalogue opens with a ringing affirmation that the Lord is the God who delivered Israel from her captivity in Egypt. Having identified himself, God lays ten conditions upon his people. The first four refer to Israel's relation with God; the remaining six to duties to other Israelites.

20:3 They Are to Have No Other Gods. Israel is to be faithful to the one and only God, who delivered her from Egypt. In practice, Israel fails to keep this command; she regularly flirts with other gods and goddesses, especially during the settlement of Canaan. The word *jealous* is used (e.g., 20:5) to refer to God's demand for total commitment on the part of his people. It does not refer to petty envy or resentment on God's part, but to his passionate love for his people and refusal to share them with any other gods.

20:4 Idols Are Forbidden. Many of the pagan nations in the region worshiped idols—that is, stone, wooden, or metal images of gods. Israel is utterly forbidden to do this. Only the Lord is to be worshiped. Scripture also condemns other idolatrous practices, including the worship of the sun, moon, and stars. Many of the practices associated with idolatry, such as sexual deviancy and the burning of children, are also forbidden. Despite these warnings, Israel lapses into idolatry at many points in her history, including the time of the patriarchs and Moses, the period of the judges, and the period of the monarchy. In addition to identifying the spiritual dangers of idolatry, the Old Testament also brings out the absurdity of the practice. How, it asks, can anyone seriously treat something made of wood as if it were a god?

Underlying this prohibition is another consideration: there is no way in which the Lord can adequately be repre-

The Israelites camped at the foot of Mount Sinai, about where St. Catherine's Monastery is located today. It was on Mount Sinai that God gave Moses the Ten Commandments.

sented by any human object. It is fatally easy to confuse the creator and the creation and end up worshipping the latter rather than the former. This commandment ends with a powerful affirmation of the total faithfulness of God to his covenant.

20:7 The Name of the Lord Must Not Be Misused. God's holy name is not to be abused, as in the swearing of false oaths.

20:8–11 The Sabbath Is to Be Kept Holy. This commandment establishes the seventh day as holy. According to the Old Testament account of creation (Genesis 1), God rested from his work of creation on the seventh day. For this reason, the seventh day of the week (Saturday) was ordained to be a day of rest, a custom which continues in modern Judaism. No manual labor of any kind was permitted on this day, which was to be observed as an occasion for physical rest and giving thanks to God. As Jesus Christ pointed out (Mk 2:23–28), the Sabbath was ordained for the benefit of humanity.

By the time of the New Testament, however, the regulations concerning the Sabbath had become expanded considerably. The Sabbath was now subject to various kinds of legalism, with its original intention being overshadowed. Jesus Christ, who openly broke some of the more restrictive Sabbath regulations, declared that the Sabbath was made for humanity, not humanity for the Sabbath. Christ's resurrection from the dead on the first day of the week (Sunday) established this day as being of especial importance for Christians. As a result, Christians observe "the Lord's day" (Sunday) as a period of Sabbath rest, rather than the original Saturday. Christians can maintain the Sabbath principle without obeying the letter of the Old Testament law.

20:12 Israelites Are to Honor Their Parents. As Paul points out (Eph 6:2), this is the first commandment with a promise attached to it. Respect for parents is linked with the well-being of Israel in the land God has promised her. There is a very strong sense of family obligation here, which is especially noticeable to modern Western readers, who are more accustomed to a very individualist way of thinking. The Old Testament, here as elsewhere, emphasizes the responsibilities of the people of God toward each other, and has little time for the ethic of pure self-fulfillment and self-indulgence that is so common in Western society today.

20:13 Murder Is Forbidden. The Hebrew word used here would normally have the sense of a deliberate and premeditated act of killing. A distinction was drawn between murder and manslaughter, the chief difference being that the former is deliberate, and the latter accidental. However, the commandment was not understood in Old Testament times to prohibit the execution of serious offenders or the taking of human life in warfare.

20:14 Adultery Is Forbidden. This practice is explicitly and repeatedly condemned by Scripture as a breach of trust. It is portrayed as something that is a snare to the unwary and destructive of both individuals and societies. The Old Testament often compares forms of spiritual faithlessness, such the worship of other gods or idols, to adultery. The Lord is treated as the husband of his people Israel. Israel's flirtations with other gods, especially Canaanite fertility gods (whose rituals included sexual elements), is therefore regarded as a violation of the covenant between God and his people in much the same way as adultery is the violation of a marriage covenant.

20:15 Stealing Is forbidden.

20:16 False Testimony—Telling Lies—Is Forbidden.

20:17 Coveting Is Forbidden. The word *covet* is a little old-fashioned and could perhaps be translated as "be envious about" or "feel jealous about." The basic thing that is condemned is longing to have something that belongs to someone else. There is a need to be prepared to accept what we have without being envious of others, for envy can all too easily lead to violence and murder, and can allow sin to express itself in dangerous ways.

The Ten Commandments are then supplemented by a series of additional laws, which expand some of the ideas expressed in the Commandments themselves. These laws relate to the prohibition of idolatry (20:22–26), the way servants are to be treated (21:1–11), the way personal injuries are to be compensated (21:12–36), the protection of personal property (22:1–15), care for the community at large (22:16–23:9), and regulations for the keeping of the Sabbath rest (23:10–13) and annual festivals (23:14–19).

God affirms his faithfulness to his side of the covenant, provided that Israel continues faithful on her side. In many ways, as we have noted above, there is a direct parallel between the covenant between God and Israel and a marriage covenant, with faithlessness on the part of Israel compared to adultery or prostitution. God promises that he will give Israel her Promised Land and that he will go ahead of her to sow confusion and terror within the lands she is to possess (23:20–33). Nevertheless, there is a warning here: Israel can easily become corrupted by the religious beliefs and practices of the peoples already living in that region. The covenant is then confirmed by the people, who declare that they are ready to receive and obey it (24:3). In a great ritual ceremony, Moses reads the Book of the Covenant to the people (24:7), who swear to obey it. Moses then returns with Joshua to Sinai, "the mountain of God," where Moses will remain for forty days and nights (24:18).

EXODUS 25:1 – 31:18

The Tabernacle

Having learned of God's covenant requirements of his people, Moses is now told of the practical details for the worship appropriate for Israel. The fine details of this section are complex. For a full appreciation of their functions and importance, they need to be read with care in the light of a technical commentary. What follows here focuses on the importance of these provisions for Christian readers.

Having called his people and established them as a "kingdom of priests and a holy nation" (19:6), God now declares that he will dwell among them in a *sanctuary* (literally, "a holy place") which is to be known as the *tabernacle* (literally, "a place of dwelling": 25:8–9). The two stone tablets on which the Ten Commandments were engraved are to be an important component of this sanctuary (25:10–22). The box in which the stones are to be transported during the period of Israel's wanderings is to be known as the "ark of the Testimony," although it will also be referred to as the "ark of the LORD" elsewhere in the Old Testament (as at 2Sa 6:11). The covenant between God and Israel will thus be physically present with Israel as she undertakes her journey through the wilderness. The ark will finally rest in the temple at Jerusalem after the conquest of this formerly Jebusite city by David.

26:31–35 The Curtain of the Temple. Of the remaining details of the tabernacle and its furnishings, some aspects of the design of the tabernacle itself should be noted. The "curtain of the temple" was an especially important feature of the tabernacle. It was included in order to provide a means of restricting access to the "most holy place," the region of the tabernacle that was regarded as sacrosanct. Although the curtain served an important practical function in relation to the worship of Israel, it came to have a deeper significance. The fact that the curtain prevented ordinary worshippers from entering the "most holy place" came to be seen as pointing to a much deeper separation between God and sinful humanity. The curtain thus came to be a symbol of the barrier placed between God and humanity by human sinfulness. At the time of the crucifixion of Jesus Christ, the curtain of the temple was torn (Mt 27:51). This dramatic event, noted in the Gospels, is seen as a symbol of one of the chief benefits brought about by the death of Christ: the barrier between God and humanity caused by sin has been torn down, so that for believers there is now free access to God on account of Christ's death.

28:1–29:46 The Priesthood. The selection of Moses' brother Aaron and his sons as priests ensures a continuous supply of people for the priesthood within Israel. The details of the priesthood extend to the clothes that are to be worn by priests (28:1–43). It is clear that the priests are to have an especially important and revered position within Israel, with the task of ensuring that Israel remains a holy people. For this reason, special attention is paid to the manner in which priests are to be consecrated (29:1–46) and the care that is to be taken over every aspect of Israel's worship.

30:1–31:18 Israel's Worship. Israel is a holy nation chosen by a holy God, and her future depends upon her remaining holy. The passage under study is a powerful affirmation of Israel's need to remain holy, even as God is holy, if she is to remain the people of God.

For Christians, many of the details described in these passages come under the general category of ceremonial or cultic law, dealing with the precise way in which Israel ordered its worship and sacrifice. Christian writers draw a distinction between the moral law (such as the Ten Commandments), which remains valid for and binding upon Christians, and the ceremonial or cultic law, which is seen as belonging to a specific period in Israel's history and as no longer being binding for Christians. Christ came to fulfill the law in such a way that the cultic law of the "old covenant" is no longer binding, having been superseded by the "new covenant" of Jesus Christ. This theme is especially clearly stated in the letter to the Hebrews.

EXODUS 32:1 – 34:35

Rebellion Against God and the Renewal of the Covenant to Moses

32:1–35 The Golden Calf. We have seen how the theme of human sin recurs throughout the narrative of God's redemption of his people. It now makes itself felt in one of the best-known episodes of Israel's wilderness wanderings: the making of the golden calf (32:1–4). During Moses' absence, Israel begins to rebel against the leading themes of the covenant with the Lord. Notice how the people attribute the exodus from Egypt to Moses, not to the Lord (32:1). Despite the total prohibition of idols within Israel, the Israelites make themselves a golden calf (probably designed to look like the Egyptian bull-god Apis, representations of which they would certainly have come across during their time in Egypt). They worship this idol, declaring that it represents the gods who brought them out of Egypt (32:4). Aaron tolerates this lapse into idolatry and does nothing to prevent the excesses that follow (32:5–6).

While Moses was up on Mount Sinai, talking with God, the Israelites again disobeyed God. They made and worshiped a golden calf, giving the credit for their escape from Egypt to the gods represented by the calf. This figurine of a similar idol is on display in the British Museum.

God is angered by the disobedience of Israel (32:7–10) and makes it clear that he wishes to disown her for so flagrantly violating his covenant. Moses, however, pleads the case for his people. He asks God to remember his covenant with Abraham, Isaac, and Jacob and his promise to make their descendants numerous so that they may inherit the Promised Land. The Lord agrees to withhold the judgment on his rebellious people (32:11–14). On descending the mountain,

Moses is rejoined by Joshua. As they enter the camp of Israel, they realize that they are witnessing a total breakdown of the covenant. As a powerful symbol of this violation of the covenant, Moses breaks the two tablets of stone upon which God had engraved the Law (32:19).

Moses is furious at Israel's rebellion. His first action is to destroy the calf by burning it. (This suggests that the calf may have been a thin layer of gold, mounted on a wooden frame.) He confronts Aaron and demands to know how the calf came into being. Aaron's reply is unconvincing: he threw lots of gold ornaments into the fire, and out popped a golden calf (32:24). The sinful people made him do it. This sly evasion of responsibility merely confirms how deeply ingrained sin has become, even at the highest levels of the people of God. Moses responds by purging Israel of those who had rebelled against God, putting some three thousand idolaters to the sword (32:25–35).

33:1–11 The Faithfulness of the Lord. The consequences of sin now become clear. God will not withdraw his promises to the descendants of Abraham, Isaac, and Jacob. They will still possess the land that he promised on oath to their forefathers. But he himself will not accompany them. His presence will be withdrawn from his people on account of their sin (33:1–3). This dismays the people, who strip off their ornaments as a sign of mourning and repentance (33:4–6). Moses pleads once more with God to remain with Israel. Despite all their faults, she is still his people (33:13). What point is there in going to the Promised Land without the presence of the one who promised it to them? What will be different about Israel, if she lacks the presence of her God? The Lord agrees to be present with his people, because he is pleased with Moses (33:17).

33:12–23 Moses and the Glory of the Lord. Moses then requests a personal favor. He wants to see God in all his glory (33:18). Yet no one is capable of seeing God in his full radiance and glory. God will pass by Moses, allowing him to catch a glimpse of him from the rear as he does so. But neither Moses nor anyone else will ever be allowed to see the face of God (33:19–23). Only Jesus Christ has seen the full glory of God and made this glory known to sinful humanity (Jn 1:18). Having revealed himself in this way, God confirms his covenant with Moses. He will go with his people into the Promised Land.

34:1–35 The New Stone Tablets. However, God's people are to avoid any form of compromise with the pagan beliefs of that region (34:1–14). In what follows (34:15–28), the main points of the Ten Commandments are restated. This time it is Moses who engraves the letters. As a result of his encounter with God, Moses' face is transfigured. Having been in the presence of the glory of God, Moses himself is radiant, reflecting that glory (34:29–35). There are important anticipations here of the transfiguration of Jesus Christ (Mt 17:3–4; Mk 9:4–5; Lk 9:30–32) when Moses will be radiant on account of the glory of Christ.

EXODUS 35:1 – 40:38

Further Regulations and Conclusion

Exodus concludes with a restatement of the regulations that will preserve her distinctive character as the people of God. The basic features of these regulations for the construction of the tabernacle and worship connected with it have already been set out (see 25:1–28:43; 30:1–5; 31:1–11), and they are repeated here for the purpose of ensuring that they will be remembered and acted upon.

Exodus closes by leaving us with a picture of the people of Israel journeying through the desert as they move onward to the land God has promised them. Despite their sin and rebellion, God remains present in their midst. Reassured by the visible presence of God (40:38), Israel presses onward to her goal. The story of the wilderness wanderings will be continued in the book of Numbers. There is now a brief pause in the narrative, as we learn more of the will of God for his people at this stage in their pilgrimage in the book of Leviticus.

LEVITICUS

The book of Exodus ended with the building of the tabernacle, which would become the focus of Israel's worship as the people journeyed through the wilderness on their way to the Promised Land. The story of how Israel moved from Mount Sinai to the land of Moab on the borders of Canaan is taken up again in the book of Numbers. Between these two books, in Leviticus, attention now shifts to the tabernacle itself, focusing on the laws and regulations for its worship. These are also supplemented by detailed instructions concerning such matters as ritual cleanliness.

The book of Leviticus takes its name from the Levites, who, along with Aaron and his sons, were given the responsibility for the conduct of worship in the tabernacle and the general maintenance of holiness among the people. A central theme of Leviticus is *holiness*. The people of God must be holy, just as God is holy. The detailed regulations set out in Leviticus bear witness to the need for every aspect of life to be subjected to the will of a holy God.

Of particular importance is the theme of sacrifice. This theme is taken up and developed in the New Testament, which affirms that Jesus Christ is the perfect atoning sacrifice for human sin. His perfect sacrifice supersedes the Old Testament sacrificial system, as well as many of the ceremonial or ritual laws associated with it. As the letter to the Hebrews comments, it is impossible for the blood of bulls or goats to take away sins (Heb 10:4). For this reason, Christian readers of Leviticus often find themselves bewildered and confused by its detailed stipulations concerning sacrifice and ritual cleanliness.

So does this mean that Leviticus has no value for the Christian reader? No! Reading Leviticus brings home to Christian readers the utmost importance of holiness on the part of the people of God. It stresses the seriousness of sin and its damaging effect upon our relationship with God. It emphasizes the need for atonement for sin and affirms God's goodness and faithfulness to his covenant in forgiving such sin. All these themes find their ultimate focus in the sacrificial death of Jesus Christ through whose blood believers are redeemed. To read Leviticus is to appreciate more fully the background to the coming of Jesus Christ and the full meaning of his atoning sacrifice (Heb 8:1–6; 10:1–7). With these points in mind, we may begin to explore its themes.

LEVITICUS 1:1 – 7:38

Types of Offerings to the Lord

Leviticus opens by detailing different types of offerings that may be presented to the Lord. Five are identified and explained.

1:1–17 The Burnt Offering. This takes the form of a male animal (such as a bull, ram, or goat). However, in the case of poorer people, a male bird (such as a dove) is an acceptable alternative. This type of offering serves a number of purposes. It can be an expression of dedication or commitment to God, an act of worship, or a form of atonement for some type of sin committed unintentionally. (See also the further details at 6:8–13; 8:18–21).

Leviticus stresses the need for the offering to be perfect, without defect of any kind (1:3). The idea of a perfect sacrifice without any blemish reaches its fulfillment in the New Testament in the obedient death upon the cross of the sinless Jesus Christ in order that human sin might finally be forgiven, and forgiven fully (see Heb 9:14).

2:1–16 The Grain Offering. This form of offering does not involve the taking of any form of animal life, but it takes the form of offering agricultural produce of various kinds. Items regarded as suitable include grain, flour, and olive oil. Although this type of offering does not involve the shedding of blood, it is intended to accompany some of the other types of offerings (see 6:14–15; Nu 28:3–8). Because these other offerings do involve the shedding of animal blood, it will be clear that every offering ultimately involves the taking of life. (See also the further regulations at 6:14–23.)

3:1–17 The Fellowship Offering. This offering involves the sacrifice of a male or female animal, usually as an expression of the worshipper's thanksgiving toward the Lord. This type of offering is unusual in one respect, in that the person offering the sacrifice is allowed to eat part of the animal that has been sacrificed (apart from the fat and blood). (See also the further regulations at 7:11–34.)

4:1–5:13 The Sin Offering. This type of offering is of major importance in relation to obtaining forgiveness for unintentional sins. Four general classes of individuals are referred to, each of which is required to make a specific sacrifice: priests, the community, leaders, and individual members of the community. In each case, the sacrifice has to be perfect and without blemish. When a priest or the entire community sins, a young bull is to be sacrificed. In the case of a leader, a lesser sacrifice is laid down: a male goat. (Sins on the part of priests were regarded as especially serious, for they brought guilt on the entire people whom he represented.) In the case of a member of the community sinning unintentionally, a sliding scale of sacrifices comes into operation. Most are required to offer a female goat or lamb. The poor are required to offer a dove or pigeon. Those who are very poor are required to offer "a tenth of an ephah" (that is, about two liters) of fine flour. (See also the further regulations at 6:24–30; 16:3–22.)

5:14–6:7 The Guilt Offering. This sacrifice is obligatory for any unintentional sin that breaks any of the commandments. The sinner is required to sacrifice a ram, make any restitution necessary, and also pay an additional twenty percent to the priest. Once this has been done, he can rest assured of his forgiveness. (See also the further regulations at 7:1–6.)

LEVITICUS 8:1 – 10:20

The Priesthood and Its Tasks

This section documents the ordination of Aaron and his sons to the priesthood (8:1–36) and their initial period of ministry (9:1–10:20). A central task of the priesthood relates to the distinction between the clean and unclean. As part of its commitment to holiness, Israel is required to avoid ritual uncleanness of any kind, through the warnings of the priesthood. Where ritual uncleanness does arise, it is to be cleansed in the appropriate manner by the priests.

LEVITICUS 11:1 – 15:33

Uncleanness

11:1–47 Clean and Unclean Food. The first major area to be discussed focuses on types of food. Certain animals are declared to be unclean. They are not to be eaten, nor should their dead bodies be approached. Examples of such unclean animals include camels, rabbits, pigs, and rats. Persons who become ritually unclean by accidentally touching their carcasses must be ritually cleansed by washing their clothes.

12:1–8 Purification After Childbirth. Ritual uncleanness can also arise in other manners. A woman is unclean after childbirth and needs to offer a sacrifice to be ritually cleansed (12:1–8). The normal offering would be a lamb; however, a poor woman could offer two young pigeons. We thus discover that Mary, the mother of Jesus Christ, was poor, for this was the sacrifice she offered after the birth of her son (Lk 2:24).

13:1–14:57 Infectious Skin Diseases. A major source of uncleanness is infectious skin diseases. In biblical times, the term *leprosy* was used to refer to a group of highly contagious skin diseases that resulted in swellings, rashes, or sores. The leprosy in Leviticus and other Old Testament references is thus not identical with the disease now known by this name (Hansen's disease). The NIV uses the general term *infectious skin disease* as a means of avoiding this misunderstanding. The Old Testament lays down regulations designed to minimize the risk to society, including the banning of those with leprosy from society in general and from Levitical service in particular. The priests are charged with the identification of leprosy and the enforcing of the isolation of those suffering from it. It is only possible for lepers to return to a normal social life once they have been declared to have been healed of the disease. This declaration has to be made by a priest after a careful inspection of the leper's skin. Once more, an offering is required before cleansing is complete (13:1–14:57).

15:1–33 Discharges Causing Uncleanness. Any form of bodily emission is regarded as making someone temporarily unclean. A male with any kind of discharge is to be regarded as unclean, as is anyone or anything who comes into direct physical contact with him (15:1–18). Similarly, a woman is to be regarded as unclean during menstruation (15:19–30). In all this, the priests are required to prevent any form of defilement to the tabernacle (15:31–33).

LEVITICUS 16:1 – 34

The Day of Atonement

One Old Testament ordinance is of particular importance for Jews. This is the Day of Atonement, which is ordained as an annual event for the removal of sin from the people of God. The full ritual is complex, involving the high priest ritually cleansing himself and then offering a bull as a sacrifice for himself and the other priests. After this, two goats are brought forward. One is selected by lot as a sacrifice, while the other becomes the scapegoat. ("Choosing by lot" refers to the practice of throwing lots—similar to modern dice—and allowing the result of the throw to determine a decision in much the same way as people today toss coins to make decisions.) The first goat is then sacrificed as an offering for the sins of the people. Afterwards, the dead bull and goat are taken outside the camp and burned. The high priest then lays his hands on the head of the second goat and transfers all the sins of the people to the unfortunate animal. The scapegoat is then driven out into the wilderness, carrying the guilt of the sins of Israel with it. (The "scapegoat" was so called because it took the sins of the people on its shoulders.)

The Day of Atonement is of major importance as a background to understanding the death of Jesus Christ, a point brought out especially clearly in the letter to the Hebrews (Heb 8:1–6; 10:1–18). Jesus Christ is seen as the perfect high priest, who makes a perfect sacrifice once and for all (instead of the annual ritual of the Day of Atonement). The sacrifice he offers is himself. By his death, the sins of the people are transferred to him and removed from his people. Note especially the fact that Jesus is put to death outside the walls of Jerusalem just as the bull and goat were finally burned outside the camp of the Israelites. The Levitical ritual sets the scene for the greater and perfect sacrifice that is yet to come and that brings about what the Old Testament sacrifices could merely point to, but not deliver.

LEVITICUS 17:1 – 27:34

Further Regulations

The remainder of Leviticus lays down a series of regulations designed to ensure that Israel retained its distinctive identity. Some of these are linked with the sacrificial system; others concern personal morality; others relate to festivals Israel is commanded to observe as a means of recalling the events that gave her a distinctive identity and purpose.

17:1–16 Eating Blood Forbidden. The first major regulation concerns blood. A fundamental principle that is of importance in understanding the Old Testament sacrificial system is laid down: "the life of a creature is in the blood" (17:11). For this reason, the people of Israel were forbidden to eat or drink blood. However, this idea also allows us to understand the importance attached to blood in Old Testament sacrifices. On the Day of Atonement, for example, the blood of the animal sacrifices was sprinkled over the atonement cover (16:15). The considerable emphasis placed by New Testament writers on the blood of Christ reflects the fact that the shedding of his blood was an atoning sacrifice by which Christ give up his life in order that human sin might be forgiven.

18:1–20:27 Unlawful Sexual Relations; Various Laws; Punishments for Sin. A series of regulations follows concerning forbidden sexual relationships (18:1–30) and other regulations (19:1–37). Once more, the concern is to keep Israel holy, just as God himself is holy. The seriousness with which sin is to be taken can be seen from the punishments laid down for sin (20:1–27). Israel must maintain her distinctive character and avoid becoming like other nations: "You must not live according to the customs of the nations I am going to drive out before you ... I am the LORD your God, who has set you apart from the nations" (20:23–24). The importance of these regulations would become especially clear as Israel entered the promised land and encountered the religious practices and beliefs of the pagan peoples already present.

21:1–22:22 Rules for Priests. The priests, as has already been noted, will play an especially important role in upholding Israel's holy calling. For this reason, special attention is paid to ensuring the holiness of the priests (21:1–22:16) and the correctness of the sacrifices to be offered (22:17–33). A sinful priest will contaminate his people; the priesthood must therefore be free from any such contamination. The emphasis on the need for a sacrifice without any blemish (22:17–22) anticipates the perfect sacrifice offered by Jesus Christ, who was himself without blemish or sin.

LEVITICUS 23:1 – 25:54

Major Festivals

A substantial section now deals with the major festivals of Israel. The main ones are the following:

23:3 The Sabbath. The seventh day of the week is to be observed as holy.

23:4–8 The Passover. It commemorates Israel's delivery from Egypt and is celebrated annually on the fourteenth day of the first month (March–April in modern calendars).

23:4–8 The Feast of Unleavened Bread. This feast, which recalls the haste in which Israel left Egypt, is celebrated annually on the following seven days of the first month immediately after the Passover (March–April in modern calendars).

23:9–14 The Feast of Firstfruits. Celebrated annually on the sixteenth day of the first month (March–April in modern calendars), this festival celebrates God's goodness in making the land fertile.

23:15–22 The Feast of Weeks. Celebrated annually on the sixth day of the seventh month (May–June in modern calendars), this feast, which would later become known as Pentecost, was basically a form of harvest festival, giving thanks for God's provision for food in the land.

23:23–25 The Feast of Trumpets. Celebrated annually on the first day of the seventh month (September–October in modern calendars) as a form of New Year Festival, this festival was subsequently known as *Rosh Hashanah.*

23:26–32 The Day of Atonement. As noted earlier, this holy day, observed on the tenth day of the seventh month (September–October in modern calendars), is concerned with the ritual cleansing of priests and people from their sins.

23:33–44 The Feast of Tabernacles. Celebrated for a period of seven days beginning on the fifteenth day of the seventh month (September–October in modern calendars), this festival commemorates the journey of Israel from Egypt to the promised land of Canaan. It would later be known as the Feast of Booths.

25:1–7 The Sabbath Year. Every seventh year, land is to be allowed to rest and recover during this fallow period.

25:8–54 The Year of Jubilee. The year after a period of seven Sabbath years—in other words, every fiftieth year—is the Year of Jubilee. In this year, all debts are to be canceled and all slaves given their freedom. The purpose of this festival appears to have been to prevent the development of long-term poverty within families.

In the midst of these regulations, further details are provided concerning the "bread of the presence" (24:1–9) and the use of capital punishment (24:10–23). This section includes the famous phrase "an eye for an eye, a tooth for a tooth" (24:20). The point being made here is that there must be a correspondence between the offense and the punishment. Someone who deliberately takes the life of another can be justly sentenced to death. The death sentence, however, would be totally out of place for someone who damaged another person's eye or tooth, or fractured his leg. This famous phrase, which is often misunderstood as implying the need for vengeance, is actually a plea for moderation in punishment. The punishment must be of comparable severity to the offense.

LEVITICUS 26:1 – 27:34

Reward for Obedience and Punishment for Disobedience

Leviticus ends with a series of regulations, reaffirming the need for Israel to be holy and to observe the commandments the Lord has given to her. The reward for obedience to these commands will be prosperity, the maintenance of national identity and integrity, and the continuing presence of God among his people (26:1–13). However, a failure to remain faithful to these commands will lead to a loss of identity, with Israel being scattered among the nations (26:27–39). Promises and warnings thus converge to remind Israel that her very existence is totally dependent upon obedience to the God who led her out of Egypt and who has promised to lead her into the promised land that lies ahead. And with that thought in mind, we return to the narrative of Israel's journey to Canaan, which we left off as Israel was camped at Sinai. The book of Numbers now takes up that narrative again.

NUMBERS

The book of Exodus ended with Israel still in the region of Sinai. Numbers now picks up the narrative and guides us through the wanderings of Israel as the people proceed on their way to Canaan.

NUMBERS 1:1 – 4:49

Details of the Tribes

Numbers opens with an account of the numbers of the tribes. (The concern for numbers in the opening chapters of the work gives rise to its title, Numbers.) Aware that the conquest of Canaan will involve military preparations, a census is taken so that Israel's military capability can be established (1:1–45). Arrangements are also made for the specific regions of the camp that are to be occupied by each tribe, with the tabernacle located at the center of the camp (2:1–34).

The resulting census indicates that some 603,550 men were available for service in the army (1:46), which would suggest a total Israelite population in the region of two million. This, however, causes a difficulty, in that the number of the firstborn is elsewhere stated to be 22,273 (3:42), which points to a much lower population. If the larger figure is correct, it would point to a huge increase in the size of Israel since her small beginnings in Egypt. It would be a clear confirmation of God's promise of fruitfulness to Abraham and his posterity.

There is, however, a difficulty with the Hebrew here, which is worth noting. The Hebrew of, for example, 1:41 reads "forty-one thousands and five hundreds." The word translated as "thousands" can also bear other meanings in Hebrew. For example, it can also mean "chief" (Ge 36:15), or "family division" (Jos 22:14). It is possible that 1:41 should therefore be translated as "forty-one chiefs and five hundred men." However, it is not clear what the ultimate explanation of the numbers recorded in these early chapters might be.

3:1–4:49 The Levites. The Levites were not treated as other tribes, but were allocated specifically religious duties (such as those set out earlier in Leviticus). Initially, the Levites were the assistants of Aaron and his sons and were given specifically religious tasks. During the period of the wilderness wanderings, for example, the Merarites (one branch of the Levites) were responsible for carrying the framework of the tabernacle (4:31–32), while the Kohathites (another branch of the family) were to carry the articles used for ministering in the sanctuary (4:12). In a later section (8:5–26), the role of the Levites is clarified further; they are to be representatives of the people before God. By their ministrations, the community will be kept holy, and thus it will be free from harm of any kind.

NUMBERS 5:1 – 10:10

Further Regulations

The next section of the work sets out detailed regulations that are concerned to ensure the religious and moral purity of Israel. This concern is of central importance; if Israel loses her distinctive character, she will cease to be the people of God. The precise regulations are ceremonial, moral, and legal (5:1–31). The blessing set out at 6:24–26 is well known to many Christians:

> The LORD bless you and keep you;
> the LORD make his face shine upon you
>   and be gracious to you;
> the LORD turn his face toward you
>   and give you peace.

6:1–21 The Nazirite. Of particular interest are the regulations concerning the Nazirites (6:1–21). The word *Nazirite* is derived from the Hebrew word meaning "to consecrate" or "to separate from." The term was used to refer to men and women who had taken the decision to consecrate themselves to God by separating themselves from certain things through a special vow. This vow could be of a limited duration; occasionally, it was for life. The vow was sealed through certain sacrifices and by ritual acts performed by a priest. Among the requirements of the Nazirite vow, the following are of special importance: to abstain from all products of the vine, to refrain from cutting their hair, and to avoid touching dead bodies. The most important Old Testament figure to have taken such vows was Samson (Jdg 13:1–5), who undertook his vows for life. Other figures chose to obey their vows for shorter periods of time.

7:1–89 Offerings at the Dedication of the Tabernacle. The earlier account of the setting up of the tabernacle (Exodus 40) is now supplemented with the precise details of all the offerings made at the dedication of the tabernacle and a further account of the continuing visible presence of God in the form of a cloud (9:15–23).

9:1–14 The Passover. The regulations concerning the Passover are now clarified further, especially in the case of those who have become unclean (for example, by touching a dead body). The Passover celebration described here is the second in Israel's history—the first had been celebrated a year earlier, while Israel was still in Egypt. The festival would not be observed again until the entry into Canaan (Jos 5:10).

One of the Passover regulations has special significance for Christians. Moses commands that the bones of the Passover lamb are not to be broken (9:12). The gospel accounts of the crucifixion of Jesus Christ make it clear that none of his bones were broken (Jn 19:36). Jesus Christ is seen as the true Passover lamb (1Co 5:7), who brings to fulfillment and completion the great act of divine redemption that the Passover marked.

NUMBERS 10:11 – 12:16 ─────────────

On the Borders of Canaan

After eleven months at Sinai, Israel finally sets out for the land of Canaan (10:11–36). Expectations are clearly high. Moses invites his brother-in-law Hobab "son of Reuel" (Reuel is another name for Jethro) to join them as they prepare to enter the Promised Land (10:29). As we discover later, he seems to have accepted this invitation; his descendants are among those present in Canaan (Jdg 1:16).

11:1–12:16 Fire and Quail From the Lord; Opposition to Moses. The atmosphere of optimism soon begins to evaporate. The people begin to grumble (11:1–35). "Things were better in Egypt! We're tired of eating manna! Let's have some meat!" The Lord responds by providing droves of quail, blown in from the sea. Moses' problems are made worse by a row with his brother Aaron and sister Miriam (12:1–16), allegedly over the issue of Moses' Cushite wife. (As Moses married Zipporah, a Midianite, it would seem that she may have died, and that Moses had subsequently remarried.) The real issue, however, is that of authority. Who has the right to speak in the name of the Lord? In what follows, a firm distinction is drawn between the Lord's revelation to his prophets in visions and dreams, and his relationship with Moses. God speaks to Moses face to face (12:6–8). (After the death of Moses, Israel looked for the coming of a messiah, who, like Moses, would know God in this close manner. This expectation is finally fulfilled in the coming of Jesus Christ "who is at the Father's side" [Jn 1:17–18].)

13:1–33 Exploring Canaan. Israel now finds herself in the wilderness of Paran, northeast of Sinai, on the borders of the Promised Land (13:1–25). Moses sends out spies to reconnoiter the territory that lies ahead. His briefing to the reconnaissance party of twelve (which includes Joshua and a man named Caleb from the tribe of Judah) is thorough: he wants full details of the peoples, land, and cities that lie ahead of them, so that they can prepare for their advance. The spies enter Canaan through its southernmost region (the Desert of Zin) and penetrate as far north as Hebron. Returning to Moses after forty days, they report on what they have discovered (13:26–33): Yes, the land does flow with milk and honey! But we can never take possession of this land. Its inhabitants are giants and will overwhelm us.

14:1–45 The People Rebel. The people take fright (14:1–4). Deciding that they were better off in Egypt, they announce their intention to choose someone to lead them back to its safety. Joshua and Caleb plead with the people: The land is good, and the Lord will be with Israel (14:5–9). Why should they hold back? But Israel has had enough. The people rebel against Moses, to the anger of the Lord (14:10–19). Moses pleads successfully for his people to be spared, despite their disobedience. But there is a price to pay for Israel's disobedience, as the Lord's response (14:20–38) makes clear.

This section is dramatic and represents a turning point in the history of Israel. It should be read carefully. As a result of her disobedience on the brink of the Promised Land, not one of the present people of Israel will live to take possession of the land. Only those who were faithful to God's command (Joshua and Caleb) will live to enter Canaan. Israel will remain in the wilderness for forty years. Only then will she be allowed to enter into Canaan. By that time, a new Israel will have been born, and a disobedient Israel will have been buried in the desert.

Israel is shocked by this decision (14:39–45). It is clear that the people deeply regret their decision not to obey Moses. They acknowledge their sin and declare that they are, after all, willing to enter into the Promised Land. But Moses refuses to listen to them. They would be disobeying the Lord—again. As a result, he will not be with them. What chance would

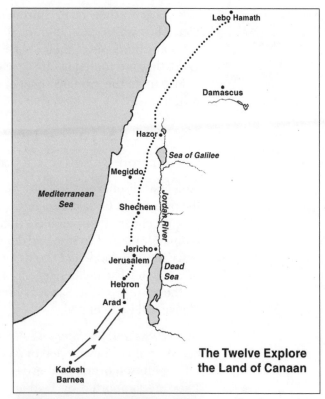

The Twelve Explore the Land of Canaan

Moses sent twelve men to explore the Promised Land. It is not certain how far north they went. They returned forty days later, bringing with them a huge cluster of grapes carried on a pole by two men. The symbol, at left, is used by a tourist agency in Israel.

they have on their own? But many are not prepared to tolerate this verdict. They will trust in their own strength. Numbers duly records the catastrophic outcome of their abortive attempt to invade Canaan without the Lord; they are routed by the Amalekites and Canaanites. Israel then begins to face up to the grim prospect of enduring forty years of wandering in the wilderness.

NUMBERS 15:1 – 19:22 —————————————

Continued Rebellion Against Moses

Israel has disobeyed the Lord; yet, as what follows makes absolutely clear, the promise of Canaan remains open. The regulations now delivered to the people concern their sacrifices in the Promised Land itself, which Israel will ultimately enter. Promise and demand are set side by side—the promise of entry into the land, and the demand to do as the Lord commands (15:1–31). Anyone who deliberately disobeys God must be cut off from his people. As the episode of the Sabbath-breaker makes clear (15:32–36), no disobedience will be tolerated.

16:1–50 Korah, Dathan, and Abiram. But rebellion against Moses continues. A group of Levites, led by Korah and two colleagues, accuses Moses of setting himself over and above everyone else. What right has he to do this? They are supported by Dathan and Abiram, who claim that Moses has totally failed to lead them into a land of milk and honey. If anything, all he has managed to do is lead them *out* of a land flowing with milk and honey, into the desert. The memory of slavery in Egypt seems to have faded, to be replaced by a nostalgic hankering after an idealized Egypt, rich with food and drink. Moses is angered by their attitude. In the end, Korah, Dathan, and Abiram perish in an earthquake shortly afterward (16:25–40).

The death of Korah, Dathan, and Abiram gives rise to new discontent within Israel. Moses and Aaron are accused of having "killed the Lord's people." This complaint is not just attributed to a few individuals, but to the whole Israelite community (16:41). It is clear that there is widespread discontent and demoralization within Israel. An outbreak of a plague is only ended when Aaron makes atonement for his people. Yet discontent remains. It is quelled to some extent by the budding of Aaron's staff (17:1–13), which is seen as a sign of God's approval of Aaron against his critics. Once more, the future hope of Israel is seen as lying in her faithfulness to the Lord. In order to ensure the continuing well-being of Israel, the priests and Levites are given religious responsibilities intended to prevent the rebellion and disobedience of the past (18:1–19:22).

NUMBERS 20:1 – 21:9 ————————————————

Preparing to Move On

It is clear that some time has elapsed. The reference to the "first month" (20:1) is actually the first month of the fortieth year after the exodus from Egypt (see Nu 33:38). Nothing has been recorded of the period Israel spent in the wilderness rediscovering her identity, purpose, and commitment to the Lord. We know nothing of any events that took place during this period, not even the locations at which Israel camped in the course of her wanderings. At the time of her rebellion against the Lord, Israel was at Kadesh. Now she is reported as arriving at Kadesh, the scene of that original rebellion. We do not know where Israel has been in-between. It is clear that a new Israel is in the process of being formed. Those who rebelled at Kadesh are now old or have already died. The deaths of Miriam (20:1) and Aaron (20:22–29) are a sign of the passing away of the old Israel. Only Moses remains.

20:1–13 Water From the Rock. But Moses will not be allowed to enter the Promised Land. Israel, as we soon discover, is still prone to grumble (20:2–13). A water shortage causes anger among the community of Israel, who once more express their grievances against Moses and Aaron. Moses is commanded to speak to a rock, and it will give forth water for the people. Yet Moses disobeys and instead strikes the rock twice with his staff. This disobedience, perhaps prompted by exasperation with the continual grumbling of Israel, angers the Lord, who declares that neither Moses nor Aaron will be allowed to enter the Promised Land (20:12). Only Joshua and Caleb will have this privilege.

20:14–21 Edom Denies Israel Passage. Moses then asks permission for his people to pass through the land of Edom (20:14–21) on their way to Moab. Moab was situated on the east bank of the river Jordan, directly east of the southern region of the land of Canaan and bordering the eastern shores of the Dead Sea. Instead of entering Canaan from the southwest, which had been Moses' intention before the rebellion at Kadesh, they will now enter the land by crossing the southern section of the river Jordan, approaching it from the east. The land of Edom lay between Kadesh and the Jordan. Hardly surprisingly, the king of Edom is less than happy about allowing such a vast group of people to pass through his land. He refuses—twice. Aware that words might not be enough, he puts together a large army and blocks their path. Israel avoids entering Edomite territory, skirting its borders.

At Mount Hor (whose location is uncertain), Aaron dies and is mourned by Israel. However, this sadness does not last long. A marauding Canaanite king based in the Negeb attacks Israel and captures some of their number (21:1–3). Israel retaliates and defeats him. This reversal of fortunes compared with a generation earlier would have been good news for Israel.

21:4–9 The Bronze Snake. Despite this military success, Moses takes the decision to go around, rather than through, Edom. That involves delay and provokes further grumbling among the people (21:4–9). An outbreak of poisonous snakes adds to their problems and provokes a mood of repentance among the people. Moses makes a bronze snake and erects it upon a pole. This offers salvation to those who have been bitten. For Christians, this incident has considerable importance, because it is alluded to by Jesus Christ (Jn 3:14–15). Just as Moses saved Israel by raising up a snake, so Christ will redeem the world by being raised up on the cross for its sake.

NUMBERS 21:10 – 25:18

From Edom to Moab

21:21–35 The Amorites Defeated. Carefully avoiding Edomite territory, Israel traces the course of the Arnon, a dried-up riverbed (or *wadi*) that flows into the eastern shores of the Dead Sea and serves as a border between the Amorites and Moabites. Israel is thus able to avoid Moabite territory altogether. Moses then requests Sihon, king of the Amorites, for permission to travel through his territory (21:21–35). Like the king of Edom, Sihon refuses and sends an army to meet the Israelites. However, Israel engages with the Amorites and routs them. As a result, Israel takes possession of a considerable amount of territory north of Moab, stretching as far north as the Jabbok, where Jacob had earlier wrestled with an angel. Finally, Israel prepares to travel across the plains of Moab in readiness to cross the Jordan and enter Canaan (22:1).

22:1–24:25 Balak Summons Balaam. The Moabites, however, have no idea that Israel intends to do nothing more than pass through their land. Having seen what Israel had done to the Amorites, they are terrified (22:2–4). This fear leads to Balak, the king of Moab, summoning the assistance of a well-known pagan expert in divination, Balaam the son of Beor. Balak wishes to persuade Balaam to place a curse on the Israelites, and so invites him to Moab for consultation (22:5–35). On his way to Moab, however, an angel of the Lord blocks Balaam's path. Despite his international reputation as a spiritual expert, Balaam cannot see the angel. The donkey, however, recognizing the presence of the angel, refuses to go any further. Finally, the Lord opens Balaam's eyes and allows him to see the angel, who commands him to tell Balak only what he is told to.

Meanwhile, Balak journeys to meet Balaam, firmly believing that he will place a curse on Israel and stop the people in their tracks. Balaam then delivers four oracles (22:36–24:25) in which he blesses Israel, to the fury of Balak. The fourth oracle is the most powerful of all, speaking in strongly messianic terms of a coming victory of the descendants of Jacob over the

Moabites (24:17–19). The authority and sovereignty of the Lord is thus demonstrated in his ability to use a pagan diviner in declaring his ultimate victory over paganism in the region.

Yet Balaam must not be thought of as a friend of Israel or the Lord. He may have refused to curse Israel at the command of the Moabites, yet he is able to exercise influence over her in other manners. As becomes clear later (31:16), Balaam advises that the best way of destroying Israel is through allowing her men to have sexual relationships with the female worshippers of local Canaanite gods. This is exactly what happens next.

25:1–18 Israel Seduced. At the military level, Israel sees herself as being favored by the Lord. Yet sin continues to be a major problem within Israel. A theme that emerges as important throughout Israel's early period in Canaan is the destructive influence of pagan beliefs and practices on the faith of the people of God. This is the case even before Israel crosses into the Promised Land (25:1–18). While still waiting at Shittim, on the other side of the river Jordan from the Canaanite city of Jericho, Israelite men become involved in various Canaanite fertility cults involving sexual immorality. The Midianites, who had allied themselves with the Moabites against Israel (22:4), were implicated in this spiritual seduction of Israel. As a result, they are declared to be enemies of Israel, despite the historic links of Moses himself with that region.

NUMBERS 26:1 – 30:16

The Census and Further Regulations

26:1–27:12 The Second Census. Some thirty-eight years have passed since a census was last undertaken. As preparation for the military campaigns that lie ahead, a second census is now undertaken to establish Israel's potential military strength in the light of the forthcoming invasion (26:1–65). A new generation has arisen since the last census; only Moses, Joshua, and Caleb remain of those who had originally left Egypt (26:65). The resulting census shows a slight decrease in the numerical strength of Israel during the forty years of wandering in the wilderness. It is clear, however, that Israel is well prepared for any military campaign that may lie ahead. Nevertheless, success or failure in such operations is firmly understood to be dependent on the continuing presence and favor of the Lord himself, rather than upon purely human strength.

27:12–23 Joshua to Succeed Moses. But who is to lead Israel into the Promised Land? The privilege and task would once seem to have belonged to Moses. However, Moses' disobedience at Kadesh (20:1–13) had disqualified him. Neither Moses nor Aaron will be permitted to enter Canaan: Aaron was already dead (20:22–29), and Moses will die before the crossing

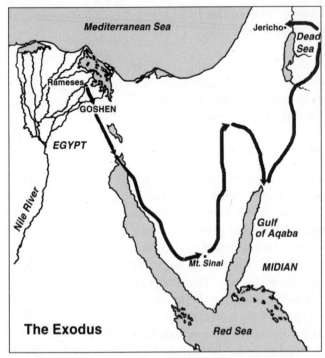

The Exodus

(Map labels: Mediterranean Sea, Jericho, Dead Sea, Rameses, GOSHEN, EGYPT, Nile River, Mt. Sinai, Gulf of Aqaba, MIDIAN, Red Sea)

of the Jordan near Shittim. He is, however, allowed to view the land from a mountain range across the Jordan before he dies (Dt 34:1–5). So who will lead Israel? We have already been introduced to Joshua the son of Nun, who has been presented as a man of integrity, courage, and obedience. The Lord declares that Joshua is the leader of his choice. The succession is thus settled and safeguarded (27:12–23).

28:1–30:16   Various   Regulations. Shortly before, we are introduced to a dispute about inheritance rights (27:1–11). This leads to the introduction of new regulations concerning these issues, which broadens out into a reaffirmation of regulations concerning various kinds of offerings (28:1–15) and the observance of festivals (28:16–29:40). Some of these regulations have already been encountered in the book of Leviticus and are repeated here to ensure that they are remembered. A final set of regulations deals with vows (30:1–16).

> Moses never entered the Promised Land. He died just before the Israelites crossed the Jordan River and conquered Jericho under the leadership of Joshua.

NUMBERS 31:1 – 36:13

Final Details

31:1–54 Vengeance on the Midianites. Earlier, the alliance between the Midianites and Moabites was noted. Moses' last act is to take vengeance on the Midianites for their actions (31:1–24). Even though Moses has family connections with Midian, he orders a thousand fighting men from each of the twelve tribes to destroy the Midianites in the region. After the division of the spoils (31:25–54), two of the twelve tribes (Reuben and Gad) request permission to remain in the region. They are attracted by the fertility of the lands and wish to remain on the east bank of the Jordan. This land, they argue, has been given to Israel by God. They should be allowed to remain there, rather than forced to cross the Jordan and enter into Canaan.

32:1–42 The Transjordan Tribes. Moses is uneasy about this proposal. The command to conquer and possess Canaan was given to *all* of the descendants of Abraham, Isaac, and Jacob. The refusal of two of the twelve tribes to cross the Jordan could lead to a general refusal on the part of the remainder to enter into Canaan, with unwelcome similarities to the earlier revolt at Kadesh. Israel had been obliged to wander in the wilderness for a generation after that rebellion. In addition, Israel will need all the fighting men at her disposal to conquer and subdue the land.

Eventually, a compromise is reached. Provided that the fighting men of Gad and Reuben go with the main body of Israel to subdue Canaan, their families may remain behind in fortified cities in the region of Gilead. After Canaan has finally been conquered, they will be free to rejoin their families on the other side of the Jordan (32:1–28). So Moses gives the land formerly occupied by Sihon, king of the Amorites, and Og, king of Bashan, to the tribes of Reuben and Gad and also to the half-tribe of Manasseh, who proceed to build safe cities in the region (32:29–42).

33:1–49 Stages in Israel's Journey. This episode is followed by a detailed account of the stages in Israel's journey from Egypt to the plains of Moab on the borders of the Promised Land (33:1–49). Forty locations are identified. Most of these are impossible to locate, because they refer to obscure regions where camps were erected, rather than to existing towns whose location can be established. But the list is important, for it allows the chronology of the later part of the exodus journey to be established (see, for example, 33:37–38, which identifies the dates of the camp at Kadesh and of Aaron's death).

33:5–34:29 Boundaries of Canaan. Moses is then commanded to take possession of Canaan and drive out all its existing inhabitants (33:50–56). The four main boundaries of the land they are to occupy are carefully defined (34:1–29). Moses then assigns regions of the Promised Land to each of the remaining nine and a half tribes. Reuben, Gad, and the half-tribe of Manasseh had already been allocated territory "on the east side of the Jordan of Jericho, toward the sunrise." Particular provision is made for the Levites (35:1–5).

> Six towns were established as "cities of refuge." Anyone who accidentally killed someone could go to one of these cities and be safe from the relatives of the dead person who wanted to avenge the death.

35:6–34 Cities of Refuge. A feature of considerable interest is the identification of "cities of refuge." Six towns, three of which were to be located in Canaan and three on the east bank of the Jordan, are to be designated in this way. The purpose of these cities is related to the accidental killing of an individual, which, by tradition, had to be avenged by someone within the family (the "avenger of blood"). Someone who finds himself in the position of having accidentally killed another person can take refuge in one of these six cities and remain there in safety. On the

Cities of Refuge

death of the high priest, there will be a general amnesty, as a result of which the person in question can return to his own people without fear of further reprisal.

Further regulations provide safeguards against false accusations of murder by insisting that more than one witness is required before anyone can be put to death on such a charge. As Israel prepares to change from being a nomadic to a settled people, she can be seen as going through a process of transition from tribal customs of revenge (in which families or clans are responsible for avenging a murder) to government by civil law (in which the state or an assembly of elders is responsible for punishing the guilty and deterring others from doing the same).

36:1–12 Inheritance of Zelophehad's Daughters. Numbers ends (36:1–12) by returning to an issue of inheritance rights, which had arisen earlier (27:1–11). The questions involve whether property or goods may be transferred from one tribe to another in the event of intermarriage between the twelve tribes. Moses declares that intermarriage between the tribes is perfectly acceptable. Tribal land, however, cannot be transferred from one tribe to another, even as an inheritance. In this way, the original allocations of territory within Canaan will be preserved.

36:13 Conclusion. Israel is now assembled on the plains of Moab, ready to enter the Promised Land. Moses, however, is still alive. The next book of the Bible, Deuteronomy, can be seen as a renewal of the covenant between God and his people before they go across the Jordan to possess the land that awaits them.

DEUTERONOMY

The title of this book is unusual. The word *Deuteronomy* comes from two Greek words literally meaning "the second law," or perhaps "the repetition of the law." This unusual title refers to the copy of the law that Deuteronomy required the king to make for himself (17:18). The work reiterates the law first delivered by the Lord to Moses at Mount Sinai and recorded in the books of Exodus and Leviticus. Deuteronomy is virtually entirely composed of addresses by Moses to Israel during the final months of his life, recounting the law given to Israel during the period of her nomadic wanderings in the desert. For this reason, it is best appreciated by reading the first four books of the Bible (or at least Exodus and Numbers) as background material.

In addition to significant sections relating to the law, Deuteronomy also includes historical sections. These summarize Israel's journey from Sinai to the borders of the Promised Land and take the story up to the death of Moses and the final confirmation of Joshua as his successor. Deuteronomy brings the first major section of the Bible (sometimes referred to as The Five Books of the Law or The Pentateuch) to an end.

DEUTERONOMY 1:1 – 4:43

The Historical Background

1:1–2:6 The Command to Leave Horeb; Rebellion Against the Lord. The book opens with Israel assembled on the plains of Moab. Forty years have passed since Israel left Egypt. After the rebellion against God's command that she enter Canaan some thirty-eight years earlier (Nu 14:33–34), Israel had been told that a period of forty years would elapse between the exodus from Egypt and her entry into Canaan. None of those living at the time of the rebellion against Kadesh, except Joshua and Caleb, would live to enter the Promised Land. Even Moses is denied that privilege. The mention of the fortieth year (1:3) immediately raises the reader's excitement; this is the year in which Canaan will be entered!

Moses begins by reminding his people that they have been called by God, who gave promises to Abraham, Isaac, and Jacob and their descendants. He relates how God finally gave them permission to move on from Sinai (also known as Horeb, as here) and to go into the Promised Land (1:6–8). He relates how spies were sent out from the camp at Kadesh to explore Canaan (1:19–25) and how they came back with good reports of what they found. But Israel refused to go in and possess the land, rebelling against the Lord (1:26–46). Moses also relates the story of his own failure to obey the Lord, which has led to his being excluded from entering the Promised Land. Thus Israel was condemned to wander around the "hill country of Seir" (2:1), just south of the Dead Sea, for a further thirty-eight years. But then the word of the Lord had come: "You have made your way around this hill country long enough; now turn north" (2:2–3).

2:7–3:29 Division of the Land; Moses Forbidden to Cross the Jordan. Moses relates to his people the great story of their triumphs as they marched northwards, defeating all who came between them and their goal (2:7–3:11). This great recital reminds the people of all that God has done for them in the past and encourages them to have great expectations for what he will do for them in the future. Canaan has been promised to them by the Lord. He is faithful to his promises and will do what he purposes for an obedient and trusting people.

Moses then relates his own part in the story: how he divided the land conquered east of the Jordan amongst the tribes of Reuben and Gad (3:12–20). Finally, he relates how on account of his failure and disobedience, he was not allowed to enter into Canaan. He was allowed to see it from a distance and was assured that his descendants would possess it; however, he would not enter into it himself (3:21–29). The constant emphasis on *possession* of the land is a major theme. Abraham, Isaac, and Jacob never possessed the land on which they lived. They were nomads, wanderers who lived off the land without ever being able to call it their own. Canaan is to be the possession of their descendants—a land that will belong to them forever.

4:1–43 Obedience Commanded; Idolatry Forbidden. Moses urges his people to remember these great acts of God. Indeed, the call to remember the Lord's great saving deeds is a common theme throughout Deuteronomy. Israel is to remember her days in slavery in Egypt and how the Lord delivered her from that oppression with a mighty hand (4:1–14). Israel's God is unique and alone can save. "Has any god ever tried to take for himself one nation out of another nation, by testings, by miraculous signs and wonders, by war, by a mighty hand and an outstretched arm, or by great and awesome deeds, like all the things the LORD your God did for you in Egypt before your very eyes?" (4:34). He alone is to be obeyed and trusted.

DEUTERONOMY 4:44 – 28:68 ————————————

The LORD's Demands for Obedience

4:44–6:3 The Law and the Covenant. The next section opens with a declaration that what follows is the law given to Israel by Moses, as she waited in the Moabite region near Beth Peor to enter the Promised Land (4:44–49). The section begins (5:1–5) with a powerful reminder of the covenant made with Israel at Sinai (here referred to by its alternative name of Horeb). The Ten Commandments (5:6–21) have already been explored (pp. 51–58), and the reader should refer back to this discussion for full details. Moses affirms that the law and the covenant are closely connected (5:22–6:19). God has promised to be with his people; his people are required to obey his laws. Moses clearly states that Israel's safety and prosperity in the Promised Land depend upon obedience to the law (6:1–3).

6:4–25 Love the Lord Your God. The passage that follows has had considerable impact on both Jewish and Christian thought (6:4–9). Moses declares that there is only one God and gives Israel this commandment: "Love the LORD your God with all your heart and with all your soul and with all your strength." The commandments are to become part of Israel's way of thinking, to be taught to her children, and to be talked about whenever possible. We see here a forceful declaration of the importance of the law of God as a means of ensuring the continuing identity and safety of God's people (a point also stressed in 6:13–19).

Moses stresses that Canaan is God's gracious gift to Israel (6:10–12). It is something that Israel by herself could never have gained. For this reason and others, Israel must never be allowed to forget God and all that he has done for his people. He has brought them out of slavery into Egypt and will give them cities they did not build, vineyards they did not plant, and wells they did not dig. These are all part of God's gracious and undeserved provision for his people. So when, in years to come, the children of those who are now living ask about the meaning of the laws that have just been given, they can be told of how these laws are a reminder of all that God has done for his people and of their need to remain faithful to him (6:20–25).

7:1–6 Driving Out the Nations. God's gracious provision for his people will also be seen in the forthcoming military campaign. Israel's victories will not be due to the might of her armies, but to the presence and power of the Lord. All pagan religious objects are to be destroyed when Israel possesses the land on account of the threat they pose to the holiness of the people of God. As the subsequent history of Israel makes clear, these warnings were well founded.

7:7–10:22 God's Chosen People. One of the most powerful themes of the Bible now becomes apparent: the election or choice of the people of God.

God did not choose Israel because of her size or strength. He chose her simply because he loved her (7:7–9). The theme of God showing his love for his people will occur time and time again in Scripture, even where God is correcting his people for their waywardness or rebellion against him. God's love is seen in action in the promises he made to Abraham, Isaac, and Jacob. The love of God for his people is an important ground for hope, especially in the light of the threat posed to Israel by other nations (7:9–26).

That love is seen at work in the chastising or correction of Israel in the desert (8:1–20). The rebellion and pain of the desert period is recalled here. God only disciplines those whom he loves, and his chastisement of Israel during its forty years in the desert is to be seen as a token of his love and care for her. She needed to learn that we do "not live on bread alone, but on every word that comes from the mouth of the LORD" (8:3). Those lessons had to be learned the hard way. Israel may find that she once more becomes proud and forgets her God (8:12–14). The lessons from her past should warn her of the dangers of forgetting the God who will never forget her.

Israel will possess the lands across the Jordan, not on account of her own righteousness or merits, but on account of the love of God for his people and his faithfulness to his promises (9:1–6). Israel's past sin, especially the making of the golden calf (9:7–10:22), is so great that she could never expect favors from God as a result of her holiness, but only on account of God's love. Israel is thus commanded to remain faithful to the Lord and obey his commands.

11:1–32 Love and Obey the Lord. This point is repeated so often (e.g., at 11:1–12) that the reader may feel wearied by it. However, the importance of the issues cannot be overstated. The very existence of Israel depends on her faithfulness to God. Without God, she will fail, lose sight of her reason for existence, and cease to exist as a nation. The frequent repetition of these promises and demands is an indication of how serious the issues are and how easily Israel can forfeit her inheritance. Moses stresses how lovely and good the land of Canaan is (11:10–12) and how Israel needs to remain faithful to the Lord if she is to possess and remain in this fertile land. Israel is thus confronted with a choice (11:26–32): she can obey the commands of God and be blessed, or she can disobey them and be cursed. Moses pleads with his people to obey God and receive the riches of God's blessing through their obedience.

12:1–13:18 True Worship. The importance of right worship is evident. Moses makes it clear that there is a real danger from syncretism—that Israel will simply take over existing Canaanite religious buildings, objects, beliefs, and practices, and by doing so, forget the Lord their God. The people must maintain their distinctiveness (12:1–32). In particular, they must resist any temptation to worship other gods (13:1–18). Any prophet, visionary or seer who declares that God wishes them to follow other gods is to be rejected as a false prophet. So serious are the dangers of worshipping other gods that anyone—even a close relative—who encourages such worship is to be put to death and his property destroyed.

14:1–27:26 Rules for Life and Worship. A series of regulations then follows—generally restating or extending regulations already given in Exodus or Leviticus. The reader may find it helpful to read these through, noticing their very precise and practical nature. Israel will be distinct, not simply on account of her religious beliefs, but on account of the way these are put into practice. External practice reinforces internal belief and faith. Examples of these regulations include the practice of tithing (14:22–29; 26:1–15). Israel was to set aside one tenth of her produce (the word *tithe* comes from the Old English word for "a tenth") for the purpose of maintaining the Levites, aliens, widows, and orphans.

One passage of special importance within this section of detailed regulations is worth particularly close attention. Moses declares (18:14–22) that after he has died, the Lord will raise up other prophets, who will declare the word of the Lord to his people. This promise may be seen fulfilled in the Old Testament prophets, who ministered to Israel at times of political and religious crisis. However, it also came to have strongly messianic overtones (see Jn 1:21, which refers to this expectation). These hopes are finally fulfilled in the coming of Jesus Christ himself, who declares God's will to his people at firsthand, as God himself.

28:1–68 Blessings for Obedience, Curses for Disobedience. This section ends with a further assurance that obeying God will bring blessing (28:1–14). The consequences of disobeying God are then made clear (28:15–68). Israel will be ruined. She will be uprooted from the land of Canaan and scattered among the nations. Moses therefore offers Israel, as she prepares to enter the Promised Land, the opportunity to renew the covenant with the Lord. This forms the subject of the next section of the book.

DEUTERONOMY 29:1 – 34:12 ────────────

The Consecration of Israel as the People of God

29:1–30:20 Renewal of the Covenant. In a ceremony of great solemnity, Moses and Israel renew their covenant with the Lord. Moses begins by reminding the people of Israel of all that God has done for them (29:1–8). The same God who made promises to Abraham, Isaac, and Jacob will continue to be the God of Israel. But Israel must be faithful to the Lord and refuse to worship any other gods (29:9–29). Obedience will lead to prosperity in Canaan and to security in the face of the many enemies they can expect to encounter. But all this is conditional upon obedience to God.

Moses declares that two options have been set before the people: life and death. The choice is theirs. If they love God and keep his commands, they will prosper and increase. If they rebel against him and abandon him, they will not live long in the land they are about to possess (30:1–20).

31:1–13 Joshua to Succeed Moses. Moses explains that he is not to be allowed to lead Israel across the Jordan into Canaan. In his place, Joshua will take command of Israel, and the Lord will go ahead of the people and give them victory. In the presence of Israel, Moses reassures Joshua of the continuing presence and favor of the Lord in the future. Moses may be taken from them; the Lord will always remain at their side.

31:14-29 Israel's Rebellion Predicted. Even with this assurance of the presence of God, Moses declares that Israel will continue to rebel against him. Despite all the warnings to the contrary, Israel will be attracted to other

In this stained-glass window in a church on Mount Nebo, Moses is depicted blessing the Israelites before they entered the Promised Land. Moses could only look at the land that God had given to his people, not enter it.

gods and will worship them. Yet although the Lord foretells this failure and sin, this does not mean that he is prepared to tolerate such rebellion. In order to deal with this situation, Moses is instructed to write down the Book of the Law and to place it alongside the ark of the covenant (31:25–26).

The truth of this prophecy may be seen from events of centuries later. It seems that this Book of the Law lay unnoticed for many years, during which Israel periodically lapsed into paganism. In 622 B.C., during the reign of Josiah, it was rediscovered (2Ki 22:1–20). When Josiah realized how much Judah had departed from the terms of the covenant, he ordered that the covenant be renewed immediately, and reforms were introduced to eliminate the pagan practices and beliefs that had crept into Israel in the period between the death of Moses and his own accession (2Ki 23:1–27). Yet the reforms introduced under Josiah were not enough to save Judah from exile. The theme of the exile begins to become of importance for the first time in 2 Kings, with the forthcoming deportation of both Israel and Judah being seen as the direct consequence of the disobedience and apostasy of their kings.

31:30–33:29 The Song of Moses and the Blessing of the Tribes. After passing over all these instructions, encouragements, and warnings to his people, Moses sings of confidence in the Lord (31:30–43) and bids Joshua, his chosen successor, to write the words of his song down for posterity (32:44–47). In the blessing of the tribes that follows (33:1–29), Moses speaks of his hopes for each of the tribes in much the same way as Jacob had earlier blessed his sons (Ge 49:1–28).

In the meantime, Moses has been allowed to have one last glimpse of Canaan. The Lord tells him that he will die on Mount Nebo (32:48–52). On account of his rebellion against God at the waters of Meribah, Moses "will see the land only from a distance," and will not be allowed to enter into it (32:52).

34:1–12 The Death of Moses. After blessing the tribes, Moses ascends Mount Nebo and is allowed to survey all the land around—land which Israel will possess. Moses has been allowed to see it before he dies. On his death, he is buried in Moab and greatly mourned by the people he has led from Egypt to the border of the new country that awaits them (34:1–9).

Deuteronomy closes with an assessment of the significance of Moses (34:10–12). There has never been anyone like him, who knew the Lord face to face. Yet with the coming of Jesus Christ, someone greater than Moses came. "For the law was given through Moses; grace and truth came through Jesus Christ" (Jn 1:17). Moses was indeed the "servant of the LORD" (34:5); Jesus Christ was his Son (Heb 3:1–6).

JOSHUA

The book of Deuteronomy brought the first major section of the Old Testament, often known as the Five Books of the Law, to an end. But the history of Israel has only just begun. During the period of wandering in the desert, Israel was given her distinctive identity as a people. Israel knew who she was, who had called her into being, and what she had to do. The narrative now moves on to the conquest of the Promised Land, as we learn how the people of God, who have wandered for forty years, enter and set down roots in the Promised Land.

JOSHUA 1:1 – 18

The Commissioning of Joshua

With the death of Moses, a new day dawns in the history of Israel. Israel is now free to enter the Promised Land and to claim at last the land that the Lord promised to their forebears many generations ago. It is clear that events now move very quickly. Joshua, the chosen successor, is formally commissioned by the Lord to lead Israel across the Jordan. (1:1–9). Joshua is commanded to remain faithful to the laws given to Moses. If he does so, his success and prosperity are assured.

Joshua wastes no time (1:10–18). Allowing three days for mobilization, he prepares to move across the Jordan. He reminds the Israelites of the great promises made to them and of their responsibilities to ensure that these promises are fulfilled. In the case of the tribes of Reuben and Gad and the half-tribe of Manasseh, he reminds the men that they must take part in the conquest of the Promised Land before they will be allowed to return to the eastern side of the Jordan and rejoin their wives and families (for the background to this, see pp. 74–75). The Israelites acclaim him as their leader and wish him the same success as that enjoyed by Moses. That success is not long in coming.

JOSHUA 2:1 – 5:12

The First Days in Canaan

2:1–24 Rahab and the Spies. Following a precedent established by Moses thirty-eight years earlier (see Nu 13:1–25), Joshua sends out spies to report back on what lies ahead of them in Canaan. The two spies are requested specifically to provide information concerning the city of Jericho, the first major Canaanite settlement lying in the path of the proposed invasion route. Like most cities of the time, Jericho was a city-state, comparable to the Greek city-states of the classical period. It was defended by substantial walled fortifications, making it a difficult military objective. As the text indicates later on, some houses were built on, or into, these walls, including the house of Rahab.

It is clear that people in the region are aware of the presence of Israel in Moab and fearful of what her intentions might be. When the presence of Israelite spies in the city is suspected, a prostitute named Rahab offers them safety and shelter (2:1–7). She explains that everyone is afraid of the Israelites and affirms her own belief that the Lord has given the land over to Israel. And just as she has shown kindness to the representatives of Israel, so the Israelites are asked to show kindness to her when they take possession of the city (2:8–14). The spies agree and ask that a scarlet cord be hung in her window. She and all inside the house will be spared. Just as the red blood of the Passover lamb marked the houses of the people of God at the time of the exodus from Egypt, ensuring that they were spared from destruction, so Rahab's scarlet cord will ensure her safety. Then the spies

God helped the Israelites cross the Jordan River. When the priests, carrying the Ark of the Covenant, stepped into the water, the river stopped, as if a giant dam had suddenly been built. The priests stood on dry ground in the middle of the riverbed until everyone was across.

are allowed to escape down a rope lowered from her window, which was set in the city's walls. After eluding their pursuers, they report back to Joshua that everyone is terrified of Israel (2:15–24; see also 5:1).

3:1–5:12 Crossing the Jordan; Circumcision at Gilgal. Encouraged by this knowledge, Joshua issues orders to cross the Jordan, with the ark of the covenant in the lead (3:1–17). There are obvious similarities between this event and the crossing of the Red Sea, not least the strong sense of expectation that something dramatic is about to happen. Having marked the site of this crossing with twelve stones (4:1–24), Joshua makes arrangements for two of the most central religious practices of Israel to be performed on Canaanite soil. First, all the males within Israel are circumcised. During the period of wandering in the desert, this rite had not been performed; now, this act of obedience to the covenant is carried out in Canaan (5:2–8), followed by the first celebration of the Passover for thirty-eight years (5:9–12). As Israel prepares to take the first steps towards conquering Canaan, she recalls how the Lord has delivered her from captivity in Egypt for this very reason.

JOSHUA 5:13 – 12:24

The Invasion of Canaan

5:13–6:27 The Fall of Jericho. Jericho now lies ahead. Encouraged by a vision of a heavenly figure who identifies himself as the "commander of the army of the LORD" (5:13–15; note the parallels with the incident of Moses at the burning bush), Joshua prepares to take the city. The story of how he orders his army to march around the city, followed by the ark of the Lord, is one of the best-known incidents in the Bible (6:2–27). On the seventh day of the siege, the walls of the city collapse, allowing Israel to gain total control. Rahab and her family are spared, but the remainder of the city, including all its inhabitants, irrespective of age, is destroyed.

This aspect of the conquest of Canaan causes concern to many reading the story, especially for the first time. How can a loving God permit such slaughter? Why are entire cities put to the sword? Did not God declare that he would spare even Sodom for the sake of a few righteous people in its midst? There are no easy answers to these questions. The ethics of warfare in the ancient world were often fairly basic: kill or be killed. However, one aspect of this matter that helps to set it in its proper context must be noted.

> Jericho was the first city conquered by the Israelites. They marched around the city for six days. On the seventh, the walls of the city collapsed, allowing them to enter. But at Ai the Israelites lost the battle because of one man.

The Canaanite people, whose land God was giving to the Israelites, worshiped the moon and other gods. The stone on the left represents a seated god. Another carving shows two hands reaching to the moon.

Israel was entering into a unique situation in her history, which she had never faced before and would never face again. She was entering into a region populated by peoples of pagan beliefs that could easily destroy the faith of Israel. As a result, it was regarded as necessary to purge such pagan beliefs and cultures from the land. In no way, then, does what happened at the time of the conquest of Canaan justify the slaughter of innocents at any other time in history. With the coming of Christ, we may rejoice that such episodes are no longer regarded as necessary or justifiable. The situation confronted by Israel as she entered Canaan will never arise again.

Sprawling modern Jericho is very different from the walled city that fell to the Israelites. The mound where the old city was located is visible on the left.

7:1–26 Achan's Sin. Success is immediately followed by sin. Despite all their pledges and oaths of obedience, Israel disobeys God at the first available opportunity. The sin in question is the theft of some of the booty from Jericho, which was meant to have been dedicated to the Lord. The theft only comes to light on account of a military failure. A band of several thousand men is dispatched by Joshua to take the nearby town of Ai, about twenty-five kilometers away. The town was not heavily populated and ought to have been an easy objective. In fact, the Israelites suffer serious losses in their abortive attempt to take it. Joshua is devastated. Has God ceased to be faithful to his covenant? Then the truth dawns: it is not God, but Israel, who has been faithless (7:1–15).

Joshua undertakes a major investigation, throwing lots until the guilty party is identified. First, the search is narrowed to the tribe of Judah, then to the Zerahite clan within Judah, then to the family of Zimri within the Zerahite clan. Achan, a member of this family, comes forward and admits his guilt. He had stolen some of the booty from Jericho and hid it under his tent. For this attempt to deceive both Israel and the Lord, he and his family are stoned to death (7:16–26). Only in this way could the guilt of their crime be purged from the people as a whole.

8:1–29 Ai Destroyed. After this purging of the guilt of the people, Joshua turns his attention again to Ai. The town is here described as having a population of 12,000 (8:25), against which Joshua commits 30,000 armed men (8:3). Archaeological evidence suggests that Ai was not a major center of population around this time and may even have existed in a ruined or semi-ruined state. There is, however, some slight doubt as to the identification of the archaeological site traditionally identified with the city. At any rate, the attack on the city (which is described in detail) is successful. Once more, the total destruction of the city and its inhabitants raises moral questions noted earlier.

8:30–35 The Covenant Renewed at Mount Ebal. The story of how Israel subdued the remainder of the land west of the Jordan will be taken up presently. Even as Israel prepares to engage in warfare with the peoples of the region, Joshua makes space for the people to renew the covenant with the Lord as Moses had commanded. This would have been a risky affair, for Israel is surrounded by hostile forces, anxious to destroy her in order to neutralize the threat she poses to their security. It is possible, however, that some local peoples have made peace with Israel. The reference to the presence of "aliens" (8:33) may refer to the presence of Gibeonites or Hivites from the region, anticipating the developments fully narrated in chapter 9.

> In the midst of the warfare necessary to take over the Promised Land, Israel renewed her covenant with God in a ceremony on Mount Ebal.

The importance of the renewal of the covenant at Mount Ebal is enormous. An altar has been built to the Lord in Canaan, establishing his claim to authority over the land and its peoples. By remaining faithful to the commands of Moses (Dt 27:1–8), Joshua ensures the continuing favor and presence of God in the forthcoming struggle to gain the ascendancy in the region.

9:1–27 The Gibeonite Deception. Three major sections now follow, dealing with the way in which Israel is able to emerge from her bridgehead in the region of Jericho and take possession of the land west of the Jordan. The sections deal respectively with the campaigns in the central, southern, and northern regions of Canaan. The first section deals with the Gibeonites (9:1–27), a group of peoples to the north of Jerusalem. Realizing that they are in danger from the advancing Israelites, the cities send emissaries to Israel. They pretend that they are from a distant region, well away from Canaan. Without consulting the Lord, Joshua agrees to enter into a treaty with them. When it

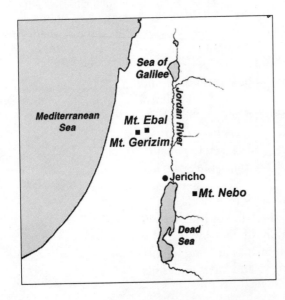

turns out that he has unwittingly made a solemn oath of peace with nearby towns, the people are furious. They will not be allowed to destroy the Gibeonites. Indeed, as it turns out later, they will even have to defend them if they come under attack. However, Joshua deals with the Gibeonites' deceit by pressing them into service as suppliers of wood and water for the altar of the Lord.

10:1–43 Southern Cities Conquered. The second section relates how Joshua deals with a coalition of kings from the southern regions of Canaan, including the cities of Jerusalem and Hebron (10:1–43). Armies from five Amorite cities lay siege to Gibeon, obliging Joshua to respond to their urgent plea for assistance. After an all-night march from his camp at Gilgal, Joshua takes the Amorite besiegers by surprise and routs them. The five Amorite kings are tracked down and executed. In a series of assaults, Joshua then lays siege to and sacks the major cities of the southern region of Canaan. In a single campaign, the entire region is subdued. It is important to notice that Joshua's sacking of the region is in response to an attack initiated from its peoples. That same pattern emerges in the account of the subjugation of the northern region of Canaan, which now follows.

11:1–23 Northern Kings Defeated. After Joshua returns to Gilgal, a coalition of city-states in the northern region of Canaan forms with the single purpose of neutralizing the threat posed by Israel (11:1–23). Armies drawn from the Galilean hill country assemble at a site referred to as Merom, which is thought to be some twelve kilometers to the northwest of Lake Galilee. Joshua defeats the armies, pursuing them to the north, and eventually turning south again to take and destroy the important city of Hazor. Joshua

The remains of a four-room home, uncovered at Hazor. This is said to have been a typical home of the Israelites. Hazor was a large Canaanite city that was conquered by Joshua.

completes his conquest of the region by defeating the Anakites. With this, the military campaigns end, and "the land had rest from war" (11:23). Joshua can now divide the land among the tribes, following the allocations laid down by Moses as described in some detail in later chapters.

This account of the conquest of Canaan is followed by a detailed list of those defeated in the campaigns of Moses and Joshua (12:1–24). As will become clear in the following chapter, there are still substantial areas of land to be taken over; however, Israel has now established a firm power base in the region from which it can expand when the time is right.

Joshua divided the land among the twelve tribes. A few received land east of the Jordan River. The map shows the territory each received, even though some of the territory had not yet been conquered.

JOSHUA 13:1 – 22:34

The Allocation of Territory to the Tribes

13:1–19:51 Division of the Land. This large section deals with the specifics of the allocation of Canaan to the tribes of Israel, giving precise details of the towns and regions they are to occupy. The account opens with details of the regions that remain to be conquered (13:1–7). It then shifts to the land east of the Jordan, which had been allocated to the tribes of Reuben and Gad and the half-tribe of Manasseh (13:8–32). In accordance with the assignment made by Moses, this allocation is confirmed and broken down by region. It must be appreciated that this territory west of the Jordan was not thought of as the "Promised Land." Attention then shifts to the Promised Land in the strict sense of the term—the areas conquered west of the Jordan, which are now allocated by lot to the remaining nine and a half tribes (14:1–19:48). Joshua himself is allocated a town in the hill country, where he will later be buried (19:49–50; 24:30).

20:1–21:45 Cities of Refuge; Towns for the Levites. The text in this part of the book of Joshua reads rather like a legal document and may seem a little uninteresting to many readers. However, it must be recalled that this section of Joshua represents the final confirmation of the promise that Israel will possess the land of Canaan. Each tribe is being allocated more than living space or grazing rights: they are being given the right

Land of the Twelve Tribes

to possess the regions assigned to them. This long section is the concrete fulfillment of the Lord's promise to give the land to the descendants of Abraham, Isaac, and Jacob. Now that promise is being fulfilled. Every region and town that is named, including the cities of refuge (20:1–9) and towns for the Levites (21:1–42), is a tangible demonstration of God's faithfulness to his promises:

So the LORD gave Israel all the land he had sworn to give their forefathers, and they took possession of it, and settled there . . . Not one of all the LORD's good promises to the house of Israel failed; every one was fulfilled (21:43–45).

22:1–34 Eastern Tribes Return Home. Finally, with the wars over, Joshua gives permission to the fighting men of the tribes of Reuben and Gad and the half-tribe of Manasseh to return home to their families, who had settled on the east bank of the Jordan. However, a misunderstanding develops, which nearly leads to war between the tribes on the east and west banks of the Jordan. Joshua had set up the tabernacle at Shiloh (18:1), about fifteen kilometers northeast of Bethel, where it would remain until the time of Samuel (see 1Sa 4:3). However, as the fighting men of Reuben, Gad, and Manasseh return to Gilead, they decide to build an altar near the Jordan, on Israelite territory. This provokes an immediate and angry response from the remaining tribes, who interpret this action as an attempt to set up a rival altar to that at Shiloh. This would have been an act of rebellion against the Lord, which would have to be punished. A delegation is sent in an attempt to avert the war that would inevitably have followed.

However, the issue is resolved. The eastern tribes had been concerned that their right to worship the Lord might have been forgotten or denied by those on the western side of the Jordan (22:24–29). Because the altar was at Shiloh, in the west, there was a danger that the eastern tribes might have been excluded from any right to worship the Lord or be part of the covenant community of Israel. Strictly speaking, the land east of the Jordan was not part of the land the Lord had promised to Israel. A case could therefore have been made for suggesting that the tribes that had settled in Gilead were not part of the people of God. The purpose of the altar at Geliloth (22:10) is to assert both their loyalty to the Lord and their right to worship him and share in his blessings to his people. Satisfied with this explanation, the delegation returns to Shiloh.

JOSHUA 23:1 – 24:33

The Death of Joshua

23:1–16 Joshua's Farewell to the Leaders. Several years of peace pass, during which Israel is able to consolidate her position. It seems that at least a decade has passed since the wars that led to Israel establishing her permanent presence in Canaan. Now Joshua is becoming old and is close to death. Using words that recall his own commissioning by the Lord to lead Israel into Canaan (1:7–8), he reminds Israel of the need to remain faithful to the Lord. He forbids intermarriage or any form of association between Israel and the peoples of Canaan on account of the potential impact that their pagan religions might have on the faith of Israel.

24:1–28 The Covenant Renewed at Shechem. Joshua then summons the tribes of Israel to Shechem to formally and solemnly renew the covenant that had been established at Mount Ebal shortly after Israel's entry into the Promised Land (8:30–35). In a powerful and moving speech, Joshua reminds his people of their origins and history (24:1–13). He recounts the calling of Abraham, Isaac, and Jacob and the migration of the people to Egypt. He reminds them of their affliction and misery in that land and of how the Lord delivered them from their bondage and led them safely to the Promised Land.

Joshua then asks all who are assembled to renew their pledges to the Lord. Those who do not wish to do so are free to serve other gods (24:14–15). Joshua affirms his own commitment to the Lord, which is echoed by the people. They freely choose to continue to serve the Lord, with all that this implies (24:16–27). Sadly, as subsequent events will show, they will prove to be as prone to rebellion and disobedience as their forefathers in the desert. Yet this lies in the future. For the moment, the talk is only of commitment and obedience. Joshua is able to dismiss the people, who return to their own regions of Canaan (24:28).

24:29–33 Buried in the Promised Land. Just as Deuteronomy ended with the death of Moses, so Joshua ends with the death of Moses' faithful successor. Joshua, having been one of the twelve spies sent out by Moses to explore Canaan half a century earlier at the time of the abortive invasion attempt (Nu 13:16–30), is now buried in his own property in the Promised Land, in fulfillment of the Lord's promises. The bones of Joseph, brought up from Egypt, are also buried in the Promised Land, so that he too might find rest in the land promised to his descendants (24:32). And so the account of Israel's wanderings ends. She has found her rest in the Promised Land. The book of Joshua is thus a story of fulfilled promises and realized hopes.

Yet Joshua has designated no successor. What will happen after his death? Who will lead Israel as she faces the new dangers which lie ahead? Will Israel ever conquer the remaining areas of Canaan? One chapter of the history of Israel now closes; another prepares to open.

JUDGES

The book of Judges deals with the history of Israel from the death of Joshua to the rise of Samuel, before there is any permanent centralized administration in the land. It chronicles the decline in religious faith and obedience in the land after the death of Joshua, especially its lapse into idolatry and pagan practices. Despite all the warnings and encouragement of Joshua, Israel fails to remain faithful to the Lord.

One of the most noticeable differences between the books of Joshua and Judges concerns the situations that confront Israel. In Joshua, Israel has to occupy and subdue Canaan, facing threats from the various peoples already living there. Israel is portrayed as a people acting and working together against these threats from within Canaan. In Judges, however, the main threats come from outside Canaan—from peoples from the east side of the Jordan, such as the Ammonites, Midianites, and Moabites. Only on one occasion is there any reference to a threat from within Canaan itself. Israel is no longer a single centralized body of people, but a settled group of tribes who have now established themselves in various regions of Canaan. Although the people share a common faith and a common story, they increasingly tend to think of their identities in terms of individual tribes and clans, rather than being members of Israel as a whole.

The word *judge* needs a little explanation. During the course of this book, we shall meet a number of individuals, such as Deborah and Samuel, who are referred to as "judges." In modern days, this would be understood to mean something like "an impartial arbitrator in legal debates," or "someone who passes judgment." However, the word is used in a very different sense in this book. Its basic meaning is "a charismatic leader raised up by God to deliver his people from danger." The emphasis is upon deliverance from danger rather than impartial legal administration! The judges are actually figures of salvation, rather than judgment. And, as will become clear from what follows, Israel certainly needs that kind of help, as she lapses into sin and rebellion.

JUDGES 1:1 – 3:6

Introduction

1:1–2:5 Israel Fights the Remaining Canaanites. Judges opens with a survey of the situation within Canaan after the death of Joshua. Large tracts of the Promised Land remain in the hands of the Canaanites. The first assault on these remaining territories is made by the fighting men of Judah (1:2–10), who make substantial advances. Of particular importance is the capture of the Philistine cities of Gaza, Ashkelon, and Ekron and their surrounding territories (1:18). Each of these cities is of major commercial and strategic importance, being located on major trade routes leading from Egypt to the north.

Other successes are scored by other tribes, including the "house of Joseph," a reference to the tribe of Ephraim and the half of the tribe of Manasseh, which chooses to settle on the west, rather than the east, of the river Jordan (1:21–26). However, the predominant pattern which emerges is that of establishing an Israelite presence in the midst of a Canaanite population. Time after time, Judges records Israel's failure to drive out the Canaanites (1:27–36). It seems that Israel's program of expansion has run out of steam. This is a clear case of failure on the part of Israel, which provokes anger from the Lord (2:1–5).

2:6–3:6 Disobedience and Defeat. The narrative then changes pace. An important bridging section deals with events after the death of Joshua and lays the foundations for an understanding of what goes wrong within Israel during the period of the judges. How can a nation that has shown such dedication and devotion under Joshua lapse into a state of lethargy or rebellion? After the death of Joshua, a generation emerges who know neither the Lord nor what he has done for Israel (2:10). As those who had been present dur-

Acco, one of the oldest known seaports in the world, was assigned by Joshua to the tribe of Asher. Many years later, the first paved road built by the Romans in Palestine went from Acco (then called Ptolemais) north to Antioch. The walls in the photograph below were built by the Crusaders about a thousand years later.

ing the nomadic period of Israel's history die, they are replaced by those who know nothing at firsthand of the great events that have led to Israel's becoming established in the Promised Land.

Disobedience and apostasy set in. Israelites begin to experiment with native Canaanite pagan religions. In particular, they worship Baal (2:13). Baal is a local god worshiped by the Canaanites and linked with fertility, both human and agricultural. Linked with Baal is the goddess Ashtoreth (also mentioned at 2:13), who is also linked with fertility cults. Worship of Baal or Ashtoreth often involved cultic prostitution and is also thought to have involved child sacrifice on occasion. By adopting these forms of worship, Israel clearly abandons her commitment to the Lord. As a result, Israel loses the protection and favor of the Lord, and becomes vulnerable to the attacks of marauders of various kinds. Judges establishes a pattern of rebellion and restoration: Israel worships other gods and finds herself in distress as a result; she returns to the Lord, and her fortunes are restored. The narrative provided by Judges illustrates this pattern many times.

Israel's misfortunes are thus seen as the direct result of the Lord's decision to try Israel and see whether she is prepared to remain faithful to him (2:20–23). In particular, the continuing presence of Canaanites in Israelite territory is seen as a result of God's withholding victory from his increasingly wayward and disobedient people (2:23). Yet Israel gradually falls away from God, allowing intermarriage with local peoples, despite Joshua's total prohibition of this practice (3:1–6).

JUDGES 3:7 – 16:31 ——————————————

Apostasy and Deliverance

3:7–5:31 Disobedience and Deborah's Song. The result of this is neatly summarized by the opening of the next section: "The Israelites ... forgot the LORD their God and served the Baals and the Asherahs" (3:7). As a result of their loss of God's favor, Israel finds herself under the oppression of a local Canaanite king. Deliverance only occurs when she repents and calls on the name of the Lord (3:8–11). The same pattern is repeated with a Moabite king (3:12–31), and with Jabin, a king of Canaan (4:1–24). In this final case, at least six tribes of Israel are rallied by the prophetess Deborah and given victory over Sisera, the commander of the forces of Jabin. Sisera himself is eventually killed by a blow from a tent peg by Jael, the wife of Heber (4:17–22). Israel subsequently overcomes Jabin (4:23–24). Deborah's song of triumph (5:1–31) is known to be one of the oldest poems in Scripture, containing many very ancient Hebrew words and expressions. It lays emphasis on the righteousness of God, which is publicly demonstrated in his victory over the enemies of his people.

6:1–40 Gideon. The narrative moves on to deal with one of the better known episodes in the Old Testament—the story of Gideon. Once more, the same pattern is noted: Israel's promises of obedience to the Lord, followed by a lapse into disbelief and disobedience. As a result, Israel finds herself being oppressed by other peoples. In this case, the oppressors are the Midianites, acting in what appears to have been a loose and shifting alliance with other peoples from the east of the Jordan, such as the Amalekites. Eventually, the Israelites are driven to despair, and, realizing that they cannot manage unaided, call upon the name of the Lord (6:1–6). They are then reminded of their failures and rebellion, and are called to repentance, despite their obstinacy (6:7–10).

The Israelites again disobeyed God and began to worship some of the pagan gods of the Canannite's. God no longer protected them. Finally a woman, the prophetess Deborah, rallied six tribes and helped to defeat one of the enemies. She used Mount Tabor to assemble her forces. The enemy was caught on the flat land.

The appointed deliverer of Israel is Gideon (6:11–24), a member of the Abierzite clan of the tribe of Manasseh. Gideon's father, Joash, illustrates well the manner in which Israel has abandoned her faith in the Lord. We learn that he has constructed an altar to Baal, along with an adjoining Asherah pole (6:25). Gideon cannot believe that he is being called by the Lord. Is he not the least important member of a rather insignificant clan? But, as Scripture makes clear, God is in the

habit of taking people who regard themselves as being insignificant and doing great things through them. Gideon is a case in point.

Gideon's mission begins at home. He must purge his family of Baal worship before he can go any further. He destroys his father's altar to Baal and replaces it with an altar to the Lord. A popular outcry results, indicating how deeply Baal worship has taken root in the region (6:28–32). However, his real mission relates to the deliverance of Israel from the Midianites and their allies. Gideon rallies first his own clan, then his own tribe, then neighboring tribes, as he prepares to deliver Israel. Yet he has genuine hesitations over his calling. Is God really with Israel? The celebrated account of how Gideon lays out a fleece to reassure himself of the Lord's intentions is too well known to need further comment (6:36–40). Its point is clear: Gideon wants to be sure that he will be acting with God's authority and support, not simply on account of some vague feeling that he is being called in this way.

7:1–8:21 Gideon Defeats the Midianites. In the end, Gideon's famous victory over the Midianites (7:1–25) does not depend on human strength, but upon the strength of the Lord. The manner of the victory makes this very clear and prevents Israel from becoming overconfident and arrogant about her own ability and power. Gideon is told to use only 300 of the 10,000 armed men who accompany him in the final assault, which (like his destruction of the altar to Baal) will take place by night. Confused by the darkness, the Midianites gain the impression that a huge Israelite army is in their midst. They scatter and are subsequently set upon and picked off by the larger Israelite force in the vicinity, as well as by others who enter the conflict once they see it is going their way. However, Gideon's success causes resentment and irritation elsewhere (8:1–21).

8:22–9:57 Gideon Dies; Abimelech Is Made King. Despite this resentment in some quarters, Gideon is recognized as the deliverer of Israel, and the people offer to make him and his descendants kings over them. Gideon refuses: only the Lord will rule over Israel (8:22–27). During the remainder of Gideon's lifetime, Israel enjoys relative peace on account of her obedience to the Lord. However, once Gideon is dead, Israel returns once more to Baal worship (8:28–35). Even Gideon's son Abimelech revolts against the memory of his father, murdering his sons and attempting to establish himself as king (9:1–7).

10:1–12:7 Tola, Jair, and Jephthah. The pattern of disobedience followed by oppression continues. After relative security under Tola and Jair (10:1–5), rebellion again breaks out. Judges records many local gods being worshiped by the Israelites (10:6–14), with a resulting destabilization in the region. Israel finds herself under attack from the Philistines to the west and the Ammonites to the east. In their situation, they again call upon the Lord, and ask for his help (10:10, 15).

The Lord raises up Jephthah the Gileadite (11:1–12:7), who routs the Ammonites. In doing so, he provokes an unfortunate feud with the Ephraimites (12:1–6). This passage is of importance historically in that it allows us to date the events in question. The reference to Israel having occupied the region for three hundred years (11:26) fits in well with what we know of the chronology of this period.

12:8–13:25 The Birth of Samson. After Jephthah, Israel enjoys relative security for a quarter of a century (12:8–15) before the cycle of rebellion and oppression begins once more. This time the oppressors are the Philistines, based on the western coastal regions of Canaan (13:1). In this case, the deliverer is to be Samson.

From the moment of his birth, it is clear that Samson is to be a Nazirite (13:5). The word *Nazirite* is derived from the Hebrew word meaning "to consecrate" or "to separate from." The term was used to refer to men and women who had taken the decision to consecrate themselves to God by separating themselves from certain things through a special vow (Nu 6:1–21).

14:1–16:31 Samson's Vengeance on, and Final Victory over, the Philistines. Samson hardly seems to be qualified as a judge of Israel. Far from being an obedient servant of the Lord, he is prone to do whatever is right in his own eyes—such as marrying a Philistine wife (14:1–3). However, the hand of the Lord is at work in a hidden manner, setting up Samson as the deliverer of his people (14:4). The story of Samson is very well known and should be read to be enjoyed.

The story has many themes of relevance to Israel, not least the way in which Samson is apparently overwhelmed by the Philistines (16:23–30). This can be seen as reflecting the way in which many Israelites think that the Lord has been overwhelmed by local pagan gods, such as Dagon. As the ultimate victory of Samson demonstrates, the Lord is still present with his people, even if they choose to rebel against him.

A further important aspect of the account of Samson is the reference to the "spirit of the LORD" coming on him in power (14:19)—an important anticipation of the manner in which God empowers his people to meet the challenges they face. In the New Testament, the coming of the Holy Spirit at Pentecost (Ac 2:1–47) may be seen as standing in a direct line of succession to this incident in the life of Samson.

JUDGES 17:1 – 21:25

Epilogue

Samson's tendency to do his own thing, rather than be openly obedient, now proves to be typical of the people of Israel as a whole, as the closing remark of this section makes clear (21:25). Israel is portrayed as lacking any centralized administration. The country has no king (18:1; 19:1) and is in the process of degenerating into moral anarchy. The series of incidents related as the book comes to a close are clearly intended to illustrate the moral and religious degeneration of this period in Israel's history. Something has to be done. Israel must be delivered from this state of decay. However, at this stage, it is far from clear what can be done about the state of things.

17:1–18:31 Micah and the Danites. Two incidents are singled out for special mention, one focusing on religious and the other on moral degeneration. First, the story is told of how a man named Micah sets up a local place of worship in Ephraim, dedicated to some local gods. A Levite is installed to preside over this paganized form of worship (17:1–13), which is taken up and spread by the tribe of Dan as they conquer neighboring territory, including the city of Laish (18:1–31). The incident, which is not specifically dated, is clearly intended to illustrate how easily pagan practices are picked up by Israel. Even though the altar at Shiloh is the only legitimate site of worship in Canaan, Micah and the tribe of Dan have no difficulty in establishing their own sites of worship, and paganized forms of worship of the Lord.

19:1–30 A Levite and His Concubine. The second incident deals with the moral corruption of Israel at the time. In terms that parallel the account of Lot's visit to Sodom (Ge 19:5), local Israelites of the tribe of Benjamin attempt to homosexually rape a traveler in the town of Gibeah, before instead raping a woman, who dies from the shock of the attack. The woman in question was the concubine of a Levite.

20:1–21:25 Israelites Fight the Benjamites. Israel is appalled at this deed and determines to take her revenge against those in Gibeah who were responsible for the act. However, the tribe of Benjamin defend their city and its inhabitants, despite the fact that it leads directly to the slaughter of their army by the remainder of Israel and the sack of their cities (20:1–48). The few remaining Benjamite males are obliged to seize young girls from the region of Shiloh to ensure the continued presence of Benjamite males in Israel (21:1–23), for no other tribe will allow them to marry their women.

This, then, is the sorry state of Israel at the end of the period of the judges. Religious and moral decay is evident. Everyone does as he pleases; there is no king to enforce authority (21:25). So will Israel become like the Canaanites and lose her distinctive beliefs and practices? Or will something happen to restore the true worship of the Lord and obedience to him? The story will be taken up in 1 Samuel.

First, we are asked to pause in the midst of this gripping historical narrative and listen to a love story set in the period of the Judges. It is a story that will play no small part in the solution of Israel's problems, as will become clear as we turn to the story of Ruth.

RUTH

The book of Ruth, which takes its name from one of its central characters, is set at the time of the Judges. As will be clear from the book of Judges, this was a time of political instability and moral and religious corruption. The background to the book of Ruth is the continuing hostility between the people of Moab and the Israelites, reflecting Moab's lingering resentment against Israel during the period of the conquest. At this time, many Moabite regions and towns had been occupied by Israel. The lands allocated to Judah were directly opposite the land of Moab, on the far side of the Dead Sea.

1:1–22 Naomi and Ruth. The story opens with an account of a famine in Israel, which obliges a family (Elimelech and his wife Naomi with their two sons) to move to Moab and find work there. While they are in this region, Elimelich dies; and both sons marry Moabite women, Ruth and Orpah. Eventually both sons die, leaving Naomi alone with her two daughters-in-law (1:5–6). Hearing that the famine has ended, Naomi decides to return home to Bethlehem, and she urges Ruth and Orpah to return to Moab and their own gods. Orpah complies with this wish, but Ruth does not (1:7–15). Even though Ruth can expect nothing from Naomi, she insists on remaining by her side. She will share Naomi's faith as well as her people (1:16–17). As a result, the two women return together to Bethlehem just in time for the barley harvest.

2:1–23 Ruth Meets Boaz. We are now told that Naomi has a relative on her husband's side named Boaz, a person of importance locally. Ruth asks permission of Naomi to go to the local fields and pick up the leftover grain (2:1–2). Without knowing either that these fields belong to Boaz or that Boaz is a kinsman of Naomi, she begins to work in some local fields. The code of law given to Moses had made provision at several points for the welfare of the poor, widows, orphans, and aliens. One such provision was the insistence that harvesters should leave behind some produce for aliens, orphans, and widows (Dt 24:19–22). Thus sheaves of wheat, olives, and grapes would remain in the fields after the harvest and could be taken and used by those less fortunate than the landowner and his workers. Boaz, on hearing of how Ruth left Moab to remain with Naomi, ensures that she is well cared for (2:3–19).

Returning to Naomi with a substantial amount of grain as a result of her labors, Ruth tells her mother-in-law about the day's events. On learning that Ruth had worked in Boaz's fields, Naomi tells her that Boaz is "one of our kinsman-redeemers" (2:20). The importance of this statement needs to be explained in a little detail. The kinsman-redeemer was a relative who had the privilege or duty to restore or preserve the full community rights of family members who had fallen on difficult times. An example of such difficulty is a family member who has had to sell himself into slavery to pay off a bad debt. The word *redeem* here means "to buy back." The particular duties of the kinsman-redeemer included the responsibility of redeeming family land where this had to be sold, redeeming enslaved family members, providing an heir for the family, avenging the death of murdered family members, and acting as a trustee for family business.

The kinsman-redeemer is of particular importance in the book of Ruth. The most likely explanation of what happens here is that Elimelech had been obliged to sell his land in Judah before leaving for Moab. Naomi would have retained the right to buy the land back, thus keeping it within the family; however, lacking the funds to do so, she is dependent upon someone in the family buying it back on her behalf. Without this redemption, she cannot possess the land to which she has rights or benefit from it in any way.

3:1–18 Ruth and Boaz at the Threshing Floor. Naomi then instructs Ruth to go to the threshing floor and sleep at Boaz's feet (3:1–6). The actions in question would probably be interpreted as indicating that Ruth wishes to marry Boaz, although it is clear that she also wishes to draw attention to the fact that he is her kinsman-redeemer. Boaz is clearly flattered by Ruth's attention (3:10). However, he points out that there is someone else who has priority over him as the kinsman-redeemer (3:12–13). Boaz nevertheless promises to intervene if things do not work out well. Satisfied, Ruth returns to Naomi.

4:1–17 Boaz Marries Ruth. Later, Boaz goes to the town

Another famine in Israel sent a family out of the country, to Moab. There were marriages and deaths, as in any family. But one son's widow, a Moabite woman named Ruth, moved to Bethlehem, marries again, and became the great-grandmother of David, the greatest king Israel has ever had.

gate, the traditional place for transacting local business and legal matters. The other kinsman-redeemer eventually turns up, and Boaz raises the subject of the redemption of Elimelech's land. The kinsman-redeemer, who is never identified by name, agrees in the presence of witnesses to buy back the land (4:1–4). Boaz then asks him to take Ruth into his home as his wife. The kinsman-redeemer declines, probably worried of the legal consequences of any male children he might have by her, who would have had certain inheritance rights concerning the property (4:6). As a result, the kinsman-redeemer declines to redeem the property and hands over all his rights in this matter to Boaz. Boaz publicly declares his intention to redeem the property and to marry Ruth (4:8–12). And so the story ends happily. Ruth marries Boaz, and they have a son named Obed.

4:18–22 The Genealogy of David. We then learn the full significance of this love story. Obed will himself marry and have a son named Jesse. And Jesse will have a son named David—the greatest king Israel will ever have. Through David, Boaz and Ruth are ancestors of Jesus Christ himself (Mt 1:5). What may read simply like a love story turns out to be God's providence at work, preparing the way for the renewal of Israel under David and its redemption through Jesus Christ.

1 AND 2 SAMUEL

The book of Judges gave a graphic account of Israel's degeneration into political, religious, and moral corruption after the golden period of Joshua. It left its reader wondering what would happen next. How could order be restored to this situation? How could Israel be brought back to the worship of the Lord? The answer is provided in 1 and 2 Samuel, which was originally one larger book, but was divided into two halves by early translators. The two works together document the development of kingship in Israel. The division (which cannot be regarded as part of the original inspired text of Scripture!) is not entirely helpful and disrupts the flow of the work. To make the reading of the work easier and to bring out the continuity of the story, we shall treat the two volumes as one work (a practice that will also be adopted in the case of 1 and 2 Kings and 1 and 2 Chronicles).

One of the developments that should be noted in this narrative is the emergence of the terms *Israel* and *Judah* to refer to the northern and southern regions of the land that was originally Canaan. The term *Israel* was originally used to refer to the whole area, up to and during the reign of Saul. However, after the death of Saul, open warfare resulted between the supporters of Saul in the north and the supporters of David in the south of the country. Because David was himself a member of the tribe of Judah, it was probably only to be expected that the term *Judah* came to refer to both the southern tribes of Simeon and Judah (Jos 19:1–9), who backed David against the house of Saul.

The house of Saul regarded itself as continuing the rule of Saul over all Israel and thus retained the term *Israel* to refer to its sphere of influence, despite the fact that this now referred only to the northern region of the country. David is initially proclaimed king of Judah at the southern city of Hebron. It is only as a result of his military campaigns that he becomes king of all Israel. Up to the time of Saul's death, there had been a non-Israelite corridor separating the northern tribes from the southern tribes. This corridor included the city of Jerusalem, which was held by the Jebusites, and the city of Gezer, which was under Egyptian control. David's conquest of Jerusalem united the two halves, a process that was finally completed when Gezer was given to Solomon as a wedding present by Pharaoh (see 1Ki 9:16–17).

When the united kingdom was divided into two after the death of Solomon (930 B.C.), it was natural that the northern kingdom should retain the name *Israel*, and the southern kingdom, centering on Jerusalem, the name *Judah*. But this lies far ahead. We must now return to the story of how the monarchy came to be established in the first place.

It will be recalled that the closing chapters of the book of Judges frequently reiterated that "in those days Israel had no king" (Jdg 17:6; 18:1; 19:1; 21:25). So how did the kingship come to be established? We shall begin to explore the story of how this happened, which begins with the birth of Samuel.

1 SAMUEL 1:1 – 7:1

The Call of Samuel

1:1–2:11 The Birth of Samuel and Hannah's Prayer. The story of the beginnings of Israel's kingship opens by introducing us to Elkanah and his two wives, Hannah and Penninah (1:1–20). Hannah has no children and is deeply distressed by this fact, not least because Penninah has had children by Elkanah and taunts Hannah over her infertility. Hannah prays for a child and promises that she will dedicate him to the Lord as a Nazirite (see Nu 6:1–21). A local priest named Eli hears of her plight and assures her that the God of Israel will grant her this wish. In due course, she conceives and gives birth to a son named Samuel.

As she had promised, Hannah dedicates Samuel to the Lord (1:21–27) and exults that the Lord has remembered her in her distress and affliction (2:1–10). This remarkable song of thanksgiving and trust is similar in many ways to the song of thanksgiving associated with Mary, on learning that she is to bear a child who will be the Savior of the world (Lk 1:46–55).

2:12–36 Eli's Sons. Samuel ends up serving in the household of Eli and assisting in the service of the sanctuary at Shiloh. The state of religious and moral degeneration in Israel is brought home vividly by the account of the behavior of Eli's sons. The sons were in the habit of sleeping with servant women in the Tent of Meeting in a way that seems to reflect practices current at pagan Canaanite sanctuaries. Samuel, however, is untainted by this abuse, and "continued to grow in stature and favor with the LORD" (2:26). A turning point is reached with the visit of an unnamed "man of God" to Eli, who passes judgment on Eli and his family and declares that the Lord will raise up a future "faithful priest," who will begin to put things to rights (2:27–36).

3:1–21 The Lord Calls Samuel. From what we know of Israel's corruption at this stage, it is no cause for surprise that "in those days the word of the LORD was rare" or that "there were not many visions" (3:1). Yet something now happens. Samuel, although perhaps only twelve years of age, is called by name by the Lord as he lies near to the ark of God. Initially thinking that it is Eli who is calling, Samuel wakes the older man up. Realizing that Samuel is being called by the Lord, Eli urges Samuel to reply to the Lord and listen to what is said. The message that is then delivered to Samuel by the Lord is uncompromising: something major is about to happen at the same time as his judgment against Eli will be carried out. Eli accepts this news calmly. It is not long before Samuel is widely recognized as a prophet. God continues to make himself known to Samuel at Shiloh.

4:1–22 The Philistines Capture the Ark. The Israelites, finding themselves in one of their periodic disputes with the Philistines, have just received a mauling in their latest engagement. Recognizing that their failure is a mark of God's displeasure, the people decide to ensure that God will be with them on their next expedition. They resolve to bring the ark of God into battle with them, assuming that where the ark goes, the Lord is sure to follow. However, as events prove, things are just not that simple. Pagans might believe that their gods are present everywhere their symbols are displayed. The same is not true of the Lord, whose presence is conditional upon obedience, trust, and repentance. (It will be recalled how God threatened to allow Israel to enter into the Promised Land without his presence, on account of her disobedience in the desert.) The Philistines utterly rout the Israelites, capture the ark of God, and slay the two sons of Eli.

On hearing the news, Eli is so shocked that he falls off his chair and dies of a broken neck. His daughter-in-law goes into premature labor from which she dies (4:12–20). The name she chooses for her newborn son—Ichabod (which literally means "no glory")—as she dies is an apt comment on the state of Israel at the moment. As she remarks, the glory of the Lord has departed from Israel (4:21–22).

5:1–7:2 The Ark Returned to Israel. The Philistines find that the presence of the ark in their midst brings them no advantages. It is moved from one city to another as misfortune falls on them (5:1–12). Finally, fed up with their misery, the Philistines arrange for the ark to be returned to Israel. It eventually finds it way to Kiriath Jearim, where it remains for twenty years (6:1–7:2). Eventually, it will be brought to Jerusalem in triumph by David. That, however, lies far in the future.

7:3–17 Samuel Subdues the Philistines at Mizpah. At the moment, Israel's worries focus on the Philistines. Realizing that their misfortunes reflect their own disobedience, the people call on Samuel for advice. He demands that they recommit themselves to the Lord and get rid of their Baals and Ashtoreths (pagan Canaanite gods and goddesses). Once this has been done,

Samuel makes a sacrifice to the Lord. The subsequent victory of Israel over a Philistine sneak attack confirms that the Lord is with her once more.

1 SAMUEL 8:1 – 12:25

The Establishment of Kingship in Israel

8:1–22 Israel Asks for a King. Samuel judges Israel for many years. Finally, he hands this job over to his sons, whom he appoints as judges. Their failings lead to discontent and to a growing popular demand for a king. Israel demands to be like the other nations around them in this respect. However, this request displeases the Lord. He is their king. Why should the people set up anyone else in his rightful place? Through Samuel, he gives a warning of what the establishment of a kingship in Israel may lead to—exploitation and centralized domination. But the people have made up their collective mind. They want a king like all the other nations. The idea of the distinctiveness of Israel has lost its appeal for them. They want to be like everyone else. And so the Lord reluctantly allows them their way. But who is to be king?

9:1–10:8 Samuel Anoints Saul. Samuel is told by the Lord to await the arrival of a young man (who we later learn is aged thirty) from the tribe of Benjamin and to anoint him as king. He will deliver Israel from the oppression of the Philistines. In due course, Saul arrives and is told that he is to be king (9:1–27). Samuel then anoints Saul with oil as a sign of his being chosen and equipped by God for the task of leadership (10:1–8). This is a private event; the public aspects of his election will come later. So important is the practice of anointing that it needs further comment.

Anointing with oil was a practice widespread in Old Testament times. In everyday contexts, anointing with oil was a form of personal cleansing or a mark of honor to a distinguished guest. Corpses were also anointed prior to burial, sometimes with very expensive perfumed oils and ointments. In a religious context, anointing was a practice associated with both purification and healing. The practice also had a religious significance that was of major importance in relation to figures of public office. Kings, priests, and prophets were all anointed as a sign of their having being chosen and appointed by God for these specific ministries. The word *Messiah* (literally, "one who is anointed") came to have the sense of "the one appointed by God" for the redemption of his people. In this developed sense of the word, the term refers to Jesus Christ (the word *Christ* is the Greek form of *Messiah*).

10:9–11:15 Saul Made King. Shortly after his anointing, Saul receives the promised Spirit of the Lord (10:9–11). Samuel then summons all Israel to formally announce the choice of king. There is widespread, yet not universal, rejoicing over the selection of Saul (10:12–27). However, the choice of

Saul does not mean that he is installed in a palace with servants and rich furnishings. When we next meet him, he is out in a field behind his oxen. Initial misgivings concerning his selection are soon overcome: Saul leads a successful offensive against an invading Ammonite army (11:1–11). Saul is then publicly confirmed as king of Israel at Gilgal, the site of Joshua's

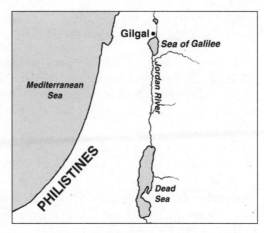

Because the people wanted a king, God told the prophet Samuel to anoint Saul as the first king of Israel. His 42-year reign began with a minor attack against the Philistines, who came after Saul's army at Gilgal.

campaigns during the period of the conquest of Canaan (11:12–15).

12:1–25 Samuel's Farewell Speech. In a farewell speech, Samuel then reminds Israel of all that God has done for her, drawing the people's attention to his great acts of deliverance and faithfulness. He warns them of the consequences of having a king. The well-being of Israel is dependent on the obedience of both king and people to the Lord. A king is no defense against anything or anyone if Israel does evil in the sight of the Lord.

1 SAMUEL 13:1 – 31:13

The Reign of Saul

13:1–15 Samuel Rebukes Saul. So the 42-year reign of Saul begins. It opens with an attack made by Saul's elder son, Jonathan, against a Philistine outpost, which causes outrage against Israel in Philistia. A huge Philistine army is mustered, equipped with chariots—formidable weapons of war, which Israel will not possess until later in her history. The Israelite army, based at Gilgal, begins to shrink as men desert in the face of this threat. Finally, after seven days, Saul offers a sacrifice to God, which ought to have been offered by Samuel. Samuel is furious. Saul's disregard of his instructions is tantamount to rebelling against God, whose representative Samuel is.

13:16–14:22 Israel Without Weapons. Philistia's advantages over Israel are considerable. Their armies are equipped with chariots and other advanced weapons of war to which Israel will not have access until the time of Solomon. The Philistines have also mastered the production of iron. Realizing its military potential and concerned to ensure that their enemies should not have access to the iron needed to make spears and swords, they have prohibited the setting up of iron works anywhere in Israel. As a result, Israel is at a considerable disadvantage over her enemy (13:16–22). Despite this disadvantage, Israel is able to defeat the Philistines by surprise. In the resulting confusion, the Philistines end up using their iron swords against each other rather than against Israel (13:23–14:22).

14:23–15:35 The Lord Rejects Saul as King. Israel's victory is carefully attributed to the Lord, not to Saul or Jonathan (14:23). In what follows, we begin to realize that Saul has a number of serious failings that call into question his competence as king (14:24–48). We learn of his ill-considered oath, which leads to his army first becoming weary with hunger, then gorging itself on blood (something prohibited by the Law of Moses). Even Saul's decision to build an altar to the Lord—the first time he has done such a thing, as the text notes (14:35)—is something of an afterthought. Despite all Saul's failings, Israel manages to expel the Philistine invaders from her land. Nevertheless, throughout Saul's reign there is continuing war between Israel and the Philistines (14:49–52).

Saul's obedience to the Lord also begins to waver substantially. Samuel, who had anointed Saul as king over Israel, instructs him to rid the land of the Amalekites. Saul deliberately disobeys Samuel over one issue (15:1–35). In the course of a bitter exchange between the two men, Samuel makes it clear that the Lord no longer supports Saul. Saul has rejected the word of the Lord; now "the LORD has rejected you as king over Israel" (15:26).

16:1–14 Samuel Anoints David. Just as Samuel had earlier anointed Saul in secret as king of Israel in obedience to the Lord, so he is now led to find his replacement. Samuel is told that the Lord has chosen one of the eight sons of the Bethlehemite Jesse (who is, it will be recalled, the grandson of Boaz and Ruth) as future king. To his surprise, it turns out to be David, the youngest son, whom Jesse did not even think worth calling over to meet Samuel. The story of how the Lord chooses David to be king over Israel is packed with important insights. Of these, probably the most important is that it is not outward appearance that matters in the service of the Lord. For example, it is clear that Jesse's son Eliab was strong and tall (16:6); but in the end, Samuel is led to choose David, the youngest of Jesse's sons, as the future king of his people:

The LORD does not look at the things man looks at. Man looks at the outward appearance, but the LORD looks at the heart. (16:7)

Samuel anoints David with oil, and the Spirit of God comes upon him in power. He is not yet king of Israel. He is, however, the man whom God has called and equipped for the task that lies ahead of him. Simultaneously, we learn that the Spirit of the Lord has departed from Saul.

16:14–23 David in Saul's Service. In the meantime, Saul is still king. David becomes part of Saul's court circle (16:15–23). Unaware of the Lord's intentions, Saul brings within his inner circle the man whom the Lord has chosen to be his replacement. It is clear that David's court appointment is not permanent, with the result that he is often to be found tending his father's flocks. It is during one such occasion that the incident takes place that propels David into the forefront of Israel's life.

17:1–58 David and Goliath. In one of his periodic battles with the Philistines, Saul finds himself confronted with the giant Goliath, who is reported as being "six cubits and a span" high—roughly nine feet or three meters. Goliath terrifies the Israelites, not least by demanding that they send out someone from the Israelite side to face him in single combat. There is a noticeable absence of enthusiasm on the Israelite side about this offer. David, who has been sent by Jesse to ensure that his older brothers are well, volunteers to fight Goliath. Discarding the heavy military armor he is offered for protection, he approaches Goliath armed only with his sling and five smooth stones as projectiles. Confident that the Lord will deliver him (17:37), he fells Goliath with his first shot. Taking Goliath's sword out of its scabbard, he kills the giant with his own weapon. Panic results within the Philistine camp, and the Israelites are able to wreak havoc as the invaders flee.

18:1–30 Saul's Jealousy of David. Perhaps the outcome is inevitable. Saul becomes jealous of David on account of his greater fame. The fight with Goliath has captured everyone's imagination. It is David, not Saul, that they are talking about. Afraid of him, Saul can do nothing to stop his growing reputation (18:1–16). His attempt to send David to his death in a further confrontation with the Philistines merely leads to David's gaining his daughter Michal in marriage and becoming even more celebrated in his subsequent victories (18:17–30).

19:1–24:22 Saul Tries to Kill David. Finally, Saul decides to have David killed. Saul's elder son, Jonathan, who is very fond of David, alerts him to the plot. At one point, Saul attempts to kill David himself. As a result, David becomes a fugitive and seeks refuge with Samuel at Ramah (19:1–24). He seeks Jonathan's advice and guidance. In a moving scene, the two men swear friendship before going their separate ways (20:1–42). David now lives a nomadic existence, pursued by Saul (21:1–23:29). At one point, David even has an opportunity to take Saul's life, but he decides to spare him.

After David killed the Philistine giant Goliath, King Saul became jealous. He even tried to have David killed. Saul was wounded when the Philistines attacked him at Mount Gilboa. He committed suicide rather than be captured.

On discovering how close he has come to being killed by David, Saul repents. However, David, suspecting that the repentance may not be genuine, continues to be wary of Saul and his men (24:1–22).

25:1–26:25 Samuel Dies. In the midst of this situation, Samuel dies (25:1). It is a moment of considerable uncertainty. Who will succeed him? Who will act as a prophet to Israel in the times ahead? The question remains unanswered. Our attention is immediately drawn back to the continuing feud between Saul and David (25:2–44), which has reached the stage at which Saul has given his daughter Michal, who was earlier married to David, to another man. Once more, Saul's pursuit of David leads to a situation in which is David is in a position to take Saul's life. Again, he spares it, with the result that Saul repents—at least, for the time being (26:1–25).

27:1–28:25 David Among the Philistines. Aware that Saul's repentance tends to evaporate after a few days, David moves to the territory of the Philistines themselves, in the belief that Saul is hardly likely to pursue him in those hostile regions. Taking a small army of six hundred men with him, David settles in the city of Ziglag, whose precise identity and location remain unknown. A condition of safe conduct in the region is that he and his men must serve in the Philistine army on demand (27:1–28:2).

Saul, his mood of repentance having duly spent itself, consults a witch to learn of his own future. In a scene that demonstrates Saul's abandonment of the Lord in favor of the occult, the figure of Samuel speaks of Saul's forthcoming doom. Terrified, Saul returns to his camp at Mount Gilboa to await the inevitable (28:3–25).

29:1–30:31 Achish Sends David Back to Ziglag. Meanwhile, David's relationship with the Philistines becomes problematical. Although serving in the Philistine army, David and his men are relieved of their duties on account of the Philistines' fear that David's men may turn against them when they go to war against Saul (29:1–11). When they return to Ziglag, they find it in ruins as the result of an attack by the Amalekites. Eventually, David and some of his men track down the raiding party and recover all the people and items that have been carried off (30:1–31).

31:1–13 Saul Takes His Life. The planned Philistine attack against Saul's forces at Mount Gilboa now takes place. In what is clearly a ferocious attack, the Philistines kill three of Saul's sons, including Jonathan. Saul himself is mortally wounded by an arrow, and he commits suicide to avoid further humiliation. Panic sets in within Israel as the news of the defeat and deaths becomes known. In a moving gesture, the men of the town of Jabesh Gilead, which Saul had earlier defended against the Ammonites (see 11:1–11), recover the bodies of Saul and his sons and bury them at Jabesh. So how can Israel recover from this catastrophic defeat? Will David ever succeed Saul as king of Israel? Is there any Israel left over which he can be king? Second Samuel immediately takes up the story.

2 SAMUEL 1:1 – 5:5

David's Accession to the Throne

1:1–27 David's Lament for Saul and Jonathan. While at Ziglag, David learns of the death of Saul and Jonathan from an eyewitness to the events who claims to have delivered the death blow to Saul. The eyewitness, who is an Amalekite, presumably expects David to be delighted with his alleged action. Instead, David orders the man to be executed and goes into mourning for Saul and Jonathan. Personal grief, however, soon gives way to a sense of duty. If Saul is dead and he, David, has been anointed king of Israel, should he not be back in Israel instead of hiding in the territories of the Philistines? The Philistines regard David as an enemy of Saul. They are ignorant of his secret anointing by Samuel to be king of Israel. Had they known of this, they would have moved against him.

2:1–3:38 War Between the Houses of David and Saul. David seeks advice from the Lord before setting out for the city of Hebron, where he is publicly acclaimed and anointed as king over Judah (2:1–7). However, Saul's family have no intention of handing the monarchy over to Saul's enemy David. A surviving son of Saul is given the kingship by one of Saul's commanders, without any authority to do so from the Lord (2:8–10). The scene is thus set for a major confrontation between two claimants to the throne of Israel. Initially, there is a small-scale confrontation between the two parties at Gibeon, a town well away from the Philistine armies. This battle is won by David's men (2:11–32).

This battle turns out to be an indication of the way things will develop in the future. The war between the house of Saul and the house of David, as the two parties are known, goes on for some time, with the house of David gradually gaining the upper hand (3:1–5). A turning point is reached when Abner, the commander who had installed Saul's son Ish-Bosheth as king over Israel, defects to David. An agreement is reached between David and Abner (3:6–21). Unaware of this, Joab, one of David's more successful commanders, murders Abner (3:22–38). David, who had no part in this plot and had promised Abner his life, is outraged by this development and goes into public mourning.

4:1–5:5 David Becomes King Over Israel. However morally bankrupt the murder of Abner may have been, it certainly had the effect that Joab probably calculated it would. The house of Saul is totally demoralized. Sensing the way things are moving, two of Ish-Bosheth's commanders murder him and bring his head to David. David has the commanders killed and buries Ish-Bosheth's head with Abner in Hebron (4:1–12). With this development, the resistance of the house of Saul to David collapses, and David is publicly anointed as king over the entire people of Israel (5:1–5). He has already been accepted as king by the southern region of Judah; his authority now extends over the entire area.

2 SAMUEL 5:6 – 10:19

The Early Successes of David's Reign

5:6–25 David Conquers Jerusalem. Once he has been established as king of Israel, David moves to consolidate Israel's position. In a major advance, he captures the Jebusite city of Jerusalem (5:6–16), which he renames as the "City of David." It will be his capital throughout his reign and will become heavily reinforced to ensure its safety. Having established his base at Jerusalem, David is able to deal with the threat still posed by the Philistines. As they advance to find and eliminate David (whom they have, of course, earlier harbored on their own territory), David seeks the guidance of the Lord as to how to deal with them. Following the guidance given, he is able to rout them and force them to retreat to their own territory (5:17–25).

6:1–23 The Ark Brought to Jerusalem. With his military situation now stabilized, David arranges for the ark of God, which has been left in the house of Abinadab for the last two decades, to be brought to Jerusalem. There is resistance to this transfer from Abinadab's family. However, the ark eventually arrives to be placed inside a tent in Jerusalem, to great rejoicing (6:1–23).

7:1–29 God's Promise to David. David feels that it is quite inappropriate for the ark of God to rest in a tent, while he himself lives in a richly furnished palace (7:1–3). He consults Nathan, a prophet, who receives a message from the Lord about both the ark of God and the future of David's descendants (7:4–17). David does not need to build God a house. Rather, God will build David a house—that is to say, a dynasty. It is David's descendants who will build the house of the Lord. The Lord promises through Nathan to establish David's throne forever, and to be his father, just as he would be the Lord's son (7:14). This strongly messianic prophecy will be the basis of Israel's future messianic hopes, which will eventually find their fulfillment in the coming of Jesus Christ as the son of God. David responds with a prayer of thanksgiving and adoration (7:18–29) in which he recalls and praises the Lord's goodness and faithfulness.

8:1–10:19 David's Victories. God's faithfulness is seen at work further in the great victories David subsequently achieves, in which a series of enemies is defeated. In many ways, David's string of victories—including the defeat of the Jebusites, Philistines, Moabites, Arameans, and Ammonites—can be seen as extending the victories won by Joshua at the time of the conquest. Under David, Israel will reach its pinnacle of power, territory, and influence. Yet all is not well. In the midst of his military triumphs, David is beginning to show personal weaknesses that will ultimately cause division and weakness within Israel.

2 SAMUEL 11:1–20:26

David's Later Failures

11:1–27 David and Bathsheba. The first sign of any disapproval on the part of the Lord for any of David's actions now makes its appearance. The victory against the Ammonites is being followed up by Joab, one of David's most effective commanders. David himself remains in Jerusalem. There he notices Bathsheba, the wife of Uriah the Hittite. (Although the Hittites had long since left the region of Canaan, some had remained behind and settled there, including Ahimelech, noted at 1Sa 26:6.) David, attracted by her, sends for her, and ends up sleeping with her. Soon afterwards, Bathsheba discovers that she is pregnant by David. Under the Mosaic law, this development means that both David and Bathsheba are liable to the death penalty (Dt 22:22). David summons Uriah home, apparently in the hope that he will sleep with his wife, so that the pregnancy will not be regarded as suspicious or attributed to him. But Uriah does not sleep with his wife (11:1–13).

Adultery is now supplemented by David's deliberate decision to murder Uriah. David arranges for Joab to ensure that Uriah is given a dangerous task and placed in a position in which he is certain to be killed. The strategy succeeds. By taking totally unnecessary risks, Joab ensures the death of Uriah, as well as others. David learns of this news and sends a brief message of condolence to Joab. Then he takes Bathsheba as his wife and she bears him a son. Yet "the thing David had done displeased the LORD" (11:14–27).

12:1–30 Nathan Rebukes David. This leads to a confrontation between the prophet Nathan and the king. Nathan, who had earlier pronounced God's blessing upon David, now chastises him by telling a parable. In this story, a rich man with many sheep killed the little pet lamb of a poor man and offered it to his guests as food. David is outraged at the story. Anyone who behaves like that deserves to die! Nathan informs him that he, David, is that man. He has taken Uriah's wife and delivered him over to a certain death. The Lord is angered by his actions and will bring disaster upon him in consequence. The death of the son of this adulterous relationship follows, to David's intense distress (12:1–23). However, things then seem to begin to go better for David. Bathsheba eventually gives birth to another son, who is named Solomon. And the military campaign against the Ammonites reaches a successful conclusion (12:24–31).

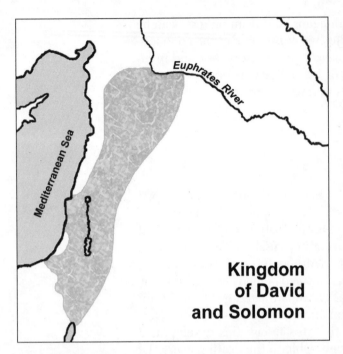

Kingdom
of David
and Solomon

The kingdom of David and Solomon stretched from the Euphrates River in the north to the Gulf of Aqaba in the south.

13:1–14:33 *Absalom Kills Amnon.* Other events point to degeneration and moral decay within David's circle. Amnon, David's eldest son, rapes Tamar, David's daughter by another wife. This leads to serious friction between Amnon and Tamar's brother, Absalom, which culminates in Absalom killing Amnon some time later (13:1–39). Absalom flees Jerusalem, but eventually returns through the good offices of Joab. Despite his great love for his son, David initially refuses to see him on account of his murder of Amnon. Eventually, however, he relents and kisses Absalom (14:1–33). There is no hint of the treachery that is to come.

15:1–12 *Absalom's Conspiracy.* It soon becomes clear that Absalom is ambitious. Not only does he take possession of a chariot (an advanced weapon of war that has not been used in Israel up to that point), but he waits by the city gate for those arriving from outside Jerusalem seeking justice and gains their affection by promising justice if he is ever to become judge of Israel. After four years, Absalom returns to Hebron with the objective of proclaiming himself as king. While there, he is joined by one of David's closest advisers, Ahithophel (15:1–12).

15:13–16:14 *David Flees.* Finally, David hears of Absalom's growing popularity and realizes that a conspiracy is under way. Aware of the danger he is in and appalled that his own son has betrayed him in this manner, David flees Jerusalem. However, David requests Hushai the Arkite, a member of David's inner circle, to go back to Jerusalem, insinuate himself within Absalom's advisers, and attempt to frustrate his plans (15:32–37).

16:15–17:29 *The Advice of Hushai and Ahithophel.* When Hushai arrives in Jerusalem, he discovers that Absalom is already totally dependent upon Ahithophel for advice (16:15–23). Absalom's chief concern is to eliminate his father and his armies; he therefore asks both Ahithophel and Hushai (who he believes to have rebelled against David) what he should do. Ahithophel has no doubts: Absalom should send out 12,000 men immediately with the specific mission of killing David alone. Once David is dead, his supporters will return to Jerusalem and transfer their allegiance to Absalom. Hushai advises Absalom to mobilize all Israel and wipe out both David and his army. (This will take time and will give David time to escape.) To ensure that David knows what is happening, Hushai sends word by messengers to David, so that he can avoid the action that is being planned against him (17:1–22).

Ahithophel, on realizing that his advice is not being followed, hangs himself (17:23). This can be seen simply as a piqued response to the rejection of his advice. However, a much more probable explanation is that he realizes that if Hushai's advice is followed, Absalom's revolt will fail, with the result that all the conspirators, including himself, will be killed. In the meantime, David makes plans to deal with the impending conflict.

18:1–19:8 Absalom's Death. By dividing his army into three independent sections, it will be difficult for Absalom to work out which, if any, is protecting David. David urges his commanders to be gentle with Absalom if they find him. In the event, the dispersion of David's forces leads to Absalom's army being spread out over a wide area, including forests (18:6–8). As a result, Absalom himself becomes detached from his own forces. Absalom's end is somewhat squalid. He gets stuck in a tree and is finished off (without David's knowledge or permission) by Joab and his companions (18:9–18).

David is deeply distressed by the news of his son's death and weeps bitterly (18:19–33). This throws his army into confusion, to the intense irritation of Joab, their commander (19:1–8). The army expects David to be grateful to them for delivering him from Absalom. Instead, David is distressed at their achievements. It is clear that Joab is convinced that David has lost his stamina and is no longer fit to be king.

19:9–20:26 David Returns to Jerusalem. David seems to become increasingly incompetent as a king in the period that follows. On his return to Jerusalem, he appears, apparently unwittingly, to favor the men of Judah over the men of Israel by allowing the former to escort him over the Jordan, leading to serious tensions developing between the two groups of men (19:9–43). This tension is exploited by Sheba, who incites the men of Israel to desert David. As a result, David is forced to rely totally on Joab and the men of Judah for support (20:1–5). Joab tracks Shimri down to the northern city of Abel Baeth Macaah. Having laid siege to the town, he offers to lift the siege and spare the city, providing its citizens hand over Sheba. In response, the citizens behead Sheba, and throw his head to Joab outside the city (20:6–26).

2 SAMUEL 21:1 – 24:25 ——————————————

Conclusion

21:1–22 The Gibeonites Avenged; Wars Against the Philistines. At this point, the strictly chronological arrangement of material in the books of Samuel ends. The final sections of 2 Samuel contain a number of reports concerning

The Citadel, or Tower of David, in Jerusalem, above, was built long after David had died. It was one of the towers of Herod's palace.The minaret was added in the 1500s. But the tomb on the right may be David's. He was buried in the City of David—the oldest part of Jerusalem— where this tomb is located.

David's reign, arranged as an appendix to the main body of the text. The incident relating to the Gibeonites (21:1–14) clearly dates from before the rebellion of Absalom. There is no reference to the original incident between Saul and the Gibeonites (21:1) that lies behind this episode and that is understood to be the root cause of the famine. The fate dealt to the remaining members of the house of Saul can be seen as confirming the rejection of Saul by the Lord. Once Saul's guilt has been purged, the famine ends. This is followed by an account of four incidents in the wars against the Philistines (21:15–22). Once more, it is very difficult to date these with any degree of precision.

22:1–23:7 David's Song of Praise; the Last Words of David. David's song of praise to the Lord (22:1–51) clearly dates from before his adultery with Bathsheba. It is also included in the Psalms (see Ps 18).

The "last words of David" (23:1–7) are probably not to be understood as the last words that David uttered before his death, but as the last piece of poetry that David composed before his death. David, as will become clear elsewhere, was a noted poet (see 23:1); and the words that follow are poetry, rather than prose. This section is important in allowing us to see David as a man filled with the Spirit of God (23:2), who knew that the Lord had established an eternal covenant with his house (23:5). The poem looks forward to the day when a king will "rule over men in righteousness . . . in the fear of God" (23:3). Perhaps David saw this hope fulfilled in himself; however, the narrative provided by the books of Samuel suggests that David was far from such an ideal king. Only with the coming of Jesus Christ as the true king of

Israel would this righteous ruler arise. Yet, as the Gospels make clear, Israel chose to reject and destroy this ruler when he finally entered Jerusalem.

23:8–24:25 David's Census; an Altar to the Lord. The list of thirty-seven of "David's mighty men" (23:8–39) is clearly drawn from an archive and may also be found in an expanded form at 1 Chronicles 11:11–41. This is followed by an account of the census of Israel and Judah (24:1–25; also found, with differences, at 1Ch 21:1–17). The dating of the incident referred to in this passage is also uncertain. What is clear is that David decides to determine the number of his troops. Joab, their commander, cannot understand the reason for this. It serves no useful purpose. As the narrative proceeds, it seems that the underlying motive may have been pride on the part of David. Perhaps David wished to gain a sense of personal achievement in the vast number of fighting men he was able to muster—800,000 in the northern region of Israel and 500,000 in the southern region of Judah. Subsequently, David regrets this action, which he recognizes to have been sinful. The results of this sin are seen in a plague on Israel, which only ends when David erects an altar to the Lord.

David is thus portrayed as an ideal king, embodying the virtues that were so conspicuously absent in Israel's first king, Saul. The books of Samuel make it clear, however, that his successes are to be attributed to the Lord, rather than to David's own wisdom. Nevertheless, David is portrayed in a strikingly honest and direct manner, with no attempt being made to hide his failings and weaknesses. His personal life is shown to be corrupt and his judgment seriously flawed at points. Yet despite these weaknesses and failures, the Lord is able to take and use David in such a way that his reign will be a standard for later generations.

1 AND 2 KINGS

As with 1 and 2 Samuel and 1 and 2 Chronicles, the two books of Kings were originally one long work, which was divided into two for convenience by translators. The two books of Kings follow on directly from the two books of Samuel, with the result that the four books together provide a continuous account of the development and history of the kingdom of Israel (and subsequently of Israel and Judah) from the establishment of the monarchy until the exile in Babylon. This continuity is brought out more clearly in the title given to the books in the Greek translation of the Old Testament, usually referred to as the *Septuagint*. In that translation, 1 and 2 Samuel are referred to as "1 and 2 Kingdoms," while 1 and 2 Kings are given the titles "3 and 4 Kingdoms."

In this commentary, the two books will be treated as a single unit. This has the advantage of allowing the ministry of Elijah to be studied as a continuous unit. Otherwise, it has to be broken into two halves at an unhelpful point in the story. The reader needs to be reminded that the division of Kings into two parts was not part of the original text of Scripture!

A central feature of 1 Kings is the division of the united kingdom of Israel into two parts after the reign of Solomon. What was originally one kingdom, usually referred to as Israel, breaks into two components in 930 B.C.. The northern kingdom of Israel proved to be unstable and went through a series of political and military crises until it finally fell to the Assyrians in 722–721 B.C.. The southern kingdom of Judah, which included the great city of Jerusalem, fared somewhat better. It would remain more or less intact until it fell to the Babylonians. With the fall of Jerusalem in 586 B.C., the nation that had been united and given stability under David ceased to exist. Only as the exiles began to return from Babylon in 538 did the nation of Judah begin to take shape once more.

KINGS 1:1 – 12:24

The Succession and Reign of Solomon

1:1–27 Adonijah Sets Himself Up as King. The opening section of this book paints a rather unflattering picture of David. Once the great king of Israel, he has now become an old man who cannot keep warm at night (1:1–4). It is obvious that David cannot live much longer. The question therefore arises: Who will succeed him as king over Israel? David had many wives and a considerable number of sons. There were thus several leading contenders for the succession. Adonijah, one of these sons, decides that he is the most suitable candidate and begins plotting to ensure that the kingship passes to him on his father's death (1:5–10). From what follows, it seems that he proclaims himself as king, following a pattern established earlier by Absalom. The next step would inevitably be the elimination of the king himself, as well as other possible claimants to the throne.

1:28–53 David Makes Solomon King. The prophet Nathan, who played a prominent role in David's early reign, seeks to ensure the succession in a manner pleasing to the Lord. He asks Bathsheba to speak to David about developments, in order to stop them before it is too late. David, on hearing of these developments from both Bathsheba and Nathan, makes immediate arrangements for Solomon to be anointed as king over both the northern peoples of Israel and the southern peoples of Judah (1:11–40). Adonijah, realizing that he has been outmaneuvered, submits to the newly anointed king (1:41–53).

2:1–46 David's Charge to Solomon; Solomon's Throne Established. Finally, David dies, having solemnly charged Solomon to remain faithful to the Lord. He is buried in his own city of Jerusalem, after reigning for a period of forty years, usually dated 1010–970 B.C. (2:1–12).

With Solomon firmly established on the throne of Israel, Adonijah begins another attempt to gain the throne. He asks from Bathsheba the right to be married to Abishag, a member of David's harem. Although Bathsheba regards the request as unimportant, Solomon recognizes it as an attempt by Adonijah to enhance his credentials as a future king and orders his execution (2:13–25). More bloodshed follows as Solomon moves to purge the guilt of past excesses (such as those committed by Joab) and to ensure that potential threats to the throne are eliminated (2:26–46). An alliance with Egypt prevents any likely invasion from that region during his reign (3:1).

3:1–28 Solomon Asks for Wisdom. Once his position is secure, Solomon moves to begin fulfilling the promises he made to his dying father. He asks the Lord to give him wisdom, a request which is gladly granted on the condition that he remains faithful to the Lord during his reign (3:2–15). The wisdom for which Solomon thus becomes famous is to be seen as a gift from the Lord, rather than a natural endowment. That wisdom is immediately shown in action in the famous case of the two women who claim to be the mother of the same infant (3:16–28). We later learn that, on account of his wisdom, Solomon is sought out by rulers throughout the world (4:29–34).

4:1–5:18 Solomon's Administration. Solomon also proves to be a successful administrator. The names of those who assist him in this task are noted (4:1–19), as are the ways in which this wisdom leads to prosperity for his people (4:20–28). This prosperity leads to the fulfillment of a major promise: the building of the temple. Nathan's prophecy to David had spoken of one of his successors building a fitting house for the Lord at Jerusalem. Solomon now fulfills that promise, committing substantial resources to the project (5:1–18). He is assured by the Lord that this project will be regarded with great favor and will lead to the Lord's continuing presence among his people Israel (6:11–13).

6:1–7:51 Solomon Builds the Temple and His Palace. The building of the temple appears to have begun around 966 B.C., four years into Solomon's reign. It took seven years to complete. The detailed descriptions provided of the building and ornamentation of the temple indicate that it was a substantial and important building, clearly pointing to the importance attached to the Lord by Solomon (6:1–10, 14–38; 7:13–51). Nevertheless, we are told that Solomon spent nearly twice as much time building his palace as he did building the temple (7:1–12). The implied criticism is clear: perhaps Solomon cared more about the majesty of his own residence than he did about the Lord's. We can see here the beginnings of some concerns that become more of a problem as Solomon's reign continues.

8:1–9:9 The Ark and the Dedication of the Temple. With great ceremony, the ark of the Lord is brought from the tent in which it had been placed by David and is installed in the temple (8:1–11). In his great prayer of thanksgiving and dedication, Solomon praises the Lord for his faithfulness (8:12–21) and asks for continuing favor and mercy upon his people (8:22–53). Finally, he reaffirms the need for Israel to remain faithful to the Lord (8:54–61). These prayers are then followed by sacrifices on a huge scale, reflecting the large numbers of people from throughout the region who turn out to witness this major moment in the history of their nation (8:62–66). The ark, which had been with Israel from the time of the covenant at Sinai to the present day, is finally given the permanent dwelling place of honor it deserves. The Lord appears to Solomon, confirming his presence with his people at Jerusalem and reminding Solomon of the continuing need for obedience and faithfulness on the part of Solomon and his sons if the Lord is to remain with his people. Failure to be obedient in this way will inevitably lead to rejection and disaster (9:1–9).

9:10–11:13 Solomon's Wealth; Solomon's Foreign Wives. We are then provided with further information about Solomon's immense wealth and the respect in which he is held internationally (9:10–28). The visit of the Queen of Sheba is ample confirmation of this international status and fame (10:1–

13). To make sure that we have fully appreciated his status, we are told of his many possessions and achievements (10:14–29) and his many wives (11:1). Here, however, the note of criticism hinted at in an earlier section becomes much more specific and focused: Solomon's foreign wives led him astray through their pagan religious beliefs and practices. We are told that Solomon genuinely loved his many wives. Nevertheless, as he grew older, his commitment to the Lord wavered. We are told explicitly that Solomon began to experiment with foreign gods such as Ashtoreth and Molech. Worship of the latter is known to have involved child sacrifice on occasion (11:2–8).

Solomon's rebellion against the Lord allows us to see David's weaknesses in their true light. David was prone to all kinds of temptations and misjudgments, as 1 and 2 Samuel make clear. Yet he never abandoned the Lord for foreign gods. The result of Solomon's faithlessness to the Lord is unequivocal. The Lord becomes angry with Solomon for his flagrant violation of the covenant. On account of David's faithfulness to him, the Lord declares that he will not take the kingdom away from Solomon during his lifetime. After his death, however, the kingdom will be divided (11:9–13).

11:14–40 Solomon's Adversaries. Solomon's problems now begin. It is clear that his flagrant disobedience in relation to the most fundamental of all of God's commands—to have no other gods—leads to God's withdrawing of his favor and support. We are told not simply that Hadad and Rezon rise against Solomon; we are told that the Lord raises both of them up against Solomon. This is no historical accident. This is the judgment of the Lord in action (11:14–25). Jeroboam, one of Solomon's officials, also leads a revolt against Solomon on the basis of a prophecy delivered by Ahijah, which speaks of the tribes of Israel being divided on account of Solomon's sin. Following an unsuccessful attempt to kill Solomon, Jeroboam seeks refuge in Egypt until it is safe for him to return. Once more, it is made clear that the forthcoming division of Israel into two kingdoms is the direct result of Solomon's disobedience (11:26–40).

11:41–12:24 Solomon's Death. Finally, Solomon dies and is succeeded by his son Rehoboam (11:41–43). Jeroboam now deems it safe to return to Israel and offers his own and his people's allegiance to Rehoboam on condition that he and Israel are treated well by the Judahites. Despite the advice of his court, Rehoboam refuses. If anything, he will make life harder for the northerners. The northerners are outraged and decide to rebel against the house of David. They install Jeroboam as their king (12:1–24). Aware of the possibility of attack from the south, he fortifies the town of Shechem and makes it his base.

1 KINGS 12:25 – 16:34

The Divided Kingdoms to the Ministry of Elijah

12:25–33 Golden Calves at Bethel and Dan. A problem now arises. Under David and Solomon, the Judahite city of Jerusalem has become the center of Israel's worship. If northerners were to go south to worship, they might end up by submitting to the authority of Rehoboam. To avoid this, Jeroboam establishes his own religious cult in the north, borrowing elements from the authentic worship of the Lord, but adding local elements apparently drawn from Canaanite traditions. Jeroboam's concern that Israelites should not attend religious worship in Jerusalem leads to his introducing religious ideas and forms of worship that are totally unacceptable to the Lord. The scene is thus set for the growing influence of paganism in Israel. This is seen initially in the incident of the golden calves at Bethel and Dan (12:25–33).

These ruins at Dan show the broad, flat altar, below, and far right, where the golden calf of King Jeroboam would have been placed. The wooden framework, near right, is a reconstruction of a canopied throne or an area for offerings to a city god. Dan was the northernmost area controlled by Joshua.

13:1–14:20 The Man of God From Judah; Ahijah's Prophecy Against Jeroboam. Condemnation of this lapse into paganism is not slow in coming. An unnamed "man of God" pronounces judgment against the idolatrous pagan practices now going on within Israel, causing consternation and dismay within Jeroboam's circle (13:1–34). Nevertheless, Jeroboam refuses to alter his practices and continues to appoint priests at the "high places" from outside the traditional priestly family of the Levites. The high places in question were basically local sanctuaries outside Jerusalem, where the Lord was worshiped, often along with other gods, using forms of worship that had pagan overtones. These high places will feature prominently in the prophetic criticism of Israel from now on. They will only finally be destroyed under the reforms introduced by Josiah (foretold at 13:2), some three hundred years later. The prophecy of impending disaster against the kingdom of Israel for its lapse into paganism continues with the prophecy of Ahijah against Jeroboam (14:1–20).

The Kingdom Divides

After Solomon died, his kingdom was divided. The northern kingdom, consisting of ten of the twelve tribes, was now called Israel. The southern kingdom of two tribes, Judah and Benjamin, was called Judah.

14:21–15:24 Israel and Judah Lapse. Our attention then turns to the southern kingdom of Judah and its king Rehoboam, the son of Solomon. We discover that Israel is not alone in its lapse into the paganism characteristic of Canaan before the conquest (14:21–31). Judah's lapse into paganism continues under Rehoboam's successor Abijah (15:1–8). However, an attempt at reform is introduced under Asa (15:9–24), who eliminated at least some of the pagan practices that had crept in under his predecessors.

15:25–16:34 Sin and Rebellion Under Successive Kings. The narrative then returns to deal with events in the northern kingdom of Israel. Jeroboam is succeeded as king by his son Nadab. However, Nadab is assassinated by his rival Baasha, who subsequently becomes king. His first major act is to slaughter all of Jeroboam's remaining family in fulfillment of the prophecy of disaster pronounced against Jeroboam and his family by Ahijah. Yet Baasha continues to encourage pagan beliefs and practices, with the result that the prophet Jehu pronounces condemnation against his household (15:25–16:7).

This pattern of continuing sin and rebellion is repeated under successive kings (16:8–28). It reaches a climax under Ahab, who intensifies the introduction of paganism into Israel through his marriage to Jezebel. This marriage was arranged during the reign of Ahab's father, Omri, and seems to have been seen as a means of consolidating an alliance between Israel and the region of Tyre and Sidon. Jezebel, a Phoenician, brings her worship of Baal (probably in some form specific to her region) to Israel at the time of her marriage. Once Ahab becomes king, he constructs a temple and altar dedicated to Baal, apparently as a counterpart to the temple and altar dedicated to the Lord at Jerusalem (16:29–34).

So Israel has degenerated into paganism. What can be done about it? The answer lies in the ministry of the prophets Elijah and Elisha, to which we now turn.

1 KINGS 17:1 – 2 KINGS 8:15

The Ministries of Elijah and Elisha

We are introduced to Elijah the Tishbite without any prior warning. Nothing in the text has prepared the way for his arrival. The scene has been set for the dramatic escalation in Baal worship in Israel under Ahab. Nothing, however, has prepared us for opposition to it. Up to this point, Israel has been departing further and further from the worship of the Lord under successive kings. Only now do we realize that something is about to happen to check this development.

17:1–24 Elijah's Early Miracles. Our introduction to Elijah makes it clear that he is a man favored by the Lord (17:1–24). His early miracles are seen by those who encounter him, such as the widow of Zarephath, as confirmation of his credentials as a man of God. There are interesting parallels here between Elijah and Moses, and between Ahab and Pharaoh. Note, for example, how Ahab refuses to believe in Elijah's warnings of judgment despite all his signs, just as Pharaoh refused to believe in Moses.

18:1–15 Elijah and Obadiah. As the story of Elijah proceeds, we discover the full intensity of Ahab's campaign against the worshippers of the Lord. Jezebel has initiated a campaign of slaughter by which the prophets of the Lord will be systematically located and killed (18:4, 13). However, there is resistance to this campaign. Obadiah (not the same individual as the prophet who also bore this name), a senior official in Ahab's palace, has hidden away a hundred prophets in two secret locations in order that they may escape the massacre.

18:16–46 Elijah on Mount Carmel. In a moment of danger and drama, Elijah confronts Ahab and delivers his message of judgment. He demands a showdown at Mount Carmel between himself and the prophets of Baal, supported by Jezebel (18:16–20). Elijah demands that the people worship either the Lord or Baal. He does not allow any alternative. Syncretism (worship of several different gods at the same time) is excluded: either the Lord or Baal is truly God (18:21–25). The prophets of Baal attempt to invoke Baal through various ritual acts of self-mutilation. Nothing happens (18:26–29). Elijah then calls down the fire of the Lord on the altar he had built (18:30–39). The reaction of the people is immediate and furious. At Elijah's call, they slaughter the prophets of Baal. And in the land that had languished under famine for years, the sound of heavy rain is suddenly heard (18:40–46). The famine had clearly been the Lord's judgment for Israel's disobedience.

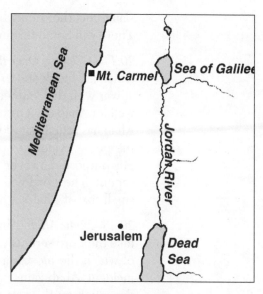

19:1–18 Elijah Flees to Horeb. Yet this great victory brings more danger for Elijah. Infuriated by Elijah's slaughter of her prophets, Jezebel vows to ensure that Elijah himself will not live. Realizing his danger, Elijah seeks refuge in the southern kingdom of Judah, beyond Ahab's sphere of authority. Tempted to despair of his situation, Elijah asks that he may be allowed to die. However, he receives an assurance from the Lord, on the basis of which he journeys for forty days and nights to Mount Horeb (probably another name for Mount Sinai). Just like Moses before him and Jesus Christ after him, Elijah is encouraged and strengthened by God during this period (19:1–8).

The prophet Elijah proved in a showdown on Mount Carmel that Baal, the Canaanite god, was no match for God. When God sent fire down from heaven, Elijah's offering, the altar, and even the stones were burned. The bull sacrificed to Baal was left untouched.

At Horeb, Elijah confesses his despair to the Lord. He is the only one left in Israel to remain faithful to the Lord, and his own life is in danger. What can be done about it? In a famous passage, we learn of how the Lord assures Elijah that he is just as much present in the weakness of a gentle whisper as he is in the power of a windstorm, earthquake, or fire. The Lord will be able to speak through Elijah, despite his weakness. Furthermore, Elijah is mistaken in his belief that he is entirely on his own; in fact, he is reassured that there are seven thousand people who have not yet submitted to Baal. We see here the theme of a *faithful remnant*—that is, a small group of faithful people within a much larger group of faithless people, through whom God is able to carry out his saving purposes (19:10–18). This theme of a faithful remnant is of major importance in the prophecies of Jeremiah and Isaiah as well as in Paul's understanding of the fate of Israel (Ro 9–11).

19:19–21 The Call of Elisha. The first such person who is made known to Elijah is Elisha, who is busy plowing fields. Elijah calls him to serve the Lord. Elisha leaves everything to follow Elijah just as the first disciples will leave their nets behind to follow Jesus. In a highly dramatic gesture, Elisha slaughters the oxen who were drawing his plow and burns the plow itself. There will be no turning back. His commitment is total (19:19–21).

20:1–34 Victory Over the Arameans. A number of incidents now take place, which are incidental to the ministry of Elijah. We learn that Israel has been at war with the Arameans and that things have not been going particularly well for Ahab. As a result, when he is offered a settlement by the Arameans, Ahab has little hesitation in accepting, despite the high price demanded for the peace. A new prophet is now introduced. We do not know his name. His purpose, however, is unmistakable. Ahab is being offered a chance to repent. The Lord will give him a victory over the Arameans, despite the small size of Ahab's army. This duly takes place (20:1–34).

20:35–22:40 Ahab. Ahab, however, continues to show himself reluctant to take the Lord seriously. A number of incidents illustrate this (20:35–21:28), of which the most important is the episode of Naboth's vineyard. In this incident, Ahab gains possession of Naboth's vineyard through a deliberate deception on the part of his wife, Jezebel. For this, Ahab and his descendants are condemned by Elijah, although judgment will be postponed until after his death and executed during the days of his son. This prophetic judgment is reinforced through the ministry of Micaiah (22:1–28), and confirmed through the death of Ahab in battle (22:29–40).

22:41–2Ki 1:18 Decline Into Paganism. Yet paganism continues in both Judah (22:41–50) and Israel (22:51–53). Ahab's son, Ahaziah, takes no steps to reverse Israel's decline into paganism. In fact, he even contributes significantly to the worsening of the situation. Finding himself injured during a rebellion by the neighboring region of Moab, Ahaziah decides to seek divine guidance about his prospects of recovery. Instead of consulting the Lord, however, he sends messengers to the northernmost Philistine city of Ekron to consult its local deity, Baal-Zebub. (This name, which literally means "the lord of the flies," was used by Israelites as a derogatory reference to Baal-Zebul, which literally means "Baal the exalted one.") Elijah is outraged. Why does the king need to ask anything of the gods of the Philistines? "Is it because there is no God in Israel?" Elijah sends a message back to Ahaziah: for his disobedience, he will die (2Ki 1:1–18).

2:1–25 Elijah Taken Up to Heaven. With this episode, Elijah's ministry comes to an end. He is succeeded by Elisha, who immediately demonstrates that he is in possession of the same signs of authority and power that were associated with Elijah (2:1–25). Elijah himself is taken up into heaven in a whirlwind. In later times, the return of Elijah was awaited as a sign that the Lord would again remember and redeem his people. Elijah would appear before the coming of the Lord (Mal 4:5–6). The ministry of John the Baptist was seen as directly following on from that of Elijah (Lk 1:17). One understanding of the identity of Jesus Christ reported in the Gospels is that he was Elijah (Mt 16:14). The appearance of both Moses and Elijah at the transfiguration of Christ (Mt 17:1–13; Mk 9:2–13; Lk 9:28–36) was further confirmation that Jesus Christ came to continue and extend the prophetic ministry of Elijah to his people.

3:1–8:15 Elisha. The account of Elisha's ministry continues with details of the miracles by which he confirms his spiritual authority (3:1–8:15). These incidents, which point to Elisha having the same spiritual authority and insight as his predecessor, make for fascinating reading. The account of how the Aramean commander Naaman is cured of his leprosy (5:1–18) is especially important, as it shows how the Lord, the God of Israel—despite often being ignored and disobeyed by Israel itself—is worshiped and acknowledged by significant people from outside Israel.

2 KINGS 8:16 – 17:41

The Divided Kingdoms to the Fall of Israel

What follows is an account of the events that take place in the kingdoms of Israel and Judah up to the time of the fall of Israel herself through the invasion of the Assyrians. The narrative can be a little difficult to read unless its structure is appreciated. The basic structure is that of a survey of events under the kings of Judah and Israel, arranged in a chronological order. This means that the narrative switches from Israel to Judah and back again. The NIV makes the task of reading these sections relatively simple by identifying each section according to king and kingdom. Thus the section entitled "Pekah King of Israel" (15:27–31) is followed by "Jotham King of Judah" (15:32–38), making it quite clear that the narrative has shifted from Israel to Judah.

The situation is made somewhat more complicated on account of *co-regencies*—periods when Israel or Judah were reigned over by two kings. For example, Jeroboam II was king of Israel during the period 793–753 B.C.. However, for the first period of his reign (793–782) he reigned alongside Jehoash. A further feature of this section of the work is its frequent use of the formula "As for the other events of the reign of——, and all he did, are they not written in the book of the annals of the kings of Judah/Israel?" Although this formula can be found earlier (e.g., at 1Ki 14:29; 15:7), it is especially noticeable in this later section, on account of the large numbers of kings being surveyed. In addition to the annals of the kings of Judah and Israel, a third source is also noted: the annals of Solomon (1Ki 11:41). The reference is to three collections of documents that have obviously been drawn upon by the writer of 1 and 2 Kings. Some readers make the mistake of confusing this collection of documents, which we no longer possess, with the biblical books 1 and 2 Chronicles. This is especially likely to happen if using versions of the Bible other than the NIV, which often use the word *chronicles* to translate the Hebrew word here translated as "annals."

8:16–9:13 Jehoram King of Judah; Jehu Becomes King of Israel. The narrative opens in the year 848 B.C. and focuses on the southern kingdom of Judah. We discover that Judah continues to displease the Lord through her rebellion against him (8:16–29). In Israel, however, things begin to change. Elisha orders that Jehu be anointed as king over Israel, despite the fact that Ahaziah is actually king at that time (9:1–13). Just as David was anointed king of Israel while Saul, who had incurred the Lord's displeasure, was reigning, so Elisha indicates that Jehu is the Lord's choice to replace the disobedient Ahaziah, and the instrument of the Lord's judgment against the house of Ahab (see 1Ki 21:21–24).

9:14–10:35 Jehu and the House of Ahab; Baal Worship. Events then move quickly. Jehu first kills Ahaziah and Joram (another of Ahab's sons) and then Jezebel herself (9:14–37). Finally, the remainder of Ahab's family and supporters are wiped out in a series of purges (10:1–17). Having eliminated the power base of the house of Ahab, Jehu turns his attention to the Baal worship which Ahab had been responsible for encouraging. In a piece of calculated deception, Jehu declares that he will worship Baal to a far greater extent than Ahab ever did. To celebrate his "conversion" to Baal worship, Jehu invites the prophets, ministers, and priests of Baal to a feast in the temple Ahab had built to Baal some time earlier (10:18–24). Once Jehu is sure that all these are safely inside the temple, he orders them to be wiped out and the temple itself to be destroyed. Baal worship is thus eliminated from Israel. However, despite this development, Jehu continues some of the practices of Jeroboam and thus fails to restore the proper worship of the Lord to Israel (10:25–36).

11:1–12:21 Athaliah and Joash. Our attention now returns to the southern kingdom of Judah. and events that follow the death of its king Ahaziah (not, by the way, to be confused with the king of Israel to bear that same name, who ruled some thirty years earlier). Ahaziah is eventually succeeded by Joash, despite an attempt by Athaliah, the mother of Ahaziah, to secure the throne for herself by the simple expedient of wiping out the entire royal family (11:1–21). Like Moses, the infant Joash survives the attempt to assassinate him. Finally, he succeeds to the throne at the age of seven, after the assassination of Athaliah. Once more, an attempt at reform is made: the temple at Jerusalem is eventually repaired. However, the high places remained intact and continue to attract worshippers (12:1–21).

13:1–15:26 Israel and Judah Remain Disobedient. The sections that follow document a saga of continuing laxity and disobedience on the part of the kings of Israel and Judah (13:1–15:26). Three points stand out as being of

The "high places," as these stones were called, were places of pagan worship and sacrifice for many people in both Judah and Israel.

special importance. First, the continuing references to the "high places" remaining intact and continuing to attract worship and sacrifice (14:4; 15:4). It is clear that pagan practices continue in both Israel and Judah throughout the period surveyed in this section. Second, there is an important reference to Elisha, in which his final illness is briefly mentioned (13:14–20). On the basis of the chronology suggested by this section, it would seem that Elisha's public ministry has either ceased or not been recorded for a period of nearly forty years. And third, we find the first reference to an attack on the region by Tiglath-Pileser III, who reigns over the Assyrian empire for the period 745–727 B.C., during which the empire expands considerably in the region of Israel (15:19). (The name *Pul* is used in the text, which is the Babylonian form of this Assyrian name.)

15:27–31 Threat From Assyria. A new and ominous period then opens in the history of Israel. In 740 B.C., Pekah ascends the throne of Israel and continues the pagan practices of his predecessors. Now the threat from Assyria has become of major importance with devastating results for Israel. Tiglath-Pileser invades part of the territory of the northern kingdom and deports its inhabitants to Assyria. The policy of deportation was designed to minimize the risk of rebellion on the part of conquered peoples by resettling them far from their homelands. Pekah is assassinated by Hoshea, who takes the throne in his stead in the year 732.

15:32–16:19 Jotham and Ahaz, Kings of Judah. In Judah, things remain quiet, even though the steady deterioration into paganism continues. A relative lull is recorded during the reign of Jotham (15:32–38). In 735 B.C., Ahaz assumes full authority as king of Judah (it seems that there may have been a co-regency with his father Jotham up to this point). It is immediately made clear that Ahaz is more like the kings of Israel than of Judah. His lapses into paganism are ruthlessly identified, including his entering into an alliance with Assyria against Israel. Ahaz ransacks the temple treasury to secure enough treasure to gain a favorable response from Tiglath-Pileser III. Favorably impressed with a pagan altar he has seen at Damascus, Ahaz orders a similar altar to be built in the temple at Jerusalem. He also tampers with other aspects of the temple furnishings, suggesting a deliberate decision to rebel against the traditional faith of Judah (16:1–19).

17:1–6 Hoshea, Last King of Israel. The narrative now returns to Israel and King Hoshea. Having gained the throne through assassination in 732, Hoshea fails to stop Israel's slide into paganism. Tiglath-Pileser III is succeeded by Shalmanesar V in 727; this latter invades the region of Samaria in 725 B.C. and lays siege to it for three years. When the fighting is over, a substantial section of the population of the region is deported to regions deep within the Assyrian empire. Israel no longer exists as a nation in its own right.

17:7–41 Israel Exiled Because of Sin. We are left in no doubt that this deportation and loss of nationhood is a direct result of the disobedience of Israel. The full scale of Israel's rebellion against the Lord is documented. Deportation is God's punishment of a disobedient people who have failed to honor, respect, and obey him. The region of Samaria is then resettled with peoples from other regions of the Assyrian empire (17:24–41) who mingle pagan beliefs with some elements of the traditional faith of Israel. As a result, Samaria becomes the center for a degenerate form of worship of the Lord. This factor goes some considerable way to explaining the severe tension between Jews and Samaritans that is encountered in the New Testament period. The Jews may be seen as the descendants of Judah, and the Samaritans as the descendants of the mixed-race population that came into being in Israel as a result of Assyria's conquest of the region.

2 KINGS 18:1 – 25:30

The Last Days of Judah

18:1–16 Hezekiah King of Judah. Israel, then, ceases to exist as a nation in 722 B.C.. But what of the southern kingdom of Judah? It is clear that a new era in Judah's history opens with the reign of Hezekiah in 729 B.C.. Initially reigning alongside his father Ahaz, Hezekiah takes full control in 715. Hezekiah introduces a major program of reform, which is only briefly described here (a fuller account is provided at 2 Ch 29–31). The high places are destroyed, as well as a range of other pagan objects of worship. Among these are the bronze snake held up by Moses (18:4). Once an image of salvation, this has now degenerated into an object of idolatrous worship and superstition.

18:17–19:37 Sennacherib King of Assyria. Yet the Assyrian threat cannot be ignored. Once Israel has been conquered, the Assyrian king Sennacherib turns his attention to the southern region, to attack Jerusalem. Initially, the Assyrians try to use verbal persuasion. Speaking in Hebrew (which the ordinary inhabitants of Jerusalem understand) rather than Aramaic (the international language of diplomacy, which was not understood by ordinary people), the Assyrians tell Hezekiah that he is doomed unless he surrenders. It is clear that they hope to provoke popular pressure against the king's intention to resist them. Yet Hezekiah insists on placing his trust in the Lord. The Assyrians scoff at this. No city has ever been saved from them by its god before.

At this stage, we are introduced to the prophet Isaiah, whom we will encounter in considerably greater detail later (see pp. 185–198). Isaiah urges Hezekiah to resist the Assyrians, who have incurred the Lord's displeasure. Hezekiah agrees and prays for guidance and courage. Isaiah then delivers a detailed prophecy against Sennacherib, prophesying his downfall (19:20–34; see also Isa 37:21–38). That same night, a disaster falls upon the encamped Assyrian army. Badly shaken, Sennacherib withdraws to Nineveh, where he will eventually die at the hands of his sons (18:35–37). The prophecy is fulfilled.

20:1–20 Hezekiah and Babylon. Hezekiah receives further encouragement and reassurance from the Lord through Isaiah (20:1–11). However, Hezekiah appears to overstep the limits of caution in his dealings with some envoys from Babylon. At a time when the world's horizons are dominated by Assyria, Hezekiah is unreasonably positive towards the Babylonians. As a result, Isaiah prophesies the future downfall of Jerusalem at the hands of the Babylonians (20:12–21).

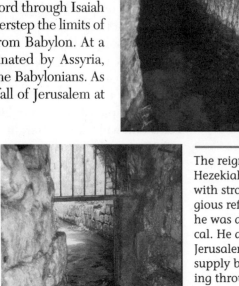

21:1–25 Manasseh, King of Judah. Hezekiah is succeeded by his son Manasseh, who lapses into paganism, even to the extent of rebuilding the high places that his father had destroyed and importing pagan objects of worship into the temple. The prophets denounce this sin and declare the coming of the judgment of the Lord. Judah will suffer the same fate as Israel (21:1–18). Things do not improve under Manassah's successor Amon (21:19–26).

22:1–20 Josiah and the Finding of the Book of the Law. Yet things do improve under Josiah, who begins to reign in 640 B.C.. In the course of some work on the

The reign of Hezekiah began with strong religious reforms. But he was also practical. He assured Jerusalem's water supply by tunneling through rock to divert water from Gihon Spring outside the city to Siloam Pool inside the city walls. The tunnel still carries water.

temple, the "Book of the Law" is rediscovered (22:1–10). It is thought that this is a reference to the book of Deuteronomy, or at least to its central chapters. On hearing it read, Josiah is appalled. He realizes that Israel has departed radically from the Law of Moses and that something will have to be done about it. This conclusion is reinforced by a prophesy from Huldah, which speaks of the forthcoming destruction of the city and temple (22:11–20). A major program of reform is set in motion (23:1–25). The catalogue of pagan items removed from the temple in itself is an indication of how compromised the worship of the Lord has become—even at Jerusalem itself, supposedly the central location for the true worship of the Lord by his people. Notice that Josiah even extends his program of cleansing to the region of Samaria. The pagan holy places of this region are demolished and desecrated.

23:1–30 Josiah Renews the Covenant. A central aspect of the program of reform undertaken by Josiah is the renewal of the covenant—the declaration on the part of king and people that they will remain faithful to the law of the Lord (23:2–3). The Passover, which has been neglected since the days of the judges, is reinstated and celebrated at Jerusalem (23:21–23).

Josiah unquestionably finds favor in the sight of the Lord. Yet his obedience is not regarded as an adequate atonement for the sin of Manessah, who had violated the covenant between God and his people at every turn. The Lord's anger does not focus on Josiah himself, but on Judah. She will suffer the same fate as Israel (23:26–27). It is now merely a matter of time. The reader has been prepared for the fate that will befall Judah. Like Israel, she will be punished for her disobedience. However, that punishment, as it turns out, will take a different form. The exile of Jerusalem will be seen as a time of purification and penance, in which the people of God can rediscover their identity and obligations. But this lies in the future. We turn back to the narrative, knowing that the end of Judah is in sight.

23:31–24:7 Jehoahaz and Jehoiakim, Kings of Judah. After Josiah's death in battle (23:28–30), he is succeeded by Jehoahaz and Jehoiakim (23:31–36). It is during the latter's reign that the first tolling of the bell that marks the end of Judah is heard. In 605 B.C., the Babylonian emperor Nebuchadnezzar defeats the massed Egyptian armies at Carchemish, establishing Babylon as the leading military and political power in the region. Along with many other territories in this region, the land of Judah becomes subject to Babylonian rule, possibly in 604 (24:1). Jehoiakim, who clearly fails to remain faithful to the Lord (23:37), decides to rebel against Babylon. It is possible that he may have been encouraged in this move by a successful Egyptian counterattack against Babylon in 601, which may have seemed to suggest that Babylon's power was on the wane. It proves to be a terrible misjudgment. Judah is invaded by Babylonian forces (24:2–4), which is clearly interpreted as the execution of the promised judgment of the Lord against his faithless people and king. Egypt, once the hope of Judah, is also defeated and neutralized as a military power (24:7). (These same events are also vividly described and analyzed by Jeremiah, the later chapters of whose prophecy should be read in the light of this historical narrative.)

24:8–25:30 Jehoiachin, Zedekiah and the Fall of Jerusalem. Jehoiakim is succeeded by Jehoiachin (the close similarity of these names being a constant source of confusion to readers) toward the end of 598 B.C., shortly before the Babylonians finally lay siege to the city (24:8–20). Early the following year (597), the king, the royal family, and the circle of royal advisors give themselves up to the besieging forces (25:1–12). They are deported to Babylon, along with several thousand captives. (Interestingly, a Babylonian ration document mentioning Jehoiachin was discovered some 2,500 years later, during excavations of 1899–1917, confirming this ignominious fate of a king of Judah.) The Babylonians place Zedekiah, a relative of Jehoiachin, on the throne as their vassal and seem happy to leave things like that for the present.

Yet Zedekiah has other ideas. Probably encouraged by the accession of a new pharaoh, who seems to offer a real threat to the Babylonians, Zedekiah determines to rebel against Babylon. The Babylonian response is massive and decisive. In January 588, they lay siege to the city. In July 586, they break through its walls and take the city. The defending army attempts to flee, but is routed. The next month, a Babylonian official arrives in Jerusalem to supervise the destruction of the defenses of the city and its chief buildings, and the deportation of its people (25:1–12). The furnishings of the temple are dismantled and taken to Babylon as booty. It is distressing

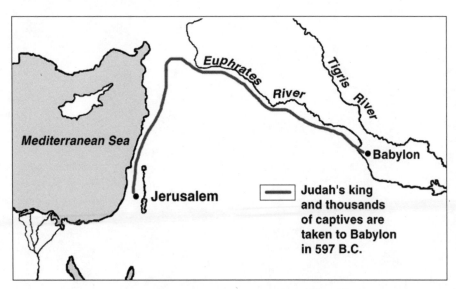

The fall of Jerusalem came in 597 B.C., when the king surrendered to the Babylonians and the king and many of the people were deported to Babylon. They followed, in reverse, more or less the same route followed by Abraham many centuries before.

to read this account of the destruction of the temple in the light of the account of its erection and ornamentation during the reign of Solomon (25:13–17).

Any hope of a quick end to the exile soon passes. Anyone capable of leading a revolt or taking charge of a government is taken and executed (25:18–21). The assassination of Gedaliah, the governor appointed by the Babylonians, sends shock waves through the remaining inhabitants of the city. Fearing Babylonian reprisals, many flee to Egypt (25:22–26).

Yet this dismal account of the fall of Judah ends on a positive note. In the later period of the exile (from 561), Jehoiachin is treated with increasing kindness by his captors. It is clear that he is to be allowed to live (25:27–30). The house of David will not be wiped out. It will live on in exile, in hope of restoration. It is widely thought that 1 and 2 Kings were written during the period of exile in Babylon. The people had no knowledge that their captivity would one day come to an end. They could only live in hope that the Lord, the God of Israel, would remember and finally deliver his people.

1 AND 2 CHRONICLES

As with 1 and 2 Samuel and 1 and 2 Kings, the two books of Chronicles were originally one long work, which was divided into two for convenience by translators. In this commentary, the two books will be treated as a single unit, as were the two books of Samuel and Kings.

In view of the repetition of material that has been encountered earlier, the commentary on these books will focus on its distinctive interpretation of this material, rather than on the historical details themselves. The reader who has been working through the books of the Bible in their canonical order will already know the historical details underlying the book, thus making their repetition unnecessary. Reading Chronicles in isolation is discouraged because it is clear that the writer of the work assumes that his readers will already be familiar with the background to the material in question. Reading the books of Samuel and Kings first, before trying to tackle Chronicles, is strongly recommended.

Before looking at the text in more detail, it will be helpful to take an overview of Chronicles. We have already seen how what was originally one kingdom, usually referred to as Israel, broke into two components in 930 B.C.. The northern kingdom of Israel went through a series of political and military crises until it finally fell to the Assyrians in 722–721 B.C.. The southern kingdom of Judah, which included the great city of Jerusalem, remained more or less intact until it fell to the Babylonians. With the fall of Jerusalem in 586 B.C., the nation that had been united and given stability under David ceased to exist. Only as the exiles began to return from Babylon in 538 did the nation of Judah begin to take shape once more.

The two books of Chronicles are clearly written with the needs of the restored community in mind. The work is concerned to demonstrate the continuity between the past and the present and to reassure its readers of the continuing validity of God's covenant promises to his people. In many ways, the books of Chronicles can be regarded as bringing together material that is spread out across the books of Samuel and Kings. However, additional material is provided in many cases, probably from archive resources. Part of the additional material relates to a much earlier period in Israel's history. Its inclusion stresses the continuity of God's presence and promises throughout the history of his people.

It is also noticeable that Chronicles tends to portray both David and Solomon in a much more favorable light than that found in the books of Samuel and Kings. The incidents that highlight David's weaker side (such as his adulterous relationship with Bathsheba) are not referred to. David's final period as a shivering, bedridden old man is not referred to. Similarly, Solomon is portrayed in a very flattering manner. Any mention of debate or conflict over the succession of Solomon is omitted. The impression could easily be gained that Solomon was the only and the obvious successor to David. No mention is made of his foreign wives or the pagan practices or beliefs they encouraged.

It is clear that one of the purposes of Chronicles is to stress the importance of David and Solomon and the example and encouragement they provide for the restored community that has now returned from exile in Babylon. They are also seen as pointing ahead to the coming of the Messiah, the ideal king of Israel, who will bring to final fulfillment all that David and Solomon tried to achieve. The work aims to encourage and inspire the nation at a time when its fortunes were often low and to reassure Israel that the God who entered into a covenant with David and Solomon remains faithful to that covenant to this very day.

The temple is seen as a major focus for Israel's hope and faith, and particular attention is paid to this theme throughout the work. Thus the account of Solomon's reign is dominated by the building of the temple, which is seen as his major contribution to the well-being of his people.

1 CHRONICLES 1:1 – 9:44

The Genealogies of Israel

The work opens with a detailed analysis of the people who connect God's work of creation and the establishment of the monarchy in Israel. No attempt is made to explore the historical issues involved, such as the way in which Israel made its way from Egypt to the Promised Land or how the people took possession of Canaan. The central point being made is that there is a direct and unbroken line of continuity within the people of God between creation and the monarchy. There are also other sections of interest, including details of the descendants of David (3:1–24).

The reader of this section may find much of this material uninteresting, due to the manner of its presentation. Being confronted with list after list of names is not especially inspiring. However, the reason for these genealogies must be appreciated. This is the family history of Israel, demonstrating the development and continuity of the people of God from the act of creation itself to the restoration. There are also moments of important theological interpretation—for example, the explicit assertion that "the people of Judah were taken captive to Babylon on account of their unfaithfulness" (9:1). These interpretations help the reader make sense of the history of God's people and discern the purposes of God behind and within the flow of history itself.

1 CHRONICLES 10:1 – 29:30

The Reign of David

The scene then changes radically. We are plunged into the world of the early monarchy. No background information is provided as to how the monarchy comes into being in the first place, nor of the role of Samuel in its creation and direction. We are given a very brief account of how Saul takes his life, and thus how the kingship of Israel becomes vacant (10:1–14). The death of Saul is firmly attributed to his disobedience, especially his use of mediums. As a result, the kingdom of Israel passes to David. The struggle David confronts as he fights to become king of Judah, and then king of all Israel, is passed over. The important point for the writer is the theological interpretation of what happens, rather than the precise historical event—a pattern that will be repeated throughout this work. Historical details are set aside in order that the religious significance of events may be fully appreciated. In some cases, as we have hinted, this leads to incidents being passed over. It is the message that is of primary importance.

11:1–16:43 David Becomes King. David is acclaimed as king of all Israel. His successes and power are attributed directly to his obedience and faithfulness (11:1–12:40). The episode of the bringing of the ark of the Lord to Jerusalem is given a position of considerable prominence within David's reign, and its spiritual significance is emphasized (13:1–16:43).

17:1–15 God's Promise to David. Having brought the ark to Jerusalem, David finds it unacceptable that he, as king, should live in a fine palace, while the ark of the Lord is placed under the shelter of nothing more splendid than a tent. On consulting the prophet Nathan on this matter, he is assured of God's promise to him and his descendants (17:1–15). There is a strongly messianic flavor to this passage, which speaks of one of David's descendants being the "son of God" and his kingdom being established forever. This passage underlies some New Testament thinking on the significance of Jesus Christ. It allows us to understand the importance of the opening of Matthew's gospel, which stresses that Jesus Christ was a descendant of David, as was required of the Messiah.

17:16–20:8 David's Victories. David responds to this promise with prayer and delight (17:16–27). As if to demonstrate that these promises are effective immediately, we are told of David's victories in a series of major engagements during his reign (18:1–12). The great victories for which David is renowned are unequivocally attributed to the Lord (18:13). A series of such engagements are singled out for more detailed discussion, including the war with the Ammonites (19:1–20:3) and the Philistines (20:4–8).

21:1–30 David Numbers the Fighting Men. The "census of Israel" assumes a major place in Chronicles. A virtually identical story is told elsewhere (see 2Sa 24:1–25), with one major difference among several minor ones. In 2 Samuel, David's decision to take a census of Israel is attributed to the Lord. Here, it is attributed to Satan (21:1). It is not clear quite how this difference is to be explained. In any case, the Old Testament regarded Satan as an agent who was ultimately responsible to God. Yet it is the location of the story that is of particular interest. In 2 Samuel, the story is part of a group of narratives gathered together at the end of the work. Here, it is placed in the main body of the work, explaining the specific location of the future temple in Jerusalem. Chronicles' particular focus on the temple leads to this narrative being placed directly before the account of the preparations for the building of the temple, rather than being relegated to an appendix.

22:1–29:30 Preparations for the Temple. Attention then shifts to preparations for the erection of the temple. The responsibility for building the temple will lie with Solomon, who is identified here as David's chosen heir (22:1–19). David is unable to undertake this task himself. His hands are stained with blood as a result of the wars he was obliged to wage to ensure Israel's continued safety (22:8–9). Nevertheless, although David is not permitted to begin the building himself, it is clear that he has laid down the basic principles of its administration and worship. Solomon, therefore, will be responsible for putting into effect the vision and instructions of his father.

Those instructions, along with other details, are then set out in some considerable detail (23:1–27:34). The material in this section is unique to Chronicles, indicating access to archive material not reproduced elsewhere in the Old Testament. The considerable attention given to the fine details of the planned worship and administration of the temple would have been of particular importance to the restored community as they sought to restore continuity with the worship of the golden age of Israel under David and Solomon. These precise details would have given postexilic Judaism a much-needed sense of direction as they sought to restore the temple and its worship after years of neglect and disuse.

A major section now follows (28:1–29:30), detailing the transition from the reign of David to that of Solomon. David sets out his plans for the temple and makes it clear that Solomon, his intended heir among his sons, will bring his vision into being. There is a clear parallel here with Moses (especially from the material at 28:12). Just as Moses received the plans for the tabernacle from the Lord, so David receives from the Lord the plans for the temple at Jerusalem. Solomon is acknowledged as David's successor by the people (29:21–25) with the result that with David's death, Solomon succeeds him as king (29:28).

2 CHRONICLES 1:1 – 9:31 ——————————

Solomon and the Building of the Temple

Attention now shifts to the reign of Solomon. This account focuses virtually entirely on Solomon's building of the temple at Jerusalem. Chronicles proceeds directly to Solomon's request for wisdom from the Lord (1:1–17)—a wisdom that is demonstrated especially in the building of the temple. The preparations for this are noted in some detail (2:1–18). A full account of its building is also provided, indicating its massive dimensions and its fine furnishings (3:1–5:1). Although Solomon actually spends longer building his own palace than he does building the temple, all details of the building of the palace are omitted from this account.

The account of how the ark of the Lord is brought to the temple from its lowly position beneath the tent erected for it by David is documented (5:2–6:11), along with the great affirmation of the faithfulness of the Lord to his people. The dedication of the temple to the Lord (6:12–7:10) is clearly a moment of great joy and celebration. It is followed by the Lord's reaffirmation of his commitment to the house of David and to his people on condition that they remain faithful to the law (7:11–22).

So what else did Solomon do during his reign, apart from build the temple? Chronicles seems to have little interest in anything other than the religious aspects of his reign. In a closing section, the work notes some public building works and a military expedition (8:1–10), but does not make much use of them. The religious aspects of Solomon's reign predominate. Indeed, our attention is then immediately redirected to his religious activities, as we learn of his regular sacrifices to the Lord (8:12–15) in obedience to the directives laid down by Moses. Chronicles explicitly brings out the continuity between Solomon and Moses at this point.

Solomon's wisdom, which was a direct gift from God, becomes legendary and attracts many visitors. Chronicles notes the visit of the Queen of Sheba, who testifies to the wisdom of the Lord in placing Solomon on the throne of Israel (9:1–12). It also records his fabulous wealth (9:13–28). Finally, Chronicles records the death of Solomon after a reign of forty years (9:29–31) and his succession by his son Rehoboam.

2 CHRONICLES 10:1 – 36:23 ——————————

The History of Judah to the Exile

A new section now opens, chronicling the history of Judah from the death of Solomon to the time of the exile in Babylon. There are obvious parallels here with the material found in 1 Kings 12–2 Kings 25. Nevertheless, important differences must be noted. For example, Chronicles draws upon sources not used by the writers of the books of Kings, with the result that we have additional material in our possession relating to the history of Judah.

However, the most important and obvious difference is that Chronicles focuses on the southern kingdom of Judah alone. It must be recalled that one of the purposes of the work appears to have been to help the restored community in Jerusalem gain an understanding of its own history and purposes. In that Israel had ceased to exist as a nation after the Assyrian invasion and deportation of 722, there was no point in referring to the history of the northern kingdom of Israel, except when it related to events in Judah. Thus, despite the importance of Elijah, he is only mentioned here indirectly (as the author of a letter: 21:12–15). Chronicles is generally thought to have a special concern to trace the faithfulness of God to his promises to David through the great king's descendants to the time of writing. Because this succession takes place only within the kings of Judah, it is natural that the work should focus on this kingdom alone.

10:1–11:4 Israel Rebels Against Rehoboam. The new section opens with an account of the division of the kingdoms, which explains how a serious disagreement between Rehoboam and the Israelite Jeroboam leads to the two nations going their separate ways (10:1–4). The origins of the tension between the two is not explained here. The reader should consult the more detailed account in 1 Kings for the background (1Ki 11:29–33).

11:5–27:9 Rehoboam King of Judah. The history of Rehoboam and his successors is then documented (11:5–27:9). It broadly parallels the account in the books of Kings, although there are differences in details or evaluation at points of interest. For example, according to 1 Kings 15:14, Asa did not remove all the high places from Judah during the course of his reforms; according to 2 Chronicles 14:3, he did. The difference is almost certainly due to the persistence of the paganism that the high places represented at the time, by which Asa's determined attempts to remove them totally were ultimately frustrated. Furthermore, Chronicles provides a generally positive evaluation of Abijah, whereas the briefer account in 1 Kings 15:1–8 is much more negative in tone. Given the complexity of the lives of some of the kings of Judah, this divergence in evaluation is not entirely surprising.

28:1–27 Ahaz King of Judah. The figure who is criticized the most severely is Ahaz (28:1–27). The incident that caused particular concern—Ahaz's decision to build an altar in the Jerusalem temple, based on a pagan model he had seen at Damascus (see 2Ki 16:10–16)—is not recorded. Nevertheless, his apostasy is fully documented. Ahaz is presented in totally negative terms as a totally unworthy king of Judah who lapses into paganism and threatens to destroy his kingdom in doing so. Jerusalem is packed with pagan altars, and high places are reestablished in every town in his kingdom. So great is his rebellion against the Lord that on his death he is not placed in the tombs of the kings of Israel.

29:1–32:33 Hezekiah King of Judah. Ahaz's successor, Hezekiah, is treated in considerable detail (29:1–32:33) and is clearly identified as a major religious reformer who is able to reverse the lapse into paganism that took place under his father. Although Hezekiah is heavily involved in a conflict with Sennacherib at this time, Chronicles focuses specifically on his religious activities. As with Solomon, it is matters of faith and worship that attract the Chronicler's main attention. The restoration of the celebration of the Passover (30:1–27) is of particular importance to the Chronicler, for it stressed the continuity of the Lord's action and presence with his people. The celebration of the Passover would have been an important focus for the identity of the restored community after the end of the Babylonian exile. This full account of the celebration of the Passover at Jerusalem would have been of considerable importance to the returned exiles as they sought to reestablish their sense of identity and purpose.

Other events in Hezekiah's reign are noted, including his confrontation with the Assyrian army (32:1–22). Nevertheless, it is clear that it is Hezekiah's faithfulness and obedience that are of special importance here. Hezekiah is portrayed as a worthy king of Judah, a fact that is reflected in his being buried alongside the descendants of David—an honor denied to his faithless father (32:23–33).

33:1–25 Manasseh and Amon, Kings of Judah. Hezekiah is succeeded by Manasseh, who is portrayed in unequivocally negative terms elsewhere (2Ki 21:1–18). Chronicles is kinder to him and suggests that, despite his disobedience, he has some redeeming features (33:1–20). For example, his attempt to eliminate pagan practices is noted, and their persistence is put down at least in part to the disobedience of the people. Manasseh is recorded as repenting of his earlier sins, an insight not found elsewhere. His successor, Amon, however, continues with the evil ways of his father and is assassinated (33:21–25).

34:1–35:27 Josiah's Reforms. The reforming reign of Josiah is treated at great length. The narrative tells of the discovery of the Book of the Law (presumably Deuteronomy, or at least part of that book) and its impact on Josiah. Yet even before its discovery, Josiah has engaged in a program of reform in which various pagan altars and images are destroyed. In response to the discovery of the Book of the Law, Josiah formally renews the covenant between the Lord and the people, swearing to follow obediently the law of the Lord (34:29–32). This is followed by a detailed account of Josiah's celebration of the Passover (35:1–19). Once more, the importance of this event to the returned exiles should be noted.

35:20–36:14 The Death of Josiah; His Successors. After an extended account of the death of Josiah (35:20–36:1), his immediate successors are given very brief treatment (36:2–14). The surrender of Jehoiachin to the besieging Babylonian army in 597 B.C. is noted, but is described in terms that avoid mentioning that Jerusalem was under siege in the first place (36:10). Similarly, the fall of Jerusalem in 586 is not explicitly mentioned in the very brief account of the reign of Zedekiah (36:11–14). The destruction of the city is passed over in silence, perhaps as being too painful to mention explicitly.

36:15–23 The Fall of Jerusalem. This silence is ended in a concluding section, which provides a succinct theological analysis of the final days of Jerusalem (36:15–21). The exile to Babylon is God's judgment on his people for their disobedience. Yet this note of judgment is also mingled with a note of hope. While the writer of the book of Kings did not know that the exile would not be permanent (however great his hopes may have been, and however much he may have trusted in the Lord), the Chronicler had the benefit of hindsight: he could record the events of the exile, knowing that they would end in deliverance and restoration to Judah. As a result, Chronicles ends on a powerful note of assurance and hope (36:22–23). The people of Jerusalem will be restored to their city, and the temple of the Lord will be rebuilt.

And on that note, we turn to the account of how that restoration and rebuilding take place, as we prepare to read Ezra.

The book of Ezra opens with an electrifying declaration: the exiles in Babylon are to be allowed to return home! The exile is over. Now the inhabitants of Jerusalem can begin to rebuild their lives, their faith, and their city. Written in a style very similar to that of Chronicles and Nehemiah (which suggests that the same person, possibly Ezra himself, wrote them all), the book of Ezra deals with the renewal of worship in Jerusalem and the decision to rebuild the temple.

EZRA 1:1 – 6:22

The Return from Exile

1:1–11 Cyrus Helps the Exiles to Return. The opening verses of Ezra clearly follow on directly from the end of 2 Chronicles, making it clear that they are to be read together as a continuous narrative. Although we are told little of what happened to the people of Jerusalem during their time in exile, we can nevertheless gain at least some understanding of the difficulties they faced and their longing to return home. Ezra opens by publishing the proclamation of Cyrus, the founder of the Persian empire who defeated the Babylonians in 539, which set the exiles free (1:1–4). The proclamation dates from 538 B.C., and shows a spirit of generosity and tolerance toward the religion of Israel that had been conspicuously absent from the Babylonians.

2:1–70 The List of the Exiles Who Returned. As a result, many of the inhabitants of Jerusalem and Judah prepare to return home, taking the captured treasures of the temple at Jerusalem with them (1:5–11). A long list of exiles who return home in this first major exodus from Babylon is presented at 2:1–70. While this list may seem irrelevant to modern readers, it must be remembered that it would have been of vital importance to the people of God after their return to Judah. It allowed them to trace their family trees back to the time of the exile and stressed their continuity with an earlier generation of the people of God.

3:1–6 Rebuilding the Altar. By September or October 537, the returning exiles have settled down in their hometowns and have begun to renew their old patterns of worship. Note that not all the exiles return to Jerusalem; other towns in Judah receive returning exiles. The Feast of Tabernacles is celebrated with an altar built especially for that purpose, despite the risk of alienating peoples in the region around them. There is still no temple at Jerusalem. However, by building an altar dedicated to the Lord, the returning exiles can begin the process of restoring worship to what it had been before the exile.

3:7–13 Rebuilding the Temple. But sooner or later, the temple will have to be rebuilt. The ruins of Solomon's temple, which had been razed to the ground by the Babylonians, will act as the foundations of the new building. Under the direction of Zerubbabel, who emerges as the natural leader in Jerusalem during this period, preparations are made to rebuild the temple in the spring of 536 B.C.. While many are overjoyed when the foundations are laid, older people (who can remember the great edifice built by Solomon) are distressed. It is clear that the new temple will not be on the same scale as its predecessor.

4:1–24 Opposition to the Rebuilding of the Temple. The texts here bring together problems that emerged over a period of several years, spanning the reigns of three Persian kings (Cyrus, Xerxes, and Artaxerxes). The first problem noted was clearly a continuing one. As part of the Persians' general strategy for keeping Israel under control, part of the population of the northern kingdom of Israel had been deported to Assyria and replaced with peoples from elsewhere in the Assyrian empire. These peoples had brought their pagan practices to the region of Samaria and had combined them with worship to the Lord. As a result, the Samaritans had evolved a form of religion that combined the worship of the Lord with pagan elements.

Some Samaritans now offer to help rebuild the temple, but are rebuffed by Zerubbabel, who does not wish their degenerate form of worship to have any association with the rebuilt temple. Piqued, the Samaritans do all that they can to prevent the rebuilding of the temple. Their most successful strategy is to inform the Persians that the Jews are rebuilding the walls of Jerusalem in order to turn it into a fortified city from which they can defy the Persians (4:12–16). As a result, work on the temple is halted for a period of more than fifteen years. It will not be until 520 B.C., when a new Persian king (Darius) has ascended the throne, that rebuilding can recommence.

5:1–6:12 Tattenai's Letter to Darius and Darius' Decree. The decision to go ahead with rebuilding at this stage is linked with the ministry of the prophet Haggai, which we will consider in detail later (see pp. 250–51). The local Persian governor objects to the rebuilding, asking what authorization the

Jews have to proceed with such a project. In reply, he is told that Cyrus had explicitly permitted such a project. On consulting his superiors, the governor is told that such a decision had indeed been taken by Cyrus, and that Darius requires the governor to give all assistance to this project.

6:13–18 Completion and Dedication of the Temple. With this royal backing, work on the temple proceeds. On 12 March 516, the temple is finally completed and dedicated to the Lord. The first major festival to be celebrated in the new building is the Passover (6:19–22), a festival with strong associations of deliverance from bondage and the commemoration of the faithfulness of the Lord. It is a fitting moment at which to celebrate the exiles' deliverance from bondage in Babylon and to recall the Lord's faithfulness to his people.

One point that is worth commenting on here is the use of the term *Jews* to refer to the returned exiles (4:23; 5:1). Up to this time, the people of God have been referred to as Israelites or Judahites. The term *Jew* comes to be used in the postexilic period to designate the people of God and will be used regularly in later writings for this purpose.

EZRA 7:1 – 10:44

Ezra's Program of Reform

7:1–8:14 Ezra and the Exiles Return. A new stage in the religious renewal of Judaism after its return from exile begins some sixty years later with the arrival of Ezra in the city of Jerusalem. Although the new section of the book that now opens does not give details of the precise dates involved, it would seem that Ezra sets out from Babylon in April 458 and arrives in Jerusalem in August of that same year. It is clear from the description provided that Ezra is deeply versed in the Law of Moses and well placed to ensure that the Jews remain faithful to its instructions (7:1–10). It is also clear that Ezra has full backing from the Persian authorities, as the text of the letter from Artaxerxes makes clear (7:11–28). Returning with Ezra is a sizable body of exiles, detailed at 8:1–14.

8:15–36 The Return to Jerusalem. After his journey from Mesopotamia to Palestine (8:15–36), Ezra relates what happens on his arrival at Jerusalem. The sudden switch to the first person at 8:1 indicates that Ezra's personal memoirs are being drawn upon at this point and in what follows. The book of Ezra draws extensively on such documents at several points. Of particular interest is that fact that the section 4:8–6:18, which involves extensive citation from official documents of the period, is written entirely in Aramaic, the international language of diplomacy during this period. Ezra has clearly incorporated these documents directly into his narrative without feeling the need to translate them.

9:1–10:44 Intermarriage. On his arrival in Jerusalem, Ezra is approached by various representatives of the ordinary people, who are deeply anxious concerning the way things are going. They report that their leaders and priests have lapsed from the high standards expected of them by marrying foreigners. Ezra is appalled by this development, seeing it as a direct violation of the law of God (9:1–15).

Why was intermarriage seen as such a serious matter? The answer lies in the need to preserve the distinctive identity of the people of God. As can be seen from the history of Israel and Judah prior to their exile, the marriage between Jews and non-Jews almost invariably led to the importation of foreign pagan religious practices and beliefs into the worship of Israel. Ezra himself identifies eight groups of people whose religious beliefs found their way into Israel on account of intermarriage (9:1). Because the Exile was to be seen as God's purification of his people on account of their lapse into paganism, it is hardly surprising that Ezra is outraged. One of the problems that led to the exile being imposed on Jerusalem seemed to be about to occur once more. It is clear that others were also aware of the seriousness of these developments (10:1–4).

Ezra acts to prevent this from taking place (10:5–17). Though the people of Jerusalem have sinned, the harm that has been done can be remedied through repentance. Ezra summons the people of Jerusalem and all Judah together to the city of Jerusalem. The period in question (November–December 458) would have fallen during the rainy season (10:9). Ezra sets the issue before the assembly and receives overwhelming support for his proposals to put things right (10:9–15). A committee of investigation is set up (10:16–17). After three months, it publishes its findings (10:18–44). The report suggests that just over one hundred men in the region, including a number of Levites, have married foreign wives. These men would have been required to divorce their wives, even in the case of those with children.

10:44 Conclusion. Here the book of Ezra ends abruptly. One of the reasons for this sudden ending has to do with the relationship between the books of Ezra and Nehemiah. Although these two books are treated as separate in English versions of the Bible, there is evidence that they were originally a single book. The final event recorded in Ezra (the publication of the committee of investigation) is to be dated to March 457. The narrative is then taken up again in 445, as the contribution of Nehemiah to the rebuilding of Jerusalem is documented. As will become clear, Ezra's ministry continues under Nehemiah and leads to a major religious revival. How that happens is the subject of the book of Nehemiah, to which the book of Ezra can be seen as an introduction.

NEHEMIAH

The book of Nehemiah continues the story, begun in the book of Ezra, of the rebuilding of Jerusalem and the reestablishment of the worship of the Lord in Judah after the release of the exiles from their captivity in Babylon. It depicts the many discouragements and difficulties faced by Nehemiah and the way he dealt with them. Nehemiah himself, like Ezra, came to Jerusalem from elsewhere in the Persian empire. Ezra had traveled from Babylon, whereas Nehemiah journeyed from the major city of Susa, some three hundred kilometers east of Babylon. Nehemiah's decision to journey to Jerusalem is to be dated to the spring of 445, some thirteen years after Ezra had set out for the same destination.

NEHEMIAH 1:1 – 7:73

Nehemiah's Arrival and Administration

1:1–2:10 Nehemiah Returns to Jerusalem. It is clear that Nehemiah is moved to travel to Jerusalem on account of reports he has heard concerning the city walls (1:1–11)—almost certainly a reference to the abandoning of construction work in response to Samaritan agitation (Ezr 4:7–23). Nehemiah, as cupbearer to Artaxerxes, was a trusted member of the court, responsible for ensuring that the king's wine had not been drugged or poisoned. He is able to take advantage of this privileged position to request permission to take temporary leave of absence in order to return to his family city of Jerusalem and to rebuild it (2:1–10). This is given, although the temporary leave in question appears to have become extended to a period of twelve years, during which he is granted the status of governor by Artaxerxes.

2:11–20 Nehemiah Inspects Jerusalem's Walls. On his arrival in Jerusalem, Nehemiah makes a nocturnal inspection of the southern section of the city's walls. Unwilling that anyone should know of his purpose in coming to Jerusalem, he carries out his inspection in secret under the cover of darkness (2:11–16). Finally, he feels able to let the leading figures of the city

The walls and gates of Jerusalem were rebuilt in 445 B.C. under the direction of Nehemiah. The project took fifty-two days. None of those gates remain. The Golden Gate, or East Gate, shown here, was built about 450 years ago, after the Turkish conquest of Jerusalem

know of his purposes (2:17–20). They greet his suggestion with delight. But Sanballat, who is clearly Nehemiah's leading political opponent, pours scorn on the idea.

3:1–4:23 Builders of the Wall; Opposition to the Rebuilding. Despite this hostility from Sanballat, work begins on the rebuilding of the walls and gates of the city. Each of the city's ten named gates is identified, along with those who were responsible for their reconstruction (3:1–32). Opposition to the rebuilding of the walls and gates grows, particularly from potential rivals of a rebuilt Jerusalem. Nehemiah learns of their plans to disrupt the work and posts armed guards to ward off assaults (4:1–23).

5:1–19 Nehemiah Helps the Poor. However, the labor-intensive demands of rebuilding the walls and guarding them from assault begin to take their toll. Popular discontent begins to grow as financial difficulties begin to mount. The situation is complicated by a food shortage, which leads to the price of basic foodstuffs such as grain rising significantly. In the end, Nehemiah can no longer ignore the outcry (5:1–5). He demands—and receives—promises that those who are benefiting financially from the situation pay back interest charges and restore property and goods that have been mortgaged to secure loans (5:6–13). To show his own seriousness, Nehemiah refuses his traditional right as a Persian governor to have superior food. He will share in the situation of his people (5:14–19).

6:1–7:3 The Completion of the Walls. Opposition to the rebuilding continues in other quarters. Sanballat spreads a rumor that Nehemiah proposes to use Jerusalem as the fortified base for a rebellion against Artaxerxes (6:1–14).

However, Nehemiah pays no attention to this rumor and presses ahead with the program of reconstruction. By October 445, the walls are rebuilt. The entire project has taken 52 days (6:15–19). Shortly afterwards, the gates are installed, and Jerusalem is once more a city that can protect itself (7:1–3). As a precaution against a surprise attack, Nehemiah orders that the gates not be opened until the heat of the day, thus making it difficult for an enemy to enter without being seen well in advance.

7:4–13 The List of the Exiles Who Returned. Now that the city can defend itself, attention can be paid to reconstructing its interior, especially its houses. As a preliminary step in this process, Nehemiah decides to establish who is present in the city. In the course of setting up this registration process, he encounters the list of people who returned from exile with Zerubbabel (7:4–73; see Ezr 2:1–70). There are minor differences between the lists provided in each case, suggesting that both accounts draw on the same original source, which may have included abbreviations or ciphers that were interpreted slightly differently at certain points.

NEHEMIAH 7:73 – 10:39

Ezra and the Dawn of Religious Revival

7:73–9:5 Ezra Reads the Law. It is interesting to notice how often religious revival and reform are linked with the public reading of the law. The public reading of the Book of the Law under Josiah in the period before the Babylonian exile (see 2Ki 23) was one such occasion. The reading of that same book by Ezra is another. It is clear that the reading in question involved the actual public reading of the Law, as well as the exposition of its meaning and implications by Ezra and a team of Levites (8:1–18). The people "now understood the words that had been made known to them" (8:12). As a result, they are moved to confess their sins and worship the Lord (9:1–3).

9:5–38 The Israelites Confess Their Sins in Prayer. The extended prayer used on this occasion is worth detailed study (9:5–8). It surveys the gracious dealings of God with his people from the time of Abraham through to exodus from Egypt and wandering in the wilderness, through the conquest of Canaan, up to the present day. The prayer includes powerful affirmations of the graciousness of God and his total faithfulness to his promises. Yet the continuing sin of God's people is also openly and fully admitted. Despite God's goodness, his people turned away from him, rebelled against him, and disobeyed him.

9:38–10:39 The Agreement of the People. As a result of these considerations, the leaders of the people put in writing their agreement to a commitment to reform and renewal (9:38–10:27). This agreement includes a number of major commitments, including a promise not to intermarry (10:30). This is a major concern to Ezra, who has earlier severely criticized the Jews for allowing this practice to continue (Ezr 9:1–15). However, this pledge of obedience goes far beyond this and includes a commitment to the upkeep of the temple and its ministers (10:31–39).

NEHEMIAH 11:1 – 13:31

Nehemiah's Later Reforms

11:1–12:26 The New Residents of Jerusalem. The narrative now returns to Nehemiah's concern to repopulate the city of Jerusalem. The walls and gates have been rebuilt. It is now necessary to rebuild the population of the once ruined city. It is agreed that the leaders of the people will live within the city. These will be joined by families chosen by lot, who will be required to live in the city rather than remain in the rural areas of Judah. While it is clear that some families volunteered to settle in the city, the majority had to be compelled (11:1–2). The names of the leading Jews who settled in Jerusalem are noted (11:3–36), along with the priests and Levites (12:1–26).

12:27–13:31 Dedication of the Wall of Jerusalem; Nehemiah's Final Reforms. In what is clearly an extract from his personal memoirs, Nehemiah records the great event of the dedication of the wall of Jerusalem (12:27–47) and the public reading of the Book of Moses (a reference to Deuteronomy). The section that excludes Ammonites and Moabites from being admitted to the assembly of God is noted (this points to Dt 23:3–6 being among the passages read), and then acted upon (13:1–3). It is clear that there is a new determination to remain faithful to the letter of the law.

So what had initially seemed an impossible task has been successfully accomplished. Jerusalem is a city once more, with walls and gates. Nehemiah can now rest in the knowledge that he has achieved what he set out to do. He now returns to the court of Artaxerxes (13:6), at some point between 433 and 432 B.C., having spent twelve years (see 5:14) as governor of Jerusalem.

However, for reasons that are not made clear, Nehemiah requests permission to spend a further term as governor of Jerusalem and returns within a year of his departure. On his return, he learns of a deliberate flouting of his regulations. One of the storerooms, which he had ordered to be set aside specifically for the safe keeping of tithes and temple offerings, has been reallocated for the personal use of Tobiah. Nehemiah is furious at the manner in which Tobiah has gained such a privilege and instantly revokes it (13:4–9). But this proves merely to be the tip of an iceberg. The provisions he had made to ensure the smooth running of the temple have fallen into disuse, with the result that the Levites have gone back to their fields to support themselves. Nehemiah moves to restore the arrangements so that worship at the temple can proceed as he had intended (13:10–14). Yet other abuses soon emerge. The Sabbath regulations are being openly flouted (13:15–22), and intermarriage is again becoming a major problem (13:23–31).

So the book of Nehemiah ends on a note of caution. Nehemiah is able to list many achievements of his time in Jerusalem. In addition to the rebuilding of the walls and gates of the city, he has instigated religious reforms that have eliminated many of the pagan practices that had begun to creep back into Jewish worship. But the reader is left with a sense of uneasiness. If such a significant departure from the law of the Lord can take place so soon after the triumphant return from exile, what will the future be like? Can the new community of Israel remain faithful to the law if its first period in the restored Jerusalem has seen so many lapses? It seems that one of the most characteristic aspects of human sin is a tendency for people to rebel against God—or at best, to serve him only when this happens to coincide with their own interests.

The history of Jerusalem in the first years of the postexilic period shows how deeply ingrained sin has become in human nature. And it raises the question: What can be done? How can Israel remain faithful to the Lord, let alone ensure that his name is known and honored throughout the world? These questions set the context for the coming of Jesus Christ as both Lord and Savior.

But that lies in the future. The biblical narrative now switches to the city of Susa, from which Nehemiah originally came, as we learn the story of Esther and the fate of a Jewish community that remained in that region of the Persian empire.

ESTHER

The book of Esther deals with the fate of a Jewish community in the city of Susa in the Persian empire during the reign of Xerxes (486–465 B.C.). While other Old Testament books dealing with the period tend to focus on events back in Jerusalem at this time, Esther deals with the events happening to the Jews who remained in the eastern region of the empire. The central character, from whom the book takes its name, is Queen Esther, a Jewess who is able to intervene on behalf of her people at a moment of crisis.

Esther is an unusual book in one respect. There is no explicit mention of God, nor any obvious reference to any aspect of worship or prayer. This absence of explicit reference to God should not, however, be interpreted to mean that Esther is a purely secular writing. It is clear that the work is intended as an illustration of God's providential guiding of his people as they face difficult circumstances. There is no need to draw explicit attention to the presence or activity of God. These are both assumed throughout.

1:1–2:23 Queen Vashti Deposed and Esther Made Queen. The work opens by setting the scene for its action, vividly depicting the power of Xerxes and the grandeur of his court (1:1–8). We are then introduced to his queen, Vashti (referred to in Greek records of the reign of Xerxes as Amestris). Vashti was deposed in 483 or 484 B.C., although the reasons for this are not clear. Her refusal to obey Xerxes' command probably reflects a power struggle within the court, which is only hinted at in this narrative (1:9–22). Eventually, she is replaced by Esther, a beautiful Jewess (2:1–1). However, Esther does not let the fact that she is Jewish be known (2:10, 20).

The dangerous world of court intrigue is then introduced. Mordecai, Esther's adviser and friend, uncovers a plot to assassinate Xerxes, which Esther duly reports to the king (2:19–23).

3:1–4:17 Haman's Plot to Destroy the Jews. Mordecai himself then becomes a cause of a plot on the part of Haman, a Persian nobleman, who becomes irritated by Mordecai's failure to pay him due respect. Haman contrives a scheme to eliminate Mordecai and the remaining Jews from the Persian empire. After casting lots (for which the Hebrew term is *Purim*), a day is selected for the deed (3:1–7).

Haman persuades Xerxes to issue an order for the annihilation of the Jews (3:8–15). Mordecai, learning of this development, asks Esther to intervene to prevent the massacre, hinting that she may well have been placed in such a prominent position for precisely this purpose (4:1–17). This clear hint at the providence of God in action spurs Esther to take action.

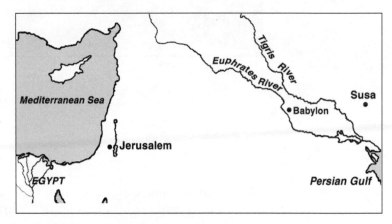

5:1–7:10 Esther's Request to the King; Mordecai Honored and Haman Hanged. Esther asks the king if he will grant her a favor, which she will explain at a banquet she proposes to give the following day to which only he and Haman will be invited (5:1–8). Haman is delighted at this honor and decides to make his happiness complete by hanging Mordecai on a purposely-built gallows the following day (5:9–14).

Fortunately, things do not turn out quite as Haman had expected. Xerxes, while browsing through some court records, discovers a record of Mordecai's uncovering a plot against him and honors him for this service (6:1–14). At the banquet she has prepared for Xerxes and Haman, Esther reveals that she is a Jewess and asks Xerxes to punish the man who has brought the threat of death to her people. Xerxes declares that the man who has perpetrated such an outrage deserves to die. On learning that it is Haman, he orders his immediate execution (7:1–10).

Esther lived in the city of Susa and became queen of the Persian Empire, though she told no one that she was a Jew. When there was a plot to massacre the Jews, she was able to help her people and see to it that the man responsible for the plot was punished.

8:1–10:3 Purim Celebrated; the Greatness of Mordecai. Following this, the Jews are given special privileges by Xerxes (8:1–16) and gain vengeance against those who had wished to destroy them (9:1–17). A festival, known as Purim after the lots which were thrown to decide the day of their death by Haman, is inaugurated by the Jews to commemorate their deliverance. The work ends by noting Mordecai's rise to power at the side of Xerxes (9:18–10:3). There are similarities between these happenings and those recorded in the story of Joseph (see Ge 39–47), in which a Jew also rises to authority in a Gentile—that is, non-Jewish—court.

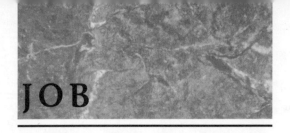

JOB

The Old Testament includes a number of different types of writings, including works of history (such as 1 and 2 Samuel), prophecy (such as Isaiah) and wisdom. The book of Job (rhymes with *robe*) belongs to this final category of writings. It is one of the most remarkable writings in the Old Testament. It focuses on a question of continuing interest and importance: Why does God allow suffering? Or, more precisely, does the fact that someone is suffering mean that he or she has fallen out of God's favor? Is suffering the direct result of sin? Important though these issues are, the Christian reader of this book may find that this work does not quite answer these questions. There are two reasons for this.

First, the problem of suffering has become of major importance in Western culture since the time of the Enlightenment—that is, since about 1750. The problem tends to be stated in a very specific form, focusing on the question of the goodness and omnipotence of God. How can a loving, good, and all-powerful God allow suffering in his world or among his people? This specific question is not addressed by the book of Job, which is primarily concerned to affirm that God is there, despite all the contradictions and confusion of life. The book makes it clear that nobody can hope to master the mysteries of life, including the apparent prosperity of the wicked and the sufferings of the righteous. Nevertheless, in the midst of all this anxiety, we can be reassured that God is present. There is a sense in which the book of Job must be read from the standpoint of the cross and resurrection of Jesus Christ in order to appreciate the manner in which a truly righteous person can undergo suffering.

Second, the literary form of the book involves an extensive amount of repetition and restatement, which makes its arguments quite difficult to follow. In what follows, we shall aim to identify the main lines of argument and exploration. It is, however, beyond the scope of this work to give a detailed analysis of the at times quite complex ideas that are being set out in the highly poetic speeches of the five contributors.

The problem of suffering is frequently raised in the Old Testament. Why do the righteous seem to be worse off than the unrighteous? Why is life so unfair? The book of Job explores some of these issues. But in many ways, the book is best seen as pointing ahead to the suffering of another righteous person—Jesus Christ. Why did Jesus have to suffer? Why did he have to die? As the New Testament makes clear, the answer to that question is not that Jesus deserved to suffer and die, but that he chose to suffer and die in order that others might live and be forgiven.

The book of Job has a distinctive structure, which needs to be understood before it can be fully appreciated. The book opens by setting the scene for Job's sufferings and allowing us to overhear Job's own understanding of his situation. We are then introduced to his three well-meaning friends, Eliphaz, Bildad, and Zophar. As the well-known phrase "Job's comforters" implies, these end up causing Job more misery and confusion than he had in the first place. Their basic assumption is that Job's suffering results from sin—an assumption that the reader, on account of the information supplied in the opening chapters of the work, knows to be incorrect.

The first part of Job consists of three cycles of speeches by the comforters, to which Job replies. This is then followed by some comments by Elihu, who seems to have been an onlooker who wished to contribute to the discussion at this point. Finally God himself responds, clearing up the confusion that has been generated by the theological ramblings of the disputants.

JOB 1:1 – 2:13

Introduction

The book opens with a powerful description of the character of Job himself. It is left beyond doubt that Job is an upright person of integrity and faith. It is also clear that Job is prosperous (1:1–5).

1:6–22 Job's First Test. The scene then shifts dramatically to a discussion between the Lord and Satan. The word *Satan* needs a little clarification. In the book of Job, the term is not treated as a proper name, and it is always preceded by the definite article. The Hebrew is thus better translated simply as "the accuser" or "the opposer," and does not have the associations of evil and rebellion against God that are traditionally associated with the proper name Satan. The figure in question is best understood as an angel or member of the heavenly court of the Lord who offers to test Job's faith and integrity (1:6–12). What would happen if Job were to lose all his outward signs of righteousness and integrity—his herds, for example? How would Job interpret such a development? The response is clear (1:13–22). Job has no hesitation in declaring that the Lord has the right to take away what he has given.

2:1–13 Job's Second Test. But what would happen if Job were to suffer physically? Once more, Job refuses to criticize God. He is prepared to accept whatever God wishes him to have, whether it is good or trouble (2:1–10).

Job's troubles are now, however, made considerably worse by the arriving of his three well-meaning friends. There can be no doubt that they cared for him greatly and wished to help him in his time of trouble (2:11–13). Initially, they simply sit beside him in silence, their presence being a sign of their care and sympathy. As events prove, however, they might have been well advised to remain silent. Their words of comfort proved to be distinctly unhelpful.

JOB 3:1 – 14:22

First Cycle of Speeches

3:1–7:21 Job Speaks and Eliphaz Replies. The first cycle of speeches opens with Job finally giving expression to his sense of frustration and distress (3:1–26). His misery is such that he wishes he had never been born. Eliphaz then intervenes in an attempt to cast light on things. It is quite clear, he argues, that Job's misery results from his sin. God would never allow a righteous person to suffer in this manner. The best course of action would be for Job to be honest about things and admit that he has sinned. Anyone who experiences the discipline of God ought not to despise it, but should learn from it. The same God who wounded Job will also bind up his wounds and heal him (4:1–5:27). Job's reply to this shows the full extent of his misery and confusion. Why does God create people, when they end up so miserable and unhappy? (6:1–7:21).

8:1–10:22 Bildad and Job. Bildad then enters the discussion (8:1–22). Picking up on Job's comment about God's apparent unrighteousness (6:29), Bildad stresses that God is just in all his ways. The fate of Job's children reflects the fact that they were sinners. Yet Job points out in reply that experience suggests that the strong triumph over the weak. It seems to him that there is no real justice underlying what he sees happening in the world (9:1–10:22).

11:1–14:22 Zophar and Job. The third comforter, Zophar, then makes his presence felt (11:1–20). It becomes clear that he lacks the gentleness and compassion of Eliphaz and Bildad. His contribution opens with what is clearly a direct criticism of Job for his lack of piety. He should not cast aspersions on God in this manner, nor be allowed to get away with some of his more intemperate statements. Job doesn't know what he is talking about. What does he know about the mysteries of God? Job ought to confess his sin and put an end to his misery.

If Zophar hoped to reduce Job to silence by this speech, he is soon disappointed. Job reiterates his basic conviction that there is a real tension between this view and his own experience. It is very difficult for him to discern the justice of what is happening to him (12:1–14:22). This speech contains some deeply moving statements concerning the frailty of human life (e.g., 14:1–2) and statements of the unbearable nature of human life without hope (e.g., 14:7–14).

JOB 15:1 – 21:34

Second Cycle of Speeches

15:1–17:16 Eliphaz and Job. The second cycle of speeches inevitably involves at least a degree of repetition. If the first set of speeches from the comforters was based upon the nature and character of God himself, the second set tends to focus more on the experience of life. Eliphaz' second speech (15:1–35) opens by reminding Job that he is not the first person ever to have wondered about the questions they are discussing. He concedes that the wicked may indeed seem to prosper. However, they are troubled by their consciences and live in fear of the consequences of their deeds. Job replies that his comforters are not the first people ever to have given the world the same unsatisfactory answers to the questions he has raised (16:1–17:16). Again, we find some moving statements concerning the need for hope in the face of death (17:14–16). These statements will bring home to Christian readers the importance of the resurrection of Jesus Christ, and the new hope it brings to those who know that they will share in its power and glory on the last day.

18:1–21:34 Bildad, Zophar, and Job. Bildad emphasizes the plight of the wicked, who are portrayed as lacking any hope or permanence (18:1–21). Job responds with an assertion of his bewilderment, both at the inconsistencies of the world and at the attitude adopted by his comforters, who seem intent on breaking him down (19:1–29). Zophar suggests that it may seem that the wicked escape unpunished, yet this is simply due to a temporary stay of execution. They will get what they deserve in the end, even if for the moment they seem to prosper. Zophar's graphic picture of the fate of the wicked in this life draws out both the material and psychological aspects of their suffering (20:1–29). In reply, Job suggests that this is simply not the case. The wicked are safe in their homes, and their families and flocks prosper. Where is the justice in that? Zophar seems to lack any real experience of the world in making such nonsensical statements (21:1–34).

JOB 22:1 – 31:40

Third Cycle of Speeches

22:1–25:6 Eliphaz, Bildad, and Job. The third set of speeches, which is limited to contributions by Eliphaz and Bildad, are noticeably more aggressive than the first two sets. Eliphaz argues that Job is wicked and that his wickedness is the direct cause of his present misfortune. If Job will only submit to God, he will find prosperity once more (22:1–30). Job's reply to this does not really address the issues raised by Eliphaz, but focuses once more on the seemingly senseless riddle of life. The wicked seem to prosper and get away with their evil (23:1–24:25). Bildad's very brief contribution to the debate (25:1–6) adds nothing new.

26:1–31:40 Job Speaks. This is followed by an extended series of speeches by Job, which generally recapitulate some of the points he has already made (26:1–31:40). Within this section, 28:1–28 is of special interest and is worth reading closely. The basic argument is that true wisdom is found only in the fear of God. The section opens with a summary of ancient mining methods, which underscores the difficulty of obtaining the most precious metals and gems. These are located deep within the earth, and their acquisition is both difficult and costly (28:1–11). Yet wisdom is not found in any such mines, nor can it be purchased with any of the precious products of these mines (28:12–19). It is only found in the fear of God. Only God understands everything. He alone views the ends of the earth and sees everything beneath the heavens (28:24). This insight sets the debate in its proper context, for it brings out that human minds are simply unable to fathom the deepest mysteries—including those under discussion at that moment.

This chapter is followed by Job's nostalgic recollection of his days of happiness and prosperity (29:1–25), reflections on his current miserable state (30:1–31), and a firm declaration of his personal integrity (31:1–40). Job is convinced that despite all his difficulties and temptation, he has remained faithful to what God requires and expects of him. If anyone can prove otherwise, they must say so. But Job believes, passionately and pathetically, that he is blameless. He cannot understand what is happening.

JOB 32:1 – 37:24

Elihu's Speeches

We have not been introduced to the fifth contributor to this discussion, who suddenly makes his appearance. In a series of four speeches, Elihu, who is clearly younger than the four other men (32:6–7), expresses his feeling that what has been said thus far does not really meet the issues. In particular, it is clear that he believes Job has managed to justify himself, but failed to justify or explain the ways of God himself (32:12).

The basic theme of Elihu's four speeches seems to be that suffering such as that experienced by Job is to be seen as God's way of disciplining his people. It is unthinkable that God should do anything that is in any way unjust (34:10–15). Nothing in the world is hidden from God (34:21–30). Therefore God must be aware of the fact that Job is suffering. The reason for such suffering can only be that Job has sinned (36:5–21). Suffering is thus linked with human hardness of heart and disobedience and can only be alleviated by repentance and amendment of life. In many ways, Elihu's arguments pick up themes that have already been found in the earlier speeches of the three comforters and add little that is new to the discussion. This discussion is now drawn to its close by the Lord himself.

JOB 38:1 – 42:17

God's Affirmations and Job's Response

38:1–41:34 The Lord Speaks to Job. The Lord now answers Job with a series of questions. In one of the most beautiful pieces of poetry in the Old Testament, the Lord speaks of the wonder and intricacy of creation (38:1–40:2). Aspect after aspect of the created order is explored, as the wonderful complexity of the world is made clear. The survey takes in every aspect of the creation, from the raging of the sea to the wonder of the constellations of the night sky, from the thundering of the rain clouds to the richness of the world's animal life. All of these were created by the Lord. Did Job create these? Does he understand the way the world is? Is he in a position to criticize God?

Job's answer is unequivocal. He has nothing to say. He knows that he has spoken out of turn. He is in no position to argue with the creator of the world (40:3–5).

The Lord then speaks again (40:6–41:34), affirming his own righteousness and his firm intention to ensure that righteousness prevails within his creation. No explanation is offered for the perplexities of life. Instead, there is a ringing declaration that all is subject to the sovereign justice of the Lord. Job may not understand, but he may trust. Using highly figurative poetic language, the Lord again speaks of his sovereignty over every aspect of his creation. The implication is clear: God may be trusted to take care of every aspect of his world. It is not something that humanity can or need understand. The important thing is to be reassured that the Lord is God and that all things are ultimately subject to him.

42:1–17 Job Speaks and Prays. Job accepts this (42:1–5). He is clearly aware that he has raised questions that are not going to be answered, and that he has ventured into regions where human understanding falters on account of the mysteries it confronts. Yet Job is reassured. The Lord is there, even in the midst of the riddles of life. As a result, he prays for his friends, who had tried to comfort him (42:10), and he is restored to prosperity.

The misery of Job caused him to wonder and want to question God, though he never lost his faith. God finally answered by pointing to the beauty and complexity of creation, even to the birth of a mountain goat, such as this ibex.

The overall message of the book of Job is clear. God does not allow his people to suffer without good reason. They may not fully understand what that reason may be. Nevertheless, they may rest assured that the Lord will do what is right. Righteousness does not exempt anyone from suffering. For the Christian, the suffering of Jesus Christ is a powerful reminder that even those who are righteous in the sight of God suffer. Yet it is also a reminder that God is able to do something through apparently pointless suffering. Will not the one who brought about the redemption of the world through the suffering of Christ bring about some good from his people's sufferings?

PSALMS

The book of Psalms, sometimes also known as the *Psalter*, is composed of a series of collections of psalms, which was probably arranged in its final form in the third century B.C.. The Psalter as we now have it includes a number of smaller collections, including the Psalms of Asaph (Psalms 73–83), the Psalms of the Sons of Korah (Psalms 84–85; 87–88), and the Psalms of David (Psalms 138–145). The 150 psalms brought together in this collection of collections are arranged in five books, as follows:

Book 1: Psalms 1–41
Book 2: Psalms 42–72
Book 3: Psalms 73–89
Book 4: Psalms 90–106
Book 5: Psalms 107–150

Although the book probably took its final form in the third century B.C., most of the material brought together dates from much earlier, generally in the period of 1000–500 B.C.. The task of dating individual psalms can be difficult, although some can be assigned to dates with a reasonable degree of certainty.

Before commenting briefly on individual psalms, some general comments on the collection of psalms as a whole will be helpful. Many psalms have titles attached to them. For example, Psalm 30 is entitled "A psalm. A song. For the dedication of the temple. Of David." This would naturally suggest that this psalm was written by David for the occasion of the dedication of the property and building materials for the temple, as recorded at 1 Chronicles 22:1–23:6. Although the reliability of the individual psalm titles have often been challenged, there are good reasons for believing that they are original and authentic. For example, psalms recorded outside the Psalter are generally given titles (such as those found at 2Sa 22:1; Isa 38:9; and Hab 3:1). Furthermore, the historical information preserved in the titles accords well with the content of the psalms in question.

Terms Used

It is known that at the time of the earliest Greek translation of the Psalter (around the second century B.C.), Jewish scholars were no longer familiar with the meanings of some of the technical terms used. This suggests that by this stage the titles were already long established and that they were retained by reason of tradition even at this early stage. Examples of these terms include *shiggaion* (a lament?), *maskil* (a meditation?), and *miktam* (a song of expiation?). One term of especial interest is *selah*, which occurs seventy-one times in the Psalter and is only found elsewhere in Habakkuk. The meaning of this word is not entirely clear. The most commonly accepted understanding of the term is that it denotes a pause, perhaps to allow for reflection on what has just been sung. However, it is also possible that it refers to the singing of a refrain, or to the raising of voices while that section of the psalm is sung. (It should be appreciated that the psalms were written to be sung, which explains the numerous musical directions that are often incorporated into the title.)

Authorship

The authorship of the Psalter is a complex issue. The psalm titles themselves mention various people, including David, Asaph, and the Sons of Korah. There are also fifty-five references to an unidentified "director of music." The Hebrew text of the titles is often ambiguous. For example, the Hebrew phrase translated as "a psalm of David" could mean a psalm (a) written by David; (b) written for or dedicated to David; (c) written about David; or (d) written for the use of David. Nevertheless, the association of so many psalms with David is entirely in keeping with the idea that he was "Israel's singer of songs" (2Sa 23:1). It is therefore reasonable to conclude that he must have been responsible for the composition of many, if not all, of the psalms that name him in the title.

Structure

The psalms, like much of the Old Testament, are written in poetic form. Unfortunately, there is still considerable debate over the precise nature of Hebrew poetry. Since the original pronunciation of the psalms is no longer known with any degree of certainty, attempts to recover the rhythm or meter have so far proved unconvincing. As a result, scholars have tended to focus on *parallelism*—the way one line of poetry is balanced by another, often either by repeating the same point using slightly different words (synonymous parallelism) or by stating the opposite (antithetic parallelism). An example of synonymous parallelism is provided in Psalm 104:33:

> I will sing to the LORD all my life;
> I will sing praise to my God as long as I live.

Other patterns can also be discerned. For example, a number of psalms are structured using an acrostic pattern, based on the letters of the Hebrew alphabet (e.g., Psalms 25, 34, 37, 111, 112, 119, 145).

Categories of Psalms

Psalms may be categorized in various ways. Most psalms fall into one of two major categories: psalms of petition (often referred to as *laments*), and psalms of praise. Other minor categories, such as wisdom psalms (such as Psalms 1, 37, 49, 73, and 112) and liturgies (such as Psalms 15, 24, 68, 82, and 115), may also be noted. We shall concern ourselves with the first two major categories.

Over a third of the psalms take the form of *prayers of petition*, the largest category within the Psalter. These are mainly prayers addressed to God reflecting thoughts and emotions arising out of human suffering. This category of psalms may be divided into two general types: plea and complaint. *Pleas* are prayers for help, made either by individuals (such as Psalms 3, 5, 7, 14, 17, 25, and 26) or by communities (such as Psalms 12, 58, 83, 94, and 123). *Complaints* are laments that God has failed to act when he might have been expected to, and are again made by individuals (such as Psalms 6, 13, 22, 35, and 39) or by communities (such as Psalms 9, 10, 44, 60, 74, and 77).

Psalms of praise, like modern hymns, express delight in God as creator and savior. Such psalms can be divided into two general categories: those that praise the greatness of God as it is revealed in nature and history (often referred to as *hymns*, such as Psalms 8, 19, 29, 33, and 47); and those that express gratitude to God for intervening in a situation of great distress or suffering (often referred to as *songs of thanksgiving*). Such songs of thanksgiving may be on behalf of individuals (such as Psalms 18, 30, 32, 34, and 92) or of communities (such as Psalms 67, 75, 107, and 124).

The harp was an important instrument in the temple orchestra. It had twelve strings and was played with the fingers. This man plays for tourists on the streets of Jerusalem.

Themes

A number of related themes give unity to the rich diversity of material found in the Psalter. At its heart is the theme of the sovereignty of God over his creation, reflected not only in the psalms of praise, which proclaim his many qualities and virtues, but also in the psalms of petition. These latter psalms reflect the belief that God alone is able to meet every request. From beginning to end, the psalms thus stress, explicitly or implicitly, the universal sovereignty of the Lord God. This theme is often linked with the kingship of God, especially in those psalms celebrating his enthronement (such as Psalms 47, 93, 95, 96, and 97). Other aspects of God's character that are of major importance within the Psalter include his holiness, righteousness, and goodness.

The Psalter also focuses on the royal monarchy, either of David himself or of one of his descendants. This reflects the unique position occupied by David and his dynasty. Not only did God choose David to be the shepherd of his people, but he also designated him as "son" (see Ps 2:7; 89:26–27). This is linked with the selection of Jerusalem, or more precisely Mount Zion, as the location for the temple. The temple was widely regarded as God's dwelling place on earth. God's presence was understood to ensure protection and peace for those living under his rule. The continued prosperity and security of Jerusalem thus became the theme of much praise.

It is not surprising that the themes of praise and prayer should be of major importance within the Psalter. These are often linked with specific references to music and musical instruments and to the human thankfulness and joy that lies at the heart of such praise.

In what follows, we shall explore some of the themes of each of the psalms. In view of the limitations on space, it will be impossible to explore these themes in the detail or to the depth that they so clearly deserve. The psalms are probably best read in an attitude of devotional meditation. The notes provided here are intended to help pick out the points that may be particularly helpful in using the psalms in this manner.

BOOK 1:

Psalms 1–41

Psalm 1. This psalm may be intended to act as an introduction to the Psalter as a whole. It stresses the importance of taking a delight in the law of the Lord and the benefits that result from this. A particularly powerful image—that of a tree planted by streams of water (1:3)—is employed to illustrate the way in which a close relationship with God leads to spiritual refreshment and renewal. The contrast with those who reject or ignore God will be clear: these are like dried-up chaff, which is blown away by the wind (1:4). A theme that will occur many times in the Psalter is that of the Lord watching over his people (1:6), ensuring their well-being, even in the face of all kinds of adversity.

Psalm 2. This psalm belongs to the general category of *royal psalms*, celebrating both the coronation of a new king of Judah as well as the kingship of the Lord over his people. The king is anointed by the authority of God, not by human authority. It is impossible to read this psalm without being reminded of, for example, the anointing of David as king over Israel by Samuel. For this reason, other earthly kings and rulers are warned to be on their guard; the king enjoys the protection of the Lord, so attack on him is futile and misguided.

However, there is also a strongly messianic element to this psalm, which speaks of the king as the "Son" of God (2:7), who enjoys the special protection and favor of the Lord. There is a clear echo here of the great promise made by the Lord to the house of David (2Sa 7:14) that he will raise up a king from one of his descendants. For the Christian, this psalm has a special significance in this respect. It is seen by New Testament writers as pointing to the coming of the son of God, Jesus Christ. This psalm is hinted at on the occasion of the baptism of Jesus Christ (Mt 3:17). Through his resurrection from the dead, Christ is declared to be the son in whom God is well pleased (Ac 13:33). Similarly, in relation to both the superiority of Jesus over angels and his role as the true High Priest, the letter to the Hebrews singles out this verse as having major relevance (Heb 2:7; 5:5).

Psalm 3. The title points to its having been written at the time that David was facing a serious rebellion from his son Absalom (2Sa 15:13–17:22). The psalm affirms the care and protection of the Lord in the face of enemies and speaks powerfully of the peace of mind this knowledge brings to God's people. This is the first psalm in a collection that is explicitly attributed to David.

Psalm 4. This psalm, also attributed to David, is again addressed to a situation of distress. It speaks of the assurance of believers that the Lord will hear them in their time of need (4:3). Even though it may seem that all is lost, the Lord may be relied upon to remain faithful to those whom he loves. The psalm includes a particularly fine prayer for the light of the face of God to shine upon his people (6:6), which echoes the great thanksgiving of Israel during its period of wandering in the desert (Nu 6:25).

Psalm 5. The fifth psalm is also a plea for help from the Lord in the face of an enemy. The believer can have confidence in the Lord on account of the righteousness of God, which will ultimately triumph over the evil of the godless. The ungodly have rebelled against God and therefore will be dealt with by God himself. There is a clear idea here that the psalmist's difficulties at this moment are caused by his faithfulness to the Lord. In that he has been faithful to the Lord, he can expect the Lord to be faithful in return and to deliver him from his situation. The believer can wait in expectation (5:3), knowing of the protection of the Lord, which is compared to a shield (5:12) that wards off the attacks and missiles of an enemy.

Psalm 6. Psalm 6 represents another prayer for the Lord's deliverance in a situation of some difficulty. The psalm sounds a note of anguish on account of the uncertainty of things (6:3), and it depicts the psalmist as being in great distress on account of his sorrow (6:6–7). When will the Lord act? The psalm stresses that the only hope of the believer lies in the Lord, not in human strength (6:2), and emphasizes the importance of the "unfailing love" of the Lord in relation to that hope (6:4).

Psalm 7. To judge by its title, Psalm 7 would seem to relate to the period in David's life when he was pursued by Saul and seemed to be continually in danger of his life. (The term *shiggaion* in the title is not understood, although it seems to be related to an Akkadian word for "lament." Its inclusion certainly points to the antiquity of the psalm.) The psalm speaks of David's decision to take refuge in the Lord in the face of his dangers, knowing that the Lord will shield and defend the righteous. The psalm ends on a note of confidence, reflecting the faithfulness of God to his covenant. Even in their darker moments, the people of God may seek refuge in his compassion.

Psalm 8. Psalm 8 strikes a very different note. It is a celebration of the place of honor accorded to humanity in the purposes of God. It opens with a ringing declaration of the majesty of God. Yet, as David reflects on the wonder of God's creation, he cannot help but wonder about his own place. It is amazing that God should have given such a place of honor to people such as himself in his great work of creation. For God has set humanity only a little lower than the angels and given them authority over the world and its remaining creatures. And he cares for them! This is truly a psalm of celebration and meditation on the wonderful love of God for his creation.

Psalms 9 and 10. These psalms should be read together, for they appear to have originally been a single psalm celebrating the steadfast love of the Lord in times of distress and need. The two psalms, together and individually, stress the total faithfulness of the Lord to his people and his willingness to hear them in their moments of distress.

Psalms 11–14. These psalms continue the theme of the threat posed by outside enemies and the need to look to the Lord for help. In their different, yet complementary ways, these psalms identify the threats posed to faith and the manner in which the Lord is able to meet those threats. Psalm 14 is of particular interest on account of its recognition that there are those who deny the existence of God (14:1). It is important to note, as the French philosopher Pascal pointed out many years ago, that Scripture nowhere feels the need to prove the existence of God!

Psalm 15. This psalm strikes a different note. It represents a fine and poetic analysis of the need for holiness and purity on the part of those who wish to draw near to the Lord. The original reference is specifically to the temple and relates to those who wish to worship. However, it can also be read from a specifically Christian standpoint as referring to the need for such holiness on the part of all who wish to gain access to God. Such access is made possible by the atoning death of Christ, which cleanses and purifies sinners and allows them access to God.

Psalms 16–18. These psalms once more focus on the idea of the Lord as a place of refuge in times of difficulty. Note especially the images used to refer to God that express the idea of stability and permanence. God is a rock and a fortress (18:2)—in other words, a secure place in which one may seek and find safety. Each of the psalms speaks of God's ability to redeem those who turn to him.

Psalm 19. This psalm deals with the glory of the Lord, especially as this is made known through the law. The opening verses (19:1–6) speak of the way in which the glory of God is revealed in the natural order, especially the heavens. This natural knowledge of God is then supplemented and refined through a knowledge of God through his law, which is declared to be "more precious than gold . . . sweeter . . . than honey from the comb" (19:10). This is an especially fine psalm to meditate upon on a starry night, or after thinking about the compassion of God as revealed in his Word.

Psalms 20 and 21. These psalms are generally thought to belong together and to represent the prayer of an army on the eve of battle (20:1–9) and its song of thanksgiving on the day of victory (21:1–13). It is not clear whether the two psalms relate to the same battle, or precisely which battle they refer to. However, given the violent nature of David's reign and the events which preceded it, the two psalms fit in neatly with what we know of the events of that period.

Psalm 22. This psalm is of considerable importance and needs to be discussed in more detail. The importance of this psalm can be judged from the fact that Jesus Christ cited its opening words as he was dying on the cross (Mt 27:46; Mk 15:34). It is the song of a righteous sufferer in response to the attacks of enemies, who at present are gaining the upper hand. He awaits deliverance from the Lord—yet at present there is no sign of any such deliverance. While the original situation refers to one of David's many difficulties, the psalm is of special importance in casting light on the crucifixion of Christ as the righteous suffering servant of God.

Although the psalm clearly relates to the events of David's lifetime, it is also prophetic, pointing ahead to events that would only be fulfilled in the coming of Jesus Christ. It speaks of the righteous sufferer being scorned and despised, surrounded by those who mock him (22:6–7)—a perfect description of the fate of Jesus Christ on the cross (Mt 27:41). Those around him taunted him: "He trusted in the Lord; let the Lord rescue him" (22:8)—some of the words of the scoffing crowd who surrounded the dying Christ (Mt 27:43). The description of the sufferer's anguish (22:12–16) corresponds well to the pain experienced by Christ on the cross. The piercing of Christ's hands and feet at crucifixion are prophesied here (22:16; see Jn 20:25), as is the casting of lots for his clothes (22:18; see Mt 27:35; Lk 23:34).

Yet the psalm ends on a note of hope. All is not lost. The Lord has neither forgotten nor despised his suffering servant, but will allow him to live to praise his name (22:24–26). The hope of the resurrection shines through this psalm even in the midst of all this suffering and anguish.

Psalm 23. The twenty-third psalm is one of the most familiar of all the psalms, on account of the metrical version. It is a beautiful statement of the goodness, guidance, and care of the Lord for those who trust and obey him. Even in life's darkest moments, believers can rest secure in his tender care.

Psalm 24. This psalm is a psalm of celebration, clearly written with the needs of some great religious occasion in mind. The most natural such occasion is David's bringing of the ark of the Lord into the city of Jerusalem (2Sa 6:12–19), an occasion of great rejoicing and praise. The psalm affirms the lordship of God over all his creation and his continuing presence among his people.

Psalms 25–28. These psalms return to the theme of the need to trust the Lord in situations of difficulty, however hopeless the odds against the faithful might be. Each represents a statement of trust in the Lord and a plea for deliverance from trouble. Psalm 27, with its powerful use of images of the Lord (27:1–3) and its prayer to be allowed to dwell in the house of the Lord and contemplate his beauty (27:4), is perhaps the finest of this group of psalms. It concludes with a powerful statement of hope. We need not wait until death to see the goodness of the Lord. We can begin to see it while we remain in the land of the living (27:13). With this hope, the uncertainties of the future may be faced, and faced with confidence and trust.

"The Lord is my sherpherd, I shall not want. ..." The beginning of Psalm 23 is one of the most familiar verses of the Bible, offering comfort, even in the dark moments of life.

Psalm 29. Psalm 29 exults in the lordship of God over his creation. Despite the great power and vast size of the creation, God is still greater and more powerful. The psalm is a powerful statement of the sovereignty of God over the universe, giving believers reason for hope in the face of the great and often frightening forces of nature.

Psalm 30. This is a psalm of dedication, which recalls the great saving acts of God and the radical difference that God's favor makes to the lives of believers. The most likely occasion for the composition of the psalm would seem to be David's dedication of the building material for the temple at Jerusalem (1Ch 22:1–6).

Psalm 31. Psalm 31 is an appeal to God in his righteousness to deliver believers from their difficult situations. This psalm refers to God as "rock" and "fortress," highlighting the strength and stability the Lord brings to life and faith (31:3). The appeal to the righteousness of God (31:1) is important: in the Old Testament, God's righteousness is primarily understood as his faithfulness to his promises to redeem his people.

Psalm 32. This psalm focuses on the importance of God's not counting sin against individuals, in order that they may experience his saving power (32:1–2). There is a particular emphasis on the way God's love surrounds the faithful (32:10), suggesting the image of a protective shield.

Psalm 33. This is a psalm of praise, which recalls God's greatness in creation and redemption and declares the great benefits which result to his chosen people (33:12). The importance of the fear of the Lord is made clear: those who fear the Lord will know his protection both in this life and in the life to come (33:19). Again, the image of a shield is used to bring out the strongly protective character of knowing God. To know God is to experience his salvation and protection at all times (33:20–22).

Psalm 34. This psalm continues the emphasis on the importance of the fear of the Lord (34:9) while also noting the benefits of faith. Once more, the Lord is depicted as protecting the faithful (34:7). Whatever the troubles that the righteous may find themselves going through, they may rest assured of the continuing presence and care of the Lord (34:19–22).

Psalms 35–41. These psalms focus on the theme of deliverance. It will be clear that this theme is of major importance throughout this collection of psalms attributed to David, reflecting the enormously difficult situations in which he found himself as he fled for his life from Saul and subsequently had to evade assassination attempts as king. Each of the psalms, in different ways, represents an acknowledgment of human need and divine graciousness. God alone is a refuge in times of trouble. He alone is a place of safety. Yet in the midst of all these dangers and threats, David knows that his true security lies with the Lord. Nothing can take this from him.

BOOK 2:

Psalms 42–72

Psalms 42–43. These psalms were originally a single psalm, which speaks of a real sense of the absence of God, linked with a confidence that a sense of his presence will one day be renewed. Its opening verse, which likens the soul seeking for God to a deer which pants for streams of water (42:1), is widely recognized as one of the most beautiful verbal pictures painted by Scripture. The basic message of this great vision of hope is that a knowledge of the presence of God will return, despite its present absence. The decision to remember the great moments of the past (42:4) is an encouragement to hope that these moments will return. God is compared to a rock (42:9) and a stronghold (43:2). The psalms end with a confident declaration that the struggling believer will praise God again and be reassured of his presence and love (43:5).

Psalm 44. Psalm 44 clearly envisages that Israel has been defeated in battle. It is a lament for past failure and a statement of hope that things will change in the future. Notice how Israel's failure is attributed directly to rejection by God (44:9–16). Just as Israel's victories are due to God's favor (44:4–8), so her failures are due to God's displeasure. Throughout the psalm, there is a sense of bewilderment, comparable to that which permeates the speeches of Job in the book that bears his name. Why has this happened? If Israel had been disobedient, or had forgotten God or rebelled against him, then this calamity could be understood (44:17–22). But it remains a mystery. Israel can only lament her failure and wonder what the future holds. The psalm ends with a prayer for future deliverance.

Psalm 45. This is a festival psalm, clearly written for the occasion of a great royal wedding.

Psalm 46. In contrast to the previous psalm, this is a declaration of total confidence in God, who is able to meet all our needs. It calls upon its hearers to be still and know that the Lord is God. Believers may rest in the fortress of the Lord, finding a security there which is denied to them everywhere else. The themes of this psalm underlie Martin Luther's famous hymn "A Mighty Fortress Is Our God."

Psalms 47–48. The theme of the praise of God, which is hinted at in Psalm 46, is picked up and developed in Psalms 47–48. These two psalms take delight in the knowledge of the universal reign of God as king and his power over all nations and peoples. The psalms are saturated with a boldness and confidence that would be unthinkable were they not grounded securely in the nature and purposes of God.

Psalms 49–50. Related ideas are developed in Psalms 49–50, which note the need to trust in God rather than in the counsel of the wicked. Psalm 49 stresses the danger of any form of assurance that is grounded in wealth or self-confidence. It points out the inexorable fate of the wealthy and urges its hearers to avoid these snares. Psalm 50 brings out the need for Israel to acknowledge its dependence on God, particularly through keeping the covenant and offering sacrifices as a token of dependence (50:14).

Psalm 51. According to its title, Psalm 51 was composed by David in the aftermath of his adultery with Bathsheba (see 2Sa 11:1–12:25). It is a psalm of remorse and repentance, which calls upon God to forgive a contrite sinner. The psalm brings out the devastating effects of serious sin on David's relationship with God and his longing to be restored to fellowship with the Lord (51:10–12). The psalm affirms both David's sinfulness and the Lord's willingness to forgive those who truly turn to him in penitence and trust.

Psalms 52–55. These psalms represent a group of psalms, each of which is referred to as a *maskil*. The term is not fully understood, as noted earlier; it is possible that it may refer to the meditative nature of the psalms in question. Psalm 52 is a firm statement of confidence in the Lord, even in times of great difficulty. Psalm 53 focuses on the folly of wickedness and looks forward to the day when the Lord will restore the fortunes of his people. Psalm 54 again focuses on the importance of trusting in God at moments of distress and anxiety. Psalm 55 develops this theme, expanding both on the seriousness of the threat from the wicked (55:9–14) and the joy of being able to cast one's cares upon the Lord (55:22). The particular danger of a close friend becoming an enemy is noted—a hint of the treachery that would be experienced by Jesus Christ, who was betrayed by one of his close circle, Judas Iscariot.

Psalms 56–60. These psalms represent a group of *miktams*. It is not clear precisely what this term refers to, but it may denote a type of lament. Once more, the theme of deliverance in times of trouble is evident at every point. At several points, the psalmist expresses himself with total honesty, asking God to destroy his enemies (e.g., 59:5). Some readers find such sections distasteful. However, they are an important witness to David's willingness to be totally honest and open in his prayers to the Lord, hiding nothing from him. There is some wisdom in this insight. Too often we hold things back from God, when we ought to be more open.

Psalms 61–65. This group of psalms are all described as "psalms of David," and focus once more on the ability of God to meet all needs, even in the most difficult of situations. Some of the poetic language used to describe the security God's presence brings should be noted—for example, the image of resting in the shadow of God's wings (63:7) or of lying awake, thinking about God in the watches of the night (63:6).

Psalm 66. Psalm 66 gives indications of having been composed to celebrate Jerusalem's deliverance from the Assyrians due to Hezekiah's obedience to the word of the Lord delivered through the prophet Isaiah (2Ki 19:9–36). The great saving acts of God in the past, including the crossing of the Red Sea (66:5–6), are recalled, as thanks are given for the latest deliverance from the threat of an enemy (66:8–9). Notice how the dangerous experience from which Jerusalem was delivered is referred to as "refining" (66:10). The experience is like a fire that purifies precious metal, leaving behind a purer and more valuable resource. A similar note is struck in Psalm 67, which opens (67:1) by recalling the great blessing given to Israel in the wilderness (Nu 6:24–26).

Psalm 68. This is a major psalm of praise and celebration, which recalls the great events of Sinai during the desert wanderings of Israel (68:7–10), the conquest of Canaan (68:11–18), and the establishment of Zion (or Jerusalem) as the capital of Israel under David. The psalm seems to have been written for the occasion of a great procession to celebrate the triumphs of God. Paul picks up the theme of this psalm in speaking of the resurrection and ascension of Christ (Eph 4:8–13).

Psalm 69. This psalm again reflects a sense of despair and sorrow in the face of threats from enemies. If this psalm dates from the time of David, it is not clear precisely what threat it concerns. It is more likely that the psalm deals with a dangerous moment in the life of one of David's successors, such as Hezekiah. The psalm's frequent references to suffering at the hands of one's enemies were seen by New Testament writers as pointing ahead to the suffering and death of Jesus Christ (see, for example, Ro 11:9–10, which takes up the themes of 69:22–23).

Psalms 70–71. Similar themes are found in Psalms 70-71, which represent further pleas for God's help in situations of danger and despair. Once more, an appeal is made to the righteousness of God (71:2)—that is, the covenant faithfulness and compassionate love of the Lord.

Psalm 72. Psalm 72 takes the form of a royal psalm, linked with Solomon, which represents a prayer for the well-being of the king and his people.

BOOK 3:

Psalms 73 – 89

This new book of Psalms opens with a series of eleven psalms ascribed to, or somehow associated with, Asaph, one of the leaders of the choirs established by David to provide music for the temple at Jerusalem (1Ch 6:39; 15:17–19; 16:4–7). Psalms 73–83 can thus be seen as a single collection with a series of common themes providing continuity across the individual psalms. One of the most important themes to be associated with this collection is that of God's sovereign rule over his people and the nations, which is seen as the ground of Israel's hope in the face of anxiety and uncertainty.

Psalm 73-83. The first psalm in the series, Psalm 73, returns to the theme of the apparent prosperity of the wicked. The ease and wealth of the life of the wicked, which drive the psalmist to despair, are depicted in a series of poetic images (73:4–12). He only regains a sense of proportion by returning to the sanctuary of God and realizing the importance of his relationship with God (73:23–28). Other psalms focus on different themes, including expressions of hope that the Lord will deliver his people from oppression by foreign powers (74, 79, 80, 83), acknowledgment that the Lord is the God and savior of Israel (75, 76), a recollection of the great deeds by which the Lord delivered his people in the past (77, 78), and the judgment of God upon his people and the nations (81, 82).

Psalm 84. Psalm 84 is a beautiful meditation on the loveliness of the house of the Lord and the comfort and solace it brings to those who come there. The image of the swallow finding its nest (84:3) points to the natural resting place of God's people being with the Lord who has redeemed them and offers them rest.

Psalm 85. This psalm may reflect the situation encountered by Ezra or Nehemiah on their return from Babylon to Jerusalem to begin the long process of rebuilding and spiritual renewal. It represents a plea for revival and restoration in order that the glory of the Lord may once more dwell in his own land (85:9).

Psalm 86. This psalm represents another prayer for help in a time of distress, which combines a strong sense of confidence in the Lord with a sense of urgency over the seriousness of the situation in which the psalmist finds himself.

Psalm 87. This psalm is a celebration of the special place of Zion as the "city of God," which looks forward to the day when all nations will acknowledge its status.

Psalm 88. This psalm returns to the themes expressed in Psalm 86. It is an open admission of the terror experienced by the psalmist in the face of his enemies and the sense of bewilderment he is experiencing. Like Job, he cannot understand what is happening to him or why God should allow it to take place. Yet he will continue to trust in and pray to the Lord (88:13). The Lord has humbled him. Eventually, the same Lord will restore him.

Psalm 89. A similar theme is developed in Psalm 89, which may well date from the time of the Babylonian attack against Jerusalem, which led to the exile of King Jehoiachin (2Ki 24:8–17). The psalm represents a prayer that the Lord will restore his people in fulfillment of the covenant made with David. The psalmist cannot understand why the Lord seems to have abandoned his people in this way, and he pleads for restoration.

BOOK 4:

Psalms 90 – 106

Psalms 90–95. The fourth book of Psalms includes some marvelous songs of praise to the Lord. *Psalm 90* depicts the hopeless state of sinful humanity apart from God, particularly stressing the brevity of human life. *Psalms 91–94* draw attention to the great benefits of knowing the Lord. *Psalm 95* represents a call to worship, which stresses the authority and majesty of God as creator and notes the consequences of disobedience and rebellion against him.

Psalms 96–101. A series of psalms then follows that focus on the praise of God as the creator of the world and the sustainer of his people. *Psalms 96–101* survey the deeds and majesty of God, and exult in his greatness and faithfulness. *Psalm 101* is the briefest of these psalms, but expresses well their general content. God is the one who is to be praised and worshipped, and whose great acts are to be responded to with thanksgiving by his obedient and joyful people.

Psalms 102–103. The mood changes abruptly at *Psalm 102*, which is basically the prayer of someone in considerable distress. It is not clear who wrote this psalm, nor under what conditions. But it is clear that it is written in confidence that even in the deepest misery and unhappiness, confidence may be placed in the steadfast love of the Lord. This note of confidence is also sounded in *Psalm 103*, which identifies the grounds of such assurance in the deeds of God in the past (103:7) and his inherent nature and character (103:2–5). The psalm rejoices in God's willingness and ability to deal with human sin, so that it need no longer disrupt the relation between God and the believer (103:8–12). The compassion of the Lord for his children is spoken of in the most moving terms: despite our frailty, God still loves us and cares for us (103:13–18).

Psalms 104–106. These psalms continue this note of confidence and praise and ground this comprehensively in God's great acts of salvation in the past. *Psalm 104* focuses on the whole area of creation, surveying the greatness of the Lord as this is revealed in the works of his creation (104:5–26). *Psalm 105* itemizes the great acts of redemption which led Israel out of Egypt into the promised land (105:5–45). By recalling God's faithfulness to his covenant in the past, believers can be reassured of his faithfulness to them in the present. *Psalm 106* undertakes a similar survey, although noting the rebelliousness of the people during the period of the desert wanderings. This faithlessness on the part of God's people is seen as a warning for the present. God's faithfulness to his covenant must not be abused or taken for granted. There is a need for Israel to keep its side of the covenant.

BOOK 5:

Psalms 107–150

The final book of Psalms includes some of the finest psalms of praise in this collection. The themes of God's greatness in creation and redemption, especially as shown in his great acts of deliverance, are referred to frequently. *Psalm 107*, with its brilliant, comprehensive recitation of the great divine acts of deliverance in Israel's history, illustrates this superbly. Who can fail to appreciate the greatness of the love of the Lord by considering these great deeds? *Psalm 108* also focuses on the theme of the love of God, drawing on material from Psalms 57:7–11 and 60:5–12 in doing so.

Psalms 109–110. These psalms deal with the trustworthiness of God in the face of difficulties and threats. *Psalm 109* envisions a case of false accusation and calls upon the Lord to deliver the writer from this situation. *Psalm 110* is of considerable importance to the writers of the New Testament. It focuses on a messianic king or priest, who will be crowned by the Lord. For New Testament writers, this great prophecy is fulfilled in the coming of Jesus Christ as the king of Israel and its true high priest (Heb 6:16–20; 7:20–22). The significance of Melchizedek (first mentioned at Ge 14:18) is the subject of extensive reflection in the letter to the Hebrews, which sees this priest as holding the key to a right understanding of the role of Jesus Christ as high priest. It is also referred to by Jesus Christ himself (Mt 22:44–45).

Psalms 111–118. This group of psalms forms a small collection within this book often referred to as the "Hallelujah Psalms" on account of their frequent use of the Hebrew term *hallelu yah,* which literally means "praise the Lord." The theme of the goodness of the Lord is constantly stated and explored, especially with reference to his great deeds in the past (surveyed in general terms, for example, at 111:2–9) and the continued experience of his blessings in the present (see 112:2–8; 113:7–9; 115:9–15). *Psalm 117,* the shortest of all the psalms, provides a brilliantly neat summary of the leading themes of this group of psalms.

Psalm 119. This collection is immediately followed by the longest of the psalms. Psalm 119 has a complex structure of 176 verses, arranged into 22 groups of 8 verses. There are 22 letters in the Hebrew alphabet, and each of the groups is allocated one letter from this alphabet. Thus 119:1–8 is allocated to *aleph*, the first letter of the Hebrew alphabet, and 119:25–32 to *daleth*, the fourth letter, and so on. The basic theme of this great psalm is the wonder and greatness of the word of God. The word of God is seen as something that both demands and offers. It demands obedience, and it offers promises of salvation and well-being. This psalm is worth reading at a single session, with a view to appreciating the full richness of the law of God and all it can mean to believers. To mention just two of the poetic images used to emphasize the importance and pleasure of the law of God: it is like a lamp to guide our feet (119:105), and it is something that tastes sweeter than honey (119:103).

Psalms 120–134. This is followed by a collection of fifteen psalms known as the "songs of ascents." Psalms 120–134 are generally thought to have been used in connection with the great yearly pilgrimages to Jerusalem, culminating in entry into the Lord's temple. The collection seems to have been arranged in such a way that the opening psalms deal with threats and difficulties of various kinds, such as those one might encounter on a long journey when far from the comforts and safety of home. The collection concludes with entry into the sanctuary itself (134:2), as the purpose of the journey has been triumphantly achieved. The most famous psalm in this collection focuses on the difficulties of the long journey to Jerusalem and the comfort that the Lord brings to those undertaking such a journey. *Psalm 121* represents a powerful promise of God's presence and protection during the journey to Jerusalem. As the pilgrims contemplate the hills they must ascend before they can reach their goal, they can draw comfort from the continual care of the Lord.

Psalms 135–136. These psalms focus once more on the Lord's great acts of redemption in the past. The deliverance of Israel from slavery in Egypt is of particular importance in each case (135:8–12; 136:10–22). However, God's work in and sovereignty over his creation (135:6–7; 136:4–9) and the calling of his people (135:4) are also singled out as important in this respect. Meditation on the works of God in the past gives hope for the present and calls to mind the great love of God for his people, which endures for ever.

Psalm 137. This is one of the most famous psalms to focus on the painful exile of Jerusalem in Babylon. The psalm evokes the poignancy of those who are cut off from their homeland and long for restoration. It ends with a curse, which many find offensive. Nevertheless, it is an important testimony to the total honesty of the psalmist, who is prepared to bring his true feelings before the Lord, rather than conceal them in platitudes. Honesty before God concerning one's feelings is one of the hallmarks of the Psalter. It is something that should be treasured. In contrast, *Psalm 138* returns to the theme of the troubles of the righteous, focusing on God's faithfulness to his revealed purpose.

Psalm 139. Psalm 139 is a powerful declaration of the ability of the Lord to see everything within the human heart. Nothing is hidden from the Lord. Nothing and nobody can escape from his presence. The psalmist invites the Lord to search him and expose anything within him that is false. There are clear parallels between the ideas of this psalm and some of Job's speeches, in which he asks God to point out his failings and sins to him.

Psalms 140–144. These psalms are psalms of distress, which call to the Lord for deliverance from danger of various kinds. The theme of the constancy of God's love and faithfulness recurs throughout these psalms.

Psalms 145–150. The final set of psalms focuses on the theme of praise, expressing thanksgiving to God for all that he is and all that he has done for his people. *Psalms 145–147* recite all the blessings that knowing the Lord brings to his people. It is clear that identifying God's blessings is seen as one of the most effective causes of praise as each of these psalms ends with outbursts of praise and adoration. *Psalm 148* takes a different form, simply inviting all of creation to join in the praise of its great and wonderful creator. *Psalm 149* has an element of "praise the Lord and pass the ammunition" about it. It acknowledges that the praise of God is always set in the real world, which threatens to destroy the people of God unless they defend both themselves and their God. Finally, the Psalter is brought to a glorious end with *Psalm 150*, one of the finest songs of praise in the Psalter, which summons every musical instrument to sound the praise of the great God of Israel, who has done such wonderful things for his people.

PROVERBS

The Old Testament includes a number of different types of writings, including works of history (such as 1 and 2 Samuel), prophecy (such as Isaiah) and wisdom. The book of Proverbs belongs to this final category of writings, which also includes Job and Ecclesiastes. Wisdom was a much-valued resource in the ancient world, and Solomon was fabled for his God-given wisdom. Wisdom should not be confused with prophecy. The purpose of the proverbs is to cast light on the practical side of life, and to pass down to later generations the accumulated wisdom of earlier generations. This wisdom is often based on shrewd observation of everyday life.

The main body of Proverbs (10:1–22:16) consists of a collection of short proverbial sayings, attributed to Solomon. The Hebrew word here translated as "proverbs" has a much broader range of meaning than the corresponding English word and can also have the meaning of "parable" or "oracle" (both of which suggest God's involvement in the gathering of human wisdom). According to biblical tradition, Solomon was a man of outstanding wisdom. He is credited with having "spoken" some three thousand proverbs (1Ki 4:32). The sayings collected together in the main body of Proverbs would amount to less than one seventh of these. This suggests that the bulk of Proverbs was written in the tenth century B.C., at a time of relative peace and stability suitable for the production of literary works. However, there are indications that not all the material collected in Proverbs may be due directly to Solomon. For example, there is reference to the sayings of two unknown writers, Agur son of Jakeh and King Lemuel. Although the work gives every indication of having been written in the tenth century B.C., there are indications in the text itself that it may have received its final form at some point during the reign of Hezekiah (c. 715–686 B.C.).

The proverbs are not intended to be treated as laws that must be adhered to strictly. They are intended to provide practical guidance as to how someone might act in a particular situation. The complexities of human relationships are such that true discernment and wisdom are required to deal with them. Most of the proverbs consist of only two lines, although slightly longer sayings are also encountered occasionally. Frequent use is made of comparisons, often on pictures drawn from everyday life. Their basic theme could be as follows: act wisely, and you will prosper; act foolishly, and you will fail.

PROVERBS 1:1 – 9:18

The Importance of Wisdom

1:1–7 Prologue. The work opens by declaring the importance of wisdom for life. It then makes it clear that wisdom is not some purely secular wisdom, but is grounded in the fear of the Lord (1:7). The "fear" in question should not be understood as a terror inspired by the thought of divine vengeance. It is best understood as a respectful submission to the word and will of God, in the full knowledge of his great power.

1:8–4:27 Exhortations to Embrace Wisdom. Not everyone is prepared to accept wisdom. Folly and sin are depicted as things that are enticing and attractive, yet that merely lure people to their doom (1:8–19). In a powerful passage, the dangers of folly are compared with the benefits of wisdom (1:20–2:18). The final section of this passage is especially important (2:13–18): wisdom is something for which it is worth giving up everything. There are interesting parallels with Jesus' comparing the gospel to the pearl "of great value" (Mt 13:45–46)—something that satisfies as nothing else can.

By pursuing wisdom and keeping clear of the dangers of the temptations of the world, a young person may rest assured of future happiness and contentment (2:19–3:18). Wisdom is like a "tree of life" (3:18), which will nourish and refresh those who find her and hold fast to her.

The theme of wisdom is now developed in a new direction. Wisdom is declared to have been at God's side during the great work of creation (3:19–20). This theme will be developed later. The passage now returns to explore the further benefits of wisdom (3:21–35). The person who has wisdom will "inherit honor" and have security in the Lord. Parents are understood to have a particularly important role to play in the process of imparting wisdom to their children (4:1–27). This is not to be seen as a paternalistic "the older know best." Rather, it is a declaration that parents have a responsibility to ensure that their children benefit from their accumulated wisdom and experience.

5:1–7:27 Warnings Against Adultery and Folly. An extended section now deals with examples of stupidity. Adultery is condemned because of its negative effects on people (5:1–23). The argument here is not really moral or theological in character. The tone adopted is practical and pragmatic: adultery will just make you miserable. After a series of warnings (6:1–19) against other kinds of stupidity (such as the negative effects of laziness or telling lies), the text returns to its main theme (6:20–7:27).

8:1–9:18 Wisdom's Call. The nature of wisdom herself now comes to the fore. Wisdom is spoken of in personal terms (8:1–36), a process that is often described as *personification* or *hypostasization*. Wisdom is portrayed as a woman who seeks to attract people to her in order that they may benefit from her counsel. Wisdom is the basis of true human government and underlies all just laws. The role of wisdom in the creation of the world is then described (8:22–31). Wisdom is once more personified and is depicted as God's assistant and skilled craftsman in the process of creation. Wisdom came into being before anything else. Anyone who has wisdom has access to the secrets of the creation and will be able to find favor in the sight of the Lord (8:32–36).

The personal aspects of wisdom are further emphasized in the following section (9:1–18), which compares wisdom and folly to two women. Wisdom calls to all who hear her voice and invites them to enter her house and feast at her table (9:1–6). Whoever accepts that invitation will find life. In contrast, folly seeks merely to lure fools to their death (9:13–18).

PROVERBS 10:1 – 22:16

The Proverbs of Solomon

The collection of Solomonic proverbs that follows cannot easily be summarized and is best read through to gain an understanding of the kind of wisdom that is being commended. The proverbs generally take the form of single statements, one verse in length, in two parts. For example, "Better a little with righteousness, than much gain with injustice" (16:8). The two parts of the proverb often express a contrast, with the word *but* joining the two parts to make this contrast clear.

The proverbs are often written in the form of commands. For example:

> Stay away from a foolish man,
>   for you will not find knowledge on his lips (14:7).

These proverbs, it must be stressed, are not to be placed on the same level as the Old Testament law! The force of the proverb cannot be compared with the absolute prohibition of, for example, the worship of idols or murder. The general status of such proverbs is best understood along the lines of "anyone who is wise will stay away from a foolish man." The proverbs are about human advice, not commands from the Lord. Hence, to give one especially interesting example, the authority of God cannot be sought for the physical punishment of children (13:24).

PROVERB 22:17 – 31:31 ⎯⎯⎯⎯⎯⎯⎯⎯⎯⎯⎯⎯⎯

Further Collections of Proverbs

22:17–24:34 Sayings of the Wise. The remainder of the book of Proverbs is taken up with shorter collections of proverbs, not all of which are attributed to Solomon himself. The "Sayings of the Wise" and its appendix (24:23–34) are snippets of worldly wisdom, generally longer in form than the shorter and pithier sayings of Solomon himself. While some of the proverbs represent worldly wisdom (e.g., 23:6–8), at other points spiritual insights are clearly involved (e.g., 22:22–23). The reference to "thirty sayings" (22:20) could be understood to refer to the remainder of this section (22:22–24:22), which breaks down into thirty parts, most of which are two verses long.

25:1–29:27 More Proverbs of Solomon. This further collection of proverbs, attributed to Solomon himself, consists of pithy sayings of wisdom, generally one verse in length. Many of these proverbs focus on issues of government and management.

30:1–31:31 Sayings of Agur and Lemuel; Epilogue. The short collection of "Sayings of Agur" and "Sayings of King Lemuel" is drawn from collections of material attributed to these writers, about whom nothing is known for certain. The book ends with a poem extolling the virtue of "a wife of noble character" (31:10–31), which consists of 22 verses, each of which begins with a successive letter of the Hebrew alphabet.

ECCLESIASTES

The book of Ecclesiastes is perhaps the most pessimistic in the Old Testament. Like Proverbs and Job, it belongs to the category of wisdom literature. The book takes the form of a collection of proverbs and observations, some long and some very brief. Many readers find the book puzzling, because it seems to be dominated by views that do not fit easily into the general pattern of biblical outlooks. The book is best understood as a powerful and convincing commentary on the meaninglessness of life without God and the utter despair and cynicism that will inevitably result from lacking a biblical faith. It represents a graphic portrayal of the misery and futility of human life without God and the inability of human wisdom to discover God in all his fullness.

The author of this work introduces himself as "the teacher" (*Ekklesiastes* in the Greek translation of the Old Testament) and is traditionally identified as Solomon on account of the reference to "son of David, king of Jerusalem" (1:1). This designation could, however, be used of any descendant of David. The book itself occasionally indicates that it was written by a subject, rather than a ruler; and the style of Hebrew used suggests that the book dates from later than the time of Solomon. There is no general consensus on any particular date, and it is probable that we shall never know with certainty when the book was written.

1:2–3:22 Everything Is Meaningless. The book opens with a dramatic declaration of the meaninglessness of life (1:2). This is illustrated by an analysis of all kinds of happenings (1:3–11). What is the point of it all? Death brings life to an end and extinguishes the memory of those who once lived. So why go on? To the Christian reader, these deeply gloomy and bleak words are transcended by the hope of the resurrection to eternal life in Jesus Christ. Ecclesiastes provides an agonized picture that allows us to understand how utterly hopeless is life without God or without hope in eternal life. It is a powerful reminder of the importance of the Christian hope.

However, the work continues its gloomy analysis. It is not merely the events of life that seem devoid of any meaning. Human wisdom is a waste of time. What use is it? If anything, it just creates more misery (1:12–18). The same goes for pleasure (2:1–16). The writer's experiments with the seeking of pleasure were disastrous. Everything proved to be little more than a meaningless "chasing after the wind" (2:11). In fact, just about every human achievement is pointless. What is the point in becoming wise, when wisdom cannot save anyone from death (2:12–16)? And what is the point in laboring over something, when everything is a waste of time (2:17–26)? It is all utterly and totally useless (3:1–22). Humans are just like animals: they live and die, and that is the end of the matter. Once more, the Christian reader of these words will turn with joy to the hope of the resurrection and the sense of purpose and peace this brings.

4:1–9:12 A Common Destiny for All. Having painted this bleak picture, the writer now fills it out with further details and examples of the futility he has in mind. The oppression of the world (4:1–12), the pursuit of promotion (4:13–16), the accumulation of riches (5:8–12), and the pursuit of wisdom are all a waste of time (7:1–8:1). Even wisdom has its limits. While acknowledging that wisdom is worth possessing, the writer raises a serious doubt. Can anyone really possess wisdom in the first place? Wisdom seems very far away and very elusive (7:23–25). People might as well eat, drink, and be happy (8:1–17); there is nothing else to look or hope for. Everyone, whether wise or foolish, sinner or saint, will meet the same miserable end: death (9:1–12).

9:13–12:8 Remember Your Creator While Young. The writer then returns to his musings on the nature of wisdom (9:13–10:20). While wisdom may well be an excellent thing, why is it that fools seem to end up in all the best positions? In the end, all these things are beyond human understanding (10:1–6). The work ends with a sustained reflection on the futility of life. Youth passes very quickly, leaving nothing but memories in the midst of present futility (11:7–12:8).

The white blossom of the caper. In ancient times the caper berry was considered an aphrodisiac. In Ecclesiastes 12:5 "desire" is the metaphysical translation of "caperberry."

12:9–14 The Conclusion of the Matter. The work closes with some final reflections on the hopelessness of things (12:9–14). The "teacher" himself was wise—but his wisdom led him only to despair and a deep sense of meaninglessness. In the end, the only source of real wisdom is the fear of the Lord. The "whole duty of man" is to "fear God and keep his commandments" (12:13). If there is any hope or meaning, it lies in God alone.

The Christian, reading this work from the standpoint of God's wonderful act of deliverance and hope through Jesus Christ, can end a study of this bleak and gloomy work by echoing some words of Peter: "Praise be to the God and Father of our Lord Jesus Christ! In his great mercy he has given us new birth into a living hope through the resurrection of Jesus Christ from the dead" (1Pe 1:3). If only the writer of this book had lived to see that glorious day!

SONG OF SONGS

This brief work, sometimes referred to as the Song of Solomon, is generally regarded as an outstanding love poem. The title literally means "the greatest of songs." The work is traditionally understood to have been written by Solomon, although there is insufficient evidence within the text of the work itself to confirm this with certainty. The book is loosely structured around five meetings between the lover and the beloved, with reflection on the periods during which they are obliged to be apart.

Many Christian writers have seen this work as an allegory of the love between Christ and his church. Others have seen it as a figure (that is, a sign or symbol) of the relation between Christ and individual believers. In other words, the work was not interpreted as a celebration of human love, but as a poetic or figurative way of speaking of the spiritual love of Christ for the church or for individual believers. More recently, however, there has been an increased willingness on the part of most Christian interpreters of this book to see it simply as a superb account of human love—a love that echoes the love of God for his people, but that focuses on the deep feelings of love between a man and a woman.

The song is divided into a number of sections, of which the most well marked are the five meetings (1:2–2:7; 2:8–3:5; 3:6–5:1; 5:2–6:3; and 6:4–8:4). The most helpful way to read this work is to take each of the five meetings at a time, and try to appreciate the anticipation of meeting and joy of fulfillment. There is an unquestionable parallel between the joy of the meeting of lovers and the believer coming home to God, and there is no reason why the book should not be read as an allegory of the love of God for his people, if the reader finds this useful.

ISAIAH

The book of the prophet Isaiah is the first of the four Major Prophets (the other three being Jeremiah, Ezekiel, and Daniel). Isaiah lived and worked in Jerusalem in the latter part of the eighth century B.C.. His call to prophecy came in 740 B.C., the year of King Uzziah's death (6:1), and he is known to have prophesied up to at least 701 B.C., when the northern kingdom of Israel fell to Assyria. At this stage, Judah and Israel were both moving out of a longer period of peace and prosperity into one of uncertainty and danger. Assyria was becoming aggressive in the region; and Israel, Judah, and Syria were uncertain as to how to react to this threat. It is against this context of political and military uncertainty that Isaiah's ministry is set. The reader will find it helpful to read the story of Jerusalem during this period, as set out in 2 Kings and summarized in this commentary (pp. 130–34). This will provide important background material to the earlier parts of this major prophecy.

The prophecy is not restricted to this period in the history of Jerusalem, however. The later parts of the book concern prophecies of hope and restoration for the Babylonian exiles. The early parts of the prophecy cover the period between the fall of the northern kingdom of Israel in 722 and the extreme danger to Judah from Assyria in 701 B.C.. An important section of the work (chapters 36–39) deals with Judah's survival of this threat. A major later section (chapters 40–55) goes on to prophesy Judah's later enslavement to Babylon and its eventual deliverance from exile in that land. The final perspective of the book looks beyond events in Judah's immediate future to a glorified Jerusalem, set amidst "new heavens and a new earth."

ISAIAH 1:1 – 12:6

Prophecies of Hope and Judgment

The work opens by declaring that what follows represents the prophecies of Isaiah concerning both Judah and Jerusalem during the reigns of several kings that span the period 792–686 B.C.. Note that Isaiah's ministry is to the southern kingdom of Judah and its capital city Jerusalem only. No mention is made of the northern kingdom of Israel (1:1). At this stage, we have no idea who Isaiah was or how he came to be called as a prophet. Those details will be provided later.

1:2–31 A Rebellious Nation. It is clear that Isaiah sees his role as declaring the word and will of the Lord to a people who are generally inclined to disobey him. This is made clear from the first major prophetic oracle recorded in this book (1:2–31), which stresses that the Lord's own people have rebelled against him. Israel—a term used throughout this prophecy to refer to the people of God, rather than to the northern kingdom of the same name—has forsaken the Lord (1:3). Even dumb animals show more sense than the people of God. Israel may offer all the right sacrifices and do all the right things at the temple, but the heart of the people is far from the Lord (1:10–17). Outward observance of the religious cult is not accompanied by love for the Lord and obedience to him. Note carefully the refrain: "Hear the word of the LORD" (1:10), a characteristic prophetic turn of phrase, indicating that the prophet is speaking under inspiration on behalf of the Lord, not for his own sake. Yet this opening oracle of judgment ends on a note of hope. God will refine his people (1:25–26), removing all their impurities as a furnace refines a precious metal and restoring his people to their former glory.

2:1–5 The Mountain of the Lord. The second major oracle reaffirms the rebelliousness and disobedience of the people of God. This oracle opens with a remarkable vision (the essentials of which are also found at Mic 4:1–3) concerning the "mountain of the LORD" (2:1–4). This refers to Mount Zion, which will become a focus of worship, peace, and prosperity when the Lord's saving work has been accomplished. This passage includes a famous reference to beating "swords into plowshares" (2:4), as it graphically portrays the reign of peace that the Lord will usher in.

2:6–4:1 The Day of the Lord. But that is in the future. In the present, the "house of Jacob" (a reference to the people of God) have rebelled against the Lord in all kinds of ways. Particular criticism is directed against the increasing influence of paganism in Jerusalem (2:6–8), which the Lord is not prepared to tolerate. The prophet then speaks of a coming "day of the LORD" in which all these practices will be swept away, as the Lord comes in majesty and power to purify his people (2:12–22). This judgment is depicted graphically (3:1–4:1) as the future fall of a proud and haughty Jerusalem is predicted. By failing to obey the Lord, both Judah and Jerusalem have condemned themselves.

4:2–6 The Branch of the Lord. The judgment will be stated more specifically presently, but a brief passage promising redemption now breaks in. The thorough-going message of judgment that is now being delivered is tempered with the future hope of salvation for those who remain faithful to the Lord.

5:1–30 The Song of the Vineyard. A major passage of judgment now opens, focusing on the image of a vineyard (5:1–7). Israel is compared to a vineyard that is established, planted, and protected at great trouble by its owner. Not unreasonably, he expected the vineyard to produce some good grapes; in the end, however, all he got for his trouble was bad fruit. The story is a parable of Israel, which God called into being, loved, and tended. He expected Israel to be righteous and obedient, but found only bloodshed and distress. Things have gone very seriously wrong. This verdict is then amplified (5:8–30), as the crimes and injustices that give rise to the Lord's anger with his people are documented. For their lack of obedience and understanding, the people of God must face exile (5:13).

6:1–13 Isaiah's Commission. At this point, we finally discover more about Isaiah himself. The year of King Uzziah's death was 740 B.C.. In that year, Isaiah had a vision of the Lord in all his holiness and majesty. It is possible that the prophet had this vision in the temple itself. The vision, which centers on the holiness of the Lord, terrifies Isaiah. As a sinner, how can he live after seeing God? In an act of purification, he is touched with a burning coal by one of the seraphs (a term used only in this passage; its full meaning is not clear). His guilt has now been removed, and he is free to speak of the Lord to his people. He is then called and commissioned to bring the word of the Lord to the people in the full knowledge that they will be hardened by what they hear and refuse to respond to it.

It is not clear why this account of Isaiah's call as a prophet occurs so late in this work. It might have seemed more natural to place it at the beginning. However, its present location within the book heightens the importance of the preceding material and prepares the reader for more oracles yet to come.

The image of a vineyard that is planted and tended carefully but yields only bad fruit is a parable on Israel itself. And Isaiah warns what will happen to God's people because of his anger.

7:1–25 The Sign of Immanuel. A new historical section now opens, set at the time of the Syro-Ephramite war of 735 B.C.. In the face of growing Assyrian expansion, Aram and the northern kingdom of Israel (often referred to as Ephraim) try to persuade Judah to join an anti-Assyrian coalition. Ahaz, who is then king of Judah, is tempted to side with the Assyrians. As a result, Jerusalem finds itself under attack from the north.

Isaiah urges Ahaz to stand firm in the knowledge that the Lord will deliver him from this threat (7:1–12). As a sign, Isaiah speaks of a virgin giving birth to a son who will be called Immanuel. In this specific historical context, Isaiah probably meant primarily that within nine months, the threat posed to Jerusalem would be ended. It is possible that the events of 8:3 are related to this. However, the great prophetic implications of the passage cannot be ignored. It clearly points ahead to the birth of another child called Immanuel (Mt 1:23), who would deliver his people from sin.

8:1–9:7 To Us a Child Is Born. After a discussion of the role of Assyria in the purposes of the Lord (8:1–22), Isaiah returns to the coming salvation promised by the Lord. He focuses attention on the region of Galilee. It is there that "the people walking in darkness have seen a great light." Here, Isaiah uses a literary device sometimes referred to as the *prophetic perfect*, by which an event that has yet to happen is spoken of as it has already come to pass. A child will be born, who will be the prince of peace. The famous passage speaks of hope in the coming of a deliverer at a dark moment in the life of the people of God (9:1–7). For New Testament writers, this great prophecy finds its fulfillment in the coming of Jesus Christ (see Lk 2:14), and his ministry in the region of Galilee.

9:8–10:34 The Lord's Anger Against Israel; the Remnant of Israel. Yet this message of hope is again set in the context of judgment and condemnation for Israel's sins (9:8–10:4). Although Isaiah is clear that God will judge Assyria (10:5–19), it is clear that he proposes to use Assyria as his "rod of anger" by which the people of God will be punished for their disobedience and rebellion. In its turn, Assyria will rebel against God and refuse to recognize that he has the right to use it as his instrument (10:15–19). Only a faithful remnant of Israel will remain, who will trust in the Lord (10:20–34).

11:1–12:6 The Branch From Jesse; Songs of Praise. From this remnant, a redeemer will emerge and will usher in a new period of hope in the history of the people of God (11:1–10). This strongly messianic prophecy finds its ultimate fulfillment in the coming of Jesus Christ, who is filled with the Spirit of God. When this redeemer finally arrives, the people of God will be exultant (12:1–6), just as Simeon was exultant when he realized that Jesus Christ was the long-awaited savior of Israel (Lk 2:25–32).

ISAIAH 13:1 – 23:18

Judgment Against Israel's Neighbors

Thus far, Isaiah's judgment has been directed primarily against Judah and Jerusalem. While Assyria has been judged, it is on account of its future and foreseen refusal to accept its limited role as the agent of God's judgment, and its attempt to set itself up as a supreme power in itself. Attention now shifts to the surrounding nations. Each of these nations comes under the righteous survey of God and is condemned for its failings.

The series of international condemnations is interrupted only to deliver a prophecy concerning Jerusalem (22:1–25). The date of the events referred to by this prophecy is unclear. It could refer to the attack mounted on Jerusalem by the Babylonians shortly before its fall and the deportation of much of its population in 586 B.C.. However, it is also possible that it refers to the earlier siege against Jerusalem mounted by Sennacherib in 701 B.C.. The latter siege is referred to explicitly at several points later in this work, and it is possible that this passage anticipates these later sections. However, the prophecy could also be seen as anticipating the devastation wrought on Jerusalem by Babylon over the period 588–586 B.C., initially during the siege and subsequently during the occupation and destruction of the city.

The reader of this section should read each prophecy carefully, noting the fundamental theme that underlies them all: in the end, only the Lord will triumph, and they will pass into the dust of history. The structure of the sections is as follows.

13:1–14:23	Babylon
14:24–32	Assyria and Philistia
15:1–16:14	Moab
17:1–14	Syria and Israel
18:1–20:5	Ethiopia (also known as Cush) and Egypt
21:1–10	Babylon
21:11–17	Edom and Arabia
22:1–25	A Prophecy concerning Jerusalem
23:1–18	Tyre

The basic theme of the ultimate victory of the Lord over all earthly and spiritual powers is then asserted in the following section, to which we now turn.

ISAIAH 24:1 – 27:13

The Lord's Final Victory

24:1–25:12 The Lord's Devastation of the Earth. The section opens (24:1–23) with a survey of the total victory that the Lord will gain over every force that opposes him, both in heaven above and on earth below (24:21–23). The judgment is universal, and none can hope to escape. Yet this judgment will bring deliverance for the people of God, who have been subjected to oppression by the forces whose comprehensive and total rout has just been foretold. Isaiah can see the jubilation and delight that these great events will bring (25:1–12). The people of God will finally find that their trust in the Lord has been totally vindicated.

26:1–27:13 *A Song of Praise and Deliverance of Israel.* A song of praise, to be sung on that day, portrays the faith of Israel as a fortified city that can withstand all assaults upon it through the faithfulness of the Lord. Israel will be delivered from all her turmoil and suffering and can rest assured that the Lord will watch over her and safeguard her in the future (26:1–21). The guilt of the people of God will be purged in an act of atonement. This atonement is almost certainly the coming period of exile, which is seen as God's way of punishing the guilt and purging the stain of the sin of his people (27:1–13). All pagan practices and beliefs will finally be removed from the people of God. As becomes clear in the following section, Jerusalem badly needs exactly that sort of purging.

ISAIAH 28:1 – 35:10

Judgment Against Jerusalem

28:1–30:33 *Woe to David's City.* The next section opens with a clear declaration (28:1–29:24) that the Lord will punish unbelief among his people. The religious life of Jerusalem has become totally debased, even to the point that its priests and prophets stagger in a drunken state through drinking too much wine and beer (28:7–8). If Jerusalem will not hear the word of the Lord in their own language, they will have to listen to the language of foreigners (28:11–13)—a clear reference to the coming of the Assyrians and the threat of deportation. The fact that Jerusalem is David's own city does not excuse the degeneration within its walls and will not save it from the coming judgment (29:1–10). This message of condemnation continues (30:1–33) by describing the miseries that await Jerusalem on account of its disobedience. Nevertheless, this prophecy of judgment is softened by the promise of restoration (30:19–26).

31:1–9 *Woe to Those Who Rely on Egypt.* As the following section makes clear, Isaiah is insistent that Israel trust in the Lord, not in its own strength or in alliances with foreign nations. Isaiah's particular concern focuses on Egypt, which was seen by many as the only source of help against the Assyrian menace at this stage. Isaiah's point is clear: "the Egyptians are men and not God; their horses are flesh and not spirit" (31:3). Jerusalem's ultimate hope and security do not lie in foreign powers, but in obedience and trust in the Lord. In the end, Isaiah declares, Assyria will fall—but it will fall before a sword that is ultimately not mortal (31:8), a clear reference to the action of God to deliver his people.

32:1–35:6 The Kingdom of Righteousness; Joy of the Redeemed. This is followed (32:1–33:24) by the promise of a future king who will reign with peace and righteousness in Jerusalem. This reign will be accompanied by the outpouring of the Holy Spirit (32:15). The prophecy also includes a message of judgment directed against a "destroyer" (33:1–9), which is probably to be identified with Assyria. This is followed (34:1–17) by an oracle of judgment against Edom and a prophecy of salvation for those restored to Jerusalem (35:1–10).

This final prophecy looks ahead to the day when all nature will rejoice with the entry of the Lord's redeemed people into Zion. The prophecy includes mention of several signs of the messianic age (35:5–6), which the New Testament indicates as having been brought to fulfillment in the ministry of Jesus Christ (e.g., Mt 12:22).

ISAIAH 36:1 – 39:8

Jerusalem and the Siege of Sennacherib

Prophecy now gives way to history, as we learn of the events which took place during the reign of Hezekiah. This section, which can also be found in a similar version at 2 Kings 18:13–20:19, explains the political crisis against which part of Isaiah's ministry is set. The occasion is the major assault mounted by the Assyrian king Sennacherib against a series of cities in Judah. The background to this event is important and needs to be explained a little.

The Assyrian king Shalmanezar V invaded Samaria, the capital of the northern kingdom, in 725 B.C. and laid siege to it for three years. When the fighting was over, a substantial section of the population of the region was deported to regions deep with the Assyrian empire. The northern kingdom of Israel no longer existed as a nation in its own right. Shortly before this catastrophe, a new era in Judah's history opened with the reign of Hezekiah in 729 B.C.. Initially reigning alongside his father Ahaz, Hezekiah took full control in 715. Once Israel had been conquered, the Assyrian king Sennacherib, who had succeeded Shalmanezar, turned his attention to the southern region of Judah. In the course of this, he decided to attack Jerusalem. It is this development which forms the background to this section of Isaiah.

36:1–37:20 Sennacherib Threatens Jerusalem; Hezekiah Prays. It is clear that the Assyrians intend to take Jerusalem by the simplest means possible. Initially, the Assyrians try to use verbal persuasion. Speaking in Hebrew (which the ordinary inhabitants of Jerusalem understood) rather than Aramaic (the international language of diplomacy, which was not understood by ordinary people), the Assyrians tell Hezekiah that he is doomed unless he surrenders. It is clear that they hope to provoke popular pressure against the king's intention to resist them. Yet Hezekiah insists in placing his trust in the Lord. The Assyrians scoff at this. No city has ever been saved from them by its god before (36:4–22). Hezekiah is distraught and prays for guidance (37:1–20).

37:21–38 Sennacherib's Fall. Isaiah urges Hezekiah to resist the Assyrians and delivers a detailed prophecy against Sennacherib, predicting his downfall (37:21–35). That same night, a disaster falls upon the encamped Assyrian army. Badly shaken, Sennacherib withdraws to Nineveh, where he will eventually die at the hands of his sons (37:36–38). The prophecy is fulfilled.

38:1–39:8 Hezekiah's Illness; Envoys from Babylon. At the time of an apparently fatal illness, Hezekiah receives further encouragement and reassurance from the Lord through Isaiah (38:1–22). But Hezekiah appears to overstep the limits of caution in his dealings with some envoys from Babylon. At a time when the world's horizons were dominated by Assyria, Hezekiah is unreasonably positive towards the Babylonians (39:1–4). As a result, Isaiah prophesies the future downfall of Jerusalem at the hands of the Babylonians (39:5–7). Hezekiah believes these events to lie far in the future. He seems unaware that his own failings will contribute to the punishment and purification of his people through exile in Babylon.

ISAIAH 40:1 – 55:13

Prophecies of Restoration from Exile in Babylon

The situation now changes radically. The grim prophecies of coming exile have been fulfilled. Jerusalem is in exile in Babylon. The great prophecies of restoration found in this new section may be the work of a prophet active during the time of the Exile, and speaking directly to the exiled community. Alternatively, they may be the words of an earlier prophet, foretelling both the Exile and subsequent restoration. Some scholars believe that we are dealing with a new writer at this point, speaking the Lord's words of comfort and hope to a exiled community whose exile was shortly to end, by the grace of God. If this is the case, we are dealing with a Second Isaiah, to be distinguished from the prophet who operated earlier during the reign of Hezekiah.

The exile of the people of Jerusalem began in 586 B.C., and ended nearly fifty years later in 538 B.C., when the first group of exiles returned to Jerusalem—an event described in the opening chapters of the book of Ezra.

40:1–41:29 Comfort for God's People. The new vision of hope opens with words of comfort (40:1–2). Jerusalem's time of exile is over. Her sin has been paid for. She is free to return home. The prophet sees the Lord going ahead of his returning people, making a highway in the desert for the people of the Lord to travel along on their way back (40:3–5). All the obstacles to their path will be swept away as the Lord guides his people home. The frailty of human power, evident in the forthcoming collapse of Babylonian power, is proclaimed. Only the word of God remains forever. Everything else will fade away (40:6–8).

The prophet now relates his glorious vision of the Lord returning in triumph to his own city of Jerusalem, and the excitement this return will bring to its inhabitants (40:9–11). The Lord will act like a shepherd, gathering up his tired flock and carrying them home. The prophet reflects on the greatness of God (40:12–26). No one can rival him. Jerusalem can rest assured that her God is beyond comparison. So why, he asks, does Jerusalem believe that the Lord has forgotten her? Does she not know that the Lord will comfort and support her? (40:27–31). The whole world will see this great act of deliverance and appreciate the greatness of the God of Israel. No idol ever achieved redemption in this manner! There is no other redeemer (41:1–29).

42:1–25 The Servant of the Lord; Song of Praise to the Lord. The prophet's attention now turns to the figure of the "servant of the LORD," who will possess the Spirit of God and bring justice to the nations (42:1–4). Further details of this servant will be provided in later chapters. The prophet returns to his theme of the greatness of the Lord and the wonderful nature of the redemption that will soon come to the exiled people of Jerusalem (42:5–25).

43:1–44:28 Israel's Only Savior; Israel the Chosen. The following sections stress that the Lord is the redeemer and savior of Israel. There is no other savior apart from the Lord (43:1–28). This point is especially important in relation to the New Testament, which unhesitatingly declares that Jesus Christ is the savior of the world—in the full knowledge that only God is savior. As God, Jesus Christ is indeed the true savior of the world.

Alongside the theme of redemption, we find that of election. God has chosen Israel as his own people (44:1–8). This is followed by a superb critique of idolatry (44:9–20). How can idols be taken seriously, when the same piece of wood can be used both to make an idol for worship and to light a fire by which to keep warm? It is too ridiculous to be taken seriously. Jerusalem must remember that it is the Lord, and no idol, who has done all these great things for her (44:21–28).

So how is this great act of deliverance to be achieved? Earlier, we learned that Assyria was the rod of the Lord's punishment against Israel. In other words, Assyria was the human agency through which Jerusalem was punished for its disobedience. In that it exceeded its authority (note how

Jerusalem is said to have suffered twice as much as was necessary [40:2]), Assyria itself must now be humbled.

45:1–48:22 The Fall of Babylon and Israel Freed. We are now introduced to the human agency by which this humbling will come about: Cyrus the Great, king of Persia (559–530 B.C.), who conquered Babylon in 539 B.C.. Cyrus has been chosen and anointed by the Lord to break Assyria and set his people free (45:1–7).

The prophet reflects on the joy and delight that this deliverance will bring to the patiently waiting people of God (45:8–25). All the gods of the nations will be shown up for what they really are. The gods of Babylon proved to be powerless to prevent the downfall of their city and empire. But the Lord will lead his people home in triumph (46:1–13). The fall of Babylon will be as spectacular as it is certain (47:1–15). Jerusalem's captivity was not the result of any weakness on the part of the Lord; it was due to the stubbornness of Israel, which required that she should be punished and refined (48:1–22).

49:1–7 The Servant of the Lord. We now learn more about the coming "servant of the LORD" (49:1–7). This servant, chosen by the Lord, will carry on the mission of Israel where Israel herself had failed. The servant is clearly a messianic figure with a mission to restore the people of God. He is also to be "a light for the Gentiles," through whom salvation will be brought to the ends of the earth (49:6). This remarkable prophecy was seen by Simeon as having been fulfilled through Jesus Christ (Lk 2:32).

49:8–26 Restoration of Israel. The theme of the restoration of Israel is then explored in some detail as the prophet foresees the great joy that this news will bring to the people of God and the consternation it will cause their enemies. This passage also uses a very powerful and moving image to emphasize the Lord's love for his people. Just as a mother can never forget the infant to whom she gave birth and that suckled at her breasts, so the Lord can never forget his own people, the people he brought into being and loves (49:15–16). This theme is then developed further.

50:1–52:12 The Servant's Obedience; Everlasting Salvation for Zion. The exile in Babylon did not mean that God had abandoned his people, broken his covenant bond with them (a process that is here compared to a divorce), or sold them to anyone. They remain his people (50:1–3), whom he will redeem and lead to their proper home.

We are then told more about the "servant of the Lord" (50:4–9). In this third of the four Servant Songs (as the pieces in question are generally known), we learn that he is to be mocked and despised. This theme will be developed most fully in the fourth Servant Song, which occurs soon after this in the text. In the meantime, the prophet's thoughts turn back to the joy that the return of the exiled community to their homes in Jerusalem will bring and the effect this will have on those who once tormented them (50:10–51:23).

This theme is then intensified as the prophet pictures in his mind the overwhelming pleasure that forthcoming events will bring to Jerusalem (52:1–12). The Lord will be seen in all his strength and power. The watchmen of Jerusalem will hear the bearers of the good news of Jerusalem's release and will shout for joy at what they learn (52:7–10). Perhaps they never expected to hear such joyous news in their lifetimes. Perhaps they never expected the exiled people Jerusalem to return. Yet suddenly the realization will dawn: they are coming home! (This same image is used at Na 1:15, in the prophet's vision of the great rejoicing that will accompany the fall of the city of Nineveh.)

52:13–53:12 The Suffering and Glory of the Servant. We now come to the fourth Servant Song, which is generally regarded as one of the most important pieces of Old Testament prophecy concerning Jesus Christ. It opens by describing the total transformation of the way in which people view this servant. Once he was despised, having a disfigured appearance. Yet now he is seen in a totally new light. Something has happened to change the way he is seen (52:13–15). So what is this all about? Who is this disfigured and despised servant? The full details are then provided (53:1–12). The reader should take this passage very slowly and savor the powerful manner in which this most moving of passages finds its fulfillment in the suffering, death, and resurrection of Jesus Christ.

The servant is someone who possessed no physical beauty. He was despised and rejected by others. He knew what it was like to suffer. Yet he did not suffer for himself; he bore the suffering and pain of others. He was pierced (just as Christ's body was pierced by the nails of the cross) for the sins of others. His wounds brought healing for others. Everyone else had lost their way. Yet the Lord laid upon this servant the iniquity of the human race. The servant suffers for others and bears their iniquities or sins. Although righteous, nevertheless he is "numbered with the transgressors." It is of the utmost importance that Jesus Christ was crucified between two criminals (Lk 22:37; 23:32–33). Could there be any more powerful demonstration that he, in fulfillment of this prophecy, was "numbered with the transgressor"? He bore their sin and ours. The servant even prayed for those who sinned, just as Jesus Christ prayed for those who were crucifying him as he died on the cross (Lk 23:34).

54:1–55:13 The Future Glory of Zion. The prophecy then moves on to dwell once more on the forthcoming wonderful reunion between God and his people (54:1–17) and the reliability of the word of God. Having promised that this would happen, the Lord will bring it all to fulfillment (55:9–11).

This wonderful prophecy of restoration would soon be fulfilled, demonstrating the faithfulness of the Lord to his word and encouraging believers to take God's promises more seriously and trustingly.

ISAIAH 56:1 – 66:24

The Vision of the Restored Community

The prophecy now changes tone slightly. The great prophecies of the coming of restoration come to an end. In their place, we find a series of prophecies that set out a vision for the future of the restored community, describing its role in the future plans of the Lord.

56:1–8 Salvation for Others. This new section opens by describing the return from Babylon in terms which suggest that it is a counterpart to the exodus from Egypt (56:1–8). The set of regulations that are laid down parallel those given to Israel after she had left her bondage in Egypt. Emphasis is placed on the need for Jerusalem to maintain covenant faithfulness with the Lord if she is to benefit fully from his blessings.

It is not only Jerusalem who is to benefit from the Lord. All nations will be blessed by him. The temple at Jerusalem will become a house of prayer for all nations, not just for Judah. And just as the Lord gathered together the exiles of Israel, so he will gather to them other peoples (56:7–8). In other words, Israel has a mission to bring a knowledge of the Lord to the nations, in order that all might find blessing in him. Yet, as we learn from the history of Israel in later years, quite the reverse would actually happen. Israel would become increasingly exclusivist, regarding the Law of God as a charter of national privilege for the Jews, rather than as a manifesto of grace for the world.

56:9–57:21 God's Accusation Against the Wicked; Comfort for the Contrite. The Lord's criticism is now directed against the wickedness of his people, who have deserted him for other lovers. Strongly critical though this passage is, the hope of grace is firmly stated (56:9–57:13). Those who are lowly and sincerely contrite will know the comfort of his grace and forgiveness (57:14–21).

58:1–59:21 True Fasting, Sin, Confession, and Redemption. The importance of true worship, obedience, repentance, and confession on the part of Jerusalem is emphasized. Human sin is a barrier to God's blessing. Yet the Lord will remain faithful to his covenant and will provide both a redeemer for his people and the gift of the Holy Spirit.

60:1–22 The Glory of Zion. Zion (another term for Jerusalem) will be greatly honored and revered throughout the world on account of the greatness of its God. The material prosperity of its people will be matched by the consolation of knowing that the Lord, the God of Israel, will remain with her forever (60:1–22). Israel will draw the nations to herself, so that they may learn of her God. Israel thus has a mission to the nations.

61:1–11 The Year of the Lord's Favor. This theme is developed further in a great passage of prophecy, which proclaims the "year of the LORD's favor." The prophecy speaks of a messianic figure on whom the Spirit of the Lord will rest, who will come to bring liberation and health to his people. The opening verses of this great prophecy were cited by Jesus Christ when he preached in the synagogue at Nazareth (Lk 4:16–21). In his ministry, the great signs and wonders spoken of in this prophecy were brought to fulfillment. The prophecy is especially focused on the restoration and rebuilding of Jerusalem, perhaps with the situations of Ezra or Nehemiah in mind. But the passage has a much wider significance, pointing to the dawning of a new era of consolation and joy for those who hitherto had known only sadness and despair. For the Christian, the references to Jesus Christ are unmistakable.

62:1–63:6 Zion's New Name. The prophecy continues with a great vision of the future greatness of Zion (62:1–12), in which Jerusalem will be acknowledged throughout the world as the place in which the Lord's redeemed dwell. The Lord stresses his total commitment to Jerusalem and her people. Yet that commitment reflects his intentions for both city and people. They are to be a light that will illuminate the nations and draw people to the Lord their God. The Lord affirms that he will deal with the enemies of his people, symbolized by Edom, one of the historic enemies of both Israel and Judah (63:1–6). The Lord will take his revenge against those who oppress his people, and none will be able to resist him.

63:7–64:12 Praise and Prayer. The prophet then turns to a glorious rehearsal of the great deeds of the Lord in history, focusing especially on the way the Lord delivered his people from captivity in Egypt. He alone is the God of history. The people are moved to repentance at the realization of their failure to remain faithful to him (64:6–7). Their hope lies solely in the goodness and mercy of the Lord by which he takes compassion upon his suffering people.

65:1–25 Judgment and Salvation; New Heavens and a New Earth. The prophecy of judgment against those who have forsaken the Lord continues (65:1–12). Yet the promise of restoration of those who remain faithful to him is affirmed once more (65:13–16). A time is coming when the Lord's faithful people will know peace. It will be a time of renewal (65:17–19) in which tranquillity will reign in the land. People can build houses and know that they will live in them. They can plant vineyards, knowing that they will eat their fruit. The wolf and the lamb will lie down together (65:20–25). As Christians know, this great vision of hope and encouragement will find its fulfillment only when the Lord brings history to an end, and his faithful people rest in the new Jerusalem (Rev 21:1–14).

66:1–24 Judgment and Hope. This great prophecy comes to an end with a final vision of restoration and hope. The Lord will execute judgment against those who oppose him and show mercy and compassion to those who trust and obey him. There will come a day when all people will acknowledge the Lord as God—including the nations of the world. In this new era, Gentiles—non-Jews—will be chosen to be priests of the Lord.

So we leave Isaiah, in the full knowledge that many of the great themes, promises, and privileges of the gospel of Jesus Christ have been anticipated by his faithful people during the time of the old covenant. Christians can rejoice that they have had the privilege of seeing many of these great promises and hopes finally come to fulfillment in and through Jesus Christ.

JEREMIAH

The book of the prophet Jeremiah is the second in the series of four Major Prophets. It is not just the longest of these major prophets. It is the longest book in the whole Bible. Jeremiah was called to be a prophet to Jerusalem in the year 626 B.C.. He would continue his ministry during the remainder of the reign of Josiah (who died in battle against the Egyptians in 609 B.C.), and during the reigns of Jehoahaz (609), Jehoiakim (609–598), Jehoiachin (598–597), and Zedekiah (597–586 B.C.). These were turbulent years. The reader wishing to know more about these events in some detail is recommended to read the story of the last days of Judah as presented either in 2 Kings or 2 Chronicles. This will provide an understanding of the historical events that form the backdrop to Jeremiah's prophetic ministry.

The basic sequence of events during the period of Jeremiah's ministry can be summarized as follows. Josiah, who has instigated a series of religious reforms that lead to a purification and refining of Judah's religious life, dies in 609, attempting to oppose an Egyptian advance to aid the ailing Assyrian forces, who are about to fall to the sustained attacks of the Babylonians and their allies the Medes. The capital city of Assyria, Nineveh, falls to their armies in 612. It is just a matter of time before Babylon establishes itself as supreme in the region. The death of Josiah is something of a personal tragedy for Jeremiah, for it is clear that the king has been sympathetic to both the prophet and his message from the Lord. Josiah's successors are consistently hostile toward him and often openly contemptuous of his prophetic message.

On the international stage, the power of Babylon continues to grow. The Egyptians, the only remaining power of importance in the region, are routed by Babylonian armies at Carchemish in 605 B.C.. The Egyptians withdraw to lick their wounds and will play no further role of importance in international politics during the time of Jeremiah. In 605, during the reign of Jehoiakim, the Babylonians lay siege to Jerusalem and subdue it for a while. Following further unrest within the city, the Babylonians attack it again in 598–597 B.C., taking away Jehoiachin, who has succeeded the king of similar name at that time.

The Babylonians install Zedekiah as king, but he rebels against Babylon, possibly believing that a new Egyptian pharaoh may be able to overthrow the Babylonian domination of the region. It is a disastrous miscalculation. The Babylonians attack Jerusalem in 588 B.C. and take full possession of the city two years later. Gedaliah is appointed governor. Jeremiah finds himself within the circle of the governor, which is shattered by his assassination shortly afterwards. Jeremiah seeks refuge in Egypt, where he is believed to have died. According to a Jewish tradition reflected in Hebrews 11:37, he was killed by being stoned while in exile in Egypt.

The general argument of the book of Jeremiah is difficult to follow at points because of the arrangement of the material within the book. The work is not arranged in a strictly chronological order, making it difficult to follow events through from one reign to another. For this reason, considerable care will be taken to ensure that readers appreciate the approximate date and historical context of key passages, so that their full significance can be appreciated. For example, if a purely chronological arrangement were adopted, chapter 26 would come between 7:15 and 7:16, and chapter 45 between 36:8 and 36:9. The book is, in fact, a complex collection of documents, requiring some patience to follow at points. However, the effort involved is unquestionably justified by the results.

JEREMIAH 1:1 – 17

The Call of Jeremiah

The book opens with events that take place in 626 B.C., the thirteenth year of the reign of Josiah, the great reforming king of Judah whose rediscovery of the Book of the Law had led to one of the greatest religious shake-ups in Judah's history (1:1–2). The call of Jeremiah is described in terms of the coming of the word of the Lord (1:2, 4). Jeremiah is told that he has been set apart by God and appointed as a prophet to the nations. Two visions follow in rapid succession as part of the calling itself. First, Jeremiah sees the branch of an almond tree. The Hebrew word for "almond tree" is very similar to that for "watching," and leads to the interpretation of this vision in terms of the Lord's concern for his people (1:11–12).

Second, he sees a boiling pot or cauldron, which is tilted away from the north. The Hebrew word for "boiling" is very similar to that for "will be poured out," leading to this vision being interpreted as a future disaster befalling Judah from the north (1:13–14). Jeremiah is asked to remain faithful to the Lord despite the great opposition he will face (1:17–19). The great loneliness and sense of isolation experienced by Jeremiah during his ministry are here put down to his faithful proclamation of the word of God against people in Judah who do not wish to hear it.

JEREMIAH 2:1 – 6:30 ———————————————

Jeremiah's Earliest Prophecies

2:1–3:5 Israel Forsakes God. The first set of Jeremiah's prophecies dates from the reign of Josiah himself. The basic message is as simple as it is uncomfortable for the inhabitants of Judah. Judah has fallen away from the Lord. As a result, God will punish and refine his people through an invasion by foreigners. The prophecy opens by recalling the close relationship that existed between God and his people in their early period. But something has gone wrong. Jeremiah reproaches his own people for abandoning the Lord without any good cause and asserting their own independence. They have forsaken the Lord and done what pleased them (2:1–30). But what has the Lord done to deserve this? What has he failed to do for his people? Why has Israel forgotten her God? Israel has behaved like a prostitute (2:31–3:5).

3:6–4:4 Unfaithful Israel. A substantial section now deals with the specifics of Judah's faithlessness. Judah has become just like her sister Israel, the northern kingdom that was wiped out by Assyria on account of its apostasy and disobedience. Judah has forgotten the Lord. The imagery of prostitution and adultery is used extensively to highlight the full extent of Judah's faithlessness to her faithful God. The Lord begs her to return to him in repentance, for he will gladly have her back (3:21–4:4).

4:5–6:30 Disaster From the North. If Israel will not repent and return, she will suffer disaster from the north. Even now, a mighty army is on the move, intent on laying waste the land and cities of Judah (4:5–31). Yet Jerusalem is full of wicked and deceitful people who have rejected the Lord. As a result, a distant nation will overwhelm them. Yet even in the face of this threat, Jeremiah knows he will not be heard. People prefer to ignore God rather than to face up to the truth of what is happening (5:1–31).

This section ends with a prophetic vision of Jerusalem under siege from an aggressor from the north, with the Lord urging the besiegers on as they punish his disobedient people (6:1–30). The image of the Lord encouraging those who seek to destroy Judah would have been deeply distressing to his audience, who imagined that they had special privileged status in the sight of the Lord that somehow exempted them from the requirements of faith and obedience to him.

JEREMIAH 7:1 – 35:19 ———————————————

Further Judgment Against Judah

7:1–29 False Religion Worthless. Jeremiah's prophecy continues with a cutting critique of the religious life of Judah. The first set of oracles focuses on the temple, the great center of the religious life of Judah (7:1–10:25). The word of the Lord comes to Jeremiah, telling him to prophesy at the gate of Solomon's temple (7:1–2). The basic theme of his temple oracles can be summarized like this: Jerusalem cannot trust in the temple for its salvation and continued favor in the sight of God. The tabernacle had been established in Shiloh at the time of the conquest of Canaan. Yet the presence of the tabernacle did not prevent Shiloh from being overrun by the Philistines. The house of the Lord has become little more than a den of robbers (7:11)—a theme to which Jesus Christ returns in his ministry in Jerusalem during the final week of his life (Mt 21:13).

7:30–9:26 The Valley of Slaughter; Sin, and Punishment. Jeremiah ruthlessly exposes the deep inroads made by paganism in the religious life of Judah. Pagan idols have been placed in the temple. High places have been reestablished. Even the pagan practice of child sacrifice has been introduced (7:30–34). The Lord will not tolerate this state of affairs and will bring judgment to his rebellious and disobedient people. Yet the people seem unaware of the seriousness of their situation. They pretend that their wounds are not serious, when they are in fact fatal. They talk about peace, when there is no peace to be had at all (8:11).

Jeremiah takes no pleasure in his own prophetic denunciation of his people. He is horrified by the extent of their sin and by the punishment that will be its inevitable and just reward. He is moved to weep over the state of his people (8:21–9:6). A time of refinement and purification must follow in which the dross of paganism and sin will be removed from Judah (9:7–9). The devastation wrought will be terrible. In a series of curt and blunt images, Jeremiah portrays the carnage that will result when Jerusalem is laid waste (9:17–26).

10:1–25 God and Idols. Jerusalem's lapse into idolatry is as senseless as it is pointless. Idols cannot save anyone, nor did they create the world. So why trust them? By abandoning the Lord, Jerusalem has brought judgment upon her head. A storm is brewing in the north that will eventually bring ruin to the towns of Judah and leave them as heaps of ruins, populated only by marauding jackals.

11:1–17 The Covenant Is Broken. The style of writing now alters. Prose may replace poetry, but the message remains the same. Judah has broken her covenant with the Lord and will herself be broken in consequence. This passage stresses the conditionality of the covenant. The Lord will remain faithful to his people. Yet the people must remain faithful to him—something they have conspicuously failed to do in the past (11:1–17). By their lapse into paganism, the people of Judah have provoked the righteous anger of the Lord.

11:18–13:27 Plot Against Jeremiah; His Complaint and God's Answer. At this point, we learn once more of the personal cost to Jeremiah of his ministry of judgment on behalf of the Lord. We learn of an attempt on his life (11:18–23) and of the prophet's bewilderment at the events taking place around him (12:1–4). Yet the Lord reassures Jeremiah that there is no alternative: Judah has sinned grievously, and will suffer disaster as a result (12:5–17). If she continues to behave in this way, she will be uprooted, abandoned and forsaken by the Lord himself. Jeremiah is then given a sign, in the form of a linen belt that was initially new, yet then become rotten (13:1–11). In the same way, the people of God have lost their initial cleanness in the sight of God and become soiled and stained by sin. Once more, Jeremiah proclaims the coming of judgment from the north (13:20), bringing with it devastation and destruction.

14:1–15:21 Drought, Famine, Sword. The prophecy then shifts slightly in its tone and focuses on what was clearly a severe drought in the land (14:1–5:9). Jeremiah sees in this further confirmation of the anger of the Lord against his people. To those false prophets who speak of lasting peace in the land, Jeremiah issues a rebuke on behalf of the Lord: there will be no peace—only destruction, famine, and plague. Escape from this ordained destruction is utterly impossible. Jeremiah is distressed at this thought, as can be seen from the "confession" that follows (15:10–21), in which he admits to his personal pain. However, the Lord assures Jeremiah of his presence and support, as the prophet seeks to remain faithful to his calling and not to speak the soothing and comforting words that the people want to hear.

16:1–17:18 Day of Disaster. The Lord gives Jeremiah a bleak message of judgment, dominated by the theme of disaster. Although moments of comfort may be discerned within this prophecy of doom, its dominant theme is that of forthcoming distress and destruction. Judah will be thrown out of her own land and placed in a foreign land (16:13). If Judah has forsaken the Lord, then the Lord is perfectly free to forsake Judah. Yet even as this somber note of future exile is sounded, a promise of restoration is placed alongside it (16:14–15). Just as the Lord brought his people up out of Egypt, so he will also gather them in from their places of exile and banishment.

17:19–19:15 At the Potter's House. After a brief section reiterating the importance of keeping the Sabbath as a sign of the covenant between the Lord and his people (17:19–27), we come to what is probably the most famous series of incidents in Jeremiah's ministry.

At the bidding of the Lord, Jeremiah visits the house of a potter and watches him at work. The first of the incidents, and the best known, focuses on the way the potter reworks his clay. Dissatisfied with the first attempt at making a pot, he breaks down the clay and refashions it until he is finally content with the outcome. In this action, Jeremiah sees a parable of God's dealings with his people. Just as the potter is at liberty to do what he pleases

God sent Jeremiah to a potter's house. There he noticed that the potter reworked clay that didn't come out right the first time, or even the second or third time. That was God's message: "Like clay in the hand of the potter, so are you in my hand, O house of Israel." These ancient Philistine bowls, bottles, and flasks were found at Ekron.

with his clay, so the Lord is equally at liberty to break and remold the people of Judah (18:1–17).

Meanwhile, Jeremiah faces increased hostility and criticism, which he clearly feels keenly (18:18–23). Yet he remains faithful to his commission to proclaim the word of the Lord. The next episode again centers on a visit to the potter's house, this time to purchase a clay jar. He is ordered to smash the jar in public as a sign of the way the Lord will smash his people for their disobedience. Both Judah and Jerusalem will be broken to pieces on account of the paganism of their peoples (19:1–15).

20:1–18 Jeremiah and Pashhur; Jeremiah's Complaint. This action irritates one of the priests, who arranges for Jeremiah to be beaten and humiliated (20:1–6). Although Jeremiah prophesies exile in Babylon for his assailant, he is unnerved by the experience. In a passage that reveals great self-questioning and uncertainty (20:7–18), Jeremiah speaks of his deep-seated feeling that he has been deceived by the Lord. His prophecies have brought him nothing but ridicule and ruin. Yet he knows that he cannot remain silent. He must speak the word of the Lord, in the knowledge that this is the Lord's will. Yet the whole process has made him so miserable that he wishes he had never been born.

21:1–14 God Rejects Zedekiah's Request. A new section now opens. Much of the previous material has concerned the reign of Josiah. The new material now abruptly moves forward, to deal with events in the reign of Zedekiah, the final king of Judah. Zedekiah has been installed by the Babylonians as their ruler in Jerusalem. Zedekiah, perhaps misreading the military and political climate, feels the time has come to rebel against Babylon. It is to prove a disastrous judgment on his part. The situation envisaged in this passage suggests that it dates from around 588 B.C., when the Babylonians laid siege to Jerusalem in response to Zedekiah's rebellion.

Zedekiah asks Jeremiah for a favorable response from the Lord in response to this situation of emergency. But Jeremiah will have none of this. The Lord will use the Babylonians to punish Jerusalem for its disobedience and rebellion. Resistance will lead only to death. Submission to exile in Babylon will lead to life. Jerusalem will be laid waste.

22:1–23:8 Judgment Against Evil Kings; the Righteous Branch. Jeremiah sees future travelers going past the ruins of the city and talking about the disobedience of its people and the response of their God to these things (22:1–9). Jeremiah's prophecy condemns both present and past kings of Judah for their failures (22:10–30).

A note of hope is sounded in the midst of this unrelenting prophecy of doom. A remnant will remain, and a new king will rise in the line of David, who will redeem his people (23:3–8). This passage only reaches its ultimate fulfillment in Jesus Christ.

23:9–24:10 Two Baskets of Fruit. After a powerful passage denouncing false prophets, who merely say what people want to hear (23:9–40), we come to another prophetic vision. This time, the vision concerns two baskets of figs, one containing good fruit, and the other rotten fruit. Jeremiah interprets the former as a symbol of the people of Jerusalem who have been carried off into exile in Babylon and the latter as Zedekiah and his court, who have remained behind in Jerusalem. The former will one day return to their home city, but the latter have no further place in the purposes of God (24:1–10).

25:1–14 Seventy Years of Captivity. Jerusalem must face seventy years of exile in Babylon, after which the Lord will punish Babylon in its turn and set his people free. Babylon, who has enslaved so many nations, will in turn be enslaved by others. The period of seventy years can be regarded as beginning with the limited deportations of 605 B.C. and ending with the first return of the exiles in 538 B.C..

25:15–26:24 The Cup of Wrath; Jeremiah Threatened With Death. A further vision follows, in which Jeremiah sees the cup of God's wrath. The nations drink of it and stagger. While they are drunk, they will die by the sword (25:15–38). A storm is gathering, which will sweep away the nations—a clear reference to the advances of the Babylonians. Jeremiah once more faces threats as a result of the unremittingly negative nature of his prophecy. These threats come from the highest level, and it is clear that Jeremiah is in serious danger of being killed (26:1–24). The threat is averted, but it is obvious that Jeremiah's words are not finding either favor or attention at the highest levels in Jerusalem. The false prophets (including Hananiah and Shemaiah, whom we shall meet presently), who proclaim that Jerusalem will be spared from Babylon and enjoy a period of peace, have the ear of the king. Perhaps the Lord wants Jerusalem to rebel against Babylon and regain its freedom?

27:1–22 Judah to Serve Nebuchadnezzar. The prophecies that follow make it clear that Jeremiah knows of these false prophecies and the false and unjustified sense of security they bring to the royal court. Jerusalem will be forced to submit to Babylon. There is no alternative. Exile is a God-given punishment for Jerusalem. The people's only hope lies in accepting what God has ordained for them in the knowledge that it will eventually lead to restoration.

28:1–17 The False Prophet Hananiah. The false prophets will have none of this. One of their number is now mentioned specifically by name: Hananiah declares that the Lord will soon break the power of Babylon and restore all the items from the temple which had been taken there by the Babylonians. Jeremiah, who is wearing a yoke as a symbol of the need to submit to Babylon, opposes Hananiah's prophecy, to the latter's intense annoyance. Hananiah breaks Jeremiah's yoke as a protest. Yet Jeremiah clearly wins the argument. Within two months, the false prophet is dead.

29:1–31:40 A Letter to the Exiles. Jeremiah then writes to those in exile in Babylon, urging them to settle down, buy land and houses, and marry. Their exile will be long-term (29:1–23). This flatly contradicts the optimistic utterances of the false prophets, including Shemaiah. Although we are not told the precise nature of his prophesying, we learn that Shemaiah has falsely claimed to be a prophet and sought to discredit Jeremiah (29:24–32). Israel will indeed be restored from exile and the Lord will establish a new covenant with them (30:1–31:40)—but not yet. There must be a time of purification and refinement.

32:1–44 Jeremiah Buys a Field. To demonstrate his God-given conviction that the Lord will indeed restore his people to Jerusalem, Jeremiah purchases a plot of land in his hometown of Anathoth. To the curious and bewildered onlookers, this would have seemed absurd. Why buy a field, when the Babylonians are about to capture Jerusalem? Yet Jeremiah's conviction remains firm: although exile is fast approaching on account of Judah's sin, the people will one day again own land in their own country.

33:1–35:19 Promise of Restoration; a Warning to Zedekiah. Restoration will follow exile (33:1–26). The messianic prophecy of 23:5–6 is repeated to underscore the reliability of what has been said (33:15–16). The covenant will be restored and renewed. This major section ends with further warnings of the seriousness of the situation of Judah and Jerusalem (34:1–35:19). None can escape—not even Zedekiah.

JEREMIAH 36:1 – 38:28 ————————————

The Woes of Jeremiah

36:1–32 Jehoiakim Burns Jeremiah's Scroll. It is clear that Jeremiah's message is deeply unpopular, especially in court circles. This is reflected in the way he is treated, documented in this section of the book. The first incident recorded relates to 605 B.C., the fourth year of Jehoiakim's reign. During this year, Jeremiah openly speaks of Jerusalem going into captivity for a period of seventy years (25:1–14). Jeremiah is ordered by the Lord to write down all his prophecies. He does so, making use of Baruch both as his secretary and his public spokesman. Jeremiah's prophecies are thus written down on a scroll. After reading out Jeremiah's prophecies aloud from a room near the temple, Baruch is invited to read it again to a group of court officials. Terrified by the judgments they hear pronounced, they insist that the king should hear them.

The king, however, is not impressed. As each section of the prophecy is read, he cuts off that section of the scroll and throws the pieces onto a burning brazier. Neither the king nor his inner circle are in the least moved or concerned by Jeremiah's prophecy. In fact, their immediate reaction is to arrest and silence both Jeremiah and Baruch. In the meantime, Jeremiah has to repeat his prophecies so that Baruch can copy them down once more. No copy has been taken. At this dictation session, it seems that Jeremiah adds additional prophecies to those originally delivered (see the "many similar words" at 36:32).

37:1–21 Jeremiah in Prison. This pattern of studied indifference to Jeremiah's prophecies continues under Zedekiah. Initially, Zedekiah allows Jeremiah a considerable degree of freedom (37:1–5), perhaps assuming that, with Egyptian troop movements forcing the Babylonians to withdraw, he has no need to be anxious about the future. However, the Babylonians repel the Egyptian advance and are soon able to resume their siege of Jerusalem. At this point, which is generally dated to 588 B.C., Jeremiah delivers a prophecy of judgment that speaks of the end of Jerusalem (37:6–10). Perhaps unwisely, he then attempts to leave the city during the period of the Babylonian withdrawal and attend to family property matters in the region of Benjamin, where his home town of Anathoth is located. He is accused of deserting to the Babylonians and thrown into prison (37:11–21).

The situation resembles the story of Joseph in many ways, especially in relation to the period spent languishing in prison. Zedekiah eventually summons him from prison and asks him whether there had been any word from the Lord. He expects to hear good news. The word of judgment that follows, speaking of his own capture by the Babylonians, is clearly not what he had expected. However, Zedekiah arranges for Jeremiah to be held under more humane conditions and to receive a supply of fresh bread.

38:1–28 Jeremiah Thrown Into a Cistern. Jeremiah's new style of imprisonment involves being obliged to remain within the courtyard of the guard. Although he is not allowed to leave, he is nevertheless allowed visitors. It is clear that the visitors ask him for his words of prophecy and pass them on to

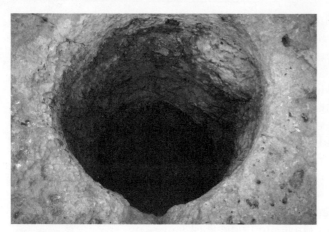

Jeremiah, who kept predicting that Jerusalem would fall and its people would be exiled, was first thrown into prison to keep him quiet, then into a cistern. A cistern is a hollowed out area used to collect water. What you see here is the opening to the cistern. Some cisterns have huge underground areas that can hold a great deal of water.

those outside. Jeremiah urges his hearers to submit to Babylon as the only hope of salvation (38:1–3). Alarmed at the result of these prophecies on the morale of the city, the officials ask for him to be silenced, preferably permanently. Eventually, they settled on a course of action that allows the prophet to live, at least for a while, but not to prophesy. He is thrown into a deep, muddy cistern within the courtyard of the guard (38:4–6).

The king, on hearing of Jeremiah's fate, arranges for him to be released from the cistern. Jeremiah once more informs the king in private that the only course of action open to him is to surrender to the Babylonians. He is then returned to the courtyard of the guard, where he remains until the city finally falls. Zedekiah has ignored his advice (38:7–28).

JEREMIAH 39:1 – 45:5

The Fall of Jerusalem

39:1–40 The Fall of Jerusalem; Jeremiah Freed. The next major section of the book chronicles the final fall of Jerusalem in July 586. It is the most detailed account of the fall of the city to be provided anywhere in the Old Testament and should be read carefully. Zedekiah is killed. The main buildings of the city are set on fire. The people of the city and all those who have already surrendered are carried off to exile in Babylon (39:1–10). Some are left behind in the land and the city, mostly poor people who will cause no problems for the occupying Babylonians.

Jeremiah is held back, however, for different reasons. He has come to the attention of Nebuchadnezzar (39:11–18), for reasons which are not clear. Perhaps he has learned of Jeremiah's advice to surrender to the Babylonians and regards him as an ally. At any rate, Jeremiah is not to be allowed to leave Jerusalem. Instead, he is to live in the house of Gedaliah, who the Babylonians have appointed as governor. Gedaliah is based at the town of Mizpah, north of Jerusalem. The events leading up to this transfer from prison to the governor's house are then related in more detail, from the standpoint of the Babylonian commander Nebuzaradan (40: 1–6).

40:7–43:13 Gedaliah Assassinated and the Flight to Egypt. It might seem that all is now well for Jeremiah. But disaster is about to befall him. Gedaliah is assassinated, along with a small detachment of Babylonian soldiers who are responsible for his safety (40:7–41:15). There are fears of a massive Babylonian reprisal against the Jews remaining in the region. Many want to leave the region immediately and seek safety in Egypt. Jeremiah is asked to pray for guidance. His prophecy speaks of doom for those who abandon their country to flee to safety in Egypt. If they remain where they are, they will not face the wrath of Babylon (41:16–42:22).

This is not what many of the senior military figures want to hear. They accuse Jeremiah of lying and prepare to set out for Egypt. It is clear from what follows that Jeremiah, Baruch, and the remaining Jews in the region are given no choice in this matter. They are forced to leave Judah for Egypt (43:1–7).

So there are now two remnants of Judah: one which has been deported to Babylon, and the other which has fled to Egypt. It is clear that Jeremiah continues to act as a prophet to the exiled Jewish community in Egpyt, predicting the destruction of Egypt itself at the hands of the Babylonians (43:8–13).

44:1–30 Disaster Because of Idolatry. Jeremiah's final recorded prophecy focuses on the new threat of idolatry that arises in Egypt. Jeremiah reports the anger of the Lord against his people. Not only have they abandoned Judah, where they should have remained as a remnant, but they have adopted the pagan religious practices and beliefs of the Egyptians themselves. As a result, they will face disaster (44:1–14).

Jeremiah's Jewish audience is not impressed. They argue that their problems began when they were forced to stop sacrificing to pagan gods by Josiah. Everything was going well while they worshiped the Queen of Heaven (a Babylonian term used to refer to the goddess Ishtar). When Josiah put a stop to that, things went disastrously wrong (44:15–19). Jeremiah is outraged at these suggestions and prophesies the total destruction of the Jewish community in Egypt (44:20–30).

45:1–6 A Message to Baruch. Nothing more is heard of Jeremiah. He is assumed to have died in Egypt. This section of the book then ends with a brief account of Jeremiah's words to Baruch, although he had written down the prophet's words many years earlier.

JEREMIAH 46:1 – 52:34

Oracles Against the Nations

The book of Jeremiah concludes with a series of oracles against the nations (46:1–51:64). The dating of these prophecies is unclear. Although the location of the oracles might suggest that they were delivered during the time that Jeremiah was in Egypt, the general content of the oracles suggests that they date from an earlier period in his career. The general theme of impending disaster at the hands of the Babylonians suggests that they date from around 605 B.C., the date of the battle of Carchemish, at which the Egyptians were totally routed by the Babylonians. They have probably been gathered together in this section of the book on account of the similarities between each of the oracles, which survey a range of nations, beginning with Egypt and ending with Babylon.

By far the greatest attention is paid to Babylon itself (50:1–51:64), but the same themes can be discerned throughout these chapters: destruction is on its way for the nations around Babylon. Babylon is the Lord's instrument of vengeance and judgment against the nations of this region, yet Babylon herself will not escape judgment. She too will fall.

The work ends with a further account of the fall of Jerusalem (52:1–34), which seems to draw upon the same source as 2 Kings 24:18–25:30. However, at several points (such as the account of the fate of Zedekiah [52:10–11]), the account in Jeremiah is more detailed. It is generally thought that this section of the work was compiled by Baruch to provide further historical information concerning the events around the time of the fall of Jerusalem, showing how Jeremiah's prophecies were fulfilled by events. It also means that this book ends on a positive note, with the hope of restoration. Jeremiah and the second wave of exiles may have disappeared into Egypt. But the hope for restoration of the Babylonian exiles is kept alive.

LAMENTATIONS

The book of Lamentations consists of five poems or "laments" over the destruction of Jerusalem by the Babylonians in 586 B.C.. Four of the five poems take a very similar form and are based on the twenty-two letters of the Hebrew alphabet. According to an ancient tradition, they were written by Jeremiah himself. Although this cannot be proved, the book certainly seems to have been written at some point between 586 and 538 B.C.. The fact that the book provides such a graphic portrayal of the destruction of Jerusalem suggests that most of the material is to be dated shortly after the fall of the city in 586 B.C., when the events described would still have been vivid in the memory of those who lived through them.

1:1–22 The First Lament. The first lament focuses on the Lord's rejection of Jerusalem. It conveys a vivid picture of a desolate city. Once a great nation, Judah has been utterly humiliated and trodden under foot. There is nobody present to comfort her at the moment of her downfall. Even the Lord seems to have abandoned his own people to the wrath of the Babylonian invader. This is no accident of history. This is the deliberate and considered infliction of punishment upon a disobedient people by the God who has once loved them. The rebellion of the people is openly acknowledged. God, in his righteousness, has every right to do this. The lament emphasizes the misery that Judah's disobedience has brought in its wake. In this first lament, no note of hope is sounded. The dominant theme is that of merited punishment and the shame and pain it has brought to a once proud people.

2:1–22 The Second Lament. The second lament deals with a related theme. It is a meditation on the Lord's anger against Jerusalem. The destruction of Jerusalem is a result of her justly incurring the anger of the Lord. He has laid waste his own dwelling place. Jerusalem's prophets and priests have failed her. They did not warn her of the seriousness of her sins, or of the future devastation that she would suffer in consequence. (Jeremiah was very much the exception to this rule; most of the "prophets" expected Babylon to fall and leave Judah in peace.) Yet why does the Lord treat his people in this way? The pain and sadness of the situation is impossible to bear.

3:1–66 The Third Lament. The third lament strikes a different and much more positive tone. It deals with the need for personal and corporate repentance and the resulting hope of renewal. This section is substantially longer than the other four laments and takes the form of three groups of twenty-two verses. Within each group, the verses are again arranged according to the order of the Hebrew alphabet. Although this lament is presented as the words of an individual, it is clear that the individual in question (who may well be Jeremiah himself) is speaking on behalf of his people. The lament reflects on the affliction the people have suffered, their need to return to the Lord, and the wonderful compassion of the Lord to those who return to him (note especially 3:21–33).

4:1–22 The Fourth Lament. The fourth lament turns to deal with the sin of the leaders of the people. After reviewing once more the distress of the people, the lament turns to allocate blame for this misery. The fault lies with the prophets and priests (4:13–14), who ought to have known better. Their failure has led to the downfall of the nation. Yet a wider failure on the part of the people themselves is also acknowledged (4:17). However, this lament also ends on a note of hope: although Zion is being punished for her sins, that punishment will come to an end (4:22).

5:1–22 The Fifth and Final Lament. The fifth and final lament takes the form of a prayer for the restoration of the people of God. It builds on the hints of hope found in the previous two laments. While once more pointing to the devastation of Jerusalem, the lament pleads with the Lord for restoration and renewal (5:21). Nevertheless, the compassion of the Lord cannot be taken for granted. The lament ends with an acknowledgment that the just anger of the Lord may lead to his total rejection of his people. Lamentations thus ends on a dark note. However, as history will show, that rejection is not total. The day is not that far ahead when the Lord will again turn the fortunes of Zion and restore his people to their homeland.

EZEKIEL

The book of Ezekiel is the third of the four Major Prophets and centers on the great issues of apostasy, sin, and exile that also dominated both Isaiah and Jeremiah. Ezekiel deals with the period in the history of Judah in which the threat of exile became both real and urgent. Following the Babylonian defeat of the Egyptians at the battle of Carchemish (605 B.C.), the way was clear for the Babylonians to dominate the entire region, which included Judah. This development is the background to some of Jeremiah's major prophecies concerning the threat of exile. That threat would be fulfilled in its totality in 586 B.C., when the besieging Babylonian army would finally conquer Jerusalem and deport its population. However, an earlier deportation took place in 597 B.C., when Jehoiachin and a group of about ten thousand of the population were deported. This group included Ezekiel.

Ezekiel thus prophesies about the state of affairs in Jerusalem from his exile near Babylon. There is no evidence that Ezekiel himself ever left Babylon. The exiles settled in Babylon along the Kebar River (1:1), which was actually an irrigation canal. We learn that Ezekiel had been born into a priestly family and would normally have expected to serve in the temple at Jerusalem. In 593, when he would normally have begun his priestly duties in the temple, Ezekiel is called to be a prophet to the exiles. This prophetic ministry is carried out entirely in Babylon and covers the period 593–573 B.C..

During the first period of his ministry, the temple at Jerusalem is still standing. The bulk of the book relates to this phase. Ezekiel's initial visions center on the idolatrous worship that has been introduced into the temple. His message is simple: Jerusalem will fall for her sins. With the final fall of the city and the destruction of the temple (586 B.C.), a new phase begins in his ministry (33:21–22). A ministry characterized by condemnation and judgment gives way to one of encouragement and reassurance. He gives the exiles oracles concerning the future restoration of his people. There will be a new temple and a new land for the people of God.

EZEKIEL 1:1 – 3:27

The Call of Ezekiel

1:1–28 The Living Creatures and the Glory of the Lord. In his thirtieth year, Ezekiel is called by the Lord to be a prophet while in exile in Babylon (1:1). His age is significant; thirty was the age at which a priest would expect to begin service in the temple. Ezekiel thus begins a service to the Lord of a rather different kind than he would have expected. The deportation that took Ezekiel to Babylon took place in 597 B.C.; his call to be a prophet dates from 593 (1:2). His calling is set in the context of a vision of God (1:4–28) that some skeptics have unconvincingly interpreted as the landing of a spaceship. The vision brings out clearly the glory of God, a major theme for Ezekiel.

2:1–3:15 Ezekiel's Call. The Lord then calls Ezekiel, referring to him as a "son of man"—a term that will be used frequently (some 93 times) in this work. The Lord commands Ezekiel to tell the people exactly what he is told, whether they like it or not (2:7). As a token of his calling, he is given a scroll on which are written words of "lament and mourning and woe." Ezekiel is told to eat this scroll and discovers that it tastes sweet. But the words Ezekiel is commanded to speak to the exiles at this stage are far from sweet. They are words of judgment and condemnation concerning Jerusalem. Overwhelmed by this vision and calling, Ezekiel rests for seven days. Then he is given details of what he is to say.

3:16–27 Warning to Israel. Ezekiel is to be a "watchman for the house of Israel" (3:17). Just as men were posted on the walls of Jerusalem to warn of impending attack or the arrival of messengers, so Ezekiel is to warn of impending judgment for his people through the word of the Lord. If Ezekiel fails to warn his people of this judgment, he will be held responsible for the consequences. If he warns them and they refuse to listen, their subsequent fate is their own responsibility (3:18–21). Ezekiel thus prepares for his prophetic ministry, forewarned that he will be dealing with a "rebellious house," who are unlikely to listen to his words, however much authority they may possess.

EZEKIEL 4:1 – 24:27

The Judgment Against Jerusalem

4:1–5:17 Siege of Jerusalem Symbolized. The oracles of judgment against Jerusalem now begin. A series of dramatic symbolic acts conveys the seriousness of the sin of Jerusalem. First, Ezekiel is asked to draw a clay tablet on which Jerusalem is depicted as being under siege (4:1–3). He is then asked to lie first on his left, and then on his right side (4:4–8). This action symbolizes the sin of the northern kingdom of Israel and the southern king-dom of Judah. It is not quite clear what the numbers 390 and 40 signify. It is possible that 390 refers to the number of years between Solomon's lapse into disobedience and the fall of Jerusalem, and that 40 refers to the num-ber of years for which Manasseh encouraged pagan practices in Judah.

The next image involves Ezekiel imitating the conditions that exist inside a city under siege (4:9–17), in which the population is reduced to eat-ing a diet of grain and vegetables and using dung as fuel. This is followed by the shaving of Ezekiel's head, in which a third of his hair is burnt, a third cut with a sword, and a third scattered in the wind (5:1–4). This action sym-bolizes the fate of the population of Jerusalem. For the benefit of those who see these actions but fail to understand their meaning, a detailed explana-tion is then provided (5.5–17). Jerusalem will be besieged. A third of her population will die of the plague or famine, a third will be killed, and a third will be scattered among the nations.

6:1–7:27 Prophecy Against the Mountains of Israel. Ezekiel turns his atten-tion to the mountains of Israel, where the high places and other sites of pagan worship and practices are located (6:1–14). These will all be destroyed, along with those who worship at them. Only some of the people will be allowed to survive. A disaster is about to happen, and the popula-tion of Judah will be carried off in chains (7:1–27). The detestable pagan practices that are going on in Judah at this moment will be the cause of her downfall and total humiliation.

8:1–9:11 Idolatry in the Temple; Idolaters Killed. Detestable practices are not found merely in the high places of the mountains of Israel. They are even taking place inside the temple at Jerusalem, supposedly the most holy place in Judah (8:1–18). Ezekiel relates how he is caught up by the Spirit and taken to Jerusalem, where he sees the glory of the Lord in the temple. Yet around the temple, all kinds of pagan rites are taking place. The inhab-itants of Jerusalem are even worshipping Tammuz, the Babylonian fertility god (8:14). Ezekiel is appalled. However, he is not alone. It is clear that some in Jerusalem are shocked at what has happened. In his vision, Ezekiel sees these faithful people being marked on the forehead with the letter *taw*—the last letter of the Hebrew alphabet, which looks like a cross (9:4). (This represents a fascinating anticipation of the Christian practice of mark-ing believers with a cross in baptism.) They will be spared from the destruc-tion which follows.

10:1–11:25 The Glory Departs From the Temple, but the Return of Israel Is Promised. Ezekiel then sees the glory of the Lord departing from the temple (10:1–20). In a series of images that recall the opening vision of the prophecy by the Kebar River, Ezekiel sees the glory of the Lord filling the temple. But it does not stay there. Slowly and majestically, it crosses the threshold of the temple. The Lord has left his temple. No longer is it protected through his presence.

As if to confirm the appalling spiritual state of Jerusalem, Ezekiel is then allowed to overhear the leaders of the city talking. They are confident that the threat of Babylonian attack has receded. They can build houses once more. However, the reality is utterly different. Destruction is on its way to the house of Israel (11:1–15). Nonetheless, a note of consolation creeps in at this point (11:16–25). Israel will be scattered amongst the nations, but the Lord will bring the people back home. Their hearts of stone will be replaced by hearts of flesh. The covenant will be renewed once more.

12:1–14:23 The Exile Symbolized; Judgment Inescapable. However, the theme of exile comes to the fore once more. Ezekiel is commanded to perform a symbolic act to bring home the ultimate fate of his people. He is told to pack his belongings and put them over his shoulder. This will be a symbol of the long trudge into exile on the part of his people (12:1–28). Despite all the platitudes and smooth words of the false prophets, there can be no escape from the punishment of exile. These false prophets speak of peace when there is no peace. They have no authority to speak on God's behalf (13:1–16), and idolatry cannot be tolerated. The people of Jerusalem have deserted the Lord for foreign idols. Now the Lord will cut off such people from himself (13:17–14:11). There can be no escape from the forthcoming judgment. There will be survivors, but the resulting devastation will make it undeniably clear that the Lord is in control (14:12–23).

15:1–8 Jerusalem, a Useless Vine. A series of prophecies then focus on Jerusalem itself. Jerusalem is likened to a vine—an image often used to refer to Israel (Ps 80:8–13; see also the related image of Israel as an unproductive vineyard in Isa 5:1–7). Where other prophets, such as Isaiah, at least allowed that Israel brought forth some fruit (even if it was poor in quality), Ezekiel seems to treat Jerusalem as utterly useless. At best, the vine of Jerusalem will make good firewood.

16:1–63 An Allegory of Unfaithful Jerusalem. A further parable follows, which likens Jerusalem to an infant abandoned at birth, without any proper after-birth care or attention. Yet the Lord took compassion on this abandoned child, gave her good food, and tended her throughout her youth. And the Lord's reward for all this? The child he tenderly nourished has become a prostitute (16:1–19). The implication of this prophecy seems to be that Jerusalem's origins lay in paganism. The city was only captured from the Jebusites by David (2Sa 5:6–9). Ezekiel's prophecy seems to suggest that her pagan past is reasserting itself. This is certainly the implication of the description of Jerusalem's infidelity to the Lord with surrounding nations (16:20–34).

The result of this degeneration is then made unambiguously clear: Jerusalem will be stripped naked in front of her lovers, so that they may see her in all her shame. The nations in whom she trusted will see her besieged and destroyed. What Jerusalem has done makes Sodom look respectable (16:35–52). Yet even in this prophecy of judgment, a ray of hope appears. Jerusalem will eventually be restored—but not before these things have happened (16:53–63).

17:1–24 Two Eagles and a Vine. This prophecy is followed by a parable of two eagles and a vine (17:1–24). The two eagles in question are Nebuchadnezzar (17:3) and an Egyptian pharaoh (17:7; the most likely candidate is Hophra). Ezekiel's vision is that of the Babylonians carrying off some of the inhabitants of Jerusalem (the "Lebanon" of 17:3) to Babylon (the "city of traders"). There they flourish. But the remaining inhabitants of Jerusalem become involved with Egypt and will wither. The meaning of the parable is explained in detail (17:11–21). However, the Lord himself will ensure that his people prosper. He will replant them and ensure their security and prosperity (17:22–24).

18:1–19:14 The Soul Who Sins Will Die. A powerful affirmation of individual responsibility and the reality of the Lord's forgiveness follows. Sons will not be punished for the sins of their fathers. And those who truly repent will live. Ezekiel makes it clear that the Lord is pleased when the wicked turn from their ways and live (18:1–32). The Lord takes no pleasure in the death of sinners. He wishes them to repent and to enjoy the privilege of continued life. The implication is clear. Jerusalem has only herself to blame for her present sorry state. There is little point in listing the sins of the past. It is the disobedience of the present that matters. Yet repentance remains a real possibility if only they will realize the extent of their sin and turn away from it. Otherwise, their princes will be uprooted and destroyed (19:1–14).

20:1–49 Rebellious Israel; Judgment and Restoration. The rebellious nature of Israel is again asserted in uncompromising terms (20:1–29). The prophecy in question dates from 591 B.C. and takes a familiar form. Ezekiel traces the history of Israel's rebellion against the Lord from the time of their stay in Egypt to the entry into the Promised Land. It is a continuous catalogue of failure and rebellion on the part of Israel, and pity and compassion on the part of the Lord. But now the time has come for judgment. Yet, once more a note of hope is sounded. There will be restoration after this judgment (20:30–49).

21:1–23:49 Babylon, God's Sword of Judgment. Babylon is now unambiguously identified as the sword by which the Lord will punish his people (21:1–32). Even now, the sword is about to be drawn from its scabbard and used against both the righteous and the wicked in Jerusalem. Ezekiel's vision of destruction suggests that all will perish in the consuming wrath of the Lord. The house of Israel has sinned to such an extent that she has become dross in the sight of the Lord. The precious metal of the people of God will be refined in a fierce heat in order that she may be purified (22:1–31). In the parable that follows (23:1–49), Judah's political alliances with foreign powers are compared in detail with prostitution. Judah and Israel, who seem to be represented by the sisters, have abandoned the Lord in favor of other lovers. Now the price must be paid.

24:1–27 The Cooking Pot. The next prophecy dates from early in 588 B.C.. The news from Jerusalem is grim. The Babylonians have laid siege to Jerusalem. Ezekiel's prophecy makes use of the image of a cooking pot. The pot represents Jerusalem, which was earlier congratulating itself on the very small scale of the deportations of 597 B.C.. All the best pieces of meat were left in the pot. But now the heat has been turned up. The pot will boil dry. The remaining meat will burn. In other words, Jerusalem will be destroyed (24:1–14). This section ends with the death of Ezekiel's wife (24:15–27).

EZEKIEL 25:1 – 32:32

Oracles Against the Nations

The next major section of the prophecy deals with the nations around Judah. This pattern of oracles has already been found in the prophecies of Isaiah and Jeremiah. Judgment on Judah does not in any way mean that her neighbors are exempted. The basic theme set out in the prophetic writings is that judgment begins within the household of faith, but is not restricted to it.

The seven oracles here presented deal with traditional enemies of Judah—the nations of Ammon (25:1–7), Moab (25:8–11), Edom (25:12–14), Philistia (25:15–17), Tyre (26:1–28:19), Sidon (28:20–26), and Egypt (29:1–32:32). The oracles against Tyre and Egypt are substantially more lengthy than the remainder. The basic theme is that the nations shall know that God is the Lord through his mighty acts, including the devastation that will come to them. Babylon is not included in this list of nations. It is, however, referred to as the agent through which the Lord will bring punishment to these proud nations, such as Tyre (26:7–14) and Egypt (30:10–12).

It is important to notice that Ezekiel, in common with the other great prophets, sees the Lord as working out his purposes through pagan nations. Even though they do not acknowledge him as Lord, they are nevertheless instruments of his providence. For Isaiah, Assyria was the rod of God's wrath against his faithless people; yet when Assyria become arrogant, she was punished by Babylon. Once more, a pagan nation served to bring about God's purposes in history. Likewise, when Babylon had exceeded its usefulness to the Lord, it in turn was brought down by Cyrus the Great—again, seen as the instrument of God's justice. Indeed, Isaiah even went so far as to declare that Cyrus was "his anointed" (Isa 45:1), using language normally reserved for the kings and priests of Israel. Jeremiah also sees Babylon as God's chosen instrument for the discipline and purification of his people.

EZEKIEL 33:1 – 39:29

The Promise of Future Comfort and Restoration

33:1–20 Ezekiel a Watchman. The next major section of the book is to be dated from after the fall of Jerusalem. Up to this point, Ezekiel's prophecies have been dominated by the themes of judgment and exile. Now, the themes of hope and restoration begin to gain the ascendancy. Although a number of passages are of a more critical and judgmental nature, there is a distinct change of mood. The section opens with a call for repentance on the part of the people. The Lord takes no pleasure in the death of anyone and would much rather that sinners turn to him in repentance and live. The tone of the prophecy is still critical, however.

33:21–33 Jerusalem's Fall Explained. Up to this point, there has been no confirmation of any of the events Ezekiel has prophesied. Jerusalem was at a great distance from Babylon. It took Ezra some four months to make the journey (Ezr 7:8–9) under what were clearly regarded as good conditions. The only means by which news of the fall of Jerusalem could reach Babylon was by messenger. The two key events are the fall of the city walls and the burning of the temple (2Ki 25:3–4; 8–9), which can be dated to 18 July and 14 August 586. The earliest that any confirmation of these events could be expected to reach the exiles in Babylon would thus have been in December 586. In a prophecy that is to be dated to 8 January 585, nearly five months after the destruction of the temple, Ezekiel receives confirmation that these events have indeed taken place from someone who has managed to escape from Jerusalem (33:21–22). Now that the fall of the city is public knowledge, Ezekiel is free to speak of the hope of restoration.

34:1–31 Shepherds and Sheep. The first major prophecy of restoration soon follows. The Lord declares that the "shepherds of Israel" (a term that clearly includes Israel's kings, priests, and prophets) have failed her utterly. As a result, the Lord's people (who are here compared to sheep) have been scattered. After severely criticizing the shepherds for their lack of responsibility, the Lord declares that he himself will be the shepherd of his people. He will gather them from the places to which they have been scattered and restore them. He will lead them to safe pastures, bind up their wounds, bring back the strays, and strengthen the weak. This great passage echoes themes that will be developed elsewhere (such as Ps 23:1–6), especially in the coming of Jesus Christ as the good shepherd, who will lay down his life for his sheep (Jn 10:11–18).

35:1–36 A Prophecy to the Mountains of Israel. The prophecy then turns to condemn Edom for rejoicing over the fate of Israel (35:1–15). In a great prophecy of restoration addressed to the "mountains of Israel," the Lord promises that he will again restore them to their former state. They will be inhabited again, and their ruins will be rebuilt (36:1–12). The Lord will bring his people home from the places to which they have been scattered. National restoration will be accompanied by personal renewal, as hearts of stone are replaced by hearts of flesh (36:13–38).

37:1–14 The Valley of Dry Bones. The great theme of the restoration of the people then reaches a climax with the most famous passage in Ezekiel: the vision of the dry bones. The prophet receives a vision of a valley full of dry bones. It is clear that they are totally dead and seem to be beyond any hope of coming back to life, in much the same way as the people of God seem to be beyond any hope of resuscitation. Yet the Lord has other ideas. In a remarkable act, which has direct parallels with the account of the creation of Adam (Ge 2:7), the Lord assembles the bones into bodies and breathes life into them. In the same way, the Lord will breathe new life into his people and restore them. The situation may seem hopeless; nevertheless, the same Lord who can restore life to dry bones will also restore his people.

Although the primary focus of this prophecy is the rescue of Jerusalem from Babylon and its restoration to its homeland, it is impossible to read the later parts of this passage (37:12–14) without anticipating the great gospel hope of resurrection to eternal life.

37:14–39:29 One Nation Under One King. The vision is then supplemented with a prophecy concerning a future king who, like David, will rule over his people. Under his rule, Jerusalem will again know all the benefits of the covenant of the Lord, including the presence of the Lord among his people (37:15–28). This section concludes with a detailed prophecy against Gog (38:1–39:29). It is not clear who this figure is. What *is* clear, however, is the firm commitment on the part of the Lord to bring his people back from captivity and to pour out his Spirit upon them (39:25–29).

EZEKIEL 40:1 – 48:35 ───────────────

The New Temple and the New Land

40:1–42:20 The New Temple. The final part of this great prophecy now opens. Dating from 573 B.C., the prophecy centers on visions of the restored temple and people. The first vision concerns the temple. Ezekiel's vision of the temple suggests a building comparable to Solomon's great architectural achievement, but with an expanded courtyard area. It is clear that Ezekiel's vision points to the restoration of a temple at least as impressive as Solomon's, but devoid of all the pagan influences that had crept into the temple area and worship under successive kings of Judah.

43:1–48:35 The Glory Returns to the Temple. The climax of this vision is now reached. Earlier, Ezekiel had suffered the pain of seeing the glory of the Lord leaving the temple, as a sign of the Lord's forsaking his rebellious people (10:1–22). He had spoken of the restoration of that presence (e.g., 37:27). Now, in his vision, Ezekiel sees that presence being restored. The glory of the Lord returns to the new temple (43:1–5). The Lord will again dwell among his people. The vision of the restored temple now continues (43:6–48:35), embracing every aspect of the life of the nation—its princes, priests, and boundaries. But it is clear that the central theme is that the Lord once more will dwell among his people. And that is why, the prophet concludes, the city of Jerusalem shall henceforth be called by a different name: THE LORD IS THERE (48:35).

DANIEL

The book of Daniel is the fourth and final part of the Major Prophets. It deals with events that take place while Jerusalem is in exile in Babylonia. Under successive Babylonian kings, a series of deportations takes place from Judah. The most significant is in 586 B.C., when Jerusalem is laid waste after the final fall of the city. However, there have also been earlier deportations, including that of 597, when Jehoiachin and about ten thousand people (including the prophet Ezekiel) were deported. Although this would seem to be the most natural date for the deportation of Daniel and his colleagues, the book of Daniel itself suggests that there were limited deportations in the aftermath of the battle of Carchemish in 605 B.C.. The Babylonians, having heavily defeated the Egyptians, turned their attention to subduing what they termed "Hatti-land," which included Judah. This policy of subjugation may have included deportation.

The book of Daniel emphasizes the importance of remaining faithful to God, even under difficult circumstances, and illustrates this from the story of Daniel and his three companions in Babylon. The later part of the book consists of visions of coming judgment and retribution, which often include symbols of peoples and nations. This style of writing, which is usually referred to as *apocalyptic*, emphasizes God's sovereign control over history and his ultimate victory over forces that may seem to have gained the upper hand for the time being.

The final chapters of the book have been the subject of considerable speculation, with many writers finding in them precise prophecies of modern events, such as the rise of Nazi Germany or the Soviet Union. It is, however, best to see these visions as relating to the rise and fall of empires in the ancient world, rather than attempting to use them to predict the future. The primary purpose of these visions is to reassure those who received them initially.

DANIEL 1:1 – 6:28

The Story of Daniel

1:1–21 Daniel's Training in Babylon. We are introduced to Daniel and his three companions, who have been deported to Babylon during recent Baby-

lonian attacks on the region by Nebuchadnezzar. There are obvious similarities between the stories of Joseph and Daniel. Both concern Jews who
find themselves carried off to foreign countries and eventually manage to
work their way into important positions within the royal administration of
these countries. Despite their refusal to compromise their obedience to the
God of Israel by eating the royal food and wine (which could well have been
offered to idols), Daniel and his friends are valued on account of their wisdom and are consulted regularly by the king.

2:1–49 Nebuchadnezzar's Dream. Like Pharaoh before him, Nebuchadnezzar has a dream that neither he nor his pagan astrologers can make sense
of. And, just as Pharaoh consulted Joseph, so the king eventually consults
Daniel (2:1–26). Daniel's interpretation of the dream is prophetic: the great
power and authority of Nebuchadnezzar will eventually give way to a series
of lesser realms. In the end, God himself will establish a kingdom that will
not be destroyed (2:27–45). This interpretation of the dream pleases the
king, and he rewards Daniel for his efforts (2:46–49).

3:1–30 The Image of Gold and the Fiery Furnace. Yet the favor found by
Daniel in the sight of the king seems to have been relatively short-lived.
The king orders an enormous image of himself to be made and set up near
Babylon. He requires all his officials to bow down and worship the image
as a sign of obedience to the king himself (3:1–7). All do—except Daniel
and his companions, who remain faithful to the command not to worship
any image (Ex 20:3–5). This failure to comply with the king's instructions
is reported by the astrologers, who are presumably piqued at Daniel's success at interpreting the dream that had baffled them. As a result, Daniel's
companions (here referred to by their Babylonian names, Shadrach,
Meshach, and Abednego) are summoned before the king and ordered to
comply. (Daniel himself is not mentioned in this narrative.) On their
refusal, they are condemned to death and thrown into a furnace. Their
deliverance from its heat moves the king to acknowledge the greatness of
their God (3:8–30).

4:1–5:30 Nebuchadnezzar's Dream of a Tree and the Writing on the Wall.
Daniel now shows himself once more to be a divinely inspired interpreter of
dreams (4:1–37). The dream relates to the downfall of Nebuchadnezzar and
his insanity. A further instance of Daniel's God-given ability to interpret
things that baffle everyone else then follows.

The event in question is a banquet, thrown by Belshazzar, Nebuchadnezzar's successor as king (5:1–30), which is disrupted by the appearance of a hand
writing on the wall. Deeply shocked, the king invites the astrologers and magi-
cians to interpret the words the hand has written. They fail. Daniel is then
summoned, and he interprets the words as referring to God's judgment on the

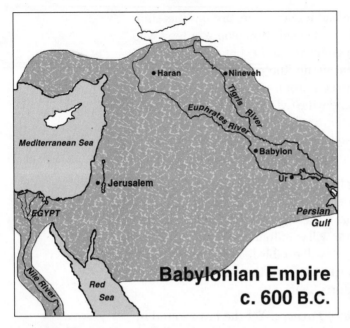

Babylonian Empire c. 600 B.C.

Haran • Nineveh •
Euphrates River
Tigris River
Mediterranean Sea
• Babylon
Ur •
• Jerusalem
EGYPT
Persian Gulf
Red Sea
Nile River

The Babylonians conquered many lands; Daniel and three of his friends were among their hostages. Daniel could interpret dreams and so came to the notice of the king. He and his friends also received special protection from God. Daniel was thrown into a pit of lions, yet was not harmed. His friends also were unhurt despite being put in a fiery furnace. Daniel stayed in Babylonia, serving three kings and witnessed the conquest of Babylonia by the Persians.

king. The words are *mene, mene, tekel,* and *parsen,* ambiguous terms that Daniel interprets as referring to the overthrow of Belshazzar by the Medes and Persians. The subsequent assassination of the king and the rise of "Darius the Mede" (possibly the name by which Cyrus the Great was known in Babylon) demonstrates once more the extent of Daniel's wisdom.

6:1–28 Daniel in the Den of Lions. Under Darius, Daniel continues to prosper, being appointed as one of a triumvirate who is to administer his extensive realms. So successful is Daniel that it seems likely that he will become the king's favorite. However, professional jealousy puts an end to all this. His rivals attempt to end his promotion prospects (not to mention his life). The only grounds for accusation lie in his worship of God. In all other respects he is blameless (6:1–5). There is an important point here, also echoed in 1 Peter: believers must ensure that the only charges that the world can lay against them relate to their faith in God and not to their moral conduct.

Without alerting the king to their vendetta against Daniel, his rivals gain the king's approval for a new law that will lay down that no one may worship any god other than Darius himself. Daniel duly disregards this order and prays to God. (Notice, however, that he does so in private, so as not to draw public attention to his actions and render himself guilty of some kind of public posturing.) However, knowing that he will pray to God in this way, his enemies burst in on him, discover him at prayer, and demand that the king throw him into the lion's den. The king is clearly reluctant to do so and demonstrates his affection for Daniel, but it must be done (6:6–18). However, to the evident relief of the king, Daniel is delivered from certain death by God. Moreover, there is an evangelistic dimension to this action: Darius, deeply impressed with the power and faithfulness of the God of Daniel, orders that this God should now be worshiped in his realm (6:19–28).

DANIEL 7:1 – 12:13

The Visions of the End

The style of the book now changes. A series of visions received by Daniel is set out at some length. In reflecting on these images, we must be careful not to misinterpret them or to apply them without thought to other periods in history, such as our own. The prophecies here recorded were given to Daniel with his own situation in mind. They cannot be treated as a detailed prediction of every major event of world history up until the present day. Rather, they are to be seen as allowing Daniel a vision of the future of the empire that has taken him captive, so that he may face the present in the knowledge of what God has prepared for him and his people.

7:1–28 Daniel's Dream of Four Beasts. The first major vision is of four beasts: a lion, a bear, a leopard, and an unidentified beast that is clearly terrifying in its appearance. Each of the beasts represents an empire: the lion corresponds to the Babylonian empire, the bear to the Medo-Persian empire, the leopard to the empire established by Alexander the Great, and the fourth beast appears to symbolize the Roman empire. The basic point being made is that Babylon will give way to other empires, which will eventually all be succeeded by the reign of God himself, who will give victory to his people.

This vision is of particular importance to Christian readers for two reasons. First, the vision speaks of "one like a son of man" (7:13–14), who comes on the clouds and is given authority by God (here referred to as the "Ancient of Days") to rule over the nations, who worship him. Jesus Christ understood this to refer to himself, especially his coming in triumph to judge the world at the end of time (see Mt 24:27–31; Mk 14:62; Rev 1:17). Second, the reference to the fourth beast appears to be a reference to the Roman empire—the empire that persecuted the followers of Jesus Christ. The Christian reader of this prophecy can see the fulfillment of this prophecy of a reign of terror, but also has the assurance that such terror will not triumph over the people of God.

8:1–27 Daniel's Vision of a Ram and a Goat. The second vision features a ram and a goat. The ram represents the Medo-Persian kings; and the goat, the king of the empire established by Alexander the Great (here referred to as the "king of Greece"). The latter will overwhelm and displace the former. A later part of the prophecy (8:23–25) refers to the coming of Antiochus IV, one of the most vicious persecutors of the Jews.

9:1–11:1 Daniel's Prayer. The impact of these visions is clearly considerable, especially when the news of the fall of Jerusalem comes through. In response, Daniel prays one of the most thoughtful and helpful prayers of the Old Testament (9:1–27). The prayer is an affirmation of the compassion, greatness, love, and faithfulness of God, even in the face of the sin and rebellion of his people. The prayer appeals to God in his righteousness and mercy to deliver his people from their predicament. Daniel makes it clear that the grounds of this prayer lie, not in any appeal to human righteousness, but to the great mercy of God himself (9:18). In response, Daniel receives an assurance concerning the future of Jerusalem and the coming of the "Anointed One" (9:25). This sense of hope is confirmed by a vision (10:1–11:1), in which he feels himself to be strengthened and encouraged by God.

11:2–12:13 The Kings of the South and the North; the End Times. Finally, Daniel receives another vision, focusing on later kings who will reign during the period of Greek rule in the region (11:2–12:13). Of particular importance is the reference to the "abomination that causes desolation" (11:31). This is widely regarded as a prophecy of destruction within the Jerusalem temple or acts of desecration against it, such as those that took place under Antiochus IV in 169 B.C.. This is followed by prophecies concerning an unknown king (11:36–45) and a final assurance that whatever may happen in the future, the Lord will remain faithful to his people (12:1–13).

Daniel himself can rest assured that even though he is in exile in Babylon, he will one day receive his "allotted inheritance" (12:13). This passage is particularly important on account of its clear references to a resurrection to life. In his closing words, the prophet looks ahead to the secure knowledge of resurrection and eternal life, one of the greatest joys of the Christian gospel.

HOSEA

A new section of the Old Testament now opens, usually referred to as the Minor Prophets. This term does not in any way imply that their prophecies are of lesser value than those of the Major Prophets, such as Isaiah. It simply refers to the fact that the twelve books that now follow are shorter than works such as Isaiah or Jeremiah.

Hosea, the first of these writings, dates from the middle of the eighth century B.C.. It is clear that Hosea, like Amos, comes from the northern kingdom of Israel and prophesies to it during its final days before it is destroyed by the Assyrians and its peoples are taken off into exile. Despite this, however, the book itself appears to have been written in the southern kingdom of Judah, suggesting that Hosea may have fled to the safety of this region after the fall of Israel.

HOSEA 1:1 – 3.5

The Faithlessness of Israel

1:1–11 Hosea's Wife and Children. The book opens by describing Hosea's family life. In response to the Lord's prompting, Hosea marries Gomer, a woman who is already guilty of adultery. After bearing Hosea a son, she subsequently has two further children. The wording of the passages referring to these two later children is significant (1:6, 8); they are not attributed to Hosea. It seems that they are the children of another man. In this story of past and present unfaithfulness, we are to see a symbol of Israel's unfaithfulness to the Lord. Each of the children is given a name that symbolizes the problems that have arisen between the Lord and his people. In particular, *Lo-Ruhamah* (which literally means "not loved") points to the utter exasperation of the Lord at the rebelliousness of his own people, which leads to his decision to reject them—a decision that can be seen summarized in the name of the third child, *Lo-Ammi* (which literally means "not my people").

The covenant formula is thus reversed. Where the Lord once declared that he was Israel's God and they were his people, we now find a terse statement to the effect that "you are not my people, and I am not your God"

(1:8). However, this is immediately followed by a promise of future restoration (1:9–11). This follows a pattern, which is evident in the writings of the Major Prophets, of tempering anger with compassion. Even though Israel is being judged for her unfaithfulness, she is being promised that restoration lies on the far side of that judgment.

2:1–23 Israel Punished and Restored. Hosea is totally dominated by the theme of the unfaithfulness of the northern kingdom of Israel to her Lord. This is clear from the song that follows, which speaks of Israel's abandonment of the God who loves her in order to chase after other gods—a clear reference to Israel's frequent lapses into paganism, which are such a conspicuous feature of her national life at this stage. Canaanite religious practices and beliefs have crept into every aspect of national life and have compromised her special relationship with the Lord. Yet the Lord speaks of his intention to woo Israel once more. He will court her in an attempt to bring back the days of their first love in Egypt (2:14–19).

3:1–5 Hosea's Reconciliation With His Wife. Hosea's final reconciliation with his wife is thus to be seen as more than the happy resolution of a domestic situation. It is a symbol of the reconciliation the Lord desires to have with his faithless people Israel. Indeed, it is more than that. It is also a statement of hope that what once seemed an impossible outcome in the context of a personal relationship might also be possible between the Lord and his people.

HOSEA 4:1 – 10:15

Israel's Disobedience and Punishment

4:1–5:15 The Charge Against Israel. The prophecy of Hosea is dominated by the accusation that Israel has flouted her covenant relationship with the Lord. Gomer's adultery is to be seen as a symbol of the state of Israel's relationship with the Lord. She has abandoned him for other short-term relationships, in which instant gratification has overshadowed all other considerations. What follows documents in some detail Israel's religious adultery and faithlessness. They have deserted the Lord for idols and pagan altars (4:1–19). Their priests have failed to stop this lapse into paganism. Their leaders have even turned to Assyria for help, when they ought to have trusted in the Lord (5:1–15).

6:1–7:16 Israel Unrepentant. One of the most beautiful passages in Hosea's prophecy then follows. It speaks of the Lord's love for his people and his passionate desire to bind their wounds and restore them. It is the Lord who has wounded his people. It is he who will restore them. The coming of the Lord is compared to the arrival of the rains that water the earth and give it nourishment. In this passage, the prophet envisages his people turning in repentance to the Lord (6:1–3). However, this is only a dream. We are immediately returned to the harsh reality, in which Israel stubbornly refuses to do anything of the sort (6:4–7:16). Judgment must therefore follow.

It is interesting to notice the asides to Judah in this prophecy. Although the prophecy is directed against the northern kingdom of Israel, every now and then reference is made to Judah—usually along the lines "and this applies to you as well, Judah." An example of this is seen at 6:11; others can be found at 4:15; 5:5, 10; and 11:12. In no way is Judah being allowed to gloat over either the misfortune or the sins of her northern neighbor. She is just as vulnerable.

8:1–10:15 Israel to Reap the Whirlwind. Israel's violation of the covenant with the Lord is then detailed. Israel has lapsed into idolatry, chosen kings whom the Lord did not want, and forgotten the God who has so clearly not forgotten her (8:1–14). A day of reckoning is at hand (9:1–9). Even so, the Lord returns to tender memories of Israel in her youth, when she first came out of Egypt (9:10). She was young and innocent in those days. Then she entered Canaan and lapsed (9:11–17). As Israel increased in prosperity, she came to rely more and more on that prosperity and on her material resources, and less and less on the Lord. The people turned to worship tangible gods, such as idols (10:1–15).

HOSEA 11:1 – 14:9

The Promise of Restoration

11:1–11 God's Love for Israel. This alienation makes the memory of the first period of the love between the Lord and his people, as they left Egypt together, all the more difficult to bear. In those days, the Lord and his people were close (11:1). Like a growing child, however, Israel grew away from the Lord and forgot the Lord's kindness during its youth (11:2–4). Why has Israel forsaken the Lord for such things? Justice demands that Israel be punished. Yet the Lord, in his compassion, is reluctant to do so. How can he turn against his own people? The Lord thus looks forward to the restoration that lies beyond the punishment that must inevitably come to his disobedient people (11:5–11).

11:12–14:9 Repentance to Bring Blessing. Israel's sin is then affirmed once more (11:12–12:14), with further illustrations of its nature and extent. Israel has gained in wealth, not always through honest means; and the people have used their wealth to pay tribute to foreign powers. What about the Lord? Why do they not pay tribute to him? Israel has become crippled through its worship of foreign gods and its submission to foreign powers. The people of Israel demanded a king of the Lord; and when the Lord granted them that request, they ended up by trusting in kings rather than in him (13:1–16).

Yet this catalogue of sin and proclamation of judgment is not the last word of the Lord to his people. In a tender vision, the prophet can still see his people declaring their intention to return to the Lord, having admitted that they need him badly. In his compassion, the Lord will heal their wounds and restore them to fellowship with him (14:1–9).

JOEL

Little is known about Joel apart from the name of his father. The prophecy contained in this book is difficult to date because there are no clear references to any historical events that would allow even a provisional date to be assigned to this work. Some have suggested that the work may date from as early as the ninth century. Others point to a later date, suggesting that the work may have been written after the return from exile.

1:1–2:11 An Invasion of Locusts. The central theme of the work is the coming of the "Day of the LORD." The occasion of the opening prophecies can be found in a disaster that had taken place. A rural economy, which was heavily dependent on crops for both human and animal feed, would be devastated through a plague of locusts. Joel describes the havoc and misery caused by the locusts in some detail and interprets this as a sign of a coming judgment in which the Lord will devastate his people (1:1–20). A day of darkness is at hand in which destruction will come to Zion (2:1–11). Although the reference is primarily to the coming of a vast cloud of locusts, it is clear that Joel sees in this catastrophe a sign of the Lord's judgment.

Joel describes an invasion of locusts and the devastation that they cause. But his real message is telling people to repent, for the day of the Lord is coming, a day of salvation for all those who call on the Lord.

2:12–27 The Lord's Answer. This disaster is intended to move a complacent people to repentance. This repentance must be heartfelt and thorough. The Lord does not want outward signs of repentance (such as the tearing of clothes). What is being demanded is inner transformation: "Rend your heart and not your garments" (2:13). Even at this late stage, with the threat of judgment and destruction there for all to see, it is not too late to repent. This section is followed by a prophecy of restoration, which is clearly related to the demand for repentance. The land may have been devastated, but it will be restored. The

ground will once more produce grain, wine, and oil. The army of locusts will die and rot (2:18–20). Soon the misery and shame of the years of the locusts will be forgotten.

2:28–32 The Day of the Lord. This promise of restoration is then supplemented with a still greater hope: the Spirit of the Lord will be poured out on all people—male and female, old and young. This will be a day of salvation, on which everyone who calls upon the name of the Lord will be saved. This prophecy of Joel provides one of the most important pointers to the great work of God that lay ahead as a result of the coming of Jesus Christ. This great prophecy would be fulfilled at Pentecost, when the Holy Spirit came with great power and inaugurated the public ministry and preaching of the Christian church (Ac 2:16–21). On account of the resurrection, Jesus Christ has been publicly declared to be Lord. As a result, anyone who calls upon his name will be saved.

3:1–21 Blessings for God's People. The final chapter of the book looks ahead to the restoration of both Judah and Jerusalem in which all nations will be brought to judgment (3:1–3). The sins of the enemies of Israel are listed, including selling children into prostitution and Jews to the Greeks. With the restoration of Israel, the achievements of her enemies have been undone. The enemies of Israel will be routed and destroyed by the Lord in his judgment (3:4–16). So the prophet turns to contemplate the future in which a restored Jerusalem, delivered from the fear of all her enemies, reigns supreme (3:17–21). Her material prosperity contrasts with the sterility and poverty of her enemies. The nations will be punished for their guilt; Jerusalem, however, will be pardoned. The Lord will dwell in Jerusalem, ensuring its safety and well-being.

This prophecy might seem to be little more than a nationalist aspiration in which a Jewish prophet looks ahead to the domination of the world by Jerusalem; however, this is clearly not so. The gift of the Spirit is clearly intended to be made to all nations—a prophecy that was fulfilled in the coming of the Spirit at Pentecost. Although the Spirit did indeed descend upon people at Jerusalem, it was given to people of all nations and not simply to Jews. Reading this prophecy from the standpoint of the New Testament, we may see it as a glorious anticipation of the coming of the Holy Spirit upon the entire people of God—that is, those for whom Jesus Christ died and who respond to his saving death in repentance and faith. Far from being a nationalist manifesto, the book of Joel looks ahead to the universal gifting of all believers.

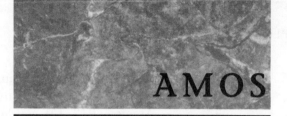

AMOS

Although born in the southern kingdom of Judah, Amos appears to have ministered primarily to the northern kingdom of Israel during the reigns of Uzziah, king of Judah (792–740 B.C.), and Jeroboam II, king of Israel (793–753). Although little is known about Amos for certain, we know that he was from the region of Tekoa in Judah and is referred to as both a shepherd (1:1; 7:14–15; note, however, that the Hebrew term may mean "a sheep breeder") and someone who takes care of sycamore-fig trees (7:14). He was probably a wealthy farmer who left his home in Judah to prophesy to the northern kingdom of Israel. The main part of his ministry was most likely carried out over a two-year period at some point during the years 767–753, centering on the shrine at Bethel. There is not enough archaeological information available to allow the date of the earthquake mentioned in the opening verse to be established with any degree of certainty.

The prophecy takes the form of judgment against both the nations and Israel for their sins. Israel is declared to be no better than the surrounding nations. In fact, she bears an even greater responsibility for her sins on account of being God's chosen people. It is clear from several references in the prophecy that this was a time of national prosperity. There were few indications of the disaster that Israel would suffer at the hands of Assyria in 722–721, which would lead to the fall of the northern kingdom. The prophecy particularly complains about the lack of social justice in Israel and her failure to remain faithful to the covenant. Although the dominant theme of Amos's prophecy is that of condemnation and judgment, the book ends with an assurance of restoration for a remnant of the people.

AMOS 1:1 – 2:16

Oracles Against the Nations

1:1–2:5 Judgment on Israel's Neighbors. The prophecy opens with a series of declarations against Israel's neighbors. To appreciate the impact this series of oracles would have made on his audience, the reader should appreciate that

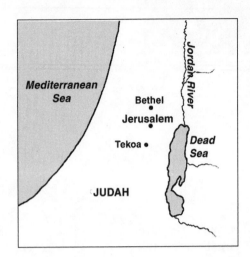

The prophet Amos, who warned of devastation and destruction because of sin, also saw Israel restored, rebuilt, never to be uprooted again. He was from the region of Tekoa in Judah.

the condemnation of Damascus (1:3–5), the Philistine city of Gaza (1:6–8), Tyre (1:9–10), Edom (1:11–12), Ammon (1:13–15), and Moab (2:1–3) would have met with widespread approval on the part of Amos's audience. These were the historic enemies of the people of God, who had made life difficult for them during the period of the united kingdom and afterwards. The fact that they were being condemned for their arrogance would be widely applauded by those within Israel who heard them.

Yet a distinct feeling of unease would have resulted from the next oracle, which pronounces judgment against Judah (2:4–5). In this oracle, we find the southern kingdom being condemned in almost exactly the same way as Tyre and Moab, yet Judah was part of the people of God. And the city of Jerusalem, which is here declared to be marked for destruction (2:5), was the site of the temple, the house of God. This sense of unease would have been replaced by a sense of despair or outrage as the prophet turned his attention to Israel itself.

2:6–16 Judgment on Israel. The judgment against Israel is longer and more detailed than the condemnation against the other nations. Amos declares that there has been a breakdown of social justice within Israel with a series of lamentable sins given as illustrations. Israel has become just as bad as her pagan neighbors. The consequences of this failure to keep the law of the Lord will be severe: Israel is to be crushed, and not even her finest soldiers or weapons of war will save her.

AMOS 3:1 – 6:14

The Condemnation of Israel

3:1–15 Witnesses Summoned Against Israel. The charges made against Israel are now pursued with vigor. First, Israel's privileged position is emphasized. What other nation did the Lord bring out of Egypt? What other people did he choose as his own (3:1–2)? Although both Judah and Israel are included in this understanding of the privileges of being the people of God, it is clear that Amos's message is directed specifically against Israel. Being the people of God has its obligations—and Israel has failed to honor them. The Lord summons all the nations around to hear his judgment against Israel. The particular sins singled out for mention here are the reversion to pagan practices associated with the shrine of Bethel under Jeroboam I (1Ki 12:26–33) and the excessive wealth of Israel's merchants, which led to the building of extravagant mansions (3:13–15).

4:1–5:17 A Lament and Call to Repentance. The basic theme of Amos's message then develops further, with mention of the sins that have arisen within Israel and that give rise to the Lord's judgment against his people (4:1–12). Israel may have kept many of the covenant requirements but boasted about doing so. To humble his people, the Lord sent famine and drought upon them, but to no apparent avail. Once more, the Lord urges his people to return to him, to repent, and to live (5:1–17). The message "seek the LORD and live" recurs throughout this passage. Israel has turned away from him. The time has come to turn back, before the Lord adopts more drastic ways of forcing his people to return to him.

5:18–6:14 The Day of the Lord. The prophet now turns to the theme of the "Day of the LORD." This phrase is used extensively in the prophetic writings of the Old Testament to refer to the great day of victory in which the Lord will triumph over his enemies and establish his rule over the nations. It is clear that many in Israel were looking forward to that day, seeing it as a clear sign of hope. The Day of the Lord would be good news for Israel. Not so, declares Amos (5:18–27). The Lord will judge Israel just as he will judge everyone else. That day will be "darkness, not light." Why does Israel long for this day? Does she not realize what it will bring to her?

Amos exposes the complacency and smugness of Israel, who seems to think that her great religious festivals and sacrificial offerings are enough to ensure her continued good standing in the sight of God. However, the favor of God depends upon social justice and righteousness in his eyes, not mechanical observance of cultic rituals. If the Day of the Lord brings anything to Israel, it will be exile in a land beyond Damascus. The complacency (6:1–7) and pride (6:8–14) of Israel are further explored, giving added weight to the severity of this judgment.

AMOS 7:1 – 9:10

Visions of Judgment

7:1–17 Locusts, Fire, and a Plumb Line. The next section of the prophecy centers on a series of visions in which Amos is shown what the future holds for Israel. The first set of visions begins with a swarm of locusts, which the Lord has prepared as a judgment on his people (7:1–3). In response to Amos's plea for mercy, this judgment is withheld. The same thing happens concerning another judgment, this time by fire (7:4–6).

This is followed by a vision of a plumb line (7:7–9), which shows how far out of line Israel has become. Israel was called into being by the Lord, true to what he intended for her. But now the plumb line shows up the extent to which she has departed from her intentions. This message of judgment is not well received by Amaziah, the priest in charge of the sanctuary at Bethel. It is clear that Amaziah feels that his professional status is undermined by the words of this amateur (the word *seer* seems to be used contemptuously). Amos replies that he is not a professional prophet; he is just someone the Lord has called to speak to the people of Israel, and that message is about forthcoming exile. Amaziah may want him to be quiet. The Lord, however, wants him to speak out (7:10–17).

8:1–9:10 A Basket of Ripe Fruit. This program of declaring what the Lord has made known to Amos continues with the vision of the basket of ripe fruit (probably figs). The ripe fruit points to the time being ripe for the judgment of Israel (8:1–14), whose sins are again identified and commented on.

The nature of the judgment involved is clarified through a further vision (9:1–10), in which Amos sees the Lord ready to begin judging his people from the altar of his temple. Israel expected the altar to be a place of security; instead, it turns out to be the starting point for the Lord's punishment of his people. His rebellious people will be ruthlessly hunted down, wherever they may seek to escape from the coming judgment. Israel cannot depend upon her special status in the sight of God to save her from this judgment. Israel might feel that she is safe on account of the Lord having brought her out of Egypt. However, the Lord was responsible for other major migrations of people in history (9:7) and no longer chooses to regard Israel as being special in this respect.

9:11–15 Israel's Restoration. This unrelenting movement toward judgment, however, will ultimately lead to restoration. In a strongly messianic passage, Amos looks ahead to the coming of another day that will dawn after the dreadful day of judgment. In this day, the ruined cities of the land will be rebuilt, and the countryside will again bring forth wine and produce in abundance. A restored Israel will once more be planted in the land, never to be uprooted again. In particular, the house of David (here referred to as a "tent" or "hut" to indicate the sorry state into which it has declined) will be restored, with new authority over the nations (9:11–12). Israel's enemies (of which only Moab is mentioned) will be subject to the reign of this restored house of David. With the coming of Jesus Christ as the king of Israel and the lord of all nations, this prophecy can be seen finally to have been fulfilled.

OBADIAH

Very little is known about either this prophet or the circumstances under which he prophesied. There are no references to historical events within the prophecy that can be dated with absolute certainty. The most likely date for the prophecy would seem to be some point during the period 605–586 B.C.. This period saw Babylonian attacks on Judah and Jerusalem, culminating in the fall of Jerusalem and the deportation of its people in 586—presumably to the delight of the people of Edom, historic enemies of Judah, who feature prominently in this prophecy. However, it must be stressed that we can only guess that this is the most likely background to the book, which is the shortest in the Old Testament.

Vv. 1–14. After the fall of Jerusalem, Edom had taken possession of some territories once belonging to Judah (Eze 35:3–15). Now, Edom itself has been ravaged by foreigners. Obadiah sees in this a just punishment of Edom for her pride. On account of her pride, Edom will be humbled (2–4) and utterly destroyed through the complicity of her former friends and allies (5–7). The nation that refused to assist Judah in her hour of need and that benefited from the fall of Jerusalem will now itself feel the pain of defeat and humiliation (8–14).

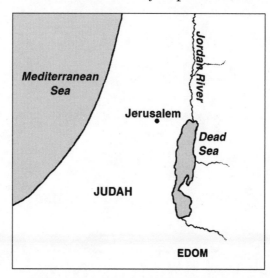

The prophet Obadiah considered it just punishment when Edom, an old enemy of Judah, would itself be attacked by foreigners.

Vv. 15–21. Obadiah then takes up the theme of the coming "Day of the LORD"

(15–21). Amos had seen this coming day as bringing judgment, rather than hope, for Israel (Am 5:18). Obadiah, however, sees it in much more positive terms. Jerusalem has paid for her sins. The coming of the Day of the Lord can now only mean restoration and deliverance for Jerusalem, and the punishment of those who have ravished and humiliated her. The Lord is both just and powerful. Therefore his people may rely upon him.

JONAH

The book of the prophet Jonah differs significantly from the remaining eleven Minor Prophets. Whereas the other eleven books are primarily concerned with the *words* of the prophet in question, the book of Jonah is much more concerned with his *deeds*. There is a sense in which it is what Jonah does, rather than anything he says, that is of importance to the reader of the book. Indeed, we are given virtually no indication of exactly what Jonah says. It is the story that really matters—a story that is among the best known in the Old Testament and that features prominently in collections of Bible stories for children.

The book indicates that the events to which it refers probably took place in the period 800–750 B.C.. The city that features so prominently in the narrative is Nineveh, a leading city of Assyria, which became the capital of the Assyrian empire at some point around 700 B.C.. By the later stage of the ninth century, Nineveh was widely thought of as the hub of the civilized world on account of its military importance. The book itself was probably written at a later stage and may even date from the postexilic period. However, the dating of the book is not of central importance to its message.

1:1–16 Jonah Flees From the Lord. The book opens with an account of the call of Jonah to go to Nineveh and preach to it. Jonah's response is immediate: he promptly boards a ship heading in precisely the opposite direction. ("Tarshish," usually thought to be the city of Tartessus, which was established in Spain by the Phoenicians, would have represented the most distant place on earth from Babylon for the writer of this prophetic book.) The voyage is disrupted by a violent storm, which causes panic among the pagan sailors. By throwing lots, they identify Jonah as the cause of their predicament and throw him overboard (1:1–16). It is important to notice how the pagan sailors refer to God by the specific title "the LORD" (1:14), thus acknowledging his sovereignty in this matter.

Jonah took a boat to Tarshish, which is in the opposite direction from Nineveh, where God told him to go to preach. During a storm at sea he was thrown overboard by the sailors. Swallowed by a giant fish, maybe a whale, Jonah had three days to rethink his decision. He decided to obey God, even though he knew that God may have mercy on Israel's enemy, Nineveh.

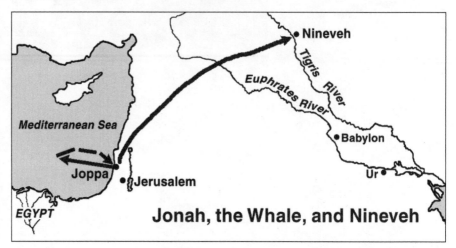

Jonah, the Whale, and Nineveh

The practice of casting lots was a means of reaching decisions that was widespread in the ancient Near East and was used by Old Testament believers wishing to have divine guidance—for example, in allocating territory to Israel within Canaan (Jos 18:10). However, it was also used specifically to identify guilty individuals, as in the case of exposing the sin of Achan (Jos 7:13–18, where the reference is to "being taken by the throwing of lots"). Even though the lots were thrown by pagans, the Lord was responsible for the selection of Jonah.

1:17–3:3 Jonah's Prayer. Jonah has not been abandoned to destruction, however. He will be given an opportunity to reconsider his actions and repent. He is swallowed by "a great fish" (1:17), which may have been a whale. The period of three days during which Jonah remains inside the fish foreshadows Jesus Christ remaining in the bowels of the earth until his resurrection on the third day (Mt 12:40). During this period, Jonah reflects on his situation, his thankfulness for deliverance being mingled with repentance for his own failure. As the prayer comes to an end, Jonah comes to his conclusion: he will make good his failures and do what he had promised. As a result, Jonah finds himself back on dry land. When the Lord's call comes again asking him to go to Nineveh, he obeys (2:1–3:3).

3:4–10 Jonah Goes to Nineveh. We are given no indication of the manner in which Jonah proclaims the Lord to the people of Nineveh. The words he uses and the occasions on which he speaks are not indicated. The real point of the account of Jonah lies elsewhere. The point is that the pagan people of Nineveh respond to the Lord. Although they do not use the special name "the LORD" to refer to God, it is clear that they acknowledge him. The Lord accepts their repentance. There are clear parallels here with two other Old Testament books, Esther and Daniel, both of which document Gentiles responding positively to the claims of the Lord.

4:1–11 Jonah's Anger at the Lord's Compassion. Jonah, however, is irritated at the Lord's compassion. The reason for this is not made clear by the text itself. But it is highly likely that Jonah's attitude reflects a form of Israelite nationalism that believed the great benefits of knowing the Lord should only be available to the people of God—in other words, to the Jews. Why should the Lord have compassion on Gentiles, especially when they are hostile towards Israel? On the basis of this nationalist theology, the Lord should be compassionate towards Israel and punish those outside its bounds. The Lord has little time for Jonah's rather petulant attitude (4:1–4).

The account of Jonah ends, perhaps a little abruptly, with the incident of the vine (or, more likely, a castor oil plant). The point being made in this concluding section of the work seems to be this: Jonah is hot and uncomfortable. In his grace, the Lord alleviates his discomfort by providing a shady plant. When it dies, Jonah becomes angry with the Lord. Yet his situation is precisely the same as before the plant's arrival. He is uncomfortable once more.

There is no hint of gratitude on Jonah's part for the temporary comfort the plant brings to him. As the story makes clear, Jonah seems inclined to complain, no matter what happens. If the Lord was compassionate enough to alleviate Jonah's discomfort for a while, would not that compassion also demonstrate itself in forgiving the repentant people of a great city? We can see in this concluding section a powerful statement of the universal love and forgiving grace of God, from which we have all benefited (4:5–11). The universality of the grace and compassion of God is proclaimed to the full in the New Testament, with its passionate plea to make disciples of all nations (Mt 28:17–20).

MICAH

Micah, who came from a village in the Judaean foothills, prophesied in the southern kingdom of Judah at some point during the period 750–686 B.C.. His clear prediction of the fall of Samaria, the capital of the northern kingdom of Israel, points to at least part of his ministry having taken place before 722–721 B.C., when the Assyrians finally ended the independent existence of Israel. There are important parallels between Micah and parts of Isaiah, which partly reflect the fact that both were prophesying around the same time. In particular, both prophets mingle prophecies of destruction with prophecies of hope, as a means of pointing to the restoration that lies beyond the inevitable punishment of Judah for her sins.

1:1–16 Judgment Against Samaria and Jerusalem. The work opens by identifying the reigns during which Micah prophesied and noting that his oracles concern both Samaria (the capital of Israel) and Jerusalem (the capital of Judah). What follows is a powerful and spirited attack on the corruption of life in the great cities of the two kingdoms. Perhaps Micah's origins in a small village lead him to be especially critical of the way of life in cities. Nevertheless, the sins he identifies and opposes represent serious violations of the covenant between the Lord and his people. The Lord's judgment on his people is coming.

2:1–3:12 False Prophets. For Micah, both Judah and Israel are guilty of a series of unacceptable offenses, including the oppression of the weak by the strong, the dispossession of people from their lands by powerful landowners, and the enslavement of helpless children (2:1–5). The priests and prophets, who ought to have been speaking out against these events, have totally failed to do so. They have taken comfort from the unacceptable idea that no harm can come to the people of God. Anyone who promised plenty of wine and beer would be acceptable as a prophet to this smug people. The leaders of the people are just as complacent, preferring reassuring prophecies of peace to the harsh realities of the coming judgment that the Lord will bring upon his people (2:6–3:12).

4:1–13 The Mountain of the Lord. This oracle of judgment is supplemented by a vision of hope. It is significant that Micah echoes some words of his near-contemporary, Isaiah (Isa 2:2–5), as he looks forward to a golden age in which peace and prosperity will reign. Does this mean that Micah is akin to one of the false prophets whom he condemns for speaking of peace? No. It means that Micah is looking beyond the calamity of impending judgment and seeing the hope that lies beyond. In those days, people will be drawn to the "mountain of the LORD" and will turn their swords into plowshares. There will be an end to war (4:1–5). The remnant of Jerusalem will be brought home in triumph. Even though Jerusalem will lose her monarchy (an event that took place as a result of the fall of Jerusalem in 586), she will be redeemed out of the hands of all her enemies (4:6–13).

5:1–4 A Promised Ruler From Bethlehem. This leads Micah to speak of the coming ruler of Judah and Israel. This ruler will arise from the town of Bethlehem, in the region of Ephrathah, and will give peace and security to his people. For Christians, this great prophecy has finally been fulfilled in Jesus Christ. Christ, himself a descendant of David, was born in this royal city. His origins are indeed "from of old"; in fact, he was present with God at creation. We can see here a clear anticipation of the coming of Jesus Christ as the shepherd of his people, leading them to a safety that transcends any peace the world can give them.

This watchtower in Samaria is the type used to keep an eye on sheep grazing on the hillside. The prophet Micah refers to the "watchtower of the flock," saying the kingdom will be restored. He speaks of the ruler from Bethlehem who will bring peace. Micah lived about seven hundred years before Jesus was born.

5:5–6:16 Deliverance and Destruction. The need for this coming deliverer is then clearly indicated. The Assyrian is coming and will devastate the land. The remnant of Jacob (in other words, those who survive within Israel and who remain faithful to the Lord) will be scattered among the nations. By scattering them in this way, through the Assyrians, the Lord will put an end to their pagan forms of worship (5:5–15). The Lord does not want elaborate sacrifices, but humility and obedience, from the people whom he loves (6:1–8). Israel must abandon her fraudulent use of inaccurate weights and measures and pursue justice for her people. If she does not, Israel will not survive to benefit from her own produce. An intervening act of judgment will allow others to benefit from the food, wine, and oil she has produced and stored (6:9–16).

7:1–20 Israel Will Rise. In the midst of all this misery and corruption, Micah's faith in the Lord remains firm. He will watch in hope for the coming of the Lord (7:1–7), just as he finally expects Israel to be delivered and restored (7:8–13). For this reason, the work ends on a note of praise, as Micah sees the Lord shepherding his people to the envy of all those surrounding them. The Lord will show compassion to his people. His anger does not last for ever, and he will finally deliver his people from the sins and iniquities that have ensnared them (7:14–20). Here again, we may see a glorious prophetic hint of the gospel of Jesus Christ and all the benefits it brings to the people of God.

NAHUM

Little is known about Nahum. He operated in the southern kingdom of Judah in the period following the fall of the northern kingdom of Israel to the Assyrians. The book may be dated with a reasonable degree of certainty to the period between the fall of the Egyptian city of Thebes (663 B.C.) and the fall of the Assyrian capital of Nineveh (612 B.C.). The former is treated as a past event, and the latter as something yet to happen. Although the book is clearly written with the needs of Judah in mind, a substantial part of its prophecy is actually directed against Nineveh itself. It is clear that Judah felt increasingly threatened by the Assyrian empire in the period following the fall of Israel and its capital city Samaria.

1:1–15 The Lord's Anger Against Nineveh. It is against this background of fear and anxiety that Nahum's prophecy is to be set. The opening prophecy envisages the joy that will accompany the overthrow of Nineveh. Using an image that is used by Isaiah to stress the joy of the restoration of Jerusalem from captivity in Babylon (Isa 52:7), Nahum looks ahead to the rejoicing that will accompany the news that Nineveh has fallen (1:15). The Lord will break the stranglehold of Assyria over his people and deliver them from its threat. Unlike Isaiah and Jeremiah, who saw Assyria as the Lord's appointed instrument of judgment and punishment of his rebellious people, Nahum treats Assyria simply as a foreign oppressor whose yoke must be cast off.

2:1–3:19 Nineveh to Fall. The second prophecy (2:1–13) looks forward both to the restoration of Israel to its former glory and also to the awe-inspiring fall of Nineveh. In his vision, the prophet can see the terror that falls upon the once-great city as its inhabitants flee for their lives, realizing that the greatness and security of the past has vanished forever. The Lord is against Assyria. Therefore it will fall. In the third section of the prophecy (3:1–19), Nahum compares the coming fall of Nineveh to the past fall of Thebes, the capital of Upper Egypt (referred to here by its Hebrew name *No Amon*). So hated is Assyria that there will be nobody to mourn her end. The world, and not just Judah, will be a better place without the tyranny of Assyria.

HABAKKUK

Habakkuk prophesied in the southern kingdom of Judah at some time around the battle of Carchemish (605 B.C.). This battle, which resulted in the total defeat of the Egyptian armies, marked the end of any serious resistance to the Babylonian advances in the region. It was not long before Judah found itself under threat from Babylon—a threat that would lead to an attack on Jerusalem and partial deportation of its inhabitants in 597 B.C. and a final onslaught in 588, eventually leading to the fall of the city and deportation of most of its population in 586 B.C.. The text of the book itself does not allow us to date the prophecy with any great precision.

1:1–11 Habakkuk's Complaint. The book opens with a complaint: Why does the Lord allow so much evil to take place within Judah? It seems that justice is not observed and that violence has become an everyday occurrence (1:1–4). The Lord's response to this complaint is dramatic. Something is indeed about to be done about this unacceptable state of affairs. He will summon the Babylonians as agents of his punishment. The Babylonians are not righteous. Indeed, they are people who regard their own strength as a god. But they will be his agent of punishment for the sins of Judah.

1:12–2:20 Habakkuk's Second Complaint. Habakkuk's second complaint picks up on this point (1:12–2:1): how can a righteous God use such a wicked people as the agent of his punishment? After all, Judah is sinful—but the Babylonians are even worse. So why use an evil nation to punish a people who, though sinful, are more righteous than they are? The answer given focuses on the fate of Babylon (2:2–20). The Babylonians will also be punished for their wickedness. A series of woes is directed against Babylon, making it clear that the Lord in no way condones any aspect of their behavior. The righteous must learn to live by faith (2:4; see also Ro 1:17). In other words, they must learn to put their trust in the Lord and realize that his ways, although apparently lying beyond human understanding, are nevertheless righteous and will achieve their goals. The knowledge of the Lord will cover the earth, just as the waters cover the sea (2:14).

3:1–19 Habakkuk's Prayer. The prophecy ends with a prayer of Habakkuk in response to all that he has learned. Like many of the psalms, the prayer takes the form of a song. It recalls the great deeds of the Lord in the past and the devastation that was caused by his presence. The song focuses on the ways in which the Lord has acted to deliver his people from their oppressors, such as in the crossing of the Red Sea (3:13–14). No matter what happens, Habakkuk declares that he will continue to praise and trust the Lord. He alone is Savior and Lord and gives hope to his people.

ZEPHANIAH

It is clear from his own description that Zephaniah belonged to the royal family of Judah, being a direct descendant of Hezekiah, king of Judah (715–686 B.C.). Zephaniah prophesied during the reign of Josiah (640–609 B.C.), which was one of the most important periods of religious reform in Judah. The rediscovery of the Book of the Law led to a major religious reformation and a corporate renewal of the covenant with the Lord, which had been violated by the paganism that flourished under earlier monarchs.

1:1–13 Warning of Coming Destruction. It would seem that Zephaniah's prophecies were delivered before these reforms. It is quite clear from their general tone that the religious life of Judah has reached an all-time low and that the threat of imminent divine judgment is required to spur the king and nation into any kind of reform and renewal. The great warning of destruction in Judah speaks of a continuing legacy of Baal worship, worship of the stars, and devotion to the god Molech, who was chiefly noted for the cult of child sacrifice associated with his name. These practices are totally unacceptable.

1:14–2:3 The Great Day of the Lord. The prophet then turns to the "Day of the LORD," a common theme among many of the prophets of this period. The coming of the Lord to such a corrupt and rebellious people can only bring judgment. It will be a time of distress and anguish, as the Lord brings a long overdue punishment to his disobedient people. Nothing can stand in the way of this judgment: wealth and power are useless. Only righteousness and humility on the part of Judah offer any hope of this dreadful judgment not being inflicted.

2:4–3:20 The Future of Jerusalem. This prophecy is followed by a series of oracles against the nations around Judah (2:4–15), detailing the judgment that will surely come against these nations. Yet Jerusalem itself, supposedly the site of the house of God, is also condemned (3:1–8). The Lord is angered that Jerusalem refuses to fear him or to accept his correction. As a result of her refusal to take any notice of him, she will be punished for her sins.

That punishment, however, will be followed by a new period in her history. She will be purified, purged both of her pagan ways and of her inhabitants, who were proud and haughty. The purification of the city will result in its being inhabited only by the meek and the humble, who trust in the Lord (3:9–13). These people will rejoice, knowing that the period of their punishment is over and that they can again be an object of delight and love to their Lord (3:14–17). They will be brought home from the lands to which they had been sent in shame and will have the satisfaction of seeing themselves restored in the full gaze of the surrounding nations.

HAGGAI

The prophet Haggai is specifically mentioned by name in the account of the rebuilding of the temple at Jerusalem after the return from exile. Along with Zechariah, Haggai belongs to the period of postexilic prophecy, in which the Lord made his ways and will known to his people after their return from exile in Babylon. The background to Haggai's ministry lies in the decision of Cyrus the Great, the conqueror of the Babylonian empire, to allow peoples who had been deported to return to their homelands (Ezr 1:2–4). In the case of the inhabitants of Jerusalem, permission was given to begin the rebuilding of the temple. Yet work soon stalled for various reasons. Haggai's prophecy concerns the need to begin the work of rebuilding as a matter of obligation to the Lord.

1:1–14 A Call to Build the House of the Lord. The date of the prophecy, which consists of four messages from the Lord, can be established with accuracy. The call to prophesy (1:1) can be dated to the end of August 520. The last message is dated from the middle of December 520, nearly four months later. The first message (1:2–11) is a command to rebuild the temple. Why are the people of Jerusalem building expensive houses for themselves, while failing to build a house for the Lord? Is it any wonder that Jerusalem is in such a miserable state, when the people treat their God in such a way? Until the Lord's house is rebuilt, Jerusalem will remain a wilderness. It is clear that this message has its desired effect. The rebuilding of the temple begins under Zerubbabel (1:12).

2:1–9 The Promised Glory of the New House. The second message is as remarkable as it is simple: The Lord is with his people. This deeply reassuring affirmation can be—and is almost certainly meant to be—interpreted in two ways. First, it is a declaration that the Lord is on the side of his people. No longer is he against them, as he was when he summoned the Assyrians or Babylonians as the agents of his wrath against Israel and Judah. And second, it is an assurance of the physical presence of the Lord among his people. Just as Ezekiel's vision of the restored temple included a dramatic moment in which the glory of the Lord returned to the temple it had earlier deserted, so Haggai is assured that the Lord will be with his restored people. The new temple will surpass in glory the old building, which had been destroyed by the Babylonians. It will bring peace to the people.

2:10–19 Blessings for a Defiled People. The third message concerns the defilement of the people. It seems that some among the returning exiles may have gained the impression that on account of their exile in Babylon, they are now free from sin. If such an idea had gained widespread assent, it would have ultimately led to lack of concern for the law of the Lord and a failure to be concerned about obeying him. Haggai demonstrates that sin is spread far more easily than holiness. There is a real danger that the people of God will become defiled through a lack of interest in holiness. Yet holiness on the part of the people is, Haggai argues, an essential precondition for blessings from the Lord. By rebuilding the temple, the people will demonstrate their commitment to the Lord. He will then return the compliment and bless the people.

2:20–23 Zerubbabel the Lord's Signet Ring. The fourth and final message is brief. It affirms the Lord's commitment to Zerubbabel. The Lord has chosen Zerubbabel and will make him "like my signet ring"—an apparent reference to Zerubbabel himself being seen as a pledge or guarantee of the faithfulness of the Lord to his people. That faithfulness is not in question, but it is clear that the people need to be reassured of it and to have physical signs of the promises of the Lord. Here we can see an important anticipation of one of the many purposes of the work of Jesus Christ—to reassure us, by both his words and his work, of God's faithfulness. As Paul points out, all of God's promises find their "Yes!" in him (2Co 1:20)—and him alone.

ZECHARIAH

Like his contemporary Haggai, Zechariah is to be dated to the period immediately after the return to Jerusalem from exile in Babylon. Haggai's calling can be dated to August 520 B.C.. Zechariah's calling took place a few months later, in October or November of the same year. Although Haggai's visions lasted only over a few months, Zechariah's prophetic ministry was spread out over a much longer period. Zechariah was among the large group of exiles who returned to Judah in 538 B.C. under the leadership of Zerubbabel. Like Ezekiel, he was also a priest. However, Zechariah was born during the Babylonian captivity. He had never seen Jerusalem before 538.

Like Haggai, Zechariah wishes to encourage the people of Jerusalem to rebuild the temple. Alongside these messages of encouragement and rebuke for inaction, there are to be found a series of strongly messianic prophecies.

ZECHARIAH 1:1 – 6:15

The Eight Night Visions

1:1–6 A Call to Return to the Lord. The work opens by identifying its author as the grandson of Iddo, who is named in Nehemiah's list of those returning from Babylon (Ne 12:4). The date of the call of the prophet can be placed in October or November 520, some time after the initial return of the exiles. The opening words of the prophecy declare both the need and the possibility of returning to the Lord. Israel may have returned to Jerusalem, but she has yet to return fully to the Lord who exiled her as a punishment and then restored her. Surely the people's experience of exile would have taught them to listen to the prophets of the Lord?

1:7–21 The Man Among the Myrtle Trees. There then follows a series of night visions, the first of which dates from about three months after the call of the prophet. The first vision (1:7–17) is that of a horseman among a group of myrtle trees. The Lord had punished his people by sending them into exile for seventy years. Yet Judah has been punished more than she deserves by the nations about her (1:14–15; a similar idea is found at Isa 40:1–2). Now the Lord's tender mercy and compassion will be made known to his people. Their towns will prosper, and the house of the Lord will be rebuilt at Jerusalem.

The second vision (1:18–21) demonstrates that the great powers who were responsible for the chaos that descended on Judah, Israel, and Jerusalem will themselves be overthrown.

2:1–3:10 A Man With a Measuring Line. The third vision is that of a man with a measuring line (2:1–13). This extended vision points to the city of Jerusalem being rebuilt. The Lord himself will dwell with his people. The Lord has chosen Jerusalem as his dwelling place and will be its chief glory. In addition to its declaration that Jerusalem will be rebuilt, the vision also points to Zechariah's relative youth (2:4).

The fourth vision (3:1–10) points ahead to the cleansing of the sin of Israel and her restoration as a priestly nation to the Lord. The symbolism involved in the vision is especially important. Joshua, the high priest who with Zerubbabel had brought the people back from Babylon (Ezr 2:2; Ne 7:7)—not the earlier leader who supervised the conquest of Canaan—is initially seen wearing filthy clothes. Then the high priest's filthy clothes are removed and replaced by clean ones. In the same way, Israel's sins will be removed by the Lord and replaced with his righteousness.

4:1–14 The Gold Lampstand and the Two Olive Trees. The fifth vision is of a solid gold lampstand. The "seven channels" are best understood as referring to channels through which the supply of olive oil for the lamp is fed. The image then emphasizes the constancy and abundance of the oil that keeps the lamp alight. This is reinforced by the reference to the two olive trees, which will provide a constant source of oil. However, there is a deeper meaning to this vision. Oil was used for anointing, especially for the anointing of priests and kings, who had a special role to play in the history of the people of God. The vision identifies Zerubbabel and Joshua as continuing the kingly and priestly functions of earlier generations, which will ultimately be fulfilled in the coming of the Messiah.

Olives on a tree and an ancient olive press from Capernaum illustrate one of the night visions of Zechariah. He saw a gold lampstand and two olive trees that provided a constant source of oil for the lampstand. Oil was also used for anointing priests and kings.

5:1–6:15 Further Visions. The final visions are briefer. The sixth vision takes the form of a flying scroll (5:1–4), symbolizing the universal validity of the law of the Lord and the condemnation it will bring to those who ignore or disobey it. The seventh vision (5:5–11) focuses on a basket in which the sins of the nation will be removed from the land and transferred to Babylon. The eighth and final vision (6:1–8) repeats the basic themes of the first vision, stressing the ultimate victory of the Lord over all his enemies.

In what follows, Zechariah sees Joshua, the high priest, being crowned (6:9–15). This action identifies him as the one who will be responsible for the rebuilding of the temple. However, there are strongly messianic overtones to this passage, which points to the coming Messiah being both a priest and a king (6:13)—a prophecy that is fulfilled in the coming of Jesus Christ as the perfect high priest and the true king of Israel.

ZECHARIAH 7:1–14:21

Repentance and Restoration

7:1–9:8 The Lord Promises to Bless Jerusalem. Some two years after the eight night visions related above, the word of the Lord comes to Zechariah again. After condemning Jerusalem for a lack of true justice, mercy, and compassion (7:1–10), the Lord declares the importance of listening to and obeying him (7:11–14). Yet despite all her faults, Jerusalem remains special in the sight of the Lord. He has chosen her and loved her. In an important turn of phrase, the Lord declares that he is "jealous for Zion" (8:1)— meaning that his love for her is such that he cannot bear the thought of Jerusalem loving anyone else.

In the past, Jerusalem has been the object of cursing. Now she will be the object of blessing. The same Lord who ordained exile as a punishment for his people now ordains blessing for her. Those around will notice and will want to discover this Lord for themselves so that they may share in her joy (8:1–23). Her enemies will be destroyed. In a panoramic survey of the region, the prophet identifies all the historic enemies of God's people and sees their downfall (9:1–8).

9:9–11:17 The Coming of Zion's King. A strongly messianic passage now opens (9:9–13). In a great vision of hope, the prophet sees the great messianic king, the descendant of David, entering into the city in triumph, bringing salvation with him. Markedly, he will not enter on a warhorse, but with humility. He will be seated on a donkey, just as David and his sons were content to ride on mules (2Sa 18:9). This great passage will reach its ultimate fulfillment in the triumphant entry of Jesus Christ into Jerusalem (Mt 21:1–11). The Lord will come and save his people (9:14–11:3). Furthermore, the messianic oracle just noted is now supplemented by another, in which the messianic shepherd-king is deemed to be worth a mere thirty pieces of silver (11:4–17). The fulfillment of this prophecy in the betrayal of Jesus Christ by Judas Iscariot is a reminder of what Israel thought of her long-awaited Messiah when he finally appeared.

12:1–9 Jerusalem's Enemies to Be Destroyed. The book comes to a close with a vision of the end, in which Jerusalem is once more under siege. The besiegers are no longer the Babylonians, but are great armies drawn from all over the earth. Perhaps this prophecy refers to the siege of Jerusalem in AD 70, when the city was destroyed by the Romans. However, the references to the victory of Jerusalem over her enemies can also be understood in terms of the final establishment of the New Jerusalem in heaven, which none can overthrow.

12:10–13:6 Mourning for the One They Pierced; Cleansing from Sin. Two themes now appear, which can only be understood in their full sense in the light of the New Testament. The first is the reference to the inhabitants of Jerusalem looking on the "one they have pierced" and whose death is mourned as that of a firstborn son or an only child (12:10). These themes are fulfilled in the crucifixion of Jesus Christ, who was pierced by his executioners as they nailed him to the cross (Jn 19:34, 37), surrounded by onlookers. Here was the death of the only son of God (Jn 3:16), the firstborn of all creation (Col 1:15, 18).

The second is the prophecy of a fountain that will cleanse the descendants of David from all their sin and impurity (13:1). This is linked with a future prophet who is wounded by his friends (13:6). These verses clearly anticipate the betrayal of Jesus Christ, whom many recognized as a prophet (Mk 8:28; Jn 4:19), by one of his friends. It also points ahead to the cleansing from sin that is possible through the death of Christ (Ac 22:16; 1Co 6:11; Rev 22:14).

13:7–9 The Shepherd Struck; the Sheep Scattered. The strongly messianic prophecies continue as Zechariah looks ahead to the coming of a future shepherd who will be struck down, with the result that his sheep are scattered. The shepherd is a favorite messianic image, pointing to the coming of a shepherd-king like David. Once more, the Christian reader of this passage will immediately recognize the fulfillment of this prophesy in the events surrounding the death of Jesus Christ. At the time of the crucifixion, his disciples were scattered like sheep without a shepherd (Mt 26:31, 56; Mk 14:27, 49–50).

14:1–21 The Lord Comes and Reigns. Finally, the prophecy returns to the theme of the "Day of the Lord." On that day, there will once more be assaults on Jerusalem and her people. Yet the Lord will triumph in the midst of this calamity and will finally overcome all the enemies of Jerusalem.

Although it is possible to see this prophecy as a piece of crude nationalism, looking forward to the Jewish domination of the world, it is clear that this is not the intended sense of the words at all. From a Christian perspective, the prophecy is clearly pointing ahead to the tribulation of the

Christian church in the world and assuring believers of the final victory of the Lord over the enemies of faith. Zechariah's vision of the purity of the temple (14:21) will only be fulfilled in the New Jerusalem. There is no temple in the New Jerusalem, because the Lord dwells there in all his fullness. But no impurity of any kind will be found there (Rev 21:22–27). God will reign supreme, and his people will rest from their labors and their fears.

MALACHI

Like Haggai and Zechariah, Malachi appears to have prophesied in the postexilic period, at some point soon after the return of the exiles from Babylon to Jerusalem. This is suggested by a number of considerations, including the close similarity between the sins condemned in this book and those singled out for condemnation by Nehemiah. It is generally thought that Malachi (whose name literally means "my messenger") was the final prophet of the Old Testament period. If this is the case, the work represents an important point of transition between the old covenant and the new, pointing ahead to the coming of the Lord to his people in Jesus Christ.

1:1–5 Jacob Loved, Esau Hated. The prophecy opens with an affirmation of the love of God for his people Israel. (It should be noted that the term *Israel* is used here to mean "the people of God" rather than "the northern kingdom." Long after the collapse of the northern kingdom through the Assyrian conquest in 722–721 B.C., the term *Israel* continued to be used in this inclusive sense by some of the later prophets and also in the writings of the New Testament.) That love is contrasted with the Lord's rejection of Esau and his descendants, the Edomites (see Obadiah's prophecy, vv. 1-14). Israel is special in the sight of God in a way that other nations and peoples are not.

1:6–2:9 Blemished Sacrifices. Despite this special relationship between the Lord and Israel, all is not well. Israel is beginning to show a degree of contempt for the Lord by cheating on her sacrificial regulations. Who cares what kind of animal is sacrificed? Anything will do. The Lord declares his disgust at the emergence of such attitudes within his own people (1:6–14). The priests of Israel are severely criticized for their failures in this respect (2:1–9). Israel has violated the covenant with the Lord in many ways, of which two are singled out for special comment.

2:10–16 Judah Unfaithful. In the first place, Israelite men are marrying foreign women. By doing so, they are introducing people with alien religious beliefs into Israel. To marry a foreign woman is to import her gods into the land of the Lord. Nehemiah had vigorously opposed this practice (Ne 13:23–29) and enforced a strict policy that prohibited such intermarriage. In the second place, Israelite men are divorcing their wives, despite the solemn covenant of commitment that undergirded the marriage. Indeed, it is possible that these two issues are related. Perhaps Israelite men were divorcing their Israelite wives in order to marry foreign women instead.

2:17–3:5 The Day of Judgment. Israel's sins thus anger and weary the Lord. Something will have to be done about it. The Lord proposes that he will send "my messenger" (for which the Hebrew, *Malachi,* is used as the title of the prophecy) to prepare the way for a great and dramatic event: the coming of the Lord himself to his temple. On account of her sin, Israel will not be able to cope with this development. The coming of the Lord will not bring consolation, but a refiner's fire, which will indeed purify—but will hurt as well. The coming of the Lord will lead to the purification of his people, a process that will be as painful as it is necessary.

3:6–4:6 Robbing God; the Day of the Lord. Nonetheless, the promise of forgiveness and restoration still stands. Despite Israel's obvious sin, the promise of reconciliation remains real and open. If Israel returns to the Lord, he will return to Israel (3:6–18). If Israel will only keep to what is required of her (for example, in respect of tithes), all will be well. However, the signs are not good. As a result, the Lord proclaims the coming of the "Day of the Lord" (4:1). In that day, the arrogant will be wiped out, while the righteous will bask in the light of the sun of righteousness (4:2).

When will this great day be? When will the Lord visit his temple? When will the Lord come? Malachi does not say. What he does say, however, is that the Lord will send the prophet Elijah before that day comes, to prepare the way for his coming (4:5–6). So if Elijah should come again, people will know that a great day is about to dawn—a day that offers both a threat and a promise. Many years later, perhaps when some had given up hope, John the Baptist appeared by the Jordan, dressed in the manner of Elijah and declaring that he had come to prepare the way for someone greater than himself. You can understand the reason for the great sense of anticipation that developed.

This brings us to the great event of the coming of Jesus Christ and its implications for the world—the subject of the New Testament, to which we may now turn, eagerly awaiting the fulfillment of the great hopes of Israel.

NEW TESTAMENT

MATTHEW

Matthew is the first of the four Gospels, each of which has distinctive characteristics. Perhaps the most noticeable feature of Matthew's gospel is its concern to demonstrate the way Jesus Christ fulfills both the prophecies and expectations of the Jewish people. It seems that Matthew was especially concerned to show his readers how Jesus Christ was exactly the person toward whom the Old Testament was pointing.

The first three Gospels include a lot of material in common. It is widely believed that all three draw on several common sources, such as collections of the sayings of Jesus that were committed to memory at a very early stage. Some material is common to all three Gospels. Some is common to Matthew and Luke (which are much longer than Mark). And some is found only in Matthew or Luke. In each case, the Evangelist (as the gospel writers are known) has drawn on his own set of historical sources to allow his readers access to the details of the central figure of the Christian faith. The overlap between the first three Gospels is reflected in the name that is sometimes given to them: Synoptic Gospels, from the Greek word *synopsis*, or "summary."

The earliest written documents of the Christian church are not the Gospels themselves, but some of the letters of Paul. So why should the Gospels have been written later than the letters? For the first few decades of its history, the Christian church relied on memorized accounts of the words and deeds of Jesus. Mark's gospel is usually regarded as the first to have been written down, probably in the mid 60s. Matthew is often thought to have been written in the 70s, although the case for it having been written earlier is still upheld by some scholars. Luke's gospel is also dated in the 70s by many scholars, although the possibility of an earlier date remains open.

MATTHEW 1:1 – 2:23 —————————————————————————

The Birth of Jesus Christ

1:1–17 The Genealogy of Jesus. Matthew's immediate concern is to tell his readers about the background to the central figure of the gospel—Jesus Christ. He therefore opens by considering the background to his birth.

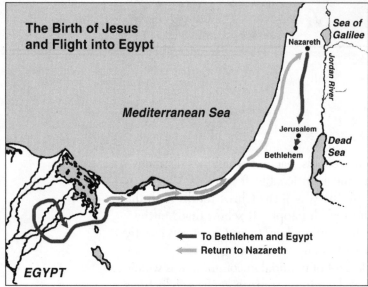

The Birth of Jesus
and Flight into Egypt

Sea of
Galilee

Nazareth

Jordan River

Mediterranean Sea

Jerusalem

Dead
Sea

Bethlehem

⟵ To Bethlehem and Egypt
⟵ Return to Nazareth

EGYPT

Mary and Joseph traveled all the way from Nazareth to Bethlehem, about a hundred miles, just before Jesus was born. They soon had to flee to Egypt when King Herod tried to kill Jesus by killing all boys in Bethlehem who were two years old or younger. After Herod died, they returned.

First, he traces the family tree. Jesus is shown to be descended from the great Old Testament figures David and Abraham. This point would have been especially important to Jewish readers of this gospel. They would realize that Jesus had the necessary family connections to be the Messiah—that is, "God's anointed one," who would bring in a new period in the history of God's people. Jesus is identified (1:1) as "the son of David" (a strongly messianic title), and as "the Christ" (1:17). Notice also that Joseph is referred to as the "husband of Mary" (1:16), rather than as the father of Jesus. Matthew is preparing his readers for the unusual circumstances surrounding the birth of Jesus, to which he will turn presently.

There are some interesting differences between the genealogy presented here and that in Luke's gospel (Lk 3:23–37). Matthew tends to trace Jesus' descent through Joseph, whereas Luke's preference is to trace it through Mary. This corresponds with Matthew's particular interest in Joseph, and Luke's in Mary. Matthew tells the story of the birth of Jesus, for example, from Joseph's perspective; whereas Luke relates it from Mary's (see p. 304–5). Matthew thus brings out the fact that, legally speaking, Jesus is the son of David.

Notice also that Matthew points out how the birth of Jesus is strategically located in the history of the people of God (1:17). Abraham marks the origins of Israel. God called him to leave his home and become "a great nation" (Ge 12:1–3). Fourteen generations later, the history of Israel entered a glorious new phase with the reign of King David. This was followed fourteen generations later by the exile of Jerusalem to the great city of Babylon. This was seen by the Old Testament prophets as another turning point in the history of Israel, marking a new period in God's dealings with his people. It was a time of renewal, purification, and judgment. And fourteen generations after this exile, Jesus Christ was born. The implication is clear: another turning point in God's dealings with his people is about to take place.

The word *Christ* is worth further thought. Too often it is treated as a surname, so that "Jesus Christ" seems to be on the same level as "John

Smith." Yet the second word is actually a title. The best translation of the name of the central figure of the Gospels is "Jesus the Christ" or "Jesus the Messiah." (The Greek word *christos*, from which we get the word *Christ*, means "anointed one" or "Messiah".)

The claim that the Messiah has finally come (1:17) would indeed be good news to many Jews. It is therefore important to demonstrate the grounds of this belief. What is there about the life of Jesus that points to this conclusion? In many ways, Matthew's gospel can be thought of as aiming to help its readers appreciate that the long-awaited Messiah has finally come in the person of Jesus of Nazareth.

1:18–25 The Birth of Jesus Christ. The story of the birth of Jesus is well known, but it is worth reading again, savoring its details. Mary is "pledged to be married" to Joseph, but has never had any sexual relations with him. When she is found to be pregnant, Joseph obviously fears the worst and prepares to have the necessary divorce papers drawn up in private. Out of kindness to Mary, he resolves to avoid a public trial, which would have led to her being stoned to death (Dt 22:23–24). Yet even as he considers this course of action, an angel of the Lord speaks to him in a dream and sets out the facts of the matter. Mary is with child through the Holy Spirit. The child who is to be born is no ordinary child. He is to be called Jesus, "for he will save his people from their sins" (1:21). Note that Joseph is not allowed to choose the name of the child. For biblical writers, to name someone is to have authority over them (as when Adam was allowed to name the living creatures, Ge 2:19–20). Joseph is told to name the child *Jesus,* because the name is a vital indication of the significance of the child who will bear it. He is to be a savior.

Matthew then introduces us to a major theme of his gospel: the fulfillment of prophecy. At twelve points, Matthew shows how the events of Jesus' life and death fulfill the great prophetic hope of the Old Testament. Here, Matthew points out how the birth of Jesus fulfills Isaiah 7:14, which speaks of a virgin bearing a child as a sign to God's people. Again, the name given to the child is enormously significant. He is called *Immanuel,* which means "God with us" (1:23). This name conveys two vital ideas that are central to the gospel: "God with us" means both that God is on our side in our struggle against sin, despair, and death and that God is among us in that he has chosen to dwell with men and women in the world. This central Christian idea (usually known as the *Incarnation*) is of special importance in John's gospel (see Jn 1:14). By fulfilling this great prophecy (and the others that follow), Jesus shows himself to be the culmination of the great hopes and expectations of the Old Testament.

2:1–12 The Visit of the Magi. Matthew then details further events surrounding the birth of Jesus, which continue the theme of the fulfillment of prophecy. The birthplace of Jesus is identified as "Bethlehem in Judea" (2:1), a village about eight kilometers south of Jerusalem. The significance of this location, which points to the prophecy (Mic 5:2) of a future ruler and shepherd of God's people being born in this royal city, is explained later (2:4–6). Yet the first worshippers of the new-born Christ are not Jews. They are Gentiles. Although they bring three gifts (2:11), we do not know that there were "three wise men," as the old Christmas tradition has it. The Magi (2:1) were almost certainly astrologers from lands east of Judea, such as Persia. The reference to the star (2:1, 9–10) is important. It clearly points to an unusual and significant heavenly event, possibly a supernova, or perhaps two or more planets occupying positions very close to each other. But it also picks up the great Old Testament theme of the star that "will come out of Jacob" (Nu 24:17), widely seen as a messianic prophecy.

Both the future worship of Jesus Christ by the Gentiles and God's victory over the worship of heavenly objects is anticipated in this marvelous account of how the Magi "bowed down and worshiped him" (2:11). The gifts they offer him are precious, an entirely appropriate means of honoring a future king. Yet King Herod (also known as Herod the Great) is deeply threatened by this development, which he clearly feels will lead to a loss of his own authority. If the real "king of the Jews" (2:2) has now been born, what place will there be for Herod, who had been installed as king of Judea by the Roman authorities? Herod moves to have Jesus eliminated and orders the massacre of all young boys in Bethlehem under the age of two (2:16). This incident can remind readers of the story of Moses, who was also delivered from the massacre of young boys ordered by a frightened king (Ex 1:22–2:10).

2:13–18 The Escape to Egypt. Warned in a dream of Herod's intention to kill Jesus, Joseph takes Mary and Jesus to Egypt for safety. Matthew points out how this action fulfills another Old Testament prophecy (Hos 11:1). Israel went into Egypt at the time of Joseph, and would finally be led out by God at the time of the Exodus. Matthew sees the same pattern in the life of Jesus. So the second chapter of this gospel ends with an account of how Joseph, Mary, and Jesus settle down in the small village of Nazareth, in the region of Galilee.

MATTHEW 3:1 – 4:11

The Opening of the Ministry of Jesus

3:1–12 John the Baptist Prepares the Way. Some years now pass. Matthew opens his introduction to the ministry of Jesus by introducing John the Baptist, the son of Zechariah and Elizabeth (Lk 1:5–80). It is obvious that John creates a sensation, with crowds streaming out into the deserts to hear him speak. John is recognized as the forerunner of Jesus. In fulfillment of Old Testament prophecy, John comes as the one who was promised to "prepare the way for the Lord" (3:3, citing Isa 40:3 and Mal 3:1). John, who clearly meets with considerable resistance from the Jewish religious authorities (3:7–10), sees his role as preparing the way for someone greater than himself. John can only baptize with water. The one who is to come will baptize with the Holy Spirit (3:11). So who is this mysterious person?

3:13–17 The Baptism of Jesus. Matthew does not keep us in suspense for long. When Jesus appears on the scene (3:13), John refuses to baptize him. The sinless Jesus does not need baptism, a symbol of repentance. But Jesus insists. The result is one of the most powerful moments in the ministry of Jesus: the Holy Spirit descends upon him as he receives an endorsement from God, who affirms that Jesus is his well-beloved son (3:17). Note that Jesus does not *become* the son of God at his baptism. God confirms what is already the case.

A modern-day baptism in the area of the Jordan River where Jesus was baptized by John the Baptist. The Holy Spirit descended upon Jesus, and a voice from heaven said, "This is my Son, whom I love; with him I am well-pleased."

4:1–11 The Temptation of Jesus. Just as Israel spent forty years in the wilderness being tested and prepared for their final entry into the Promised Land, so Matthew tells us how Jesus is prepared for his mission to Israel through his temptation—a period of forty days and nights in the wilderness in which Jesus confronts and successfully resists temptation. The testing centers on whether Jesus will use his power and authority as the Son of God for his own advantage or for the ends for which they have been given. There are important anticipations of the cross in this passage, especially the section dealing with the temptation to throw himself from the highest point of the temple, knowing that he would be saved (4:6). Will Jesus come down from the cross and escape death? Or will he remain there, faithful to the end, and redeem those for whom he came to die? By the end of this period, it is clear that Jesus will be obedient to the will of his Father. He is ready to begin his public ministry.

MATTHEW 4:12 – 13:58

Jesus' Ministry in Galilee

4:12–17 Jesus Begins to Preach. Jesus' ministry now begins in the region of Galilee. In fulfillment of Old Testament prophecy (4:14), Jesus begins to preach his message in this region. It has two central themes (4:17): the need for repentance, and the coming of the kingdom of God. Matthew relates how this message finds a response in the calling of the first disciples: Peter, Andrew, James, and John (4:18–22). They are fishermen—not academics, not religious teachers, not even educated people. They illustrate superbly the remarkable attraction Jesus proves to have over people—an attraction that Matthew then documents from the early healing ministry of Jesus (4:23–25). Even at this early stage, Jesus creates a sensation.

5:1–7:29 The Sermon on the Mount. But Jesus is not a mere healer. He has come to bring the good news of the kingdom of God. Immediately, Matthew introduces us to a major section of the teaching of Jesus, which is generally known as the Sermon on the Mount (5:1–7:29). One of the most distinctive characteristics of Matthew's gospel is the way the teachings of Jesus are conveniently arranged into five blocks of material, of which this is the first. Each block ends with similar words (7:28; 11:1; 13:53; 19:1; 26:1). The fivefold division may suggest that the author sees his work as a new Law, reflecting the five books of the Pentateuch—Genesis through Deuteronomy—and Jesus as a new and greater Moses. The sermon stresses the high demands that Christians are called to work toward, while realizing that it is impossible to meet them without the grace of God himself.

For many commentators, the sermon sets out a series of standards that Christians should aim toward, even if they ultimately fail to reach them in their own lives. This does not mean that the demands are perfectionist or hopelessly idealistic. It just points to the fact that being a Christian makes a difference in the way people live and indicates the goals they should be aiming at, even if they cannot achieve them all. It is like being set on the right road and encouraged to begin walking down it. Even if believers don't reach

According to tradition, Jesus gave the Sermon on the Mount from this hillside, overlooking the Sea of Galilee. The sermon on the mount begins with "Blessed are ..."

the end of that road, at least they know that they are walking in the right direction.

5:1–12 The Beatitudes. The sermon opens with a set of pronouncements that are widely known as the Beatitudes. Each pronouncement opens with the words "Blessed are . . . ." The word *blessed* is easily misunderstood. It does not really mean "happy" or "fortunate." It is possible, as Jesus points out, to be blessed even if you are unhappy. Someone is *blessed* if he or she has found favor and acceptance in the sight of God. Even if the believers' worldly status or situation is humble or distressing, they can know that they have found favor in the sight of God—which is much more important. Notice how many of the Beatitudes emphasize that a lowly situation (such as meekness), or a situation of need (such as mourning or persecution) is seen as leading to blessing.

5:13–16 Salt and Light. Believers are then compared to salt (5:13) and light (5:14–16). Believers are the "salt of the earth," in that they can bring a new quality to the world. Perhaps with rock salt in mind (where water could easily wash out the salt, leaving only rock behind), Jesus stresses how easily believers can lose their "saltiness" unless they take care to preserve it. Believers are also like lamps, able to bring light to a dark world, leading people to find and praise God.

5:21–48 The Fulfillment of the Law. The coming of Jesus Christ is then declared to be in fulfillment of the law, not contradiction of it. In no way does the coming of Jesus abolish the law. He has come to fulfill it (5:17–20). In Christ, the purposes and intentions of the law reach their climax and final fulfillment. He is the one to whom the Law and the Prophets point. While in no way endorsing the precise and detailed interpretations of the law that prevailed in the Judaism of the time, Jesus is clearly indicating that the Old Testament continues to play an important role in the life of believers. The relation between the Old Testament law and the life of faith is explored in some detail in the writings of Paul, and will be returned to later in this work.

Indeed, far from abolishing the law, Jesus intensifies it. Murder is not simply about the physical action of killing. It is about the motivation that underlies this action. Adultery is not simply about the physical action of sleeping with someone else's partner. It is about the motivation for that action. If someone is asked to walk one mile, Jesus asks them to walk two. The basic theme is clear: the righteousness that is the ultimate goal of the new covenant actually exceeds that of the old covenant. There is thus no basis in the teaching of Jesus for any accusation of *antinomianism* (that is, a disregard or contempt for the moral law) in the Christian life. Christians are obliged to do good. Yet Jesus insists that the motivation for doing such good deeds must not be to gain public favor, but to please God, who sees and rewards in secret (6:1–4). This also applies to prayer. Jesus is critical of loud, long, and pompous public prayers and declares that the prayers of individuals (by which he does not mean the public worship of the church) should ideally be in private to avoid this temptation. In any case, the effectiveness of prayer is not dependent upon its verbosity (6:5–8)!

6:9–15 *The Lord's Prayer.* Having set the context in which prayer should be offered, Jesus hands down a model prayer that has become an integral part of the life of Christian believers down the ages. It is generally known as the Lord's Prayer. Its simplicity, brevity, and intimacy set a model for the kind of prayer Jesus wishes his followers to adopt. The prayer affirms the fatherhood of God, reminding us that we owe our origins to him and that he cares for his children. It reminds us that God is holy (the term *hallowed* has the basic meaning of "keep holy") and that this holiness must be reflected in the way believers address God in prayer, speak of him to the world, and worship him. It asks God to bring about his sovereign will in the lives of believers—a dangerous prayer, given what God sometimes wants his people to do for him. The prayer then turns to the needs of believers—their physical need for food and their spiritual need for forgiveness, comfort, and protection from temptation.

At this point, the prayer ends. However, some later versions of the text of Matthew's gospel add a final concluding section offering glory to God, which reads as follows in the Authorized or King James Version: "For thine is the kingdom, and the power, and the glory, for ever. Amen." This longer version has found its way into the traditional forms of public worship of many Christian denominations. Yet although the prayer has ended, Jesus' comments on its importance have not. In a passage that must not be overlooked, Jesus makes the point that God's forgiveness of our sins is linked with our forgiveness of the sins of others (6:14–15), a point illustrated by a famous parable later in this gospel (18:21–35).

6:16–34 *Fasting and the Providence of God.* Jesus now returns to the theme of giving glory to God, not currying favor with religious people (6:16–18). Underlying this point is the basic principle that it is more important to lay up an imperishable treasure in heaven than to labor for something here on earth that will not endure (6:19–24). Believers must learn to trust in the providence of God, a lesson Jesus illustrates from the birds of the air and the lilies of the field. The important thing is to look toward God, not the world, and to trust in his goodness and seek his righteousness (6:25–34).

7:1–23 *Judging Others; Answers to Prayer; Right Behavior.* The sermon continues with a reminder of the sinfulness of human nature, which leads us to criticize others when we ought to be examining ourselves (7:1–6). Jesus affirms both the importance of prayer and God's goodness in responding to our needs. Just as human fathers, inadequate though they are, still want to do good for their children, so God takes delight in answering the requests of his children (7:7–12). The importance of right behavior is stressed in a number of ways (7:13–23). Just as the good tree brings forth good fruit, so the person who has really come to faith will naturally produce good works.

7:24–29 The Wise and Foolish Builders. The sermon ends with the *parable of the house built on the rock and the house built on the sand* (7:24–27). Jesus here makes it clear that it is vitally important that the house of faith is built on a solid foundation, that will survive the worst storms life can produce. Only by building on Jesus Christ and his gospel can we be sure of the stability and peace that God intends for our lives.

The crowd, deeply impressed by this teaching, recognize Jesus as someone who, unlike their own teachers, teaches with authority (7:28–29). That authority is now confirmed by a series of remarkable events before we come to the second major section of teaching (10:5–42). In several healings, Jesus demonstrates that there is something about him that distinguishes him from everyone else. All the signs of spiritual authority and power are present in his ministry—both in what he says and in what he does. The Sermon on the Mount focuses on what Jesus says; our attention is now drawn to what he does.

8:1–17 Jesus Heals Many. The healing of the man with leprosy (8:1–4) illustrates the ability and willingness of Jesus to heal, as well as his affirmation of the Old Testament law—note how the healed leper is sent to the priest for confirmation of the healing. The healing of the centurion's servant (8:5–13) demonstrates the importance of faith for healing. As Jesus' words make clear, it also shows both that Gentiles are drawn to Jesus Christ and that they can benefit from his ministry. (As a senior officer, the centurion would have been a Roman, not a Jew.) All these healings, together with many others, are in direct fulfillment of Old Testament prophecy (8:14–17).

8:18–9:8 Jesus' Authority. After stressing the cost of following him, Jesus continues to demonstrate his authority over the natural and spiritual order—whether by stilling a storm, casting out demons, or healing someone who is paralyzed (8:18–9:8). The crowds are amazed at his authority. Significantly, the demons also recognize his true identity, hailing Jesus as the Son of God (8:29).

9:9–13 The Calling of Matthew. The calling of Matthew (widely regarded as the compiler of this gospel) is of especial interest (9:9–13). Matthew—referred to by his original name of Levi son of Alphaeus in Mark's account of the same incident (Mk 2:13–17)—was a tax collector and thus a member of a group of Jews who were widely despised and regarded as outcasts by their fellows. At this time, the region of Palestine was occupied by the Romans. Not only did the tax collectors associate with the Gentile occupying power, but they also charged more taxes than they were entitled to as a way of ensuring their own well-being. As a result, they were detested by Jews and regarded as traitors. Yet Jesus calls one of them to his inner circle. In this action, we can see one of the most important aspects of Jesus' ministry—his acceptance of those regarded as beyond hope of redemption by Judaism, including prostitutes, Gentiles, and tax collectors. Jesus summarizes this with his declaration that he has come "to call sinners, not the righteous" (9:13). There is unquestionably a strong trace of irony in this declaration. Perhaps those, such as the Pharisees, who think they are righteous are merely self-righteous? The glorious new wine of the gospel cannot be contained by the tired old wineskins of Judaism (9:14–17).

9:18–38 Jesus Heals. A series of further healings is then recorded. One is of particular interest. The woman who had been bleeding for twelve years (9:20) would have been regarded as unclean by Jews, on account of the discharge of a bodily fluid. Yet Jesus has no hesitation in healing her. What Judaism regards as unclean, Jesus sees as someone worth saving.

10:1–42 Jesus Sends Out the Twelve. A new phase in Jesus' ministry now develops. Jesus gives his twelve disciples authority to continue his ministry (10:1–4) and instructs them as he sends them out. They are to bring the good news of the coming of the kingdom of God, along with its attendant signs of healing and renewal, to the people of Israel (10:5–42). Notice that initially Jesus sends his disciples only to the Jews and instructs them to avoid others, such as Samaritans. It is clear that Jesus regards the Jews as the people of God, who have the right to hear the good news of what God is doing for his people before anyone else. As events prove, the rejection of Jesus and the gospel by Judaism leads to the opening up of the gospel and its benefits to *all* peoples, a theme that is especially important for Paul. Anticipating this rejection, Jesus makes it clear that his disciples can expect to have a tough time as they preach this good news in Israel. But he reassures them of the continuing protection and provision of God as they set out. In moments of great stress, the Holy Spirit will even give them the words they need to speak.

11:1–19 Jesus and John the Baptist. The story now shifts back to John the Baptist, who had been thrown into prison by Herod (see 14:3–4). John sends his followers to ask Jesus whether he is the long-expected Messiah or whether they will have to wait for someone else (11:2–3). In reply, Jesus lists the great signs of the coming of the Messiah, which had been prophesied in the past (Isa 35:4–6; 61:1). As can be seen from his ministry at this stage, they have all been fulfilled. It is clear that the Messiah has indeed arrived. Jesus declares that John marks the end of an age. He is the Elijah, who the Old Testament promised would come before the coming of the

Lord himself (Mal 4:5). Jesus' words leave us with no option but to conclude that he himself is the Lord.

11:20–12:14 Lack of Repentance; Sabbath-Rest. Although many respond to Jesus, it is clear that many refuse to repent (11:20–24). But for those who do repent, Jesus offers rest and refreshment (11:25–30). This theme of rest is developed in the account of Jesus breaking the Sabbath laws by picking corn and healing people on the day of rest (12:1–13). Two points are brought out clearly here. First, Jesus has authority over the Sabbath; and second, the Sabbath was instituted in order to give people refreshment, rather than to add still further to their burdens.

12:15–50 Old Testament Prophecy; Jesus' Authority Over Evil Spirits. The theme of the relation of Jesus to Old Testament prophecy is then taken up once more. Matthew shows how Jesus' ministry fulfills one of the great messianic prophecies of the Old Testament (12:15–21; see Isa 42:1–4). He also reports how the resurrection of Jesus will bring to fulfillment the "sign of Jonah" (12:38–42) through his resurrection from the dead. Yet the theme of the authority of Jesus over evil spirits is also significant in this section (12:22–37, 43–45). It is clear that Jesus has authority over such spirits. The question then arises concerning the basis of this authority. The crowds attribute this authority to his messianic status. His opponents attempt to cast aspersions on Jesus by suggesting that he has authority over demons because he is in league with "Beelzebub, the prince of demons" (12:24). This assertion is the unforgivable sin—the blasphemy against the Holy Spirit, by which the great acts of God are attributed to Satan.

13:1–52 Parables of the Kingdom. A third major section of teaching now opens (13:1–58), which includes some of the most famous "parables of the kingdom." The fact that Jesus teaches in parables is itself significant, as it points to the fulfillment of another Old Testament prophecy (13:35; see Ps 78:2; Hos 12:10). The Hebrew word that is hinted at here has a number of meanings, including "riddle" or "dark saying." As becomes clear, these "dark sayings" can only be understood by those who have been given the privilege of understanding them. Some may hear them and yet totally fail to understand what they are all about. They will see, but not perceive (13:10–17).

The first such parable is the *parable of the sower* (13:1–9, 18–23). This parable notes how the same seed falls on different kinds of ground. What eventually happens to it depends on the quality of the soil. In the same way, Jesus sows the seed of the word of God through his preaching. The effect it has on people depends on how they respond to it. If someone should fail to respond or fall away, it is not on account of any failure on the part of the seed.

The second parable focuses on a *field of wheat* in which an enemy of the farmer has sown some weeds (13:24–30, 36–43). Wheat and weeds thus grow alongside one another. Rather than risk damaging the wheat by getting rid of the weeds at this stage, the farmer decides to wait until the harvest. They will be separated out then. Just so there will be good and evil people in the world that will only be separated out at the Last Judgment. Rather than risk injuring the righteous, God will wait until the end to sort things out—and then sort them out permanently. The same point is also made in the *parable of the net* (13:44–50).

Two brief parables—the *growth of a seed* and the *spread of yeast in dough*—illustrate the way the kingdom of God can expand from small beginnings (13:31–33). The value and attraction of the gospel are then illustrated by the *parables of buried treasure* and the *pearl of great price* (13:44–45).

13:53 A Prophet Without Honor. This section of Matthew's gospel concludes by reporting the rejection of Jesus by his own people at Nazareth. Despite all the signs of spiritual authority and power, the people of Nazareth are dismissive of him. Because of their lack of faith, Jesus performs no miracles in his hometown. This points to an important general principle: no faith, no miracles. Faith is the precondition of benefiting from Christ.

MATTHEW 14:1 – 20:34

The Final Phase of Jesus' Ministry

14:1–36 John the Baptist Beheaded; the Popularity of Jesus. A new phase begins with the execution of John the Baptist (14:1–12). As a result of this, Jesus attempts to withdraw from his public ministry. However, the crowds will not allow him to be on his own. The feeding of the five thousand (14:13–21) illustrates the huge size of the crowds now following him, as much as it points to the compassion and power of Jesus. His authority over the natural order is again emphasized through his walking on the water and the ensuing stilling of the storm. Again, we learn of the huge interest in Jesus, evident in the large crowds that gather everywhere he moves (14:22–36).

15:1–39 Jesus and Judaism. The relationship of Jesus to the Judaism of his day now comes into focus once more. The issue of ritual cleanliness emerges as important, with the Pharisees protesting against the disciples' failure to observe ritual cleanliness traditions (15:1–19). Jesus argues that the Pharisees are putting human traditions above the word of God. It is not eating food with unwashed hands, but the evil thoughts of the heart that make a person unclean. This rebuke directed against the traditionalism of the Pharisees is followed by an incident that shows how people outside Judaism (in this case, a woman from the region of Tyre and Sidon) were attracted to Jesus and put their faith in him (15:21–28). The feeding of the four thousand (15:29–39), which is very similar to the earlier account of the feeding of the five thousand, once more points to both the appeal and authority of Jesus.

6:1–12 Pharisees and Sadducees Demand a Sign. But not everyone is prepared to accept the authority of Jesus. The Pharisees and Sadducees (the two main religious parties within Judaism) put him to the test and demand a sign by which this authority can be verified (16:1–4). Jesus points them to the "sign of Jonah," a clear reference to his forthcoming resurrection (see 12:39–40). After warning his disciples against the influence of the Pharisees and Sadducees (16:5–12), Jesus and his disciples press on to the region of Caesarea Philippi. It is here that one of the most important incidents in the ministry of Jesus takes place. This time, however, it is the disciples, rather than Jesus, who are the focus of attention.

16:13–20 Peter's Confession of Christ. Jesus asks his disciples the basic question: Who do people say that I am? (He uses the technical term *Son of Man* to refer to himself in this case.) The disciples report back on the various opinions that they have heard: Jesus is one of the prophets, or John the Baptist come back to life, or perhaps Elijah. But Jesus presses them: What about you? Who do you say that I am? This is a vitally important question. Unlike the crowds, the disciples have been with Jesus throughout most of his ministry. They have watched him and listened to him. Now they are being asked what their conclusion is.

Peter speaks for them all when he replies that he believes that Jesus is the Christ (that is, Messiah), the Son of the living God (16:13–20). In other words, Jesus is the long-awaited Messiah, who has come to his people. Jesus declares that Peter is correct. This is not a conclusion that he could have reached unaided. He has been assisted by God himself in reaching this momentous conclusion. Presumably anxious that the title *Messiah* might be understood in a purely political sense, Jesus asks the disciples not to tell anyone of their realization of his true identity. The Messiah could too easily be misunderstood as a triumphalist political leader, concerned only to liberate the country from its Roman occupying force.

16:21–28 Jesus Predicts His Death. But it is clear that the disciples themselves also have misunderstandings concerning Jesus. Immediately after their confession that he is the Messiah, Jesus declares that he must go to Jerusalem, suffer, be put to death, and finally rise from the dead. He is under compulsion to do this. It is part of his calling. He must do it. But the disciples cannot cope with this. It was no part of their traditional view of the Messiah that he should suffer and die. Peter protests—and is rebuked by Jesus (16:21–28).

17:1–13 The Transfiguration. An important anticipation of the Resurrection now follows. The account of the Transfiguration (17:1–13) demonstrates the continuity of Jesus with the ministries of Moses and Elijah, while at the same time providing an anticipation of the resurrection glory of

Christ. An endorsement of Jesus' identity and authority from heaven confirms his ministry and mission.

17:14–18:20 Humility and Sin Within the Church. After reports of further healing and teaching in the region (17:14–27), we come to the fourth major block of teaching in this gospel (18:1–35). This teaching focuses on the importance of humility (18:1–9), and the importance of individual Christian believers (18:10–14). Jesus makes clear the way sin within the church is to be handled, and he affirms that where two or three are gathered together in his name, he himself is present among them (18:15–20).

18:21–35 The Parable of the Unmerciful Servant. This section of teaching includes a major parable relating to forgiveness. Jesus speaks of a servant to a king who runs up a huge debt. So great is the debt that he and his entire family will have to be sold into slavery in order to meet his obligations. The servant begs for his debt to be canceled. In his mercy, the king agrees. Yet the servant promptly demands immediate payment of a trivial debt owed him by another servant. When this unfortunate man proves unable to pay, he is thrown into prison. The king is outraged by this behavior, and revokes his forgiveness of the huge debt. This parable supplements the important concluding sections of the Lord's Prayer (6:14–15) and speaks of our forgiveness depending upon our forgiving others "seventy-seven times" (or perhaps "seventy times seven"). In other words, forgiveness is to be offered time and time again, without any limits.

19:1–30 Divorce; Little Children; the Rich Young Man. After this, Jesus crosses the Jordan and undertakes a teaching and healing ministry in the area. Part of that teaching ministry includes clarification on Moses' teaching concerning divorce (19:1–12), and an important affirmation of young children (19:13–15).

This is followed by a meeting with a rich young man (19:16–30), in which the question of the conditions for salvation are discussed. After discovering that the young man has faithfully kept the commandments, Jesus asks him to sell all he has and follow him. This dismays the young man, who departs with great sadness. Notice that Jesus does not make any attempt to compromise his position. It is difficult for someone who is rich to enter the kingdom of God. But Jesus does not say that it is impossible. It is clear that wealth poses a real obstacle to coming to God; nevertheless, as Jesus makes clear, with God anything is possible. Nobody lies outside the saving purposes of God, who has promised salvation to those who put their faith in Jesus Christ.

20:1–16 The Parable of the Workers in the Vineyard. This theme of the faithfulness of God to his promises is taken up in the *parable of the workers in the vineyard* (20:1–16). The parable focuses on a landowner who offers some workers a denarius—the usual daily wage—to work in his vineyard for a day. Later, he hires some more, promising them the same wage even though they will work for a shorter period. He does the same again at noon, and again in the middle of the afternoon. At dusk, he pays all the workers the same wage, despite the fact that some have labored all day and some for only a matter of two or three hours. The workers who had been hired at the beginning of the day are furious. It's not fair, they declare. Yet the landowner had remained faithful to his promises.

The importance of the parable for believers lies at two different levels. First, it allows them to see that even though God called the Gentiles later than the Jews, both are still entitled to the same reward of salvation. And it also reminds them that the promise of forgiveness and salvation remains open, even though some may only respond to that offer late in the day.

20:17–19 Jesus Predicts His Death as a Ransom for Many. Readers are then reminded once more of the high price of that salvation, as Jesus once more predicts his betrayal, suffering, and resurrection. These passages remind us also that Jesus' death is no accident. It is something that has been purposed and foretold. Jesus dies because he has to die—there is no other way in which sinful humanity can be redeemed. The crucifixion has to happen.

This prediction of suffering and death is followed by a deeply moving declaration on the part of Jesus. He has come to serve and to give his life as a ransom for many (20:20–28). The word *ransom* indicates a payment made by which freedom is gained. Through the death of Jesus, believers are liberated from bondage to sin. Secular rulers may lord it over people. Christian leaders, however, are to serve their people as Christ served before them. The compassion of Jesus in his ministry is then further demonstrated by his healing of two blind men (20:29–34).

MATTHEW 21:1 – 28:20

The Final Week

21:1–11 The Triumphal Entry. While all this has been going on, Jesus and his disciples have been drawing nearer and nearer to Jerusalem. According to Deuteronomy 16:16, all Jewish men were required to celebrate the Passover feast in Jerusalem itself. On this occasion, the Passover would take on a special significance for Jesus, who turns out to be the true Passover lamb, sacrificed for the sins of the world. Jesus has told his disciples that he must go to Jerusalem, to be betrayed and crucified. Now he prepares to enter the great city itself (21:1–4).

Jesus enters in humility, mounted on a donkey, in fulfillment of a great messianic prophecy of the Old Testament (Zec 9:9). He enters Jerusalem as its king, an event especially celebrated by Christians on Palm Sunday. It is clear that there were many who were looking forward to this event. He is greeted by crowds, honoring him and singing his praises (21:5–11). Although Jesus is treated as a king, the crowds refer to him as a prophet (21:11). They have yet to discover that he is both prophet and king—and also a savior.

21:12–22 Conflict With the Religious Authorities. The final week of Jesus' life is packed with teaching and conflict with the religious authorities. The first major incident is the celebrated "cleansing of the temple," in which Jesus ejects the merchants and overturns the tables of the money changers and sellers of doves (21:12–17). The protest is probably only partly against the commercialization of the temple areas. It almost certainly represents Jesus' anger that any form of payment or purchase is necessary before an individual may worship God. The cursing of the fig tree (21:18–22) represents Jesus' anger against the Judaism of his time, which was barren when it ought to have borne much fruit.

This model of the Temple in Jerusalem shows what the entrance to the temple may have looked like when Jesus threw out the merchants and turned over the table of the money-changers.

21:23–46 Jesus Is Questioned and Rejected. Controversy now develops with increasing intensity. Once more, the authority of Jesus is questioned by his critics (21:23–27), who prove unable to give an adequate response to Jesus' challenge to them. Jesus stresses that it is more important to do the will of God than to talk about it. Prostitutes and tax collectors will be given preference over the Pharisees for this reason (21:28–32). This point is reinforced

by the *parable of the tenants* (21:33–46), which is a superb and distressing illustration of the way Judaism had rejected the prophets of God and was also about to reject the son of God. The final killing of the son reminds us of Jesus' predictions of his own death in Jerusalem, through which his final rejection by Judaism will be sealed.

The question of who shall enter the kingdom of God is then addressed through the *parable of the wedding feast* (22:1–14). A great wedding feast is prepared, and a select few invited. When these refuse or fail to turn up, the invitation is extended to all around. The point of the parable is simple. The gospel invitation is first offered to Israel. When she fails to respond, or rejects the invitation, it is thrown open to the Gentiles. Yet the invitation is not unconditional. Just as the wedding guests must dress in an appropriate way for the feast, so repentance and faith are needed to enter the kingdom of God.

22:15–46 More Controversial Questions. Jesus then addresses a series of controversial questions raised by the Pharisees and Sadducees, who attempt to outwit him. An initial attempt is made by the Pharisees to trap Jesus by embroiling him in a controversy that relates to the Roman authorities (22:15–22). Should Jews pay taxes to the Romans or not? The Pharisees are opposed to paying such taxes. The Herodians (who are strongly pro-Roman) are in favor. Both groups are opposed to Jesus. Whichever way he replies, Jesus will lose out, either by supporting treason or by supporting the Romans. Jesus takes neither option, evading the trap set for him. He draws attention to the image of Caesar on the coins used to pay the tax. What is Caesar's should be given to Caesar. What is God's should be given to God. As humanity is created in the image of God (Ge 1:26–27), this reply is actually a declaration of the need for people to dedicate themselves to him.

This is followed by a question raised by the Sadducees concerning marriage at the resurrection (22:23–33). In an attempt to trap Jesus into conceding that there is no resurrection, they ask a question, based on marriage in heaven, designed to demonstrate the logical impossibility of resurrection. Jesus points out that because there is no marriage in heaven, their argument falls to the ground. Since the Sadducees are reduced to silence over this, the Pharisees quiz him over which of the commandments in the law is the greatest (22:34–40). This is not specifically a question about the Ten Commandments. The law was generally regarded as having 613 commandments. Jesus was being asked to single one out as being of supreme importance. By bringing together Deuteronomy 6:5 and Leviticus 19:18, Jesus provides a succinct answer to this question—and then puts one of his own to the Pharisees (Mt 22:41–46). As stated, the question has no easy answer, and it reduces Jesus' opponents to silence.

23:1–39 Seven Woes. Jesus continues his controversial ministry in Jerusalem by condemning the religion of his day for its many faults (23:1–39). Particular criticism is directed against the external and formal character of the religion of the Pharisees. All too often, they have become preoccupied with trivial matters and have neglected the great issues of justice and faith. They "strain out a gnat but swallow a camel" (23:24). (The reference here is to the smallest and largest types of unclean creatures.)

24:1–35 Signs of the End of the Age. Jesus now opens the fifth and final section of his teaching. This section focuses on the end of the age (24:1–25:46). This section, which is sometimes referred to as the "Olivet discourse," alerts the disciples to the troubles that lie ahead. The distress and pain that lie in the future are vividly described. Many of these sayings will find at least partial fulfillment in the destruction of Jerusalem by the Roman armies in A.D. 70. This will be a time of betrayal, of persecution, and of false teaching. It is clear, however, that Jesus' ultimate reference is to the end of the world itself, at a time and date that are unknown to all save the Father. Not even the Son knows this (24:36). It will come like a thief in the night (24:42–44)—a saying of Jesus that Paul picks up and uses in 1 Thessalonians 5:2.

24:36–25:13 The Day and Hour Unknown. The sudden coming of the end leads Jesus to place a particular emphasis upon the need for watchfulness. Unlike the householder who was not prepared for the thief who broke into his property, believers must not be taken unawares by the coming of the Lord. This point is made with clarity in the *parable of the ten virgins* (25:1–13), which exhorts its hearers to "keep watch, because you do not know the day or the hour."

25:14–30 The Parable of the Talents. The theme of the return of the Lord is also explored in a different direction in the *parable of the talents* (25:14–30). Attention here focuses on what the servants do during the master's absence. The parable tells of a master who entrusts his *talents* (quantities of silver, which act as money) to his servants during his absence, and of the variety of ways in which the servants make use of that money. The main point being made is that the master will return, without warning, to see what has happened in his absence.

Yet in addition to this, three other points are made by this parable. First, talents are gifts from God. The servants had no claim on the money; it was their master's, entrusted to them during his absence. They were stewards, rather than possessors, of the money. They were responsible for its wise use during the master's absence. Second, God's gifts are given in order to be used. The returning master is furious with the servant who buried his talent and refused to use it. Believers are responsible thus for using these gifts in the world and will be held accountable for the way they are used. And third, God's gifts increase through being used. The parable tells of three servants, two of whom use their talents, and the third who buries it in the ground. This final talent remains unaltered in its hole in the ground. It was not used and therefore did not grow. The two other servants, however, found that the money with which they had been entrusted increased through being used wisely. Faith does not deepen through being allowed to stagnate, but through being applied.

25:31–46 The Sheep and the Goats. This is followed by the *parable of the sheep and the goats,* which develops the theme of judgment. The parable points to the ultimate separation of the good and the wicked, developing the ideas already found in the parable of the weeds (13:24–30; 36–43) and the net (13:47–50). The parable brings out clearly the importance of good works in the Christian life as a mark of true commitment to Christ.

26:1–13 Preparations for Jesus' Death. The pace of the narrative now quickens dramatically. It is two days from the Passover, and Jesus once more foretells his forthcoming crucifixion. In the meantime, arrangements are made by the Jewish authorities for the arrest of Jesus, culminating in Judas Iscariot's decision to go to the chief priests and offer to hand Jesus over to them. Jesus himself is anointed in preparation for burial as this is happening.

26:17–30 The Last Supper. Having hinted at the forthcoming death of Jesus in many ways, Matthew now narrates the events of the Last Supper. This event is a Passover meal, which takes place the evening before the crucifixion. For Jews, the meal acted as a reminder of the great act of deliverance through which God led his people out of Egypt. Jesus celebrates this meal with the twelve disciples.

It is clearly an occasion of great intimacy. Yet Jesus announces that one of them—one of his closest colleagues—will betray him. The disciples are shocked at this, but Jesus insists that this must happen. It has been foretold in Scripture (as in Isa 53:1–12) and so must come to pass. But this does not in any way excuse his betrayer, who is now publicly identified as Judas. (Note how Judas refers to Jesus merely as *Rabbi* or "teacher," while the others refer to him as *Lord*.) Jesus then offers his disciples broken bread as a sign of his soon-to-be-broken body, and wine as a sign of the new covenant to be established through his blood, and through which forgiveness of sins will be possible. By continuing to eat bread and drink wine in remembrance of Jesus Christ, Christians ensure that the full significance of his saving death will never be forgotten.

26:31–46 Peter's Denial; Jesus and the Disciples at Gethsemane. The group then moves to the Mount of Olives, where Jesus explains that in fulfillment of the messianic prophecy of Zechariah 13:7, the disciples will fall away on account of the events that are about to take place (26:31–35). Yet in this moment of darkness and gloom, a ray of light shines. Jesus declares that after he has risen, he will go ahead of the disciples to Galilee. Peter refuses to believe this. No matter what happens, he will stand by his Lord. Yet Jesus gently rebukes him: that night, Peter will deny him three times. The weakness of the disciples immediately becomes apparent when they move on to Gethsemane (26:36–46). Clearly deeply distressed at the knowledge of what lies ahead, Jesus turns to prayer. The disciples just fall asleep.

Jesus' prayer is especially important. He prays that, if possible, "this cup" may be taken from him. In this context, the cup is a symbol of sorrow and suffering. It is clear that the full humanity of Jesus expresses itself in this prayer. He does not want to die. But if God has purposed that he should die, then he will bear its pain. Many commentators see in this prayer evidence that the full weight of human sin is beginning to bear down upon Jesus, cutting him off from his Father. On the cross, he will experience a sense of being totally abandoned by God on account of the burden of human sin. Here in Gethsemane, we can begin to see our sin being transferred to Christ.

26:47–56 Jesus Arrested. Finally, the moment of betrayal arrives. The fact that it has been foretold in no way diminishes its tragedy and pathos. Judas, again greeting Jesus as a mere "Rabbi," betrays him with a sign of love—a kiss. Jesus is resigned to this. Scripture must be fulfilled. Obedient to the will of his Father, here as always, Jesus allows himself to be led away, as his disciples scatter—like sheep whose shepherd has been struck down (26:47–56).

26:57–68 Before the Sanhedrin. Jesus is then dragged before representatives of the Jewish religious establishment. (A religious trial before the high priest will be followed by a civil trial in front of the Roman governor Pontius Pilate.) He is followed, at a safe distance, by Peter. Under Jewish law, two male witnesses were required to secure a conviction of any kind. This poses some problems, for no witnesses are forthcoming. Eventually, two come forward with a somewhat garbled version of some of Jesus' words. It might have been possible to convict him on the basis of this obvious distortion. However, the high priest asks Jesus specifically whether he is "the Christ, the Son of God." In answer to this direct question, Jesus replies in the affirmative. Notice that Jesus himself never himself claims to be the Messiah (which is what the Greek term *Christ* means). But when others realize who he is (as with the disciples at Caesarea Philippi, 16:13–17), or ask him specifically whether he is the Messiah, he admits to being so. The high priest is outraged that anyone should make such claims, and declares that he is guilty of blasphemy. And so anyone doing so would be—unless they were the Messiah and Son of God. The penalty for blasphemy was death. However, with one exception, the Romans had deprived the Sanhedrin (that is, the 71-member supreme Jewish court, consisting of the chief priests, elders, and teachers of the law) of the right to sentence anyone to death. This was a matter for the Roman authorities. And so Jesus is taken to the Romans. They will decide what to do next.

26:69–75 Peter Disowns Jesus. The narrative now switches to Peter, who has been waiting outside in the courtyard, keeping his distance from what is going on inside the house. It is obvious that he is very apprehensive. He is noticed by some of the servants, who challenge him. Hasn't he been with Jesus? Surely he is one of his followers? But Peter denies having anything to do with Jesus—three times. After the third denial, the cock crows, and Peter realizes that he has not only failed Jesus, but that Jesus' prediction of his failure has come true.

It is worth making a comment on the "cock crowing." The Romans divided the night into four watches—evening 6:00–9:00 P.M., "midnight" 9:00–12:00 P.M., "when the cock crows" 12:00 midnight–3:00 A.M., and "dawn" 3:00–6:00 A.M. These four watches are referred to at Mark 13:35. The "cock crowing" may in fact be a reference to the trumpet blast that marked the end of the third watch of the night, rather than to the cry of a cockerel.

27:1–10 Judas Hangs Himself. But Peter's failure is totally overshadowed by that of Judas, who has betrayed Jesus for thirty pieces of silver, in fulfillment of Old Testament prophecy (the prophecy in question seems to bring together both Jer 19:1–13 and Zec 11:12–13). He is burdened down with his guilt and clearly wants to repent and receive forgiveness for what he has done. But the Jewish leaders, who here may be taken as a symbol of Judaism at that time, have no forgiveness to offer. They tell Judas that it is his responsibility. We see in this passage one of the greatest paradoxes of the gospel. Judas, who probably needs forgiveness more than anyone, is the one who brings about the death of the one through whom forgiveness ultimately comes.

27:1–31 Jesus Before Pilate. The narrative now returns to Jesus, who has been brought before Pontius Pilate, Roman governor of Judea A.D. 26–36. Pilate confronts Jesus with the charges brought against him and is amazed when Jesus makes no reply. However, we may see in this the fulfillment of an important Old Testament prophecy: that the suffering messiah would be silent before his accusers (Isa 53:7). Pilate's inclination, which would have been reinforced by his wife's belief in Jesus' innocence, would probably have been to order some token punishment, but take things no further. However, the crowd is whipped up into a frenzy by agitators. They demand that Jesus be crucified.

Pilate, who has the right to release a prisoner at Passover, offers to release either Jesus or a convict named Barabbas. The crowd demands the release of Barabbas and the death of Jesus. Barabbas is thus the first to benefit directly from the death of Christ. He ought to have died. Jesus dies in his place. Washing his hands of the whole affair, Pilate sends Jesus off to be flogged and crucified. Jesus is then humiliated by the Roman soldiers, who dress him up in a caricature of royal costume, including a crown of thorns.

The floggings administered by the Romans were vicious. They had been known to cause the death of victims before they were crucified. Under Jewish law, victims were only allowed to be flogged with forty strokes. This was invariably reduced to 39, as an act of leniency. But under Roman law, there were no limits to the extent of the suffering to be inflicted. The whips used for this purpose generally consisted of several strands of leather with small pieces of metal or broken bones at the end. These tore apart the skin of those being whipped, with the result that many did not survive the ordeal.

27:32–43 The Crucifixion. Jesus, clearly severely weakened by his beating, proves unable to carry his own cross, and Simon from Cyrene is forced to carry it for him. Finally, they reach Golgotha, the place of execution. This place is also often referred to as "Calvary," from the Latin word *Calvaria* meaning "the skull"—the literal meaning of Golgotha. As Jesus hangs on the cross, he is mocked by those watching him die, while the Roman soldiers cast lots for his clothes. These events fulfill the great Old Testament prophecy of the fate of the righteous sufferer of Psalm 22 (see Ps 22:7–8, 18). The identity of Jesus with this sufferer is confirmed by his cry of utter desolation (27:46), which draws upon the opening verse of this important psalm. It is here that Jesus experiences the sense of the absence of God. The sin that he is bearing on behalf of his people has now cut him off from his Father.

27:45–56 The Death and Burial of Jesus. Finally, Jesus dies. Darkness settles over the land, perhaps pointing to the fact that the "light of the world" (Jn 8:12) has been extinguished. A series of events then takes place, pointing to the significance of what has just happened. The opening of the tombs points ahead to the resurrection of Christ. However, the tearing of the "curtain of the temple" is of particular interest. The curtain of the temple was an especially important feature of the Old Testament tabernacle (Ex 26:31–35). It provided a means of restricting access to the "most holy place," the region of the tabernacle that was regarded as sacrosanct. Although the curtain served an important practical function in relation to the worship of Israel, it came to have a deeper significance. The fact that the curtain prevented ordinary worshippers from entering the most holy place came to be seen as pointing to a much deeper separation between God and sinful humanity. The curtain thus came to be a symbol of the barrier placed between God and humanity by human sinfulness. The tearing of this curtain at the crucifixion (27:51) is a symbol of one of the chief benefits brought about by the death of Christ: the barrier between God and humanity caused by sin has been torn down, so that there is now free access for believers to God on account of Christ's death (Ro 5:1–2).

The disciples, we now discover, are nowhere to be found. Matthew carefully identifies some witnesses of the death of Jesus, but not a single disciple is mentioned. It seems that they, like sheep without a shepherd, have scattered—just as Jesus had predicted. The witnesses who are identified are the Roman centurion, who declares that Jesus is the Son of God (27:54)—a vitally important testimony, coming from a Gentile. The chief priest, symbolizing his own Jewish people, has refused to accept that Jesus is the Son of God. Yet here we can see the acceptance of this fact among the Gentiles, anticipating both the mission to the Gentiles, and the enormous appeal which the gospel would prove to have to those outside Judaism. The other witnesses are women. Notice how Matthew names them (27:55–56), so that they will not be forgotten. Finally, Jesus is buried in a borrowed tomb (27:57–61). The women are still there, keeping vigil by the tomb, at the end of this long day—the first Good Friday.

The prophecy of resurrection has not been forgotten, however—at least, not by the Jewish leaders. In order to forestall any attempt on the part of the disciples to steal the body of Christ and thus spread false rumors of his resurrection, they request Pilate to place a guard on the tomb (27:62–66).

28:1–15 The Resurrection. And so we come to the third day—Sunday. In a brief account of the discovery of the empty tomb, we learn that Jesus has risen from the dead and has gone ahead of his disciples to Galilee. The women who were the first to discover the empty tomb are afraid at what has happened (28:1–10). So are the Jewish leaders, who realize the implications of the resurrection: that Jesus, whom they have accused of blasphemy and demanded to be crucified, will have turned out to be the Messiah and their Lord. Rumors are planted to attempt to discredit the resurrection (28:11–15). Yet, as we learn from the other gospels and from Acts, it is all to no avail.

28:16–20 The Great Commission. And so Matthew's gospel comes to its famous conclusion. Even though some disciples continue to doubt that he has been raised from the dead, Jesus reassures them both of the reality of his resurrection, and of his continuing presence until the end of time itself. The Great Commission is entrusted to the disciples: they are to go and make disciples of all nations, reaching out beyond the bounds of Israel to the farthest places of the earth. The fact that you are reading this gospel is a testimony to their effectiveness in doing just that. There is a link between Christian faith today and that Great Commission all those years ago. Believers may preach the gospel with the full authority of the risen Christ, resting assured of his presence and power until he comes again.

MARK

Mark's gospel is the second of the three Synoptic Gospels and is widely regarded as being the first to have been written down. The gospel of Mark is generally accepted to have been written by the John Mark who is known to have accompanied both Peter (1Pe 5:13) and Paul (Ac 12:12, 25). It is thought to have been written in Rome, drawing extensively on the memories of Peter. The vivid details that are such a distinctive feature of this gospel (such as the specific reference to the cushion in the boat at 4:38) and the occasionally critical portrayal of the disciples (as at 8:14–21) are best understood if Peter was the source of the stories in question. For these and other reasons, scholars tend to regard Mark's gospel as the first of the Gospels to be written down, with Matthew and Luke expanding his accounts of the life of Jesus on the basis of additional sources available to them. Peter was executed during the Roman emperor Nero's persecution of the Christians during the period A.D. 64–68, and it is possible that the death of Peter was the stimulus Mark needed to ensure that the gospel was committed to writing.

One of the most noticeable features of the gospel of Mark is its emphasis on the deeds of Jesus, rather than on his teaching. Mark's focus on Jesus' cross, rather than his teachings, gives his gospel a distinctive emphasis. Nevertheless, Mark passes down some major parables and sayings of Jesus.

MARK 1:1 – 6:29

The Galilean Ministry of Jesus

1:1–8 John the Baptist Prepares the Way. Whereas Matthew and Luke provide details of the birth of Jesus, Mark plunges us directly into the events of his ministry, beginning with its background of John the Baptist. The great prophecy of the coming of the Lord to his people is recalled, especially as it points to the coming of someone in advance to prepare his way. We are then introduced immediately to John the Baptist, who is to be seen as fulfilling this Old Testament prophecy. The description of John is significant; there are strong similarities with that of Elijah (2Ki 1:8). Because Elijah was expected to return before the final coming of the Lord to his people (Mal 4:5) in order to prepare the way for this great event, this description has considerable importance. As John himself makes clear, he is only here to prepare the way. Someone greater than himself is coming.

1:9–13 The Baptism and Temptation of Jesus. Although we can guess who he is talking about, Mark then confirms what we suspect. Jesus appears and is baptized by John in the Jordan (1:9). With breathless pace, Mark takes us through the events of Jesus' preparation for ministry. Matthew and Luke provide far greater detail (for example, about the temptation of Jesus, to which Mark devotes only a line). Mark rushes on, as if he is anxious that we should waste no time in discovering who Jesus Christ is and why he is of such great importance.

1:14–20 The Calling of the First Disciples. It seems that the stimulus to the ministry of Jesus is the imprisonment of John the Baptist. Once this has happened, Jesus begins to proclaim the "good news of God." The kingdom of God is drawing near. There is an urgent need to repent. The phrase *kingdom of God* should not be understood in a geographical or territorial sense. It does not refer to an area of land ruled by God, but to the kingly rule of God himself. The first evidence of the breaking through of this kingly rule of God can be seen in the calling of the first disciples. In response to Jesus' call, the disciples leave everything and follow this man. There seems to be something about him which draws them. He has authority, which they obey.

1:21–45 Jesus Drives Out an Evil Spirit and Heals Many. The narrative now moves from Galilee to Capernaum, where the first public recognition of his true identity takes place. The reader already knows that Jesus is the Son of

"They went to Capernaum, and when the Sabbath came, Jesus went into the synagogue and began to teach." This synagogue was built in the third or fourth century A.D., long after Jesus taught in Capernaum, but perhaps on the same spot as the synagogue of Jesus' time.

God (1:1, 11). This fact is now publicly acknowledged by an evil spirit (1:21–28), over whom Jesus clearly has authority. This incident makes a deep impression on those looking on. Quickly, word spreads. Something dramatic is happening. This is confirmed by a series of healings, through which Jesus becomes much sought after (1:29–45). No matter how much Jesus may try to avoid publicity, his name is on everyone's lips.

2:1–12 Jesus Heals a Paralytic. But who is Jesus Christ? And what authority does he possess? This question comes to the fore in the following chapter. What at first seems to be another healing turns out to have major implications for a right understanding of the identity of Jesus. As part of his healing of a paralytic, Jesus declares that the man's sins are forgiven. The teachers of the law are outraged by this. Only God can forgive sins! They accuse Jesus of blasphemy. And, in one sense, they are right to do so. Only God can forgive sins. By claiming this authority, Jesus puts himself in the place of God. But the Christian reader of this passage will notice two things. First, that the man is healed. Jesus clearly possesses the ability to heal—and hence the authority to forgive. And second, the later resurrection of Jesus from the dead affirms that he is indeed the Son of God (Ro 1:3–4) and thus possesses the necessary authority to forgive sin. But at this early stage in his ministry, there is no hint of what is to come. That will soon change—but not yet.

2:13–17 The Calling of Levi. Jesus then adds a tax collector to his inner circle of disciples, to the outrage of the onlookers. (Mark and Luke both refer to the person concerned by his original name, Levi or "Levi son of Alphaeus." In Matthew's account of the same incident, the apostolic name *Matthew* is used.) Tax collectors were widely despised and were regarded as outcasts by their fellows. At this time, the region of Palestine was occupied by the Romans. Not only did the tax collectors associate with the Gentile occupying power, but they also charged more taxes than they were entitled to as a way of ensuring their own well-being. As a result, they were detested by Jews and regarded as traitors. Yet by calling one of them to his inner circle, Jesus demonstrates his acceptance of those regarded as beyond hope of redemption by Judaism, including prostitutes, Gentiles, and tax collectors. Jesus summarizes this with his declaration that he has come to call sinners, not the righteous (2:17). There is unquestionably a strong trace of irony in this declaration. Perhaps those, such as the Pharisees, who think they are righteous are merely self-righteous?

2:18–22 Jesus Questioned About Fasting. The criticism continues. Not only does Jesus call outcasts into his inner circle, but he also does not impose rigorous fasting requirements on them. Jesus responds by pointing out that there is no need for fasting while the bridegroom—an obvious reference to himself—is still among his guests. The glorious new wine of the gospel cannot be contained by the tired old wineskins of Judaism (2:22).

2:23–3:6 Lord of the Sabbath. Yet the criticism goes on relentlessly. The Pharisees criticize Jesus for picking corn on the Sabbath. Jesus retorts that the Son of Man (a reference to himself) has authority over the Sabbath. The clear implication is that the Creator has authority over his creation. In any case, Jesus points out that the Sabbath was ordained for the benefit of people, not the other way around, and cites the example of David to show that his actions have excellent precedents. He also insists that he has a right to heal on the Sabbath, and he challenges any who think otherwise to prove it. There is a long silence. Furious at this, the Pharisees (who are generally nationalistic and anti-Roman in their politics) and the Herodians (who are strongly pro-Roman), who normally have nothing to do with each other, begin to plot to destroy Jesus.

3:7–19 The Appointing of the Twelve Apostles. Yet while they are doing so, the crowds are gathering around Jesus, who is acknowledged as Son of God by the evil spirits over whom he has authority (3:7–12). At this point, Jesus calls to himself twelve disciples (3:13–19), whom he designates as *apostles*—a word that literally means "those who are sent." These twelve are given authority to speak and act in Jesus' name and will play a central role in the ministry of Jesus. Even at this stage, the grim act of future betrayal is noted (3:19). After Judas had betrayed Jesus and committed suicide, he was replaced with Matthias (Ac 1:15–26), thus keeping the number at twelve. Why is this number so important? One possibility is that it picks up the theme of the Twelve Tribes of Israel, with Jesus being the one who will restore the people of God to what God intended them to be.

3:20–35 Jesus and Beelzebub. The question then arises concerning the basis of Jesus' obvious authority. Finding it impossible to deny that such authority exists, his opponents suggest that this authority over demons is grounded in some link with Beelzebub, "the prince of demons." Jesus declares that this is the unforgivable sin—the blasphemy against the Holy Spirit, by which the great acts of God, seen in and through the ministry of Jesus, are attributed to Satan.

4:1–34 A Series of Parables. A series of parables then follows, focusing on the image of seeds. The first in the series is the *parable of the sower* (4:1–20), which draws on the image of a sower scattering seed on the ground as an image of the preaching of the word of God in the world. Jesus notes how it is the same seed that falls onto different kinds of ground. What eventually happens to it depends on the quality of the soil. In the same way, Jesus sows the seed of the word of God through his preaching. The effect it has on people depends on how they respond to it. If someone should fail to respond, or should fall away, it is not on account of any failure on the part of the seed.

The second parable, about *a lamp on a stand*, departs briefly from the theme of seeds and draws on the imagery of light (4:21–25). Just as a lamp is allowed to illuminate a room, so the effects of the gospel are to be felt in the world. The theme of *growing seeds* then returns, allowing two points to be made. First, the absence of any sign of growth does not necessarily mean that the seed has failed to establish itself (4:26–29). The kingdom of God may grow in secret, before its presence becomes visible to the world. Second, a small seed, such as a *mustard seed*, may give rise to a very large plant (4:30–34), just as the kingdom of God will grow from its small beginnings.

4:35–5:20 Jesus' Authority Confirmed. A series of events then takes place in quick succession, confirming Jesus' authority over the natural and supernatural order. In a story packed with fine detail, suggesting that Mark had access to a firsthand account of the incident, we learn of Jesus' authority over the wind and the waves, to the astonishment of his disciples (4:35–41). And in the healing of a man who was possessed by demons (5:1–20), we see once more that evil spirits recognize the identity of Jesus as Son of God and submit to his authority. Once more, amazement and fear mingle among the onlookers, who are stunned by what they see taking place before their eyes.

5:21–43 A Dead Girl and a Sick Woman. Finally, by bringing the young daughter of Jairus, a prominent member of the local synagogue, back to life, Jesus demonstrates that he has authority over death itself (5:21–24, 35–43).

Jesus healed two demon-possessed men in this region east of the Sea of Galilee. The evil spirits from one man moved into a herd of pigs, which ran squealing down the hillside into the lake and were drowned.

Alongside this miracle, we also learn of another healing incident. Jesus heals a woman who had been bleeding for many years and who was widely regarded as being beyond any hope of cure. Yet this is more than an act of healing. It is also an important act of affirmation. The woman would have been regarded as unclean by Jews on account of the discharge of a bodily fluid. Yet Jesus has no hesitation in healing her. What Judaism regards as unclean, Jesus sees as someone worth saving. This is one of the few gospel passages that records—and explains—the precise Aramaic words used by Jesus (another being Mk 7:34).

6:1–13 A Prophet Without Honor; Jesus Sends Out the Twelve. Yet despite all these great happenings and acts of spiritual authority and power, Jesus finds that he is not accepted by his own people (6:1–6). Despite all the signs of spiritual authority and power, the people of Nazareth are dismissive of him and refuse to acknowledge him. Jesus himself is amazed at their lack of faith. Because of their lack of faith, Jesus performs no miracles in his hometown. This points to an important general principle: No faith, no miracles. Faith is the precondition of benefiting from Christ. The faith of the disciples, however, is then affirmed. The Twelve are sent out to preach the gospel, with the result that demons are driven out and the sick healed (6:7–13). This clearly points to faith on the part of both the disciples and those to whom the good news is proclaimed.

6:14–29 John the Baptist Beheaded. The narrative then returns to John the Baptist. In one of the best-known incidents in the Gospels, we learn of the manner in which the daughter of Herodias (named Salome, according to the Jewish historian Josephus) secures the execution of John the Baptist by putting Herod under obligation to her. Her mother Herodias disliked John on account of his opposition to her marriage to Herod. She had left her first husband, Philip, in order to marry his brother, who was Herod himself. John had pointed out that this was strictly against the Law of Moses, thus causing considerable resentment on Herodias's part.

6:30–56 Jesus Feeds the Five Thousand and Walks on the Water. We then return to the ministry of Jesus (6:30–44). After the disciples return from their mission, Jesus attempts to find time to be alone with them. However, the crowds will not allow them to be on their own. The feeding of the five thousand illustrates the huge size of the crowds now following him, as much as it points to the compassion and power of Christ. The

One day, in a remote area, a crowd gathered to hear Jesus. For hours he taught them. Then he fed them all, with only the five loaves of bread and two fish that a boy had with him. Five thousand men plus women and children were fed. This mosaic was found at Tabgha, on the western shore of the Sea of Galilee.

authority of Jesus over the natural order is again emphasized through his walking on the water and the ensuing stilling of the storm (6:45–56). Again, we learn of the huge interest in him, evident in the large crowds that gather everywhere he moves.

This major section of Mark's gospel thus ends by demonstrating the remarkable authority of Jesus. This authority is obvious in his teaching and in his ability to command both the natural and supernatural orders. It is clear that Jesus is someone very special. But is he just a wonder worker? Is he just a great teacher? Or is there something more to Jesus than this? As Mark's gospel continues to unfold, the full significance of his identity begins to emerge.

MARK 7:1 – 10:52

The Later Ministry of Jesus

7:1–23 Clean and Unclean. The relationship of Jesus to the Judaism of his day now comes into focus once more. The issue of ritual cleanliness emerges as important, with the Pharisees protesting against the disciples' failure to observe ritual cleanliness traditions. Jesus argues that the Pharisees are putting human traditions above the word of God. It is not eating food with unwashed hands, but the evil thoughts of the heart, that make a person unclean. Mark emphasizes that Jesus declares all foods to be clean.

7:24–37 The Faith of a Syro-Phoenician Women. This rebuke directed against the traditionalism of the Pharisees is followed by an incident that shows how people outside Judaism (in this case, a Syro-Phoenician woman from the region of Tyre and Sidon) are attracted to Jesus and put their faith in him (7:24–30). The important point of this incident is the reality of the woman's faith. Despite not being a Jew, the woman is able to benefit from Christ. After leaving this region and returning to Galilee, Jesus continues to heal and demonstrate his authority (7:31–37). Nothing that Jesus does silences the crowds, who continue to proclaim his deeds across the country.

8:1–26 The Authority of Jesus Demonstrated and Questioned. The feeding of the four thousand (8:1–10), which is very similar to the earlier account of the feeding of the five thousand, once more points to both the appeal and authority of Jesus. But not everyone is prepared to accept that authority. The Pharisees put him to the test and demand a sign by which this authority can be verified (8:11–13). Jesus refuses to give them any such sign and warns his disciples against the malevolent influence of the Pharisees and the Herodians (8:14–21). A further healing miracle then takes place in which the sight of a blind man is restored (8:22–26).

7:27–30 Peter's Confession of Christ. Jesus and his disciples then press on to the region of Caesarea Philippi. It is here that one of the most important incidents in the ministry of Jesus takes place. This time, however, it is the disciples, rather than Jesus, who are the focus of attention. Jesus asks his disciples the basic question: Who do people say that I am? The disciples report back on the various opinions that they have heard: Jesus is one of the prophets, or John the Baptist come back to life, or perhaps Elijah. But Jesus presses them: What about you? Who do *you* say that I am? This is a vitally important question. Unlike the crowds, the disciples have been with Jesus throughout most of his ministry. They have watched him and listened to him. Now they are being asked what their conclusion is.

Peter speaks for them all when he replies that he believes that Jesus is the Christ (8:27–30). In other words, Jesus is the long-awaited Messiah, who has come to his people. Presumably anxious that the title *Christ* or "Messiah" might be understood in a purely political sense, Jesus asks the disciples not to tell anyone of their realization of his true identity. The Messiah could too easily be misunderstood as a triumphalist political leader, concerned only to liberate the country from its Roman occupying force.

8:31–9:1 Jesus Predicts His Death. But it is clear that the disciples themselves also have misunderstandings concerning Jesus. Immediately after their confession that he is the Messiah, Jesus declares that he must go to Jerusalem, suffer, be rejected, be put to death, and finally rise from the dead. It is an integral part of his calling. He must do it. But the disciples cannot cope with this. It was no part of their traditional view of the Messiah that he should suffer—and die. Peter protests against what Jesus tells them and is rebuked by Jesus. It is clear that the cross is going to be a major theme in Mark's account of the ministry of Jesus.

9:2–13 The Transfiguration. Yet an important anticipation of the resurrection now follows. The account of the Transfiguration demonstrates the continuity of Jesus with the ministries of Moses and Elijah, while at the same time providing an anticipation of the resurrection glory of Christ. An endorsement of Jesus' identity and authority from heaven confirms his ministry and mission. Notice the reaction of the disciples: they are frightened (9:6). Precisely this same emotion is aroused by the Resurrection itself (16:8), of which the Transfiguration is a foretaste.

9:14–32 The Healing of a Boy With an Evil Spirit. After a further demonstration of the power of Jesus over evil spirits (9:14–29), the theme of the coming suffering of Jesus reappears (9:30–32). The disciples continue to be bewildered by this prediction. It does not accord with their expectations of what the Messiah will be like. The Messiah was expected to be a figure of triumph, not suffering. Yet Jesus makes it clear that the forthcoming triumph of the Resurrection can only take place through the cross.

It must also be appreciated that the references to Jesus "rising" would have been incomprehensible to the disciples. It is easy to suppose that the disciples were accustomed to the idea of resurrection. In fact, however, neither of the two main Jewish beliefs about it of the period bear any resemblance to the resurrection of Jesus. The Sadducees denied the idea of a resurrection altogether (a fact that Paul was able to exploit at an awkward moment [Ac 23:6–8]). But the majority expectation was of a general resurrection on the last day, at the end of history itself. The resurrection of Jesus simply did not conform to contemporary expectations. The disciples would probably have interpreted Jesus' words as referring to his final resurrection on the last day—not to his resurrection in history. That would have been incomprehensible. We have gotten used to the idea of Jesus' resurrection, but we need to appreciate how difficult it would have been for the disciples to take this idea in at the time.

9:33–50 Status, Temptation, and Being Like Salt. A section of teaching then opens. After noting the unimportance of matters of status and the importance of servant leadership (9:33–41), Jesus deals with the problem of sin and the need to be alert to the issue of temptation (9:42–49). Care should be taken to avoid temptation in one's own life, as well as to avoid causing others to stumble through temptation. The disciples are said to be like salt, in that they can bring a new quality to the world (9:50). Perhaps with rock salt in mind (where water could easily wash out the salt, leaving only rock behind), Jesus stresses how easily believers can lose their "saltiness" unless they take care to preserve it.

10:1–31 Teaching and Healing in Judea. After this, Jesus undertakes a teaching and healing ministry in the region of Judea. Part of that teaching ministry includes clarification of Moses' teaching concerning divorce (10:1–12) and an important affirmation of young children (10:13–16). This is followed by a meeting with a rich young man (10:17–31), in which the question of the conditions for salvation are discussed. After discovering that the young man has faithfully kept the commandments, Jesus asks him to sell all he has and follow him. This dismays the young man, who departs with great sadness.

Notice that Jesus does not make any attempt to compromise his position. It is difficult for someone who is rich to enter the kingdom of God, as the famous comparison between the rich man entering the kingdom of God and the camel passing through the eye of a needle makes clear. But Jesus does not say that it is *impossible*. It is clear that wealth poses a real obstacle to coming to God. Nevertheless, as Jesus makes clear, with God anything is possible. Nobody lies outside the saving purposes of God, who has promised salvation to those who put their faith in Jesus Christ.

10:32–34 Jesus Again Predicts His Death. Readers are then reminded once more of the high price of salvation, as Jesus once more predicts his betrayal, suffering, and resurrection. These words remind us once more that Jesus' death is no accident. It is something that has been purposed and foretold.

Jesus dies because he has to die—there is no other way in which sinful humanity can be redeemed. The crucifixion has to happen. This is the third prediction of his passion in Mark's gospel.

10:35–52 The Request of James and John; the Healing of Blind Bartimaeus. This prediction of suffering and death is followed by a deeply moving declaration on the part of Jesus. In response to a petty squabble among the disciples over who is the greatest, Jesus points out that rank in the kingdom of God is determined by God and is gained through the suffering he is about to undergo himself. Jesus also affirms the importance of servant leadership. He has come to serve and to give his life as a ransom for many (10:35–45). The word *ransom* indicates a payment made by which freedom is gained. Through the death of Jesus Christ, believers are liberated from bondage to sin. Secular rulers may lord it over people. Christian leaders, however, are to serve their people as Christ served before them. The compassion of Jesus in his ministry is then further demonstrated by his healing of a blind man. Although physically blind, he is possessed of spiritual sight; he immediately acknowledges Jesus as the son of David (10:46–52).

Throughout this, Jesus and the disciples have been drawing nearer and nearer to Jerusalem—the city in which Jesus predicted that his own betrayal and death would take place. The healing of the blind man took place at Jericho, a mere twenty kilometers from Jerusalem. The entry into Jerusalem, with all that this implies, is now imminent.

MARK 11:1 – 16:8

The Passion, Death, and Resurrection of Jesus

11:1–11 The Triumphal Entry. Jesus now prepares to enter the great city itself (11:1–1). Jesus enters in humility, mounted on a donkey, in fulfillment of a great messianic prophecy of the Old Testament (Zec 9:9). Jesus enters Jerusalem as its king, an event especially celebrated by Christians on Palm Sunday. It is clear that there were many who were looking forward to this event. He is greeted by crowds, who honor him and sing his praises. However, Mark makes it clear that Jesus is concerned about the temple. Immediately after the entry into Jerusalem, Jesus goes to the temple and examines it (11:11). Nothing happens that evening, however. Jesus is tired and goes on to Bethany, about three kilometers away. But on the next day, the action begins.

11:12–25 Jesus Clears the Temple; the Withered Fig Tree. A hint of the origins of Jesus' anger against the temple may possibly be gained from the incident of the fig tree (11:12–14). As he walks from Bethany to Jerusalem, Jesus sees a fig tree that gives the impression of being in fruit but, on closer inspection, turns out not to be so. Perhaps we can see in this incident the grounds of Jesus' anger against the temple. The tree that is meant to bear fruit has only borne leaves. The temple, which is meant to be a house of prayer for all nations—pointing to the coming of the good news of God to the Gentiles—has degenerated into a symbol of Jewish nationalism and religious privilege.

Entering the temple, Jesus ejects the merchants and overturns the tables of the moneychangers and sellers of doves (11:15–17). The protest is probably only partly against the commercialization of the temple areas. It almost certainly represents Jesus' anger that any form of payment or purchase is necessary before an individual may worship God. But at a deeper level, we may see Jesus proclaiming the failure of Israel to bring the good news of her God to the world—a point affirmed by the citation of Isaiah 56:7. As Jesus and the disciples return to Bethany that evening, they notice that the fig tree has withered (11:20–25), just as Israel has withered spiritually by failing in her responsibilities.

11:27–12:12 The Authority of Jesus Questioned. Controversy now develops with increasing intensity. Once more the authority of Jesus is questioned by his critics (11:27–33), who prove unable to give an adequate response to Jesus' challenge to them. The *parable of the tenants* (12:1–12) illustrates the way Judaism had rejected the prophets of God, and it is a prediction of the way they will also reject the Son of God. The killing of the son reminds us of Jesus' predictions of his own death in Jerusalem.

12:13–17 Paying Taxes to Caesar. Jesus then addresses some controversial questions raised by the Pharisees and Sadducees, who attempt to trap him into making incautious remarks. An initial attempt is made by the Pharisees to trap Jesus by involving him in a long-standing controversy that relates to the Roman authorities. Should Jews pay taxes to the Romans or not? The Pharisees are opposed to paying such taxes. The Herodians (who are strongly pro-Roman) are in favor. Both groups are opposed to Jesus. Jesus will either end up supporting treason or supporting the Romans—either of which will result in his being discredited in the eyes of many and in his possible arrest for sedition.

Jesus takes neither option, evading the trap set for him. He draws attention to the image of Caesar on the coins used to pay the tax. What is Caesar's should be given to Caesar. What is God's should be given to God. As humanity is created in the image of God (Ge 1:26–27), this reply is actually a declaration of the need for people to dedicate themselves to him.

12:18–27 Marriage at the Resurrection. This is followed by a question raised by the Sadducees, who do not believe in the resurrection, concerning marriage at the resurrection. They attempt to trap Jesus into conceding that there are insuperable logical difficulties associated with the idea of a resurrection. The question focuses on marriage in heaven, raising the issue of what happens to a woman with many husbands. Jesus points out that since there is no marriage in heaven, their argument falls to the ground.

12:28–34 The Greatest Commandment. Jesus is then challenged by one of the teachers of the law over the issue of which of the commandments in the law is the greatest. It should be appreciated that this is not a question about the Ten Commandments, but about the much larger range of commands contained in the Law of Moses. The law was generally regarded as having 613 commandments. Jesus is being asked to name the one that is of supreme importance. In his famous answer, Jesus combines Deuteronomy 6:5 and Leviticus 19:18, to provide a brilliant statement of the fundamental purpose and goal of the Old Testament law.

12:35–44 Whose Son Is the Christ? The Widow's Offering. Having met the challenges of his opponents, Jesus then puts a question of his own to the Pharisees (12:35–40). The question focuses on the interpretation of one of the messianic psalms (Ps 110) and proves to be unanswerable. Having baffled his opponents, Jesus then criticizes the teachers of the law for their all too human weaknesses—in contrast with a poor widow, who is highly praised for her generosity and selflessness (12:41–44). The widow places two "very small copper coins" in the chests that are along the walls of the Court of the Women. The point Jesus makes is simple, yet fundamental: the woman, although giving little, nevertheless gave "all she had."

13:1–31 Signs of the End of the Age. Jesus continues his ministry in Jerusalem by focusing on the end of the age. This section, which is sometimes referred to as the "Olivet discourse," alerts the disciples to the troubles that lie ahead. The future distress and pain are vividly described. Many of these sayings will find at least partial fulfillment in the destruction of Jerusalem by the Roman armies in A.D. 70. This will be a time of betrayal, of persecution, and of false teaching. It is clear, however, that Jesus' ultimate reference is to the end of the world itself, at a time and date unknown to all save the Father. Not even the Son knows this (13:32). The sudden coming of the end leads Jesus to place a particular emphasis on the need for watchfulness.

14:1–26 Jesus Anointed at Bethany; the Lord's Supper. It is only two days from the Passover, and Jesus once more foretells his forthcoming crucifixion. As this is happening, Jesus is anointed by an unnamed woman in preparation for burial (14:1–11). The disciples are outraged at the extravagance of this gesture. Jesus, however, rebukes them. The woman's action will be remembered wherever the gospel is preached. As Judas prepares to betray Jesus—the first indication we have had that this predicted action is about to take place—Jesus returns to the theme of remembrance, as he celebrates a Passover meal with his disciples (14:12–26).

Having hinted at the forthcoming death of Jesus in many ways, Mark now presents his account of the Last Supper. This is a Passover meal, which takes place the evening before the crucifixion. For Jews, the Passover meal was a reminder of the great act of deliverance through which God led his people out of Egypt (see Ex 12:42-49). Jesus celebrates this meal with the twelve disciples in an upper room, which has been prepared for them in advance. To the dismay of the disciples, Jesus declares that one of them— one of his closest colleagues—will betray him. This must happen. It has been foretold in Scripture (as in Isa 53:1–12) and so must come to pass. But this does not in any way excuse his betrayer.

Jesus then turns to the theme of remembrance. The Passover meal included both bread and wine. Jesus now gives a new meaning to each of these two elements. The bread is declared to be his body, and the wine his "blood of the new covenant, which is poured out for many." There is a clear reference here to Jesus' earlier declaration that he will give his "life as a ransom for many" (10:45). This passage is rich in allusions to the establishment of the covenant between God and Israel at Sinai, and it points to the establishment of a new covenant between God and his people through the death of Christ.

14:27–42 Jesus Predicts Peter's Denial; Gethsemane. The group then moves to the Mount of Olives, where Jesus predicts that the disciples will fall away on account of the events that are about to take place, in fulfillment of the messianic prophecy of Zechariah 13:7 (14:27–31). Peter refuses to believe this. No matter what happens, he will stand by his Lord. Yet Jesus gently

This hill outside the old city of Jerusalem is the Mount of Olives, where Jesus and his disciples went after they had eaten the Last Supper. It is where Jesus predicted that all of his disciples would leave him, even deny knowing him. The Garden of Gethsemane, where Jesus went to pray that night, is at the foot of the hill.

rebukes him: that night, Peter will deny him three times. The weakness of the disciples immediately becomes apparent when they move on to Gethsemane (14:32–42). Clearly deeply distressed at the knowledge of what lies ahead, Jesus turns to prayer. He asks his disciples to keep watch; however, they fall asleep. They lack the physical strength to stay awake.

Jesus' prayer is especially important. The intimacy of the prayer is evident from the use of the word *Abba* (14:36), an Aramaic word for "Father" found only at this one point in the Synoptic Gospels. Jesus prays that, if possible, "this cup" may be taken from him. In this context, the cup is a symbol of sorrow and suffering. It is clear that the full humanity of Jesus expresses itself in this prayer. He does not want to die. But if God has purposed that he should die, then he will bear its pain. Many commentators see in this prayer evidence that the full weight of human sin is beginning to bear down upon Jesus, cutting him off from his Father. On the cross, he will experience a sense of being totally abandoned by God on account of the burden of human sin. Here in Gethsemane, we can begin to see our sin being transferred to Christ.

14:43–52 Jesus Arrested. Finally, the moment of betrayal arrives. The fact that it has been foretold in no way diminishes its tragedy and pathos. Judas, greeting Jesus as a mere "Rabbi," betrays him with a sign of love—a kiss. Jesus is resigned to this. Scripture must be fulfilled. Obedient to the will of his Father, here as always, Jesus allows himself to be led away as his disciples scatter. The tantalizing reference to a young man who flees naked from the scene is seen by some commentators as a possible reference to Mark himself, who may well have been present at the scene of betrayal.

14:53–65 Before the Sanhedrin. Jesus is then forcibly taken before the Sanhedrin (that is, the 71-member supreme Jewish court, consisting of the chief priests, elders, and teachers of the law), representing the Jewish religious establishment. This religious trial before the high priest would be followed by a civil trial in front of the Roman governor Pontius Pilate, if this proved necessary. Under Jewish law, two male witnesses were required to secure a conviction of any kind. This poses some problems, for no consistent witnesses against him are forthcoming. Eventually, two come forward with a distorted version of some of Jesus' words. It might have been possible to convict him on the basis of this obvious misrepresentation. The high priest asks Jesus to respond to these vague accusations and is amazed when Jesus makes no reply. However, we may see in this the fulfillment of an important Old Testament prophecy: that the suffering Messiah would be silent before his accusers (Isa 53:7).

However, the high priest then asks Jesus specifically whether he is "the Christ, the Son of the Blessed One." In answer to this direct question, Jesus replies in the affirmative. Notice that Jesus himself never claims to be the

Messiah (which is what the Greek term *Christ* means). But when others realize who he is (as with the disciples at Caesarea Philippi, Mt 16:13–17), or ask him specifically whether he is the Messiah, he admits to being so. The high priest, outraged that anyone should make such claims, declares that he is guilty of blasphemy. And so would anyone doing so be—unless they *were* the Messiah and Son of God. The penalty for blasphemy was death. However, with one exception, the Romans had deprived the Sanhedrin of the right to sentence anyone to death. This was therefore a matter for the Roman authorities.

14:66–72 Peter Disowns Jesus. The narrative now switches to Peter, who has been waiting outside in the courtyard, keeping his distance from what is going on inside the house. He is noticed by one of the servant girls, who challenges him. Hasn't he been with that Nazarene Jesus? Surely he is one of his followers? But Peter denies having anything to do with Jesus—three times. After the third denial, the cock crows and Peter realizes that he has not only failed Jesus, but that Jesus' prediction of his failure has come true. He breaks down and weeps.

The reference to the cock crowing is important. The Romans divided the night into four "watches"—evening, 6:00–9:00 P.M.; midnight, 9:00–12:00 P.M.; "when the cock crows," 12:00–3:00 A.M.; and dawn, 3:00–6:00 A.M. These four watches are referred to earlier in this gospel (13:35). The cock crowing may, in fact, be a reference to the trumpet blast that marked the end of the third watch of the night, rather than to the cry of a cockerel. Although some versions of the text of Mark make reference to the cock crowing twice, many early manuscripts refer to it only as crowing once.

15:1–32 Pilate and the Crucifixion of Jesus. The narrative now returns to Jesus. It is early in the morning of the Friday that is to prove to be the last day of Jesus' life. The Sanhedrin finally reaches its decision and hands Jesus over to Pontius Pilate, Roman governor of Judea from A.D. 26 to 36. Pilate confronts Jesus with the charges brought against him. Initially, he demands to know if Jesus is the "king of the Jews." Pilate's interest in this question was probably political. If Jesus had been making any kind of claims to be a Jewish king, it would probably have amounted to an open call to the Jews to rebel against Rome. Pilate then turns to the specifically religious charges brought against Jesus by the chief priests. To his amazement, Jesus refuses to respond to these accusations. Again, we may see in this the fulfillment of the crucial Old Testament prophecy that the Messiah would be silent before his accusers (Isa 53:7). It is clear that Pilate can find nothing about Jesus that merits the death penalty. However, he is placed under enormous pressure by the crowd, who insist upon his crucifixion.

Pilate has the right to release a prisoner at Passover. He offers to release either Jesus or a convict named Barabbas. The crowd demands the release

of Barabbas and the death of Jesus. Barabbas is thus the first to benefit directly from the death of Christ. He ought to have died, but Jesus died in his place. Pilate sends Jesus off to be flogged and crucified. Jesus is then humiliated by the Roman soldiers, who dress him up in a caricature of royal costume, including a crown of thorns. He is ritually humiliated as the "king of the Jews" (15:16–20), a title that will also be included in the charge against him, which would have been written on a wooden board and placed above his head on the cross.

This is Gordon's Calvary, the site some believe is where Jesus was crucified because the rocks vaguely resemble a skull. "Golgotha" is from the Hebrew, and "Calvary" from the Latin word for "the skull." The site is shown in the model of Jerusalem in the photo on the left. The Garden Tomb, an alternate burial site, is nearby. Church of the Holy Sepulchre stands on the traditional site of the Tomb.

The floggings administered by the Romans were vicious; they had been known to cause the death of victims before they were crucified. Jesus, severely weakened by his beating, proves unable to carry his own cross; and Simon of Cyrene is forced to carry it for him. Finally, they reach Golgotha, the place of execution. This place is also often referred to as "Calvary," from the Latin word *Calvaria* meaning "the skull"—the literal meaning of *Golgotha*. As Jesus hangs on the cross, he is mocked by those watching him die, while the Roman soldiers cast lots for his clothes. These events fulfill the great Old Testament prophecy of the fate of the righteous sufferer of Psalm 22 (see Ps 22:7–8, 18). The identity of Jesus with this sufferer is confirmed by his cry of utter desolation (15:34), which draws upon the opening verse of this important psalm. It is here that Jesus experiences the sense of the absence of God. The sin that he is bearing on behalf of his people has now cut him off from his Father. The crowds around Jesus demand that he come down from the cross and save himself. However, he remains there and saves sinful humanity instead (15:21–32).

15:33–41 The Death of Jesus. Finally, Jesus dies. Darkness settles over the land, perhaps pointing to the fact that the "light of the world" (Jn 8:12) has been extinguished. The "curtain of the temple" is torn from top to bottom, an event with important significance in the light of the saving significance of the death of Christ. The curtain of the temple was an important feature of the Old Testament tabernacle (Ex 26:31–35). It was included in order to provide a means of restricting access to the "most holy place," the region of the tabernacle that was regarded as sacrosanct. Although the curtain served a practical function in relation to the worship of Israel, it came to have a deeper significance. The fact that the curtain prevented ordinary worshippers from entering the most holy place came to be seen as pointing to a much deeper separation between God and sinful humanity. The curtain thus came to be a symbol of the barrier placed between God and humanity by human sinfulness. The tearing of this curtain at the crucifixion is a symbol of one of the chief benefits brought about by the death of Christ. The barrier between God and humanity caused by sin has been torn down, so that for believers, there is now free access to God on account of Christ's death (Rom 5:1–2).

Mark now draws our attention to the testimony of the Roman centurion, who declares that Jesus is the "Son of God" (15:39)—a vitally important testimony, coming from a Gentile. As Mark's gospel is often thought to have been written in Rome (notice, for example, the reference to the "Praetorium" at 15:16), the importance of the testimony of this Roman officer would have been of special relevance to his intended readership.

15:42–47 The Burial of Jesus. Mark also draws our attention to the role of three women: Mary Magdalene, Mary the mother of James and Jesus, and Salome (15:40–41). Although the disciples are nowhere to be seen, the women remain as witnesses to the death of Christ—just as these same women would be the first witnesses to the Resurrection. Finally, Jesus is buried in a borrowed tomb (15:42–47). The disciples are not mentioned. The burial arrangements are made by a prominent Jewish religious leader, Joseph of Arimathea, who is clearly sympathetic toward Jesus. Two of the three women are still there, keeping vigil by the tomb, at the end of this long day—the first Good Friday.

16:1–8 The Resurrection. Early on the morning of the following Sunday, the three women go once more to anoint the body of Jesus at the tomb. The previous day had been the Sabbath, on which such activity would have been disallowed. Once more, there is no mention of the disciples, who are clearly totally demoralized. As they draw near to the tomb, the women realize that it is empty and learn that Jesus has been raised. Terrified, they run away (16:1–8).

It should be noted that all four gospels attribute the discovery of the empty tomb to women. The only Easter event to be explicitly related in detail by all four of the gospel writers is the visit of the women to the tomb of Jesus. Mark tells us the names of these women witnesses—Mary Magdalene, Mary the mother of James, and Salome—three times (Mk 15:40, 47; 16:1). Yet Judaism dismissed the value of the testimony or witness of women, regarding only men as having significant legal status in this respect. The greatest news the world has ever known is thus first disclosed to people whose status as witnesses was negligible! This point is of considerable importance in relation to the historical reliability of the Gospels. Would anyone invent a story in which its climax was first witnessed by people whose testimony would carry so little weight at the time? Yet the Gospels have no hesitation in reporting the facts as they were, without doctoring them to make them more acceptable and credible.

16:9–20 Ending of the Gospel According to Later Manuscripts. At this point, Mark's gospel breaks off. Some later versions of the text include the section 16:9–20, which relates the appearance of Jesus to his disciples and includes, at 16:12, a reference to the incident on the road to Emmaus (described in detail at Lk 24:13–35). But most scholars are agreed that the text ends at 16:8. The women are terrified at their discovery. What can it mean? Just as the disciples were terrified at the Transfiguration, so the Resurrection initially evokes fear. That will give way to joy—but only once the full reality of what has happened has been appreciated.

LUKE

Luke, the third of the Synoptic Gospels, is the first part of a two-part work, the second being the Acts of the Apostles. Taken together, these two works constitute the largest piece of writing in the New Testament. Both works are dedicated to a man named Theophilus (literally meaning "a lover of God"), who may well have been a wealthy and influential Christian sympathizer at Rome. Luke himself was probably a Gentile by birth, with an outstanding command of written Greek. He was a physician and was the traveling companion of Paul at various points during his career. Luke's gospel has clearly been written with the interests and needs of non-Jewish readers in mind, apparently with a special concern to bring out the relevance of the "good news" for the poor, oppressed, and needy.

It is not clear when Luke's gospel was written. The abrupt ending of the account of Paul's imprisonment in the Acts of the Apostles suggests an early date for the two-part work, such as some time in the period 59–63. However, many scholars argue that Luke draws on Mark's gospel at points, suggesting that the third gospel is to be dated later than the second, and pointing to the 70s as a possible time of writing.

LUKE 1:1 – 2:52

The Birth of Jesus Christ

1:1–4 Introduction. Luke opens his gospel by setting out his intention of giving as accurate as possible an account of the events that lie behind the Christian gospel, drawing on eye-witness accounts. The same method will be used in Acts; reliable sources are checked out and brought together to create a coherent account of both the foundations and the subsequent spread of the Christian gospel.

1:5–25 The Birth of John the Baptist. Luke, drawing on sources not available to the other Evangelists (as the writers of the Gospels are known), then provides us with detailed information concerning the birth of John the Baptist (1:5–25). John is born into a priestly family. There are clear similarities between the situation of Zechariah and Elizabeth and that of Elkanah and Hannah (see 1Sa 1:1–2:11). In each case, a child, born through the providence of God, becomes a prophet. There are also similarities between John the Baptist and the prophet Samuel. For example, both take Nazirite vows of obedience, which include a vow to abstain from alcohol (Nu 6:1–4; Jdg 13:4–7; 1Sa 1:11).

Even before he is born, John is thus marked out as a special figure within the providence of God. He will be like Elijah (1:17) and go before the Lord to prepare his way. The Old Testament prophet Malachi had declared that the Lord would send the prophet Elijah to prepare the way for his coming (Mal 4:5–6). So if Elijah should come again, a great day would be about to dawn in which the Lord would come to his people with judgment and salvation. Thus, even at this early stage, we have a strong indication that the coming of the Lord to his people is not that far away.

1:26–45 Jesus' Birth Foretold; Mary Visits Elizabeth. This is confirmed shortly afterward by the visit of the angel Gabriel to Mary, in which he announces that she will bear a child (1:26–38). In a message that brings together many of the great messianic hopes of the Old Testament, the angel tells Mary that she has found favor in the sight of God and will bear a son who is to be named Jesus. He will stand in succession to David as the ruler of his people. Though Mary is a virgin, she will have a child through the power of the Holy Spirit. Mary then visits her relative Elizabeth, and they share the news of all that has happened to them both (1:39–45). From what follows (1:56), it is clear that Mary remains with Elizabeth until the ninth month—that is, until the birth of John.

1:46–56 Mary's Song. In the great song of praise which follows, Mary expresses her joy at the news she has had and all that it will mean for Israel (1:46–55). The song, often referred to as the *Magnificat* (from its opening word in the standard Latin translation of the text), bears a strong resemblance to the great song of praise of Hannah, as she exulted in the knowledge that she would bear a child (1Sa 2:1–10). Mary's song dwells on the great faithfulness of God to his people and on his mercy and favor to those who, like her, are humble and meek. It is clear that a great act of divine deliverance lies at hand.

1:57–66 The Birth of John the Baptist. This sense of anticipation is heightened by the birth of John the Baptist and the realization on the part of the people that the hand of the Lord is upon him. In his song, which celebrates the birth of his son, Zechariah proclaims the great faithfulness of God to his people (1:67–80). The song—often referred to as the *Benedictus* (from the opening word of the standard Latin translation of the text)—declares that, in his great faithfulness to his people, the Lord God of Israel has raised up a new hope of salvation within his people. His son, John, will go before the Lord to prepare the way for his coming. Salvation and forgiveness are near at hand.

The city of Bethle-
hem, in the Judean
hills, as it looks
today.

This aerial view
shows Manger
Square, built on the
place according to
tradition where Jesus
was born. Mary and
Joseph had traveled
the hundred miles
from Nazareth
because a census
was being taken. But
Bethlehem also ful-
fills the prophecy of
Micah from many
centuries before.

2:1–20 *The Birth of Jesus.* Luke now leads directly into the climax of these first two chapters: the birth of Jesus himself. The section opens by relating the events of salvation history to those of world history (2:1–7). Luke dates the birth of Jesus with reference to the reigns of two figures. First, it took place during the time of Caesar Augustus, the first Roman emperor, whose reign spanned the period 31 B.C.–A.D. 14. Second, it occurred during the governorship of Quirinius in Syria. This is slightly more difficult to date, with a range of dates a few years before and after A.D. 1 being suggested. At this time, a census was held, presumably for taxation purposes, as a result of which Joseph and Mary went to the royal city of Bethlehem. While they were there, Jesus was born. The action of the imperial authorities thus led to the fulfillment of the great messianic prophecy of Micah 5:2. Traditionally, the site of his birth has been identified as a stable on the basis of the reference to a "manger" (2:7), which is basically a feeding trough for animals.

The narrative now shifts to a group of shepherds in nearby fields at night (2:8–20). An angel declares the birth of a Savior, who is Christ the

Lord. Luke's Greek text is quite complex at this point, and it is probably best interpreted as follows: a child has been born, who at one and the same time is Savior, Messiah, and Lord. In other words, the angel is proclaiming that one who will save his people, who is the long awaited Messiah, and who is Lord, has been born. As a result, they go and find the newborn child and spread the word of his birth.

2:21–40 Jesus Presented in the Temple. The child is named Jesus, in obedience to the message of the angel to Mary (2:21–24). In obedience to the law of Moses, he is circumcised, and, as the firstborn male of the family, is dedicated to the Lord. Mary offers a sacrifice for her purification after the interval of forty days specified by the law is complete (Lev 12:2–8). The sacrifice in question is that specified for the poorest of people, pointing to the state of poverty in which Mary and Joseph live.

Two incidents now take place that further confirm the spiritual significance of the child Jesus. Simeon, who has been granted a special gift of discernment through the Holy Spirit, recognizes Jesus as the coming Messiah (2:25–35). His song of praise, often referred to as the *Nunc Dimittis* (from its opening words in the standard Latin translation of the text), speaks of the Lord finally allowing him to see the coming of salvation to Israel, for both the glorification of God's people and the revelation of God to the Gentiles. This is followed by an encounter with the prophetess Anna (2:36–40), who proclaims the significance of Jesus to "all who were looking forward to the redemption of Jerusalem."

2:41–52 The Boy Jesus at the Temple. This section of Luke's gospel concludes with an account of how Mary and Joseph lose Jesus during a visit to the temple some twelve years later (2:41–50). The story, which is told from the perspective of Mary and Joseph, reflects their bewilderment at Jesus' wisdom and his statement that he had to be in his Father's house. Only later will the full significance of this statement become clear. This pattern is encountered throughout the Gospels. Jesus' words and deeds often only assume their full significance and meaning in the light of his cross and resurrection—for example, his comments about the rebuilding of the temple (Jn 2:19–22) and his prediction of his own betrayal and death (Mk 9:31–32). Yet even at this early stage, the clues are there for those with the wisdom to see them.

So where does Luke get all this information? Who is his source? The most obvious source is Mary herself, who would have been an eyewitness to much of what we read about in this section. The remarks that Mary "treasured up all these things and pondered them in her heart" (2:19) and that she "treasured all these things in her heart" (2:51) are a clear hint that Mary committed everything to memory, and that Luke has drawn upon her memories in compiling these two opening chapters of his narrative. Where

Matthew tends to tell the story of the birth and early life of Jesus from Joseph's point of view, Luke relates it from Mary's.

LUKE 3:1 – 9:62 ─────────────────────────────

Jesus' Ministry in Galilee

3:1–20 John the Baptist Prepares the Way. Luke once more takes care to relate the events of salvation history to those of world history. Following the tradition of ancient historians, including those of the Old Testament, the opening of the ministry of Jesus Christ is dated with reference to the years of the reign of regional and international rulers (3:1–2). Some of these are relatively easy to date. Pontius Pilate was Roman governor (or, more strictly, procurator) of Judea in A.D. 26–36. The "fifteenth year of the reign of Tiberias" can be dated to the period A.D. 28–29. Other dates are more difficult to fix, due to the imprecision of our knowledge concerning the people involved. Although they would be well known to Luke's readers, whether Jews or Gentiles, there is now some difficulty in ascertaining the dates with certainty. Nevertheless, it is clear that Jesus' ministry begins, according to Luke, just before A.D. 30. Luke later notes that Jesus was "about thirty years old" when he began his ministry (3:23).

This ministry begins with an encounter with John the Baptist. Luke provides a substantial degree of background information concerning John (3:3–20). It is obvious that John creates a sensation, with crowds streaming out into the deserts to hear him speak. John is recognized as the forerunner of the Messiah; indeed, there is even a suggestion—which John is quick to refute—that he himself might be that Messiah (3:15–17; the Greek word *Christ* means "Messiah"). In fulfillment of Old Testament prophecy, John comes as the one who was promised to "prepare the way for the Lord" (3:4, citing Isa 40:3 and Mal 3:1). John sees his role as preparing the way for someone greater than himself. John can only baptize with water; the one who is to come will baptize with the Holy Spirit (3:16). In an aside, Luke then informs us of what will later happen to John as a result of his criticism of Herod's seduction of Herodias, his brother's wife (19–20).

3:21–38 The Baptism and Genealogy of Jesus. Luke then tells us that Jesus was among those who were baptized by John (3:21–22). When he is baptized, a voice from heaven affirms the identity of Jesus as the Son of God in fulfillment of the great messianic hope set out in Psalm 2:7. Jesus does not *become* the Son of God at his baptism. God confirms what is already the case. Yet although Jesus is in reality the Son of God, Luke points out that most people just think of him as the son of Joseph.

In his genealogy of Jesus, Luke makes the point that Jesus traces his descent from Adam, not just from Abraham (3:23–28). Where Matthew stresses the Jewish origins of Jesus, Luke points to his wider significance for the human race as a whole. While not in any way denying Jesus' special importance for Judaism, Luke wants to bring out his universal significance. There are differences between the genealogies presented here and in Matthew's gospel (Mt 1:2–16). The differences in the genealogies from David onwards are best explained on the basis of the assumption that Matthew traces Jesus' descent after David through Joseph, whereas Luke's preference is to trace it after David through Mary. As we noted earlier, this corresponds with Luke's particular interest in Mary, and Matthew's in Joseph.

4:1–13 The Temptation of Jesus. Just as Israel spent forty years in the wilderness being tested and prepared for their final entry into the promised land, so Luke tells us how Jesus is prepared for his mission to Israel through his temptation—a period of forty days and nights in the wilderness in which Jesus confronts and successfully resists temptation. The testing centers on whether Jesus will use his power and authority as the Son of God for his own advantage or for the ends for which they have been given. By the end of this period, it is clear that Jesus will be obedient to the will of his Father. He is ready to begin his public ministry.

4:14–44 Jesus Rejected at Nazareth. That ministry now opens with Jesus' public rejection by his own people at Nazareth. Luke has emphasized that Jesus was filled with the Spirit (4:1, 14). Thus inspired, he returns to Nazareth, already the object of intense discussion, to worship at the local synagogue. Although the text does not explicitly state this, it seems that Jesus has already ministered extensively before coming to Nazareth. By this stage, he has become well known and is clearly a frequent teacher in synagogues throughout the region. But at Nazareth, he finds open rejection. Reading the great messianic prophecy of Isaiah 61:1–2, he declares that this prophecy has been fulfilled in himself.

The prophecy makes reference to the preaching of good news and the healing of the blind—essential elements of Jesus' ministry. This suggests strongly that Jesus applies these words to himself in the knowledge that the details of his public ministry will confirm them. But instead, he finds outrage and rejection. As the following episodes make clear, Jesus is even accepted as the "Holy One of God" (4:31–37) and "Son of God" by demons (4:38–44), whereas his own people will not hear him. Despite this rejection, Jesus continues to preach in synagogues, clearly receiving a warm welcome by others.

5:1–11 The Calling of the First Disciples. Jesus then calls his first disciples. Although it is clear that he has been greatly admired by many people to date, he now invites some to assume a specially favored position alongside him. The first disciples are ordinary fishermen, who, Jesus declares, will be made into "fishers of men."

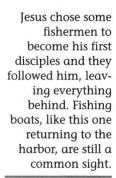

Jesus chose some fishermen to become his first disciples and they followed him, leaving everything behind. Fishing boats, like this one returning to the harbor, are still a common sight.

5:12–26 Jesus' Healing Ministry Continues. The healing of the man with leprosy (5:12–16) illustrates the ability and willingness of Jesus to heal, as well as his affirmation of the Old Testament law—note how the healed leper is sent to the priest for confirmation of the healing.

What at first seems to be another healing (5:17–26) turns out to have major implications for a right understanding of the identity of Jesus. As part of his healing of a paralytic, Jesus declares that the man's sins are forgiven. The teachers of the law are outraged by this. Only God can forgive sins! They accuse Jesus of blasphemy. And, in one sense, they are right to do so. Only God can forgive sins. By claiming this authority, Jesus is putting himself in the place of God. But the Christian reader of this passage will notice two things. First, the man is healed. Jesus clearly possesses the ability to heal—and hence the authority to forgive. And second, the later resurrection of Jesus from the dead affirms that he is indeed the Son of God (Ro 1:3–4), and thus possesses the necessary authority to forgive sin. But at this early stage in his ministry, there is no hint of what is to come. That will soon change—but not yet.

5:27–32 The Calling of Levi. Jesus then adds a tax collector named Levi to his group of inner disciples, to the outrage of the onlookers. (Mark and Luke both refer to the person concerned by his original name, Levi or "Levi son of Alphaeus"; in Matthew's account of the same incident, the apostolic name *Matthew* is used.) Tax collectors were widely despised and regarded as outcasts by their fellows. At this time, the region of Palestine was occupied by the Romans. Not only did the tax collectors associate with the Gentile occupying power. They also charged more taxes than they were entitled to as a way of ensuring their own well-being. As a result, they were detested by

Jews and regarded as traitors. Yet by calling one of them to his inner circle, Jesus demonstrates his acceptance of those regarded as beyond hope of redemption by Judaism, including prostitutes, Gentiles, and tax collectors. Jesus summarizes this with his declaration that he has come to call sinners, not the righteous (5:32).

5:33–6:11 The Authority of Jesus Questioned. The criticism of Jesus continues relentlessly. Not only does Jesus call outcasts into his inner circle, he does not impose rigorous fasting requirements on them. Jesus responds by pointing out that there is no need for fasting while the bridegroom—an obvious reference to himself—is still among his guests. The glorious new wine of the gospel cannot be contained by the tired old wineskins of Judaism (5:33–39).

Yet the criticism goes on (6:1–11). The Pharisees criticize Jesus for picking corn on the Sabbath. Jesus retorts that the Son of Man (a reference to himself) has authority over the Sabbath. The clear implication is that the Creator has authority over his creation. In any case, Jesus points out that the Sabbath was ordained for the benefit of people, not the other way around, and cites the example of David to show that his actions have excellent precedents. He also insisted that he has a right to heal on the Sabbath, and he challenges any who think otherwise to prove it.

6:12–19ff Sermon on the Plain. After calling the twelve disciples together (6:12–16), Jesus delivers what is sometimes referred to as the "Sermon on the Plain," which includes some of the material to be found in the "Sermon on the Mount" (Mt 5:1–7:29). The sermon, which is spoken to the disciples rather than to those Jesus has just healed, stresses the high demands Christians are called to work toward, while realizing that it is impossible to meet them without the grace of God himself.

6:20–26 Blessings and Woes. The sermon opens with a set of pronouncements, which are widely known as "the Beatitudes" (6:20–23). Each pronouncement opens with the words "Blessed are. . ." The word *blessed* can easily be misunderstood to mean "happy" or "fortunate." Yet it is possible, as Jesus points out, to be blessed even if you are unhappy. Someone is "blessed" if he or she has found favor and acceptance in the sight of God. Even if the believers' worldly status or situation is humble or distressing, they can know that they have found favor in the sight of God—which is much more important. This point is stressed in the series of "woes" which follow (6:24–26); those who have found worldly security and satisfaction may easily forfeit favor in the sight of God.

6:27–45 Love for Enemies; Judging Others; A Tree and Its Fruit. The high standards expected within the kingdom of God are then set out. The strongly self-sacrificial character of the redeemed life is brought out in a series of commands, each illustrating the radical nature of the gospel demands. For many commentators, the sermon sets out a series of standards that Christians should aim toward, even if they ultimately fail to reach them in their own lives. This does not mean that the demands are perfectionist or hopelessly idealist. It just points to the fact that being a Christian makes a difference in the way such people live and indicates the goals they should be aiming at, even if they cannot achieve them all. The sermon continues with a reminder of the sinfulness of human nature, which leads us to criticize others when we ought to be examining ourselves (6:37–42). Just as the good tree brings forth good fruit, so the person who has really come to faith will naturally produce good works (6:43–45).

6:46–7:10 The Wise and Foolish Builders; Faith in Jesus. The sermon ends with the parable of the house built on the rock and the house built on the sand. Jesus here makes it clear that it is vitally important that the house of faith is built upon a solid foundation, which will survive the worst storms life can produce. Only by having faith in Jesus Christ and his gospel can we be sure of the stability and peace God intends for our lives. As if to make this point absolutely clear, Luke then relates a series of incidents that bring out the importance of faith in Christ. The faith of the Roman centurion in the ability of Jesus to heal his servant is noted, commended, and rewarded (7:1–10), as is that of a sinful woman (7:36–50). Her faith, Jesus declares, has saved her (7:50).

7:11–32 Jesus and John the Baptist. The question of the identity of Jesus then emerges once more. After raising a widow's son (7:11–17), Jesus is approached by two disciples of John the Baptist, who is languishing in prison (7:18–32). John wishes them to ask Jesus if he is the Messiah whose coming he had proclaimed, or whether he should wait for someone else. Jesus responds by pointing out that all the great signs to be associated with the coming of the Messiah have been fulfilled through him. A list of messianic prophecies, including that quoted from by Jesus at Nazareth, are clearly seen as having been fulfilled in the ministry of Jesus (7:22; see Isa 29:18–19; 35:4–6; 61:1–2). Jesus affirms that he is indeed the one for whom John had been sent to prepare the way in fulfillment of prophecy.

7:33–50 Jesus Criticized as a Friend of Sinners. Yet criticism continues. Jesus continues to be criticized for being the "friend of sinners" (7:33–35). In response, Jesus makes the point that the greater the sin, the greater the gratitude at its forgiveness (7:36–50). In forgiving the sin of a local woman, Jesus again raises the question of his authority. Only God can forgive sins—so who, people wonder, is this "who even forgives sins?" (7:48–49; see 5:20–26).

Drawn to Jesus, the Twelve and a group of women, many of whom are specifically named (8:1–3), follow him around and minister to him.

8:4–15 The Parable of the Sower. The *parable of the sower* draws on the image of a sower scattering seed on the ground as an image of the preaching of the word of God in the world. Jesus notes how it is the same seed that falls onto different kinds of ground. What eventually happens to it depends on the quality of the soil. In the same way, Jesus sows the seed of the word of God through his preaching. The effect it has on people depends on how they respond to it. If someone should fail to respond or fall away, it is not on account of any failure on the part of the seed.

8:16–21 A Lamp on a Stand. A second parable draws on the imagery of light. Just as a lamp is allowed to illuminate a room, so the effects of the gospel are to be felt in the world. In a saying that reinforces the importance of faith, and action as a result of that faith, Jesus affirms that his brothers are "those who hear God's word and put it into practice" (8:19–21).

8:22–39 Jesus' Authority Confirmed. A series of events then take place that confirm Jesus' authority over the natural and supernatural order. Through his stilling of a storm, Jesus is shown to have authority over the wind and the waves, to the astonishment of his disciples (8:22–25). And in the healing of a man who is possessed by demons (8:26–39), we see once more that evil spirits recognize the identity of Jesus as "son of the Most High God," and submit to his authority. Once more, amazement and fear mingle among the onlookers, who are stunned by what they see taking place before their eyes.

8:40–56 A Dead Girl and a Sick Woman. Finally, by bringing the young daughter of Jairus, a prominent member of the local synagogue, back to life, Jesus demonstrates that he has authority over death itself. Jesus also heals a woman who had been bleeding for many years and who was widely regarded as being beyond any hope of cure. Yet this is more than an act of healing. It is also an important act of affirmation. The woman would have been regarded as unclean by Jews on account of the discharge of a bodily fluid. Jesus refuses to acknowledge this barrier to his ministry. No artificial human obstacles will be placed between the healer and those whom he has come to save.

9:1–17 Jesus Sends Out the Twelve and Feeds Five Thousand. The Twelve are sent out to preach the gospel, with the result that demons are driven out and the sick healed (9:1–6). This and other reports come to the attention of Herod, who had earlier beheaded John the Baptist (an incident recounted at length in Mk 6:14–29). Herod, like so many others, is confused over the identity of Jesus. Is he John the Baptist come back to life? Or is he Elijah? (9:7–9). After a brief interlude, in which Luke recounts the feeding of the five thousand (Lk 9:10–17), this theme is pursued again: Who is Jesus?

9:18–27 Peter's Confession of Christ. This is precisely the question that Jesus puts to the disciples. The disciples report back on the various opinions that they have heard: Jesus is one of the prophets, or John the Baptist come back to life, or perhaps Elijah. But Jesus presses them: What about you? Who do *you* say that I am? This is a vitally important question. Unlike the crowds, the disciples have been with Jesus throughout most of his ministry. They have watched him and listened to him. Now they are being asked what their conclusion is.

Peter speaks for them all when he replies that he believes that Jesus is "the Christ of God" (9:20). In other words, Jesus is the long-awaited Messiah, who has come to his people. Presumably anxious that the title *Messiah* might be understood in a purely political sense, Jesus asks the disciples not to tell anyone of their realization of his true identity (9:21). The Messiah could too easily be misunderstood as a triumphalist political leader, concerned only to liberate the country from its Roman occupying force. Immediately after Peter's confession that he is the Messiah, Jesus declares that he must go to Jerusalem, suffer, be rejected, be put to death, and finally rise from the dead. It is an integral part of his calling. He is to be a suffering Messiah.

9:28–45 The Transfiguration; Jesus' Power Over Evil Spirits. An important anticipation of the resurrection now follows in the account of the Transfiguration (9:28–36). This incident demonstrates the continuity of Jesus with the ministries of Moses and Elijah, while at the same time providing an anticipation of the resurrection glory of Christ. An endorsement of Jesus' identity and authority from heaven confirms his ministry and mission.

After a further demonstration of the power of Jesus over evil spirits (9:37–43), the theme of the coming suffering of Jesus reappears (9:44–45). The disciples continue to be bewildered by this prediction. It does not accord with their expectations of what the Messiah would be like. The Messiah was expected to be a figure of triumph, not suffering.

9:46–62 Who Will Be the Greatest? The Cost of Discipleship. This early period of Jesus' ministry comes to an end (9:46–62) with a discussion among the disciples as to who will be the greatest among them. Jesus' reply makes it clear that worldly standards of supremacy and rank carry no weight in the kingdom of God. This is followed by a series of uncompromising statements concerning the cost of discipleship. Everything else must take second place to following Christ (9:57–62).

LUKE 10:1 – 19:27

Jesus' Later Ministry

10:1–37 Jesus Sends Out the Seventy-two. Jesus now commissions seventy-two disciples to carry on the work of proclamation of the good news of the kingdom of God (10:1–24). They are authorized to speak in his name, and they return joyfully to report of the results of their ministry.

Asked what must be done for someone to inherit eternal life (10:25–28), Jesus allows his questioner to answer this for himself and then affirms the importance of love of God and love of one's neighbor, bringing together Deuteronomy 6:5 and Leviticus 19:18. However, the questioner has another issue to raise: Who is my neighbor? Jesus answers this question with the *parable of the good Samaritan* (10:30–37), which draws on the traditional hatred between Jews and Samaritans to make the point that mercy must not be compromised by social or national prejudices.

10:38–11:13 Mary and Martha; the Lord's Prayer. The episode with Mary and Martha (10:38–42) is generally thought to illustrate the importance of spending time with Jesus, enjoying the luxury of his presence and teaching, instead of fussing around and being anxious about other things. These can wait!

The theme of spending time with the Lord is then further developed in a section dealing with prayer. Jesus hands down a model prayer, generally known as "The Lord's Prayer." Its simplicity, brevity, and intimacy set a model for the kind of prayer Jesus wishes his followers to adopt (11:1–4). The prayer affirms the fatherhood of God, reminding us that we owe our origins to him and that he cares for his children. It reminds us that God is holy (the term *hallowed* has the basic meaning of "keep holy") and that this holiness must be reflected in the way believers address God in prayer, speak of him to the world, and worship him. The prayer then turns to the needs of believers—to their physical need for food and their spiritual need for forgiveness, comfort, and protection from temptation. Just as even sinful human fathers wish well for their children, so God will give his Holy Spirit to those who ask for it (11:5–13).

11:14–32 Jesus and Beelzebub; Sign of Jonah. His opponents then attempt to cast aspersions on Jesus by suggesting that he has authority over demons because he is in league with "Beelzebub, the prince of demons" (11:14–28). Jesus vigorously rejects this attempt to attribute his authority to Satan. The unbelief of his critics is further underscored by their demands for a sign by which his authority might be justified. Jesus points them to the "sign of Jonah," a clear reference to his forthcoming resurrection (11:29–32; see Mt 12:39–42).

11:33–12:2 Jesus Criticizes the Pharisees. A series of teachings then follows, dealing with questions that arise at this stage during Jesus' ministry. In particular, Jesus criticizes the Pharisees for their hypocritical conduct, which focuses on externals and neglects internal matters of faith and motivation. Lacking any real doctrine of grace, they merely lay burdens on others without doing anything to assist them. The disciples are to be on their guard against such people and the threat that they pose.

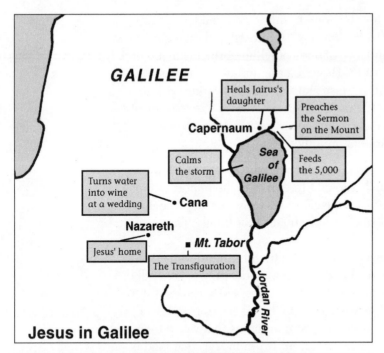

Jesus in Galilee

GALILEE

Heals Jairus's daughter

Preaches the Sermon on the Mount

Capernaum

Sea of Galilee

Calms the storm

Feeds the 5,000

Turns water into wine at a wedding

Cana

Nazareth

Jesus' home

Mt. Tabor

The Transfiguration

Jordan River

These maps list only a few of the events in Jesus' life. Much of his time was spent in Galilee. Crowds would follow him from place to place as word of his teachings and his miracles spread. Jesus' earthly ministry covered a mere three years, beginning when he was about thirty.

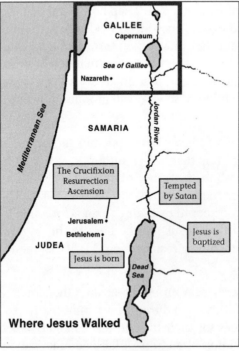

Where Jesus Walked

GALILEE
Capernaum

Sea of Galilee
Nazareth

Jordan River

SAMARIA

Mediterranean Sea

The Crucifixion Resurrection Ascension

Tempted by Satan

Jerusalem
Bethlehem

JUDEA

Jesus is baptized

Jesus is born

Dead Sea

12:13–13:9 Watchfulness. This is followed by a series of teachings focusing on the theme of watchfulness. The disciples are not to be like the rich fool (12:13–21), who stored up wealth on earth without considering the eternal dimensions of life. Nor are they to worry too much about the physical aspects of life (12:22–34). If God takes care of the birds of the air and the lilies of the field, will he not also take care of them? What the disciples should be worried about is being taken unawares by the coming of the Lord.

A series of illustrations brings out the importance of being prepared for the return of an absent master (12:35–48), pointing to the coming of Christ. This theme of "being prepared for the end" is then developed in a number of different directions. The coming of Jesus will bring division, not peace (12:49–53). The disciples are to watch for the signs of the end as people watch for signs of a change in the weather (12:54–59). The need for urgent repentance is illustrated by the incident of the tower of Siloam and the fruitless tree threatened with destruction unless it bears fruit (13:1–9).

The healing and teaching continue. Jesus' vigorous refutation of those who criticize his healing on the Sabbath meets with widespread approval. The *parable of the mustard seed* points to how the kingdom of God can grow rapidly from small beginnings (13:19). The theme of healing on the Sabbath is explored further when he is invited to eat at the house of a local Pharisee (14:1–14). He uses this occasion to emphasize the difference between worldly and spiritual understandings of rank and importance.

The theme of food leads on to the *parable of the great banquet* (14:15–24). This parable deals with a feast to which a select few are invited, but who, for various reasons, fail to attend. The invitation is then extended to all. The parable clearly deals with the extension of the good news of the kingdom from the narrow bounds of Israel to the Gentiles. Yet Jesus makes it clear that the kingdom of God is not simply about feasting. Becoming and being his disciple will involve pain, suffering, and loss. It is something that must be thought about carefully, not undertaken lightly (14:25–35).

15:1–32 Parables of the Lost. Three parables then follow, each of which focuses on the joy of recovering something that is lost and rebuts the objections of the Pharisees and teachers of the law against the welcome Jesus offered to so-called sinners. Why should not God be overjoyed at the return of the lost? The first parable centers on the recovery of a *lost sheep* (15:3–7); the second on the finding of a *lost coin* (15:8–10); and the third—the celebrated *parable of the prodigal son*—on the return of a wayward son to his father (15:11–32). This third parable superbly illustrates the joy experienced by the father at the return of his son, whom he had given up as lost. It also points to the sense of irritation felt by the father's older son, who fails to understand fully the grounds of the father's delight at the restoration of his brother.

16:1–18:14 The Parables Continue. A series of parables then follow, interspersed with accounts of incidents on the way to Jerusalem (16:1–19:27). The *parable of the shrewd manager* (16:1–15) points to the need to plan for the future, particularly in the light of coming judgment. The parable in question is difficult to interpret and is probably best understood as follows. It was common practice to overcharge buyers. The steward was in fact reducing the debts from the inflated prices charged by the master to the real price the items were worth. As a result, the master could take some comfort from what he had done, and the clients would regard the steward favorably.

The story of *the rich man and Lazarus* (16:19–31) illustrates both the evils of riches and the importance of the Resurrection in establishing the authority of Jesus. However, Jesus suggests that humanity is so sinful that it is unlikely even to listen to someone who returns from the dead in this manner. Perhaps that sin is inevitable. Nevertheless, there is a real need to avoid being the cause of sin to anyone (17:1–4).

The importance of faith is then stressed (17:5–10), illustrated by the incident in which ten men are healed of leprosy (17:11–19). Only one—a Samaritan—has the grace to thank Jesus for what he has done. Jesus commends him for doing so and assures him that his faith has restored him.

Jesus then returns to the theme of the coming of the kingdom, and especially emphasizes the need for watchfulness (17:20–37).

Two parables then illustrate aspects of the good news. The *parable of the persistent widow* (18:1–8) illustrates how even an unjust judge responds to persistent requests. How much more so, he suggests, will God—who is a good and merciful judge—respond to the persistent prayer of his people. This is followed by the *parable of the Pharisee and the tax collector* (18:9–14), which brings out the importance of humility. The Pharisee thanks God for his many virtues. The tax collector openly admits his misery and sin. There is no hint that the Pharisee was a hypocrite. It is virtually certain that he did everything he mentioned, which exceeded the demands of the law. For example, fasting was only commanded by the law on the Day of Atonement—yet he fasted twice a week. The point being made is simple: humility leads to mercy and forgiveness.

18:15–30 Little Children; Jesus and the Rich Ruler. The kind of lowliness that is commended is then illustrated through two different incidents. In the first, Jesus declares that people must receive the kingdom of God with the trust, delight, and dependence of little children (18:15–17). In the second, the meeting with the rich young ruler (18:18–30) brings out the obstacle that riches pose to acceptance in the sight of God. After discovering that the young man has faithfully kept the commandments, Jesus asks him to sell all he has and follow him. This dismays the young man, who departs with great sadness. It is clear that wealth poses a real obstacle to coming to God. Nevertheless, as Jesus makes clear, with God anything is possible. Nobody lies outside the saving purposes of God, who has promised salvation to those who put their faith in Jesus Christ.

18:31–43 Jesus Again Predicts His Death; a Blind Beggar Receives His Sight. Readers are then reminded once more of the high price of salvation, as Jesus once more predicts his betrayal, suffering, and resurrection (18:31–34). This passage reminds us that Jesus' death is no accident. It is something that has been purposed and foretold. Jesus dies because he has to die—there is no other way in which sinful humanity can be redeemed. The crucifixion has to happen.

This prediction of suffering and death is followed by the healing of the blind man (18:35–43), which illustrates both the importance of faith and the spiritual discernment of this physically blind man, who recognizes the "son of David" as he passes.

19:1–10 Zacchaeus the Tax Collector. The personal impact of Jesus is then demonstrated in the encounter with Zacchaeus the tax collector. As noted earlier, tax collectors were hated on account of their dishonesty and collaboration with the Roman authorities. Zacchaeus, however, is attracted to Jesus. Despite his despised social status, Jesus welcomes him and visits his home—to the outrage of onlookers. Yet the encounter proves to be transformative. Zacchaeus repents of his dishonesty and offers more than adequate restoration of anything he has dishonestly received. For Jesus, this provides yet another illustration of his mission to seek and reach the lost.

19:12–27 The Parable of the Ten Minas. The theme of the return of the Lord is then explored in the *parable of the ten minas*, which corresponds broadly to the more familiar parable of the talents (Mt 25:14–30). Attention here focuses on what the servants do while the master is away. The parable tells of a master who entrusts his *minas* (quantities of silver, which act as money) to his servants during his absence, and of the variety of ways in which the servants make use of that money. The main point being made is that the master will return without warning to see what has happened in his absence.

LUKE 19:28 – 24:53

The Passion, Death, and Resurrection of Christ

19:28–44 The Triumphal Entry. While all this has been going on, Jesus and his disciples have been drawing nearer and nearer to Jerusalem. Jesus had told his disciples that he must go to Jerusalem to be betrayed and crucified. Now Jesus prepares to enter the great city itself. Jesus enters in humility, mounted on a donkey, in fulfillment of a great messianic prophecy of the Old Testament (Zec 9:9). Jesus enters Jerusalem as its king, an event especially celebrated by Christians on Palm Sunday. It is clear that there are many who are looking forward to this event. He is greeted by crowds, honoring him and singing his praises, to the obvious annoyance of the Pharisees.

19:45–48 Jesus at the Temple. The final week of Jesus' life is packed with teaching and conflict with the religious authorities. The first major incident is the cleansing of the temple, in which Jesus ejects the merchants and overturns the tables of the money changers and sellers of doves. The protest is probably only partly against the commercialization of the temple areas. It almost certainly represents Jesus' anger that any form of payment or purchase is necessary before an individual may worship God.

20:1–19 The Authority of Jesus Questioned. Controversy now develops with increasing intensity. Once more, the authority of Jesus is questioned by his critics (20:1–8), who prove unable to give an adequate response to Jesus' challenge to them over the authority of John the Baptist. The *parable of the*

A sycamore tree in Jericho brought a tax collector face-to-face with Jesus. Too short to see much, Zacchaeus climbed the tree to get a better view and met Jesus. That meeting prompted a vow from the tax collector to give half of what he owned to the poor and to repay anyone he might have cheated four times the amount.

tenants (21:9–19) represents a superb and distressing illustration of the way Judaism has rejected God's prophets—and is also about to reject the Son of God. The final killing of the son reminds us of Jesus' predictions of his own death in Jerusalem, through which his final rejection by Judaism will be sealed. Yet even though he has been rejected, this will not be the end of the story, as the prophetic remark concerning the rejected stone makes clear (20:17; see Ps 118:22). (The "capstone" refers to the stone placed in an archway, which held a building together.)

20:20–26 Paying Taxes to Caesar. Jesus then addresses a series of controversial questions raised by agents of the religious authorities, who attempt to outwit him. An initial attempt is made to trap Jesus by embroiling him in a controversy relating to the Roman authorities. Should Jews pay taxes to the Romans or not? The Pharisees are opposed to paying such taxes. The Herodians (who are strongly pro-Roman) are in favor. Both groups are opposed to Jesus. Whichever way he replies, Jesus will lose out, either by supporting treason or by supporting the Romans. Jesus takes neither option, evading the trap set for him. He draws attention to the image of Caesar on the coins used to pay the tax. What is Caesar's should be given to Caesar. What is God's should be given to God. As humanity is created in the image of God (Ge 1:26–27), this reply is actually a declaration of the need for people to dedicate themselves to him.

20:27–44 The Resurrection and Marriage. This is followed by a question raised by the Sadducees concerning marriage at the resurrection (20:27–40). In an attempt to trap Jesus into conceding that there is no resurrection, they ask a question, based on marriage in heaven, designed to demonstrate the logical impossibility of resurrection. Jesus points out that since there is no marriage in heaven, their argument falls to the ground. He further adds to the embarrassment of his opponents by showing up their inability to make sense of the messianic prophecy of Psalm 110:1 (20:41–44).

20:45–21:38 Signs of the End of the Age. After stressing the importance of humility and commending the generosity of a poor widow (20:45–21:4), Jesus turns his attention to the end of the age (21:5–38). This section alerts the disciples to the troubles that lie ahead. The distress and pain that lie in the future are vividly described. Many of these sayings will find at least partial fulfillment in the destruction of Jerusalem by the Roman armies in A.D. 70. This will be a time of betrayal, of persecution, and of false teaching. It is clear, however, that Jesus' ultimate reference is to the end of the world itself, when he, as the "Son of Man" will come again in glory to judge the world. His point is that the disciples must not be frightened when these things happen. When they come to pass, it will be a sign that their hour of final redemption has arrived.

City of Jerusalem

● ● ● ● **Possible route**
of Jesus to the cross

Gordon's Calvary

Damascus Gate

Antonia
Fortress

Via Dolorosa

Lion's Gate
(Stephen's Gate)

Mount
of Olives

Golgotha

TEMPLE MOUNT

Golden
Gate

Wilson's
Arch

Temple

Citadel
Tower of David

Western
Wall

Herod's
Palace

City of David area

Kidron Valley

House of Caiaphas

Siloam
Pool

Hinnom Valley

0   100 yards

22:1–38 The Last Supper. Luke then sets the scene for the final days of Christ's earthly life at the time of the Passover, when Israel remembered the great act of deliverance by which God rescued their ancestors from bondage in Egypt (22:1–12). According to Deuteronomy 16:16, all Jewish men were required to celebrate the Passover feast in Jerusalem itself. On this occasion, the Passover will take on a special significance for Jesus, who turns out to be the true Passover lamb, sacrificed for the sins of the world. Redemption is drawing near.

As Luke begins to tell the story of Christ's final days in Jerusalem, we become aware of the power of sin in the present. Luke relates how the Jewish leaders plot to get rid of Jesus, Satan enters into Judas Iscariot, and the love of money triumphs over the love of God. The Passover was indeed a celebration of a past act of deliverance. Yet the power of sin remained. Something needed to be done to achieve a once-for-all victory over sin. In what follows, we learn of how the death of Christ holds the key to this vital development.

As the Jewish people were preparing to sacrifice their Passover lambs, Jesus prepared to die. While Israel remembered a past act of redemption, God was achieving a new work and greater work of redemption in their midst. Having gathered together in the Upper Room, Jesus and his disciples celebrate Passover (22:14–23). With great solemnity, Jesus tells the apostles that he will never celebrate Passover again "until it finds fulfillment in the kingdom of God." The Passover is seen as something that points beyond itself to something greater that is yet to find its fulfillment. And as the meal proceeds, the full meaning of his words begins to become clear. Just as the Passover lamb was slain, so Jesus will be slain. His body will be broken, and his blood shed. And through his death, a "new covenant" will be established.

Jesus' words are momentous: the Passover is about to find its fulfillment in and through him. But what does a "new covenant" mean? The Greek word used here has the sense of "testament" as in "last will and testament." It points to a set of promises and an inheritance, which become effective with the death of the testator. Jesus is declaring that through his death, the promises of forgiveness and eternal life come into effect, allowing believers to receive the inheritance of eternal life. Yet these words of promise are followed by a reminder of the reality and presence of sin as Jesus declares that one of his disciples will betray him.

Luke continues to tell the tale of Christ's final days on earth by returning to the theme of the presence and power of sin (22:24–38). Even at this solemn moment, as Christ's death draws near, the disciples begin to bicker among themselves. Is Luke telling his readers how much even the apostles needed redemption? Is he hinting at how weak unredeemed human nature is? If so, it allows us to understand and appreciate all the more Christ's death on the cross to liberate sinful humanity from the power of sin. The lingering presence of sin can be seen in Peter's confident denial that he could ever let Jesus down: "I am ready to go with you to prison and to death" (22:33). In the light of what eventually happens, those words sound rather superficial and hollow.

Jesus declares that he has come to be a servant among his people. He is a servant king, unlike the power-loving kings of the Gentiles. And that service is seen supremely in the fact that he is willing, in fulfillment of prophecy, "to be numbered with transgressors." A sense of new urgency breaks in as Jesus speaks of this great prophecy "reaching its fulfillment." This calls to mind other sections of that prophecy, such as "the Lord has laid on him the iniquity of us all" (Isa 53:6, 12). Even though Jesus is sinless, he is content to be treated as if he were a sinner, so that he can redeem sinners.

22:39–53 Jesus Arrested on the Mount of Olives. Jesus and the disciples then leave the warmth and safety of the Upper Room and go out into the night (22:39–53). Many commentators see the burden of human sin beginning to weigh on Jesus at this point. The Lamb of God has taken the weight of human sin upon his shoul-

On the Via Dolorosa, the route Jesus would have taken on his way to be crucified on Calvary.

At left is a game scratched into the stone of the pavement where Jesus is believed to have been tried. The game was played by Roman soldiers. The winner could do anything he wanted to the prisoner in their charge. The lines have been highlighted to make them easier to see.

ders and become affected by it. Does he begin to share in the human condition of being uncertain about God? Certainly, his deeply moving prayer suggests hesitation about the future mingled with total obedience: "Father, if you are willing, take this cup from me; yet not my will, but yours be done" (22:42). (The "cup" is a traditional Old Testament reference to suffering.) Luke brings out Jesus' pain and anguish at this point, noting that "his sweat was like drops of blood falling to the ground." We must not think of Christ's passion has having begun only at the moment of crucifixion. Luke makes it clear that Jesus went through mental agony as he reflected on what lay ahead of him. Part of that agony concerns his betrayal by one of his closest friends.

The story of the betrayal of Jesus by Judas's kiss is probably one of the best-known incidents from the Gospels. Many commentators have pointed to the irony of the event: a gesture of affection becomes an act of betrayal.

There is a moral here. The history of the church reminds us that those who declare love for Christ may still betray him by their actions.

Even in his moment of betrayal, the kindness of Jesus still shines through. In a moment of foolishness, one of his followers cuts off the ear of the high priest's servant. Jesus heals this man, just as he had healed so many others during his ministry. Even as his crucifixion draws near, he still shows the compassion of God for those who need healing.

22:54–62 Peter Disowns Jesus. Luke then relates another story of failure. Jesus has just been betrayed by a disciple. Now he will be disowned by another. Peter, the closest to Jesus of the apostles, has been confident of his own commitment to Christ. He has declared that he will willingly face prison or even death for him. But when things get tough, Peter discovers that he is a total failure. He repeatedly denies having anything to do with Christ. Then, in a moment of utter despair, he remembers his brave words and feels ashamed. In Luke's words, "He went outside and wept bitterly."

22:63–67 The Guards Mock Jesus; the Chief Priests Question Him. Having faced betrayal and denial, Jesus is then confronted with mockery, as his guards begin to taunt and ridicule him. All this is in fulfillment of prophecy: "He was despised and rejected by men, a man of sorrows and familiar with suffering" (Isa 53:3). Finally, he is faced with disbelief and rebellion as he is brought before the chief priests. They demand to know whether he is "the Christ" (22:67) or "the Son of God" (22:70). According to the Jewish beliefs of the time, the appearance of the Messiah would lead to his people falling down in worship before him. Yet when Jesus admits that he is the Son of God, all the chief priests do is to hand him over to the Romans for execution. Luke reminds us that sin, with its deep-seated tendency to rebel against God, had permeated to the very heart of Israel. Israel could not save itself. It needed a redeemer. The sheer tragedy of the sinful human situation is seen in this: when a redeemer finally came, he was rejected with contempt.

23:1–25 Jesus Before Pilate and Herod. Accused of being "Christ, a king" by his Jewish opponents (23:2), Jesus is now led to face the Roman governor, Pontius Pilate (23:1–12). Once more, Luke draws our attention to the irony of the situation. The Messiah's people should have knelt at his feet. Instead, they rise up. They ought to have adored him. Instead, they accuse him. The accusations brought against Jesus can be seen as deliberately slanted to make Pilate take the worst possible view of Jesus. He is charged with opposing payment of taxes to Caesar and claiming to be a king. Both of these are calculated to rouse the suspicions of a Roman governor, anxious to suppress any sedition or rebellion in his territories. By restating Jesus' religious message in political terms, the high priests hope to discredit him. In the event, they fail. Pilate has no hesitation in declaring that Jesus "has done nothing to deserve death." And when he sends Jesus to Herod, Herod mocks him but can find no basis for the charges brought against Jesus. Yet this does not satisfy the crowds, who are clearly intent on destroying him.

We are now introduced to Barabbas who "had been thrown into prison for an insurrection in the city, and for murder" (23:19). Luke presents Barabbas as a man guilty of rebellion and murder, someone who, according to the law, deserves to die. The crowds demand the death of Jesus and the release of Barabbas. Pilate repeats his firm belief that Jesus does not deserve death for any reason. Yet in the end, he is not totally in control of the situation. He finally yields to the enormous pressure that is being applied to him by the crowds. Barabbas is released, and Jesus is led away to execution.

22:26–46 The Crucifixion and Death of Jesus. And so we come to Luke's account of the suffering and death of Jesus Christ—a section of Luke's gospel that is often referred to as "the passion narrative," from the Latin term *passio*, "suffering" (23:26–46). Jesus is so tired that Simon from Cyrene has to carry his heavy cross on his shoulders (23:26). He is put to death between two criminals (23:33), praying for those who are putting him to death (23:34)—again, in fulfillment of prophecy (Isa 53:12). He is mocked and taunted by those he has come to redeem (23:35). The crowds scorn him: "Let him save himself if he is the Christ of God, the Chosen One." The soldiers mock him and call on him to save himself (23:36–37). One of the criminals curses him and demands that he save himself (23:39). But Christ remains on that cross. Instead of saving himself, he saves sinful humanity. One of the two criminals, deeply moved by what takes place, puts his faith in him, and receives an assurance of going with Christ to paradise (23:42–43).

Finally, Jesus dies. Luke notes some events accompanying his death and leaves his readers to ponder their meaning. "Darkness came over the whole land" (23:44). The light of the world had been extinguished. "The curtain of the temple was torn in two" (23:45). The curtain symbolized the barrier placed between God and humanity through sin. With the death of Christ, this barrier has been torn down.

23:47–56 The Innocence of Jesus. Luke then returns to the central theme of the innocence of Christ. Having already cited Pontius Pilate as a witness to his guiltlessness, Luke now calls on the support of the senior Roman officer present: "Surely this was a righteous man!" (23:47). The declarations of Pilate and the centurion are thought to be of vital importance for Luke. His gospel was probably aimed partly at Roman readership, which may have heard rumors of Jesus as an executed criminal or political rebel. Luke puts the record straight. Jesus did not die for his own sins, but for the sins of others. Luke also makes the point that not every senior Jewish religious figure approved of what had happened, noting Joseph of Arimathea (23:50–51) as an example of someone who was deeply uneasy over the course that events had taken.

23:50–56 Jesus' Burial. Finally, Luke records the burial of Christ. This whole passage is tinged with sadness. There is not a hint of an expectation of the resurrection. The promise of Jesus' resurrection seems to have been forgotten. The picture Luke paints for us is that of a dedicated and caring group of people ensuring that their dear friend Jesus is buried with quiet dignity. Luke stresses that "the women" were witnesses to all that he describes (23:49, 55).

24:1–12 The Resurrection. "He has risen!" (24:6). With these words, the lives of all those who saw Christ die are turned upside down. As Luke tells us the story of that first Easter Day, we can sense the total surprise and disbelief of all concerned. Here is no group of gullible disciples, determined at any cost to believe that Christ is risen. Here is a group of hardheaded men and women, confronted with evidence that throws their world into confusion as they try to take in the momentous implications of what is going on. The man that they have known and loved, the man that they have seen killed, the man that they have buried themselves, is risen! The Gospels insist that the initial reaction to the resurrection is fear (24:5). The disciples cannot take in what is happening.

Two travelers on the road to Emmaus from Jerusalem, a trip of about seven miles, were joined by a third man. It was Jesus, but they did not recognize him until later. Then they knew that Jesus had risen from the dead.

Yet the angel reminds them of the great promise Christ had made to them before his death (24:6–7). He had prophesied that he would be betrayed and crucified, and that he would finally rise again. And in a moment of wonder, the disciples remember (24:8). But again, Luke stresses that the disciples are not going to be rushed to hasty conclusions. They want time to think about things and take in their momentous implications. The words of the women "seemed to them like nonsense" (24:11). Even Peter went away, "wondering to himself what had happened" (24:12).

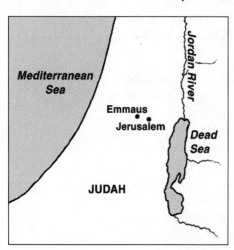

24:13–35 On the Road to Emmaus. In the midst of all this excitement and confusion, Luke leads us away to a quiet road leading from Jerusalem to Emmaus (24:13–35). Two disciples, one of whom is named Cleopas, are discussing the day's events and marveling at them (24:13–17). Again, Luke lets us know that they are still not sure what to make of them (24:19–24). As they talk, a third man joins them. The risen Christ is present with them, yet they do not recognize him.

The stranger then opens up the Scriptures to them, explaining how Jesus had "to suffer these things and then enter his glory" (24:26). Again, we encounter the theme of the necessity of Christ's death. This was no accident. He had to suffer and die to buy freedom and forgiveness for his people. And Jesus takes these marveling disciples through the Old Testament prophecies, as "he explained to them what was said in all the Scriptures concerning himself" (24:27). But they still do not realize who he is.

The moment of truth dawns shortly afterwards, when he makes himself known to them through the breaking of the bread (24:30–31). And suddenly, everything falls into place. They realize who he is and all that this implies. Two things happen as a result. They understand who he is, and make sense of all that he has told them about Scripture (24:32). And they begin to witness to the reality of the resurrection (24:33–35).

24:36–53 Jesus Appears to the Disciples; the Ascension. Luke then takes us back to Jerusalem, to the company of the apostles (24:36–53). Jesus appears to them. Once more the reaction is that of fear, rather than of joy (24:37). The apostles still cannot really believe what has happened. Yet Jesus, knowing their unspoken doubts, reassures them. It really is he. The marks on his hands and feet are there to prove it (24:39). And again, Jesus patiently explains that all this had to happen to him (24:44–47). The reality of his suffering and death is now surpassed by the power of his risen presence. Gradually, fear gives way to joy and amazement (24:41). Their doubts are resolved.

Reassurance of the resurrection then leads directly into the apostles being commissioned to proclaim this good news to the world. What has happened is not just good news for the disciples, who have regained a friend. It is good news for the world, which has gained a savior. The apostles are to go forth into that world: "You are witnesses of these things" (24:48). It is only when the disciples themselves really believe that Christ is risen, that they are told to go and tell others the news. Luke's point is clear: the resurrection of Jesus is something that is trustworthy.

Yet the disciples are not to witness unaided. The power by which God raised his Christ from the dead will be channeled into the apostles' witness and preaching. They will be "clothed with power from on high" (24:49), a reference to the promised coming of the Holy Spirit, who will empower his people to proclaim the good news of the risen Christ to all nations. And, having been blessed by their Lord at Bethany, the disciples "returned to Jerusalem with great joy" (24:52). The good news they have been entrusted with is not burdensome to share, for it brings joy. And Christians today have been called to share in the apostles' witness to the risen presence of Christ in their lives. They can turn from Luke, reassured of the trustworthiness of the gospel and the joy it can bring to a world that needs to hear it. In the second part of his work, the book of Acts, we will learn of how that world responded to this news.

JOHN

John's gospel is noticeably different from the first three gospels, both in terms of its style of writing and also in the way it presents its material. It is often thought to be the gospel that is most suited to devotional reading, because it uses powerful imagery to bring home to its readers the full impact of Jesus Christ on believers, and his significance for the world.

The gospel itself testifies that its author is "the disciple whom Jesus loved" (e.g., 13:23–26; 18:15–16). Tradition has identified this as the apostle John, although it should be noted that the text of the gospel itself does not make this statement explicitly. There are reasons for thinking that the gospel may have been written for churches in the region of Ephesus.

The date of writing of the gospel remains unclear. The text itself suggests that both Peter and the "beloved disciple" are dead (see 21:19, 22–23), thus pointing to a date at some point after A.D. 70. This is also suggested by other factors. Most scholars suggest a date toward the end of the first century (perhaps around A.D. 85), although the possibility of an earlier date remains open.

JOHN 1:1 – 51

The Background to the Ministry of Jesus

1:1–18 The Word Became Flesh. It is immediately obvious that there is something different about John's gospel. Matthew, Mark, and Luke all open their gospels by pointing to important events in history that cast light on the background to Jesus's ministry—such as his ancestors, the events surrounding his birth, or the coming of John the Baptist. But John is different. We are immediately taken behind the scene of history to learn of the background to the coming of Jesus Christ as seen from the perspective of God himself.

The gospel opens with a section that is usually referred to as the *Prologue* (1:1–18)—a sort of "foreword," which sets the scene for the coming of Christ. Even before we are introduced to any event in history, we know the background to the coming of Jesus. Jesus is none other than "the Word" become "flesh" (1:14). The Prologue opens by recalling the great words of the Genesis creation account, taking us right back to the beginning of time

(1:1; see Ge 1:1). The term *Word* (Greek: *logos*) is used to refer to Christ. The use of this word is enormously important, for it points to God's ability to communicate himself, and make himself known, through Jesus Christ— a major theme of John's gospel.

It is immediately clear that there is a direct relationship between God's work of creation and his work of redemption. The passage makes it clear that creation was the work of God through Christ (1:3), just as redemption is also the work of God through Christ. And this process of redemption involves Christ entering into the world. The imagery now shifts from word to light, as John brings out the judgment that the coming of Christ brings to the world. Light shows up things as they really are and thus brings both judgment and the hope of cleansing. Even though the world is dark, it cannot overcome the light, which now breaks into its gloom (1:3–5; note that the Greek word translated as "understood" by the NIV also has the sense of "overcome").

We are now prepared for the coming of John the Baptist (1:6–9). John was a witness to the coming of the light into the world. He himself was not that light. Nevertheless, he pointed to its coming. Yet when that light finally entered into the world, the world chose to reject it (1:11–13). His own people rejected him—a clear reference to the refusal on the part of Judaism to acknowledge the Messiah when he finally came. Yet those who did recognize and acknowledge Christ were granted the privilege of becoming children of God.

John then summarizes the importance of Jesus in his famous declaration that "the Word became flesh and made his dwelling among us" (1:14). The glory of Christ is the same as the glory of God himself—a glory that we have been allowed to see and experience through Christ. Many Christian writers use the term *Incarnation* to refer to the coming of Christ. The word means "being in the flesh" and refers to God coming into his world in the person of Jesus Christ. The testimony of John the Baptist is then anticipated: this is indeed the person to whom I was sent to bear witness. Even though nobody has seen God face to face—Moses, after all, only caught a glimpse of the back of God disappearing into the distance—God has determined to make himself known through Jesus Christ (1:15–18). And why is Jesus Christ able to make God known in this way? For John, the answer is simple and crucial: Jesus makes God known because Jesus himself is God.

1:19–28 John the Baptist Denies Being the Christ. We now enter the realm of human history. The scene has been set for the coming of Jesus Christ. Now we prepare to hear how he made his appearance on the stage of history. John opens his account by drawing our attention to the ministry of John the Baptist, who affirms that his purpose is to prepare the way for the coming of the Lord. He emphatically denies being anyone of any importance himself. He is not, for example, the long-awaited prophet, nor is he the Messiah. He is simply there to point to someone else.

1:29–34 Jesus the Lamb of God. But who? We already know the answer to this from the Prologue. We now see this answer actualized in history as Jesus comes toward John (1:29–34). John immediately bears witness to Christ, making it clear that this is the person whose coming he was sent to proclaim. This is none other than the Son of God himself. Some of John's own disciples are attracted to Jesus and spend some time with him. Although they initially refer to him as *rabbi* (the term used to refer to a teacher), as a result of their encounter with Jesus they begin to refer to him as the Messiah (1:35–42).

1:35–51 Jesus' First Disciples. Further encounters with Jesus follow, as his first disciples begin to spread the news of him around the neighborhood (1:43–51). Philip is explicitly clear about the significance of Jesus: he is "the one Moses wrote about in the Law, and about whom the prophets also wrote" (1:45). In other words, he is the fulfillment of all the great hopes and expectations of the Old Testament. Nathaniel, to whom Philip has explained all these things, is skeptical, and wonders if anything good can come out of Nazareth. Philip's reply is simple: "Come and see"—in other words, have your doubts resolved by encountering Jesus for yourself. This is an important model for evangelism, because it directs people's attention away from arguments and disputes and leads them directly to the person of Christ. And sure enough, when Nathanael meets Jesus, he is convinced. Here is the "Son of God" and the "King of Israel" (1:49).

JOHN 2:1 – 12:11

The Public Ministry of Jesus Christ

2:1–11 Jesus Changes Water to Wine. The public ministry of Jesus begins with a celebration—a wedding feast at Cana in Galilee. The occasion is remarkable on account of the miracle Jesus performs on that occasion. The feast threatens to grind to a halt because the wine is running out. Nearby are six large stone vessels full of water, which was meant to be used for Jewish purification rites. Jesus changes this water to wine, to such good effect that the master of the banquet regards it as being even better than the wine they had originally been using.

It is, of course, easy to treat this simply as a miracle. There is no doubt that it was this; John describes it as "the first of his miraculous signs" (2:11). But it is also more than that. It can be read at a number of symbolical levels. For example, the comment about the new wine being better than the old can be read as pointing to the superiority of the new covenant over the old covenant. Equally, it is important that the water thus transformed was originally to be used for the purpose of purification rites. A religion of ritual cleansing is thus transformed into a faith that "gladdens the heart of man" (as Ps 104:15 describes the effect of wine).

2:12–25 Jesus Clears the Temple. The scene now changes. It is the season of Passover, and Jesus goes up to Jerusalem for the feast. According to Deuteronomy 16:16, all Jewish men were required to celebrate the Passover feast in Jerusalem itself. Later, the Passover would take on a special significance for Jesus, whom we will discover to be the true Passover lamb, sacrificed for the sins of the world. But on this occasion, Jesus directs his attention towards the temple and the abuses that have found their way within its precincts.

John places the incident of the cleansing of the temple at the opening of the ministry of Jesus, whereas the Synoptic Gospels (that is, Matthew, Mark, and Luke) place it during the final week of Jesus' ministry. The reason for this divergence is not entirely clear, although two reasons can easily explain the difference. First, it could be suggested that we are dealing with two different attempts to clean up the temple, one that dates from the opening, and the other from the close of his ministry. This is supported by differences in detail between the accounts (for example, John mentions the selling of cattle and sheep and the use of a whip, which are not noted in the Synoptic Gospel accounts of the same incident). Alternatively, it could be suggested that John has placed the account of the cleansing of the temple at the opening of Jesus' ministry to bring out the theological importance of the event. By placing the account at the opening of the ministry, John brings out the fact that Jesus was exercising judgment throughout his ministry, and not simply at its end.

The incident is particularly important on account of a misunderstanding that arises over some words of Jesus. His reference to destroying the temple (2:19) is misunderstood to refer to the physical building in which his protest has taken place. This charge reappears at the time of his trial before the high priest (Mt 26:60–61). The onlookers protest that building the temple has taken 46 years thus far (it would finally be completed in A.D. 64, work having started around 20 B.C.—a fact which suggests that this incident took place around A.D. 26). But the real meaning of Jesus' words only becomes clear after the resurrection itself. His reference to raising it again in three

The first miracle Jesus performed was at a wedding in Cana in Galilee. When the wine was gone, Jesus had servants fill six stone jars with water. When the banquet master tasted it, he said it was better than the wine they had been serving. Normally, the better wine would have been served first.

days is a reference to himself. This is important, as it points to the way in which many of Jesus' sayings and deeds can only be understood fully and properly in the light of his resurrection.

3:1–21 Jesus Teaches Nicodemus. It is clear that many people are attracted to Jesus on account of his miraculous signs (2:23). Yet this could be little more than a superficial attraction, based on passing interest. Jesus demands a far more radical commitment than this on the part of those who wish to be his followers, as the meeting with Nicodemus makes clear. This meeting is one of the most familiar episodes in John's gospel and deserves careful study.

Nicodemus, like so many others, is attracted to Jesus. On account of his senior status within Judaism, he visits Jesus by night so that his interest will not compromise his position within the Sanhedrin, the 71-member supreme Jewish court, consisting of the chief priests, elders, and teachers of the law. He declares that he, and others, know that there is something special about Jesus. Only someone with a special relationship with God could perform such miraculous signs.

Jesus' response clearly mystifies Nicodemus. Only someone who is "born again" can see the kingdom of God. Nicodemus assumes that this refers to a physical rebirth, in which it is necessary to reenter his mother's womb. Yet Jesus' words have a deeper significance. As becomes clear, he is referring to a spiritual rebirth, in which someone who already possesses life at the physical level comes to birth at the spiritual level. One is alive already, in the sense that one physically exists. Yet one has yet to discover life in all its fullness, which comes only through being born again. The references to the "flesh and spirit" (3:6) make this point clear. Yet there is more to the idea than this. The Greek word translated as "again" (*anothen*) can also mean "from above." (We find it used in this sense in Matthew's account of the curtain of the temple being torn from "top to bottom"—literally, "from above to beneath"—at Mt 27:51.) This rebirth does not take place from below, but from God himself. To see the kingdom of God, it is necessary to be born of both water and the Spirit (3:5), a reference to both the physical and spiritual side of life. It is also possible that Jesus intends to distinguish between the external cleansing of water and the internal renewal brought by the Holy Spirit.

So what authority does Jesus have to make such statements? This question is dealt with by Jesus, who makes the point that only someone who has descended from heaven—and will ascend there again—has the authority and the ability to speak about heavenly things (3:13). Here we see a clear statement of the importance of the resurrection in establishing Jesus' authority. In the incarnation, Jesus comes down to earth, already in full possession of the authority to speak about God. The resurrection demonstrates this authority publicly, as well as being the means by which "the one who came down from heaven" will return there.

Jesus then proclaims the crucial link between his own forthcoming death and the full benefits of the gospel. In a reference to Moses delivering Israel from a plague of snakes (Nu 21:8–9), Jesus speaks of the deliverance of believers from death through the gift of eternal life, which will become possible through his death. The "eternal life" in question must not be thought of as some kind of infinite extension of everyday existence. Rather, it refers to a new *quality* of life, begun here and now through faith, which is consummated and fulfilled through resurrection. This eternal life is only made possible through the love of God, which is shown in the astonishing fact that he loves his world so much that his only Son should die for it (3:16).

There are important echoes here of the trauma experienced by Abraham when he was asked to give up his only son Isaac (Ge 22:1–14). What Abraham was not, in the end, required to do, God willingly did in order that sinful humanity might have the hope of eternal life. The death of the Son of God is thus the price of eternal life. Yet, despite the wonderful gift God offers, the world will not want anything to do with it (3:19–21). It prefers darkness to light, and the gloomy prospect of death to the glorious hope of eternal life.

3:22–36 John the Baptist's Testimony About Jesus. The story now shifts to the countryside of Judea, in which John is continuing his ministry (3:22–36). Hearing the reports of the growing fame and influence of Jesus, John stresses that this rests on the authority of Jesus to speak for God—an authority John clearly does not regard himself as possessing. Jesus speaks the words of God and has supreme authority. For this reason—and perhaps

This uncompleted church is on the site of Jacob's well, at the foot of Mount Ebal, which is just showing behind the archway. It was at Jacob's well that Jesus spoke with the woman from Samaria.

we can sense a tinge of sadness here?—Jesus must become still greater, while John himself will fade into the background.

4:1–26 Jesus Talks With a Samaritan Woman. As Jesus and his disciples move from Judea to Galilee, they are obliged to pass through Samaria, traditionally hostile to Jews (4:1–4). Jesus, tired by the journey, decides to rest by the traditional site of Jacob's well (which is not specifically identified in Scripture), while his disciples go to get some food from the nearby town of Sychar. While he rests, a Samaritan woman comes to draw water at the well. A dialogue results, which is one of the best-known in this Gospel (4:9–26).

The Samaritan woman is initially astonished that Jesus should want to speak to her. She was both a Samaritan (with whom Jews traditionally had no dealings) and a woman (and hence avoided in public by Jewish men, in order to avoid any form of sexual temptation or impropriety). The conversation initially focuses on the theme of thirst. Jesus offers to provide "living water" (as opposed to the stagnant water of the well) which would satisfy her in such a way that she would never thirst again (4:13). The woman is puzzled by this. Nevertheless, she is deeply impressed by Jesus' knowledge of the secrets of her private life (4:16–18). There is clearly something special about him. But what?

The woman draws the conclusion that Jesus is a prophet (4:19). But she soon discovers that even this is inadequate to do justice to the significance of Jesus. She speaks of her faith in the future coming of the Messiah and the insight that he would bring. Jesus then declares that he himself is none other than this Messiah (4:26). The woman thus began by finding a thirsty man, then a prophet, and finally, the long-awaited Messiah.

4:27–42 The Disciples Rejoin Jesus. On their return, the disciples are shocked to find Jesus speaking with a Samaritan woman. However, the effects of his dialogue are obvious. The Samaritans in her village have heard her report and are converging on Jesus in order to find out more about him. Initially, their interest is aroused by her reports about him. Yet, when they meet him for themselves, their faith becomes grounded in Jesus himself, rather than in the woman's testimony concerning him. They recognize that he is the Savior of the world.

4:43–5:15 Jesus Heals the Official's Son; the Healing at the Pool. This faith in Jesus as the Savior of the world is then amply justified in a healing miracle in the Galilee region involving an official's son, which leads to faith on the part of all who are witnesses to the event (4:43–54). This healing incident is then identified as the "second miraculous sign that Jesus performed," the first having been the changing of the water into wine at Cana in Galilee. It is followed some time later by a healing miracle in Jerusalem (5:1–15). This incident is important for a number of reasons. It demonstrates the authority of Jesus both to heal the infirm, and also to heal on the Sabbath—

an important echo of the theme that the "son of Man is Lord even of the Sabbath" (Mk 2:23–28).

But it is also important to notice the question (5:6) Jesus puts to the invalid: Do you want to be healed? Healing only follows once the invalid has admitted his need to be healed, recognized Jesus' ability to heal, and accepted the healing Jesus offers. In the same way, the forgiveness that Jesus makes possible can only be received by those who acknowledge their need of forgiveness, acknowledge the ability of Jesus to forgive their sins, and finally accept and receive that forgiveness.

5:16–47 Life Through the Son. This act of healing causes controversy. But Jesus continues to assert his authority, which rests on his relationship with his Father. There is the closest of relationships between Father and Son, with the result that the Son has full authority to act for the Father, especially in relation to judgment. The Father has also declared that his life—a reference to eternal life—will be made available to the world through the Son. This important statement will, of course, be fully justified through the resurrection. However, Jesus makes these declarations at this early stage in order to make it clear that he has authority to speak for God throughout his ministry.

Jesus is particularly critical of those who fail to respond to the witness borne to him by others, such as John the Baptist. John was like a lamp preparing the way for the greater light that was to come. Yet there is another testimony that Jesus believes people should have understood and acknowledged—the testimony of Scripture. Jesus is here referring to the Old Testament. Earlier, we saw how Nathanael recognized Jesus as "the one Moses wrote about in the Law, and about whom the prophets also wrote" (1:45). But why have others not done the same? Jesus points out that there are many who think that eternal life is gained by studying Scripture as an end in itself. In fact, eternal life is gained through an encounter with the one to whom Scripture points—Jesus Christ himself. If these people bothered to study Moses' writings properly, they would realize that he had written about Jesus.

6:1–24 Jesus Feeds the Five Thousand and Walks on Water. Our attention then turns again to the miracles of Jesus. John provides an account of the feeding of the five thousand, illustrating once more the authority of Jesus over the natural order (6:1–15). The response to this miracle is significant: people begin to draw the conclusion that he is "the Prophet who is to come into the world" (6:14). The reference here is to the prophet promised by Moses, whom God would raise up in the future (Dt 18:15–19). Jesus' authority over the natural order is then demonstrated once more through his walking on the water (6:16–24). However, the real importance of these passages lies in their leading into the great discourse on the "bread of life," which develops themes already raised by the miracle of the feeding of the five thousand.

6:25–59 Jesus the Bread of Life. The theme that Jesus explores focuses on *bread*. Why do people spend so much effort pursuing bread, when this will simply perish? Why not work for something that will endure for ever? Instead of eating a bread that will satisfy physically, and then only for a while, why not eat bread that will lead to eternal life? The crowds around initially think Jesus is referring to manna, the food that was providentially provided for Israel as it wandered through the wilderness. But Jesus is referring to himself, as what follows makes clear.

Jesus declares that he is the "bread of life" (6:35). This saying is of particular importance, because it is the first of the "I am" sayings. The form of these sayings is grammatically unusual, making them stand out from the remainder of the text. This point is difficult to appreciate for readers not familiar with Greek. However, the importance of the point is that there is a direct similarity between these sayings and Exodus 3:14, in which God reveals himself to Moses as "I AM WHO I AM." There is thus an implicit declaration of divinity on the part of Jesus within each of these sayings. The seven "I am" sayings in John's gospel are as follows:

6:35, 48	The Bread of Life
8:12, 9:5	The Light of the World
10:7, 9	The Gate for the Sheep
10:11, 14	The Good Shepherd
11:25	The Resurrection and the Life
14:6	The Way, the Truth, and the Life
15:1, 5	The True Vine

Jesus, then, is the "bread of life," who has come down from heaven and will give life to the world (6:33). Everyone who feeds on him will be raised up on the last day and will have eternal life. The bread that Jesus will offer the world is his own flesh. He is the "bread of life" (6:48). Those who ate manna in the wilderness died. But those who feed on Christ will have eternal life. Again and again we find Jesus reiterating that he has come down from heaven in order to bring life to the world. So how does someone benefit from this bread? What do the references to "eating" this bread mean? Jesus makes it clear that he is speaking about faith. Anyone "who believes has everlasting life" (6:47). The image of eating points to the closest of relationships between Jesus and the believer in which Christ becomes part of the believer's life.

6:60–71 Many Disciples Desert Jesus. Yet these sayings cause division. Many of those who had been attracted to Jesus cease to follow him. However, this is something to be expected. Jesus points out that only those who are enabled to by the Father will come to him. It is not a purely human choice. Yet the Twelve remain with him. As Peter points out, Jesus alone has the words of life. There is nobody else to compare with him. The theme of sin then enters briefly, as Jesus declares that one of the Twelve will betray him.

7:1–24 Jesus Goes to the Feast of Tabernacles. A major section now opens (7:1–8:59), which focuses on the growing opposition to Jesus and his response to this. The initial occasion for this is the Feast of Tabernacles, the major Jewish festival that celebrated God's providential provision for his people during the period of wandering in the wilderness as Israel moved from Egypt to the Promised Land (7:1–13; see Lev 23:33–43). Jesus' disciples go from Galilee to Jerusalem to observe the festival. Jesus follows later in secret, knowing that he will be the subject of critical scrutiny. Halfway through the festival, Jesus appears in the Jerusalem temple precincts and begins to teach (7:14–24). The initial reaction is amazement: how can this man know so much, when he has never undertaken any formal study? (A similar reaction can be seen in Luke's account of the twelve-year-old Jesus' remarkable knowledge of the law [Lk 2:46–47].) Yet Jesus declares that his wisdom does not have its origins in himself. It derives directly from God, who has sent him in the first place.

7:25–52 Is Jesus the Christ? This point is then stated with greater intensity, and it provokes considerable controversy. Jesus' claims to have been sent by God and to speak with God's authority provoke some to be tempted to physical violence against him, and others to put their faith in him. Some believe that he is the coming Prophet, others that he really is the Messiah. Others counter this suggestion. The Messiah will be a descendant of David and come from Bethlehem; Jesus, however, comes from the region of Galilee. Although Jesus indeed spent most of his life in Nazareth (which was in the region of Galilee), it is clear that these onlookers were unaware of the circumstances of his birth, or his historical pedigree (see Mt 1:1–2:1). This ignorance is also reflected in the comments of the Pharisees, who dismiss Jesus as a nonentity. No prophets will come out of Galilee (7:45–52).

The passage is also of importance on account of Jesus' references to the future coming of the Spirit (7:37–39). The Spirit will only come when Jesus has been glorified—a clear reference to the resurrection. And when the Spirit does come, he will be like "streams of living water" within believers, bringing them new life and refreshment.

7:53–8:11 A Woman Caught in Adultery. A section now follows that is not present in the earliest manuscripts of John's gospel. Those manuscripts that do include it occasionally place it at other points—such as toward the end of John 21, or even toward the end of Luke 21. The incident in question does, however, fit in entirely with what we know of the ministry of Jesus. The incident deals with a woman who is about to be put to death by stoning for adultery. Should this sentence be carried out? The question bears a close resemblance to the question about whether it was proper to pay taxes to Caesar. If Jesus declared it was not proper to do so, he would have been in open conflict with the law. As it happens, Jesus upholds the law, while imposing a condition upon its execution that makes this impossible. Whoever is "without sin" (not the specific sin of adultery, but any sin in general) may carry out the sentence. The woman's accusers slink away, beginning with the oldest (who presumably have accumulated the greatest burden of sin). The passage provides a superb illustration of the manner in which sin has permeated human nature.

8:12–59 The Validity of Jesus' Testimony. Further controversy now ensues (8:12–59). Jesus declares that he is the "light of the world" (8:12)—the second of the great "I am" sayings. The point being made is that in a world of darkness and sin, Jesus is the light by which people are saved from their lostness. Father and Son together testify that this is the truth. Human beings, even if they are the descendants of Abraham, are slaves to sin and are unable to break free from its bondage. Only Jesus himself is free from sin (8:46) and able to make known the truth that will set people free. Abraham and the prophets were great people, but they died like everyone else. But there will be something different about Jesus—a clear reference to the resurrection. His audience is shocked by the boldness of this claim.

This claim is further developed with a dramatic assertion on the part of Jesus: "Before Abraham was born, I am!" (8:58). Like the "I am" saying that opened this section (8:12), the Greek structure of this statement picks up the name of God revealed to Moses (Ex 3:14) and hints strongly at the eternity of Jesus Christ. The Christian reader of John's gospel already knows this. The Prologue (1:1–18) contains a strong statement of the preexistence of Christ and of his involvement in the work of creation itself. Before Abraham or the world came into being, Jesus Christ was already existent and active. To the Christian, this is a glorious affirmation of the divinity of Christ. However, to many Jewish onlookers at the time, it was nothing less than blasphemy. And so they tried to stone Jesus, just as they had earlier sought to stone the woman taken in adultery.

9:1–41 Jesus Heals a Man Born Blind. Jesus then continues to demonstrate his authority to heal and teach. In a fitting confirmation of his claim to be the "light of the world" (8:12; 9:5), Jesus heals a man who is born blind. This great healing becomes the focus for Jesus' declaration that the world is spiritually blind and needs to be healed if it is to see and benefit from the light of the world. Controversy results over both the healing itself and its implications. The Pharisees, who try to play down its importance, find themselves humiliated by the insistence on the part of the healed blind man, who wants to tell everyone about his healing and about the one who healed him. Totally frustrated, they "threw him out" (9:34)—a probable reference to some kind of excommunication. Yet the formerly blind man merely comes to faith in Jesus Christ and worships him (9:38)—an acknowledgment of the divinity of Christ, in that Jews were permitted to worship only God and none other (Ex 20:4–5). He had been rejected by his own people, yet he found acceptance with Jesus.

10:1–21 The Shepherd and His Flock. The narrative now shifts from a discussion of Jesus as the "light of the world" to Jesus as "the good shepherd." This section includes two of the seven "I am" sayings. The section opens by establishing the imagery of the people of God as sheep—an image that would be familiar through its extensive use in the Old Testament (e.g., see Ps 74:1; 78:52; 79:13; 100:3; 119:176). In much the same way, God himself was often portrayed as the shepherd of his people (e.g., see Ge 49:24; Ps 23:1; 80:1; Jer 31:10). Basing himself on this well-known imagery, Jesus declares, in the third of the "I am" sayings, that he is the "gate for the sheep" (10:7, 9). This powerful image makes the following point: there is only one way in which sheep can find safety, and that is through him. Only through Jesus Christ can anyone come in from the dangers of a fallen world and find safety and rest inside. Anyone who enters through Jesus will find salvation, pasture, and life (10:9–10).

The discussion then turns to the image of a shepherd. In the past, Israel had suffered from irresponsible, uncaring, and self-seeking leaders, referred to as "false shepherds." In his great prophetic vision of the future of Israel, Ezekiel looked forward to the day when the Lord himself would shepherd his people (Eze 34:1–17). In referring to himself as the "good shepherd" (10:11), Jesus declares that this moment has arrived. His care for his sheep is such that he will—and, as events will prove, does—lay down his life for his sheep. He does this willingly and voluntarily, in obedience to his Father, who will then restore him to life.

10:22–42 The Unbelief of the Jews. These sayings, and many others, anger some of his Jewish audience. They accuse him of blasphemy: "You, a mere man, claim to be God" (10:33). Jesus rejects this argument. There is no blasphemy in his declaring himself to be the Son of God if his words and deeds demonstrate that this is indeed the case. If his critics will not listen to what he says, will they not at least ask what his great miracles point to? Yet despite the official hostility, many continue to put their faith in him.

11:1–44 The Death of Lazarus. The authority of Jesus is then confirmed dramatically in one of the best-known episodes in John's gospel—the raising of Lazarus. Lazarus is the brother of Mary and Martha, two sisters from the village of Bethany, both of whom are mentioned elsewhere in the New Testament (Lk 10:38–42). It is clear that the family is known to Jesus. On hearing that Lazarus is ill, Jesus eventually travels to be with them. When they finally arrive at the village, Lazarus has been dead for four days. This period is important, because it emphasizes that Lazarus is totally past any hope of resuscitation.

On his arrival, Jesus is greeted by Martha. He assures her that her brother will rise again. Martha's reply makes reference to the general Jewish belief (not shared, however, by the Sadducees) that the dead will rise at the end of time (11:23–24). Jesus then dramatically declares, in the fifth of the "I am" sayings, that he is "the resurrection and the life" (11:25). This terse statement declares more than the central Christian belief that resurrection and eternal life are made possible through Jesus Christ. It declares that Jesus himself *is* the life that is made possible through his resurrection. Eternal life is about being with Christ. Resurrection is about being raised with Christ, to be with Christ. Jesus Christ is not simply the basis of the gospel. He is also its content.

What Jesus said here is enormously significant and needs to be looked at carefully. First, he declares that anyone "who believes in me will live," even if he dies (11:25). This part of the statement makes it clear that anyone who puts faith in Jesus Christ has the hope of resurrection and eternal life, and need no longer fear death. The second part of the statement amplifies this somewhat: anyone who "lives and believes in me will never die" (11:26). This makes a slightly different point: that to have faith in Jesus is to begin something now, so that, at least in one sense, such a person will never die. Death implies separation. Jesus' point is that a relationship may be begun with him now through faith, and that death cannot in any way separate the believer from Christ.

Martha's response to this is immediate. She puts her trust both in the messenger and the message, and she acknowledges that he is indeed the Messiah (or "Christ"), the Son of God who has come into the world (11:27). That trust is immediately justified. Jesus shows that he has authority even over death, as he brings Lazarus back from the dead to the amazement of all. Even the dead hear his voice and respond to it. And so do the living—deeply impressed by what they see, many of Mary's friends put their faith in him (11:45).

11:45–57 The Plot to Kill Jesus. However, when the Sanhedrin, the supreme Jewish court, hears of these developments, they do not respond with faith. Instead, they make plans to destroy Jesus (11:46–57). Caiaphas, the high priest at the time, is clearly worried about the threat of Roman intervention if things get out of hand and many respond to Jesus. He argues that the death of Jesus for his people would be preferable to the entire nation being wiped out. His words are a simple statement of political realism, but they have a deeper meaning than he intends or imagines. For Jesus does indeed

> Jesus received word that his friend Lazarus was ill in Bethany. But he delayed going to him and Lazarus died. Only then did Jesus go to Bethany. He went to the tomb and called Lazarus to come out. Though dead for four days, Lazarus was once again alive, and many came to believe in Jesus.

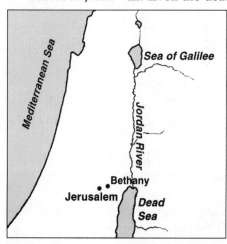

die for his people—not in order to avert the threat of Roman intervention, which came about with a massive vengeance in A.D. 70, but in order to make it possible for their sins to be forgiven.

12:1–11 Jesus Anointed at Bethany. The closeness of Jesus' death is then brought home by his being anointed with expensive oil by Mary. As the Passover draws near, Jesus prepares to die for his people.

JOHN 12:12 – 17:26

The Farewell Discourses of Jesus Christ

12:12–19 The Triumphal Entry. The triumphal entry into Jerusalem takes place against this background of threats against Jesus on the part of the Jewish religious authorities. Yet despite all their threats and criticisms, more and more are coming to faith in him. As we read the account of this entry, we again come across a theme we noted earlier—that the disciples do not fully understand what is happening at the time and only come to a full appreciation of its importance in the light of the resurrection (12:12–19).

12:20–36 Jesus Predicts His Death. Jesus then predicts his own death and declares that this is the ultimate reason for his coming into the world. When he is lifted up from the earth on the cross, he will draw everyone to himself (12:32). This verse represents a dramatic clarification of Isaiah's great prophecy of the coming of a suffering servant (Isa 52:13–53:12). This prophecy had spoken of this servant being "raised and lifted up and highly exalted" (Isa 52:13). This could have been misunderstood to mean "made important, and given an important status in the world." Now we realize that it means something rather different. The suffering servant will be raised up on a cross for all to see. The hope of resurrection for that servant is indeed there—but first, he must be raised up on the cross and die in the full gaze of a scornful public.

12:37–50 The Jews Continue in Their Unbelief. So why do so few believe in him? Why this atmosphere of pervasive unbelief? Has not Jesus shown his authority in all that he has said and done? John now draws our attention to the fact that this rejection and unbelief had been foretold in the great prophetic writings of the Old Testament. Noting the prophecies of Isaiah in particular, John declares that Isaiah had seen the glory of Jesus himself and was speaking about Christ in the prophecies in question.

13:1–17 Jesus Washes His Disciples' Feet. The section now moves on to the great "farewell discourses"—the words spoken by Jesus to his closest disciples as he prepares to be taken from them and put to death. Once Judas has left the assembled company, Jesus can speak openly to those who remain about what lies ahead. But first, John sets the scene for these discourses

(13:1–30). It is "just before the Passover," when Israel recalled God's great act of deliverance in the past, by which he set his people free from their bondage in Egypt. A Passover lamb was sacrificed in memory of this great event. With great skill, John draws his readers' attention to a central insight of the gospel. A new act of divine deliverance is about to take place, with Jesus as the true Passover lamb who gives his life as a sacrifice for the sins of his people. John stresses that Jesus knows he has to die (13:1, 3). His death is no accident, no premature end to a promising career as a religious teacher. Here is the Savior of the world, preparing to die for those whom he loves.

The passage stresses the humility of Jesus. He is prepared to wash his disciples' feet (13:4–5). At a Christian seminary in India, there is a statue of Jesus washing Peter's feet. Hindu visitors to the seminary often pause to admire it. They assume it depicts a disciple falling down in worship at Jesus' feet. They are astonished to learn that it is Jesus who is kneeling. "How he must love his disciples," some of them remark.

Having washed his disciples' feet, Jesus explains the importance of this action (13:12–17). We see here a superb illustration of the idea of a "servant king"—someone who has authority, but exercises it by serving, rather than dominating others.

13:18–30 Jesus Predicts His Betrayal. One of the great themes of the New Testament is that Jesus brings to fulfillment the great prophecies of the Old Testament. Many of these prophecies are positive in tone, speaking of the coming of the Messiah to his people, and of the marvelous things he will achieve. But some are more melancholy, speaking of the betrayal of the Messiah by one who is close to him. Once more, John makes it clear that the betrayal of Jesus is no accident. Sadly, it is something that has to happen. Jesus explains this to his disciples so that they will not be dismayed when it does (13:19). Not only is he to be betrayed, but perhaps most shocking of all, he is to be betrayed by one of those with whom he is sharing that last supper. Here, John notes Jesus' own distress (13:21) as he faces up to the grim events that lie ahead. We must never think that death was an easy thing for Jesus to face.

But which of the disciples is it to be? Who will betray him? One of themes we find earlier in John's gospel is that Jesus knows the inmost secrets of people's hearts. For example, both Nathanael and the Samaritan woman are amazed that he knows their innermost thoughts so intimately. It comes as no surprise to find that he knows who is to betray him (13:22–27): it will be Judas.

In a poignant passage, Jesus tells Judas to go and do what has to be done (13:27). As Judas leaves the room and the presence of Christ, John makes his famous comment: "And it was night" (13:30). Judas has left the presence of the Light of the World and has gone into the darkness of a fallen and sinful world. Through Judas, the Light of the World will be extinguished. Through the power of God, however, it will rekindled.

13:31–38 Jesus Predicts His Death and Peter's Denial. With the departure of Judas, Jesus can speak frankly and openly to the faithful disciples. The farewell discourses that now follow represent moments of great intimacy between Jesus and his disciples, as he explains what is going to happen and prepares them for the future. First, Jesus repeats what he had said earlier: he is soon to be taken from them (13:33). Yet this will lead both to his own glorification and to the glorification of God through him. Yet the main emphasis of this passage falls on the need for disciples to love one another (13:34–35). Jesus loves them so much that he will die for them; that same quality of love is to be evident in the lives of Christian believers. Love of this quality cannot be ignored by the world (13:35).

Peter then asks Jesus to explain where he is going and asks to be allowed to come with him (13:36–38). Jesus explains that Peter will have his wish in due course. But not yet. When Peter protests, Jesus predicts that he will be denied by Peter three times "before the cock crows." The reference to the "cock crowing" needs a little comment. The Romans divided the night into four "watches"—evening, 6:00–9:00 P.M.; midnight, 9:00 P.M.–12:00; "when the cock crows" 12:00–3:00 A.M.; and dawn, 3:00–6:00 A.M. (see Mk 13:35). The "cock crowing" may in fact be a reference to the trumpet blast that marked the end of the third watch of the night, rather than to the cry of a cockerel.

14:1–4 Jesus Comforts His Disciples. It is clear that the disciples are distressed at the thought of Jesus' leaving them. Knowing this, Jesus comforts them. The disciples must learn to trust him. He knows what he is doing and where he is going. And in the midst of this reassurance, we find the promise that where Christ goes, his disciples will follow. They will not be separated from him, but will know the joy of being reunited with him. They—and all believers—will be privileged guests in his Father's house.

14:5–14 Jesus, the Way to the Father. But how can they find their way there? Thomas raises the kind of awkward commonsense question that may have gone through the minds of others (14:5). Jesus replies with a powerful and helpful statement: "I am the way and the truth and the life" (14:6). Jesus does not show the way and then leave his disciples to make their own way unaided. He takes them there, accompanying them as they travel. He is far more than a good religious teacher, who tells his followers what to do and who to believe. He is the good shepherd, who loves, tends, feeds, and guides his sheep.

But how can we know what God is like? Once more, Jesus provides a powerful answer (14:7–13). God is Christlike. To have seen Jesus is to have seen the Father (14:9). To give an example, the love of Jesus for his disciples is shown by his being prepared to give his life for them. There is no love greater than this. And that is what the love of God is like. Jesus is like a snapshot of God, the "image of the invisible God," as Paul puts it (Col 1:15). Yet the love of Christ for believers must also be shown in the love which believers show towards each other.

14:15–31 Jesus Promises the Holy Spirit. However, the main theme of this section of the passage is the giving of the Holy Spirit. Christians will not be on their own in the midst of a disbelieving and hostile world. They will be given "another Counselor" (14:16), who will be sent by the Father. This is an enormously encouraging thought. The word *Counselor* has a number of meanings, including "comforter." The root meaning suggests someone who encourages, reassures, and stimulates believers to do things that otherwise they could never do. Without such divine assistance, Christians would be unable to live and work effectively for God in the world. When God issues a command, he also provides gifts that equip his people for the tasks that lie ahead. Christians are not like "orphans" (14:18). They can rest assured of the continuing presence and care of God as they live out their calling in the world. The Holy Spirit is God's gift to his people, to enable believers to obey Christ's commands (14:21).

But perhaps Jesus is just saying these things to encourage his disciples. Perhaps they are without any basis in reality. Possibly aware of such thoughts, Jesus moves to reassure them. These are not his own words. They are the words of his Father (14:24) who sent him. As the resurrection confirms, Jesus speaks as one who has the right to make promises on God's behalf—promises that can be trusted.

Developing the idea of the Holy Spirit as the Counselor, Jesus assures his disciples that the Spirit will bring to mind all that he has taught them (14:26). He then speaks some enormously consoling words to his disciples. "My peace I give you" (14:27). This is not peace as the world understands it. Secular ideas of peace may include an absence of conflict, but cannot bring any comfort or peace of mind in the face of death. The peace that Jesus offers brings hope in the face of death, and a reassurance that his love will never let his people go. For this reason, the disciples need not be troubled or afraid. Once more, as the resurrection makes clear, this is no wishful thinking, but an assurance based upon the power of a loving God. Finally, Jesus assures his disciples of one remaining issue. Even though "the prince of this world is coming" (14:30), he has no hold over Jesus. The reference is to Satan and his allies, such as sin and death. Jesus will die. But that is not to be the end of the story. The best wine is yet to come.

15:1–17 The Vine and the Branches. We have already noted the importance of the great "I am" sayings of John's gospel. In this passage, Jesus says "I am the true vine" (15:1, 5). The image of a vine has deep Old Testament roots. Jesus uses it to emphasize the importance of "remaining in him," perhaps more familiar in older English translations as "abiding in him." Believers are attached to Jesus as branches are attached to a vine. And just as a branch can only bear fruit if it remains attached to the vine, so believers can only bear fruit if they remain in Christ. If they fail to do so, they will wither and die (15:6). There seems to be no intended reference to eternal punishment in the image of a dead branch being "thrown into the fire and burned." The point being made is simply that there is nothing much that can be done with a dead branch except use it for firewood. But believers are not meant to be like this. By remaining close to Christ, they will bear much fruit, as God intends them to. But apart from—that is, removed from—Christ, they can do nothing (15:5).

The image of a vine is also important because of the idea of pruning (15:2). This is one of the most important New Testament ways of dealing with suffering. Just as a father disciplines only those whom he loves, so the Father only prunes those branches that he expects to bear fruit. Christians must learn to see suffering, difficulty, or adversity as a form of God's pruning, by which he will make them better Christians and more effective witnesses to him in the world. Useless branches are discarded. Only those that are worth the trouble are pruned.

We now return to the theme of the love of Christ for his disciples and the love these disciples must have for each other. If this theme seems familiar, it is on account of its importance. There is a natural connection between the love of the Father for the Son, the love of the Son for believers, and the love of believers for each other (15:9–10, 17). In much the same way, there is a close connection between obedience, love, and joy (15:10–12). Obedience to the love of Christ is the only route to lasting joy.

Jesus then speaks words that are so familiar that we need to rediscover them and savor their full meaning: "Greater love has no one than this, that one lay down his life for his friends" (15:13). There is nothing more that anyone can give than life itself. And that is what Jesus will give for those whom he loves. He can give no more, and he willingly gives his life in order that others might live. It is a deeply moving thought, which reminds believers of how precious they are in the sight of Christ. But there is more to this great affirmation. Those for whom Jesus dies are not so much his "servants," as his "friends" (15:14–16). In washing his disciples' feet, Jesus makes it clear that he is not prepared to lord it over them. They are not his menial servants, but his friends—those whom he has chosen, and those whom he loves.

Believers are not those who have chosen Jesus, but those whom Jesus has chosen (15:16). This may seem strange at first. Believers may feel: Surely we *did* choose to follow him? Surely it *was* our decision? But Jesus here points to the deeper insight—that God draws people to him, preparing the way as they come home to him. As they look back over how they came to faith, Christians can sometimes see the hand of God at work, moving them in certain ways that eventually led them to discover him. Christians are believers because they are *meant* to be believers.

15:18–16:4 The World Hates the Disciples. Jesus now turns to deal with the hostility of the world toward believers. Although the world was created by God, it has now rebelled against him, refusing to recognize his authority over it. The world thus hates Jesus, who asserts God's claims over his creation and declares it to be sinful: "If I had not come and spoken to them, they would not be guilty of sin. Now, however, they have no excuse for their sin" (15:22). And its hate for Jesus extends to the disciples: "If the world hates you, keep in mind that it hated me first" (15:18). The world's hostility toward Christ is thus transferred to his servants. To be a Christian is potentially to suffer on account of Christ, who suffered first in order that believers be called by his name. To be a Christian is to be called out of the world (15:19) and bear the force of its fury at having lost its control of us.

16:5–33 The Work of the Holy Spirit; Grief Into Joy. We now learn of the mixed feelings of joy and sadness experienced by the disciples on account of their knowledge of the imminent suffering and death of Christ. On the one hand, they are horrified that the man whom they love and adore is to be taken from them to die in such a horrific manner. On the other hand, they know that his death will bring about the salvation of the world. The "Lamb of God, who takes away the sin of the world" (1:29) must be slain before he can take that sin away. In this passage, Jesus confronts those mixed feelings and reassures his disciples: "You are filled with grief. But I tell you the truth: It is for your good that I am going away" (16:6–7).

Jesus now returns to the great theme of the coming of the Holy Spirit—the Counselor or Comforter whose presence and power will guide and empower the disciples as they face the future for Christ. The task of persuading the world of its sin is not something Christians must accomplish unaided. They will be assisted by the Spirit (16:8–9). The coming of the Spirit at Pentecost may be seen as fulfilling this prophecy.

Finally, Jesus speaks of his resurrection (16:16). It is immediately clear that Jesus' words cause his disciples some confusion. They just cannot take in all that he is saying. It doesn't seem to make sense. They are bewildered. Yet Jesus knows what they are thinking (16:19). He uses an analogy to bring out how grief can be changed to joy. The analogy is that of a woman giving birth to a child (16:20–22). The physical pain of giving birth gives way to the joy of knowing that a new life has come into the world. In the same way, the physical pain of Christ's death will give way to the joy of knowing that the hope of eternal life has dawned in a sad and dark world.

Finally, Jesus assures his disciples of his continuing love and care for them and grants them the privilege of being able to approach the Father in his name (16:23–24). Whatever they ask in his name will be given to them. This does not mean that God will give believers anything they want, providing they simply add the word "in Jesus' name" mechanically onto their prayers. Rather, it means that God will grant them all that they need to "abide in Christ," and bear much fruit in his name. The Christian tasks of evangelism and care may be great—but so are the gifts God provides to minister in his name.

The subject now changes slightly, as Jesus deals with his own mission:

> I came from the Father and entered the world; now I am leaving the world and going back to the Father. (16:28)

Christ humbled himself so that he could come into this world and redeem sinful humanity. "God so loved the world that he gave his one and only Son, that whoever believes in him shall not perish but have eternal life" (3:16). After his mission has been accomplished, he will be exalted by the Father.

But this is in the future. In the meantime, the disciples will be scattered after Jesus' death and will have trouble and sorrow in his world. But in the midst of all these difficulties, they may have the consolation of knowing that Jesus has overcome the world (16:33). Its apparent triumph is temporary. The death of Jesus seems to point to the world's victory over Christ. The resurrection shows that it is the world that has been defeated, and that Christ is the victor. Christians need that kind of perspective as they contemplate the sadness and despair of the world. This knowledge brings an assurance of peace. The world may cause all kinds of anxieties to believers as they wonder what is going on and whether God is really there. But Christ reassures his disciples: "Take heart! I have overcome the world."

17:1–26 Jesus Prays. This section is followed by an extended prayer of Jesus (17:1–26), which is often referred to as the "high priestly prayer" on account of the themes of offering and sacrifice that can be seen throughout it. The time has now come (17:1). Earlier in the gospel, Jesus had often stated that the time had not yet come (e.g., 2:4; 7:6, 30; 8:20). But now that moment has arrived. God had given Jesus the authority to bring knowledge of him to the world, and in doing so to bring eternal life. That task has now been accomplished. It is time to go.

But what of those whom he leaves behind? What of the disciples? Jesus offers a prayer on their behalf. They have put their trust in him and will remain behind in the world after he has been taken from it. Jesus prays that they might know God's protection and unity in all that lies ahead for them. They are no longer "of the world." Yet Jesus' prayer is not that they should be taken out of the world, but that they should be protected and encouraged while they witness to and in that world.

Yet Jesus also looks ahead down the great road of history, to those who will put their faith in him on account of the disciples' witness. He prays for them as well, that they might know unity and the joy of being able to go where he is about to go, and be with him. Jesus prays that the love that the

Father had for the Son might be present among them in whatever lies ahead for them (17:25–26).

JOHN 18:1 – 21:25 ─────────────────────────

The Passion, Death, and Resurrection of Christ

18:1–11 Jesus Arrested. The farewell discourses now come to an end. Words give way to actions, as Jesus prepares to meet his death. Jesus and his disciples cross the Kidron Valley to the east of Jerusalem and enter an olive grove. It is there that they are confronted by Judas and a detachment of soldiers. The moment of betrayal has come. Brushing aside a pathetic attempt on the part of Peter to prevent the arrest, Jesus affirms that he is prepared to "drink the cup" that the Father has given him. He will go through with the suffering that is an integral part of the mission for which God has sent him into the world.

18:12–21 Jesus Taken to Annas; Peter's Denial. Jesus is then forcibly taken before Annas and Caiphas, followed by Peter and "another disciple"—possibly John himself. Although Caiphas was the high priest, there appears to have been lingering popular affection for Annas, who was deposed as high priest by the Romans in A.D. 15. Although he no longer had any official position of seniority, he nevertheless continued to exercise considerable influence (18:12–14). While the process of interrogation proceeds, Peter finds himself denying anything to do with Jesus. The challenge does not come from anyone of any importance, but merely from a slave girl. Yet Peter still denies having anything to do with Jesus. He will deny him two more times before the cock crows (18:25–27; see 13:38).

18:19–40 The High Priest Questions Jesus; Jesus Before Pilate. In the meantime, Jesus is being subjected to questioning by the high priest. Initially, Jesus makes the point that the high priest and his officials had ample opportunity to question him about his teaching while he taught openly in the temple area. Why all this secrecy? Why not challenge him openly? John's gospel does not go into any detail about the precise charges that are brought against Jesus by his accusers. However, it is clear that they are sufficiently serious to warrant his being turned over to the Roman authorities (18:28–40). Pilate, Roman governor of Judea A.D. 26–36, is clearly puzzled by the charges brought against Jesus. The Jewish leaders want to avoid entering the Roman palace so that they are not affected by the ritual uncleanliness which would result from this contact with Gentiles on the eve of the major religious festival of the Passover. Pilate is therefore obliged to leave the palace and confront the crowd outside.

The issue Pilate has to determine is whether there is any basis for a death sentence against Jesus. He explores the issue of whether Jesus is a king, and receives the reply that Jesus' kingdom is "not of this world" (18:36). Pilate takes this as meaning that Jesus admits to being a king, and will now refer to Jesus, perhaps scathingly, as the "king of the Jews." Being in a position to set a prisoner free at Passover, Pilate offers to release Jesus. The crowd, however, demands the release of Barabbas, who had taken part in an insurrection against Rome.

19:1–27 Jesus Sentenced to Be Crucified. After ordering that Jesus should be flogged, Pilate brings him before the crowds again. He informs them that there is no legal basis for the death sentence. He is not prepared to crucify him. Yet the clamor increases. The crowd insists that, since Jesus claims to be the Son of God, he deserves to die. They follow up their advantage by pointing out the negative impact that any report of someone claiming to be king of the Jews would have on Caesar, the Roman emperor. At this, Pilate caves in. As the Jews declare that they have no king but Caesar, Pilate hands Jesus over to be crucified (19:1–16). Over the place of his execution, the charge against him is written for all to see: "Jesus of Nazareth, King of the Jews." In many paintings and representations of the crucifixion, this inscription is represented by four letters: INRI—the initial letters of the Latin phrase *Iesus Nazarenus Rex Iudaeorum*, meaning "Jesus of Nazareth, King of the Jews."

The soldiers in charge of the execution throw lots for his clothes. In doing so, they unconsciously fulfill the great prophecy of Psalm 22:18, which speaks of the destiny of a righteous sufferer. In drawing attention to this psalm, John also intends his readers to note the many other parallels between the prophetic description of the sufferings of this righteous person and the actual events of the crucifixion itself. And, watching from a safe distance is the disciple Jesus loved—widely regarded as a reference to the author of this gospel—John, who is thus identified as an eyewitness of the events which take place.

19:28–42 The Death and Burial of Jesus. Finally, Jesus dies (19:28–37). His final words are "It is finished." The Greek original of these words has the sense "It is accomplished," or perhaps, in certain contexts, "It has been settled or paid." This is no cry of despair. This is a cry of achievement. What had to be done is done. For John, Jesus is the true Passover lamb, who dies on the cross at more or less the moment when the Passover lambs are being slain. Just as the Passover lamb has to be perfect and without any broken bones (Ex 12:46), so it is in the case of Jesus, the sinless Passover lamb who is slain for the sin of the world. It appears to have been normal practice to break the legs of the victims of crucifixion, to hasten their end by denying them any means of supporting themselves on the cross. Yet in Jesus' case, this is not necessary—again, leading to an unwitting fulfillment on the part of the Roman soldiers of a great Old Testament prophecy. Instead, Jesus is

This tomb in Jerusalem shows the way a large round stone could be rolled into place to seal the tomb after a person had been buried. The groove in which the stone rolled sloped down so it was much harder to open the tomb than to close it.

stabbed with a spear to make sure that he is dead, as a result of which "a sudden flow of blood and water" emerges—apparently a description of clotted blood. There can be no doubt that Jesus is dead. Joseph of Arimathea, accompanied by Nicodemus, arranges for his burial in a nearby borrowed tomb (19:38–42). As the following day is the Sabbath, there is nothing more that can be done. Further arrangements will have to wait until Sunday.

20:1–9 The Empty Tomb. Sunday arrives. Mary Magdalene is the first to visit the tomb "while it was still dark." Mark's account places this visit "just after sunrise" (Mk 16:2), when darkness would gradually have been giving way to the first light of day. It is clear, however, that something dramatic has happened during the night. Mary's initial reaction is that the authorities—whether Jewish or Roman—have removed Jesus' dead body. There is no hint of an expectation of resurrection—a point that John explains to his readers (20:9). All they can see is that the dead body of Jesus is there no more. The gravecloths in which Jesus had been wrapped remain inside the tomb. Jesus, however, has gone (20:1–9).

20:10–23 Jesus Appears to Mary Magdalene and to His Disciples. The disciples return home (20:10). There is no hint of joy at the thought of the resurrection of Jesus. The atmosphere is that of utter disconsolation. Not only is Jesus dead, but they have not even been allowed to bury him properly and pay their final respects to the man who mattered so much to them. Yet Mary remains behind, lingering at the site of the empty tomb. Unaware of what has really taken place, she is astonished to find a figure behind her, who she takes to be the gardener—that is, the person in charge of the garden (19:41) within which the tomb was located (20:11–15).

The "gardener" then speaks to her. And just as the sheep know the voice of the good shepherd (10:3–5), so Mary recognizes who is speaking to her. Overjoyed, she rushes to tell the others of what—or, more accurately, who—she has seen (20:16–18). Although they are initially obliged to rely upon her testimony, they soon discover for themselves the reality of the resurrection, as Jesus stands among them in his risen glory that same evening (20:19–23). There is a fascinating parallel here with the story of the Samaritan woman. Just as the people of her village initially believed in Jesus on account of her report, but then discovered it to be true for themselves (4:42), so the disciples also trust Mary, before what she said is confirmed by Jesus himself.

20:24–29 Jesus Appears to Thomas. But not Thomas. He is absent from the meeting at which Jesus appears to his disciples and is deeply skeptical of their reports about the resurrection. He wants proof. He wants to see the nail marks in Christ's hand and to touch his wounds, both from the nails and the spear. On being confronted with the risen Christ, he kneels in adoration. His confession is of the utmost importance: "My Lord and my God." It is one of the clearest statements in the New Testament of the divinity of Jesus Christ. But it is also important to notice how Jesus looks ahead to the doubts of those who will come to faith later. Thomas has it easy. He can have his doubts dispelled by an encounter with Christ. Those who come later—including all the readers of this section—are more blessed than he, for they have believed without access to this sort of proof.

20:30–31 An Explanation. This section of the gospel ends with an explanation (20:30–31). John has had to be selective in what he included in his gospel. There is so much more that could have been included. But what we find in this gospel has been written for a reason—to bring us to faith in this same Jesus Christ, so that we might, along with those we have read about, believe that he is the Messiah and the son of God, and thus come to have the same eternal life which has been the subject of this gospel.

21:1–23 Jesus and the Miraculous Catch of Fish; His Reinstatement of Peter. The gospel as a whole now comes to a close with an epilogue, stressing once more the reality of the resurrection (21:1–14). All the doubts about the resurrection are dispelled. It is clear that Jesus has risen, and that this news, along with all that it implies for the world, must be proclaimed. But attention focuses on two disciples: Peter, and the "disciple whom Jesus loved" (almost certainly a reference to John himself). In a moving dialogue (21:15–23), Jesus both charges Peter with the responsibility of taking care of his sheep, and looks ahead to the day of Peter's own death (Peter is thought to have been martyred at Rome under the emperor Nero around A.D. 64). Despite his denial of Jesus, he is now reinstated. Jesus speaks the words of reinstatement and recommissioning: "Follow me!" It does not matter what happens to others, as Jesus' comments about the other disciple (21:20–22) make clear. The important thing is to follow Jesus, irrespective of where that same following may lead others.

21:24–25 Conclusion. John then ends his gospel. It is clear that there is so much more that he wants to tell his readers. There is simply not enough space for him to say all that he would like. But there is more than enough to give food for thought and to convey the full significance of Jesus Christ, who is the "light of the world" and the "bread of life" to a hungry people who up to now have walked in darkness.

ACTS

Acts—or the Acts of the Apostles, as it is often called—is the second installment of Luke's account of the origins of the Christian church and follows on from the gospel attributed to Luke. Taken together, Luke's gospel and history of the early church is the largest single document in the New Testament. In his gospel, Luke told Theophilus (probably a well-placed Roman official who had become interested in Christianity) about the life, death, and resurrection of Jesus. However, the story does not stop there. By the time Luke was writing, Christianity was well on the way to becoming a major force in the Roman empire. So how did Christianity progress from its humble origins in Palestine to the hub of the Roman empire? How did it come to wield such influence in so short a time?

Luke sets out to show how the gospel spread like wildfire throughout the Roman empire. He is careful to make a distinction between the divine power that lies behind the gospel (such as the resurrection of Christ and the gift of the Holy Spirit), and the human agents who served to spread it (such as Peter and Paul). Acts opens with a vivid account of the ascension of the risen Christ and the coming of the Holy Spirit in power. Although the work is entitled Acts of the Apostles, it could probably equally well be described as the "Acts of the Holy Spirit." Having allowed us to appreciate the power of the gospel, Luke moves on to deal with the people who were committed to it. The first twelve chapters focus on Peter and the dramatic series of events that led to the Christian gospel's becoming firmly rooted in Jerusalem and the surrounding regions.

Having shown how the gospel became rooted in Palestine, Luke moves on to show how it gradually became established in much of the Roman empire. The remainder of the work focuses on Paul—a figure familiar to readers of the New Testament. Luke explains Paul's background and shows how he became first a Christian, then the "apostle to the Gentiles." He gives a vivid account of the impact Paul had on the expansion of the Christian church from Palestine into the regions of modern-day Turkey and Greece. He gives details of the three missionary journeys Paul undertook in the eastern Mediterranean, and ends with a description of his final voyage as a prisoner to Rome itself. Luke gives us access to some of Paul's sermons, allowing us to appreciate the way he presented the gospel in a variety of different situations.

ACTS 1:1 – 12:25 ───────────────

The First Days of the Church

1:1–11 The Gift Provided. Luke begins his second work by reminding his readers of the great events of Easter and of Christ's command not to leave Jerusalem, but to wait for the gift God had promised (1:4). But what is this gift? And when would it come?

Immediately, Luke answers this question by reminding his readers that John the Baptist merely baptized his followers with water, whereas Jesus would baptize "with the Holy Spirit" (1:5). John's baptism symbolized regeneration. The baptism that Jesus offers brings real renewal and rebirth. The disciples have been called to be Christ's "witnesses in all Judea and Samaria, and to the ends of the earth" (1:8). This is a great and daunting responsibility. Christians are not to stand around idly, wondering where Jesus has gone (1:10–11). Their task is to make that same Christ known to the world.

However, Luke makes it clear that this great challenge is matched by an equally great enabling gift. The disciples will "receive power when the Holy Spirit comes" on them (1:8). Here we find one of the great themes of the New Testament: God gives gifts to enable his people to meet the challenges and tasks he gives them. The church still needs those gifts badly as she confronts the new challenges and opportunities awaiting her.

1:12–14 Fellowship. This opening passage closes with a vivid portrayal of the close-knit fellowship that is enjoyed by the early church (1:13–14). Though small in number, they are full of confidence and anticipation. Where once they had been a band of demoralized and dismayed men and women who had seen their leader executed, they are now an excited group of evangelists, waiting to proclaim the good news of their risen Savior to the world. And, as we shall see, they do not have long to wait.

At this stage, the Christian church is small in number. Luke mentions the figure of 120 believers (1:15). It is all too easy for the casual reader of Acts to lose sight of the importance of this point. We know from history that the church would grow enormously. But try to imagine that you don't know this. Try to imagine that you are reading this for the very first time, not knowing what is going to happen. In a period in which new religions were born every minute, what chance would so small a group of people have? Would their message survive at all? The fact that it did is, as Paul points out, a reminder that the gospel does not rest on human wisdom, but on the power of God.

1:15–26 Matthias Chosen to Replace Judas. The passage goes on to describe the search for a replacement for Judas. But why was a replacement needed? One suggestion is that the twelve apostles were the New Testament equivalent of the twelve tribes of Israel. Further, just as Peter sees the betrayal of Jesus foreshadowed in Old Testament prophecy (1:20), so he also sees there the need for a replacement. Note how the authority of Scripture is linked with the action of the Holy Spirit (1:16).

What qualifications were thought of as being necessary for someone to share in the "apostolic ministry" (1:25)? The basic requirement seems to have been that an apostle is one who was present with the remaining eleven apostles from the point at which Jesus was baptized by John to the moment of his ascension (1:21–22). Matthias is then chosen by the casting of lots (1:26). This is an exceptional course of action in exceptional circumstances, reminding believers that God must be involved in the selection of church leaders. It follows a well-established Old Testament precedent, in which matters of major spiritual importance were sometimes determined by allowing the Lord to decide things through throwing lots.

2:1–13 The Holy Spirit Comes at Pentecost. We now come to one of the most important passages in the New Testament. Earlier, we saw how the disciples would "receive power when the Holy Spirit comes" on them (1:8). In this momentous passage, the fulfillment of that promise is described. "All of them were filled with the Holy Spirit" (2:4). There is no indication that the disciples were expecting anything like this to take place. They seem to have been taken by surprise, as they gathered together "on the day of Pentecost" (2:1). Luke struggles with words as he attempts to describe what happened when the Spirit came. It was "like the blowing of a violent wind" (2:2). What "seemed to be tongues of fire" (2:3) rested on those present.

It is obvious that something dramatic and unexpected has taken place, for which no existing way of speaking is adequate. Luke has to forge new images and analogies as he tries to convey the unprecedented events that unfold. Peoples from throughout the civilized world of the time hear and understand the gospel (2:5–12). They are "amazed and perplexed" (2:12) by what they hear. It is clear that something astonishing is taking place before their eyes. The barriers of culture and language are broken down as God draws to himself a new people, drawn from every nation under heaven.

Yet even the greatest works of God are mocked by those who fail to understand. Those standing around the dying Christ poked fun at him. And those witnessing the outpouring of the Spirit do the same. The disciples have had too much to drink (2:13), they sneer. Even today, people make fun of Christians on account of their conversion experiences or religious beliefs. As Luke reminds us, this is nothing new!

2:14–41 Peter Addresses the Crowd. In the midst of the excitement and confusion, Peter preaches the first recorded Christian sermon. Because his audience is largely Jewish, he makes considerable use of Old Testament prophecy, showing how it points to both the death and resurrection of Jesus and the coming of the Holy Spirit. A similar approach is often used by Matthew in his gospel, as he draws attention to the many ways in which Jesus fulfills Old Testament prophecy.

Peter begins by disposing of the suggestion that he or his colleagues are drunk. It is, after all, only nine o'clock in the morning (2:15). Something far more significant is happening. Peter explains its meaning by appealing to one of the great prophecies of the Old Testament, Joel 2:28–32, which speaks of God pouring out his Spirit upon all people "in the last days" (1:17). To understand Peter, we need to explore this Old Testament passage in a little more detail (see p. 232). In his prophecy, Joel speaks of the coming of a future day, in which God will come to his people in power and reassure them of his presence and care (Joel 2:27). The fortunes of Judah and Jerusalem will be restored, and all nations will be gathered together (Joel 3:1–2). On that day, God will "pour out [his] Spirit on all people" (Joel 2:28). The gift of the Spirit will lead to prophecy and vision. The pouring out of the Spirit is thus seen as a sign of this long-hoped-for "day of the Lord." The coming of the Spirit is thus seen as a sign of a vitally important moment in the history of the people of God, in which "everyone who calls on the name of the Lord will be saved" (Joel 2:32). As Peter makes clear, this means that salvation is now available to all.

In the first part of this sermon, Peter shows how the coming of the Holy Spirit is in fulfillment of Old Testament prophecy. He now focuses on the person of Jesus, and on his significance for the world. Peter begins this new section of the sermon by declaring that Jesus was "a man accredited by God" (2:22). God performed a series of miracles, wonders, and signs through him—things everyone knew about and recognized as being from God. Peter stresses that Christ's death on the cross was no accident, but something that took place "by God's set purpose and foreknowledge" (2:23). While this does not remove human responsibility for the death of Christ, it nevertheless sets that death in a very different context. God purposed to achieve something through the death of Christ. What Israel rejected, God sealed with his approval through the resurrection.

The theme of the Resurrection dominates this part of Peter's sermon. Two distinct ideas can be disentangled in the midst of its rich network of themes. First, the sheer joy that Jesus is alive. Death was not able to hold him (2:24, 26, 32). Second, the realization that the Resurrection means that Jesus has been "exalted to the right hand of God" (2:33). More than that: the Holy Spirit is given through Christ. "He has received from the Father the promised Holy Spirit" (2:33). Peter brings this section of the sermon to a climax by pointing out how two messianic passages from the Psalms can only refer to Jesus (2:25–35). "God has made this Jesus, whom you crucified, both Lord and Christ" (2:36). (The term *Christ* means "Messiah"; both words mean "anointed one.") Jesus is the long-promised Messiah, who has authority over his people.

The impact of Peter's preaching on his audience is immediate and shattering. "What shall we do?" (2:37) they ask. The crowd realizes that Peter's conclusion demands a response—not just agreement with what he has been saying, but a real change in heart and mind. Two words summarize the response he asks of his hearers. First, they are to *repent* (2:38). Repentance is about an inner reorientation, a turn about in one's life away from sin and toward God. The outward and public sign of this inward change is baptism, which Peter urges upon his hearers (3:38, 41). Second, having accepted the need for repentance, the way is open to *receive* (2:38) the gift of the Holy Spirit. Repentance and renewal go hand in hand, as part and parcel of the promise of God to his people. Peter makes it clear that this promise is for all. There is no small print, restricting it to only a chosen few, a privileged elite, or a national group (2:39). The message is appealing and transforming. At nine o'clock that morning, there had been 120 believers. By the evening of that same day, 3,000 had been added to their number (2:41).

2:42–47 The Fellowship of the Believers. Luke also gives us insights into the quality of the fellowship of the converts at this time. The new believers grow through the teaching of the apostles (such as that presented in many of the sermons recorded in Acts), fellowship, the breaking of the bread, and prayer (2:42). It is a time of great excitement and expectation (2:43). People expect things to happen, and—as Luke makes clear—they do, with the result that the church grows daily (2:47). The image of believers having everything in common (2:44) has served as a model for many Christian communities. Even if it sounds idealistic today, it continues to remind believers that all that they have has been given to them by God for the common good.

3:1–10 Peter Heals the Crippled Beggar. The story now changes pace. We move away from the frenetic activity of Pentecost, to an occasion when Peter and John meet a man crippled from birth at one of the temple gates (3:2, 10). His situation is hopeless. Nothing can be done for him. His only hope for survival is to beg for money. In many ways, he can be regarded as representing the pitiful condition of fallen humanity: we are unable to change our situation, and our only hope is to cope with it. Peter, however, offers the man what he really needs—healing: "Silver or gold I do not have, but what I have I give you" (3:6). Here is a powerful and moving illustration of the hope that the gospel brings to the world.

The New Testament often uses the term *healing* to refer to the salvation that comes through Christ. The word immediately suggests the idea of a restoration to wholeness, including both physical illness and broken personal relationships. It is a word that has a deep meaning for our modern world, which is aware of its ills, yet often lacks both the resources and the will to do anything about them. It is an especially important term for Luke, who was a physician by background.

Perhaps the most powerful aspect of this incident concerns the reaction of those who know the crippled man (3:9–10). It is obvious that his situation has changed. Something has happened to him. No longer is he a sullen beggar. He is seen "walking and jumping, and praising God" (3:8).

3:11–26 Peter Speaks to the Onlookers. The impact made by the healing of the crippled beggar is enormous. A crowd gathers, curious to find out more about what has happened (3:11). The opportunity is too good to miss: Peter preaches a sermon. His initial concern is to dismiss the idea that he has some special powers that healed the cripple. There is nothing special about Peter himself (3:12). On the other hand, there is something special about the risen Christ, which led to that afternoon's spectacular event. "By faith in the name of Jesus, this man whom you see and know was made strong" (3:16). Once more, we see how personal transformation is one of the most powerful and telling forms of witness to the gospel. Arguments about whether God exists or not tend to get bogged down very quickly. However, it is difficult to argue with someone who wants to talk about the difference that Christianity has made in his or her life. Perhaps Christians today can learn from this example.

Peter again stresses the importance of the resurrection of Christ (3:15), and the way in which the suffering Messiah fulfilled the great prophetic hopes of the Old Testament (3:18–26). The Old Testament points ahead, looking beyond itself to the coming of the Messiah and "times of refreshing" (3:19) for the people of God. Peter's message is direct and simple: those times have now come. The great hopes of the prophets and patriarchs have now been fulfilled. "You are the heirs of the prophets and of the covenant God made with your fathers" (3:25). Yet this promise requires a response from those who hear it. Peter asks his audience to turn from their wicked ways (3:26). It is important to appreciate that the gospel changes people's lives, not just the way people think.

4:1–4 Preaching the Resurrection of Jesus. The events after Pentecost attract a lot of attention and ensure a ready hearing for the gospel among the people. The number of believers has by now grown to 5,000 (4:4) as a result of the preaching of the gospel. But not all are pleased about these new developments. Some are distinctly threatened by them. The religious authorities of the time are outraged by the apostolic preaching of the resurrection of Jesus (4:2). Even today, some people suggest that Christians should not preach the Resurrection, because it belittles other religious teachers (who have not been raised from the dead!). Acts reminds us that for Christians, the resurrection of Jesus is nonnegotiable, something so important that it must be proclaimed, whatever the results. "We cannot help speaking about what we have seen and heard" (4:20).

4:5–22 Peter and John Before the Sanhedrin. After a night in jail, Peter and John are hauled before a religious court to account for their actions (4:5–7). But the authorities are faced with a dilemma. Everyone knows about the healing of the crippled man. It is not something that can be denied. Arguments can be refuted, but miracles are rather more difficult to deal with. (Once more, note the importance of personal transformation as a form of witness!) Peter and John defend themselves by declaring that they can only remain faithful to what they have seen and heard:

> It is by the name of Jesus Christ of Nazareth, whom you crucified but whom God raised from the dead, that this man stands before you healed. (4:10)

He alone brings salvation (4:12). How can they remain silent? They may only be "unschooled, ordinary men" (4:13), but their testimony has a power and inner conviction that cannot be denied—not least when the healed person is at hand to back them up (4:14).

4:23–31 The Believers' Prayer. Peter and John return to the church to report on what has happened to them (4:23). It is clear that the assembled believers are deeply troubled by the reports of hostility towards the gospel (4:24); and instinctively, they turn to prayer. They recall God's sovereignty and goodness and take comfort from the fact that inspired Old Testament

Peter and John healed a lame beggar on their way to the temple, then began preaching to the people about the resurrection of Christ. Jewish leaders arrested Peter and John and took them before the high court, the Sanhedrin. The next day, after some threats, the two were set free. (This model of the temple in Jerusalem shows where the Sanhedrin met.)

writers spoke of such hostility against God and his messiah (4:25–28). Obeying God is never going to earn approval from the world. The current opposition to the gospel fits into this pattern of defiance and resistance on the part of worldly and religious rulers. So the assembled believers ask God for the necessary strength and determination to face the future with its great challenges and opportunities (4:29–30).

As Luke makes clear, they get the encouragement and reassurance they need. Luke records how they were "all filled with the Holy Spirit and spoke the word of God boldly" (4:31). Yet this is no human boldness, such as some kind of bravado. It is a secure confidence in the power and purpose of God to uphold those—then and now—who obey him and preach his gospel with conviction and steadfastness.

4:32–11 The Believers Share Their Possessions. At several points, Luke sets out the vision that fired the early Christians—a vision that can still challenge and inspire today. As we have seen, those first Christians were infectiously enthusiastic about their faith. But they were also concerned to put that faith into action, both inside and outside the church. This important section gives us a glimpse of the social concerns of the church. It challenges Christians today to consider their own attitudes to other believers and to society at large.

Luke sets out the way in which the first Christians are transformed by the gospel. Although the apostles continue faithfully to preach the resurrection of Christ (4:33), that preaching is supplemented by the fostering of Christlike attitudes inside the church: "No one claimed that any of his possessions was his own, but they shared everything they had" (4:32). Possessions were seen as a gift from God, given for the good of the church. They were to be shared for the common good. As a result, no one was in need (4:34–35). This is not communism. This is simply Christian love in action.

Luke then provides some examples, positive and negative, of Christian attitudes toward possessions. Barnabas is praised for his unselfish attitudes (4:36–37). Ananias and Sapphira, on the other hand, pretend to give all the proceeds from a land sale to the church, but secretly hold back part of the money (5:1–2). When confronted with their deceit, both die, possibly from heart attacks (5:5, 10). This passage raises anxieties for some readers, on account of its apparent harshness, and especially Peter's severe words to both. However, it is clear that Ananias and Sapphira are being criticized for their lack of honesty and their attempt to mislead the apostles.

ACTS 5:12 – 8:40

Increasing Success and Growing Persecution

As the narrative of the early church continues, it becomes clear that the gospel continues to have enormous appeal during these early days. People hold Christians in respect, yet are frightened to join them (5:13). Perhaps we see here something like the problem faced by Nicodemus. Although attracted to Jesus, he was fearful of this becoming public knowledge. As a result, he visited Jesus at night, so that none would know (Jn 3:1–16). Nevertheless, despite this reticence on the part of many, it is clear that some are able to overcome the stigma of following Christ and publicly declare their faith (5:14).

5:17–42 The Apostles Persecuted. But this success brings with it resentment on the part of the high priest and his associates, who are "filled with jealousy" (5:17) at each new success of the gospel. This theme becomes increasingly frequent in Acts, as Luke documents the growing hostility toward the gospel by the Jewish authorities at every level. Interestingly, Luke often places reports of official hostility toward believers alongside reports of popular support (5:26), indicating that the ordinary people do not share their leaders' prejudices.

The initial instinct of the religious authorities is to suppress the movement by force, throwing its leaders in prison. But this backfires. The apostles, set free by divine providence, merely move on to preach the gospel within the court of the temple itself (5:19–20), bringing the "full message of this new life" to an even wider audience.

Eventually the apostles are persuaded to appear before the Sanhedrin, an assembly of senior religious figures (5:26). The high priest's irritation with them is obvious (5:28). Why are they still talking about Jesus? Why don't they keep quiet? Life would be a lot easier for everyone. Peter's reply is important: "We must obey God rather than men" (5:29). It is impossible, he argues, to be silent about the truth of what God has done in Christ. No one can be silent about the exaltation of Christ and the promise of "repentance and forgiveness of sins to Israel" (5:31). The apostles are witnesses to these things. They cannot bear false witness!

The situation becomes nasty. The original idea was to put the apostles in the dock. However, it now turns out to be the Sanhedrin itself that is put on trial, through its apparent failure to respond to God when he came to his people. However, the tension is defused through an intervention from Gamaliel, a respected teacher of the law (5:34). His argument wins the day and is of considerable importance. If this movement is from God, he declares, it will be unstoppable (5:38–39). There have been many spurious religious teachings in the past. If this one is for real, it will survive. "If it is from God, you will not be able to stop these men; you will only find yourselves fighting against God" (5:39). As we look ahead to the further expansion of the church, as Luke describes it in this work, we can see the wisdom of his advice, and we have to reckon with the conclusion to which it points— that the gospel is indeed "from God."

6:1–15 The Choosing of the Seven. At this stage, the expansion of the church requires that further measures be taken to ensure that none of its missionary and pastoral tasks are neglected (6:1–7). The choosing of the seven is an indication of the growing appeal of the gospel to Jews outside and the resulting increase in this section of the population within the church. All seven, including Stephen, have Greek names, suggesting that all were drawn from this section of the church. However, this increasing growth is met by growing opposition from certain Jewish bodies, with the result that Stephen finds himself accused of blasphemy and is brought before the Sanhedrin—that is, supreme Jewish court (6:8–15).

7:1–53 Stephen's Speech to the Sanhedrin. In his defense, Stephen delivers an impassioned speech to the Sanhedrin (7:1–53). The speech is a remarkable summary of the manner in which God has prepared the way for the gospel. It begins with the calling of Abraham (7:1–8) and traces the development of the people of God from their descent into, and eventual exodus from, Egypt (7:9–44), through the entry into the Promised Land (7:45), and the establishment of the monarchy (7:46). It is important to note the considerable portion of this sermon that is devoted to Moses, who is seen as establishing the fact that the people of Israel are prone to disobey God. Have things changed? Israel is just the same today, Stephen declares (7:51). Whenever a prophet appeared in their midst, their instant reaction was to kill him, rather than to listen to him (7:52–53). Their killing of Jesus Christ is just the latest example in a long chain of rebellion and disobedience.

7:54–8:1 The Stoning of Stephen. This outrages the Sanhedrin, who determine to stone Stephen to death for blasphemy there and then (7:54–8:1). Before they have a chance to do this, however, Stephen declares that he has had a vision in which he saw the Son of Man—a reference to Jesus himself—standing at the right hand of God. This indicates not merely that Jesus has been accepted and vindicated by God, but it implies that Jesus now has equal status with God—which adds further to the outrage of the traditionalists. And so Stephen dies, the first Christian martyr. Luke now mentions in passing that among those who witnessed and approved of his death was a man called Saul, who will figure prominently in the remainder of Luke's account of the early church.

The Lion's Gate in Jerusalem. It is also known as St. Stephen's gate. Stephen criticized the people of Israel for disobeying God and persecuting his prophets. Angered, the members of the Sanhedrin dragged Stephen outside and stoned him. His death marked the beginning of the persecution of Christians in Jerusalem and beyond.

8:1–3 The Church Persecuted and Scattered. As a result of this martyrdom, the church is subjected to vicious persecution, leading to its

members being scattered throughout the region (8:1–40). Saul is identified as one of the ringleaders of this attempt to destroy Christianity. However, the process of persecution merely disperses the apostles throughout the region, and allows them to witness to the gospel over a far wider area than before. We read of Philip preaching in the northern region of Samaria and subsequently heading south towards Gaza. In each case, they meet with a positive response. (Later, we learn that the gospel penetrates even to Cyprus and Antioch as a result of this dispersion [11:19–21].)

8:4–25 Philip in Samaria; Simon the Sorcerer. The establishment of the gospel in Samaria leads to an incident of considerable importance—a confrontation with a sorcerer named Simon (often referred to as "Simon Magus"). As the gospel meets with an overwhelmingly positive result in Samaria, through the preaching of the word and the working of signs and wonders, Simon becomes attracted to the idea of purchasing some of the spiritual gifts of the apostles for himself. He is severely chastised by Peter for this suggestion.

8:26–40 Philip and the Ethiopian. In the meantime, Philip, who had headed south, has a meeting with a senior official in the household of the queen of the Ethiopians (8:26–40). The Ethiopian may have been a Jewish proselyte (notice how he had traveled to Jerusalem to worship, and his familiarity with the Old Testament). Now on his way home, he finds himself puzzled by a portion of the prophet Isaiah that he is reading in his chariot. The passage in question is Isaiah 53:7–8, a section dealing with the coming of the "suffering servant." Philip asks him if he can understand what he is reading. The Ethiopian invites Philip to join him and explain the text. Philip then shows how this text and others point to the good news of Jesus Christ. As a result, the Ethiopian makes the decision to be baptized there and then, and goes on his way rejoicing.

9:1–19 Saul's Conversion. But a more momentous conversion is in the offing. The narrative now returns to Saul. By his attempt to eliminate the church, Saul has succeeded merely in dispersing it, with the result that the gospel spreads far beyond Jerusalem. As he continues his attempt to eliminate Christianity, he shifts his sights from Jerusalem to Damascus (9:1–19). As he travels along the road to Damascus with a view to ridding the city of its growing Christian presence, he experiences an encounter with the risen Jesus Christ. He hears Christ speak his name and ask why Saul is persecuting him. Blinded by the vision, he is obliged to be led into Damascus by his attendants.

However, Ananias, one of the growing number of Christians in the city, receives a vision in which Saul is identified and located. He is asked to take care of Saul, who is to be the Lord's "chosen instrument ... before the Gentiles" (9:15). On finding Saul, Ananias lays his hands on him, with the result that he regains his sight. As a token of his new-found faith, Saul is baptized.

This account of the conversion of Paul is found three times, with minor variations, in Acts (see also 22:3–16; 26:9–18). It is also found in an abbreviated form in Paul's own writings (Gal 1:13–17). The brevity of this account reflects the fact that Paul clearly assumes that his readers are broadly familiar with the story of his conversion, and he wishes simply to use the account to establish his credentials as an apostle.

9:20–31 Saul in Damascus and Jerusalem. So Saul, who was once a persecutor of the church, now becomes its defender. Luke notes how Saul is able to demonstrate irrefutably that Jesus is the Messiah, to the amazement of those who know his background and the irritation of the Jewish population of Damascus. During his period in the region (which he elsewhere identifies as being three years in length [Gal 1:17–18]), he clearly grows considerably in stature and wisdom. As a result, he comes under threat of death from those whom he once supported. Learning of an attempt to kill him, Saul is lowered down the city wall in a basket and escapes from the city. He makes his way to Jerusalem, where he continues his evangelistic ministry until his own personal safety makes it imperative that he be moved to Tarsus.

9:32–42 Peter in Lydda and Joppa. Attention now shifts from Saul to Peter (9:32–43), who is continuing his work of evangelism and healing in the region to the northwest of Jerusalem, around the towns of Joppa (now the modern city of Jaffa) and Lydda. In each case, he performs miracles of healing among the Jews. But a major crisis is about to develop. Thus far, the good news has been taken to Jews, whether Grecian or Hebraic. But what about the Gentiles? Will they benefit from the gospel?

10:1–48 Cornelius Calls for Peter; Peter's Vision. This issue is raised for Peter by a message he receives from a Roman centurion named Cornelius (10:1–8). Though not a Jew, he is "God-fearing"—a term used to refer to a Gentile sympathetic to Judaism, but who has not formally become a proselyte. In a vision, Cornelius learns of the presence of Peter, and sends messengers to him to arrange a meeting. As the messengers approach Joppa, Peter himself has a vision (10:9–16; see also 11:5–14) in which he sees various creatures being lowered in what looks like a sheet. Some of these are unclean, and hence forbidden to Jews. Yet Peter hears a voice commanding him to eat them. He refuses. He will not eat anything unclean or impure. Yet he is told in return that nothing that God has created is unclean or impure. Wondering what the vision means, Peter goes to meet the messengers who are waiting for him.

The meaning of the vision soon becomes clear (10:17–48). The vision is a declaration that the Gentiles are no longer to be treated as impure or second class. When Peter arrives at Cornelius' house, he has understood the meaning of the vision. Even though Cornelius is a Gentile, and even though the law prohibits Jews from having contact with Gentiles, Peter declares that these barriers are now broken down:

> God does not show favoritism but accepts men from every nation
> who fear him and do what is right. (10:34)

As Peter speaks of the great work of God through the death and resurrection of Jesus Christ, a remarkable thing happens. The Holy Spirit descends on all who are listening to him—Jews and Gentiles. It is clear that the same Spirit is being experienced by all present. The Spirit refuses to make any distinction between Jew and Gentile, causing them all to speak in tongues and praise God. Any lingering doubts on Peter's part are now removed: he baptizes them in the name of Jesus.

11:1–18 Peter Explains His Actions. This action is not well received by the church back in Jerusalem. They call Peter to account for his actions. Why did Peter go into the house of Gentiles (something regarded as defiling by Jews)? The Jewish Christians are outraged, in that Peter has clearly violated parts of the Law of Moses (11:1–3). Peter responds by relating the vision he had at Joppa (11:4–14) and its consequences. His line of thought is clear: nobody has the right to resist God. If God has given the same gift to the Gentiles as he gave to the Jews, what right did he, Peter, have to stand in the way of its full recognition? The company of believers is not merely persuaded by this argument, but they are delighted that God has allowed the Gentiles to share in the great benefits of Christ (11:15–18).

11:19–30 The Church in Antioch. Our attention now returns to the effects of the persecution initiated by Saul some time ago. As a result of this persecution, the disciples have been scattered throughout the region, leading to the more rapid spread of the gospel than would otherwise have been the case. As so often happens, a time of persecution becomes a time of expansion. We now learn of the establishment of Christian communities in the region of Antioch (11:19–30). This development is of strategic importance. At this stage in its history, the Roman empire is dominated by three cities: first and foremost is Rome itself; second is the Egyptian city of Alexandria; and third is Antioch. In due course, the gospel will establish itself in all three cities.

We now learn of the foothold established in the city of Antioch. Luke's readers, familiar with the politics of the eastern region of the Roman empire, would immediately have realized the significance of this development and the great comfort it would have brought at a time of persecution elsewhere. We also learn of another important development associated with Antioch: it is in this city that the word *Christian* is first used to refer to believers (11:26). Up to this point, a variety of words have been used. This term will now pass into general usage.

12:1–19 Peter's Miraculous Escape From Prison. The rapid growth in the church at this stage is seen as a threat by many within the Jewish community. It is also a cause of concern to the Herodians, a group of Jews who support the Roman presence in the region. Luke now documents a number of developments that relate specifically to the Herodians (12:1–25). "King Herod" (12:1) refers to Agrippa I, a nephew of the Herod who had beheaded John the Baptist. (The term *Herod* was often used to refer to members of the Herodian dynasty without identifying which of the various family members was intended.) Having beheaded James the brother of John (Mt 4:21), it is clear that Herod intends to deal with Peter in much the same way as Jesus before him. He will be publicly tried at Passover. The inevitable result of this trial would have been death, probably by crucifixion. But it is not God's will that Peter should die at this time. In an act of deliverance, Peter is set free from his chains and escapes from imprisonment, to the outrage of Herod.

12:21–23 Herod's Death. The subsequent death of Herod is then documented (12:21–23). It is likely that this death took place some time after the escape of Peter. Luke suggests that an interval—"a while" (12:19)—separates this escape and his death. While celebrating a festival in honor of the emperor Claudius in AD 44, Herod is acclaimed as a god—an acclamation he makes no attempt to deny. He is immediately struck down with violent pains, from which he dies a few days later. Luke's account of events corresponds well with that presented by the Jewish historian Josephus, confirming Luke's reliability as a historian.

12:24–25 Christianity Continues to Spread. Yet despite all these official and semiofficial attempts to suppress the gospel, Christianity continues to spread. The remainder of Acts focuses on the ministry of one individual who, with his companions, will prove instrumental in the spread of the gospel throughout the eastern Mediterranean world—Saul, who, as we shall see (13:9), soon becomes known by his more familiar name of Paul. Having gained a foothold in the third city of the empire, the gospel now moves on inexorably to gain ground in its greatest city, Rome itself. Although Paul is not responsible for establishing the gospel in Rome, he nevertheless writes to the church in that city, probably in the spring of AD 57, and will eventually be received and supported by this church when he arrives there in the spring of AD 59. But this is to look into the future. Our attention returns to Luke's account, which now goes back to Antioch.

ACTS 13:1 – 28:31

The Spread of the Gospel from Antioch to Rome

13:1–3 Barnabas and Saul Sent Off. While the leading members of the church are worshipping and fasting, the Holy Spirit identifies Barnabas and

Paul as having a special commission to perform for the Lord (13:1–3). After the leaders of the church have laid hands on them, they begin their journey of preaching, teaching, and evangelism. This is the first of Paul's missionary journeys (13:4–15:35), which would probably have taken place at sometime around A.D. 46–48. At this stage, Paul would probably have been around forty-four years old. Some fourteen years have passed since his conversion, during which time he has been occupied primarily with missionary work in the region of Syria (Gal 1:21). Now he is called to undertake a much more ambitious missionary project. For this journey, Paul and Barnabas are joined by John Mark (referred to simply as John at 13:5, but more usually

known as Mark). Mark, a cousin of Barnabas (Col 4:10), is generally thought to have been the author of the gospel now known by his name.

13:4–52 On Cyprus and in Pisidian Antioch. So in AD 46, these three companions set out on their way to the south coast of Asia Minor, a region of the northeastern Mediterranean coast that constitutes modern-day Turkey. Their journey initially takes them to the island of Cyprus (13:4–12).

This Roman road at Perga, in ancient Pamphylia on the southern coast of modern-day Turkey, is one that Paul traveled in his missionary work. He and Barnabas passed through on their way to Pisidian Antioch.

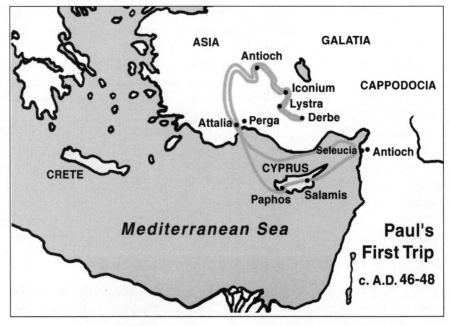

Although Luke does not mention this during his narrative, at some point early in this journey, Paul suffers from his "thorn in the flesh" (1Co 2:3; 2Co 12:7), which may have taken the form of an illness such as malaria. At this stage in the journey, Mark leaves the group and returns to Jerusalem (13:13). It is not clear why this takes place. At any rate, Paul and Barnabas then proceed alone to another city named Antioch, located in the province of Galatia, and usually referred to as "Pisidian Antioch" to distinguish it from the Syrian city of the same name (13:14–52).

During his time in Pisidian Antioch, Paul preaches a Sabbath sermon at a local synagogue, proclaiming that Jesus is the long-awaited messiah. Through Jesus Christ, God has made forgiveness of sins available in a way that the Law of Moses could never allow. The message meets with an enthusiastic response. Paul is invited to speak again on the following Sabbath at the same synagogue. Some of its members, unable to wait that long to hear more, seek out Paul and Barnabas for further discussions. This irritates some of the local Jewish leaders, who manage to have Paul and Barnabas expelled from the region.

14:1–28 In Iconium and Again in Antioch in Syria. The same pattern of events is repeated at Iconium (14:1–6). In nearby Lystra and Derbe, the apostles are received with such enthusiasm that they are taken for gods themselves—an impression that they are able to dispel, while at the same time proclaiming the good news (14:7–18). This time, however, local Jewish opposition is more violent, with an attempt being made to stone Paul to death (14:19–20). Undaunted, Paul establishes small Christian communities in the area, and then revisits those he has already planted as he traces his steps back to Antioch (14:21–28). The gospel is now firmly rooted outside Palestine.

15:1–40 The Council at Jerusalem. But inside Palestine, things are becoming difficult. Divisions are beginning to open up within the church over the issue of circumcision. A section of the church is arguing that it is essential that male Christians be circumcised. In effect, they seem to regard Christianity as an affirmation of every aspect of contemporary Judaism, with the exception of one additional belief—that Jesus is the messiah. Unless males are circumcised, they can not be saved (15:1). In Paul's absence, things have become serious, with a real threat of division within the church.

In order to resolve this issue, Paul and Barnabas set out to Jerusalem from Antioch. Luke now provides us with an account of the first General Council of the Christian church—the Council of Jerusalem in AD 49 (Acts 15:2–29). The debate is initially dominated by converted Pharisees, who insist upon the need to uphold the Law of Moses, including the circumcision requirements. Yet Paul's account of the amazing impact of the gospel among the Gentiles causes the wisdom of this approach to be questioned. If so many Gentiles are being won for the gospel, why should anything unnecessary be put in their way? Paul concedes the need to avoid food that has been sacrificed to idols—an issue that features elsewhere in his letters (1Co 8:7–13). But there is no need for circumcision. This position wins widespread support and is summarized in a letter that is circulated at Antioch (15:30–35).

Yet although the issue is resolved at the theoretical level, it will remain a live issue for many churches in the future, as the relationship between the new wine of the gospel and the old wineskins of Judaism continues to be controversial. Having sorted out this issue in Palestine, Paul determines to return to Galatia to make sure that the churches he has planted know of this decision. (Incidentally, it should be noted that Paul's letter to the Galatians is dominated by this issue.) A second missionary journey is therefore undertaken (15:36–18:22) around AD 50–52. Initially, Paul expects to be accompanied by Barnabas. However, the latter wants to take Mark along with him, which Paul refuses to countenance—again, for reasons that are not clear, but that seem to relate to Mark's premature departure from the first missionary journey.

Paul's Second Trip
c. A.D. **49-52**

16:1–15 Timothy Joins Paul and Silas. The first stage of the journey takes them overland to Galatia (15:36–41). At Lystra, they are joined by Timothy, who will become one of Paul's most trusted colleagues (16:1–5). They then proceed to the northwestern tip of Asia Minor. At Troas, close to the site of the ancient city of Troy, they are joined by Luke himself, who is unquestionably a major eyewitness source for many of the accounts relating to this part of the journey (notice the use of *we* in many of the reports from this section). Crossing the Aegean Sea, they land in the area of Macedonia, where they spend some time in the city of Philippi, a major Roman colony. For the first time, the good news is being preached on the continent of Europe. It is here that Lydia, a well-to-do business woman, is converted and baptized (16:13–15). Her house subsequently becomes a center for missionary activity in the region. Not surprisingly, Paul later writes to the church that was planted during his time in the city.

16:16–17:10 Paul and Silas Imprisoned and Released. Inevitably, opposition results from this success, with the result that Paul and Silas are thrown in jail (16:16–40). However, once the authorities have discovered that they are Roman citizens, they are hastily released; and they are able to return to Lydia's

Paul and Silas were beaten, then imprisoned in Philippi, a major Roman colony. They were put in an inner cell, their feet fastened in stocks. But an earthquake that night shook the prison and all the prisoners' chains came loose. The next day they were released. The top photo shows the interior of a cell that is said to be the one where Paul and Silas were held.

house before moving on to the region of Thessalonica. Here, Paul may have taken temporary employment as a tentmaker (1Th 2:9) to support himself while undertaking missionary work in the region. As a result of his preaching in the local synagogue (17:1–9), a church is established (to which he will later write his first two letters, 1 and 2 Thessalonians).

17:10–34 In Berea and in Athens. After passing through Berea (17:10–14), the group finally arrives in Athens, still widely regarded as the intellectual center of the ancient world (17:15–34). The city had a reputation for its short-lived interest in the latest ideas and intellectual fashions, and appears to have seen in Paul the source of some exciting new ideas. It is here that Paul delivers his famous address on the Areopagus, or "Mars Hill." Rather than get caught up in some petty theological arguments, Paul declares that it is common knowledge that there is a creator God, who

has authority over men and women. But who is this God? And how may he be known? Having noted an altar in the city dedicated to "an unknown god," Paul declares that what the Athenians worship as something unknown, he will proclaim as someone who can be known. Having thus laid the foundations for the gospel, he develops the basic Christian message of the need for repentance. The reception accorded to his address is not particularly enthusiastic. Nevertheless, the gospel has now been proclaimed in Athens.

18:1–28 In Corinth. There is no letter from Paul to the Athenians. It seems that no church was founded in this city. But in the port city of Corinth, further south, Paul gains a much more sympathetic hearing (18:1–28). At that time, Corinth was a huge seaport, with many openings for evangelism within the local Jewish community, as well as within the vastly larger Gentile population. Paul stayed there for eighteen months. It was clearly an important time. Encouraged by the reports of church growth in the region of Macedonia, Paul wrote both of his letters to the Thessalonian Christians. Aided by Priscilla and Aquila, the church grew considerably, drawing in both Jewish and Gentile converts.

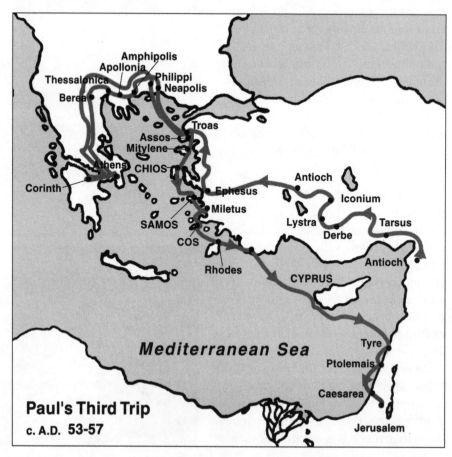

Paul's Third Trip
c. A.D. **53-57**

19:1–41 Paul in Ephesus. But Paul is anxious to move on. At some point in AD 53, Paul sets off on his third missionary journey (18:23–21:17). The conversion of Apollos, a Jew from the Egyptian city of Alexandria, leads to renewed evangelistic activity elsewhere in the region. However, Apollos seems to leave out a number of aspects of the gospel. While his preaching persuades many that Jesus is the Christ, there seems to have been no mention of the gift of the Holy Spirit. For example, baptism seems to be understood as little more than an external token of cleansing, without any real understanding of spiritual renewal. Yet once this misunderstanding is cleared up, Apollos is able to undertake a major evangelistic ministry in Corinth.

Paul, however, is now involved in evangelism in the city of Ephesus. The city is a stronghold of pagan superstition, centering on the goddess Diana. This cult is supported by the local merchants, who rely on it for their living. Yet, on account of Paul's ministry, the city will become a stronghold of the Christian church (19:8–20). However, this is not without its difficulties. A local silversmith manages to provoke a riot, which is eventually subdued by some diplomacy from a local official (19:23–41).

20:1–21:16 The Church in Jerusalem. Paul's attention now turns to the church in Jerusalem, the work of which he wishes to support. Traveling by land, Paul sets off for Jerusalem, with the object of collecting money to support the work of the church in the city (20:1–16). At the town of Miletus, near Ephesus, Paul brings members of the Ephesian church together in order to bid farewell to them (20:17–38). As he journeys on to Jerusalem, he appears to have become aware of difficulties awaiting him at Jerusalem. A series of warnings received along the way point to hostility lying ahead (21:1–16). Yet on his arrival in Jerusalem, he is warmly received by the Christians in the city (21:17–26). He is advised by local Christian leaders to show respect for the Jewish laws and to avoid giving offense. As is clear from his actions, Paul decides to adopt this advice.

But it does not work. Almost immediately, Paul is made an object of hate by some local Jewish fanatics. In a scene that at times resembles the gospel accounts of the arrest and trial of Jesus, the crowds get out of control. The local Roman commander orders Paul to be arrested (21:27–36). Paul's attempt to defend himself to his Jewish accusers, using the Aramaic language, only enrages them all the more (21:37–22:21). In this defense, Paul provides an account of his Jewish credentials and tells how his own conversion took place. Things seem to go well until Paul speaks of his own mission to bring this good news to the Gentiles (22:21). At this point, however, the crowd becomes uncontrollable. His attempt to defend himself before the Sanhedrin exposes the divisions between the Pharisees and Sadducees over the question of the resurrection and again leads to rioting.

22:22–24:1 Paul in Custody. For his own safety, Paul is placed in protective custody and sent under escort to the headquarters of the Roman procurator of Judaea, based at Caesarea (22:22–23:33). He will spend a period of two years—AD 56–58—in custody at Caesarea. The length of this imprisonment reflects the recall of the procurator Antonius Felix for alleged cruelty to Jewish rebels and his eventual replacement by Porcius Festus.

24:1–27 The Trial Before Felix. Initially, Paul is tried before Felix. But this trial is inconclusive. The account of the proceedings provides its readers with a third version of Paul's conversion and also indicates that there is no particular hostility on the part of this senior Roman citizen toward Christianity. It is clear that Felix is anxious concerning the impact of Christianity in the highly volatile region he is responsible for administering. Yet he has no quarrel with any of its basic ideas. This point would have been important for Luke's readers, many of whom—perhaps including Theophilus himself—would probably have been Roman.

25:1–12 The Trial Before Festus. The trial then seems to have been adjourned as a result of the recall of Felix. After some two years, Felix is replaced by Festus (24:27), and the trial can resume. It is clear that the Jew-

Caesarea Maritima, built by Herod the Great on the Mediterranean coast, became Israel's main seaport and the Roman capital of Palestine. Paul was secretly brought here from Jerusalem when a plot to kill him was discovered. Paul had been arrested when some Jews claimed his teachings violated the law. Visitors can still walk along the Roman aqueduct, above left, view the fortress (which is of a later date), and sit in the theater.

ish leaders regard Paul as a serious threat and wish to pursue the case against him as forcefully and rapidly as possible (25:1–12). Yet Paul outmaneuvers his opponents. Knowing that they wish him to be tried before a Jewish religious court in Jerusalem, he makes the point that he is guilty of no crime in the sight of Rome—again, an important point for Luke's Roman readers. Paul claims the right to be tried in a Roman court before the emperor or his representative—a privilege to which every Roman citizen had the right.

25:13–26:32 King Agrippa. Unsure as to how to proceed, Festus consults with Herod Agrippa II (referred to as "king" here, but in reality little more than a figurehead), who is on a goodwill visit to the region (25:13–27). Agrippa, interested in hearing Paul for himself, gives him a hearing (26:1–32). Once more, Paul relates how he had been converted, leading Agrippa to ponder whether he will become converted him-

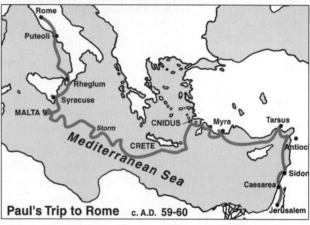

Paul's Trip to Rome c. A.D. 59-60

self. Since there is clearly nothing treasonable in what Paul says, Agrippa is in favor of setting him free. But Paul has demanded a trial in Rome. The matter is now out of their hands, and he will have to go to Rome. Once more, the impact of this development on Luke's Roman readers must be appreciated. Paul's transference to Rome is, in effect, the result of a technicality, rather than any proven guilt on his part.

27:1–28:10 Paul Sails for Rome. And so Paul sets sail for Rome, at some point in the later part of AD 58 (27:1–28:10). It is clear that Luke is present on this voyage—note the constant use of the word *we*. Luke is an honest historian, allowing his reader to understand which parts of Acts are due to his own eyewitness reporting and which are due to the reports of others. The account of the trip, with its many dangers culminating in the shipwreck on Malta, is a masterpiece of narrative in which fine detail after fine detail is woven into the tapestry of the story. After being forced to spend the winter on the island of Malta, they eventually arrive at Puteoli in the Bay of Naples in the spring of the following year. There they are greeted by members of the local churches, who have clearly been looking forward to greeting this famous Christian leader from the eastern region of the Roman empire. As they

The island of Cnidus was one of the safe harbors Paul's ship passed on his way to Rome as a prisoner. Unable to hold the course, they sailed instead for the island of Crete, then toward Rome. But they were delayed three months. Their ship ran aground near Malta.

approach Rome itself, they are joined by more Christians from the great city, who have traveled to meet him.

28:11–16 Arrival at Rome. The symbolic importance of this point must not be underestimated. Paul has already written his great letter to the Roman Christians (probably in the spring of AD 57), and hence would be known to the churches in the region. The gospel has already taken a firm hold in the "eternal city," and the compassion and care shown toward him by Paul's fellow believers is an important testimony to the growing influence of the gospel in the region.

28:17–31 Paul Preaches at Rome Under Guard. Although under restrictions, Paul is able to live a relatively open life in the city as he awaits his trial. In typical Pauline fashion, the apostle begins an evangelistic ministry to his chief critics—the Jews (28:17–28). In his address, Paul emphasizes that the coming of Jesus represents the fulfillment of the Law and the Prophets,in much the same way as the refusal of official Judaism to respond to the Messiah on his arrival was in fulfillment of the scriptural predictions of the hardheartedness and rebelliousness of Israel. For this reason, Paul has become an apostle to the Gentiles, who are prepared to listen to him.

Then, suddenly, the account ends. Luke affirms that Paul is free to move and speak, and that he exercises a successful evangelistic ministry for two years (28:30–31). Even though he is technically awaiting the arrival of charges from his accusers so that he can face trial in Rome, he is nevertheless at liberty to speak about Christ. So what happens next? Why this abrupt end to Acts?

Nobody knows. From some of his letters, we know that Paul expected to be released soon (Php 2:24; Phm 22), leaving open the possibility that, after his time in Rome, Paul traveled elsewhere, perhaps on a fourth missionary journey. For example, the letter to the Romans hints at a possible visit to Spain (Ro 15:24, 28). Early Christian writings outside the New Testament canon certainly know of a tradition that he arrived there. If Paul was indeed released in AD 61 or 62, there is no reason why he should not have undertaken such a journey. Indeed, there are references in the Pastoral Letters (1Ti 1:3; 3:14; 2Ti 4:13, 20; Tit 1:5) that point to travels in regions that Luke does not record him visiting on previous occasions—such as Crete, Nicopolis, and Colossae. Furthermore, the early historian of the church, Eusebius, states that Paul was released after his first period of imprisonment. But we do not know.

There is another explanation. During the persecution of Christians in Rome under the emperor Nero, a number of leading believers were martyred in AD 64. It is widely believed that both Peter and Paul were among them. Luke's Roman readers would have known of this, and they would have realized that Paul was guilty of no crime in the eyes of Roman law. He would have been martyred for one reason, and one reason only—his faith.

ROMANS

Paul probably wrote his letter to the Christians at Rome in the early spring of A.D. 57, during his time at Corinth in the course of his third missionary journey. No apostle had ever visited Rome before. The letter therefore provides the church at Rome with the basic elements of Christian teaching. Although most of Paul's letters were directed to churches he had personally established and taught, the church at Rome had never been instructed by anyone of his stature. For this reason, this letter is of special importance to Christians today.

1:1–7 Introduction. The letter opens with a declaration of Paul's personal authority as an apostle (1:1). The subject of his letter is to be the gospel concerning Jesus Christ. Immediately, Paul emphasizes that the gospel was promised beforehand in the Old Testament. This is no novelty, but a long-promised and long-awaited act of salvation, which brings to a climax the great work of preparation in the Old Testament (1:2). And that gospel centers on the good news concerning Jesus Christ, the Son of God, whose credentials in this respect were established first through his being a direct descendant of David, and second through his resurrection from the dead (1:3–4). Paul is entrusted with the task of calling all people to respond to this good news—a good news that he will explore during the course of this letter.

1:8–15 Paul's Longing to Visit Rome. After greeting his readers as fellow Christians, Paul tells them of his delight at the witness of the Roman church, and of his longing to be with them so that he can be of some use to them. He has been able to serve congregations elsewhere in the world. Now he longs to come to Rome itself and to proclaim the gospel in all its fullness at the hub of the Roman empire (1:8–13). Paul regards himself as being under an obligation to proclaim this good news to everyone, irrespective of nationality or social status (1:14–15).

ROMANS 1:16 – 8:39

The Main Themes of the Gospel

Paul then gives full expression to his delight at the gospel. It is difficult to avoid noticing Paul's obvious joy (1:16–17). The power of God is at work for the salvation of everyone who believes. Notice the emphasis on "everyone." There are to be no human barriers placed in the way of the gospel. Through faith, a righteousness that comes from God is made available to all who have faith—a righteousness which, as Paul will explain later in this letter, places those who believe in the gospel in a right relationship with God. Paul sees this great gospel affirmation as bringing to fulfillment the vision of the prophet Habakkuk (Hab 2:4), in which the righteous would live by faith in God.

1:18–32 God's Wrath Against Humanity. To understand the full importance of this revelation of the righteousness of God, Paul analyses the sinful situation in which humanity finds itself (1:18–32). The glory of God has been made known to all through his wonderful work of creation. Yet humanity has not merely ignored God. It has deliberately chosen to rebel against him. Instead of worshipping the Creator himself, it has worshiped aspects of his creation. Humanity has fallen away radically and totally from what God intended for it. Even those who feel they stand above such things are in reality contaminated by them. They have simply failed to realize how deeply their judgments and motives are affected by sin. Everyone, irrespective of whether they are Jews or Gentiles, has fallen short of the glory of God (2:1–11).

2:1–29 God's Righteous Judgment. Paul lays emphasis on one particular theme at this point. It is clear that he is concerned to counter the idea that seems to have gained influence among at least some Jews—the idea that the Law of Moses was some kind of charter of national privilege that exempted Israel from God's judgment; that the Gentiles would be condemned by God on account of their sin, but because Israel possessed the Law, she was immune from such judgment. Paul dismisses this kind of argument. If anything, God's judgment will be directed against the Jews first, because they ought to have known better. Circumcision does not guarantee acceptance in the sight of God. It is merely an external sign. What really matters is the inward reality of faith and trust in God—something demanded of Jews and Gentiles alike (2:12–29).

3:1–20 No One Is Righteous. This does not mean that being a Jew is without its good points (3:1–8). What it does mean is that the Jew has no privileged access to God. All—whether Jew or Gentile—are sinners. All—whether Jew or Gentile—need God's forgiveness. Paul assembles an impressive array of biblical citations to bring out the fact that humanity is totally contaminated by sin (3:9–20). The Law of Moses is powerless to deliver from sin. Although it is able to identify sin and raise human consciousness of being sinful, it cannot do anything about what it uncovers. The law is thus like a medical practitioner who has diagnosed a fatal illness, but is unable to remedy it in any way. At least it shatters any illusions we may have. But it cannot improve things.

3:2–31 Righteousness Through Faith. All this has changed through the coming of Jesus Christ. The Law and the Prophets pointed to this great development in which God's righteousness would be made known outside the limits of the law. Just as all have sinned, so all will be freely justified by the grace of God. Through faith in Jesus Christ, everyone can share in this righteousness. Jesus Christ was presented by God as "a sacrifice of atonement" (a term also translated as "propitiation"). In other words, the death of Christ is the one and only means by which the sin of humanity can be cleansed and forgiven. And just as all have sinned, so all can benefit from the death of Christ.

4:1–25 Abraham Justified by Faith. Paul then demonstrates that Abraham himself was "justified" (that is, put in a right relationship with God) through his faith. The great patriarch was not put in a right relationship with God through circumcision. That came later. That relationship with God was established through Abraham's faith in God's promise to him (Ge 15:6). Circumcision was simply the external sign of that faith. It did not establish that faith, but confirmed something that was already there. The great promise of God to Abraham was made before either circumcision or the Law of Moses were delivered. Thus all who share in the faith of Abraham are the children of Abraham. It is possible for the Gentiles to share Abraham's faith in the promises of God—and all the benefits that result from this faith—without the need to be circumcised, or be bound to the fine details of the Law of Moses. It is Christ's death and resurrection, not external observance of the law, that constitute the ultimate grounds of relationship with God.

5:1–11 Peace and Joy. Therefore, Paul affirms, believers may rejoice in the knowledge that they have been justified by faith (5:1–5). Through faith in God, believers have access to his presence, and to the hope, peace, and love which can come only through the saving work of Christ on the cross. Even though sinners were powerless to do anything about their situation, God graciously chose to intervene at the right moment. Paul exults in the amazing love of God for sinners. Maybe we could understand why someone might want to give his life for a very good person. Yet the love of God is shown through Christ's giving his life for sinners! Through his death, we now have reconciliation with God (5:6–11).

5:12–21 Death Through Adam, Life Through Christ. Having already used Abraham as an example of faith, Paul now explores the relationship between Christ and Adam (5:12–21). In this very helpful comparison, we can see the way God chose to reverse the work of Adam through the work of Christ. Adam's disobedience led to sin, condemnation, and death. Yet Christ's obedience led to forgiveness, justification, and eternal life. Just as all humanity shares in the sinful state that resulted from Adam's fall, so all those who put their faith in Christ will share in the glorious joy of grace and peace that result from his obedience to the will of his Father.

6:1–14 Dead to Sin, Alive in Christ. As a result, believers have died to sin and risen to new life in Christ (6:1–7). This change, which is symbolized in baptism, does not mean that the resurrection has already taken place. Rather, it means that the believer has "died to sin"—that is, that the power of sin over the believer has been broken, with the result that the believer can now experience a new life of faith in which it is Christ, rather than sin, who reigns. Just as Christ was crucified, so the believer's old nature, along with its bondage to sin, has been put to death, in order that a new nature might come to birth. Paul thus assures believers that they may count themselves as "dead to sin but alive to God in Christ Jesus" (6:8–14). They are no longer under law, but under grace.

6:15–7:25 Slaves to Righteousness; Struggling With Sin. There has thus been a change of allegiance through faith (6:15–23). On account of faith, believers are no longer "slaves to sin," but are now "slaves to God." Instead of being loyal to sin, which leads only to the reward of death, Christians owe their loyalty to God, who offers the gift of eternal life in Christ. Believers have died to the authority of the law on account of their faith (7:1–6). As a result, they are released from its power only to condemn, so that they can discover the grace offered through the gospel. So there is nothing wrong with the law. It does not cause sin. It simply exposes the reality and power of sin and prevents people from lapsing into a false security concerning their own situation and abilities (7:7–12).

Paul then discusses the problem of sin (7:13–25). This passage is difficult to interpret, for it is not clear whether Paul is here referring to his life as a pious Jew before his conversion, or to his life as a Christian after his conversion. His reference to being "sold as a slave to sin" (7:14) certainly suggests that he is referring to his life as a non-Christian. However, the use of the present tense throughout this section suggests that Paul is referring to something that was still applicable at the time of writing. The debate is complex and cannot easily be resolved.

Whatever the answer may be to this question, it is clear that Paul brings out the power of sin and the utter inability of human nature to break free from its stranglehold. Even if people wanted to break free from sin, they would find that their good intentions were frustrated by sin (7:17–23). So what can be done about this? If we had to rely on our own resources, the answer would be simple: Nothing. Yet, as Paul declares, we have not been left on our own. Who will rescue us? God will! Through the death and resurrection of Jesus Christ, the powerful hold of sin has been broken.

8:1–17 Life Through the Spirit. As a result, the joys of the Christian life are available to believers. There is no condemnation now for believers. They have been set free through Christ. That which the law could never do, God did through sending Christ to die for sinners. As a result, believers are "sons of God" or "children of God," a fact that is objectively grounded in Christ and that is confirmed by the internal witness of the Holy Spirit (8:1–17). Through faith, they have been adopted into the family of God; and as a result of this, they now share the full inheritance rights of the natural son of God, Jesus Christ. Christians are thus "heirs of God and co-heirs with Christ." This gives them hope, because it affirms that they will share in all that he has already received—whether it is suffering or glory.

8:18–39 Future Glory; More Than Conquerors. This glory is worth waiting and suffering for (8:18–27). Paul likens the life of faith to a woman who is about to give birth. She is in pain, but she knows that new life will result. All the suffering and pain of the present life will be seen in its proper perspective once believers have been glorified with Christ. Christians can rest assured that God works for their good in all things (8:28–30), even if they do not fully understand what is happening. Believers can know that there is nothing in all of creation or the world to come that can ever separate them from the wonderful love of God, made known in Christ (8:31–39).

ROMANS 9:1 – 11:36

The Problem of the Rejection of Israel

Having now presented the main themes of the gospel, Paul turns to deal with a difficult question that has been hinted at, but not fully dealt with, in what he has said so far. Why did Israel reject the Messiah? And why did Israel—Paul's own people—find themselves rejected by God? This question will preoccupy Paul for a substantial portion of the letter (9:1–11:36). As we prepare to explore this section of the letter, it must be understood that Paul is not dealing specifically with the issue of predestination (the question of God deciding human happiness or misery in advance, from eternity). This word is not used once throughout this section. The key question that Paul is wrestling with relates to God's purpose in raising up Israel as the bearer of his good news—and then seeming to reject Israel once the Messiah had arrived. Why did this happen?

The answer Paul gives is complex and needs to be considered carefully. Paul's mood should also be noted. He is clearly sorrowful and distressed over this issue, and he greatly wishes that his own people would be saved. After all, they have received God's covenants and law, and the Messiah has emerged from within their ranks (9:1–5). Yet being a physical descendant of Abraham does not guarantee being in a right relationship with God (9:6–18). As Paul puts it, "not all who are descended from Israel are Israel."

Yet God has raised up, guided, and preserved Israel because he intends to use her as a means of bringing knowledge of himself to all nations. This has been the reason for bringing her into being in the first place. Israel is, from beginning to end, the creation and possession of God. And just as a potter has the right to rework his creation to ensure that it does what he intended it to do, so God is entitled to refashion Israel to ensure that his intended objectives are met (9:19–29). The use of the image of the potter is significant (9:21). The same image was used by Jeremiah (Jer 18:6) to make sense of the way God was dealing with Jerusalem at the time of the Babylonian invasion.

9:30–10:21 Israel's Unbelief. Yet Israel decided to trust in her own righteousness, based on possession of the law (10:1–21). Rather than submit to the righteousness of God—which, for Paul, comes through the gospel— she chose to rely on the law, unaware that Christ was the ultimate goal of that law (10:4; the word *end* here is best understood as "goal" or "objective"). Yet Israel was meant to proclaim this righteousness of God to the world—and if Israel failed to proclaim it, how was anyone going to get to hear about it? Israel knew about the coming of Christ—but she did nothing to make this known (10:14–15). As a result, this good news has been entrusted to the Gentiles, in fulfillment of Old Testament prophecy.

11:1–10 The Remnant of Israel. Yet this does not mean that God has rejected each and every member of Israel (11:1–36). Paul is absolutely clear that the gospel is offered to Jew and Gentile without distinction. Individual Jews, like individual Gentiles, can have access to God through faith, on account of what Christ has done. Yet being a member of Israel in itself does not ensure this access. It is faith, not nationality or the external sign of circumcision, that matters. In developing this point, Paul draws on the idea of a "remnant" within Israel, an idea that is illustrated by the 7,000 Israelites at the time of Elijah who did not worship Baal (see p. 125). Despite the rejection of Christ by the leaders and institutions of Israel, many Jews have come to faith in Christ. They are the new faithful remnant.

11:11–36 The Model of an Olive Tree. So what, then, is the relationship between Jew and Gentile? Paul uses the model of an olive tree onto which new branches have been grafted. The stump of the tree is Israel, and the grafted branches the Gentiles. They have been brought into Israel on account of their faith. The church is thus what Israel was meant to be—the community of faithful people who, like Abraham, trust in the promises of God, and who will proclaim this news to the world. The church is built on the foundation of God's saving work and revelation in and through the history of Israel. Without this preparation in the history of Israel, there would be no church—so Gentiles owe their salvation to God's work in and through the Jewish people. There can be no place for Jewish nationalism or Gentile hostility toward the Jews within the church. Yet God's work has now reached far outside the narrow confines of Judaism, which has become a religion of national privilege.

ROMANS 12:1 – 15:14

Practical Advice

12:1–21 Living Sacrifices. Having dealt with this theoretical issue, which was a live concern in the church at Rome as it was elsewhere in the churches, Paul turns to give practical advice to his fellow believers at Rome. In the light of their death to sin through faith, he urges them not to be conformed to the world, but to be transformed and renewed (12:1–3). Paul then develops the qualities that he particularly expects to find in believers. These include an awareness of the various roles played by individual Christians in the life of the church (12:4–8) and the showing of love in many different aspects of the Christian life (12:9–21).

13:1–14 Submission to the Authorities. One question that was particularly important to the church at Rome was the relations between believers and the secular power. How should Christians respond to a non-Christian government? Rome was the center of the empire, and it was therefore natural that believers in the city would come face to face with this issue in their everyday lives. Paul's advice remains of fundamental importance: believers should submit to the governing authorities, in that these have been established by God to bring order to his world (13:1–7).

However, it is clear that Paul assumes that the secular government will remain within its allocated sphere of authority. What happens if the government should exceed that authority by rebelling against God and persecuting his people? Paul does not deal with this question. However, the implication of his line of thought would suggest that by doing this, the government would have exceeded its limits and could no longer expect Christians to respect or obey it.

Following Jesus Christ, Paul reaffirms the importance of the Law, and its summary in terms of loving neighbors as oneself (13:8–14; see also Mt 19:19; Mk 12:31; Lk 10:27). He also affirms that the future Christian hope gives a new meaning to life in the present. Believers are walking in the dark, in the sure knowledge that the day of salvation is nearer than when they first believed. This hope gives them confidence as they travel in the life of faith, knowing that the day of eternal life is at hand. (A similar point is made by many of the gospel parables relating to the theme of watching.)

14:1–15:13 The Weak and the Strong. Paul then turns to deal with the question of giving offense to other believers, whose faith may be weaker. This continues to be an important issue today for many Christians. What, Paul asks, can be said to someone who, for example, refuses to eat meat? The basic lines of his argument, which remains of vital importance in the life of the church, can be set out as follows: All food is clean, so there is no need for anyone to refuse to eat meat or drink wine on the grounds of faith. However, some do refuse to eat or drink such items on the grounds of conscience. So why destroy the work of God for the sake of such a trivial issue? If their faith is so weak that they feel the need for such scruples, those whose faith is strong must respect the views of those whose faith is weaker. Those who are strong in their faith must bear with the failings of those who are weak. As a result, Christians must learn to accept and respect one another, in order that God's work may be advanced.

15:14–16:27 Conclusion. The letter then draws to a close. Paul sets forth his own understanding of his special mission to the Gentiles (15:14–22) and the results of his ministry in the eastern Mediterranean region. He declares his hope to be able to visit the church at Rome in order to share in their fellowship (15:23–33).

He then commends the many Christians whom he knows (16:1–23). What is especially noticeable about this impressive list of individuals is how many of them are women. One of them—Junias (16:7)—is even described as an apostle, suggesting that she was recognized as a preacher of the gospel in the region.

The letter ends with a doxology—or exclamation of praise—in which Paul gives thanks to God for revealing his gospel to all nations (16:25–27).

1 CORINTHIANS

Corinth was one of the most important cities of Greece, often estimated as having a population of more than 500,000 people. A leading seaport and commercial center, Corinth was evangelized by Paul during his third missionary journey. The letter, written from the city of Ephesus in Asia Minor, probably dates from some point before the feast of Pentecost in A.D. 55. It was prompted by a number of factors, including a visit from some prominent members of the Corinthian church and a letter brought by some other Corinthian visitors requesting guidance at a number of points. The resulting Pauline letter is primarily pastoral in its orientation, although it includes a vigorous defense of some of the central themes of the gospel.

1:1–9 Greetings and Thanksgiving. The letter opens with Paul sending his greetings to his Christian brothers and sisters in Corinth (1:1–3), followed by a strong statement of the Christian hope of resurrection, based on the total faithfulness of God (1:4–9). Here, as elsewhere, we are reminded that the faith of believers is securely grounded in a relationship with a trustworthy and faithful God.

1:10–17 Divisions in the Church. Immediately, Paul proceeds to one of his chief causes for concern—the divisions that are emerging at Corinth. The Greeks were notorious for forming factions. While this made Greek politics much more interesting than they otherwise might have been, it was potentially disastrous in the church. The factions seemed to center on personalities. Paul here notes three—himself, Apollos (see Acts 18:24–28), and Cephas (another name for Peter, and possibly referring to Christians who placed a particular emphasis on their Jewish heritage). Paul, as one of the personalities on which this personality cult has come to center, is outraged. The gospel must not be divided by its human agents. There is a real danger that the cross of Christ will be emptied of its power as a result.

1:18–2:16 Christ, the Wisdom and Power of God. This thought leads Paul directly into a major discussion of the

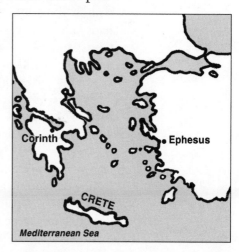

A carving of a Christian cross, found at Avdat, in the Negev, a well-preserved site from the Byzantine period. Paul discusses the place of the cross in the Christian life in the first chapter of his letter to the church at Corinth.

place of the cross in the Christian life (1:18–2:5). Paul points out how the cross lays down a challenge to human ideas of wisdom and power. The Jews insisted on looking for signs of some sort, and the Greeks demanded wisdom. But in the end, neither got what they were looking for. For Paul, Christianity is all about "Christ crucified"—a phrase that can mean either "the crucified person of Jesus Christ" or "a crucified messiah." The second interpretation of the phrase is likely, because it represents a total contradiction of the Jewish belief that the messiah would be a figure of triumph, which was totally contradicted by the cross.

For Paul, human standards of wisdom—such as those associated with the Greeks—are overturned by the cross. Christian believers need not worry when they are, by worldly standards, weak or foolish. They are only weak and foolish when judged by the world. In the light of the cross, they are strong and wise. God has actively chosen what is weak and lowly in the sight of the world in order to show up the total folly of worldly standards.

Paul also makes the important point that the gospel does not rest on human wisdom, but on the power of God. This means that the resilience and strength of the gospel do not lie in the eloquence of its preachers, but in the power of the God who upholds and sustains both the gospel and those who proclaim it (2:1–5). In the end, true wisdom comes only from God, through the Holy Spirit. Wisdom is something God reveals, rather than something human beings can hope to find for themselves (2:6–16). This emphasis on the importance of the Holy Spirit will occur many times during this letter and is of major importance to Paul. But further exposition of the role of the Holy Spirit will have to wait until later in the letter. Paul now returns to the divisions that have opened up within the Corinthian church.

3:1–4:21 On Divisions in the Church. One of the problems faced by the church at Corinth was its spiritual immaturity. It was a young church, perhaps only a few years old. As a result, Paul was only able to offer them some Christian basics, rather than a full exposition of the gospel (3:1–2). Just as a newborn child cannot cope with solid food and so relies on milk, so Paul found that he could only offer the Corinthians milk rather than solid food. They were not mature enough to cope with anything else. And this immaturity is reflected in the factions which are simply the carrying over of worldly disputes and attitudes into the church (3:3–4).

But why is this being allowed to happen? Paul and Apollos, two centers of such personality cults, have each had different roles to play in establishing the church at Corinth. Initially, the imagery is that of growing seeds. Paul got things going (Ac 18:4–11); Apollos followed things up (Ac 18:24–28). Yet they were both engaged in the same overall task. God is the one who really matters. They were just working in the background (3:5–9). So why don't the Corinthians realize this? The imagery now shifts from seeds to houses. The Christian life is ultimately grounded in Christ himself. Christ is the only foundation on which the life of faith can be built (3:10–15).

Continuing this theme of Christians as buildings, Paul affirms that individual believers are temples of God, and that the Holy Spirit dwells within them individually (3:16–23). One of the many important points made by this comparison is that the relationship with God established by conversion changes people. It is not simply something external, but a transforming relationship in which God comes to dwell within his people.

Paul now moves on to gently chasten the Corinthian church for its failure to respond fully and faithfully to the gospel that had been entrusted to it (4:1–21). Paul has no intention of humiliating his Corinthian brothers and sisters. Nevertheless, he feels that he must somehow draw their attention to these issues. They did not learn to behave in this way from him. In each case, the problems that arise result directly from the importation of secular values into the church.

5:1–6:20 Sexual Immorality. Paul begins by addressing the growth of sexual immorality within the Corinthian church (5:1–13). The church has become even worse than the world in some respects. Paul makes it clear that this kind of behavior is not to be tolerated. While believers have to live in the world despite its corruption, they should make every effort to avoid being contaminated by those who are clearly sexually immoral. Paul returns to this theme a few paragraphs later (6:9–20), where he identifies the theological basis of this immorality. Some Corinthian believers clearly believe that their faith frees them from any moral obligations. In response, Paul makes the fundamental point that they are not totally at liberty. They have been bought at a price and are therefore required to be obedient to their master, who is none other than God himself.

6:1–8 Lawsuits Among Believers. Paul then notes with despair that the secular obsession with lawsuits has found its way into the church (6:1–8). Can they not sort things out for themselves, without parading their differences in front of unbelievers? It is clear that Paul believes this to be an appalling witness to the world.

7:1–40 Marriage. The issue of marriage then arises. Paul seems to open this discussion by quoting from a letter the Corinthians have written to him. The phrase "It is good for a man not to marry" seems to be quoted by Paul, rather than endorsed by him. Paul is known to have been strongly in favor of marriage (see Eph 5:22–33; Col 3:18–19); indeed, at one point he even identifies the refusal to marry as a kind of heresy (1Ti 4:1–3). The phrase should thus probably be included in quotation marks, along with other quotations or slogans accepted at Corinth (such as at 6:12–13). In what follows, Paul offers a strong defense both of marriage and of full sexual relations within marriage. Marriage is not a sin, and nobody should be discouraged from marrying. Each believer must work out what is best for him or her, in order that they may serve the Lord as effectively and wholeheartedly as possible.

8:1–13 Food Sacrificed to Idols. Paul then deals with something that was an issue for many believers in Greek and Roman cities: food that has been offered to idols. At least twelve pagan temples were known to have been in existence around this time, although not all may have been used for worship of this kind. Paul's answer is simple. There is no problem about the food. The problem lies with the believer who has a scrupulous conscience over this issue. Although believers may eat such food without anxiety, they must respect the consciences of weaker believers, who may find this scandalizing. Faith is too precious a gift to risk compromising in this manner. Although there is nothing wrong with eating such food, it should not be eaten if doing so will give offense to other believers.

9:1–11:13 Confidence in the Christian Life; the Lord's Supper. After discussing the rights and responsibilities of apostleship, Paul turns to the theme of confidence in the Christian life (10:1–11:1). There is no room for complacency of any kind, he warns. Israel was complacent during the period of wilderness warnings—and look at what happened to her as a result. The grace of God is something that must never be taken for granted. It must not be imposed upon. However, Paul couples this warning with an assurance: although God will break down human pride, he will do so in a way that takes account of how much each believer can bear, and will allow a way out for those who need it (10:11–13).

Paul is particularly concerned about the abuse of the Lord's Supper (10:14–22) and abuses of Christian freedom (10:23–11:1). In response to the latter, he emphasizes the importance of responsibility toward others. The Christian life is corporate, and this means that individual believers must pay attention to the scruples and concerns of others—a principle that has already been stated clearly in dealing with the question of meat offered to idols.

11:2–16 Propriety in Worship. Having mentioned the Lord's Supper, Paul now turns to deal with issues of worship in general. This section offers a number of problems to its readers, which need to be noted. First, Paul lays down that women should cover their heads during public worship (11:2–16). The major question that arises here is this: Is Paul laying down a local regulation for the church at Corinth around A.D. 55, or a permanent regulation for the entire Christian church in every time and place? Most interpreters of this passage believe that Paul is laying down a local rule in response to local circumstances. Similarly, Paul's stipulations about the length of hair are widely regarded as a response to local factors at Corinth, and probably reflect the fact that long hair in a man and short hair in a woman were regarded as a sign of homosexuality—something Paul would not tolerate within his church. In this, Paul declares that he is simply following common practice.

11:17–34 The Lord's Supper. Paul then provides further explanation concerning the Lord's Supper. Concerned that this meal is being treated with disrespect, Paul explains why it was instituted in the first place. He wishes to pass on what he has received (11:23), using language that clearly implies that Paul is passing on a solemn and unalterable practice or belief, which goes back to Jesus Christ himself. The words Paul quotes bear a strong similarity to those used by Jesus Christ himself at the Last Supper (see Lk 22:17–20). Eating the bread and drinking the wine are reminders of the saving death of Christ and must not be taken lightly. In particular, there is a need for believers to examine themselves, to ensure that they do not come under judgment.

12:1–11 Spiritual Gifts. Paul now turns to deal with the charismatic aspects of worship, specifically with the role of the Holy Spirit. The gift of the Holy Spirit is given for the good and upbuilding of the church as a whole. The one Spirit works in many ways, depending on the individual in question. Each of these ways is equally valid. The important thing is that the "manifestations of the Spirit" lead to the common good, not to individual gratification.

12:12–31 One Body, Many Parts. Paul stresses this point through his analogy of the church as a body. Just as a human body has many parts, each with different functions, so the church has many members, each with their different roles to play. They are all needed. Their interdependence is considerable, with the result that when one member suffers, all suffer. There is no room for arrogance within the body, nor can one member declare that others are not required.

Having established this general point, Paul then turns to the specific issue of the "manifestations of the Spirit." Some are entrusted with the spiritual gift (or "gift of the Spirit"—the Greek can be translated both ways) of prophecy, others of teaching, others of being an apostle, and so on. All are necessary for the good of the church. Not everyone speaks in tongues—but so what? The important point is that some do, and thus contribute to the life of the church as a whole. Paul thus lays the foundation for a theology that acknowledges the great diversity of the gifts of the Spirit without declaring that any one is of supreme importance, or that any can be dispensed with as unnecessary.

13:1–13 Love. Yet Paul does draw attention to one aspect of the work of the Spirit that he regards as being of vital importance to the life of the church—

love. Paul selects four spiritual gifts (13:1–3), and makes the point that all are without real value unless they are accompanied by love. Yet love is not to be thought of as a gift of the Spirit. More strictly, it is a fruit of the Spirit (Gal 5:22)—something that is the natural result of the Spirit's presence in the life of a believer. Not all are given the gift of speaking in tongues, but all ought to show the fruit of love. The need for some of the gifts of the Spirit will pass away. However, love will remain forever. Long after prophecy has ceased and people have stopped speaking in tongues, love will continue to be of vital importance within the church.

14:1–40 Gifts of Prophecy and Tongues and Orderly Worship. Having shown the importance of love, Paul returns to the theme of the gifts of the Spirit in more detail (14:1–39). (Paul perhaps implied that the Corinthians had many gifts of the Spirit, but lacked love.) While affirming the importance of speaking in tongues and prophecy, Paul expresses some anxieties about the manner in which these take place at Corinth. The issue of good order in public worship emerges as being of major importance, not least on account of the impression that speaking in tongues might create on outsiders or visitors. There is a need to speak in words that can be understood. Otherwise, the church will not be built up in faith. Everything must be done in a fitting and orderly way (14:40).

One aspect of Paul's teaching on public worship has attracted special attention—the requirement that women should be silent in worship and ask their husbands to explain things they don't understand when they get home (14:33–40). Once more, this seems to be a local rule reflecting local conditions. Paul's concern is clearly for order in worship, which would be disrupted by talking within the congregation. Scholars have suggested that the Corinthian congregation would have included many well-educated men, but few educated woman. The need for the women to have things explained to them by their husbands should therefore be seen as specific to this congregation, rather than a universal comment on the ability of women to understand.

15:1–58 The Resurrection of Christ. But such issues are put in perspective when Paul turns to address his major concern at Corinth—the denial of the resurrection of Christ (15:1–58). Using very solemn language, Paul declares that the Resurrection is a nonnegotiable element of the Christian faith. The central affirmation of the Christian faith is that Christ died for our sins and was then raised again (15:1–4). Paul makes the point that this was a public event, to which there were many witnesses, some of whom were still living at the time he was writing.

And even he, Paul, can testify to the reality of the Resurrection (15:5–7). No matter which of the apostles people ask, they will get the same answer—Christ has been raised from the dead. The Corinthians had accepted this as well—to start with (15:8–11).

But now some of them are denying the resurrection of Christ. But why? Not only is the witness to that event highly reliable, as Paul has just shown, but without it, the Christian faith makes no sense (15:12–19). The whole Christian hope would be lacking any foundation. Without the Resurrection, there is no hope of eternal life and no forgiveness of sins (see Ro 4:24–25). An "eat, drink, and be merry, for tomorrow we die" attitude would be the only realistic approach. Yet the reality is totally different: Christ has been raised from the dead. There can be, and need be, no doubt about this. And because Christ has been raised, believers will be raised as well. Paul uses the term *firstfruits* (15:20) to refer to Christ's resurrection. In other words, Christ is the first in the great resurrection harvest, which will include all believers.

Having vigorously defended the reality of the Resurrection, Paul then moves on to discuss the nature of the resurrection body of believers (15:35–58). The point that Paul is making in this difficult passage is that there is a direct connection between earthly and resurrection bodies, even though they will be totally different. The seed that dies in the ground gives rise to a plant that looks nothing like the seed—yet there is a direct link between seed and plant. In the same way, the death of the natural body will give way to the resurrection body, which need look nothing like the present body. Yet the connection remains!

But this kind of speculation has limited importance for Paul. The vitally important thing is that the resurrection of Christ *did* occur, and that the believers' resurrection *will* occur. The Christian life may be lived in this secure and certain hope of resurrection. Christians know that God has given them the victory over sin and death through Jesus Christ. And knowing that, they may serve him with all their abilities.

16:1–18 Conclusion. Finally, Paul brings his letter to an end by asking his readers to contribute to the churches at Jerusalem (16:1–4) and by making a few personal requests relating to his future missionary plans (16:5–18). In the course of these requests, he mentions by name those who have supported and assisted him in his missionary tasks. Finally, Paul passes on greetings from the churches in the region of Asia (that is, the area around Ephesus). It is clear that many of these were house churches, including that which met in the house of Aquila and Priscilla (16:19–20).

The letter probably ended with Paul adding a few lines in his own handwriting. The bulk of the letter would have been written by a professional secretary or scribe. Now Paul added some items in his own hand (16:21–24). These final words look ahead with passionate longing for the coming of the Lord, as he commends his dear brothers and sisters to the love and grace of their common Savior and Lord, Jesus Christ.

2 CORINTHIANS

Paul's second letter to the church at Corinth was written at some point late in A.D. 55, before winter had finally set in. The letter was written from Macedonia, the region to the north of the Roman province of Achaia (in which both Corinth and Athens were located). The mood of the letter is somber, and it is clear that things have not improved all that much at Corinth since Paul's first letter of about six months earlier. Perhaps some of the difficulties noted in that first letter have been sorted out. Now, new problems have arisen in their place.

1:3–11 The God of All Comfort. The letter opens with greetings to his readers (1:1–3), which Paul clearly expects to include Christians in the whole region of Achaia, rather than Corinth itself. The theme that dominates the early verses of the letter is that of the consolation that God offers to believers (1:4–7). Terms such as *compassion* and *comfort* are used to refer to the deep sense of peace that believers are able to experience through knowing God's consoling presence in the midst of suffering. For Paul himself has been through a very difficult time (1:8–11). Although he does not identify the hardships he has experienced, it is clear that he expects his readers to have heard at least something about them.

1:12–2:17 Paul's Change of Plans. He now turns to deal with a distressing accusation being made against him by some at Corinth—that of a lack of sincerity toward the Corinthian church—through his cancellation of a planned visit to the city (1:12–2:11). Paul makes clear that it was only after great thought that he had canceled this visit. He wished to spare the church from any pain that such a visit might bring, on account of the criticisms he might have been obliged to make. However, since the church itself has taken action against his critics, he considers the incident closed. In any case, Paul clearly regards the hand of God as having been upon his travel plans (2:12–17), just as he is aware of the gracious assistance of God at every point in his ministry. He has been given the privilege of preaching the good news of Christ, allowing the fragrance of Christ to be present in the stench of a decaying world.

3:1–18 The New Covenant. Paul now turns to deal with the theme of the joyful privilege of being a minister of the new covenant (3:1–6). The contrast with the old covenant is clear at every point. Although the covenant given through Moses can be said to reflect the glory of God, that of the new covenant exceeds it at every point. The old covenant did not succeed in establishing a right relationship between humanity and God, whereas the new is able to do precisely this (3:7–11). Just as a veil was placed over the scrolls of the law in synagogues, so the law placed a veil between the people and God. But now, through Christ, that veil has been removed (3:12–18).

4:1–5:10 Treasures in Jars of Clay. Yet the treasure of the gospel has been entrusted to weak and frail human beings. This is a major theme in this letter—the sufficiency of the grace of God to compensate for the weakness of believers. For Paul, one of the great joys of the gospel is that God has chosen to make known the good news of redemption in Christ through the ministry of ordinary people (4:1–18). The treasure of the gospel has been placed in jars of clay. Even though believers are aware of their weakness and are subjected to all kinds of persecution and harassment, they can rest assured that they will be upheld by God himself. In any case, human mortality will eventually give way to immortality on account of the gospel of grace (5:1–10). The flimsy tent of earthly lives will give way to the solid building of resurrected bodies.

5:11–6:13 The Ministry of Reconciliation. Having dwelt on the weakness and mortality of the ministers of the gospel, Paul now turns to the gospel itself (5:11–21). In a superb passage, he declares that on account of the gospel, sinners become a new creation through their conversion. Something happens to transform them. And that transformation has its ground in God himself, who "was reconciling the world to himself in Christ." As a result of Christ's work, our sin has been transferred to him, and his righteousness has been transferred to us. And the ministry of proclaiming this good news has been entrusted to believers, who are called upon to be "Christ's ambassadors" in the world. They are "God's fellow-workers" (6:1–2). Paul then

Corinth was a large Roman city that Paul visited on his second trip and wrote to several times. Its commercial center was known for its wickedness. These Doric columns are from a 5th century B.C. Temple of Apollo. In the background of the picture at left is the Acrocorinth, the citadel that dominated the ancient city.

documents his own personal hardships once more (6:3–13). He has had to suffer for the gospel. Others must expect to do the same.

6:14–7:1 Do Not Be Yoked With Unbelievers. A brief passage then deals with a practical concern relating to Christian conduct. It is clear that Paul is anxious about the results of believers being "yoked with unbelievers." This could be understood as a specific reference to mixed marriages between believers and unbelievers, in line with the prophetic criticism of intermarriage between Jews and Gentiles. But it is more likely that Paul is concerned about the use of pagans within the church, including teaching roles. Just as the Old Testament prophets were anxious that pagan practices would contaminate Israel's faith through intermarriage between Jews and pagans, so Paul is concerned to ensure that Christian faith is not adulterated by paganism in the same way.

7:2–9:15 The Jerusalem Collection. It is clear that Paul is concerned that his earlier letter to Corinth may have caused some offense to its readers. If this is the case, he is saddened by the offense given, but nevertheless he believes that he was right to raise the issues with them. However, it is clear that Paul believes, to his obvious delight, that the issues that had troubled him earlier have now been resolved (7:2–16). With these issues behind him, he is able to raise once more the question of the collection that he intends to be used to help support the mother church at Jerusalem. Just as the Lord Jesus Christ became poor for the sake of believers, so believers ought to give to support the work of ministry elsewhere (8:1–15). Paul declares his intention to take every precaution to ensure that the money is administered properly, and he notes that his colleague Titus will visit Corinth presently to oversee matters (8:16–9:5). Paul also makes reference to an unnamed "brother" (8:22), who may well have been Luke or Barnabas.

Underlying this appeal for money is the belief that Christians throughout the world ought to support each other in every way possible (9:6–15). The theme of stewardship is developed here. Although Paul's concern is to raise money for the Jerusalem collection, the general principles apply throughout the Christian life. God's gifts do not *belong* to those to whom they have been given. They are *entrusted* to them, with the expectation that they will be used. In order for the gospel to be advanced, generous giving and sowing is required of all. As it is God who provides the seed in the first place, believers are simply using God's own gifts in his service. By giving generously in this way, believers are doing two things—meeting the needs of God's people, and giving thanks and glory to God. The implication of Paul's comments seems to be that the Macedonian churches, who were much less wealthy than the Achaian churches, had given generously—so why should the Corinthians not be equally generous?

10:1–11:33 Paul's Defense of His Ministry. The tone of the letter now changes abruptly. The first nine chapters are gentle in character, probably reflecting a growing appreciation of Paul and his ministry within the Corinthian church. But Paul still has opponents, and he now moves to confront them and their criticisms of his ministry. The first accusation that he confronts is that he is not "spiritual" enough to be a true apostle (10:1–6), or that he has an exaggerated sense of his own speaking ability (10:7–11). Paul rejects such criticisms. He will be judged by the effectiveness of his ministry in Corinth and elsewhere by the extent to which God has been pleased to work through him (10:12–18). There is no room for boasting here. There is, however, a real need to be honest about what God has done in and through his ministry.

Paul then makes the point that he preached the gospel in Corinth without any support from them. Would they have been more persuaded of his apostolic claims if he had lived off their generosity? He was supported by the Macedonian churches while he undertook his evangelistic ministry in Corinth. In no way can he be accused of having exploited the Corinthians (11:1–15). Paul then provides an impressive catalogue of the hardships he has suffered during his missionary journeys (11:16–33). On reading this list of hardships, we realize how little Luke has told us of Paul's personal sacrifices for the sake of the gospel. Luke's account of Paul's evangelistic ministry makes reference to some difficulties, but does not have the detail that Paul provides. Paul's point in this passage is that he has suffered greatly as he exercised his apostolic ministry. So why is he being criticized for claiming to be an apostle?

12:1–10 Paul's Thorn. Paul then mentions a particular hardship—the "thorn in the flesh." He makes the point that there are some who have something to boast about—like someone who has had a mystical experience of God, being caught up into the heavens. But boasting can lead to arrogance, rather than humility. Paul brings out the importance of humility from his own experience, making reference to the "thorn." It is not clear what this "thorn" actually was. The most likely explanation is that it refers to an illness Paul contracted during the course of his missionary journey, which severely limited his actions. An obvious possibility would be malaria.

But it is the *spiritual* relevance of the "thorn," rather than its precise identity, that really matters. It taught Paul to rely on the grace of God, rather than on his own strength. It also brought home to him that his own weakness was more than compensated for by the strength of God. Paul heard the Lord speak these words, which summarize these points superbly: "My grace is sufficient for you, for my power is made perfect in weakness" (12:9).

12:11–13:11 Paul's Concern for the Corinthians. Having failed to visit Corinth in the recent past (to the irritation of some in the church [1:15–2:1], as we have seen), Paul now affirms his intention to visit Corinth for a third time (12:14–21). His ministry will be self-supporting, and he will make no demands on the Corinthian church. In a moment of self-disclosure, Paul confesses his anxieties over this forthcoming visit: he might find things at Corinth that would distress him (12:21). Yet, no matter how difficult it may be, Paul is determined to maintain discipline within the church (13:1–10). Challenges to his apostolic authority will not deter him from insisting on the moral responsibilities of believers. Paul can live with challenges to his own personal prestige. However, he will not tolerate violations of Christian conduct.

13:11–14 Final Greetings. The letter thus comes to an end on a negative note. Paul's need to express his concern about the church at Corinth leads to the final section of this letter having a critical tone. Yet in his final greeting (13:11–14), Paul affirms the graciousness of God. Despite all human weakness, the grace of God is at work in the churches. And so Paul ends with a form of words that has passed into Christian use down the ages, and is now known simply as "the grace" (13:14). By using these words in their prayers, Christians today remind themselves of their continuity with that early Christian community in Corinth. Though they lived nearly two thousand years earlier, they share the same Lord and faith as believers today. Every time they use this prayer, Christians affirm that time and space are no barriers to sharing a common faith in Christ.

GALATIANS

Paul's letter to the Galatians dates from some point around A.D. 53. It is not clear whether the churches in question were clustered in the northern or central area of Galatia, or whether they were based in the southern Galatian cities Paul had visited during his first missionary journey, such as Pisidian Antioch, Iconium, and Derbe. Another possibility is that the letter dates from shortly after the Council of Jerusalem (see Acts 15), which raised questions very similar to those Paul addresses in this letter.

1:1–2:10 Paul's Apostleship and the Gospel. The letter opens with a greeting and an affirmation of Paul's status as an apostle (1:1–2). His apostolic authority does not derive from any human agency, but from a direct commission by the risen Christ—a clear reference to the circumstances surrounding his conversion, to which he will return presently. After a brief statement of some of the great themes of the gospel (1:3–5), including salvation from sin through Christ, Paul turns to the issue that is troubling him. The Galatian churches—churches he had planted himself—are in the process of abandoning the gospel.

Paul insists that anyone who preaches a gospel that differs from that which he delivered to them is to be ignored (1:6–10). He begins by establishing his authority as an apostle, providing details of his conversion. Paul derived the gospel directly and personally from the risen Christ. He is not guilty of repeating some purely human tradition, or of inventing a gospel to suit his own taste. He is being obedient to the same Christ whom he encountered at the moment of his conversion (1:11–12).

For the benefit of those who do not know his personal history, Paul provides a very brief account of his conversion (1:13–24). This provides a summary of the events that are documented in more detail at Acts 9:1–31. It is not intended to be exhaustive, but simply to demonstrate that Paul has authority from Christ to preach the gospel in his name, and that this authority is recognized by the other apostles (2:1–10). They acknowledge that Paul has been entrusted with the task of proclaiming the gospel to the Gentiles, just as Peter has the equally important task of preaching the gospel to the Jews. Paul is thus emphatic concerning both the divine foundations of his calling and its public recognition by the remaining apostles.

2:11–21 Paul Opposes Peter. However, he admits to differences with Peter. Paul here gives us an important insight into a real tension within the early church, which has now made its presence felt in Galatia as well. The development that Paul is worried about is the emergence of a *Judaising party*— that is, a group within the church that insists that Gentile believers should obey every aspect of the Law of Moses, including the need to be circumcised. According to Paul, the leading force behind this party is James—not the apostle James, who died in A.D. 44, but the brother of Jesus Christ who was influential in calling the Council of Jerusalem, and who wrote the New Testament letter known by his name.

For Paul, this trend is highly dangerous. If Christians can only gain salvation by the rigorous observance of the law, what purpose does the death of Christ serve? It is faith in Christ, not the scrupulous and religious keeping of the Law of Moses, which is the basis of salvation. Nobody can be *justified* (that is, put in a right relationship with God) through keeping the law. The righteousness on which human salvation depends is not available through the law, but only through faith in Christ.

3:1–14 Faith or Observance of the Law. Aware of the importance and sensitivity of this issue, Paul then explores this question in greater detail (3:1–29). The Galatians have fallen into the trap of believing that salvation came by doing works of the law, or by human achievement. So what has happened to faith? Did the gift of the Holy Spirit ever come through keeping the law? Paul then makes an appeal to the example of Abraham to make his point.

Paul argues that Abraham was justified through his faith (3:6–18). The great patriarch was not put in a right relationship with God through circumcision. That came later. That relationship with God was established through Abraham's faith in God's promise to him (Ge 15:6). Circumcision was simply the external sign of that faith. It did not establish that faith, but confirmed something that was already there. Nor does the law, or any aspect of it, abolish the promises God has already made. The promise to Abraham and his seed—which includes believers—remains valid, even after the introduction of the law.

So the basic point is that the promise of God to Abraham was made before either circumcision or the Law of Moses was delivered. Thus all who share in the faith of Abraham are the children of Abraham. It is possible for the Gentiles to share Abraham's faith in the promises of God—and all the benefits that result from this faith—without the need to be circumcised, or be bound to the fine details of the Law of Moses. It is Christ's death and resurrection, not external observance of the law, which constitute the ultimate grounds of relationship with God. Paul clinches his case by citing from the prophet Habakkuk (Hab 2:4), who declares that the righteous shall live by faith.

Yet in the middle of this detailed analysis of the relation between the law, the promise, and faith, we find an important interpretation of the meaning of the death of Christ (3:10–14). Paul notes that the law declares that everyone who dies on a tree—a category that includes execution by crucifixion—is cursed (Dt 21:23). Yet, as the Resurrection makes clear, Christ did not die under a curse. Christ therefore became a curse "for us" (3:13). In other words, the curse that affected the cross did not relate to Christ himself, but to believers, in that Christ chose to bear their curse for them. The guilt of sin was thus assumed by Christ himself on the cross.

3:15–25 The Law and the Promise. So what purpose did the law serve? Paul is clear that the law had a positive role to play. The whole world, according to Scripture, is held captive to sin, preventing anyone from achieving righteousness. But the law was able to point ahead to the coming of Christ, who would be the means by which deliverance from sin would finally be achieved. The law was thus like a guardian, teacher, or mentor, which took charge until the coming of the gospel. But now that faith has finally come, the law need no longer have this function.

3:26–4:7 Sons of God. So what, then, does faith achieve? Paul has already emphasized that the righteousness that puts believers in a right relationship with God (which is the basic meaning of the word *justification*) comes only through faith. But what are its other benefits? Paul now identifies one of the many blessings that faith brings (3:26–4:7). Faith in Christ gives believers the status of being sons of God. As a result of this new status in Christ, all other differences are totally overshadowed. They are not abolished. They are just seen in their proper light. Differences of nationality, social status, or gender are seen to be of no ultimate significance. Believers remain different from one another—but those differences are seen to be unimportant in relation to issues of salvation or Christian living.

As a result of being sons of God, believers are in full possession of all the legal rights of sonship—including both liberty and inheritance rights. The Holy Spirit confirms this, allowing believers to refer to God as *Abba*— a remarkably intimate term for a father, reflecting the close relationship between the believer and God.

4:8–5:15 Freedom in Christ. Yet the Galatians want to squander these privileges. They want to revert to being slaves to the dictates of the Law of Moses, rather than exulting in the glorious liberty of the gospel (4:8–20). Why should the fine detail of Jewish regulations get in the way of Christian living? Why should believers be obliged to observe special Jewish festivals and regulations? Paul confesses himself to be bewildered by their lapse into some form of legalism. Who wants to be a slave, when one can be a son? Paul illustrates this point by an exposition of Genesis 16:1–16 and 21:2–5, which, although difficult to follow, makes the point that there is no need for believers to lapse back into slavery, when they have the right to the privileges of sonship (4:21–31).

Paul thus declares that Christ has come in order to liberate believers. They have been set free and must never allow themselves to be lured back into slavery (5:1–15). If anyone feels that he must be circumcised, then he is under obligation to the law in its totality—and Christ might as well not have come, as far as he is concerned. The issue is that of freedom. This does not mean a freedom to indulge in sin, but rather a freedom to love without limits. As Paul puts it, the entire law can be summarized in terms of love.

5:16–6:10 *Life by the Spirit.* Yet this love does not rest upon legalism. Believers are moved by the work of the Spirit to love others (5:16–26). The command to love is necessary, as an objective statement of what it means to be a Christian. Yet the basic motivation to love in this way is subjective, arising through the renewing work of the Holy Spirit within believers. Just as the sinful nature naturally leads to all kinds of immorality, so the Spirit naturally leads to love, joy, peace, patience, kindness, goodness, faithfulness, gentleness, and self-control. Paul refers to these as "the fruit of the Spirit," meaning that they will arise naturally in the life of faith, just as fruit grows on a tree. The old sinful nature has been put to death on the cross. Now believers are able to come to life, through the renewing work of the Spirit.

Paul then carefully explains how these principles will work out in the Christian life (6:1–10). Throughout Paul's letters, we find theology being used as the basis of ethics and pastoral care. Paul's emphasis on the need for believers to lead loving lives is grounded on the belief that the Spirit of the risen Christ will assist and empower them. They will not be acting on their own!

6:11–18 *Not Circumcision, but a New Creation.* Finally, Paul brings this letter to an end. The closing sections are written in his own handwriting. The rest of the letter would have been written by a professional scribe. In these concluding remarks, he again makes the point that circumcision is useless. The important thing is to experience the new creation, which comes only through faith in Christ. And rejoicing in this thought, he commits the Galatian believers to the care of the Lord Jesus Christ.

EPHESIANS

Ephesus was the chief city of the region of Asia Minor, and the scene of some of Paul's most difficult evangelistic work. This letter does not have the usual specific greetings that are customary in Paul's letters. This has led some scholars to conclude that the letter was meant to be circulated throughout the churches of the region, rather than addressed to any one congregation. Even the specific reference to Ephesus (1:1) is omitted by many manuscript versions of the text.

The letter does not deal directly with any specific false teaching, which further suggests that the letter was intended to circulate throughout the churches of Asia Minor, rather than to deal with the specific problems of any one congregation. It is difficult to date the letter precisely, due to the lack of personal details that are usually found in Paul's letters. However, a date in the early 60s would fit in with what we know of Paul's movements and situation at this time.

1:1–14 Spiritual Blessings in Christ. The letter opens with an affirmation of Paul's credentials as an apostle (1:1–2), followed by a remarkably powerful statement of the glory of the risen Christ (1:3–14). Paul declares that believers have been chosen from the foundation of the world to be adopted as sons of God, through the death and resurrection of Jesus Christ. God's purposes have been made known through Jesus Christ so that believers might know what God intends for them. And their election is *sealed*—that is, confirmed—by the indwelling of the Holy Spirit.

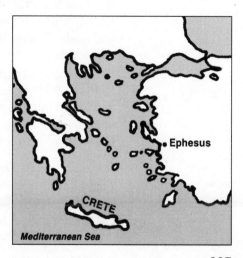

Paul uses this image to bring out the fact that the presence of the Holy Spirit represents God's seal of ownership upon believers. But the Spirit is more than this; he is also a *deposit*, which guarantees inheritance of salvation. Paul here uses what seems to have been a commercial or trading term, meaning "an initial payment that secures possession of something, with the promise to pay the full amount later." Paul is thus declaring that the presence of the Spirit in believers'

397

The Mercantile Agora, at left, built in Ephesus in the third century B.C., was one of the places Paul stopped on his trips. The ruins on Curetes Street date from the second century A.D., about a hundred years after Paul's stay.

lives is both a sign of God's ownership and sovereignty, and the confirmation of a promise to give more in the future.

1:15–23 Thanksgiving and Prayer. Having rejoiced in the wonder of the gospel, Paul now turns and gives thanks for the believers in the region. Knowing that they already believe in the Lord Jesus Christ, Paul prays that they might come to the full knowledge of his glory in every respect. Paul's language strains to its limits as he tries to express his sense of wonder at the richness of the gospel, which he and his readers have in common. The power of the risen Christ, under whose authority God has placed the present age, is available to believers through faith.

2:1–10 Made Alive in Christ. The letter then turns to celebrate the benefits of faith in Christ. Paul rejoices in the fact that the power of the rulers and spirits of the present age have been overcome through the resurrection of Christ. Through faith, believers have been delivered from the death of sin and made alive in Christ. They have begun to taste the life of heaven, as they are raised up with Christ in the heavenly realms. By this, Paul does not mean that Christians are physically removed from this world. He is simply pointing to the way in which faith allows believers to experience the presence and power of Christ in a way that anticipates their fullness in heaven. And this great hope does not rest on any human achievement, but on the workmanship of God within believers, as he works to refashion them in his service.

2:11–22 One in Christ. God has broken down all barriers in order that all might find the peace and joy that comes only through faith in Christ. There is no place for any human distinctions within the Christian community—for example, between Jew and Gentile. Christ died in order to break down once and for all such divisions, and to enable all to come to him. Both Jew and

Gentile are able to come to God through Christ. In the church, both groups are equally valued and welcome. Both are fellow-citizens within the household of God, which has been built securely upon the teaching and witness of the prophets and apostles, with Jesus Christ himself as the cornerstone.

3:1–13 Paul, the Preacher to the Gentiles. Paul continues this theme of the Jews and Gentiles being brought together in one body as he explains his own special calling to be the bearer of God's good news to the Gentiles (3:1–13). Paul stresses that he was given access to the mystery of the gospel by a special revelation, a clear reference to the events of his conversion, in which he had a personal encounter with the risen Christ. And an integral part of the gospel message is the proclamation that Jews and Gentiles alike can share in and benefit from the promises of Jesus Christ.

For Paul, the fact that he has been singled out in this way does not in any way reflect a special talent or merit on his part. His calling is purely a matter of God's grace. Even though Paul is intensely aware of his own weakness and failings, he is nonetheless called and equipped to be an apostle. He is convinced that his calling was a matter of grace, not human merit. Christians may approach God with confidence on account of his grace and the work of Jesus Christ.

3:14–21 A Prayer for the Ephesians. Paul thus prays that his readers might be strengthened through Christ's coming to dwell within their hearts in power. At this point, Paul pauses to try to put into words the full extent of the love of Christ for his people, glorying in its width, length, height, and depth (3:14–21). Human words cannot adequately express this love, and yet it is available in all its fullness to those who put their faith in Jesus Christ. Believers need to discover that God "is able to do immeasurably more than all we ask or imagine."

4:1–16 Unity in the Body of Christ. Christians also need to discover their unity. There is only one Lord, only one faith, and only one baptism. As a result, there is a need for believers to discover that beneath any differences, there is a common unity in Christ. Through the death of Christ, God has broken down all divisions. Believers must make sure that they do not create new divisions and thus undo the work Christ has already done. Paul emphasizes that despite its different component parts, there is only one church. All its various members, in their different roles, share the same common task of building up the *body of Christ* (one of Paul's favorite terms for the church), and leading each and every believer to the fullness of Christ. For it is Christ who holds the entire church together, as its head. (There is an important parallel here with the image of the vine and the branches [Jn 15:1–7].)

4:17–5:21 Living as Children of Light. One vitally important aspect of this process of maturing in Christ is maintaining Christian integrity in a fallen world. In this major section, Paul stresses that Christian faith must lead to a Christian lifestyle, in which believers stand out from the world in terms of their moral conduct. They must discard their old selves and former natures and clothe themselves with the new nature that comes through Jesus Christ. Paul identifies a series of specific failings that Christians must take care to avoid (4:25–31).

In particular, Paul emphasizes the importance of forgiveness. Just as God forgave their sins in Christ, so believers must forgive the sins of others (4:32). The church is thus to be a community of compassion and forgiveness, in contrast to the world. Here, we see Paul bringing out the need to be like God himself: believers are to be imitators of God, patterning their lives on God as he has made himself known through Christ. Anything that comes in the way of this process of becoming like God, or that threatens to make believers become like the fallen world, is to be avoided. Christians have been called out of darkness into light and must not return to that darkness. For this reason, they must encourage and support each other—for example, through song and prayer—in order that they may remain faithful and close to their risen Lord (5:1–20).

5:21–32 Wives and Husbands. Paul then turns his attention to the practical business of relationships within the church and family. His argument here is that God has ordered the world in a certain way and that this ordering must reflect itself in human relationships. The word *submit* is used several times in this section (5:21–6:9), not with the sense of "obeying an earthly superior," but rather with the meaning of "discovering and accepting God's intentions." For example, at no point are wives told to *obey* their husbands. Paul's instructions to his female readers do not employ this term at all—although he does lay down that children should obey their mothers and fathers (6:1). The mutual relationship between man and woman in marriage is defined in terms of love and submission—that is, the same quality of self-giving love that took Christ to the cross for his church, and the same committed willingness to be faithful to the demands of a relationship.

6:1–9 Children and Parents, Slaves and Masters. The relations of man and woman, children and parents, slave and master are all defined in terms that at first sight seem to be conventional first-century terms. Yet, on closer inspection, some vital qualifications are introduced. We have already noted the way in which husbands are told to love their wives. Parents are also instructed not to exasperate their children, just as masters are reminded that their superiority over slaves has an earthly, not a heavenly, basis. In all this, we may see the basic principle set out in Galatians 3:28 being explored—that in Christ there are no fundamental distinctions of race, gender, or social status. These exist on earth—but they must be seen from a heavenly perspective. Life within the church must begin to mirror the life of heaven, in which such distinctions will play no part.

6:10–20 The Armor of God. Having instructed his congregations to avoid sin and remain faithful to the Lord, Paul then provides his readers with guidance on how this may be achieved. His basic point is that it is impossible to manage these demands without the grace of God. An integral element of the Christian life is the cultivation of the practice of turning to God and using the resources God has put at believers' disposal. This leads Paul to his famous image of the "full armor of God" (6:10–18).

Paul clearly understands the Christian life to involve conflict. As will be clear from his own career, that conflict often arises through the opposition of secular and religious authorities to the message of the gospel. But it is clear that Paul also recognizes another level of conflict, which could be referred to as "spiritual warfare." The Christian is obliged to struggle, not just against "flesh and blood" (in other words, purely human opponents), but against "the powers of this dark world and against the spiritual forces of evil in the heavenly realms" (6:12).

To resist these onslaughts, Christians must make the best use of the defenses God himself provides—such as truth, righteousness, faith, and salvation. Notice that all the types of armor Paul mentions except one are defensive—that is, intended to defend the wearer against the attacks of others. The only offensive weapon is the "sword of the Spirit," which allows the Christian to launch a counterattack against such spiritual forces, armed with the Spirit of the living God.

6:21–24 Final Greetings. Finally, Paul asks his readers to pray for him, as he ends his letter by dwelling on the themes of grace and peace—two central themes of the Christian gospel that allow believers to live and work in the world, knowing that their faith rests securely on a rock that God himself has established. Whatever difficulties believers may find themselves in—and recall that Paul himself is in chains at this point (6:20)—they may know that they have peace with God.

PHILIPPIANS

P aul's letter to the church at Philippi is generally thought to have been written during a period of imprisonment, probably in Rome, around A.D. 61. The circumstances of the letter fit in well with those described in Act 28:14–31, when Paul was under house arrest, but was still permitted to see visitors and enjoy at least some degree of freedom.

Philippi was an important Roman colony in Macedonia, and was evangelized by Paul during his second missionary journey (Ac 16:11–40). It was the first European city in which Paul proclaimed the gospel. There were so few Jews in the region that there was no synagogue. (Acts 16:16 refers only to a "place of prayer," not a synagogue.) This may explain both why Paul does not cite the Old Testament at all during this letter, and also why the letter is virtually free of argument. It is one of the most positive and delightful of Paul's letters, setting out the sheer joy of the gospel to its readers.

1:1–11 Thanksgiving and Prayer. The letter opens with an outpouring of delight and thanksgiving. Paul is filled with joy at the reports he has heard of the church in the region. He speaks of their "partnership in the gospel" with him, and of his great confidence in all that God will do through them in the years that lie ahead. It is clear that Paul longs to be with them, sharing in their work and witness. But he knows that he may entrust them to the Lord, confident of his guidance and protection.

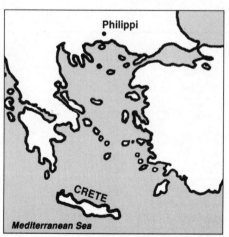

Philippi

CRETE

Mediterranean Sea

1:12–30 Paul's Chains Advance the Gospel. Just as Paul has heard reports about the Philippians, so the Philippians have clearly learned about Paul's imprisonment (1:12–14). Paul reassures them that the cause of his imprisonment is his faith. There are no other accusations being brought against him, other than the stand he has taken for the gospel. And the fact that he has taken this stand is itself a powerful act of witness for the gospel. The contingent of Roman guards from which his guards are drawn are aware of his faith in the gospel and that his imprisonment is for Christ, and Christ alone. And Paul's stand on this matter has given new confidence to other Christians as they seek to witness to the Lord. Even in this apparently miserable situation, Paul is able to bear witness to his faith.

Yet not all preach Christ from such good motives. Paul admits that some preach the gospel for questionable reasons (1:15–18). But for Paul, the important thing is that the gospel is preached. Even the most base motive can be used in the spreading of the gospel. And this thought encourages Paul as he contemplates his own situation. He may be in prison; nevertheless, the gospel continues to be preached. Paul declares his personal conviction that whatever happens to him will turn out for the good under God's grace. It does not matter whether he lives or dies. If he lives, he will be able to preach the gospel. If he dies, he will go to be with Christ—which is even better. He will be content to accept whatever the Lord wills for him, knowing that Christ will be exalted, whether through Paul's life or his death (1:19–26). Believing in Christ may lead to suffering for Christ. This is already happening in the case of Paul. It may also happen to the Philippians (1:27–30). Yet Paul declares that it is a privilege to suffer in this way (note 1:29; the phrase "it has been granted" implies a special favor).

2:1–11 Imitating Christ's Humility. With this point in mind, Paul urges his readers to think about the example of Jesus Christ, who provides a model for Christian behavior (2:1–4). The particular point that Paul wishes to bring out is the importance of humility, which he sees illustrated to perfection in the life and death of Jesus Christ. Paul now draws on a Christian hymn, which was evidently known to his readers, in making these points (2:5–11). It will be helpful to note the main features of this remarkably helpful statement of the meaning of the death and resurrection of Christ.

The hymn begins by affirming that Jesus Christ had the nature of God from the beginning. However, he chose "make himself nothing" or "empty himself," by becoming a servant in the form of a human being. We can see here a clear reference to the Incarnation—that is, to Christ becoming a human being and entering into our world of time, space, and suffering (Jn 1:14). Christ humbled himself. Not only did he set aside his majesty to come to dwell among us human beings, he was willing to subject himself to death on a cross for our salvation.

Yet God chose to exalt him to the highest place—a clear reference to the resurrection and ascension of Christ. These great events publicly demonstrated that Christ was divine, and that every knee should bow at his name and confess that he is indeed Lord. An Old Testament text that originally referred to God (Isa 45:23) is here applied to Jesus Christ. On account of the Resurrection, Jesus Christ has been demonstrated to be divine, so that this transposition is fully justified. But the main point that Paul wishes to make here is simply that this attitude of humility ought to be part of the Christian life.

2:12–18 Shining as Stars. Paul then urges his readers to "work out" their salvation (2:12–18). Yet in doing so, Paul is not implying that the Christian life is totally dependent upon human effort. A close inspection of his comments (2:12–13) reveals that there are two contributors to the Christian life—the believer and God. Paul asks his readers to do their best. He then makes the point that God is at work in the lives of believers, enabling them to desire and achieve his purposes. Christians are not on their own. God does not make demands and then leave believers to get on with them on their own. He assists them, as they do what they can for him.

2:19–30 Timothy and Epaphroditus. We then learn of Paul's plans for the future, and especially for Timothy and Epaphroditus. They have both been with Paul in Rome, and it is his intention to send them both to Philippi and then to follow them when this becomes possible. This suggests that Paul expects to be released from his house arrest at Rome in the near future and to resume his missionary and pastoral activity.

3:1–11 No Confidence in the Flesh. Having informed the Philippians of his plans for the future, Paul returns to the theme of confidence and joy in the gospel. There is no ground for confidence in any human achievement or qualification—such as being a Jew, (3:1–6). Paul makes the point that if there were any such ground for confidence, he would be a very confident man indeed, on account of his excellent standing within Judaism. But all of this is worthless in comparison with the joy and privilege of knowing Christ. To know Christ overshadows everything and shows it up in its proper light (3:7–11). Once more, we find Paul making the point that righteousness does not come by observing the law, but by faith in Christ. Yet alongside this theological argument, we can detect Paul's sense of utter delight of being able to share in the fellowship of Christ—both in his sufferings and, eventually, in his resurrection. This thought gives him comfort and hope as he contemplates the future (3:12–16).

3:12–4:1 Pressing on Toward the Goal. The fact that Philippi was a Roman colony also comes in useful to Paul. It gives him a model for his thoughts about the relationship between the present situation of believers and their future state in heaven (3:17–4:1). For believers, their "citizenship is in heaven." In other words, the church is a colony of heaven, whose people look forward to the day when they can return to their homeland. The true homeland of believers is heaven. They are presently exiled on the earth, but they have the full assurance that they will one day return home. Christ will come from heaven and gather his people to him and transform them, so that they share both his glorious likeness and also his habitation in heaven.

4:2–20 Exhortations and Thanks. The letter now begins to draw to a close. Paul asks his readers to rejoice, no matter what their circumstances (4:1–9).

All their concerns and requests can be made known to God, who will grant them peace in the midst of this turbulent world. Paul praises the Philippians for their kindness toward him, including the gifts they had sent through Epaphroditus. He reassures them that he has found the secret of being content, no matter what his situation. Wherever he is, and whatever his situation, he can draw strength from the God of peace. God will meet all his needs (4:10–20).

4:21–23 Final Greetings. The letter ends with Paul wishing God's blessing on his readers (4:21–23). Yet one little phrase in the closing paragraph merits a little closer attention. Paul sends greetings to Philippi from "those who belong to Caesar's household" (4:22)—a clear reference to the presence of Christians within the palace area itself. The gospel has not merely reached Rome. It has begun to find its way to the heart of its seat of power. It would be many years before the emperor became a Christian. Nevertheless, the foundations for this dramatic development were already being laid during Paul's own lifetime.

COLOSSIANS

Colossians, like Philippians, is a letter written by Paul while he was under house arrest in Rome, probably at some point around A.D. 60. The city of Colossae (also spelled Colosse) was located on the River Lycus in Asia Minor. Paul himself had not evangelized this city during any of his missionary journeys. However, Epaphras, one of Paul's converts during his Ephesian ministry (Ac 19:10), had traveled to the city to preach the gospel there. The letter is particularly concerned to deal with a false teaching that has arisen within this young church.

In view of the importance of this false teaching to the letter, it is important to consider what it was. Although this false teaching is never specifically expounded, its main features can be worked out from Paul's response to it. These appear to have been three: first, an emphasis on some secret or mystical knowledge (a theme that would become a major theme of the movement known as *Gnosticism*, which became especially influential in the second century); second, a strict set of rules concerning what it was legitimate to eat and drink, linked with an emphasis on asceticism; and third, a tendency to play down the importance of Jesus Christ, and to worship angels. In many ways, these ideas seem to represent a mingling of Jewish and Greek ideas. Paul counters the teaching by emphasizing that all that needs to be known about God and his purposes has been revealed supremely, uniquely, and adequately in Jesus Christ.

1:1–14 Thanksgiving and Prayer. The letter opens with the traditional greetings, and giving thanks for all that God has done in and through the church at Colossae. The main themes of the gospel are stated: God has rescued believers from darkness and brought them into the kingdom of his Son. Through Christ they have redemption and forgiveness of sins. Paul assures the believers in the city of his continued prayers for their spiritual well-being and development.

1:15–23 The Supremacy of Christ. Paul then launches into one of the major themes of the gospel, which is of

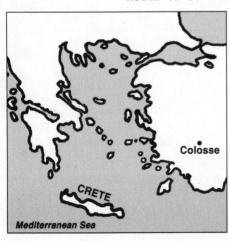
Colosse
CRETE
Mediterranean Sea

particular importance in the light of the Colossian error. The theme is that of the majesty of Jesus Christ. Christ is declared to be the image of the invisible God. In other words, although God himself cannot be seen, he has chosen to make himself known in a visible and tangible form in Jesus Christ. Everything is subject to Christ; he possesses God's total authority. God dwells fully in Christ. Through him, and through him only, we can have reconciliation with God. Throughout this section, the implication is clear: Christ is the unique bearer of divine revelation. Nobody else possesses his spiritual authority.

1:24–2:5 Paul's Labor for the Church. Paul then affirms his own authority. He has been commissioned by God (not by any human being!) to proclaim this gospel (and no other gospel!) to every living creature. It is his mission to make known this gospel in all its fullness. God has fully disclosed all that needs to be known for salvation. He, Paul, will make sure that the "glorious riches of this mystery" are known to all. The gospel is thus "perfect wisdom"—a phrase Paul has clearly chosen carefully, to make clear that it does not require addition. This wisdom has been made known fully and completely in Christ. The gospel makes available "the full riches of complete understanding." And anyone who says anything else, even in "fine-sounding arguments," is trying to deceive them.

2:6–3:4 Freedom From Human Regulations Through Life with Christ. This brings Paul directly to his concern about the false teachings that are gaining a hearing at Colossae. This section provides the real heart of the letter, and would have been read with particular care and attention by its original recipients. He urges his readers to avoid the "hollow and deceptive philosophy" that is grounded in secular human culture rather than in the self-revelation of God in Christ. In Christ, and in Christ alone, the fullness of God has been made known in physical form.

Relentlessly, Paul presses home his point. It is Christ, and Christ alone, who is supreme. Believers need look to no one and nothing else in their search for wisdom and knowledge. He alone can deliver humanity from its bondage to sin and death. Through his cross, Christ has disarmed the powers and authorities. It is possible that the Colossians were being urged by the false teachers to worship such powers and authorities. Paul, however, insists that their power has been broken by Christ. Why worship a defeated power, when one can and should worship the one who triumphed over them?

Paul declares that believers are under no obligation whatsoever to observe fussy regulations concerning food or drink. Nobody has the authority to lay such obligations on them. These are purely human commands and regulations, without any basis in the will of God. They may seem to be wise and spiritual—yet they threaten to destroy the basis of faith by diverting believers away from Jesus Christ himself.

But believers have been raised with Christ. By this, Paul does not mean that they are already in heaven. He means that their future place in heaven is assured, on account of Christ, and that the anticipation of the joy of heaven can be experienced now. For that reason, they should raise their eyes heavenward, where Christ has gone (3:1–4). Paul's point here is that this exercise will remind believers of the ultimate authority of Christ. He, and he alone, has been raised in this manner. Christ alone has been raised from the dead, and Christ alone possesses the authority that results from being raised in this way.

3:5–17 Rules for Holy Living. In the light of this, Paul asserts the need for moral behavior on the part of believers (3:5–17). Yet these moral demands differ totally from the demands of the false teachers. Paul calls believers to be like Christ. As God's chosen people, they should demonstrate Godlike qualities to the world. Interestingly, Paul notes the importance of praise in sustaining the Christian life (3:16).

In a brief section, he provides a summary of his views on appropriate Christian approaches to the relationships of wives and husbands, children and parents, and masters and slaves (3:18–4:1; for an expanded account, see Eph 5:21–6:9, where the same values are noted, but with a more detailed theological foundation being provided).

4:2–6 Further Instructions. Paul then turns his attention to his own needs. He asks for prayer in order that doors may be opened for his preaching of the gospel in their region. He asks for prayer in order that he may communicate the gospel as effectively and faithfully as possible. Once more, it seems that Paul has every expectation of being released from protective custody at Rome in the near future, so that he will again be free to travel and proclaim the gospel.

4:7–18 Final Greetings. The letter then moves to its close, with a series of personal greetings. Paul commends Tychicus to them. He will bring the Colossian believers further news about Paul, as may John Mark, if he ever gets to Colossae. The form of the reference to Tychicus suggests that he may have been the bearer of the letter (and possibly of others, such as Ephesians and Philemon, as well). Epaphras—who brought the gospel to Colossae in the first place—is mentioned to them, as is Luke. Notice the reference to the letter being "read to you" (4:16). It was the practice to read such letters aloud in the churches, so that all might hear what Paul had to say. Once more, Paul ends his letter with a concluding section in his own hand (4:18; see also 1Co 16:21; Gal 6:11; Phm 19), asking his readers to remember that he is being held captive for the sake of the gospel.

1 THESSALONIANS

Paul's first letter to the Christians at Thessalonica was written from Corinth, probably at some point in A.D. 51. The date cannot be fixed with absolute certainty. It is widely accepted, however, that this is the earliest of Paul's letters in the New Testament. Thessalonica was the largest city in Macedonia, and was evangelized by Paul during his second missionary journey (Ac 17:1–14). Paul was only able to stay in the city briefly, being obliged to flee from the city and seek refuge in nearby Berea before moving on to Athens and then Corinth. While in Corinth, Paul wrote to the Christian church at Thessalonica to offer it encouragement and guidance.

1:1–10 Greetings and Thanksgiving. The letter opens with greetings from Paul, Silas, and Timothy—the three evangelists who had founded the church in the city (1:1–2). Although all three are mentioned, what follows makes it clear that the letter is Paul's work. He begins by offering thanks and praise for the remarkable growth of the church in the city and the extent to which its reputation has spread throughout the regions of Achaia and Macedonia (1:3–10). Thessalonica was a busy seaport located on the Egnatian Way, one of the major trade routes in the region. It was thus an ideal center for mission. It is clear that many in the city had turned away from various forms of paganism in order to accept Jesus Christ, and that these developments were attracting attention throughout the region.

2:1–16 Paul's Ministry in Thessalonica. Paul's stay in Thessalonica had been brief and probably did not allow him time to say all that needed to be said to the fledgling church. This letter gives Paul the opportunity to put into writing some of the points that need to be made. The first major section of the letter deals with a series of matters relating to ministry, and especially the proclamation of the gospel.

The first major point concerns motivation. The gospel is not proclaimed from a desire to please people—the evangelist is no demagogue! Nor does it arise from greed, a desire for personal gain, or winning praise from people. The most fundamental motivation

for evangelism is a desire to please and serve God. Paul and his companions were entrusted with the gospel message by God himself and were carrying out their responsibility to him by preaching the gospel at Thessalonica.

This attitude on the part of those who proclaimed the gospel was met with a corresponding attitude on the part of those who received it. The Thessalonians realized that this was no human wisdom, having its origins in the human mind, but something grounded in the word of God itself. Despite all the opposition, whether from Jew or Gentile, the gospel had been preached and believed.

2:17–3:13 Timothy's Report; Paul's Longing to See the Thessalonians. Paul then begins to tell of his own experiences. He relates how he had to leave Thessalonica abruptly, leaving behind a church that was unsettled. Paul had sent Timothy to encourage them, and had then made inquiries about them to assure himself that all was well. But now he has learned from Timothy that all is as it should be. It is easy to see Paul's relief at the report Timothy has brought to him, both concerning the morale of the Thessalonian church, and also of their memories of him. It is clear that the Thessalonians bore Paul no grudge for his hasty departure, which left them to face opposition without any real guidance or support. He assures them of his prayers for them and his longing to see them again.

4:1–12 Living to Please God. He now turns to deal with ethical matters, stressing the importance of right conduct. It is vitally important that the Thessalonians live upright and attractive lives, so that others from outside the church might be drawn into its fellowship on account of their witness.

4:13–5:11 The Coming of the Lord. As the letter comes to a close, Paul chooses to explain some aspects of Christian belief concerning the end of all things. In a section that shows familiarity with some of the gospel passages dealing with the need for believers to ??? for the coming of the Lord, Paul stresses that Christ may come again at any moment and that his people must be ready for this event. Nobody can be sure precisely when this will happen, and there is a need to be watchful. The Day of the Lord will come like a thief in the night, when people are unprepared for it.

It is possible that some believers at Thessalonica had died since Paul's visit, leading to a discussion about their fate and that of those who were still living. Paul reassures them of the hope of resurrection, and that the great promises of eternal life are open to those who are still alive when Christ comes. It seems that the Thessa-

Thessalonica was a large Roman city in Macedonia visited by Paul on his second missionary trip. He wrote two letters to the church at Thessalonica. The city was founded in 315 B.C. and has had an eventful history ever since. The White Tower was built long after Paul's stays in the city.

lonians were convinced that those who died in faith would indeed rise again to eternal life. The problem concerned those who were still alive at the time of the Second Coming. What will happen to them? Will they be able to share in the resurrection?

Paul reassures them on this point. Whether they are alive or dead at that time, they will all be taken to be with the Lord. Both those who are "awake" and those who are "asleep" (terms Paul uses here to mean "living" and "dead") will live with Christ (5:10). Yet confusion would arise over this point at Thessalonica as a result of his letter, obliging Paul to write once more to correct a misunderstanding that resulted.

5:12–28 Final Instructions. Paul then brings his first surviving letter to a close. After offering some advice on relationships within the church, Paul reassures his readers of the total faithfulness and reliability of God. The God who has called them is faithful and will see them through to the end (5:24). After asking that the letter be read aloud in the congregation, Paul commends those who read the letter to the grace of God.

2 THESSALONIANS

Paul's second letter to the church at Thessalonica probably dates from about six months after the first. It was written from Corinth in late A.D. 51 or early 52. Like the first letter, the work opens with a dedication from Paul, Silas, and Timothy, who were responsible for establishing the church in the city in the first place (Ac 17:1–14). The bulk of the letter deals with a misunderstanding that has arisen as a result of one section of the first letter.

1:1–12 Thanksgiving and Prayer. After an opening greeting (1:1–2), Paul once more gives thanks for the growth and witness of the Christian community in the great city of Thessalonica (1:3–12). It seems that the church is going through a period of oppression, and Paul reassures them that this is to be expected. Suffering for the kingdom of God is a sure sign of being counted worthy of that kingdom. But Paul soon turns his attention to the real issue, which has to do with the second coming of Christ.

2:1–12 The Coming of the Lord. It seems that the Thessalonians were unsettled by Paul's first letter (or possibly by a different letter, circulating under Paul's name, but not written by him; however, the view Paul describes could easily arise through a misunderstanding of the contents of 1Th 4:13–5:3). Some appear to have understood Paul to mean that the day of the Lord has already come—that is, that the end time is under way, leading up to the final coming of Christ in the very near future (2:1–12).

It is possible that this belief may underlie the idleness that Paul castigates later in the letter (3:6–15). Some may have argued that since the end of the world will happen at any moment, there is no point in doing anything. Paul argues that his own ministry shows how false this attitude is. He himself was not idle, but threw himself totally into the business of preaching the gospel. The instruction regarding not allowing an idle person to eat (3:10) should probably be seen in this context of end-time speculation.

In response to this feeling that the final days have begun, Paul declares that there will be warning signs, evident to all, before this final period in the history of the world begins (2:1–12). In particular, he draws attention to the dawn of a period of open rebellion against God (see Mt 24:10–12) and to the coming of "the man of lawlessness" (2:3). This person, who seems to correspond to the "antichrists" mentioned in John's letters (see 1Jn 2:18), will claim to be God. When these events have taken place, the end days will have begun. But they have not happened yet.

2:13–15 Stand Firm. Paul is quite clear that he taught the Thessalonians these things when he was with them (2:5). They have either forgotten them or have been led astray in some way. For this reason, Paul emphasizes the need to remain faithful to the teachings he had passed on to them, whether by word of mouth or by letter (2:13–17). He asks for the prayers of his readers, so that he and his colleagues might be able to preach the gospel in safety (3:1–5). Yet Paul is careful to make it clear that his ultimate ground of security lies in the faithfulness of Christ, in whom he knows he may have total confidence (3:3–5). His prayer is thus partly that his readers may come to share that same faith and hope that is so characteristic of his own ministry as a servant of the Lord.

3:16–18 Final Greetings. And so Paul ends his letter, once more commending his readers to the "Lord of peace." As with so many of his letters, Paul ends this letter with a few sentences that he has penned himself. The rest of the letter would have been written by a professional scribe. But Paul, wanting to authenticate the letter and add a personal touch, wrote these final words himself.

1 TIMOTHY

Paul's two letters to Timothy and the letter to Titus form a special group. They are distinguished by the fact that they are written to specific individuals, rather than to churches, and also by their strongly pastoral tone. This latter is seen in their concern with issues of church government and practical Christian living. For this reason, these three letters are often referred to collectively as the "Pastoral Letters." The Pastoral Letters date from a time after the events described in Acts 28. The most obvious explanation is that Paul was released from his house arrest in Rome at some point around A.D. 63, and that these letters were written after this release.

The first two letters are written to Timothy, who had played a significant role in Paul's missionary work (especially in Achaia and Macedonia; see Ac 17:14–15; 18:5), and is referred to with great affection in several of Paul's letters (Php 2:19–22). In addition, no fewer than six of Paul's letters name him in their opening greetings (2 Corinthians, Philippians, Colossians, 1 and 2 Thessalonians, and Philemon). Paul refers to Timothy as his "true son in the faith," raising the possibility that Paul was himself responsible for Timothy's conversion.

1:1–11 Warning Against False Teachers. After greeting Timothy (1:1–2), Paul warns of the dangers that can arise through false teachings (1:3–11). The general description of the false teachings that follow suggest that Timothy has encountered doctrines similar to those that had troubled the Christian churches at Ephesus and especially at Colossae, mingling some Jewish ideas with others that had been borrowed from paganism. Paul stresses the need of remaining faithful to the basics of the gospel, which have been entrusted to him as an apostle.

1:12–20 The Lord's Grace to Paul. Paul then spends some time talking about these basics, noting with sadness that some have departed from them totally (1:19–20). He stresses the importance of grace, explaining why it is of such importance to him personally. It was only by the grace of God that he, who had been a blasphemer and persecutor, was shown mercy. This mercy results directly from the death of Christ. In fact, Christ came into the world with the specific intention and purpose of saving sinners—of whom Paul was among the worst (1:15). Paul's point is that if the grace of

God can deliver him from sin, it can deliver anyone. Paul's personal testimony is thus to be an encouragement to others to discover the depths of God's forgiving grace.

2:1–15 Instructions on Worship. Having emphasized the importance of right doctrine, Paul then explores the importance of correct forms of worship. Public prayer for people in authority is commended—even if these are not believers. Paul seems to regard such people as potential Christians, drawing attention to the fact that Christ died for them. God wants everyone to be saved, and he sent Christ into the world in order that he might be a mediator between God and the world. Paul uses the idea of a *ransom* to explain the meaning of the death of Christ—that is, Christ's death is to be seen as a payment that secures the liberation of those who were formerly in captivity.

Paul then lays down some guidelines about the roles of men and women in worship. Paul, apparently speaking in a personal capacity rather than in his capacity as an apostle, insists upon propriety in public worship. In particular, he states his opposition to women being allowed to teach. Some scholars hold that this is to be understood as meaning that Paul did not allow any woman to be an official teacher in the church. Others suggest that he has a particular type of woman (perhaps unqualified or self-appointed teachers) in mind.

This is followed by a statement that has been the subject of considerable debate on account of both its translation and interpretation (2:15). Paul states that women—Eve? A woman in general?—will be "saved" or "restored" through bearing a child. This could mean, for example, that Eve's disobedience is countered by Mary's obedience in bearing Jesus Christ (just as Adam's sin was countered by the obedience of Christ), or that any sin imputed to womankind in general has been canceled through the birth of Christ. It could also mean that a woman who has faith in Christ can find salvation simply through her calling as a mother.

3:1–16 Overseers and Deacons. Paul then turns to the issue of church order and the qualifications of those who are to minister. The change in Paul's language makes it clear that he is no longer speaking in a purely personal capacity, but is speaking for the church at large. By this stage, the need for an official ministry within the church to carry on the work of the apostles had become increasingly clear. So how were they to be chosen? Paul sets out a series of guidelines to govern the selection of ministers.

Two basic offices or ministries are identified in this section: bishops, overseers, or superintendents (to use the various English translations of the Greek word *episkopos*), and deacons. It is clear that Paul expects such people to be of exemplary conduct and character and to be strong and knowledgeable in their faith. In the end, however, Paul points out that the church rests on the foundation of Jesus Christ, not on its ministers.

4:1–16 Instructions to Timothy. Having laid down guidance for the church at large, Paul now turns to offer counsel to his much-loved coworker Timothy himself. He stresses the importance of solid doctrine and fidelity to the gospel as it has been passed down to him. Timothy is to avoid the false teachings of the age and to place his full trust in the gospel of salvation in Christ. For Paul, the doctrinal orthodoxy of the churches can be maintained in part through the public reading of Scripture, preaching, and teaching. Timothy is thus called upon to develop such a ministry, for his own benefit as well as that of his hearers.

5:1–6:2 Advice About Widows, Elders, and Slaves. Again, we find Paul returning to the practical pastoral wisdom for which these letters are especially noted. Having stressed the importance of both life and doctrine (4:16), Paul offers guidance as to how to deal with a series of pastoral issues (5:1–6:2). His emphasis on the priority to be given to the pastoral care and support of widows is particularly significant. In the pagan culture of this period, widows and orphans were often left totally without support. Paul clearly believes that the church has a duty to support its widowed female members. The advice to believers who are slaves with believing masters is also significant. Paul urges them to behave with even greater diligence toward such masters.

6:3–10 Love of Money. Yet it is the lure of possessions, especially money, that causes Paul special concern (6:3–10). "The love of money," he famously remarks, "is the root of all evil." Note that it is not money in itself. Paul treats this as something that is neutral. It is the *attitude* people have toward money that is the problem. Paul urges Timothy to seek contentment in what he has and to avoid the active pursuit of wealth with all its attendant dangers. Later, he also points out that the only riches really worth seeking are those grounded in God himself (6:17–19).

6:11–21 Paul's Charge to Timothy. Finally, Paul charges Timothy to fight the good fight that lies ahead of him, secure in the confidence of the eternal life God has promised him (6:11–16). He is to remain faithful to what has been entrusted to him—a charge that could refer both to the churches to which he is called to minister, and also to the gospel he is to preach and teach. Perhaps Paul is aware that the time is drawing near when he must pass on the work of proclaiming and defending the faith to others (6:20–21). Timothy, he is sure, will be a faithful servant in the years that lie ahead.

2 TIMOTHY

Paul's second letter to Timothy presupposes a situation rather different from his first. Paul is now in prison once more, possibly for the last time. It is difficult to assign a date to the letter, although some date during the reign of the emperor Nero, possibly A.D. 65–67, would seem to be reasonable. Perhaps Paul is aware of the death of Peter, which may have convinced him of the urgency of writing to Timothy for the last time. The letter is saturated with an atmosphere of finality. Paul clearly believes that he has not much longer to live; and as a result, he wants to pass on his final instructions to the man who would have to exercise a role of leadership in the churches Paul will leave behind. At several points during the letter, Paul hints at his loneliness. He feels abandoned by those who were once his colleagues and friends, but who have now lost interest in him or disowned him.

1:1–3:9 Encouragement to Be Faithful. The letter opens with the traditional apostolic greeting (1:1–2). It is clear that Timothy was greatly loved by Paul. He had earlier referred to him as his "true son in the faith" (1Ti 1:2), suggesting that Paul may have led Timothy to faith. Paul's detailed knowledge of Timothy's family background certainly suggests a deep affection for the younger man (1:3–5). But there is no time for sentimental reflection. Paul wants to pass on to Timothy his instructions for the churches, as they face new difficulties in the future. The implication, especially of some of the material in the final chapter, is clear: Paul will not be around to guide the churches for very much longer.

Paul begins by reminding Timothy of the main points of the gospel, especially that salvation is by the grace of God, rather than by human effort. This grace, which had been purposed from all eternity, was made known only through the coming of Jesus Christ as Savior. Paul reminds Timothy of how he had been called to be an apostle of this good news for humanity. Despite all the suffering this had brought him, including being abandoned by those whom he had thought to be his friends, he remains absolutely determined to defend and safeguard the gospel that has been entrusted to him (1:6–18). This theme of being entrusted with the gospel is of central importance in this letter. When Paul speaks of "his gospel" (e.g., 2:8), he does not mean "the gospel that he possesses and owns," but "the gospel that has been entrusted to him for safe keeping."

Paul therefore urges Timothy to be strong, and to endure whatever hardship may lie ahead of him (2:1–6). Death and suffering are not to be feared. The resurrection of Jesus Christ allows them to be seen in their true light. They will not get in the way of the believer's final reward in heaven. The example of Jesus Christ himself is of vital importance here, giving hope to believers in their present hardships. To make this point, Paul quotes from an early Christian hymn with which Timothy would have been familiar (2:11–13). This hymn affirms that those who have died with Christ will be raised to life with him, on account of his total faithfulness to his promises. The image of "dying with Christ" is used elsewhere in Paul's writings to refer to conversion and its resulting benefits (Ro 7:6) and occasionally to baptism, which is the public demonstration of this conversion (Ro 6:3–7).

Having reassured Timothy of the certainty of the reward that is awaiting him and all who believe in Christ, Paul stresses the importance of moral living and avoiding false teaching (2:14–26). Indeed, Paul declares that an outbreak of false teaching and personal greed is to be expected in the last days (3:1–9).

3:10–4:8 Paul's Charge to Timothy. Having forewarned Timothy of all the dangers and difficulties that lie ahead, Paul solemnly charges him with the responsibility of guiding the churches through the uncertain period that is coming. Paul points to his own problems as an illustration of the kind of thing that Timothy can expect to happen to him. He must be under no illusions. But he will not be without protection and guidance. In particular, Paul stresses the importance of Scripture as a God-given and God-breathed resource for ministry and teaching (3:14–17). It will protect Timothy from false teaching and equip him to meet all the challenges that lie ahead. It will be clear that this resource continues to be of vital and supreme importance to Christians today, as they try to learn more about their Savior and their salvation, and all that Scripture implies for their lives.

Having stressed the importance of Scripture, Paul charges Timothy to preach and teach, countering false teachings and reassuring believers of the grounds and nature of the Christian faith and hope. In this fickle and fallen world, people will want to hear other ideas. Timothy must be prepared to carry on preaching and teaching, even if he meets with hostility or scorn. Paul expresses his own deep sense of contentment at having fought the good fight, and being able to rest in the knowledge of the crown of righteousness that is held in store for him—and for all who share his own faithfulness to their calling.

4:9–22 Personal Remarks and Final Greetings. Finally, Paul ends with the personal remarks and greetings that are so characteristic a feature of his letters. The letter includes a commendation of John Mark (4:11), the traveling companion of Paul and Barnabas for part of the first missionary journey before his decision to leave them for Jerusalem (Ac 13:13). It is thought that Mark wrote his Gospel at some point around this time, probably in Rome. It is clear that, despite the gloomy tone of parts of his letter, Paul expects to meet Timothy again. Unlike many of the friends who failed to support him, he is confident that Timothy will remain faithful. But in the end, Paul's hopes rest on the faithfulness of God, not of any human being. And so he commends Timothy to the grace of the faithful God whom they both serve and love.

TITUS

Titus was one of Paul's many Gentile converts, and he is known to have served him well and faithfully at several major stages in his ministry. Luke does not mention Titus at any point in Acts. However, there are frequent references to him elsewhere in the New Testament, indicating his importance to the early churches. In this letter, Paul again deals with the issues of pastoral ministry and teaching that he had addressed in the two letters to Timothy. The letter seems to have been written following the release of Paul after his imprisonment in Rome, described in Acts 28, and is probably to be dated around A.D. 64. However, there are no references to events within the letter to allow more precise dating.

1:1–4 Greetings. The letter opens with a traditional apostolic greeting, linked with a vigorous statement of hope in the gospel. The total faithfulness and reliability of the gospel are affirmed in exultant tones, making it clear that despite all his difficulties, Paul remains absolutely and joyfully committed to the gospel (1:1–3). He has no doubt either of his calling to be an apostle or of the power of the gospel.

1:5–16 Titus's Task on Crete. Paul then explains the background to his decision to leave Titus on the Mediterranean island of Crete. Luke does not record Paul as having had any ministry in this region, although the visit in question may have taken place after Paul's eventual release from imprisonment in Rome. It is clear that in Paul's absence, Titus has been preoccupied with establishing and organizing the churches on the island. Paul's advice to Titus relates chiefly to the fine details of church organization, including the personal qualities that are to be looked for in the ministers of the church. He is especially concerned with the roles of elders and overseers—or, more traditionally, bishops. From Paul's comments, it seems that he expects Titus to have some difficulty in finding suitable persons within Crete, which he clearly regards to be peopled with liars and cheats.

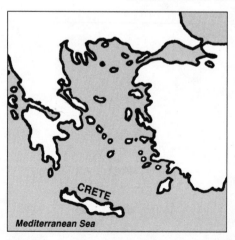

Mediterranean Sea

CRETE

2:1–3:11 What Must Be Taught to Various Groups. The strongly pastoral tone of the letter continues, as Paul advises Titus on how to deal with various groups within the church. It is important to note how one of Paul's chief concerns is to get a favorable public hearing for the gospel among potential converts and present critics. His advice to Christian slaves with unbelieving masters is particularly interesting, because it makes clear how important personal witness can be in gaining a positive response to the good news. In this context, Paul brings out how negative and unhelpful disagreements can be (3:9–11).

Underlying this pastoral wisdom is some important theological reflection. Paul emphasizes that the gospel rests upon the work of "our great God and Savior, Jesus Christ" (2:13), who gave himself up in order that believers might be saved and purified, becoming the people of God. There is a strong emphasis on the transformational aspects of the gospel: to be a believer is to be a changed person. Salvation involves washing and renewal. The themes of purification and transformation are both linked with the grace of God, the death of Christ, and the renewing work of the Holy Spirit—without these, the Christian life would be an impossibility. Believers may rest assured that they have been justified through the grace of God, and that they are heirs to all that lies ahead for them in heaven. Recognizing that some will find these ideas objectionable, Paul urges Titus to defend them, irrespective of the response they evoke from those who hear them.

3:12–15 Final Remarks. Finally, Paul sends his personal greetings to those around Titus, mentioning his travel plans. As always, we realize that the gospel is not simply about ideas—it is about men and women whose lives have been changed by the gospel and who share in a fellowship that knows no national boundaries.

PHILEMON

This short letter was written by Paul from Rome during the period in which he was held under house arrest (around A.D. 60). It is a highly unusual letter in that it deals with the fate of a runaway slave, rather than with the leading ideas of the gospel. However, the inclusion of the letter in the New Testament reminds us that the gospel is not just about ideas, but about real life and the moral decisions that are part of real life. Paul's concern is to show how the gospel bears on the situation of a single slave, who has come to put his faith in Christ. The message is simple: Every believer counts, whether slave or master.

Vv. 1–7 Greeting and Thanksgiving. The letter opens (1–3) with a traditional apostolic greeting, which identifies Philemon both as a believer and a friend. (Since the letter is so brief, references are given only by verse number, there being no chapters to refer to—a situation which is also encountered in the letter of Jude.) Paul takes great delight in the reports he has heard concerning Philemon's faith and the impact that this is having on those around him (4–7).

Vv. 8–22 Paul's Plea for Onesimus. Paul then gets down to the real purpose of the letter. He does not want to impose upon Philemon, let alone to preach at him. But he does have a favor to ask, which he believes Philemon will realize to be grounded in the love that the gospel illustrates and commends. This favor concerns Onesimus, a slave who became Paul's son—a reference to conversion—while Paul was in prison at Rome. The name *Onesimus* means "useful," and Paul exploits this meaning in a pun (11), which is clearly designed to win over Philemon to the favor in question. This favor turns out to be a request to treat Onesimus mercifully.

Onesimus clearly had stolen some property from his master and then run away. Under Roman law, the penalty for this was death. However, Onesimus has now become a Christian through the ministry of Paul, and Paul asks Philemon to be merciful. Onesimus is no longer a slave, but a brother. Paul has told him to return to his master. In response, he hopes that Philemon will forgive him for his past behavior (12–21).

Vv. 22–23 Final Greetings. After expressing his hope that he will be able to meet Philemon again (22), Paul sends his own greetings, along with those of four others, including Mark and Luke. We have no way of knowing what the outcome of this letter was. However, the letter would have been carried to Philemon by Onesimus; and the very fact that it is included in the New Testament suggests that Philemon decided to act on its contents.

HEBREWS

The Letter to the Hebrews is one of the most fascinating letters in the New Testament, stressing how Jesus Christ represents the fulfillment of the Old Testament sacrificial system. It is not clear who the intended readers of the letter would have been. The most appropriate readers would have been Greek-speaking Jewish converts to Christianity, who wanted to know the relationship between their new faith and the old ways and ideas of Judaism. This information is provided in a superb manner by this letter.

The author of the letter is also unknown. Some older English translations suggest that the author is Paul. However, the text makes no such claim. In any case, the style of the writing is very different from that of Paul. The two people who are most likely to have written the work are Barnabas and Apollos, both of whom would have had the deep familiarity with the Old Testament and the excellent command of the Greek language that this book demonstrates. However, the question of authorship is not of major importance to appreciating the importance and relevance of this letter. The writer will simply be referred to as "the author" in this commentary.

1:1–2:4 The Son Superior to Angels. The letter does not open with a greeting. Instead, it plunges directly into a declaration of the superiority of Jesus Christ over every other form of divine revelation. Noting that God has indeed revealed himself to some extent and in different ways in the past, the author declares that he has now chosen to reveal himself completely and definitively through his Son Jesus Christ. Jesus Christ is the "exact representation" of God. In other words, to see Christ is to see God. Jesus is like the mirror image or the definitive imprint of God's own nature.

Having made this point, the author proceeds to demonstrate the superiority of Jesus over a range of people who might be considered rival claimants to the title of "supreme revelation of God." In due course, he will deal with Moses, a figure of special importance to Jewish readers. But first his attention focuses on the angels, regarded by some Jews as the mediators of God's revelation. In an analysis of a series of biblical passages, he demonstrates how they point to the coming of Jesus Christ as the Son of God. God spoke to no angel like this! Angels serve God—and therefore serve Jesus Christ, to whom they are inferior.

2:5–18 Jesus Made Like His Brothers. In addition, the Son has authority over the world to come. In an important exposition of Psalm 8, the author demonstrates how the psalm's reference to the son of man being made "a little lower than the angels" is a reference to the incarnation of Jesus Christ (2:5–9). In other words, the psalm looks ahead to Jesus Christ becoming man, and hence willingly accepting a status lower than that of the angels in order to achieve the salvation of humanity. And as a result of his incarnation, Jesus was made perfect through suffering (2:10–18).

For the author, this is a vitally important point, bringing hope to any who are going through suffering or being tempted. Jesus had to become like us human beings in order to redeem us. To be an effective high priest, who would be able to deal with our sins, he must become like those he intends to redeem. Although Jesus is none other than God himself—a point the author establishes in his opening chapter—this does not mean that he is totally different from us. He is both God and a man. Being God does not prevent him from being human as well. Hence the author insists on the likeness between Jesus and ourselves, and the great spiritual comfort this brings. Jesus knows what it is like to suffer—and so can sympathize with us when we suffer.

3:1–6 Jesus Greater Than Moses. The author now turns his attention to the greatest figure of the Old Testament, through whom God gave the law to Israel—Moses. Great though Moses was, he is overshadowed and outranked by Jesus. Just as a son is superior to a servant within a household, so Jesus (as the Son of God) is superior to Moses (as the servant of God) in God's saving plans and purposes.

3:7–19 Warning Against Unbelief. The author now turns his attention to the need for redemption. He points out how even after Israel had been given the law, they continued to sin. In an important exposition of Psalm 95, the author draws attention to the devastating impact of Israel's rebellion against God and to the continued promise of a "rest" for the people of God. The idea of a "rest" is used here as a symbol of the redemption God offers to his people. Yet that rest cannot be entered on account of unbelief. So what can be done about this?

4:1–13 A Sabbath-Rest for the People of God. The author begins by stressing that the hope of a Sabbath-rest for the people of God remains open, despite all the sin of the past. The vital role of the word of God is noted. It is able to bring out the reality of human sin, penetrating to the very depths of human nature. From his brief overview of Israel's history, the author brings out the fact that those who are obedient can expect to receive this promised rest.

4:14–5:10 Jesus, the Great High Priest. Having identified the promise of rest and the problem of sin, the author now turns to the means by which this promise may be fulfilled through Jesus Christ, the great high priest. Although some aspects of this theme will be explored later, the author makes a number of points immediately, as he sets out the significance of Jesus Christ. First, he makes the point that Jesus Christ is a sympathetic high priest. He is like us in every way (except for sin), so that we can draw near to God through him with confidence. Second, he draws attention to the need to be called to the office of high priest. In the case of Jesus Christ, this calling comes directly from God himself. By learning obedience through suffering, Jesus demonstrated himself to be the perfect high priest, who would be able to make the necessary sacrifice for sin.

5:11–6:20 The Certainty of God's Promise. This theme will be taken up again presently. The author now turns to deal once more with the problem of unbelief (5:11–6:12), stressing the serious threat that it poses to a believer's relationship with God. He then returns to the theme of the promises of God and deals with their utter reliability (6:13–20). In making a promise, people swear by the authority of someone greater than themselves to bring home their commitment to the promise. But in God's case, there is no who is superior to him. As a result, God swears by himself as way of affirming his total faithfulness to his promises. God cannot lie; therefore, believers can have total trust in his promises. The author uses the image of an anchor to bring out the way the Christian life is firmly "anchored" in God himself. And the ultimate grounds of this hope? For the author, it is that believers may rest assured of their salvation on account of the work of Jesus as high priest (6:19–20).

7:1–28 Melchizedek the Priest. This leads the author to explore the high priesthood of Jesus in more detail. He begins by focusing on the mysterious figure of Melchizedek (Ge 14:18–20), who blessed Abraham on his return from defeating the five kings. This action implies the superiority of Melchizedek over Abraham, which is confirmed by Abraham's paying tithes to him. Now the Levitical priests, who were descended from Abraham, failed to deal with the sin of the people. For this reason, there is a need for a different priest, descended from Melchizedek rather than Abraham, who can deal with the sinful situation of humanity. The author then argues that Jesus Christ is a high priest after the order of Melchizedek (picking up a theme from the strongly messianic Psalm 110:4).

So what failings were there with human high priests? The author points out how these high priests had to make sacrifices for their own sins before dealing with those of their people. And this very action demonstrated that they needed forgiveness as much as everyone else. The need, therefore, is for a sinless high priest. And this is only met through Jesus Christ.

8:1–9:10 The High Priest of a New Covenant. Jesus is therefore the high priest of the new covenant, which replaces the old covenant established through Moses (8:1–13). Using a series of Old Testament passages, the author demonstrates that the old covenant had to pass away to make way for a better covenant, mediated only through Jesus Christ. And so the ceremonial regulations of the old covenant, important in their own time, are now outmoded (9:1–10). A distinction is drawn between the eternally valid aspects of the Old Testament (such as the promises of forgiveness), and those that are superseded through the coming of Christ (such as external matters of worship or regulations concerning food and drink).

9:11–28 The Blood of Christ. In a reference to the ritual associated with the Old Testament Day of Atonement (Lev 16:11–19), the author points out how the blood of bulls and goats was only able to achieve outward cleansing. But the blood of Christ is able to achieve eternal redemption, thus bringing about the internal cleansing and purification that the law had pointed to, but was unable to deliver (9:11–14). Through his blood, Christ is the mediator of a new covenant, through which those who have been called may receive their eternal heritage (9:15).

The author now draws out the parallel between the old and new covenants and human wills. (The same Greek word is used to refer to both, in much the same way as is the English word *testament*.) A will becomes operative once the person who made it has died. And through the death of Christ, the promises of forgiveness have finally been realized. At his first coming, Christ was sacrificed for us, so that he might bear our sins. At his second coming, he will bring the final salvation for those who have put their trust in him and have been sanctified through his blood (9:16–28).

10:1–18 Christ's Sacrifice Once for All. As the author continues to develop the contrast between the sacrifices of the Old Testament and the perfect sacrifice of Christ, he points out how the Old Testament sacrifices did not actually achieve what they pointed to. If the sacrifices had to be repeated year after year, it is clear that they had not achieved their objective. To put it simply: the blood of bulls and goats cannot take away sins (again, note the clear reference to the Day of Atonement ritual, Lev 16:11–19). The priest offers the same old sacrifices year after year, without ever managing to take away people's sins—but Christ made a perfect and once-for-all sacrifice, which obtains full forgiveness of sins and thus does away with any need for further sacrifices. Christ's perfect sacrifice makes the sacrifices of the old covenant obsolete. There is no need for them anymore, in that what they pointed to—but could not deliver—has now been achieved.

10:9–39 A Call to Persevere. With this thought in mind, the author urges his readers to appreciate what God has done for them and the great hope to which it leads. On account of the death of Christ, a way has been opened through the curtain of the temple—that is, through the barrier that separates the people from God on account of their sin. It is now possible to draw near to God with full assurance that sins have been cleansed and forgiven through the blood of Christ. And this thought, the author argues, ought to enable believers to persevere in the Christian life.

11:1–40 By Faith. A further stimulus to perseverance is provided by the great figures of faith of the Old Testament. In one of the most famous passages in the letter, the author provides his reader with a spectacular panorama of trust, as he surveys the great believers of the Old Testament. Faith is about being able to see through to the world of spiritual realities. It is about being certain of things that we cannot actually see, but nevertheless know to be true—such as the truth and trustworthiness of the promises of God. The author then surveys the great men and women of faith, allowing us to see that a central feature of Christian faith—a trust in the promises, presence, and power of God—was present in the past.

So what advantage does the Christian believer have over these great Old Testament figures of faith? The author is clear: they trusted in the great promises of God, but did not receive what they were promised. The Christian believer also believes in those same promises, but has the advantage both of *knowing* that they have been fulfilled in Jesus Christ, and of *receiving* the benefits that were promised (11:39–40).

12:1–13 God Disciplines His Sons. With this thought in mind, the author encourages his readers to take heart from the witness of the past. He provides believers with a powerful image to encourage them to keep going in the Christian life. He argues that it is like being in a race and being cheered on by a crowd of believers from the past. They are shouting encouragement, just as crowds urge on runners in a marathon, so that believers will make the effort to finish the course. And if that thought is not enough, the author asks believers to fix their eyes on Jesus and to appreciate how he was prepared to accomplish all that was asked of him (12:1–3). Jesus is here referred to as the "author and perfecter of our faith" (12:2). By this, the author wants to bring out the fact that Jesus has gone before believers in the life of faith, blazing a trail that they are being asked to follow. Jesus is both the basis of their faith and an example of faith. He has made the Christian life possible through his sacrificial death. He also provides an example from which believers may take encouragement.

And just as discipline is an important element in long distance running, so it is in the Christian life. In order to finish the marathon of the Christian life, believers need to be disciplined by God. The author thus asks his readers to expect and welcome discipline from God. Discipline is to be seen as a mark of commitment and love. After all, fathers discipline only their own sons. God's discipline affirms believers by informing them that they are his sons (12:4–13).

12:14–13:19 Encouragement to Keep Going. The letter now begins to draw to its close. It does so with an extended passage of encouragement, urging its readers to devote time and attention to their relationship with God, not to be discouraged by their weaknesses, and to seek comfort and strength in Jesus Christ. Life may change, but he will remain the same forever. There is a real need to advance to Christian maturity and to shake off the sin that can so easily be an obstacle to faith.

13:20–25 Concluding Prayer. The author concludes with a powerful prayer of commitment and with personal greetings. In his prayer, he entrusts his readers to the care of a greater pastor than himself, who can be relied upon to care for his sheep and to bring them safely through to their final salvation. The same God who raised Christ from the dead will work in the lives of believers and bring them through whatever lies ahead.

JAMES

The letter of James is the first of a group of letters that is sometimes referred to as the "Catholic Epistles" or "General Epistles." These unusual terms draw attention to the fact that the letters in question are not written to specific individuals or specific churches, but seem to be intended to be read by a wide range of people. Their intended readership is thus general or universal. (The word *catholic* basically means "universal" or "general.")

The letter of James was probably not written by James the apostle, but by James the brother of Jesus, who played an important role in the Council of Jerusalem (Ac 15:13). This council was especially concerned with clarifying whether Christian believers would be under any obligation to respect the Law of Moses, especially its requirement that males should be circumcised. In the end, the council decided that this should not be a requirement (see pp. 369–70). However, no reference is made to this controversy in the letter.

The absence of any reference to the controversy over whether Gentile believers should be circumcised points to an early date for the letter. However, James appears to be concerned to correct a possible misunderstanding of Paul's doctrine of justification by faith, which would suggest a date at some point in the late 50s or early 60s. We will probably never know precisely when the letter was written.

The letter is packed full of practical advice, which is as invaluable today as it was when it was first written. At a number of points, it seems to draw on, or reflect, knowledge of the themes of the Sermon on the Mount.

1:1 Addressed to Jewish Converts. The letter is addressed to "the twelve tribes scattered among the nations" (1:1). This way of referring to believers suggests that they are primarily Jewish converts. The letter is probably the most Jewish writing in the New Testament. It seems to reflect a very early period in the history of the church when a large proportion of believers were converted Jews and the meeting place of Christians is still referred to as a "synagogue" (2:2, in the Greek).

1:2–2:13 Trials and Temptations. James opens his letter by stressing the need to resist doubt and temptation. The role of riches in causing temptation is particularly noted. Believers are not simply people who hear the word of God. They are those who obey it (1:19–27). Faith is something that expresses itself in practical, not just theoretical, ways. James is particularly concerned to ensure that the standards of the world do not contaminate the church (1:27). The example he chooses to bring out the way the church can be swayed by worldly attitudes is that of a rich man who turns up for a meeting and is given preference in every way over a poor man (2:1–13).

2:14–26 Faith and Deeds. Probably the most important section of the letter now follows. It is possible that James has encountered a misunderstanding of Paul's doctrine of justification by faith, which suggested that if someone believes in Christ, he or she is freed from any obligation to do good works. Whether this is the case or not, there can be no doubt that James is concerned to emphasize the moral consequences of faith. Even the demons believe that there is a God—but that faith does not justify them!

James declares that the kind of faith that matters is a faith that shows itself in action. This does not mean that anyone is put right with God by doing good works. Rather, it means that good works are the natural result of a real faith. James appeals to two examples from the Old Testament to make this point—Abraham and Rahab. Both believed in God and did certain things as a result.

3:1–4:12 Taming the Tongue; Learning Humility. The emphasis now returns to practical wisdom. The tongue needs careful controlling (3:1–12). The tongue can just as easily praise as curse. There is a real need to take care over what is said, given the enormous consequences of careless and thoughtless words. The importance of wisdom is noted, and its true source in God affirmed (3:13–18). Believers should submit themselves to God and learn his humility (4:1–12). Once more, the dangers of worldliness are pointed out. Anyone who chooses to become a friend of the world will end up by being an enemy of God.

4:13–17 Boasting About Tomorrow. As an example of this worldliness, James gives the example of someone who confidently predicts the future course of his life. For James, this is unacceptable. Our futures lie with God, who alone knows what will take place. Anyone planning the future should add the phrase "if it is the Lord's will" to his words as a reminder as to who is in control (4:13–17). (This phrase is often represented by the letters D.V., representing the Latin form of this phrase, *deo volente*.)

5:1–12 Warning to the Rich; Patience in Suffering. The criticism of attitudes toward riches apparent earlier in the letter now emerges once more. James makes the point that riches come from somewhere and are generally gained at someone else's expense. For this reason, the Lord is angry with those who are rich (5:1–6). In marked contrast, James encourages those who are suffering in any way, in order to increase their patience. The example of Job is commended: suffering can lead to blessings (5:7–12).

5:13–20 The Prayer of Faith. The letter draws to its conclusion with some practical advice on prayer (5:13–20). The importance of prayer is noted, especially the prayers of the righteous, whether for forgiveness or for healing. The practice of anointing the sick with oil in the name of the Lord is commended. Finally, the importance of supporting and correcting each other in the faith is pointed out. And so this very practical and moral letter comes to its end.

1 PETER

The first letter of Peter is addressed to Christians scattered throughout the general region of Asia Minor, who are facing the threat of persecution. Although that persecution has yet to begin, it is clearly seen as a major threat by those to whom Peter was writing. The situation that the letter presupposes could easily fit in with what we know of the difficulties faced by Christians in the reign of Nero (A.D. 54–68). Peter indicates that he was in "Babylon" when he wrote the letter (5:13), which is widely interpreted as a reference to Rome itself (although a town of that name also existed on the River Euphrates around this time).

1:1–2 Authorship and Readership. The letter opens with an affirmation that its writer is Peter, the apostle, and that his intended readership is believers in the general area of Asia Minor. The descriptions used for believers are very important. They are "God's elect" (in that they have been chosen by God) and "strangers in the world" (in that although they live in the world, they are not of that world). Father, Son, and Holy Spirit are all identified as being involved in the salvation of believers.

1:3–12 Praise to God for a Living Hope. Peter then expresses his joy at the Christian hope (1:3–4.9). He and his readers have the enormous privilege of being born again into a hope that nothing can ever take away from them. They are being shielded by God's power so that they will finally inherit all the riches that are being stored for them in heaven. And they can rest assured of this inheritance, on account of the resurrection of Christ. Even though the threat of suffering looms on the horizon, it cannot take away their hope in Christ.

The salvation that believers now enjoy is something that the great prophets of the Old Testament longed to see. They knew that God would send a messiah, whose sufferings and glory the people of God would share (1:10–12). Many New Testament writers, especially Matthew and the writer of the letter to the Hebrews, stressed the way the coming of Jesus Christ brought to fulfillment the great hopes and expectations of the Old Testament, often allowing the true meaning of a passage to be understood for the very first time.

1:13–2:3 The Reality and Cost of Redemption. Peter then stresses both the reality and the cost of redemption. The cost of the redemption of believers cannot be measured in terms of silver and gold. These are not precious enough to compare to the true price of our redemption. The price of salvation is nothing less than the blood of Christ, "a lamb without blemish or defect"—a clear reference to the perfect lamb that had to be selected for the Passover celebration, which recalled God's great act of deliverance in which he freed his people from bondage in Egypt.

Nothing can snatch this hope away from believers. In the midst of a transient world, believers can rest assured of the reality of the hope of final redemption and resurrection. Christian faith rests securely in the word of God, which will stand for ever. And, given the total faithfulness of God to his people, Peter urges them to show an equal faithfulness to God, by dedicating themselves to his service and ridding themselves of all sinful desires. They must go on to maturity, just as infants progress from milk to solid food (2:1–3).

2:4–12 The Living Stone, and a Chosen People. Peter then explains the privileges of being the people of God. In a famous passage, he develops the image of believers as stones that are being built up into a house. Although this image differs from Paul's analogy of the human body with its various parts, the same point is being made: the Christian life is meant to be corporate, rather than individualist. Furthermore, these stones are being laid on an absolutely solid and dependable foundation, which is none other than Jesus Christ himself. Unbelievers may fail to understand how someone who was rejected by his own people could come to have such importance. But Christ, though rejected by his own people, was affirmed by God through his resurrection, and was thus declared to be the Son of God.

Believers, as a body, are called to be the people of God. Peter brings together a small galaxy of Old Testament themes and allusions as he demonstrates how the calling of believers brings to fulfillment a whole series of hopes and prophecies. They have been chosen by God. They have been made into a royal priesthood (a reference to the king-priests of the Old Testament, who were endowed with special gifts of the Spirit). They are holy, like God himself, and belong to him, in that he has purchased them through the blood of his only son. God has called them from the darkness of a sinful world into his own wonderful light. In every respect, Peter brings out the dramatic consequences of being called out of the world to serve God through Christ. But as a result of their calling, they are now aliens and strangers in the world (2:11). Although they live in the world, they look beyond it to their homeland in heaven. It is a great privilege to be a Christian.

2:13–25 Submission to Earthly Authorities. Part of that privilege is to suffer for Christ. Peter urges his readers to submit to earthly authorities, so that any resulting persecution will be obviously due to the fact that they are

Christians. Christ has already suffered and left this example for believers to follow. It is therefore important that believers be seen to suffer for Christ, and not for some civil offense for which some form of punishment would be fully merited. Peter wants to gain the maximum evangelistic potential from any persecution of Christians.

However, as he explores the theme of suffering, Peter meditates further on the death of Christ. Drawing on Isaiah's words concerning the future suffering servant of God (Isa 52:13–53:12), he shows how the suffering of Christ on the cross fulfilled this great prophecy. Christians believe that Christ bore their sins on the cross. It is by his wounds that they have been healed. They were like sheep that had gone astray, yet through Christ, they have returned to God.

3:1–7 Wives and Husbands. As we noted earlier, Peter is concerned to gain the maximum evangelistic potential for the gospel. Apparently as part of this strategy, Peter urges husbands and wives to behave toward each other in ways that would be acceptable to the world at large. Peter's plan is clear: he wants Christian wives to be able to win over their nonbelieving husbands. However, it is clear that Peter believes that both men and women have an equal share in the "gracious gift of life" (3:7). While Peter is recommending that wives adopt an attitude of submission to their husbands, this is seen as a tactic to enable them to win over their husbands to their faith. For Peter, gender has no bearing on eternal life—an attitude echoed and endorsed by Paul (Gal 3:28).

3:8–4:19 Suffering for Doing Good. The theme of suffering now returns. To be a believer is potentially to be a suffering believer. Peter begins his discussion of this somber theme by emphasizing the need to suffer for the gospel, rather than for doing wrong. What is the point of suffering for doing wrong? The important thing is to make sure that any suffering that comes the way of believers is a direct result of their faith, rather than of wrongdoing. The example of Christ is supremely important in this respect.

Peter then elaborates on some aspects of the meaning of the death of Christ (3:18–22) that deserve special attention. The death of Christ is the means by which sin is forgiven and access to the presence of God is gained. Christ is now raised on high and seated at the right hand of God, with all heavenly beings and powers in submission to him. However, before his resurrection, Christ "went and preached to the spirits in prison" (3:19). The full meaning of this passage is not clear. However, one possible interpretation is of interest and may be noted here. According to this interpretation, the passage refers to Christ preaching the good news to those who died before his coming, so that none might be deprived of hearing the gospel.

This section also includes an important interpretation of Noah's ark. The waters of the flood point both to judgment (in that they resulted from the sin of the world) and salvation (in that they offered a means of deliverance through the ark). In much the same way, the water of baptism symbolizes both the judgment resulting from sin, and the cleansing and forgiveness that result only from the death and resurrection of Jesus Christ.

Peter then encourages his readers to prepare for suffering (4:1–11), in the sure knowledge that God will sustain and support them and that their fortitude under suffering will lead to the praise of God. Believers must not be surprised by this threat of suffering. Perhaps Peter has in mind the "commonsense" view that the righteous will not suffer—a view that is contradicted by the cross, on which the only truly righteous person suffered and died. Believers must expect to suffer for their righteousness. Whatever heavenly reward it will gain, it is likely to lead only to mocking, scorn, and persecution on earth.

5:1–11 To Elders and Young Men. Peter makes it clear that he writes as someone who himself has been a witness to the sufferings of Christ (5:1). He now asks his readers to prepare themselves, as individuals and as communities, for any such ordeals. After some advice to elders and young men (5:2–5), he emphasizes that believers may cast all their cares upon the God who cares for them (5:6–7). Although the threat of satanic attack remains real, it may be resisted by standing firm in the faith in the sure knowledge that God will comfort and restore them (5:8–11).

5:12–14 Final Greetings. The letter then concludes. Peter acknowledges the assistance of Silas in writing the letter (5:12). It is highly likely that Silas did more than write the letter down. Secretaries were often given the task of putting a writer's thoughts into better Greek than the writer himself could manage. The letter is written in excellent Greek—much better than would be expected from a former Galilean fisherman! Silas may well have ensured that Peter's practical advice and theological wisdom were stated in the best possible manner. (Interestingly, 2 Peter is written in much poorer Greek, and no reference is made to Silas—perhaps we may see Peter's unaided writing style in this later letter?) Finally, Peter offers the greetings of John Mark, who is widely credited with recording Peter's memories of Jesus in the form of the gospel of Mark.

2 PETER

The second letter of Peter differs from the first in a number of ways. Perhaps the most obvious is the style of Greek used, which is noticeably less polished than that of the first letter—a point that is often explained through the involvement of Silas in the composition of the earlier letter. The letters also differ significantly in terms of their subjects: 1 Peter was especially concerned with the threat of suffering and hardship; 2 Peter is more concerned with the threat posed by false teaching.

1:1–21 Making One's Calling and Election Sure. The letter opens with a call to believers: they must work to ensure their election or salvation by pressing on toward Christian maturity. God has promised that those who remain faithful will share in his own nature and will escape from this sinful world. Believers need to press on to ensure that they benefit from this secure promise (1:1–11). Yet there is a real threat to this security of faith from false teachers.

Before providing further details of these teachers, Peter emphasizes his own personal credentials as an apostle (1:12–21). He has been an eyewitness to what he reports. He has not invented anything, but merely faithfully and truthfully reported what he has seen and heard, guided and sustained by the Holy Spirit.

2:1–22 False Teachers and Their Destruction. This contrasts sharply with the dishonesty of the false teachers. Peter makes the point that there have always been false teachers within the household of faith, even in the days of the Old Testament prophets. The rise of false teachers within the church thus falls into a well-established pattern. However, by denying or calling into question the fundamentals of the Christian faith, it also poses a serious threat to the gospel. Peter makes it clear that many false teachers are motivated by personal ambition and care nothing for the welfare of believers.

Although Peter never specifically identifies the false teachings that so concern him, it is clear that he expects his readers to know what they are. The false teachings in question are like dried-up springs, which seem to offer refreshment, but on closer inspection turn out to be arid. They offer freedom to their hearers, but in reality they threaten to enslave them once more by dragging them back into the world from which they had been liberated by the gospel (2:17–20). The hints that he provides suggest that the false teachings are related to those that emerged at Colossae and that would later find their full expression in the movement known as Gnosticism in the second century. Peter's concern is more to emphasize the fate of the false teachers than to provide an analysis and refutation of their teaching.

3:1–13 The Day of the Lord. Peter then turns to deal with a question that seems to have been troubling some of his readers. When will the Second Coming take place? It seems that many who expected to live to see this coming had died, causing bewilderment to some. Peter stresses the total reliability of the Lord's promise to return. He will return, but nobody knows for certain when this will be. In any case, there may be a disparity between divine and human understandings of time. After all, a thousand years is like a day in the sight of the Lord. The important thing, Peter argues, is to look forward with certainty to the hope of the new heaven and new earth, rather than become preoccupied with precise dates and times.

3:14–18 Trust in the Lord. Peter then asks his readers to trust in the Lord, knowing that the Lord in his patience wants people to be saved. The delay of the Second Coming will give more people the opportunity to repent. The fact that the Second Coming has not yet happened is not an indication of God's failure or faithlessness, but rather an expression of his patience, and of his desire to save as many people as possible. This point, Peter argues, is made in the writings of Paul, although he concedes that these are not as easy to understand as one might like (3:14–16).

Finally, Peter reassures his readers of the total reliability of "our Lord and Savior Jesus Christ" (3:17–18). He can be trusted—unlike the false teachers!

1, 2, 3 JOHN

The three letters of John are best taken together, because they are very similar in content and style. Their common author is the apostle John, who was also responsible for writing the fourth gospel and the book of Revelation. It is generally thought that the letters date from the end of the first century, perhaps having been written from the city of Ephesus around A.D. 85–90. The identity of the readership of the first two letters is not clear. They are addressed to believers in general, and may have been intended as circular letters for the use of traveling evangelists. The third letter is specifically addressed to Gaius, whose identity is not clear.

1 JOHN

The first letter, in addition to affirming some central features of the gospel, is concerned to deal with false teachings that had arisen within the church at this time. The basic features of the false teachings (which seem to be an early form of Gnosticism) include a denial of the incarnation of Jesus Christ, and the belief that there is no need for believers to act morally. It opens with John affirming that he is an eyewitness to the coming of Jesus Christ (1:1–4). The basic theme of the gospel is that the light of life has broken into a dark world. Through the blood of Christ, the lives of believers may be purified from the taint of sin (1:5–7).

1:8–10 Sin. Having introduced the theme of sin, John now develops it in more detail. The universal extent of sin is vigorously affirmed: nobody is free from its stains, and all need cleansing from its contamination (1:8–10). John's purpose in writing is partly to encourage believers to resist sin, but also to assure them that if they do sin, they have forgiveness through the "atoning sacrifice of Christ." In other words, the death of Christ enables God to cancel the guilt of sin and purge its stain from us (2:1–2).

2:3–14 Love. It is clear that some of John's readers have been told that there is no need for them to concern themselves with morals. John rejects this opinion and insists on the need for morality, and especially love, in the Christian life (2:3–14). This does not mean that believers should love the world, but rather love the God who created the world, and those whom God has redeemed from that world into the community of believers (2:15–17).

2:18–27 Warning Against Antichrists. The theme of false teaching is now explicitly introduced. John declares that the churches are in danger of being seduced by "antichrists" (2:18–27). The word is plural, and refers to a general category of people who oppose the claims of Jesus Christ to be the Messiah (note especially 2:22). John makes it clear that Jesus is to be acknowledged both as Son of God and as Messiah. To fail to do this is to miss out on the benefits of the gospel, including knowing the Father. (There are strong echoes of some themes of John's gospel here, especially its insistence that the Father is made known through the Son [Jn 14:6, 9].)

2:28–4:21 Love One Another. The theme of the love of God is now examined in greater detail (2:28–4:21). All those who are called "children of God" must live up to this calling, especially by resisting sin. Although at points John may seem to suggest that the life of believers is characterized by a complete absence of sin (e.g., 3:9), a closer reading indicates that his meaning is slightly different. The lives of believers must not be characterized or dominated by sin. In other words, believers must live toward God, not toward sin.

On a more positive note, John stresses the importance of love within the Christian community (3:11–24). The same love that was shown in Jesus laying down his life for his people must also be at work in the lives of believers. The world may hate believers. Believers, however, must love each other. John summarizes the gospel in a nutshell as follows: to believe in Jesus the Son of God, and to love each other as he commanded us (3:23).

In a brief digression, John now warns his readers against a further specific false teaching—the denial of the basic Christian belief that "Jesus Christ has come in the flesh" or that "Jesus is from God" (4:1–6). (This is similar to the error noted in an earlier chapter, which refused to accept that Jesus was the Christ or Messiah.) He then returns to the theme of the love of God. The reason for the digression then becomes clear.

God is love. But what is the love of God like? John declares that the love of God is shown in action (4:7–21). Everyone knows that actions speak louder than words. God, John declares, showed his love in action by sending his son Jesus Christ as an atoning sacrifice, so that believers might live through him. And it will be clear that if Jesus Christ is *not* from God, the basis of this declaration is void. Only if Jesus is from God is the love of God shown in the death of Christ on the cross. And believers can know and share in this love. God loved them first. Their love is simply a response to his.

5:1–12 Faith in the Son of God. John then emphasizes once more the importance of accepting that Jesus is the Messiah (or Christ). This is no human belief, but one that has been revealed by God himself. Believing that Jesus is the Son of God is the only basis for Christian living and hope of eternal life. This great truth is confirmed by the witness of the Holy Spirit—a reference to the Spirit's witness at the baptism of Jesus (Jn 1:32–34). God himself has declared that Jesus Christ is his Son. To fail to acknowledge this is to make God out to be a liar. The same point was made earlier, when John declared that anyone who denied his or her sinfulness made God out to be a liar (1:8–10).

5:13–21 Concluding Remarks. The first letter of John then concludes by declaring once more the total reliability of the gospel. John wants his readers to know that they have eternal life. Sin is indeed an obstacle to God—but not every type of sin leads to spiritual death or the loss of the hope of eternal life. Believers must resist sin and trust in Jesus Christ as the Son of God. By doing so, they can rest assured that God will hear and respond to their prayers and finally bring them to eternal life.

2 JOHN

The second and third letters of John are so brief that, like Philemon and Jude, references are made only to verse numbers. The second letter is probably written to a specific church and its members in Asia Minor, here referred to as "the chosen lady and her children" (1). The reference to the "chosen sister" in verse 13 is probably a reference to another local church.

After stressing the importance of love in the life of the Christian believer and community (4–6), John again deals with the false teaching that he had addressed at greater length in his first letter—namely, the denial that Jesus Christ had come in the flesh (7–11). It is clear that John's intention here is to oppose the teachers, rather than to analyze and criticize the teaching (as he did in the first letter).

3 JOHN

The third letter is specifically addressed to Gaius, who is clearly a prominent Christian believer. The letter encourages him to be faithful in his Christian work. The references to hospitality (6–8) probably reflect the care shown to traveling missionaries, who used the houses of local Christian believers as staging posts on their evangelistic journeys. After reporting unfavorably on one local believer—who is clearly something of a prima donna (9–10)—and favorably on another (12), John ends his letter by passing on his greetings to all whom he knows.

JUDE

The letter of Jude is shrouded in mystery. It is not clear who "Jude" is. The most likely contenders for authorship would be Judas the apostle—whom Luke carefully distinguished from Judas Iscariot (Lk 6:16; Ac 1:13), and Judas, the brother of the Lord (Mt 13:55; Mk 6:3). Nor is it clear for whom he was writing.

The main theme of the letter is a false teaching that has arisen and that appears to have become widespread. Variations on the same theme can be found in numerous other New Testament works, including Colossians, 2 Peter, and 1 John.

Vv. 1–16 False Teaching. The letter opens with Jude greeting his readers (1–2), followed by an immediate condemnation of false teaching. Jude had intended to write a very different letter, in which he would have written about the salvation that is the common heritage of all Christians. However, the "faith that was once for all entrusted to the saints" is under threat from false teaching. The basic themes of the false teaching, to judge from Jude's very brief analysis (4) is a denial of the lordship of Jesus Christ and the rejection of the need for morality (teachings which are also examined and rejected in 1 John).

What follows is quite difficult to understand (5–16). It is clear that Jude is well-read in Jewish writings, including a number of works that are not included in the Old Testament, and sees parallels between some of the incidents related in these works and the problems of his own day. Just as Paul occasionally quoted from secular Greek writers to illustrate a point to a Greek audience, so Jude clearly feels that his readership (presumably largely Jewish) will benefit from these comparisons and realize how serious the problems are. In a series of images, Jude emphasizes the sterility and self-serving motives of the false teachers, without going into detail concerning the nature of their teachings (12–13).

Vv. 17–25 A Call to Persevere; a Doxology. Having stressed the dangers posed by such teachers, Jude urges his readers to persevere in the true faith (17–2). The rise of false teachers is only to be expected. Believers must strengthen their own faith through prayer. As for those who are weak in faith, they are to be treated mercifully (22–23).

The letter ends with a doxology or exclamation of praise in which Jude affirms the glorious hope that the gospel offers to believers and the steadfastness of the God who has called believers to faith in his name (24–25).

REVELATION

The book of Revelation, which brings the New Testament to its close, is probably the most difficult book in the New Testament to understand. It is generally regarded as having been written by John the apostle, who was also responsible for the gospel and three letters bearing his name in the New Testament. The book seems to have been written at a late date, probably during the latter part of the reign of the Roman emperor Domitian (A.D. 81–96), when the Roman authorities were attempting to suppress Christianity in certain regions of their empire.

In many ways, the bulk of the book of Revelation resembles the second half of the prophecy of Daniel. It is composed of visions, making extensive use of symbolism and highly figurative language. In some cases, it is reasonably clear what the symbols represent. In many cases, however, the interpretation of the visions is difficult and speculative. It is no accident that the visions of Revelation have proved in recent years to be a hunting ground for some of the more bizarre religious sects and cults, who have found it easy to interpret some of the visions in line with their own highly unusual understandings of the end of the world. Readers of the visionary parts of the book must be clear that it is highly speculative to interpret any aspects of these visions in terms of the political world of today.

REVELATION 1:1 – 3:22

The Messages to the Churches

1:1–8 Greetings and Doxology. The book opens by declaring that it is a "revelation of Jesus Christ" (1:1). The word *revelation* (Greek *apokalypsis*)—which gives the book its name "The Apocalypse"—literally means "the removing of a veil." John addresses himself to the seven churches of Asia Minor, each of which will be addressed individually in the course of this section of the work. The work opens by giving thanks to God for all he has done for believers through Jesus Christ. God is declared to be "the Alpha and the Omega" (1:8), a reference to the first and last letters of the Greek alphabet. He is the beginning and end of history, its source and its ultimate goal.

1:9–20 One Like a Son of Man. John then describes the circumstances under which the revelation came to him (1:9–20). After noting that he shares in the sufferings of the churches, he relates how he experienced a vision of the risen Christ. This incident took place on a Sunday on the island of Patmos,

The peaceful island of Patmos, off the coast of Asia Minor, is where John has the visions that he describes in the Book of Revelation.

off the coast of Asia Minor, when John was "in the Spirit" (1:10)—a reference to a state of inspiration, comparable to that associated with the Old Testament prophets.

Using language that recalls the vision of the prophet Daniel (Da 7:13), John relates how he saw the risen Christ standing among seven golden lampstands, holding seven stars in his right hand. These aspects of the vision are then interpreted to him: the seven stars represent the angels associated with each of the churches to be addressed in the work, just as the lampstands represent the churches themselves.

This opening vision, however, seems to set the scene for the whole book. John is told to write of "what you have seen, what is now, and what will take place later" (1:19). This suggests a threefold structure. First, "what you have seen" is a clear reference to the opening vision (1:9–20). Second, "what is now," is a reference to the state of the seven churches, which will be addressed in the letters to the seven churches (2:1–3:22). And third, John is told to relate "what will take place later," referring to the great vision of the end, which takes up the bulk of this distinctive work (4:1–22:21).

2:1–11 To the Churches in Ephesus and Smyrna. John now relays to the seven churches of Asia Minor the messages that were entrusted to him in his vision. The church at *Ephesus* is commended for its perseverance, and also for its rejection of the "practices of the Nicolaitans" (2:1–7). This group appears to have been characterized by a doctrine of Christian liberty that allowed its adherents to become involved with idolatry and fall into various forms of moral laxity. However, the church has lost its enthusiasm for the gospel, which it needs to rediscover.

The church at *Smyrna* has been going through a hard time, apparently being discriminated against by both the Roman authorities and a large Jewish presence in the city (2:8–11). Yet their sufferings will not destroy their faith, and they may rest assured that they will inherit eternal life at the end.

2:12–29 To the Churches in Pergamum and Thyatira. The church at *Pergamum* is praised for its faithfulness in the face of the official Roman cult of emperor worship, which had a regional center in the city (2:12–17). However, the church has tolerated the presence and teachings of the Nicolaitans (see above), which has compromised its integrity. As a result, there is a need for repentance and change within the church.

The church in *Thyatira*, although commended in some ways, is criticized for allowing toleration of paganism within its ranks (2:18–29). This tendency is clearly associated with some prominent woman within the congregation, who is given the name "Jezebel" to bring out her affinity with the pagan queen of that same name, who led Israel astray at the time of the ministry of Elijah (2Ki 9:30–37).

3:1–13 To the Churches in Sardis and Philadelphia. The church in the wealthy city of *Sardis*, despite its outward appearance of strength, is declared to be inwardly weak (3:1–6). It needs to recover its vision and sense of identity by returning to the roots of its faith. This message includes the first reference in this work to the "book of life" (3:5), a register of all those who are citizens of heaven and thus have a right to reside within it. To have one's name blotted out from this book would be to imply loss of all citizenship rights—and hence the right to dwell within heaven.

The church in the city of *Philadelphia* is praised for its faithfulness and spiritual strength during what has clearly been a very difficult time (3:7–13). The "synagogue of Satan" is probably a reference to an aggressive Jewish community, intent on eliminating Christianity from the region. The church is reassured of the continuing protection and presence of God in order that it may survive what lies ahead.

3:14–22 To the Church in Laodicea. Finally, the church at *Laodicea* is addressed. This is perhaps the most celebrated of the seven messages to the churches in the region. The church in this city is declared to be lukewarm in its faith and in urgent need of repentance and revival. It has trusted in its own strength, rather than in the power of the Lord. The city was noted in the ancient world for its wealth, its textiles, and for a local eye ointment. The criticism of the church alludes to all three (3:19) in terms that make it clear that the risen Christ alone can supply what the church needs. The message concludes with the famous declaration that Christ is knocking at the door of this church, seeking readmission. If the door is opened, he will enter and eat with those inside—a clear statement of restoration of fellowship.

REVELATION 4:1 – 22:21

The Visions of the End

4:1–11 The Throne in Heaven. The tone of the book now alters radically. We are caught up in a prophetic vision of heaven. John enters into heaven as through an open door and is confronted with a glorious vision of God, very similar to that granted to Isaiah (see Isa 6:3, cited here). This vision of the worship of heaven prepares the way for the remainder of the vision, which relates events in heaven to the situation of the persecuted church on earth in Asia Minor.

5:1–14 The Scroll and the Lamb. As he contemplates the vision of God, John becomes aware of the presence of a lamb. This lamb is none other than Jesus Christ, who was slain in order to redeem sinful humanity for God. The lamb is an important symbol here. It picks up the theme of the slaughtered Passover lamb, whose blood marked off Israel from her enemies (Ex 12:1–7); the lamb who was slain for others (Isa 53:7); and the lamb who takes away the sins of the world (Jn 1:29). The use of the number seven may also be noted here: there are seven seals (5:1), seven horns, and seven eyes (5:6). The number seven is here used as a symbol of the completeness of heaven. Other examples of its use include the seven churches (1:4), seven crowns (12:3), seven hills (17:9), seven kings (17:10), seven plagues (15:6), and seven trumpets (8:2).

6:1–11:19 The Seals and the Trumpets. The scene now changes. The Lamb is granted authority to open the seven seals, setting loose forces of destruction and devastation on the earth (6:1–17). Before the opening of the final seal, all of the people of God are marked with a sign to demonstrate that they are God's own. A total of 144,000—12,000 from each tribe of Israel—are marked in this way, as well as an unnumbered multitude drawn from every nation on earth, whose sins have been washed away by the blood of the Lamb (7:1–17). This important chapter makes the point that a faithful remnant of Israel will be saved, along with countless others whose sins have been purged by the saving death of Christ. (The number 144,000 should probably be regarded as symbolic rather than actual.)

With the sealing of the people of God, the final seal is opened. Initially, there is a reverential silence. Then the forces of destruction are unleashed, to the accompaniment of seven trumpet blasts (8:1–11:19). At the sound of the seventh and final trumpet, voices from heaven declare the dawning of the reign of God.

12:1–20:15 A Series of Visions. But disbelief and rebellion against God continue. In a vivid series of visions, John sees a series of figures and beasts, symbolizing the forces of evil and Satan (12:1–13:18). The final beast to be mentioned has the mystical number 666 (13:18). It is far from clear how this number is to be interpreted. Given that seven is seen as a perfect number, it is possible that 666 is to be seen as a "trinity of imperfection" or a numerical code for an enemy of the church, perhaps spelling out the name NERO CAESAR (that is, "the emperor Nero").

The reference to the mark of the beast (13:16–17) is important, because it indicates the importance of the mark of Christ (the cross) in sealing a believer's redemption. The mark of the beast probably refers to a symbol of the emperor cult, which forced individuals to worship the Roman emperor as a god as a means of demonstrating loyalty to Rome.

Yet the end is now very near. After a vision that demonstrated that the 144,000 drawn from the twelve tribes of Israel were safe, and were intended to be the firstfruits of those redeemed from the earth (14:1–5), John is presented with a vision of the final destruction of evil and unbelief (14:6–20:15), culminating in the destruction of Satan himself. The time scale referred to in this section has been the subject of frequent speculation, particularly the "thousand years" for which Satan is bound (20:2, 7). However, the figure is best seen as symbolic, rather than as a precise indication of time. The book of Revelation is not a timetable, but a prophetic vision, concerned above all with demonstrating the final and total victory of God, despite all the trials and tribulations of his people at present.

21:1–22:21 The New Jerusalem and Final Victory. Now the tone of the book changes radically once more. John presents us with his vision of a new heaven and a new earth, and of the new Jerusalem (21:1–5). The vision can be regarded as the ultimate fulfillment of the great Old Testament prophecies of renewal and regeneration of the world, and the ushering in of a new age in which suffering and pain are abolished for ever. The vision of the new Jerusalem continues by affirming that there is no temple in the city. There does not need to be, for God himself is present in its midst (21:6–27). This must be seen in the light of the prophecy of Ezekiel, who saw the "glory of the LORD" depart from the temple as a result of Judah's disobedience. Now God's presence has been restored to his people forever. God's people will finally be granted a vision of his face, something that not even Moses was permitted on earth (22:1–6; see Ex 33:20; Jn 1:18).

So what is the value of this vision? What comfort would it bring to the seven churches of Asia Minor? The answer becomes clear in the closing section of the book (22:7–21). It is an assurance that things will not go on forever, and that the suffering of today will finally give way to the hope of heaven—which nothing can take away. Those who have been sealed by God may rest assured that whatever trials and difficulties they are facing, God will remain faithful. Believers will be delivered from the presence and threat of all those who are seeking their destruction. Behind the facade of events on earth, a train of events is being set in motion in heaven that will bring the forces of evil to an end. Christ will come again and bring all things to an end. And then:

> There will be no more death or mourning or crying or pain, for the old order of things has passed away. (21:4)

And that vision remains just as important for Christians today. Believers can take comfort in the sure and certain knowledge that whatever the woes and pains of this life, their future joy and life lies with the risen Christ.

FOR FURTHER READING

Aone-volume commentary on the Bible suffers from a number of limitations, the most important of which is space. The discussion of the meaning and relevance of any given biblical passage is limited severely by this restriction. Another difficulty is raised by the author of a commentary. No matter how good the commentator, readers will want to have access to other viewpoints. For this reason, it is a good idea to build up a library of commentaries on Scripture. Guidance on this is provided here.

Other books are also useful in helping people gain more from reading Scripture. The following work is strongly recommended to all interested in getting the most out of their reading of the Bible:

> Gordon D. Fee and Douglas Stuart, *How to Read the Bible for All Its Worth*, 2nd ed. (Grand Rapids: Zondervan, 1993).

Several sets of commentaries are of interest. *The Tyndale Old Testament Commentaries* and *The Tyndale New Testament Commentaries* (Downers Grove, IL: InterVarsity Press, and Leicester, UK: Inter-Varsity Press) are excellent "starter" commentaries, and are well worth purchasing. They include contributions by leading biblical scholars, pitched at a level suitable for the serious reader who is not (yet!) a biblical scholar.

The Bible Speaks Today series (Downers Grove, IL: InterVarsity Press, and Leicester, UK: Inter-Varsity Press) is less concerned with issues of scholarship, and focuses on the relevance of the text to the situation of today. It is an excellent addition to the bookshelf of any serious student of the Bible and is especially helpful in the preparation of addresses and sermons.

The Classic Biblical Commentary series (Wheaton, IL: Crossway Books) aims to make available some of the best commentaries of the past, edited with the needs of modern readers in mind. This series draws on the great expositors of the past, such as C.H. Spurgeon and J. H. Ryle, who still merit a hearing today.

The New International Biblical Commentary (Peabody, MA: Hendrickson) is also recommended. Currently in fourteen volumes, it uses transliterated Greek, for the serious student who does not as yet know New Testament Greek.

Volumes in all the series mentioned above give suggestions for more detailed commentaries that can be used for further study.